Lecture Notes in
Computer Science

Edited by G. Goos and J. Hartmanis

247

STACS 87

4th Annual Symposium on Theoretical Aspects
of Computer Science
Passau, Federal Republic of Germany, February 19–21, 1987
Proceedings

Edited by
F.J. Brandenburg, G. Vidal-Naquet and M. Wirsing

Springer-Verlag

Editors

Franz J. Brandenburg
Martin Wirsing
Fakultät für Mathematik und Informatik, Universität Passau
Innstr. 27, D-8390 Passau

Guy Vidal-Naquet
Laboratoire de Recherche en Informatique
Bâtiment 490, Université de Paris-Sud
F-91405 Orsay Cedex

CR Subject Classification (1987): C.1, C.2, D.2.6, D.2.m, F, G.2.1, G.2.2

ISBN 3-540-17219-X Springer-Verlag Berlin Heidelberg New York
ISBN 0-387-17219-X Springer-Verlag New York Berlin Heidelberg

Printing and binding: Druckhaus Beltz, Hemsbach/Bergstr.
2145/3140-543210

Foreword

The Fourth Annual Symposium on Theoretical Aspects of Computer Science (STACS 87) was held on February 19-21, 1987 in Passau, Germany. It was preceded by Symposia in Paris (1984), Saarbrücken (1985) and Orsay (1986).

The Symposium was organized jointly by the Special Interest Group for Theoretical Computer Science of the Gesellschaft für Informatik (GI), the special interest group for applied mathematics of the Association Française des Sciences et Techniques de l'Information, de l'Organisation et des Systèmes (AFCET), and the University of Passau. It is held alternatively in France and Germany.

In response to the call for papers 125 papers were submitted. The program committee met on October 3rd and selected 34 papers chosen on the basis of their scientific quality and relevance to the Symposium. Three invited talks were given by R. Book, G. Kahn and K. Mehlhorn.

For the first time, ten software systems showing ways and possibilities for applying results of research in Theoretical Computer Science were demonstrated at the Symposium and latest research results were informally presented as posters. This volume contains the invited presentations, the selected papers and abstracts of the systems demonstrations.

The program committee of STACS 87 consisted of

Jean Berstel, Paris
Michal Chytil, Praha
Maria Dezani-Ciancaglini, Torino
Philippe Flajolet, Rocquencourt
Jan van Leeuwen, Utrecht
Pierre Lescanne, Nancy
Burkhard Monien, Paderborn
David Park, Coventry
Rüdiger Reischuk, Darmstadt
Wolfgang Thomas, Aachen
Guy Vidal-Naquet, Orsay
Martin Wirsing, Passau (Program Chairman)
Emo Welzl, Graz

On behalf of the program committee the program chairman would like to thank all those who submitted papers and the referees who helped for the task of evaluating papers.

The support of

Fremdenverkehrsverein Passau,
IBM Deutschland GmbH, Stuttgart
SIEMENS AG, München
SUN Microsystems GmbH, München
Symbolics GmbH, Frankfurt
Volksbank Passau-Freyung eG, Passau

is gratefully acknowledged. Finally we would like to thank Mrs. C. Daniels and Ms. R. Eggerl for their help in preparing and organizing the conference, Mr. H. Hussmann for his help in installing the systems demonstrations and Springer-Verlag for their excellent cooperation concerning the publication of this volume.

Passau, February 1987 F.J. Brandenburg, G. Vidal-Naquet, M. Wirsing

Acknowledgement

Every paper was carefully reviewed by (at least) four referees. Their assistance is gratefully acknowledged.

I.J. Aalbersberg	V. Akman	H. Alt
K. Ambos-Spies	S. Anderson	K. Apt
A. Arnold	E. Astesiano	C. Attiya
F. Aurenhammer	A. Avron	B. Becker
C. Beierle	F. Bellegarde	T. Belzner
J. Bergstra	A. Bertoni	E. Best
W. Bibel	H. L. Bodlaender	M. Bonuccelli
L. Bougé	O. Boxma	F. J. Brandenburg
W. Brauer	G. Brebner	W. Bucher
R. Burstall	M. Coppo	T. Coquand
G. Costa	B. Courcelle	S. Crespi-Reghizzi
M. Dam	W. Damm	C. Delgado Kloos
B. Demo	V. Diekert	J. Doenhardt
K. Donner	H. Edelsbrunner	J. Eickel
P. van Emde Boas	J. Engelfriet	L. Fariñas del Cerro
E. Fehr	J. Flum	L. Fribourg
U. Furbach	Sh. Gao	A. Geser
I. Gnaedig	R. Gnatz	I. Guessarian
Y. Gurevich	J. Guyard	T. Hafer
T. Hagerup	H. Hansen	R. Hennicker
U. Heuter	S. Hölldobler	W. Hohberg
F. Honsell	H. J. Hoogeboom	G. Hotz
J. Hromkovic	Hungar	H. Hußmann
K. Indermark	J. Jaray	M. Jerrum
G. Jorrier	B. Josko	G. Kahn
v. Karger	M. Kaufmann	M. Kaul
C. Kirchner	H. Kirchner	H. Klaeren
P. Kleinschmidt	H.-J. Kreowski	F. Kröger
H. Kuchen	M. Kunde	K.-J. Lange
H. Langmaack	N. Levy	J. Loeckx

G. Lolli	G. Longo	R. Loogen
V. Manca	D. Mandrioli	P. Marchand
A. Marchetti-Spaccamela	A. Martelli	Marzinkewitsch
G. Mascari	M. Mauny	G. Mauri
K. Mehlhorn	A. Merceron	D. Mery
F. Meyer auf der Heide	G. de Michelis	P. Miglioli
K. Mitchell	S. Miyano	B. Möller
E. Moggi	R. Müller	F. Nickl
R. de Nicola	R. Obermeier	W. Oberschelp
P. Obipreddi	M. Ornaghi	H.G. Osthof
T. Ottmann	F. Otto	M. H. Overmars
P. Padawitz	P. Päppinghaus	L. Pagli
J. Parrow	H. Partsch	M. Paul
H. Petzsch	T. Pinegger	K. V. S. Prasad
M. Protasi	F. J. Radermacher	G. Reggio
R. Rehrmann	A. Reiser	M. Rem
J. L. Remy	B. Reusch	M.M. Richter
S. Ronchi	C. Roos	G. Rossi
G. Rote	M. Rusinowitch	N. Sabadini
L. Saitta	A. Salibra	D. Sannella
G. Schmidt	U. Schöning	A. A. Schoone
R. Schott	A. Schrijver	R. Schuster
R. Seidel	D. Siefkes	C. Simone
J. Souquières	E. Speckenmeyer	R. Steinbrüggen
C. Stirling	T. Streicher	D. Taubner
G. Tel	A. Tsakalidis	H. Tzschach
W. Unger	M. Veldhorst	B. Venneri
M. Venturini	R. Verbeek	H. Vogler
W. Vogler	A. Voss	K. Wagner
D. Walker	H. Walter	M. Warmuth
K. Weihrauch	P. Weiss	M. Wiegers
C. Wieners	A. Wight	W. Woess
M. Zacchi		

Table of Contents

Formal Languages

Abstract Data Types

Rewriting Systems

Denotational Semantics

Semantics of Parallelism

Net Theory

Fairness

Distributed Algorithms

Systems Demonstrations

TOWARDS A THEORY OF RELATIVIZATIONS: POSITIVE RELATIVIZATIONS*

Ronald V. Book

Department of Mathematics
University of California, Santa Barbara
Santa Barbara, CA 93106, USA

INTRODUCTION

When Stephen Cook [12] introduced the concept of NP-completeness, he used the notion of Turing reducibility computed in polynomial time. When Richard Karp [14] studied reducibilites between combinatorial problems, he used the notion of many-one reducibility computed in polynomial time. Since that time there have been many studies of complexity bounded reducibilities and their corresponding reduction classes with emphasis being placed on reducibilities that can be computed in polynomial time or in polynomial space. These studies have not been carried out with the sole intention of investigating reducibilities as such but rather in an attempt to shed light on the (still unknown) relationships among the corresponding unrelativized complexity classes. This has been particularly true of the various Turing reducibilities that have been considered.

Two papers that established important properties of complexity bounded reducibilites were published in 1975. Ladner, Lynch, and Selman [17] surveyed and compared the main types of reducibilities computed in polynomial time, both deterministically and nondeterministically. Baker, Gill, and Solovay [1] established the existence of sets A and B such that the reduction classes P(A), NP(A), and PSPACE(A) are equal and the reduction classes P(B), NP(B), and PSPACE(B) are pairwise unequal; these results may be interpreted as showing that computational complexity theory is not part of recursive function theory. The results suggest that one should not expect to solve problems such as P =? NP or NP =? PSPACE either by a straightforward simulation (i.e., construct a set A such that P(A) = NP(A) can be shown and then use that proof to show that P = NP) or by a straightforward diagonalization (i.e., construct a set B such that P(A) ≠ NP(B) can be shown and then use that proof to show that P ≠ NP).

---

*Preparation of this paper was supported in part by the National Science Foundation under Grant DCR-8312472.

Much of the work in this area since 1975 has been of one of two types: "separation theorems" that show the existence of oracle sets for which the corresponding reduction classes are not equal, and "collapsing theorems" that show the existence of oracle sets such that the corresponding reduction classes are equal. One of the important goals of computational complexity theory is to establish a theory of intractability as part of a general quantitative theory of complexity. Any such theory must provide the tools necessary to develop an understanding of the nature of relativized computation in the presence of resource bounds. It also must take into account the various separating and collapsing results that arise when one considers relativizations and provide an explanation, through general principles, of when and how such separation and collapsing can take place.

Many of the separation theorems regarding relativizations of classes specified by time-bounded oracle machines do not depend on time bounds as such. Rather, time bounds serve to bound the number of nondeterministic steps allowed in any computation, and hence, to bound the number of strings that can be candidates for oracle queries. Furthermore, time bounds serve to bound the number of oracle queries that can be made in any computation and, hence, the "size" of the set of queries that can be searched. If one restricts attention to these parameters, then one can establish more general separation results. This has been the theme of a previous paper [8].

One theme that has been pursued by the author and his co-workers has been the development of restricted relativizations with the property that any separation of relativized classes implies the separation of the unrelativized classes. Such restricted relativizations give rise to the notion of "positive relativizations." Consider the problem $\mathcal{C} =? \mathcal{D}$ where $\mathcal{C}$ and $\mathcal{D}$ are complexity classes. A positive relativization of this problem is a restriction R placed both on the machines of the type specifying class $\mathcal{C}$ and on the machines of the type specifying class $\mathcal{D}$ such that the following is true: $\mathcal{C} = \mathcal{D}$ if and only if for every set A, $\mathcal{C}_R(A) = \mathcal{D}_R(A)$. If such a positive relativization exists, then showing (by any means whatsoever) the existence of a set B such that $\mathcal{C}_R(B) \neq \mathcal{D}_R(B)$ amounts to a proof that $\mathcal{C} \neq \mathcal{D}$.

The restrictions R used to obtain positive relativizations of problems have been such that both the oracle machines specifying classes of the form $\mathcal{C}_R(A)$ and the oracle machines specifying classes of the form $\mathcal{D}_R(A)$ have essentially the same power to explore the query tree or space of queries. With the classes specified by polynomial bounds on time or space, this often means that for each input string x and each oracle set A, the size of the space of queries that can be explored by computations relative to A of a machine of type $\mathcal{C}$ on x is polynomially equivalent to the space of queries that can be explored by computations relative to A of a machine of type $\mathcal{D}$ on x, in the sense that each can be bounded by a polynomial in the other. In addition, the sizes of the query strings themselves must be polynomially equivalent.

In a similar way one can consider the notion of "negative relativizations." A negative relativization of the $\mathcal{C} =? \mathcal{D}$ problem is a restriction R placed both on the machines of the type specifying class $\mathcal{C}$ and on the machines of the type specifying class $\mathcal{D}$ such that the following is true: $\mathcal{C} \neq \mathcal{D}$ if and only if for every set A, $\mathcal{C}_R(A) \neq \mathcal{D}_R(A)$. If such a negative relativization exists, then showing (by any means whatsoever) the existence of a set B such that $\mathcal{C}_R(B) = \mathcal{D}_R(B)$ amounts to a proof that $\mathcal{C} = \mathcal{D}$.

If there is one restriction R that yields both a positive relativization of the $\mathcal{C}$ =? $\mathcal{D}$ problem and also a negative relativization of the $\mathcal{C}$ =? $\mathcal{D}$ problem, then the following result must hold:

(a) if there exists a set A such that $\mathcal{C}_R(A) = \mathcal{D}_R(A)$, then $\mathcal{C} = \mathcal{D}$;

(b) if there exists a set A such that $\mathcal{C}_R(A) \neq \mathcal{D}_R(A)$, then $\mathcal{C} \neq \mathcal{D}$.

This means that there is a relativization principle for the $\mathcal{C}$ =? $\mathcal{D}$ problem. In this case one can solve the $\mathcal{C}$ =? $\mathcal{D}$ problem by solving any of the relativized problems, i.e., by solving $\mathcal{C}_R(A) =? \mathcal{D}_R(A)$ for some set A.

This paper is essentially tutorial in nature and is a more detailed version of a previous report [7]. The goal is to provide guidelines for those who are seeing this material for the first time and for those who are teaching this material. Primarily, it is an overview of the results on positive relativizations of the following problems: P =? PSPACE, NP =? PSPACE, PH =? PSPACE, DSPACE(log n) =? NSPACE(log n), and P =? NP. In addition, it describes a relativization principle for the problem of whether the polynomial-time hierarchy is in fact an infinite hierarchy. Only the basic proofs from the literature are presented, and in some cases only proof sketches are provided. To a large extent the results presented are based on the work of the author and his co-workers.

Section 2

PRELIMINARIES

It is assumed that the reader is familiar with the basic concepts of complexity theory. Some of the concepts that are most important for this paper are reviewed here, and notation is established.

For a string x, $|x|$ denotes the length of x. For a set S, $\|S\|$ denotes the cardinality of S. For a set S and integer $n \geq 0$, let $S^{\leq n} = \{x \in S \mid |x| \leq n\}$. A set S is sparse if there is a polynomial p such that for all $n \geq 0$, $\|S^{\leq n}\| \leq p(n)$.

A set T is a tally set if $T \subseteq \{0\}^*$.

It is assumed, unless explicitly stated otherwise, that all sets of strings considered are taken over some fixed finite alphabet Σ that contains 0 and 1. If $A \subseteq \Sigma^*$, then $\overline{A} = \Sigma^* - A$. For sets $A, B \subseteq \Sigma^*$, the join of A and B is $A \oplus B = \{0x \mid x \in A\} \cup \{1x \mid x \in B\}$.

The notation $\langle \cdot , \cdot \rangle$ denotes a pairing function. The notation is abused by pairing finite sets A and B as $\langle A, B \rangle$ but also pairing a string x with a finite set T as $\langle x, T \rangle$.

An oracle machine is a multitape Turing machine M with a distinguished work tape, the query tape, and three distinguised states QUERY, YES, and NO. At some step of a computation on an input string x, M may enter the state QUERY. In state QUERY, M transfers into the state YES if the string currently on the query tape is in some oracle set A; otherwise, M transfers into state NO; in either case, the query tape is instantly erased. The set of strings accepted by M relative to the oracle set A is $L(M, A) = \{x \mid$ there is an accepting computation of M on input x when the oracle set is A$\}$. Also, $L(M)$ denotes $L(M, \emptyset)$.

Oracle machines may be deterministic or nondeterministic. An oracle machine may operate within some time bound T, where T is a function of the length of the input string, and the notion of time bound for an oracle machine is just the same as that for an ordinary Turing machine. An oracle machine may operate within some time bound S, where S is a function of the length of the input string; in this case, it is required that the query tape as well as the ordinary work tapes be bounded in length by S (but some exceptions are discussed in Section 4).

Of particular interest are the classes P(A), NP(A), and PSPACE(A) for arbitrary oracle sets A. Here $P(A) = \{L(M, A) \mid M$ is a deterministic oracle machine that operates in time $p(n)$ for some fixed polynomial $p\}$. Thus, P(A) is the reduction class of A under the polynomial time Turing reducibility $\leq^P_T$. For any class **C** of sets, $P(\mathbf{C}) = \cup\{P(A) \mid A \in \mathbf{C}\}$. The analogous notions are used in defining NP(A) and PSPACE(A).

The polynomial-time hierarchy as studied by Stockmeyer [28] and Wrathall [32] is defined as the structure $\{\langle\Delta^P_i, \Sigma^P_i, \Pi^P_i\rangle\}_{i\geq 0}$, where $\Sigma^P_0 = \Delta^P_0 = \Pi^P_0 = P$, $\Delta^P_{i+1} = P(\Sigma^P_i)$, $\Sigma^P_{i+1} = NP(\Sigma^P_i)$, and $\Pi^P_{i+1} = \text{co-}\Sigma^P_{i+1}$. The union $\cup_{i\geq 0} \Sigma^P_i$ is denoted by PH.

For any set A, the polynomial-time hierarchy relative to A is defined as the structure $\{\langle\Delta^P_i(A), \Sigma^P_i(A), \Pi^P_i(A)\rangle\}_{i\geq 0}$, where $\Sigma^P_0(A) = \Delta^P_0(A) = \Pi^P_0(A) = P(A)$, $\Delta^P_{i+1}(A) = P(\Sigma^P_i(A))$, $\Sigma^P_{i+1}(A) = NP(\Sigma^P_i(A))$, and $\Pi^P_{i+1}(A) = \text{co-}\Sigma^P_{i+1}(A)$. The union $\cup_{i\geq 0} \Sigma^P_i(A)$ is denoted by PH(A).

If S is a space bound, then for any oracle set A, $DSPACE^A(S)$ denotes the set $\{L(M, A) \mid M$ is a deterministic oracle machine that operates with space bound $S\}$. Classes of the form $NSPACE^A(S)$ are defined analogously. Recall that Savitch's Theorem [25] yields the fact that for any set A, $PSPACE(A) = \cup_{k>0}DSPACE^A(n^k) = \cup_{k>0}NSPACE^A(n^k)$. Recall that $A \leq^P_m B$ if there is a function f computable deterministically in polynomial time such that for all x, $x \in A$ if and only if $f(x) \in B$. A set K is $\leq^P_m$-complete for a complexity class **C** if $K \in \mathbf{C}$ and for every $C \in \mathbf{C}$, $C \leq^P_m K$.

Section 3
TIME VS. SPACE: THE POLYNOMIAL CLASSES

It appears that the first study of positive relativizations as such was carried out by Book and Wrathall in [6,11]. The specific problems considered were those of NP =? PSPACE and PH =? PSPACE. From the results of Baker, Gill, and Solovay [1], it is known that there exist sets A and B such that NP(A) = PSPACE(A) and NP(B) $\neq$ PSPACE(B), so that one cannot solve these problems by using the standard models for relativizations and constructing appropriate oracle sets. The new reduction classes introduced by Book and Wrathall were based on the notion that a Turing reduction may be computed using polynomial space but with only a polynomial number of oracle queries allowed in any computation. These new reduction classes were referred to as PQUERY(A) and NPQUERY(A) for each A, depending on whether the reductions were computed deterministically or nondeterministically. Later, Selman, Xu, and Book [26] considered the problem P =? PSPACE using these same ideas. Balcázar, Book, and Schöning [3] developed simple proofs of some of the results in [6,11,20], and it is their proofs that are presented here.

For every set A, let PQUERY(A) (NPQUERY(A)) be the class of languages L $\in$ PSPACE(A) such that there is a deterministic (resp., nondeterministic) polynomial space-bounded oracle machine M with the following properties:

(i) M recognizes L relative to A, and

(ii) there is a polynomial p such that for all x, in every computation of M on x there are at most $p(|x|)$ oracle queries.

Reduction classes of the form PQUERY(A) and NPQUERY(A) are invariant under the changes in the definition such as "in every computation" replaced by "some accepting computation," and "in every computation" replaced by "in every accepting computation."

It is easy to see that for every set A, P(A) $\subseteq$ PQUERY(A), NP(A) $\subseteq$ NPQUERY(A), and PSPACE $\subseteq$ PQUERY(A) $\subseteq$ NPQUERY(A) $\subseteq$ PSPACE(A). It is shown in [6] (also see [8]) that there exists a set B such that PQUERY(B) $\neq$ NPQUERY(B) $\neq$ PSPACE(B). Also, there exists a set C such that NP(C) is not included in PQUERY(C). The fact that there exists a set B such that PQUERY(B) $\neq$ NPQUERY(B) shows that Savitch's Theorem [25] does not apply to these classes even though it does relativize when there are no restrictions on the number of queries made in computations.

To obtain simple proofs of the main results of [6,11,20], Balcázar, Book, and Schöning developed the following facts. Let QBF be the set of "quantified Boolean formulas" so that QBF is $\leq^P_m$-complete for PSPACE [28].

Lemma 3.1. For every set A, PQUERY(A) = P(QBF $\oplus$ A) and NPQUERY(A) = NP(QBF $\oplus$ A).

Proof. Clearly, for every A, P(QBF $\oplus$ A) $\subseteq$ PQUERY(A), since QBF $\in$ PSPACE $\subseteq$ PQUERY(A), A $\in$ PQUERY(A), and P(PQUERY(A)) = PQUERY(A). To show the other inclusion, notice that for any machine M witnessing L $\in$ PQUERY(A), there is a deterministic transducer T that uses only polynomial work space and on input an instantaneous description I of M will compute the unique accepting, rejecting, or query configuration J that is reachable from I without querying the oracle. Let B = {<I, x> | I is an instantaneous description of M and x is a prefix of the unique query or accepting or rejecting configuration T(I)}. Clearly, B $\in$ PSPACE so that B $\leq^P_m$ QBF. Hence, a deterministic polynomial time-bounded transducer T' that uses binary search can simulate T by computing relative to QBF.

Since the number of oracle queries that M can make in any computation is bounded by a fixed polynomial, a deterministic polynomial time-bounded oracle machine can simulate M relative to A by using T' and making oracle queries to QBF $\oplus$ A. Hence, PQUERY(A) $\subseteq$ P(QBF $\oplus$ A).

The nondeterministic case is easier since a machine can simply guess the appropriate configuration. □

Many of the results about classes of the form PQUERY(A) or NPQUERY(A) are similar to results about classes of the form P(A) and NP(A). Placing a bound on the number of oracle queries that are allowed in a computation results in classes whose structure appears to be similar to that of classes specified by time-bounded machines, even though these classes are specified by space-bounded machines. Lemma 3.1 explains why this is the case.

Using Lemma 3.1 it is easy to prove the following fact.

Theorem 3.2

(a) NP = PSPACE if and only if for every set A, NP(A) = NPQUERY(A).

(b) P = PSPACE if and only if for every set A, P(A) = PQUERY(A).

Proof. The proof from right to left is trivial since NP(QBF) = PSPACE. If NP = PSPACE, then QBF $\in$ NP and NP = co-NP, so that for all A, NPQUERY(A) = NP(QBF $\oplus$ A) = NP(A). □

It is widely believed that P $\neq$ PSPACE and NP $\neq$ PSPACE. The results in Theorem 3.2 show that these relationships might be established by using the new relativizations: construct a set A such that P(A) $\neq$ PQUERY(A) or NP(A) $\neq$ NPQUERY(A).

The results in Theorem 3.2 illustrate the basic idea that to have a positive relativization theorem it appears necessary that the space of queries in one model must be polynomially equivalent to the space of queries in the other model. Here the results are very tight: deterministic models are compared and nondeterminstic models are compared. In both cases the limitations on the space of queries that is so generated depends only on the mode of operation: in the deterministic case, the limitations are the same because one need only consider the action of a P( ) operator; in the nondeterministic case, the limitations are the same because one need only consider the action of an NP( ) operator.

Now consider the problem PH =? PSPACE. Book and Wrathall considered the notion of iterating the NPQUERY( ) operator. This yields the following structure.

Let A be a set of strings. Define $\Sigma^{PQ}_0(A) = \Pi^{PQ}_0(A) = \Delta^{PQ}_0(A) = \Delta^{PQ}_1(A) =$ PQUERY(A), and for each integer $i \geq 0$, define $\Delta^{PQ}_{i+1}(A) = \text{PQUERY}(\Sigma^{PQ}_{i+1}(A))$, $\Sigma^{PQ}_{i+1}(A) = \text{NPQUERY}(\Sigma^{PQ}_i(A))$, and $\Pi^{PQ}_{i+1}(A) = \text{co-}\Sigma^{PQ}_{i+1}(A)$. The structure $\{(\Sigma^{PQ}_i(A), \Pi^{PQ}_i(A), \Delta^{PQ}_i(A))\}_{i\geq 0}$ is the <u>polynomial-query hierarchy relative to</u> A. Define $\text{PQH}(A) = \cup_{i\geq 0} \Sigma^{PQ}_i(A)$.

Using Lemma 3.1 as the initial step in an induction argument, it is not difficult to show the following fact.

Lemma 3.3. For every $i \geq 1$ and every set A, $\Sigma^{PQ}_i(A) = \Sigma^P_i(\text{QBF} \oplus A)$. For every set A, $\text{PQH}(A) = \text{PH}(\text{QBF} \oplus A)$.

It follows easily from Lemma 3.3 that the following positive relativization result holds.

Theorem 3.4. PH = PSPACE if and only if for every set A, PH(A) = PQH(A).

Thus, one might show that PH ≠ PSPACE by constructing a set A such that PH(A) ≠ PQH(A). Note that if B is a set that is complete for PSPACE with respect to any reducibility computed in polynomial time, then PH(B) = PSPACE(B). Also, Yao [33] has shown that there exists a set C such that PH(C) ≠ PSPACE(C). Hence, one cannot hope to solve the problem of PH =? PSPACE by using the standard models for relativizations.

Theorem 3.4 is another example of a positive relativization theorem which is based on the idea that the space of queries in one model is polynomially equivalent to the space of queries in the other model. In both cases the space of queries is generated by applying the PH( ) operator.

Theorem 3.4 will be sharpened in Section 6.

It should be noted that while Yao [33] has shown that there exists a set A such that PH(A) ≠ PSPACE(A), it does not appear that his proof can be modified to show that PH(A) ≠ PQH(A).

Section 4

SPACE CLASSES: LOG SPACE

One of the important open problems in complexity theory is that of DSPACE(S(n)) =? NSPACE(S(n)) for space bounds S(n). This problem may be viewed as an instance of the more general problem of determining the costs that are necessary to perform some nondeterministic task by using the deterministic mode of computation. The best result known today is that due to Savitch [25]: For all constructible space bounds S, $\text{NSPACE}(S(n)) \subseteq \text{DSPACE}(S(n)^2)$.

The case S(n) = log n has received a great deal of attention, partly because of the specific combinatorial problems that are complete for NSPACE(log n) with respect to reducibilites computable deterministically in log space. In addition, there are several results on this question that can be viewed as positive relativizations, and it is those that are of interest in the present context. The most basic is due to Rackoff and Seiferas [23].

Theorem 4.1. DSPACE(log n) = NSPACE(log n) if and only if for every set A, $DSPACE^A$(log n) = $NSPACE^A$(log n).

Proof. The proof from right to left is trivial.

Suppose that DSPACE(log n) = NSPACE(log n). Fix some set A, let L ϵ $NSPACE^A$(log n), and let M_1 be a nondeterministic oracle machine that operates within space bound c log n and is such that L(M_1, A) = L. Consider a nondeterministic machine M_2 that behaves in the following way. On input $x{*}y$, where $*$ is a new symbol that serves as a marker and y is a string of 0's and 1's, M_2 simulates a computation of M_1 on input x. However, in the simulated computation, when M_1 queries the oracle about a string z, M_2 views y as the initial segment of length c log $|x|$ of the characteristic sequence of an oracle set and gives the query answer "yes" or "no" according to whether or not y indicates that z is in the oracle set. The machine M_2 accepts $x{*}y$ if and only if some simulated computation of M_1 accepts x with y as the appropriate characteristic sequence. Since $|z| \leq c \log |x|$, M_2 need not consider those strings $x{*}y$ with $|y| > 2^{c \log |x|} = |x|^c$. Since M_2 needs use of at most c log $|x|$ work space, L(M_2) ϵ NSPACE(log n); by hypothesis, this means that L(M_2) ϵ DSPACE(log n), so that there is a deterministic machine M_3 that uses work space at most d log n, for some $d > 0$, and is such that L(M_3) = L(M_2). Now consider a deterministic oracle machine M_4 that on input x will simulate a computation of machine M_3 but now will use answers to oracle queries as if they were bits of the characteristic sequence of the oracle set. Clearly, M_4 need use only c log n work space and L(M_4, A) = L(M_1, A) = L. □

Thus, one might show that DSPACE(log n) ≠ NSPACE(log n) by constructing a set A such that $DSPACE^A$(log n) ≠ $NSPACE^A$(log n).

In the context of the theme of the present paper, it is important to note that in Theorem 4.1 the order of the length of the strings is the same in both the deterministic and nondeterministic modes of operation, and, up to polynomial equivalence, the size of the query space is the same in both modes.

The result of Rackoff and Seiferas is a special case of a result established earlier in unpublished doctoral dissertation of I. Simon [27].

Theorem 4.2. DSPACE(log n) = NSPACE(log n) if and only if for every space-constructible function S such that for all n, S(n) ≥ log n, and every set A, $DSPACE^A$(S(n)) = $NSPACE^A$(S(n)).

In the results considered above, the oracle machine is assumed to behave so that the space bound applies to the query tape as well as to the work tape. When the space bound is $o(n)$, then there exist examples of sets A such that A cannot be reduced to itself; e.g., there exist A such that A does not belong to $DSPACE^A(\log n)$. If one does not make that assumption, then the situation described in the above results changes.

Notation: Subscript 0 indicates that the space bound does not apply to the query tape.

It is clear that for every space bound S and every set A, $A \in DSPACE_0{}^A(S(n))$.

Consider a deterministic oracle machine that uses $O(\log n)$ work space. It is easy to see that for such a machine there is a fixed polynomial $p(n)$ such that every halting computation has at most $p(n)$ steps. Hence, the query tape may as well be bounded in length by $p(n)$ since the strings to be queried have length at most $p(n)$. On the other hand, nondeterministic oracle machines may run for much longer and hence have longer query strings. Thus, the sizes of the query spaces are not necessarily polynomially equivalent. This is what Ladner and Lynch [16] used to show the following fact.

Theorem 4.3. There exists a set A such that $DSPACE_0{}^A(\log n) \neq NSPACE_0{}^A(\log n)$.

There is a modification of the situation where the space bound does not apply to the query tape. This modification was introduced by Ruzzo, Simon, and Tompa [24].

Notation: The subscript RST indicates that while a machine may be nondeterministic, when it begins to write on the query tape it must operate deterministically until the query is made (at which time the query tape is erased).

Notice that a deterministic machine always satisfies the RST restriction whether or not the length of the query tape is bounded. Wilson [29] used this fact to strengthen Theorem 4.1.

Theorem 4.4. $DSPACE(\log n) = NSPACE(\log n)$ if and only if for every set A, $DSPACE_0{}^A(\log n) = NSPACE_{0,RST}{}^A(\log n)$.

Proof. The proof from right to left is trivial.

Suppose that $DSPACE(\log n) = NSPACE(\log n)$. Fix some set A, let $L \in NSPACE_{0,RST}{}^A(\log n)$, and let M_1 be a nondeterministic oracle machine that operates within space bound $c \log n$ and is such that $L(M_1, A) = L$, M_1 satisfies the RST restriction, and the query tape of M_1 is not bounded by the space bound $c \log n$. Consider a point in a computation of M_1 such that the machine is ready to write on the query tape. From that point until the next time that the oracle is queried, the computation is completely determined by the following information: the input string and the position of the read head on the input tape; the contents of the work tape and the position of the read/write head on the work tape; and the current state. Notice that all of this information except the contents of the input tape can be encoded in a string $\alpha \in \{0, 1\}^*$ of length $O(\log|x|)$ so that there are only $d|x|^k$ such strings, for some d and k which depend only on M_1; each such α may be considered to be an integer between 0 and $d|x|^k$. Let $A(M_1, |x|)$ denote the set of all such α. Notice that there is a log-space computable function f that from any x and any $\alpha \in A(M_1, |x|)$ will yield the unique string z such that in some computation of M_1 on x that reaches a configuration encoded by α, z will appear on the query tape the next time that M_1 is about to query the oracle.

Consider a machine M_2 that on input $x*y$, $|y| = d|x|^k$, will simulate a computation of M_1 on x but will not write on the query tape. When the simulated computation of M_1 reaches a configuration that is about to write on the query tape, say the configuration encoded by α, M_2 ignores the portion of the instructions that tell what is to be written on the query tape. When the simulated computation is about to query the oracle, M_2 uses the αth bit of y is as the oracle answer.

The machine M_2 is nondeterministic and uses $O(\log n)$ space, so by hypothesis, $L(M_2) \in DSPACE(\log n)$; let M_3 be a deterministic machine that witnesses this. Now consider a deterministic machine M_4 that on input x begins to simulate M_3. When M_3 wishes to read the αth bit of y, M_4 writes α on its work tape and computes the value of f on the pair (x, α). Then M_4 queries the oracle about the string $f(x, \alpha)$ and uses that answer as the αth bit of y. Clearly, M_4 is deterministic and uses $O(\log|x|)$ work space, and $L^A(M_4) = L^A(M_1) = L$. □

The model studied in Theorem 4.4 allows for more flexibility than that of Theorem 4.1 in constructing a set A that might have the property that $DSPACE_0{}^A(\log n) \neq NSPACE_{0,RST}{}^A(\log n)$, thus witnessing $DSPACE(\log n) \neq NSPACE(\log n)$.

The reader should notice that the proof of Theorem 4.4 is similar to that of Theorem 4.1 but, as Wilson notes, where the model studied in Theorem 4.1 has only short query strings, the model studied in Theorem 4.4 has query strings that can be computed using only a small amount of work space. What is important for the theme of the present paper is that with the RST model, the order of the size of the query strings is the same in both the deterministic and nondeterminstic modes of operation, and the computation of the query strings is carried out deterministically in both modes, so that up to polynomial equivalence the query spaces have the same size.

The interested reader should see Wilson [29] for further discussion of some of these points.

Wilson [30] also introduced a different restricted relativization of space-bounded classes using the notion of an "oracle stack" and used this notion to study how the classes in the NC hierarchy compare to DSPACE(log n). Taking still a different approach, Wilson [31] considered positive relativizations with respect to the classes in the NC hierarchy.

Section 5

TIME CLASSES: P =? NP

In this section a positive relativization of the P =? NP problem is developed.

Let M be an oracle machine. For any set D and any input string x, let $Q(M, D, x)$ be the set of strings y such that in some computation of M on input x relative to D, the oracle is queried about the string y. For any set D, any input string x, and any intesger $k > 0$, let $Q(M, D, x, k)$ be the set of $y \in Q(M, D, x)$ such that there is a computation of M on input x relative to D with the properties that M queries the oracle at least k times and, at the kth time, M queries the oracle about y.

If M is a deterministic oracle machine whose running time is bounded by the function T, then for any set D and any input x, $\|Q(M, D, x)\| \leq T(|x|)$. But for a nondeterministic oracle machine N whose running time is bounded by T, the only bound for $\|Q(N, D, x)\|$ is $2^{T(|x|)}$ unless some further restriction is placed on N. By nondeterministically "guessing" the query strings, N can nondeterministically search the set $Q(N, D, x)$ of queries in time $T(|x|)$ even though this set has size which may be as large as $O(2^{T(|x|)})$. Indeed, this is what happens in the proof by Baker, Gill, and Solovay [1] of the existence of a set A such that $P(A) \neq NP(A)$. The oracle property "$x \in L(A)$ if and only if <u>there exists</u> a string of length $|x|$ in A" plays a key role: for any set B, $L(B)$ can be recognized nondeterministically in linear time by simply guessing a query string of the same length as the input string and querying the oracle about that string's membership in B.

The phenomenon described in the last paragraph must be prevented if one wishes to have a positive relativization of a comparison between classes specified by deterministic and by nondeterministic time-bounded machines. For the case of the P =? NP problem, Book, Long, and Selman [9] defined the following restricted relativization.

For any set D, let $NP_B(D)$ denote the class of languages L such that $L \in NP(D)$ is witnessed by a machine M such that for some polynomial q and all x, $\|Q(M, D, x)\| \leq q(|x|)$.

Notice that if M is a deterministic oracle machine that runs in time $q(n)$ for some polynomial q, then for every D and every x, $\|Q(M, D, x)\| \leq q(|x|)$; this implies that $P(D) \subseteq NP_B(D)$. Thus, the restriction of $NP(D)$ to $NP_B(D)$ is a restricted relativization with the property that the size of the query space is polynomially equivalent to the size of the query space in $P(D)$.

The result (of Book, Long, and Selman) that will be shown here is that $P = NP$ if and only if for every set D, $P(D) = NP_B(D)$. Thus, if one wishes to show that $P \neq NP$ by using relativizations, it is sufficient to construct a set A with the property that

$P(A) \neq NP_B(A)$.

The main result of this section is an immediate consequence of the following lemma.

Lemma 5.1. For every set D, $NP_B(D) \subseteq P(D \oplus SAT)$, where SAT is the satisfiability problem or any other problem that is complete for NP with respect to $\leq^P_T$.

Sketch of the Proof. In order to prove Lemma 5.1, it is necessary to develop certain technical machinery. In particular, for any finite set S of strings over a given finite alphabet Σ, let $c(S)$ be an encoding of S as a single string; for example, if $S = \{s_1, \ldots, s_m\}$ and $*$ is a symbol not in Σ, then $c(S) = *s_1* \cdots *s_m*$.

Let D be any set and let $L \in NP_B(D)$. Then there are a nondeterministic oracle machine M_1 and polynomials $p(n)$ and $q(n)$ such that $L(M_1, D) = L$, M_1 runs in time bounded above by $p(n)$, and for every input string x, $\|Q(M_1, D, x)\| \leq q(|x|)$. There is no loss of generality by assuming that for each $n > 0$, M_1 has a unique accepting configuration for all strings of length n accepted by M_1 relative to any oracle set.

Define the function f as follows: For each input string x of M_1, each pair T_{YES} and T_{NO} of disjoint finite sets of strings, and each integer $k > 0$, string y is a value of $f(x, c(T_{YES}), c(T_{NO}), 0^k)$ if there is a computation C of M_1 on x such that (i) the kth time that C enters the QUERY state, y is the string on the query tape, and (ii) if w is any string queried during the first $k - 1$ times that C enters the QUERY state, then $w \in T_{YES} \cup T_{NO}$ and the answer used by C to the query about w is "yes" if and only if $w \in T_{YES}$.

It is clear that f is a partial multi-valued function that can be computed nondeterministically in polynomial time, and so the graph of f is in NP. If M_1 is computing relative to D and, for some x and k, $T_{YES} \subseteq D$ and $T_{NO} \subseteq \overline{D}$, then $f(x, c(T_{YES}), c(T_{NO}), 0^k) = Q(M, D, x, k)$ so that $f(x, c(T_{YES}), c(T_{NO}), 0^k) \subseteq Q(M, D, x)$. Hence, $f(x, c(T_{YES}), c(T_{NO}), 0^k)$ can be computed deterministically in polynomial time relative to any set that is complete for NP with respect to $\leq^P_T$ by using binary search. Recall that for $k = 1$, $T_{YES} \cup T_{NO} = \emptyset$. Hence, $\|\cup_{k>0} f(x, c(T_{YES}), c(T_{NO}), 0^k)\| \leq q(|x|)$, and it is clear that by using a recursive procedure relative to $D \oplus SAT$, the set $\cup_{k>0} f(x, c(T_{YES}), c(T_{NO}), 0^k)$ can be computed deterministically in polynomial time.

This means that there is a deterministic polynomial time-bounded oracle machine that relative to $D \oplus SAT$ first computes $\cup_{k>0} f(x, c(T_{YES}), c(T_{NO}), 0^k)$, and then simulates M_1 relative to D. Thus, L can be recognized deterministically in polynomial time relative to $D \oplus SAT$. □

Theorem 5.2

(a) $P = NP$ if and only if for every set D, $P(D) = NP_B(D)$.

(b) $NP = co\text{-}NP$ if and only if for every set D, $NP_B(D) = co\text{-}NP_B(D)$.

The proof of Theorem 5.2(a) given by Book, Long, and Selman is somewhat different from the sketch of the proof of Lemma 5.1 given here. In the original proof, the hypothesis that $P = NP$ is used to show that the function f described in the proof of Lemma 5.1 can be computed deterministically in polynomial time.

A result of Long and Selman [19] follows immediately from Theorem 5.2.

Corollary 5.3

(a) $P = NP$ if and only if for every tally set T, $P(T) = NP(T)$.

(b) $NP = co\text{-}NP$ if and only if for every tally set T, $NP(T) = co\text{-}NP(T)$.

How sharp is Theorem 5.2? That is, is it really necessary that the size of the sets $Q(M, D, x)$ be bounded by a polynomial, or can one obtain similar results with functions that majorize every polynomial? This has been answered recently by Zimand [34], who showed that the results of Theorems 5.2 are the best possible in the following sense.

Theorem 5.4. Let f be any function that is subexponential and that majorizes every polynomial. For every set A, let $NP_f(A) = \{L \mid$ there is a nondeterministic polynomial time-bounded oracle machine M that witnesses $L \in NP(A)$ and has the property that for all x, $\|Q(M, A, x)\| \le f(|x|)\}$. Then there is a set B such that $P(B) \ne NP_f(B)$.

There is a good deal of additional information that can be obtained from Lemma 5.1.

Theorem 5.5. For every $k > 1$ and every set $A \in \Delta^P_k$, $NP_B(A) \subseteq \Delta^P_k$. That is, for every $k > 1$, $NP_B(\Delta^P_k) = \Delta^P_k$.

<u>Proof</u>. By Lemma 5.1, $NP_B(A) \subseteq P(A \oplus SAT)$. By hypothesis, $A \in \Delta^P_k$, and since $k > 1$, $SAT \in \Delta^P_k$. Since Δ^P_k is closed under finite union, this shows that $A \oplus SAT \in \Delta^P_k$. Also, $\Delta^P_k = P(\Sigma^P_{k-1})$, so that $P(\Delta^P_k) = P(P(\Sigma^P_{k-1}) = \Delta^P_k$. Hence, $NP_B(A) \subseteq \Delta^P_k$. □

One interpretation of Theorem 5.5 given by Book, Long, and Selman is as follows. Let $\mathcal{C}(\,)$ be any operator defined by a class of oracle machines. The <u>least fixed point of</u> $\mathcal{C}(\,)$ is the smallest class $\mathcal{L}$ of languages such that $\emptyset \in \mathcal{L}$ and $\mathcal{C}(\mathcal{L}) = \mathcal{L}$. Now the least fixed point of the $P(\,)$ operator is the class P, and the least fixed point of each of the operators PSPACE( ), PQUERY( ), and NPQUERY( ) is PSPACE. The least fixed point of the NP( ) operator is the union PH of the polynomial-time hierarchy. Theorem 5.5 shows that the least fixed point of the $NP_B(\ )$ operator is Δ^P_2.

Since $\Delta^P_{k+1} = P(\Sigma^P_k) \subseteq NP_B(\Sigma^P_k) \subseteq NP_B(\Delta^P_{k+1})$, Theorem 5.5 yields the following characterization of classes of the form Δ^P_k for $k > 1$.

Corollary 5.6. For every $k > 0$, $NP_B(\Sigma^P_k) = P(\Sigma^P_k) = \Delta^P_{k+1}$.

If $A \in NP$, then $NP_B(A) \subseteq P(A \oplus SAT) = P(SAT) = \Delta^P_2$, so that Theorem 5.5 also allows the following conclusion.

Corollary 5.7. For every operator $\mathcal{C}(\ )$ defined by a class of oracle machines and every $k > 0$, let $\mathcal{C}^{(k)}(\ )$ denote the k-fold composition of the $\mathcal{C}(\ )$ operator. Then for every $k > 0$, $NP_B^{(k)}(NP) = NP_B^{(k+1)}(P) = \Delta^P_2$.

Corollary 5.6 yields interesting information about the polynomial-time hierarcy. For $k > 1$, if $B \in \Sigma^P_k - \Delta^P_k$, then B is not in $NP_B(\Sigma_{k-1}) = \Delta^P_k$. Thus, the definition of $NP_B(\ )$ shows that the following holds.

Corollary 5.8. For each $k > 1$, if $B \in \Sigma^P_k - \Delta^P_k$, then for every nondeterministic polynomial time-bounded oracle machine M and every set $A \in \Sigma^P_{k-1}$ such that $L(M, A) = B$, it is the case that for infinitely many input strings x, $\|Q(M, A, x)\|$ majorizes every polynomial.

Corollary 5.8 may be interpreted as saying that if M is a nondeterministic polynomial time-bounded oracle machine that witnesses $B \in \Sigma^P_k - \Delta^P_k$ as $B = L(M, A)$ for some $A \in \Sigma^P_k$, then M must search through nonpolynomial-size portions of the query space $Q(M, A, x)$ on its computations on infinitely many of the strings in B. Hence, the full power of nondeterminism is necessary to show that the polynomial-time hierarchy extends to some level $k \geq 2$ as $\Sigma^P_k \neq \Delta^P_k$.

Notice that if M witnesses $L \in NP_B(A)$, then for every x, $Q(M, A, x)$ is sparse, and so both $A \cap Q(M, A, x)$ and $\overline{A} \cap Q(M, A, x)$ are sparse. This is a stronger restriction than simply demanding that A be sparse. In fact, the set B constructed by Baker, Gill, and Solvay [1] with the property that $P(B) \neq NP(B)$ is a sparse set. In an exceptionally informative paper, Long [18] has investigated the similarities and differences between classes of the form NP(S), when S is a sparse set, and classes of the form $NP_B(A)$, for arbitrary sets A. Long has shown, for example, that there is a recursive sparse set S such that for all A, $NP(S) \neq NP_B(A)$, and that there is a recursive set A such that for all sparse sets $NP_B(A) \neq NP(S)$.

For every set D, let $NP_{PB}(D)$ denote the class of languages L such that $L \in NP(D)$ is witnessed by a machine M such that for some polynomial q and all x, $\|Q(M, D, x) \cap D\| \leq q(|x|)$.

The relativization $NP_{PB}(D)$ appears to be less restrictive than the relativization $NP_B(D)$ since the polynomial bound is placed only on those query strings that are actually in the oracle set. Clearly, for every sparse set S, $NP_{PB}(S) = NP(S)$, and for every set A, $NP_B(A) \subseteq NP_{PB}(A) \subseteq NP(A)$. Long established the following result that has the form of Corollary 5.6.

Theorem 5.9. For every $k > 0$, $NP_{PB}(\Sigma^P_k) = \Delta^P_{k+1}$.

Theorem 5.9 may be interpreted as saying that if M is a nondeterministic polynomial time-bounded oracle machine that witnesses $B \in \Sigma^P_k - \Delta^P_k$ as $B = L(M, A)$ for some $A \in \Sigma^P_k$, then M must search through nonpolynomial-size portions of the oracle set A on its computations on infinitely many of the strings in B. In particular, this means that the following holds.

Corollary 5.10. For each $k > 1$, if $A \in \Sigma^P_k - \Delta^P_k$, then for every sparse set $S \in \Sigma^P_{k-1}$, A is <u>not</u> in NP(S).

There are other results that are related to the concepts described in this section. Balcázar and Book [2] have considered the class of sparse sets S with the property that $NP(S) \subseteq P(S \oplus SAT)$ and have shown that every self-p-printable set is in this class but that there are sets in this class that are not self-p-printable. Balcázar, Book, and Schöning [5] have studied the class of sets A such that $NP(A) \subseteq P(A \oplus SAT)$ in the context of the notions of "highness" and "lowness." Hemachandra [13] has used techniques similar to those used in the proof of Lemma 5.1 to show that the strong exponential hierarchy collapses.

Book, Long, and Selman [10] extended techniques introduced by Selman, Xu, and Book [26] to obtain additional positive relativizations of the P =? NP $\cap$ co-NP problem. These techniques are referred to as "qualitative" since they restrict the type of query configurations that can be obtained, whereas restrictions yielding classes of the form $NP_B(A)$ are referred to as "quantitative" since they restrict the quantity of query strings that can be generated. The restricted relativizations based on qualitative techniques seem to offer less possibility of application than those stemming from quantitaive techniques.

Recall that the relationship between NP and DEXT = $\{L(M) \mid M$ runs within time 2^{cn}, for some $c > 0\}$ is not known (except for the fact that NP $\neq$ DEXT). Long and Selman [19] established a positive relativization of the question NP $\subset$? DEXT that can be strengthened in the following way.

Proposition 5.11

(a) NP ⊂ DEXT if and only if for every self-p-printable set S, NP(S) ⊂ DEXT(S).

(b) PSPACE ⊂ DEXT if and only if for every self-p-printable set S, PSPACE(S) ⊂ DEXT(S).

Section 6

THE POLYNOMIAL-TIME HIERARCHY

In Section 5, the role of sparse sets in the potential construction of different levels in the polynomial-time hierarchy was introduced. It was noted that this role was very restricted, in the sense that a sparse set S in Σ^P_k does not encode sufficient information to let $NP(S) = \Sigma^P_{k+1}$ unless $\Sigma^P_{k+1} = \Delta^P_{k+1}$. In fact, if we consider the polynomial- time hierarchy relative to sparse oracle sets, much stronger conclusions can be reached.

Consider the open question of whether the polynomial-time hierarchy extends to infinitely many levels, that is, whether for every integer $k > 0$, $\Sigma^P_k \neq \Pi^P_k$. If not, then the polynomial-time hierarchy collapses, that is, there exists some k such that $\Sigma^P_k = \Pi^P_k$, so that $PH = \Sigma^P_k$.

Theorem 6.1. The following are equivalent:

(a) the polynomial-time hierarchy collapses;

(b) there exists a sparse set S such that the polynomial-time hierarchy relative to S collapses;

(c) for every sparse set S, the polynomial-time hierarchy relative to S collapses.

Theorem 6.1 can be interpreted in the following way.

Corollary 6.2

(a) If there exists a sparse set S such the polynomial-time hierarchy relative to S is infinite, then the (unrelativized) polynomial-time hierarchy is infinite.

(b) If there exists a sparse set S such the polynomial-time hierarchy relative to S collapses, then the (unrelativized) polynomial-time hierarchy collapses.

Thus, to determine whether the polynomial-time hierarchy is infinite by using relativizations, it is sufficient to solve this problem for the hierarchy relativized to an arbitrary sparse set. It is not the case that the polynomial-time hierarchy relative to one sparse set extends to infinitely many levels while collapsing relative to a different sparse set.

In the form stated above, Theorem 6.1 is due to Balcázar, Book, and Schöning [4]. However, the equivalence of parts (a) and (b) of Theorem 6.1 was first observed by

Karp and Lipton [15], though in quite a different form. Furthermore, Long and Selman [19] established the equivalence of parts (a) and (c) of Theorem 6.1.

Notice that the equivalence of parts (a) and (c) of Theorem 6.1 has the form of a positive relativization. But taking the negation of parts (a) and (b) of Theorem 6.1 yields the following statement: The polynomial-time hierachy does not collapse if and only if for every sparse set S, the polynomial-time hierarchy relative to S does not collapse. This statement might be considered to be a "negative relativization." Taken together, a positive relativization and a negative relativization give rise to a "relativization principle."

Balcázar, Book, and Schöning [4] also considered other questions about the polynomial-time hierarchy, such as its relation to classes such as PSPACE, the probabilistic polynomial-time class PP, and the class D*P (= P(PP)). In each case there is a result that has the form of Theorem 6.1. These appear to be the first set of results of the following form:

(a) condition C holds if and only if for every sparse set, condition C holds relative to that sparse set;

(b) condition C does not hold if and only if for every sparse set, condition C does not hold relative to that sparse set.

In elementary recursive function thoery, a certain "relativization principle" holds: An assertion is true in the unrelativized case if and only if it is true relative to an arbitrary oracle set (or, more precisely, its proof can be extended to a proof of the corresponding assertion realtivized to an arbitrary oracle set). But Baker, Gill, and Solovay [1] essentially proved that such a relativization principle does not hold in general for complexity theory. Theorem 6.1 (and the other results having the same form in [4]) can be interpreted as showing that for certain questions about the polynomial-time hierarchy, restricting the domain of oracle sets to the class of sparse sets yields a relativization principle for these questions. It is of interest to see whether this restricted relativization principle has wider applicability.

Turning now to the proof of Theorem 6.1, notice that part (a) implies part (b) since the empty set is sparse. Also, part (c) implies both part (a) and part (b). Thus, it is sufficient to show that part (a) implies part (c) and that part (b) implies part (a).

<u>Sketch of the Proof that (a) implies (c)</u>. Suppose that the polynomial-time hierarchy collapses. Let k be the least integer such that $\Sigma^P_k = \Pi^P_k$, so that $PH = \Sigma^P_k$. Let S be sparse and let $A \in \Sigma^P_{k+2}(S)$. Let M be a Σ^P_{k+2} oracle machine that witnesses $A \in \Sigma^P_{k+2}(S)$. Let $B = \{\langle x, T\rangle \mid T$ is a finite table and $x \in L(M, T)\}$, so that $B \in \Sigma^P_{k+2} = \Sigma^P_k$ (since $PH = \Sigma^P_k$). Let $N(S) = \{\langle T, 0^n\rangle \mid T$ is a finite table, $n \geq 0$, and $T^{\leq n} = S^{\leq n}\}$. Then $\langle T, 0^n\rangle \in N(S)$ if and only if $(\forall u)_{\leq n}$ [$u \in T$ if and only if $u \in S$]. This implies that $N(S) \in \Pi^P_1(S)$.

Since S is sparse, there is a polynomial r such that for all n, $\|S_{\leq n}\| \leq r(n)$. Since M is a Σ^P_{k+2} oracle machine, there is a polynomial q such that for every n, any computation of M on any input of length n queries the oracle about strings of length at most $q(n)$. Let $p(n) = r(q(n))$.

Consider membership in A: $x \in A$ if and only if there exists a table T such that $\|T\| \leq p(|x|)$ & $\langle T, 0^{q(|x|)}\rangle \in N(S)$ & $\langle x, T\rangle \in B$. Since $N(S) \in \Pi^P{}_1(S)$, this yields $A \in \Sigma^P{}_2(S \oplus B)$. In addition, $x \in A$ if and only if for all tables T such that $\|T\| \leq p(|x|)$, if $\langle T, 0^{q(|x|)}\rangle \in N(S)$, then $\langle x, T\rangle \in B$. Thus, $N(S)$ being in $\Pi^P{}_1(S)$ implies $A \in \Pi^P{}_2(S \oplus B)$. Hence, $A \in \Pi^P{}_2(S \oplus B) \cap \Sigma^P{}_2(S \oplus B)$. Since $B \in \Sigma^P{}_k$, this means that $A \in \Sigma^P{}_{k+2}(S) \cap \Pi^P{}_{k+2}(S) \subseteq \Pi^P{}_{k+2}(S)$. Thus, $\Sigma^P{}_{k+2}(S) \subseteq \Pi^P{}_{k+2}(S)$ so that $PH(S) = \Sigma^P{}_{k+2}(S)$, that is, the polynomial-time hierarchy relative to S collapses to $\Sigma^P{}_{k+2}(S)$. □

The first proof of the above fact was due to Long and Selman [19], who proved a tighter result: If the hierarchy collapsed to level k, then the hierarchy relativized to a sparse set also collapsed to level k. The proof given here is similar to that of Balcázar, Book, and Schöning [4], who also proved the tighter version.

As noted above, the equivalence of parts (a) and (c) of Theorem 6.1 has the form of a positive realtivization. In addition, the proof given above follows the form of several of the proofs in previous sections.

To prove that part (b) implies part (a), the following notion is very useful.

A set A is <u>self-reducible</u> if there exists a deterministic polynomial time-bounded oracle machine M such that (i) on inputs of size n, M queries the oracle only about strings of length at most $n - 1$ and (ii) $L(M, A) = A$.

<u>Sketch of the Proof that (b) implies (a)</u>. Let S be a sparse set such that for some $k \geq 0$, $\Sigma^P{}_k(S) = \Pi^P{}_k(S)$ so that $PH(S) = \Sigma^P{}_k(S)$. Let A be a set that is $\leq^P{}_m$-complete for $\Sigma^P{}_{k+2}$ and that is self-reducible. Clearly the sets described by Wrathall [32] have this property. It is sufficient to prove that $A \in \Pi^P{}_{k+2}$, since this implies that $\Sigma^P{}_{k+2} \subseteq \Pi^P{}_{k+2}$, so that $PH = \Sigma^P{}_{k+2}$.

Notice that $A \in \Sigma^P{}_{k+2} \subseteq PH \subseteq PH(S) = \Sigma^P{}_k(S)$. Using the characterizations developed by Stockmeyer [28] and Wrathall [32], recall that there is a polynomial p and a deterministic polynomial time-bounded oracle machine M_1 such that for all x, $x \in A$ if and only if $(\exists y_1)_p(\forall y_2)_p \cdots (Q_k y_k)_p\langle x, y_1, \ldots, y_k\rangle \in L(M_1, S)$, where Q_k is a universal quantifier if k is even and Q_k is an existential quantifier if k is odd. Thus, there is a polynomial q such that $x \in A$ if and only if $(\exists y_1)_p(\forall y_2)_p \cdots (Q_k y_k)_p\langle x, y_1, \ldots, y_k\rangle \in L(M_1, S^{\leq q(|x|)})$.

Recall that S is sparse. Thus, there is a polynomial r such that for each $n \geq 0$, $\|S^{\leq n}\| \leq r(n)$. Let $B = \{\langle x, T\rangle \mid T$ is a finite table and $(\exists y_1)_p(\forall y_2)_p \cdots (Q_k y_k)_p\langle x, y_1, \ldots, y_k\rangle \in L(M_1, T)\}$. Since M_1 is a deterministic polynomial time-bounded oracle machine, it is clear that B is in Σ^P_k.

Recall that A is self-reducible. Let M_2 be a self-reducing machine for A. Consider the following characterization of membership in A: $x \in A$ if and only if for all tables T of size at most $r(q(|x|))$, $[(\forall u)_q[u \in L(M_2, \{y \mid \langle y, T\rangle \in B\})$ if and only if $u \in \{z \mid \langle z, T\rangle \in B\}]$ implies $\langle x, T\rangle \in B]$. All quantifiers are polynomially bounded and this predicate has the form $(\forall T)[(\forall u)R^B(u, T)$ implies $S^B(x, T)]$, where $R^B(u, T)$ represents the predicate "$u \in L(M_2, \{y \mid \langle y, T\rangle \in B\})$ if and only if $u \in \{z \mid \langle z, T\rangle \in B\}$" and $S^B(x, T)$ represents the predicate "$\langle x, T\rangle \in B$." Since $B \in \Sigma^P_k$, this characterization shows that A is in Π^P_{k+2}. □

The proof that part (b) implies part (a) is related to the proof given by Balcázar, Book, and Schöning [4]. Karp and Lipton [15] used self-reducible complete sets in this way in their proof that if NP $\subseteq$ P/poly, then the polynomial-time hierarchy collapses.

Do any of the problems considered in Sections 3-5 have relativization principles? This is one of the most interesting open problems in this investigation.

It should be noted that Plaisted [21] studied some of the problems about the polynomial-time hierarchy from a somewhat different viewpoint. While considering the characteristic sequences of oracle sets, he studied "slowly growing" oracles and "slowly utilized" oracles. While Plaisted [22,23] applied these notions in classifying the complexity of certain arithmetic problems, it does not appear that anyone has made a formal comparison of his techniques to those used in the present investigation.

References

1. T. Baker, J. Gill, and R. Solovay, Relativizations of the P =? NP problem, SIAM J. Comput. 4 (1975), 431-442.

2. J. Balcázar and R. Book, Sets with small generalized Kolmogorov complexity, Acta Inform., to appear. Also see J. Balcázar and R. Book, On generalized Kolmogorov complexity, STACS-86, Lecture Notes in Computer Science 210 (1986), 334-440.

3. J. Balcázar, R. Book, and U. Schöning, On bounded query machines, Theoret. Comput. Sci. 40 (1985), 237-243.

4. J. Balcázar, R. Book, and U. Schöning, The polynomial-time hierarchy and sparse oracles, J. Assoc. Comput. Mach. 33 (1986), 603-617.

5. J. Balcázar, R. Book, and U. Schöning, Sparse sets, lowness, and highness, SIAM J. Computing 15 (1986), 739-747.

6. R. Book, Bounded query machines: On NP and PSPACE, Theoret. Comput. Sci. 15 (1981), 27-39.

7. R. Book, Relativizations of complexity classes, in (G. Wechsung, ed.), Frege Conference 1984 - Proc. of the International Conference, Akademie-Verlag, Berlin, 1984, 296-302.

8. R. Book, Separating relativized complexity classes, in (D. Kueker, E.G.K. Lopez-Escobar, and C. Smith, eds.), Mathematical Logic and Theoretical Computer Science, Lecture Notes in Pure and Applied Mathematics, Marcel Dekker, to appear.

9. R. Book, T. Long, and A. Selman, Quantitative relativizations of complexity classes, SIAM J. Comput. 13 (1984), 461-487.

10. R. Book, T. Long, and A. Selman, Qualitative relativizations of complexity classes, J. Comput. Syst. Sci. 30 (1985), 395-413.

11. R. Book and C. Wrathall, Bounded query machines: On NP( ) and NPQUERY( ), Theoret. Comput. Sci. 15 (1981), 41-50.

12. S. Cook, The complexity of theorem-proving procedures, Proc. 3rd ACM Symp. Theory of Computing, 1971, 151-158.

13. L. Hemachandra, The sky is falling: the strong exponential hierarchy collapses, Technical Report TR 86-77, Dept. of Computer Science, Cornell University, 1986.

14. R. Karp, Reducibility among combinatorial problems, in R.E. Miller and J.W. Thatcher (eds.), Complexity of Computer Computation, Plenum Press, 1972, 85-104.

15. R. Karp and R. Lipton, Some connections between nonuniform and uniform complexity classes, Proc. 12th ACM Symp. Theory of Computing, 1980, 302-309. An extended version has appeared as: Turing machines that take advice, L'Enseignement Mathématique, 2nd Series 28 (1982), 191-209.

16. R. Ladner and N. Lynch, Relativization of questions about log space computability, Math. Syst. Theory 10 (1976), 19-32.

17. R. Ladner, N. Lynch, and A. Selman, A comparison of polynomial-time reducibilities, Theoret. Comput. Sci. 1 (1975), 103-123.

18. T. Long, On restricting the size of oracles compared with restricting access to oracles, SIAM J. Comput. 14 (1985), 585-597.

19. T. Long and A. Selman, Relativizing complexity classes with sparse oracles, J. Assoc. Comput. Mach. 33 (1986), 618-627.

20. D. Plaisted, Restricted oracles, Technical Report UIUCDCS-R-79-995, Dept. of Computer Science, Univ. of Illinois at Urbana-Champaign, October 1979.

21. D. Plaisted, New NP-hard and NP-complete polynomial and integer divisibility problems, Theoret. Comput. Sci. 31 (1984), 125-138.

22. D. Plaisted, Complete divisibility problems for slowly untilized oracles, Theoret. Comput. Sci. 35 (1985), 245-260.

23. C. Rackoff and J. Seiferas, Limitations on separating nondeterministic complexity classes, SIAM J. Comput. 10 (1981), 742-745.

24. W. Ruzzo, J. Simon, and M. Tompa, Space-bounded hierarchies and probabilistic computation, J. Comput. Syst. Sci. 28 (1984), 216-230.

25. W. Savitch, Relationships between nondeterministic and deterministic space complexities, J. Comput. Syst. Sci. 4 (1970), 177-192.

26. A. Selman, M.-R. Xu, and R. Book, Positive relativizations of complexity classes, SIAM J. Comput. 12 (1983), 565-579.

27. I. Simon, On Some Subrecursive Reducibilities, Ph.D. dissertation, Stanford University, 1977.

28. L. Stockmeyer, The polynomial time hierarchy, Theoret. Comput. Sci. 3 (1976), 1-22.

29. C. Wilson, Relativized Circuit Size and Depth, Ph.D. dissertation, University of Toronto, 1985.

30. C. Wilson, A measure of relativized space which is faithful with respect to de submitted for publication.

31. C. Wilson, Relativized NC, submitted for publication.

32. C. Wrathall, Complete sets and the polynoial-time hierarchy, Theoret. Comput. Sci. 3 (1976), 23-33.

33. A. Yao, Separating the polynomial-time hierarchy by oracles, Proc. 26th IEEE Symp. Foundations of Computer Science, 1985, 1-10.

34. M. Zimand, On relativizations with restricted number of accesses to the oracle set, Math. Syst. Theory, to appear.

Natural Semantics

G. Kahn
INRIA, Sophia–Antipolis
06565 Valbonne CEDEX, FRANCE

Abstract

During the past few years, many researchers have begun to present semantic specifications in a style that has been strongly advocated by Plotkin in [19]. The purpose of this paper is to introduce in an intuitive manner the essential ideas of the method that we call now Natural Semantics, together with its connections to ideas in logic and computing. Natural Semantics is of interest *per se* and because it is used as a semantics specification formalism for an interactive computer system that we are currently building at INRIA.

1. Introduction

During the past few years, many researchers have begun to present semantic specifications in a style that has been strongly advocated by Plotkin in [19]. The purpose of this paper is to introduce in an intuitive manner the essential ideas of the method that we call now Natural Semantics, together with its connections to ideas in logic and computing. Natural Semantics is of interest *per se* and because it is used as a semantics specification formalism for an interactive computer system that we are currently building at INRIA.

1.1. *Aim of work*

It is interesting and illuminating to present several aspects of the semantics of programming languages in a unified manner: static semantics, dynamic semantics, and translation. It has been shown in earlier work [10]that it is possible to use denotational semantics to give a satisfactory account of all these semantic aspects. What is more, several researchers, following [16]process the resulting formal descriptions to obtain actual type-checkers, interpreters, and translators. One may wonder why it should be necessary to investigate yet another semantics specification formalism.

Several difficulties come up in a purely denotational definition.

- Coding up static semantics as semantics in a domain of types turns out to be a subterfuge. Since type-checking aims at characterizing legal programs, the domain of type values has to include one (or several) values for "wrong type". In the presence of overloading, an identifier may *a priori* have several possible types. Should the overloading resolution algorithm be part of the formal specification? As discussed in [9], writing static semantics in this way is more akin to *programming* in a functional language than to writing a formal specification.
- A similar lack of abstraction and expressive uneasiness is felt when specifying translations. The need to have an extra parameter just for the purpose of generating new symbols in a denotational way and the lack of an elegant way to do backpatching are examples. A consequence is that specifying translators is again considered a programming activity and proving properties of translations is made considerably harder.
- Denotational semantics is of course much better suited to express dynamic semantics. Two techniques of denotational semantics, known as currying and continuations, are notationally difficult for most language designers, but following the ideas of Mosses [16]this difficulty could be overcome. In the case of parallelism and non-determinism, denotational semantics becomes substantially more difficult. Somehow an operational definition is easier to understand and more convincing. The semantic definitions of many new proposals for parallel languages involve axiomatizing atomic transitions, or transactions, and are easily expressed in Natural Semantics. But this is not to say that Natural Semantics should be identified with operational semantics.

This research is partially supported under ESPRIT, Project 348.

The general idea of this sort of semantic definition is to provide axioms and inference rules that characterize the various semantic predicates to be defined on an expression E. To paraphrase Prawitz [18], "the inferences are broken down into atomic steps in such a way that each step involves only one language construct".

For example in static semantics, one wants to state that expression E has type τ in the environment ρ. Hence one axiomatizes

$$\rho \vdash \text{E} : \tau$$

where the environment ρ is a collection of assumptions on the types of the variables of E. To specify a translation from language L_1 to language L_2, on gives rules of the form

$$\rho \vdash \text{E}_1 \rightarrow \text{E}_2$$

where ρ records assumptions on identifiers, expression E_1 is in the source language and E_2 is in the target language. In dynamic semantics, there is a much greater variance in style, depending on the properties of the language to describe. In the simplest languages, it is sufficient to express that the evaluation of expression E in state s_1 yields a new state s_2. This predicate is written

$$s_1 \vdash \text{E} \Rightarrow s_2$$

where s_1 records the values of the identifiers involved in E.

A semantic definition is a list of axioms and inference rules that define one of the predicates above. In other words, a semantic definition is identified with a logic, and reasoning with the language is proving theorems within that logic. Computing (e.g. type-checking, intepreting) is seen as a way to solve equations. For example, given state s_1 and program E, is there a state s_2 s.t. $s_1 \vdash \text{E} \Rightarrow s_2$ holds? Or given an initial type-environment ρ_0, is it possible for expression E to be assigned a type τ such that $\rho_0 \vdash \text{E} : \tau$ holds?

This formulation suggests several remarks.

- Other kinds of equations could be of interest. For example, given E and τ, does there exist some ρ such that $\rho \vdash \text{E} : \tau$? This is a type-inference problem.
- Since the presentation is inherently relational, rather than functional, non-deterministic computation will be the general case. Similarly, overloading in type-checking will arise naturally.
- Since several logics will be defined on the same object language (e.g one assigning types to programs and another assigning values to them), it will be interesting to examine relationships between these logics.

Now there are many ways of presenting a logic. In our experiments, on the left of the turnstile symbol $\vdash$ we always have a collection of assumptions on variables, not arbitrary formulae. This is most reminiscent of Natural Deduction. Rules for dealing with block structure, type-checking, or evaluating applications are very close to certain rules in Natural Deduction, except for the fact that our collections of assumptions or environments are not necessarily sets. Hence the name Natural Semantics was coined, rather than the more restrictive and less informative "Structural Operational Semantics" of Plotkin.

1.2. *Comparison with syntax*

The way we look at Natural Semantics is proof-theoretic: we think of axioms and rules of inferences as a way of generating new facts from existing facts. Inference rules allow the construction of new proof-trees from existing proof-trees. In this regard, our view is very close to the traditional use of context-free grammars in computer science.

A grammar is presented as a collection of grammar rules. The rules define legal parse trees, and as a consequence legal sentences. Analogously, axioms and inference rules serve in defining legal proof-trees, and hence the facts that may be derived from axioms using inference rules. A grammar may be used either as a generator or as a recognizer. There exist general algorithms to find a parse tree for a given sentence. Likewise, a semantic description may be thought of in two ways: as a generating facts or as a description of possible computations. Corresponding to the general recognizers of context-free grammars, we have the general interpreters of semantic descriptions. Grammars may be ambiguous, and this often considered a nuisance. But we *want* to model nondeterministic computations, and in a logical system it is generally the case that there are several proofs of the same fact.

There is however a major technical difference between grammars and logical systems. In a grammar, the non-terminals stand for sets of words. In an inference rule, or rule scheme, the variables stand for individuals (terms), and all occurrences of the same variable in the rule should be substituted with the same term.

2. The formalism

2.1. *Rules*

A semantic definition is an *unordered* collection of rules. A rule has basically two parts, a numerator and a denominator. *Variables* may occur both in the numerator and the denominator of a rule. These variables allow a rule to be instantiated. Usually, typographical conventions are used to indicate that the variables in a rule must have a certain type.

The numerator of a rule is again an *unordered* collection of formulae, the *premises* of the rule. Intuitively, if all premises hold, then the denominator, a single formula, holds. More formally, from proof-trees yielding the premises, we can obtain a new proof-tree yielding the denominator, or conclusion, of the rule.

2.2. *Sequents and conditions*

Formulae are divided in two kinds: *sequents* and *conditions*. The conclusion of a rule is necessarily a sequent. On the numerator, sequents are distinguished from conditions, that are placed slightly to the right of the inference rule. Conditions convey in general a restriction on the applicability of the rule: a variable may not occur free somewhere, a value must satisfy some predicate, some relation must hold between two variables. As boolean predicates, conditions are built with the help of logical connectives from atomic conditions. One may wish to axiomatize atomic conditions, for example in a separate set of rules.

A sequent has two parts, an *antecedent* (on the left) and a *consequent* (on the right), and we use the turnstile symbol $\vdash$ to separate these parts. The consequent is a predicate. Predicates come in several forms, indicated by various infix symbols. These infix symbols carry no reserved meaning, they just help us in memorizing what is being defined. The first argument of the consequent is called the *subject* of the sequent. Naturally, the subject of a rule is the subject of its conclusion.

A rule that contains no sequent on the numerator is called an *axiom*. Thus an axiom may be constrained by a condition.

2.3. *Judgements*

In a single semantic definition, sequents may have several forms depending on the syntactic nature of their subject. For example, in a typical Algol-like language, there are declarations, statements and expressions. The static semantics will contain sequents of the form

$$\rho_1 \vdash \text{DECL} : \rho_2$$

for the elaboration of declarations, of the form

$$\rho \vdash \text{STM}$$

to assert that statements are well typed, and also of the form

$$\rho \vdash \text{EXP} : \tau$$

to state that expression EXP has type τ. The various forms of sequents participating in the same semantic definition are called *judgements*. One reason for the elegance of the formalism is that several judgements are used without being given explicit names. In programming, overloading is used to the same end. Note that in our context like in programming, abuse of overloading leads to obscurity.

2.4. *Rule sets*

Some structure must be introduced in a collection of rules, if only to separate different semantic concerns. For example, in static semantics, one wishes to distinguish structural rules of consistency from the management of scope and the properties of type values. To this end, rules may be grouped into sets, with a given *name*. Sets of rules collect together rules or, recursively, rule sets. When one wishes to refer to a sequent that is axiomatized in a set of rules other than the textually enclosing one, the name of the set is indicated as a superscript of the sequent's turnstile.

2.5. *Abstract syntax, Use clauses*

Semantics tells us facts about the constructs of a language. These constructs taken together form the abstract syntax of the language, technically an order-sorted algebra. Intuitively, each construct has arguments and results belonging to syntactic categories, and some syntactic categories may be included in others. We indicate that language L is concerned with a definition by the declaration use L. In a translation, two languages are involved and we have to import two algebras. Other objects, such as environments or stores are often elements of algebras, and we will naturally modularize our definition by importing these algebras as well. When analyzing mechanically semantic rules, we will identify the various abstract syntax constructors. Ambiguity may arise if two algebras use the same name for an operator. Most of the time the context will be sufficient to resolve the ambiguity, but we may have to specify what operator we really mean.

Abstract syntax terms may occur in rules. They should of course be valid terms w.r.t their abstract syntax. Every such term is typed with a syntactic category (such as L.*expression*, or L.*statement*, or L.*declaration*). A language L includes all of its syntactic categories, and it is possible for two languages to share a given syntactic category. For example PASCAL and MODULA can share the category *expression*.

With an abstract syntax, we also import conventions on how to write abstract syntax trees in a linear fashion. Except where the notation is too ambiguous, we use systematically this readable way of denoting terms. For example, we will write

$$\text{while } \textsc{cond} \text{ do } \textsc{stm}$$

rather than use the general notation for terms

$$\text{while}(\textsc{cond}, \textsc{stm})$$

but the reader should be aware that the subject of a rule is never a string but a tree.

2.6. *Assigning types to rules*

The scope of variables is limited to the rule where they appear. Nevertheless, it is necessary to follow certain naming conventions to make a definition readable. For example, we want to assert that variables called ρ, possibly with indices or diacritical signs, are environments. For this we allow variable declarations. The scope of such declarations is the set of rules where they appear. It is not necessary to declare in this way all variables, because often their type may be inferred. In particular, it is practically never useful to declare variables that stand for abstract syntax fragments because these variables occur in the subject of rules. There, a language constructor dictates their type. Declarations and abstract syntax definitions serve then in typing sequents. It might also be wise to declare judgements, rather than merely infer how many judgement forms are involved in a definition.

2.7. *Typographical conventions*

In accordance with standard mathematical practice, it is convenient to associate different fonts to different types of variables. But it would be extremely painful to indicate these font changes as we enter the semantic definitions in a computer, with a keyboard that has a limited character set. Instead, we associate font information to types, and our type-checker is set-up to generate a text that is fully decorated with font changes. This text is then processed by TEX and either printed or examined on a high resolution display. It is clear that a sober use of fonts enhances the readability of semantic definitions.

2.8. *General strategy for execution*

As mentioned earlier, we want to use a computer to solve various kinds of equations on sequents. Typically, our unknown will be type values, states or generated code. But environments, or program fragments may also be unknown. To turn semantic definitions into executable code, there are probably many approaches. One is to compile rules into Prolog code, taking advantage of the similarity of Prolog variables and variables in inference rules. Roughly speaking, the conclusion of a rule maps to a clause head, and the premises to the clause body. Distinct judgements map to distinct Prolog predicates. Conditions, although written to the right of rules, are placed ahead of the rule body.

An equation is turned into a Prolog goal. Since pure Prolog attacks goals in a left to right manner, proofs of premises will also be attempted from left to right. This is not always reasonable, so that we need to use a version of Prolog that may postpone attacking goals until certain variables are instantiated. Conditions should be evaluated as soon as possible, to avoid building useless proof-trees. In our experiments, we have used Mu-Prolog [17]with success to that end.

2.9. *Actions*

It is useful to attach actions to rules, in a manner that is reminiscent of the way actions are associated to grammar-rules in YACC. Actions are triggered only after an inference rule is considered applicable. An action needs to access the rule's variable bindings, but it cannot under any circumstance interfere with the deduction process. Typically, actions are used to trace inference rules, to emit messages, to perform a variety of side effects. It is important to understand that searching for a proof may involve backtracking, so that if an inference has been used in a computation at some point, it does not necessarily participate in the final proof.

In terms of style, actions should be used with parsimony. For example, when specifying a translation, it is mandatory to *axiomatize it* rather than have actions generate output code. On the other hand, in the context of type-checking, it is more appropriate to have actions filter error messages, rather than introduce strange type values to handle various erroneous situations.

A significant use of actions is in debugging inference rules. We want to follow what inference rules are applied, but also *where* they are applied. In other words, when a rule is used we want to know where the subject of the rule is, with respect to the subject of the initial equation. When executing a dynamic semantics specification, we follow execution very precisely in this way.

To solve this problem, we imagine that each variable that stands for an abstract syntax tree is in fact a pair made of tree and a tree address. Our rule compiler then keeps track of the tree-offsets of the variables introduced in the subject of the rule, relative to the tree address of the subject. Within actions, the user can refer to the tree-address of the rule's subject via a standard variable.

3. A small functional language

As an example, we are going to write semantic specifications in Natural Semantics for a very small functional language. This language, called Mini-ML, is a simple typed λ-calculus with constants, products, conditionals, and recursive function definitions. Of ML [11], it retains call-by-value. The language is strongly typed, but there are no type declarations, types are inferred from the context. It is possible to define functions that work uniformly on arguments of many types: one construct introduces ML-polymorphism.

The dynamic semantics of ML is fairly simple to describe. The only difficulty resides in handling elegantly mutually recursive definitions. To illustrate compilation, we use as target code the the Categorical Abstract Machine (CAM) of Cousineau and Curien [4]. It is interesting to see how convenient Natural Semantics is to specify such a translation and some of its properties. ML typechecking is the object of numerous discussions in the literature, e.g. [6]. Using an *inference system* to describe typing goes back at least to Curry [5]. Reynolds [20]is a remarkable presentation in this spirit.

We begin with an intuitive presentation of the language.

3.1. *Sample programs*

To illustrate mini-ML, we introduce several examples in *concrete* syntax. First of course is how to write the factorial function:

$$\begin{array}{l}\mathbf{letrec}\, \mathit{fact} = \lambda x.\,\mathbf{if}\ x = 0\ \mathbf{then}\ 1\ \mathbf{else}\ x * \mathit{fact}(x-1)\\ \mathbf{in}\, \mathit{fact}\ 4\end{array}$$

Next, we define and use the higher order function *twice*:

$$\begin{array}{l}\mathbf{let}\ \mathit{succ} = \lambda x.x+1\\ \mathbf{in}\ \mathbf{let}\ \mathit{twice} = \lambda f.\lambda x.(f\ (f\ x))\\ \quad \mathbf{in}\ ((\mathit{twice}\ \mathit{succ})\ 0)\end{array}$$

The language has block structure, so that the following expression evaluates to 6:

$$\begin{array}{l}\mathbf{let}\ i = 5\\ \mathbf{in}\ \mathbf{let}\ i = i+1\ \mathbf{in}\ i\end{array}$$

Here we have both simultaneous definitions and block structure:

$$\begin{array}{l}\mathbf{let}\ (x,y) = (2,3)\\ \mathbf{in}\ \mathbf{let}\ (x,y) = (y,x)\ \mathbf{in}\ x\end{array}$$

and this last example involves simultaneous recursive definitions:

$$\textbf{letrec}(\mathit{even}, \mathit{odd}) = (\lambda x.\,\textbf{if } x = 0 \textbf{ then } \mathit{true} \textbf{ else } \mathit{odd}(x-1),$$
$$\lambda x.\,\textbf{if } x = 0 \textbf{ then } \mathit{false} \textbf{ else } \mathit{even}(x-1))$$
$$\textbf{in } \mathit{even}(3)$$

3.2. *Abstract Syntax of Mini-ML*

An abstract syntax is an order-sorted algebra. It is given by a set of sorts, a description of their inclusion relations, and the list of all language constructors, together with their syntactic types. The abstract syntax of Mini-ML is given[1] on Fig. 1. It defines a λ-calculus extended with **let**, **letrec**, **if**, and products. Furthermore, in an expression $\lambda P.e$, P may be either an identifier or a (tree-like) pattern. For example $\lambda(x, y).e$ is a valid expression and so is $\lambda(x, ((y, z), t)).e'$. The constructor *mlpair* builds products of expressions, while the *pairpat* constructor serves in building patterns of identifiers. The *nullpat* constructor is used for the unit object (), which is both a pattern and an expression.

sorts

EXP, IDENT, PAT, NULLPAT

subsorts

EXP⊃ NULLPAT, IDENT   PAT⊃ NULLPAT, IDENT

constructors

Patterns

pairpat	:	PAT×PAT	→	PAT
nullpat	:		→	NULLPAT

Expressions

number	:		→	EXP
false	:		→	EXP
true	:		→	EXP
ident	:		→	IDENT
lambda	:	PAT×EXP	→	EXP
if	:	EXP×EXP×EXP	→	EXP
mlpair	:	EXP×EXP	→	EXP
apply	:	EXP×EXP	→	EXP
let	:	PAT×EXP×EXP	→	EXP
letrec	:	PAT×EXP×EXP	→	EXP

Figure 1. Abstract Syntax of mini-ML

4. Dynamic Semantics

In Mini-ML, the evaluation of a sub-expression always yields a value, so that we have to axiomatize the single judgement

$$\rho \vdash \mathrm{E} \Rightarrow \alpha$$

where E is a Mini-ML expression, ρ is an environment and α is the result of the evaluation of E in ρ. Functions can be manipulated as any other object in the language. For example a function may be passed as parameter to another function, or returned as the value of an expression. Thus the domain of semantic values is slightly more complicated than for a traditional Algol-like language.

4.1. *Semantic values, environments*

Values in Mini-ML are either:

- integer values in $\mathbb{N}$
- boolean values *true* and *false*, in italics to distinguish them from the literals true and false.

[1] An abstract syntax may also be presented as a set of inference rules. Sort inclusions give then rise to *inheritance* rules.

- closures of the form $[\![\lambda\text{P.E}, \rho]\!]$, where E is an expression and ρ is an environment. A closure is just a pair of a λ-expression denoting a function and an environment.
- *opaque* closures, i.e. closures whose contents cannot be inspected. These closures are associated to predefined functions.
- pairs of semantic values of the form (α, β) (which may in turn be pairs, so that trees of semantic values may be constructed).

Naturally the value of an expression E depends on the values of the identifiers that occur free in it. These values are recorded in the environment. A Mini-ML *environment* ρ is an ordered list of pairs $P \mapsto \alpha$ where P is pattern and α a value. The symbol $\cdot$ separates the elements of this list. Here is an example of environment:

$$(x, y) \mapsto (true, 5) \cdot x \mapsto 1$$

The environment is intuitively scanned *from right to left* so that in this example, x is associated to 1, y is associated to 5, and no other identifier has a value associated to it. The typical equation we want to solve with the formal system in Fig. 2. is

$$\rho_0 \vdash \text{E} \Rightarrow \alpha$$

where α is the unknown and ρ_0 is an initial environment. The initial environment associates opaque closures to a few predefined operators, such as $+$, $-$, etc.

4.2. *Semantic rules*

The semantic rules of Mini-ML are shown on Figure 2. Axioms 1 to 3 state that integer and boolean literals are in normal form, i.e. yield immediately a semantic value.

$$\rho \vdash \text{number N} \Rightarrow \text{N} \qquad (1)$$

$$\rho \vdash \text{true} \Rightarrow \mathit{true} \qquad (2)$$

$$\rho \vdash \text{false} \Rightarrow \mathit{false} \qquad (3)$$

$$\rho \vdash \lambda\text{P.E} \Rightarrow [\![\lambda\text{P.E}, \rho]\!] \qquad (4)$$

$$\frac{\rho \overset{\text{val\_of}}{\vdash} \text{ident I} \mapsto \alpha}{\rho \vdash \text{ident I} \Rightarrow \alpha} \qquad (5)$$

$$\frac{\rho \vdash \text{E}_1 \Rightarrow \mathit{true} \qquad \rho \vdash \text{E}_2 \Rightarrow \alpha}{\rho \vdash \text{if E}_1 \text{ then E}_2 \text{ else E}_3 \Rightarrow \alpha} \qquad (6)$$

$$\frac{\rho \vdash \text{E}_1 \Rightarrow \mathit{false} \qquad \rho \vdash \text{E}_3 \Rightarrow \alpha}{\rho \vdash \text{if E}_1 \text{ then E}_2 \text{ else E}_3 \Rightarrow \alpha} \qquad (7)$$

$$\frac{\rho \vdash \text{E}_1 \Rightarrow \alpha \qquad \rho \vdash \text{E}_2 \Rightarrow \beta}{\rho \vdash (\text{E}_1, \text{E}_2) \Rightarrow (\alpha, \beta)} \qquad (8)$$

$$\frac{\rho \vdash \text{E}_1 \Rightarrow [\![\lambda\text{P.E}, \rho_1]\!] \qquad \rho \vdash \text{E}_2 \Rightarrow \alpha \qquad \rho_1 \cdot \text{P} \mapsto \alpha \vdash \text{E} \Rightarrow \beta}{\rho \vdash \text{E}_1\ \text{E}_2 \Rightarrow \beta} \qquad (9)$$

$$\frac{\rho \vdash \text{E}_2 \Rightarrow \alpha \qquad \rho \cdot \text{P} \mapsto \alpha \vdash \text{E}_1 \Rightarrow \beta}{\rho \vdash \text{let P} = \text{E}_2 \text{ in E}_1 \Rightarrow \beta} \qquad (10)$$

$$\frac{\rho \cdot \text{P} \mapsto \alpha \vdash \text{E}_2 \Rightarrow \alpha \qquad \rho \cdot \text{P} \mapsto \alpha \vdash \text{E}_1 \Rightarrow \beta}{\rho \vdash \text{letrec P} = \text{E}_2 \text{ in E}_1 \Rightarrow \beta} \qquad (11)$$

Figure 2. The dynamic semantics of mini-ML

Axiom 4 asserts that an expression of the form λP.E is also in normal form. The value obtained is a closure, pairing this expression with the environment. This is in sharp contrast with λ-calculus, where E would be further reduced. Axiom 5 simply says that the value associated to an identifier is to be looked up in the environment. But since the environment is somewhat complex, we choose to axiomatize this process with auxiliary rules, the set VAL_OF. These rules are described later. Evaluation of conditional expressions is specified in the next two rules 6 and 7. Note that these rules have the same conclusion but that they are mutually exclusive. They are also exhaustive provided, as we shall assume, we evaluate only expressions that are type correct. The rules show that evaluation of E_1, E_2 and E_3 takes place in the same environment, and has no side effect. Hence it could be done in parallel.

In Natural Deduction terminology, rules 2 and 3 are *introduction rules* for the boolean values *true* and *false*. Rules 6 and 7 are *elimination* rules, they tell how boolean values may be consumed. Putting together rule 2 and 6 (resp. 3 and 7)we obtain two unexciting derived inference rules

$$\frac{\rho \vdash E_2 \Rightarrow \alpha}{\rho \vdash \text{if true then } E_2 \text{ else } E_3 \Rightarrow \alpha} \tag{6'}$$

$$\frac{\rho \vdash E_3 \Rightarrow \alpha}{\rho \vdash \text{if false then } E_2 \text{ else } E_3 \Rightarrow \alpha} \tag{7'}$$

Rule 8 is the introduction rule for pairs of values. Both components of the pair must be evaluated. The lack of rules for value-pair elimination (left projection, right projection) might indicate a weakness in the design of Mini-ML. But a rule in the set VAL_OF serves that purpose.

The next rule 9 deals with function application. Because of type-checking, the operator of an application can only evaluate to a functional value, i.e. a closure. This closure is taken apart. The closure's body is evaluated in the closure's environment, to which the parameter association $P \mapsto \alpha$ has been added. Since E_2 is evaluated, Mini-ML uses call-by-value. The rule is valid whether P is a pattern or a single variable. Note that the rule is departing from denotational semantics in that E is *not* a subexpression of E_1 or E_2. It is a closure elimination rule, whereas rule 4 was the closure introduction rule. From rule 4 and 9 we deduce an interesting rule:

$$\frac{\rho \vdash E_2 \Rightarrow \alpha \qquad \rho \cdot P \mapsto \alpha \vdash E_1 \Rightarrow \beta}{\rho \vdash \lambda P.E_1\ E_2 \Rightarrow \beta} \tag{9'}$$

This rule can be added, as an optimization, to the semantics of mini-ML. In the case where the operator of an application is syntactically a λ-term, it is not necessary to build a closure that is to be taken apart immediately thereafter. If we compare this new rule with rule 10, we see that, at evaluation time,

$$\lambda P.E_1\ E_2 \equiv (\text{let } P = E_2 \text{ in } E_1).$$

Rule 10 is typical of Natural Deduction, as we can see in a logical presentation where ρ is implicit and emphasis is placed on discharging hypotheses:

$$\frac{E_2 \Rightarrow \alpha \qquad \begin{array}{c}[P \mapsto \alpha]\\ E_1 \Rightarrow \beta\end{array}}{\text{let } P = E_2 \text{ in } E_1 \Rightarrow \beta} \tag{10}$$

The last rule, rule 11, defines in one and the same way the simple recursive functions and the mutually recursive ones such as

$$\begin{aligned}\text{letrec } (f,(g,h)) = (&\lambda x.\cdots f \cdots g \cdots h \cdots,\\ &(\lambda y.\cdots f \cdots g \cdots h \cdots,\\ &\lambda z.\cdots f \cdots g \cdots h \cdots))\\ \text{in } E\end{aligned}$$

The rule is very similar to rule 10, except that expression E_2 is evaluated in the same environment as E_1, rather than in ρ. We should keep in mind that in Mini-ML only functional objects may be defined recursively, so that α is either a closure, or a tree of closures. In both cases, it will contain a reference to itself and may be understood as a regular infinite tree.

For clarity, we had omitted the rule dealing with predefined function symbols:

$$\frac{\rho \vdash E_1 \Rightarrow \text{opaque OP} \qquad \rho \vdash E_2 \Rightarrow \alpha \qquad \overset{\text{eval}}{\vdash} \text{OP}, \alpha \Rightarrow \beta}{\rho \vdash E_1\ E_2 \Rightarrow \beta} \tag{12}$$

This rule is an elimination rule for opaque closures. When the operator of an application evaluates to an opaque closure, we assume that there is an evaluator EVAL that is capable of returning a value β corresponding to the argument α. Here, we could be a little more realistic and have opaque closures contain both the name of an operator *and* the name of an evaluator, to be invoked in this rule. There is no introduction rule for opaque closures: we assume that they come solely from the initial environment.

4.3. *Searching the environment*

The separate set VAL_OF (see Fig. 3.) gives rules to associate values to identifiers, given some environment. There are two problems to solve. First, we must traverse the environment from right to left to take into account block structure. This is achieved by the rules 1 and 2. Rule 1 could be called a *tautology* rule, and rule 2 is a *thinning* rule. The second problem is that the environment contains associations of the form $P \mapsto \alpha$ where P is a pattern, i.e. a tree of identifiers. From typechecking we know that P is bound to a value of the same shape, and rule 3 traverses P.

set VAL_OF is

$$\rho \cdot \text{ident}\ \text{I} \mapsto \alpha \vdash \text{ident}\ \text{I} \mapsto \alpha \quad (1)$$

$$\frac{\rho \vdash \text{ident}\ \text{I} \mapsto \alpha}{\rho \cdot \text{ident}\ \text{X} \mapsto \beta \vdash \text{ident}\ \text{I} \mapsto \alpha} \quad (\text{X} \neq \text{I}) \quad (2)$$

$$\frac{\rho \cdot \text{P}_1 \mapsto \alpha \cdot \text{P}_2 \mapsto \beta \vdash \text{ident}\ \text{I} \mapsto \gamma}{\rho \cdot (\text{P}_1, \text{P}_2) \mapsto (\alpha, \beta) \vdash \text{ident}\ \text{I} \mapsto \gamma} \quad (3)$$

end VAL_OF

Figure 3. The ML environment rules

Rule 3 is a sort of pair elimination rule. It is an astonishingly simple method to keep rules 10 and 11 valid when P is a pattern.

4.4. *Executing the definition*

To solve the equation in the unknown α

$$\rho_0 \vdash \text{E} \Rightarrow \alpha$$

we search for the last step of the proof of this fact. The structure of E forces this step in general. Rules 6 and 7 on the one hand, rules 9 and 12 on the other can lead to backtracking. This situation is very general and analyzed in [2]. It is interesting to remark that the derived inference rules 6′ 7′ and 9′ can be added to the definition, since they can only infer valid facts. But they should systematically be preferred to 6 and 7, or to 9 and 12 because they are "faster". Intuitively, they should be preferred because their subject is more *specific*.

Non-termination in Mini-ML may occur because of rule 11. In the process of solving the initial equation, it is possible to grow the candidate proof tree endlessly from the bottom up. Then the equation will have no solution. Remark also that the Mini-ML we have described uses call-by-value. It is not difficult to write rules for a lazy Mini-ML, along the lines of [15]. The idea is to create new introduction rules for a different kind of closure called ***suspensions***, and new elimination rules for these suspensions.

The fact that we used a functional language to illustrate dynamic semantics should not leave the impression that imperative languages cannot be described. Several experiments with Algol-like languages are reported in [13].

5. Translation

Translation from one language to another is heavily guided by the structure of the source language. Hence it is clear that our formalism is well suited for specifying translations.

Recently, Cousineau and Curien have proposed a very ingenious abstract machine for the compilation of ML [4]. The complete semantics of the machine is described first. Then we specify the translation from Mini-ML to CAM.

5.1. *Specifying the Categorical Abstract Machine (CAM)*

The Categorical Abstract Machine has its roots both in categories and in De Bruijn's notation for lambda-calculus. It is a very simple machine where, according to its inventors, "categorical terms can be considered as code acting on a graph of values". Instructions are few in number and quite close to real machine instructions. Instructions *car* and *cdr* serve in accessing data in the stack and the special instruction *rec* is used to implement recursion. Predefined operations (such as addition, subtraction, division, etc.) may be added with the *op* instruction.

5.1.1. *Machine code and Machine state*

The abstract syntax of CAM code is given in Fig. 4.

sorts

VALUE, COM, PROGRAM, COMS

subsorts

COM⊃COMS

constructors

Programs

program	:	COMS	→	PROGRAM
coms	:	COM*	→	COMS

Commands

quote	:	VALUE	→	COM
car	:		→	COM
cdr	:		→	COM
cons	:		→	COM
push	:		→	COM
swap	:		→	COM
op	:		→	COM
branch	:	COMS×COMS	→	COM
cur	:	COMS	→	COM
app	:		→	COM
rec	:	COMS	→	COM

Values

int	:	→	VALUE
bool	:	→	VALUE

Figure 4. Abstract syntax of CAM code

The state of the CAM machine is a stack, whose top element may be viewed as a register. If s is a stack and α is a value, then pushing α onto s yields $s \cdot \alpha$. Several kinds of values may be pushed on the stack. Atomic values

- integers in $\mathbb{N}$,
- truth values *true* and *false*,

but also closures and environments since the machine is designed for higher-order functional languages

- closures of the form $[\![c, \rho]\!]_{cam}$, where c is a fragment of CAM code and ρ is a value that is meant to denote an environment,
- pairs of semantic values, and hence recursively trees of such values.

The pair constructor is used in particular to build environments. A special value () denotes the empty environment.

5.1.2. *Transition rules*

The rules describing the transitions of the CAM machine appear in Fig. 5. Two judgements are used. Only rule 1 involves the judgement

$$s \vdash c \Rightarrow \alpha$$

meaning that program C, started in state s returns α as result. All other rules involve only sequents of the form

$$s \vdash \mathrm{C} \Rightarrow s'$$

where C is CAM-code and s and s' are states of the CAM machine. The sequent may be read as *executing code* C *when the machine is in state* s *takes it to state* s'.

$$\frac{\mathit{init\_stack} \vdash \mathrm{COMS} \Rightarrow s \cdot \alpha}{\vdash \mathit{program}(\mathrm{COMS}) \Rightarrow \alpha} \tag{1}$$

$$s \vdash \emptyset \Rightarrow s \tag{2}$$

$$\frac{s \vdash \mathrm{COM} \Rightarrow s_1 \qquad s_1 \vdash \mathrm{COMS} \Rightarrow s_2}{s \vdash \mathrm{COM};\, \mathrm{COMS} \Rightarrow s_2} \tag{3}$$

$$s \cdot \alpha \vdash \mathit{quote}(\mathrm{V}) \Rightarrow s \cdot \mathrm{V} \tag{4}$$

$$s \cdot (\alpha, \beta) \vdash \mathit{car} \Rightarrow s \cdot \alpha \tag{5}$$

$$s \cdot (\alpha, \beta) \vdash \mathit{cdr} \Rightarrow s \cdot \beta \tag{6}$$

$$s \cdot \alpha \cdot \beta \vdash \mathit{cons} \Rightarrow s \cdot (\alpha, \beta) \tag{7}$$

$$s \cdot \alpha \vdash \mathit{push} \Rightarrow s \cdot \alpha \cdot \alpha \tag{8}$$

$$s \cdot \alpha \cdot \beta \vdash \mathit{swap} \Rightarrow s \cdot \beta \cdot \alpha \tag{9}$$

$$\frac{\overset{\mathrm{eval}}{\vdash} \mathrm{OP}, \alpha \Rightarrow \beta}{s \cdot \alpha \vdash \mathit{op}\,\mathrm{OP} \Rightarrow s \cdot \beta} \tag{10}$$

$$\frac{s \vdash \mathrm{C}_1 \Rightarrow s_1}{s \cdot \mathit{true} \vdash \mathit{branch}(\mathrm{C}_1, \mathrm{C}_2) \Rightarrow s_1} \tag{11}$$

$$\frac{s \vdash \mathrm{C}_2 \Rightarrow s_1}{s \cdot \mathit{false} \vdash \mathit{branch}(\mathrm{C}_1, \mathrm{C}_2) \Rightarrow s_1} \tag{12}$$

$$s \cdot \rho \vdash \mathit{cur}(\mathrm{C}) \Rightarrow s \cdot [\![\mathrm{C}, \rho]\!]_{cam} \tag{13}$$

$$\frac{s \cdot (\rho, \alpha) \vdash \mathrm{C} \Rightarrow s_1}{s \cdot ([\![\mathrm{C}, \rho]\!]_{cam}, \alpha) \vdash \mathit{app} \Rightarrow s_1} \tag{14}$$

$$\frac{s \cdot (\rho, \rho_1) \vdash \mathrm{C} \Rightarrow s \cdot \rho_1}{s \cdot \rho \vdash \mathit{rec}(\mathrm{C}) \Rightarrow s \cdot \rho_1} \tag{15}$$

Figure 5. The definition of the Categorical Abstract Machine

Rule 1 says that evaluating a program begins with an initial stack and ends with a value on top of the stack that is the result of the program. The initial stack *init_stack* contains a single element, the initial environment. This environment includes the closures corresponding to the predefined operators. For example, we might have

$$\mathit{init\_stack} = \big(\big(\big((), [\![\mathit{cdr}; \mathit{op}+,\ ()]\!]_{cam}\big), [\![\mathit{cdr}; \mathit{op}-,\ ()]\!]_{cam}\big), [\![\mathit{cdr}; \mathit{op}*,\ ()]\!]_{cam}\big).$$

Rules 2 and 3 specify sequential execution for a sequence of commands. Axioms 4 to 7 show that elementary instructions overwrite the top of the stack with their result. Instructions *push* and *swap*, described in rules 8 and 9 are useful to save the top of the stack. Rule 10 switches to an external evaluator EVAL for predefined operators. The external evaluator must be aware that it receives a single tree-stuctured argument.

Rule 11 and 12 define the *branch* instruction. It takes its (evaluated) condition from the top of the stack, and continues with either the true or the false part. The *cur* instruction is described in rule 13: $\mathit{cur}(\mathrm{C})$ builds a closure with the code C and the current environment (top of the stack) placing it on top of the stack. Rule 14 says that the *app* instruction must find on top of the stack a pair consisting of a closure and a parameter environment. Then the code of the closure is evaluated in a new environment: that of the closure prefixed by the parameter environment.

The last rule is the less intuitive one. The *rec* instruction is used to build the self referencing environment ρ_1. Such an environment is necessary for the evaluation of recursive definitions. Notice the remarkable simplicity of rule 15.

5.1.3. ***Remarks***

- Given some program P written in CAM code, to run it is to find an α such that $\vdash P \Rightarrow \alpha$. The general execution strategy works well and there are never any choices to build a proof. Rule 3 is the only one with two premises, and they must be treated from left to right.
- The Natural Deduction point of view does not seem to bring much insight here, but it is convenient to specify an abstract machine in the same formalism as a semantic definition. The equivalence of certain sequences of code can be proved easily and this is useful for optimisation [3].

5.2. *Generating CAM code for Mini-ML*

We are now ready to generate CAM code for mini-ML. Here is what we will produce for the factorial example in paragraph 3.1, laid out like an assembly code listing:

```
push;                                                   letrec fact =
rec    (cur   (push                                     λx. if
                     push;  cdr                         (x
                     swap;  quote(0)                    ,0
                     cons;  op =                        ) =
              branch (quote(1),                         then 1 else
                     push;  cdr                         (x
                     swap;  push;  car;    cdr          ,(fact
                            swap;  push;   cdr          ,(x
                                   swap;   quote(1)     ,1
                                   cons;   op -         )-
                            cons;  app                  )call
                     cons;  op *)))                     )*
cons                                                    in
       push;  cdr                                       (fact
       swap;  quote(4)                                  ,4
       cons;  app                                       )call
```

The rules for translating Mini-ML to CAM[1] are given in Fig. 6. In these rules, except for rule 1, all sequents have the form:

$$\rho \vdash \text{E} \rightarrow c$$

where ρ is an environment, E is an expression in Mini-ML, and c is its translation into CAM-code. In words, the sequent reads: ***in environment ρ, expression E is compiled into code c***. The notion of environment used in this translation is exactly the notion of a pattern in Mini-ML, i.e. a binary tree with identifiers at the leaves. The environment is used to decide what code to generate for variables.

Translation of an ML program is invoked, in rule 1, with an initial environment *init_pat* that is merely a list of predefined functions. The environment builds up whenever one introduces new names (rules 6, 10, and 11). It is consulted when one wants to generate code for an identifier (rule 5). Then an access path is computed in the ACCESS rule set. The access path is a sequence of *car* and *cdr* instructions (a coding of the De Bruijn number associated to that occurrence of the identifier) that will access the corresponding value in the stack of the CAM.

Rules 2, 3, and 4 generate code for literal values. Rule 5 generates an access path for an identifier. In rule 6, the body of a λ-term is compiled and then wrapped in a *cur* instruction. To understand the next rules, the following inductive assertion is useful: ***the code for an expression expects its evaluation environment on***

[1] The proof of correctness of this translation is given in [7]

$$\frac{init\_pat \vdash \text{E} \rightarrow c}{\vdash \text{E} \rightarrow program(c)} \tag{1}$$

$$\rho \vdash \text{number N} \rightarrow quote(\text{N}) \tag{2}$$

$$\rho \vdash \text{true} \rightarrow quote(true) \tag{3}$$

$$\rho \vdash \text{false} \rightarrow quote(false) \tag{4}$$

$$\frac{\rho \overset{\text{access}}{\vdash} \text{ident I} : c}{\rho \vdash \text{ident I} \rightarrow c} \tag{5}$$

$$\frac{(\rho, \text{P}) \vdash \text{E} \rightarrow c}{\rho \vdash \lambda\text{P.E} \rightarrow cur(c)} \tag{6}$$

$$\frac{\rho \vdash \text{E}_1 \rightarrow c_1 \qquad \rho \vdash \text{E}_2 \rightarrow c_2 \qquad \rho \vdash \text{E}_3 \rightarrow c_3}{\rho \vdash \text{if E}_1 \text{ then E}_2 \text{ else E}_3 \rightarrow push; c_1; branch(c_2, c_3)} \tag{7}$$

$$\frac{\rho \vdash \text{E}_1 \rightarrow c_1 \qquad \rho \vdash \text{E}_2 \rightarrow c_2}{\rho \vdash (\text{E}_1, \text{E}_2) \rightarrow push; c_1; swap; c_2; cons} \tag{8}$$

$$\frac{\rho \vdash \text{E}_1 \rightarrow c_1 \qquad \rho \vdash \text{E}_2 \rightarrow c_2}{\rho \vdash \text{E}_1 \ \text{E}_2 \rightarrow push; c_1; swap; c_2; cons; app} \tag{9}$$

$$\frac{\rho \vdash \text{E}_1 \rightarrow c_1 \qquad (\rho, \text{P}) \vdash \text{E}_2 \rightarrow c_2}{\rho \vdash \text{let P} = \text{E}_1 \text{ in E}_2 \rightarrow push; c_1; cons; c_2} \tag{10}$$

$$\frac{(\rho, \text{P}) \vdash \text{E}_1 \rightarrow c_1 \qquad (\rho, \text{P}) \vdash \text{E}_2 \rightarrow c_2}{\rho \vdash \text{letrec P} = \text{E}_1 \text{ in E}_2 \rightarrow push; rec(c_1); cons; c_2} \tag{11}$$

Figure 6. Translation from mini-ML to CAM

top of the stack, and it will overwrite this environment with its result. Thus the environment must be saved by a *push* instruction whenever necessary. If a temporary result is obtained, the *swap* instruction will push it on the stack, while bringing back on top the environment necessary for further computation. Now rule 7 and 8 become quite clear. Rule 9 builds a pair of values, the operator and the operand, and then generates an *app*. Rules 10 and 11 are very similar, just the way rules 10 and 11 were in dynamic semantics. A simple parameter binding is added to the environment in rule 10, while rule 11 adds a recursive binding. As indicated before, at execution time the *rec* instruction will build a self-referencing environment.

From the identity that is valid at run-time

$$\lambda\text{P.E}_2\ \text{E}_1 \equiv (\text{let P} = \text{E}_1 \text{ in E}_2)$$

we deduce that the following inference rule should be valid

$$\frac{\rho \vdash \text{E}_1 \rightarrow c_1 \qquad (\rho, \text{P}) \vdash \text{E}_2 \rightarrow c_2}{\rho \vdash \lambda\text{P.E}_2\ \text{E}_1 \rightarrow push; c_1; cons; c_2} \tag{12}$$

Indeed, it is shown in [3]that rule 12 may be ***deduced*** from rules 6 and 9, once a few basic lemmas on CAM code have been established. Rule 12 is a code optimization rule. It should be added to the other rules and preferred when applicable.

To generate code for identifiers, the set ACCESS in Figure 7. is used. Here again, we assume the the program that is to be translated type-checks, and in paticular that it contains no undeclared variables. The rules in this set are similar to the rules in the set VAL_OF, except that while searching for an identifier, one constructs simultaneously its access path.

6. Type-checking Mini-ML

6.1. *General framework*

set ACCESS is

$$\frac{\rho \mapsto \emptyset \vdash \text{ident}\,\mathrm{X} : c}{\rho \vdash \text{ident}\,\mathrm{X} : c} \tag{0}$$

$$\rho \cdot \text{ident}\,\mathrm{X} \mapsto c \vdash \text{ident}\,\mathrm{X} : c \tag{1}$$

$$\frac{\rho \vdash \text{ident}\,\mathrm{X} : c}{\rho \cdot \text{ident}\,\mathrm{Y} \mapsto c' \vdash \text{ident}\,\mathrm{X} : c} \quad (\mathrm{Y} \neq \mathrm{X}) \tag{2}$$

$$\frac{\rho \cdot \rho_1 \mapsto c; \text{car} \cdot \rho_2 \mapsto c; cdr \vdash \text{ident}\,\mathrm{X} : c'}{\rho \cdot (\rho_1, \rho_2) \mapsto c \vdash \text{ident}\,\mathrm{X} : c'} \tag{3}$$

end ACCESS

Figure 7. Generating access paths for identifiers

The semantic specifications of the previous sections rely on the hypothesis that they are applied to well-typed program fragments. From that angle, being well typed is a constraint on abstract syntax trees – what is sometimes called *context-sensitive* syntax. But if an expression E has type τ, it also means that the possible values that E may take during execution are characterized by τ. When axiomatizing

$$\rho \vdash \mathrm{E} : \tau$$

where ρ is a type environment, both viewpoints are present. If the sequent has no proof, then E does not type-check. If it can be proved, then E has type τ. The relationship between the type system and the dynamic semantics must be established, by showing a variant of the Subject Reduction Theorem of [5].

Before introducing an inference system that assigns types in Mini-ML, the type language has to be explained. In typed λ-calculus every object has a type. Thus the type language must be able to express ***basic types*** as well as ***functional types***. For example, the type of the successor function $\lambda x.x + 1$ is $int \rightarrow int$. In the same way the identity function $\lambda x.x$ for integers has type $int \rightarrow int$, but for booleans it has type $bool \rightarrow bool$. It is clear that the identity function may be defined without taking into account the type of its present parameter. To express this ***abstraction*** on the type of the parameter, the ***type variable*** α is bound by a quantifier: the polymorphic identity function has type $\forall\alpha.\alpha \rightarrow \alpha$.

6.2. *The Type Language*

The type language contains two syntactic categories, types and type schemes.

Types: a type τ is either

i. a basic type *int*, *bool*,

ii. a type variable α ,

iii. a functional type $\tau \rightarrow \tau'$, where τ and τ' are types,

iv. a product type $\tau \times \tau'$, where τ and τ' are types.

Type schemes: a type-scheme σ is either

i. a type τ,

ii. a type-scheme $\forall\alpha.\sigma$, where σ is a type-scheme.

Remark: quantifiers may occur only at the top level of type-schemes, they do not occur within type-schemes.

A type expression in this language may have both *free* and *bound* variables. Let us write $FV(\sigma)$ for the set of free variables of a type expression σ. We now define two relations between type expressions that contain type variables.

Definition. *A type scheme σ' is called an **instance** of a type scheme σ if there exists a substitution S of types for free type variables such that:*

$$\sigma' = S\sigma.$$

Instantiation acts on *free* variables: if S is written $[\alpha_i \leftarrow \tau_i]$ with $\alpha_i \in FV(\sigma)$ then $S\sigma$ is obtained by replacing each free occurrence of α_i in σ by τ_i (renaming the bound variables of σ if necessary). The *domain* of S is written $D(S)$.

Definition. *A type scheme $\sigma = \forall\alpha_1 \cdots \alpha_m.\tau$ has a generic instance $\sigma' = \forall\beta_1 \cdots \beta_n.\tau'$, and we shall write $\sigma \succeq \sigma'$, if there exists a substitution S such that*

$$\tau' = S\tau \quad \text{with} \quad D(S) \subseteq \{\alpha_1 \cdots \alpha_m\}$$

and the β_i are not free in σ, i.e.

$$\beta_i \notin FV(\sigma) \qquad 1 \le i \le n.$$

Generic instantiation acts on *bound* variables. Note that if $\sigma \succeq \sigma'$ then for every substitution S, $S\sigma \succeq S\sigma'$. Note also that if τ and τ' are types rather than type-schemes, then $\tau \succeq \tau'$ implies $\tau = \tau'$.

6.3. *The typing rules*

The rules for typing Mini-ML programs are given in Figure 8. Two judgements are used. The main judgement has the form

$$\rho \vdash \text{E} : \tau$$

where the environment ρ is a list of assumptions of the form $x : \sigma$. The environment is to be scanned from right to left. Concatenation of two environments ρ and ρ' is noted $\rho + \rho'$. An auxiliary judgement is necessary to handle the declaration of patterns correctly:

$$\vdash \text{P}, \tau : \rho.$$

This formula means that declaring P with type τ creates the type environment ρ. For example we have:

$$\vdash (x, (y, z)), (\tau_1 \times (\tau_2 \times \tau_3)) : x : \tau_1 \cdot y : \tau_2 \cdot z : \tau_3$$

The first three axioms are the introduction rules for basic types. Rule 4 is the introduction rule for $\rightarrow$. The environment may associate a generic type σ to an identifier, but in ML an occurrence of an identifier has a type τ. So the condition in rule 5 specifies to create a generic instance of τ of the type scheme σ.

Rule 6 is the elimination rule for the basic type *bool*. It is interesting to note that there are two occurrences of τ in the premises, so that the rule unifies the types of the two expressions E_2 and E_3. Rule 7 introduces product types. Rule 9 is the elimination rule for $\rightarrow$. It performs unification on τ' in the same way as rule 6.

From rules 4 and 8 we deduce

$$\frac{\vdash \text{P}, \tau_2 : \rho' \qquad \rho \vdash \text{E}_2 : \tau_2 \qquad \rho + \rho' \vdash \text{E}_1 : \tau_1}{\rho \vdash \lambda \text{P}.\text{E}_1\ \text{E}_2 : \tau_1} \tag{9'}$$

which differs from rule 9. So from the point of view of types,

$$\lambda \text{P}.\text{E}_1\ \text{E}_2 \not\equiv (\text{let P} = \text{E}_2 \text{ in E}_1).$$

Rule 9 is the source of polymorphism in Mini-ML: the environment ρ'' is obtained from ρ' by generalization with respect to ρ. It is important to understand that generalizing ρ' creates several independent type schemes, while generalizing τ_2 would give a single type scheme. Rule 10 defines recursively τ_2 in terms of itself and it exhibits the usual similarity with rule 9'. There is no point in trying to generalize ρ' with respect to $\rho + \rho'$.

The last two rules concern declarations. Rule 11 builds a singleton environment, rule 12 concatenates environments, while checking that they do not intersect. This is to exclude patterns with repeated occurrences of the same variable.

To search the type environment, the familiar rules of tautology and thinning are shown again in Figure 9.

$$\rho \vdash \text{number N} : int \tag{1}$$

$$\rho \vdash \text{true} : bool \tag{2}$$

$$\rho \vdash \text{false} : bool \tag{3}$$

$$\frac{\vdash \text{P}, \tau' : \rho' \qquad \rho + \rho' \vdash \text{E} : \tau}{\rho \vdash \lambda \text{P.E} : \tau' \rightarrow \tau} \tag{4}$$

$$\frac{\rho \overset{\text{type\_of}}{\vdash} \text{ident X} : \sigma}{\rho \vdash \text{ident X} : \tau} \quad (\tau = inst(\sigma)) \tag{5}$$

$$\frac{\rho \vdash \text{E}_1 : bool \qquad \rho \vdash \text{E}_2 : \tau \qquad \rho \vdash \text{E}_3 : \tau}{\rho \vdash \text{if E}_1 \text{ then E}_2 \text{ else E}_3 : \tau} \tag{6}$$

$$\frac{\rho \vdash \text{E}_1 : \tau_1 \qquad \rho \vdash \text{E}_2 : \tau_2}{\rho \vdash (\text{E}_1, \text{E}_2) : \tau_1 \times \tau_2} \tag{7}$$

$$\frac{\rho \vdash \text{E}_1 : \tau' \rightarrow \tau \qquad \rho \vdash \text{E}_2 : \tau'}{\rho \vdash \text{E}_1 \; \text{E}_2 : \tau} \tag{8}$$

$$\frac{\vdash \text{P}, \tau_2 : \rho' \qquad \rho \vdash \text{E}_2 : \tau_2 \qquad \rho + \rho'' \vdash \text{E}_1 : \tau_1}{\rho \vdash \text{let P} = \text{E}_2 \text{ in E}_1 : \tau_1} \quad (\rho'' = gen(\rho, \rho')) \tag{9}$$

$$\frac{\vdash \text{P}, \tau_2 : \rho' \qquad \rho + \rho' \vdash \text{E}_2 : \tau_2 \qquad \rho + \rho' \vdash \text{E}_1 : \tau_1}{\rho \vdash \text{letrec P} = \text{E}_2 \text{ in E}_1 : \tau_1} \tag{10}$$

$$\vdash \text{ident X}, \tau : \text{ident X} : \tau \tag{11}$$

$$\frac{\vdash \text{P}_1, \tau_1 : \rho_1 \qquad \vdash \text{P}_2, \tau_2 : \rho_2}{\vdash (\text{P}_1, \text{P}_2), \tau_1 \times \tau_2 : \rho_1 + \rho_2} \quad (\rho_1 \cap \rho_2 = \emptyset) \tag{12}$$

Figure 8. Rules for type assignment in Mini-ML

set TYPE_OF is

$$\rho \cdot x : \sigma \vdash x : \sigma \tag{1}$$

$$\frac{\rho \vdash x : \sigma}{\rho \cdot y : \sigma' \vdash x : \sigma} \quad (y \neq x) \tag{2}$$

end TYPE_OF

Figure 9. Searching the type environment

6.4. *Remarks*

- Strictly speaking, the definition above is too generous. It computes recursive types for certain Mini-ML expressions that are not supposed to have any type, such as $\lambda x.x\,x$.
- In Mini-ML, the Subject Construction Theorem is valid [5]. Consider the proof tree for

$$\rho \vdash \text{E} : \tau.$$

If we label each inference step with the constructor of its subject, we see that this proof tree is isomorphic to E. This result does not seem specific of Mini-ML.
- Many interesting ideas in type systems such as inheritance, overloading, coercions etc... are not present in Mini-ML. It is our experience that such ideas can be described fairly simply with Natural Semantics.
- The type-checker obtained from a definition in Natural Semantics is correct but not readily usable: it fails to type-check as soon as there is one type error. It is shown in [12]how to transform mechani-

cally such a definition into a friendly type-checker that emits error messages and carries on. Further mechanical transformations yield in certain conditions an incremental type-checker.

7. Conclusion

In this presentation of Natural Semantics, we hope to have shown a simple and mathematically tractable method of writing semantic descriptions. At the present time, we investigate how to incorporate these ideas in a most faithful way in the construction of a complete interactive environment [13]. Much work is still needed of course, but the results of the first few years indicate that it is possible to create an elegant and reasonably efficient system.

ACKNOWLEDGMENTS

This paper owes much to earlier contributions of D. Clément and J. Despeyroux. Th. Despeyroux has built a large part of the system that permits testing semantic definitions. G. Berry, G. Cousineau and G. Huet have given sound advice in various discussions.

REFERENCES

[1] CARDELLI L., "Basic Polymorphic Type-checking", Polymorphism, January 1985.

[2] CLÉMENT D. "The Natural Dynamic Semantics of Mini-Standard ML", to appear in *Proceedings CFLP*, Pisa, March 1987.

[3] CLÉMENT D., J. DESPEYROUX, TH. DESPEYROUX, G. KAHN, "A simple applicative language: Mini-ML", *Proceedings of the ACM Conference on Lisp and Functional Programming 1986.*

[4] COUSINEAU G., P.L. CURIEN, M. MAUNY, "The Categorical Abstract Machine", in *Functional Languages and Computer Architecture*, Lecture Notes in Computer Science, Vol. 201, September 1985.

[5] CURRY H.B., R. FEYS, Combinatory Logic, Volume I, North-Holland Publishing Company, 1958.

[6] DAMAS L., R. MILNER, "Principal type-schemes for functional programs", *Proceedings of the ACM Conference on Principles of Programming Languages 1982*, pp.207–212.

[7] DESPEYROUX J., "Proof of Translation in Natural Semantics", *Proceedings of the First ACM Conference on Logic in Computer Science, LICS 1986.*

[8] DESPEYROUX T., "Executable Specification of Static Semantics", *Semantics of Data Types*, Lecture Notes in Computer Science, Vol. 173, June 1984.

[9] DESPEYROUX T., "Spécifications sémantiques dans le système MENTOR", Thèse, Université Paris XI, 1983.

[10] DONZEAU-GOUGE V., "Utilisation de la sémantique dénotationnelle pour la description d'interprétatioı non-standard: application à la validation et à l'optimisation des programmes", *Proceedings of the 3rd International Symposium on Programming*, Dunod, Paris, 1978.

[11] GORDON M., R. MILNER, C. WADSWORTH, G. COUSINEAU, G.HUET, L. PAULSON, "The ML Handbook, Version 5.1", INRIA, October 1984.

[12] HASCOET L., "Transformations automatiques de spécifications sémantiques. Application: un vérificateu de types incrémental" Thèse , To appear, Université de Nice, 1987.

[13] HEERING J., J. SIDI, A. VERHOOG (EDS), "Generation of interactive programming environments - GIPE intermediate report", CWI Report CS-R8620, Amsterdam, May 1986.

[14] MACQUEEN D.B., "Modules for standard ML", *ACM Symposium on LISP and Functional Programming*, 1984, pp.198–207.

[15] MAUNY M. "Compilation des langages fonctionnels dans les combinateurs catégoriques. Application au langage ML", Thèse, Université Paris 7, 1985.

[16] MOSSES P., "SIS: a compiler generator system using denotational semantics", DAIMI, University of Aarhus, August 1979.

[17] NAISH L., Negation and Control in Prolog, Lecture Notes in Computer Science, Vol. 238, 1986.

[18] PRAWITZ D., "Ideas and results in proof theory", *Proceedings of the Second Scandinavian Logic Symposium*, 1971, North-Holland.

[19] PLOTKIN G.D., "A Structural Approach to Operational Semantics", DAIMI FN-19, Computer Science Department, Aarhus University, Aarhus, Denmark, September 1981.

[20] REYNOLDS J.C., "Three Approaches to Type Structure", *Proceedings TAPSOFT*, Lecture Notes in Computer Science, Vol. 185, March 1985.

[21] WARREN D.H.D., "Logic Programming and Compiler writing", *Software–Practice and Experience*, **10**, 1980, pp.97–125.

On Local Routing of Two-Terminal Nets †
(Extended Abstract)

by

Michael Kaufmann and Kurt Mehlhorn

Fachbereich 10, Informatik
Universität des Saarlandes
6600, Saarbrücken, West Germany

I. Introduction

The *planar rectangular grid* consists of vertices $\{(x,y); x,y \in \mathbf{Z}\}$ and edges $\{((x,y),(x',y')); |x-x'|+|y-y'|=1\}$. A *routing region* R is a finite subgraph of the planar rectangular grid.

In the sequel R always denotes a routing region. We call a bounded face F of R trivial if it has exactly four vertices on its boundary and nontrivial otherwise. We use M to denote the nontrivial bounded faces and $\overline{M}$ to denote M together with the unbounded face. Let B be the set of vertices of R with degree at most three. Note that a vertex $v \in B$ lies on the boundary of a face $F \in \overline{M}$.

A *local routing* is a path in the routing region R connecting two vertices of B. The endpoints of the path are called its terminals. Two local routings p and q are *elementarily equivalent* if there are paths p_1, p_2, q_2, p_3 such that $p = p_1p_2p_3$, $q = p_1q_2p_3$, and such that $p_2q_2^{-1}$(q_2^{-1} is the reverse of path q_2) is a boundary cycle of a trivial face. Two elementarily equivalent paths are hence the same except that they take two different routes around a single trivial face. Two local routings p and q are *equivalent* if there is a sequence $p_0, \ldots, p_k, k \geq 0$, of paths such that $p = p_0, q = p_k$ and p_i and p_{i+1} are elementarily equivalent for $0 \leq i < k$. Note that if p and q are equivalent then p and q have the same terminals.

We use $[p]$ to denote the equivalence class of local routing p, i.e., to denote the homotopy class of path p. A *global routing* or *net* is an equivalence class $[p]$; the terminals of the path p are also called the terminals of the net.

We are now ready to state the *Local Routing Problem* (LRP).

† This work was supported by the DFG, SFB 124, TP B2, VLSI Entwurf und Parallelität. A full version of this paper is available from the authors.

Input: A routing region R and a multi-set $\mathcal{N}$ of nets.
We assume that each net $N \in \mathcal{N}$ is given by one of its representatives.
We use n to denote the number of vertices of R plus the total length of the representatives and call n the size of the problem.

Output: A local routing $lr(N)$ for each net $N \in \mathcal{N}$ such that
1) $lr(N) \in N$ for all $N \in \mathcal{N}$
2) $lr(N_1)$ and $lr(N_2)$ are edge-disjoint for $N_1, N_2 \in \mathcal{N}$, $N_1 \neq N_2$

or an indication that there is no such set of local routings.

▮

Figure 1 gives an example.

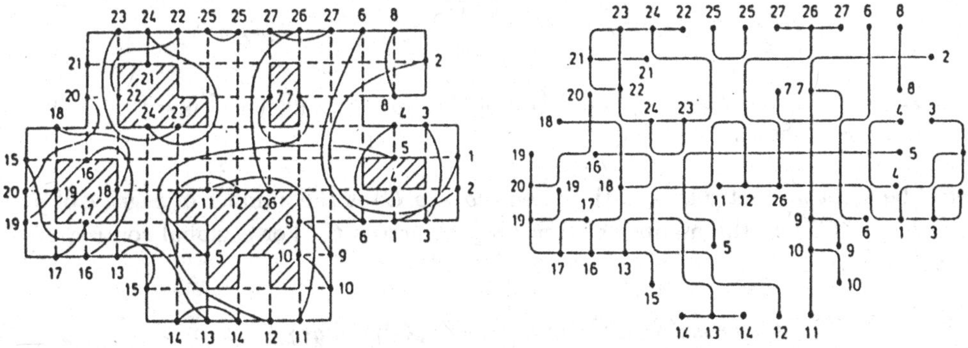

Fig. 1. A Local Routing Problem and its solution. The global routings are shown as curves for added clarity.

In this paper we will prove the following theorem.

Theorem 1: Let $P = (R, \mathcal{N})$ be an even bounded LRP of size n.

a) P is solvable if and only if the free capacity of every cut is nonnegative.
b) In time $O(n^2)$ one can decide whether P has a solution and also construct a solution if it does. ▮

It remains to define the terms "even LRP", "cut", "free capacity of a cut" and "bounded".

The *multiple-source dual* $D(R)$ of routing region R is defined as follows (cf. Figure 2). For every edge e of R there is a dual edge $d(e)$ with its endpoints lying in those faces of R which are separated by e. The endpoints of dual edges which lie in faces outside $\overline{M}$ are identified, the endpoints in faces in $\overline{M}$ are kept distinct and are called sources of the dual graph. A *cut* of R is a simple path in the dual graph connecting two sources. The *capacity* $cap(C)$ of a cut C is its length (= number of edges of R intersected by the cut) (cf. Figure 2). A cut can be viewed as a polygonal line $s_1, \ldots, s_k$ where each s_i is a straight-line segment and s_i and

s_{i+1} have different directions (one horizontal, one vertical). A cut is a *1-bend cut* if $k \leq 2$ and a *0-bend cut* if $k = 1$.

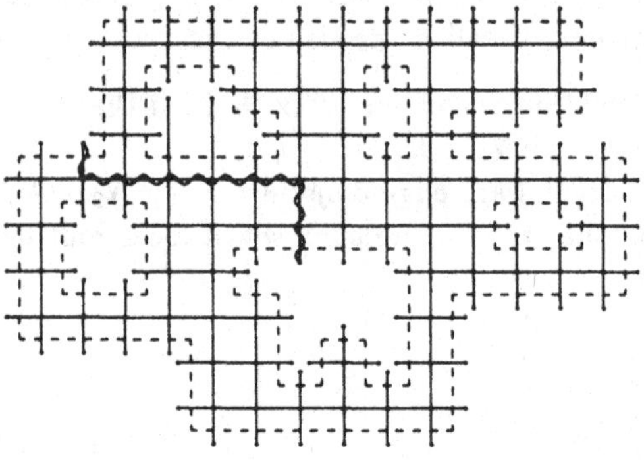

Fig. 2. The multiple-source dual $D(R)$ of the routing region of Figure 1. A cut of capacity 8 is shown wiggled.

Let C be a cut and let p be a path. Then $cross(p, C)$ is the number of edges e of p with $d(e)$ in C, i.e., the number of times p goes across C. For a global routing gr we define

$$cross(gr, C) = \min\{cross(p, C); p \in gr\}.$$

The *density* $dens(C)$ of cut C is defined by

$$dens(C) = \sum_{N \in \mathcal{N}} cross(N, C)$$

and the *free capacity* $fcap(C)$ is given by

$$fcap(C) = cap(C) - dens(C)$$

A cut C is *saturated* if $fcap(C) = 0$ and *oversaturated* if $fcap(C) < 0$.

An *LRP* is *even* if $fcap(C)$ is even for every cut C and it is *1-even* if $fcap(C)$ is even for every 1-bend cut C.

For a vertex $v \in V$, $deg(v)$ denotes the degree of v in the graph R and $ter(v)$ denotes the number of nets having v as an endpoint. An *LRP* is *bounded*, if $deg(v) + ter(v) \leq 4$ for all vertices v.

At this point all terms are defined and we can now put our work into perspective. We view the routing problem as the problem of finding edge-disjoint paths in a grid graph. This is usually called routing in *knock-knee mode*, since two solution paths may both bend in the same vertex. The mode where this is excluded is called Manhattan mode. Previous work on routing problems in knock-knee mode can be found in Preparata/Lipski [PL], Frank [F], Mehlhorn/Preparata

[MP], Nishizeki/Saito/Suzuki [NSS], Kaufmann/Mehlhorn [KM], Becker/Mehlhorn [BM], Kramer/v. Leeuwen [KvL] and Brady/Brown [BB]. The problems considered in the first five papers are special cases of the LRP considered here. They solve the routing problem for channels [PL], switchboxes ([F], [MP]), convex generalized switchboxes ([NSS]) and generalized switchboxes ([MK]), respectively. In a generalized switchbox problem we have $M = \emptyset$, in a convex generalized switchbox problem we have in addition that every two boundary vertices are connected by a path with at most one bend, and in a switchbox problem R is a rectangle. The time bounds obtained in these papers are much better than the bound in the present paper, e.g., $O(n(\log n)^2)$ for the generalized switchbox problem. The paper by Becker/Mehlhorn is incomparable with the present paper; it is more restrictive in some ways since all vertices in B have to lie on the boundary of the unbounded face and it is more general in other ways since the routing region R may be an arbitrary even (= all nodes not on the boundary of the unbounded face have even degree) planar graph, nets are simply pairs of points in B, and no homotopies are required in the input. Kramer/v. Leeuwen prove that the global routing problem is NP-complete, i.e., if we drop the condition that $lr(N) \in N$ for $N \in \mathcal{N}$ (in other words, a net is just a pair of vertices in B), then the problem becomes NP-complete. Finally, Brady/Brown treat the problem of layer assignment and show that any layout in knock-knee mode can be wired using four conducting layers.

The present paper also has sources in graph theory, most notably the paper by Okamura/Seymour [OS]. They showed that the cut condition, i.e., $fcap(X) \geq 0$ for all cuts X, is necessary and sufficient for the solvability of even multi-commodity flow problems in planar graphs provided that all terminals lie on the same face. We drop this restriction and thus generalize their result; however, our solution *only* works for grid graphs. The generalization to general planar graphs remains a major challenge. A partial result was recently obtained by v. Hoesel and Schrijver [HS]; they treat the case $|M| = 1$. An implementation of the Okamura/Seymour result can be found in Matsumoto/Nishizeki/Saito [MNS] and in Becker/Mehlhorn.

We also want to mention the papers by Cole/Siegel [CS] and Leiserson/Miller Maley [LMM]. They prove the same result as we do but for river routing instead of routing in knock-knee mode, i.e., they require that solution paths are *vertex-disjoint*. Of course, nets cannot cross in their case.

Automatic VLSI design systems, e.g., CALCOS (Lauther [L]) and PI (Rivest [R]) for integrated circuits divide the routing problem into several stages.

1) Determine a global routing for every net.

2) Cut the routing region into regions of simple shape, e.g., channels.

3) Determine for every net the exact positions where it crosses channel boundaries.

4) Route each channel.

In some systems, e.g., CALCOS, stages 3 and 4 are combined into a single stage. Channels are routed one by one and the routings in the first i channels fix the positions of the nets which leave these channels. In all stages heuristic algorithms are usually used. The result of Kramer/v. Leeuwen states that the general routing problem is NP-complete; our theorem states that the combination of stages 2) to 4) can be solved in polynomial time, at least for two-terminal nets and in knock-knee mode.

This paper is organized as follows. In section II we give the algorithm which is then proved correct in section III. Section IV, describes an implementation and its analysis. Section V is a short conclusion. Sections III and IV are ommitted from this extended abstract.

We close this section with a remark about notation. A path p is a sequence $e_1e_2\ldots e_k$ of edges where $e_i = (v_i, v_{i+1})$ for $1 \le i \le k$. We call v_1 the start vertex of p, v_{k+1} the end vertex of p and v_1 and v_{k+1} its terminals, i.e., we view a path as being oriented from v_1 to v_{k+1}. The reverse path $p^{-1} = e_k \ldots e_2e_1$ is then oriented from v_{k+1} to v_1. A net $N = [p]$ is an equivalence class of paths and therefore also oriented. The start vertex of N is the start vertex of p. The reverse net N^{-1} is the equivalence class $[p^{-1}]$. Of course, a routing problem changes only in an inessential way, if the orientation of some nets is changed. We will tacitely use this fact in the following sections.

II. The Algorithm

In this section we describe an algorithm for solving local routing problems.
Let $P_0 = (V_0, E_0, \mathcal{N}_0)$ be an even local routing problem which satisfies the cut condition, i.e., $fcap(C) \in 2 \cdot \mathbb{N}_0$ for every cut C. Here $2 \cdot \mathbb{N}_0$ denotes the set of even nonnegative integers. Our algorithm constructs a solution for P_0 iteratively by transforming P_0 into simpler and simpler routing problems. We will maintain the invariant that *the current routing problem $P = (V, E, \mathcal{N})$ is good with respect to P_0*.

Definition 1: A routing problem $P = (V, E, \mathcal{N})$ is *good* with respect to $P_0 = (V_0, E_0, \mathcal{N}_0)$ if

a) P is a routing problem with $V \subseteq V_0$ and $E \subseteq E_0$.

b) $fcap(Y) \in 2 \cdot \mathbb{N}_0$ for all 1-bend cuts Y, i.e., the cut condition for 1-bend cuts is satisfied and the problem is 1-even.

c) P is bounded.

d) If P is solvable then P_0 is solvable. ∎

Remark: For the problems P constructed by our algorithm the connection between a solution of P and a solution of P_0 is very simple. For every net $N \in \mathcal{N}_0$ there will be a set $\mathcal{N}(N) \subseteq \mathcal{N}$ of nets of the current problem P and a set $E(N) \subseteq E_0 - E$ of edges such that local routings for the nets in $\mathcal{N}(N)$ together with the edges in $E(N)$ form a local routing for N. In other words, the set $E(N)$ of edges has already been reserved for the net N and the fragments $\mathcal{N}(N)$ of net N still have to be routed. When P is trivial, i.e., $\mathcal{N} = \emptyset$, then a solution for P_0 was found. ∎

We will mostly use the phrase P is good instead of P is good with respect to the basic problem P_0.

Definition 2: An *LRP* P is *reduced* if $ter(v) < deg(v)$ for all $v \in V$, and there is no cut with capacity one. ∎

In each iteration of the algorithm (cf. Prog. 1) the routing problem is simplified in two phases (procedures Simplify1 and Simplify2). Procedure Simplify1 eliminates all cuts with capacity one and all vertices v with $deg(v) = ter(v)$ and turns the routing problem into a reduced routing problem. Procedure Simplify2 works on reduced routing problems and either discards some edges in the left upper corner of the routing region (if there is no saturated cut through the left upper corner) or it chooses a particular net to be routed through the left upper corner. In the second case a vertex v with $deg(v) = ter(v)$ is created and hence Simplify1 applies in the next iteration. Thus at least one edge will be eliminated in each iteration and hence $O(n)$ iterations suffice to find a solution.

```
(* P0 = (V0, E0, N0) is an even local routing problem
satisfying the cut condition *)
P = (V, E, N) ← P0
while E ≠ ∅
do (* P is good *)
    Simplify1;
    (* P is good and reduced *)
    Simplify2;
    (* P is good *)
od
```

Prog. 1

Lemma 1. *Let P be a 1-even local routing problem. Then $deg(v) = ter(v)$ mod 2 for all v. In particular, if P is bounded then $deg(v) = 3$ implies $ter(v) = 1$ and if P is reduced then $deg(v) = 2$ implies $ter(v) = 0$. Also there are no vertices of degree one.*

We will next describe procedures Simplify1 and Simplify2, cf. programs 2 and 3. In Simplify1 we distinguish two cases, namely the existence of a cut X with $cap(X) = 1$ or the absence of such cuts and the existence of a vertex v with $deg(v) = ter(v)$. Assume first that there is a cut X with $cap(X) = 1$. Since P is good and hence is

1-even and satisfies the cut condition for X we must have $fcap(X) = 0$. Thus there is a unique net N with $cross(N, X) = 1$. Let $e \in E$ be the edge intersected by X and let $N = [p_1 e p_2]$ where $cross(p_1 e p_2, X) = 1$. We remove edge e, reserve it for net N, and replace net N by the two nets $[p_1]$ and $[p_2]$. A solution for P is readily obtained from a solution for the modified problem which we denote by P'. We only have to combine the local routings for $[p_1]$ and $[p_2]$ with edge e and obtain a local routing for N.

---

procedure Simplify1
begin (* P is good *)
    while there is a cut X with $cap(X) = 1$ or a vertex v with $deg(v) = ter(v)$
    do (* P is good *)
        if there exists a cut X with $cap(X) = 1$
        then let X be a cut with $cap(X) = 1$ and let N be the unique net with $cross(N, X) = 1$;
            let e be the edge intersected by cut X and let $N = [p_1 e p_2]$ where $cross(p_1 e p_2, X) = 1$;
            remove edge e, reserve it for net N and replace net N by nets $[p_1]$ and $[p_2]$.
        else let v be a vertex with $deg(v) = ter(v)$;
            let e_i, $1 \leq i \leq 2$, be the edges incident to v and
            let N_i, $1 \leq i \leq 2$, be the nets incident to v where the edges are numbered as shown in Figure 3 and N_i is *right-of* N_{i+1};
            let $N_1 = [e_1 p_1]$, where p_1 does not use edge e_1;
            remove edge e_1, reserve it for net N_1 and replace net N_1 by net $[p_1]$
        fi
        (* P is good *)
    od
    (* P is good and reduced *)
end

Prog. 2

Lemma 2. *The problem P' defined above is good, i.e., the then-case of procedure Simplify1 maintains the invariant.*

Assume next that there is no cut with capacity one but that there is a vertex v with $deg(v) = ter(v)$. Then $deg(v) = 2$. We will now define two orderings, one on the d edges incident to v and one on the d nets incident to v. We will then assign the i-th edge in the ordering of edges to the i-th net in the ordering of nets and simplify the routing problem in this way.

The ordering on the edges incident to v is easy to define. Let e_i, $1 \leq i \leq 2$, be the edges incident to v ordered counterclockwise around v and numbered such that the faces between e_1 and e_2 is trivial. cf. Figure 3.

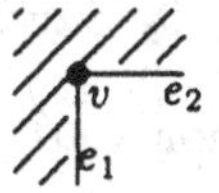

Fig. 3. A vertex v with $deg(v) = 2$ and the edges incident to it. The face in $\overline{M}$ is shown hatched.

We turn to the ordering on nets next. We define this ordering in three steps. We first define an ordering on paths, then define the concept of a canonical representative of a net and then order nets via their canonical representatives.

Definition 3: a) Let p_1 and p_2 be local routings with a common start vertex v. Then p_1 is *right-of* p_2 if either

- $p_1 = p_2$ or

- p_1 is a proper prefix of p_2 and p_2 enters the endpoint t_1 of p_1 through edge e_i and leaves it through edge e_j where $i > j$ and $e_1, \ldots, e_d$, $d \in \{2,3\}$ is the ordering of the edges incident to t_1 defined above or

- p_2 is a proper prefix of p_1 and p_1 enters the endpoint t_2 of p_2 through e_i and leaves it through edge e_j where $i < j$ and $e_1, \ldots, e_d$, $d \in \{2,3\}$ is the ordering of the edges incident to t_2.

- p_1 and p_2 differ in their first edges, p_1 starts with edge e_i, p_2 starts with edge e_j and $1 \leq i < j \leq d$ or

- p_1 and p_2 have a maximal non-trivial common prefix p, i.e., $p_1 = pq_1$ and $p_2 = pq_2$ and the first edges of q_1 and q_2 are distinct, and the three edges "last edge of p", "first edge of q_1", "first edge of q_2" are ordered counterclockwise around their common endpoint.

Figure 4 illustrates this definition.

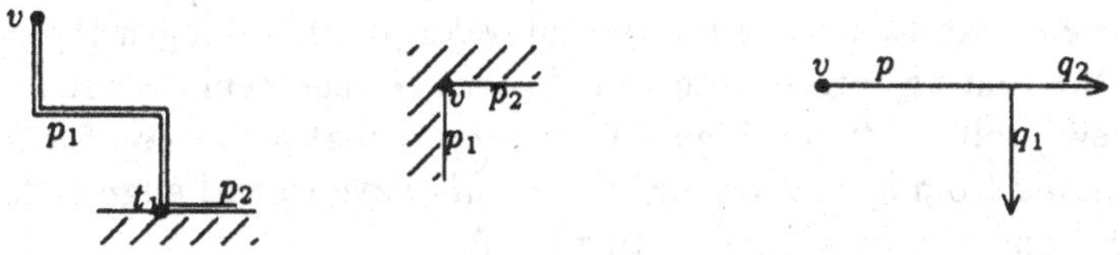

p_1 is a prefix of p_2 $\qquad$ p_1 and p_2 have a common prefix p

p_1 and p_2 differ in their first edges

Fig. 4. The various cases of definition $3a$. The local routing p_1 is *right-of* local routing p_2.

b) Let N be a net. A path $p \in N$ is *the canonical representative* of net N if p is a shortest path in N and if p is *right-of* all other shortest paths in N. We denote the canonical representative of net N by $can(N)$, cf. Figure 5.

c) Let N and N' be nets with a common start vertex terminal v. Then N is *right-of* N' if $can(N)$ is *right-of* $can(N')$. ∎

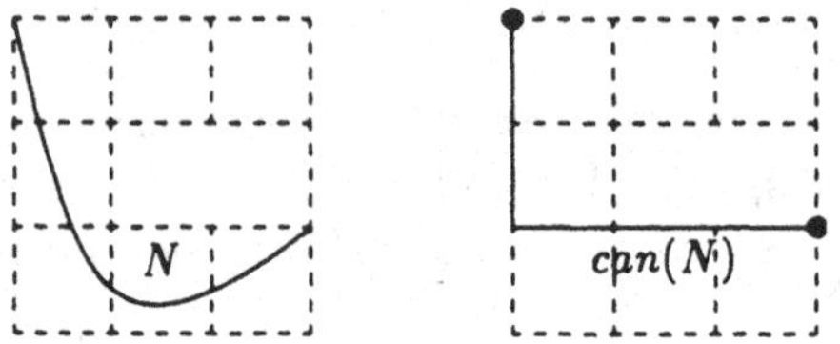

Fig. 5. A net and its canonical representative.

Remark: Definition 3a is long but there is a simple idea behind it. Follow the paths p_1 and p_2 starting in their common start vertex v. When they separate one will proceed to the right of the other one. The special cases (one prefix of the other or no common nontrivial prefix) reduce to the general case if one artificially introduces a pseudo-edge at each vertex $w \in B$ entering w from the nontrivial face and extends all paths by pseudo-edges at both ends. The relation *right-of* clearly totally orders the paths with a common start vertex and hence a net has a *unique* canonical representative. ∎

We are now ready for the else-case of procedure Simplify1. Let $e_i, 1 \leq i \leq 2$, be the edges incident to v in the ordering defined above and let $N_i, 1 \leq i \leq 2$, be the nets incident to v, where N_1 is *right-of* N_2. (Here we implicitly assumed that the nets N_i incident to v have v as their start vertex. This might require to change the orientation of some nets. If there is a net N which has v as its start and end vertex then both orientations have to be considered, i.e., N is some N_i and N^{-1} is some N_j, $i \neq j$.) Write $N_1 = [e_1 p_1]$ where p_1 is a path not using edge e_1. N_1 can be written this way because e_1 can be replaced by an equivalent path of length three. Remove edge e_1 from the routing region, reserve it for net N_1 and replace net N_1 by net $[p_1]$. Call the new problem P', cf. Figure 6. It is clear that a solution for P can be immediately derived from a solution for P'; we only have to add edge e_1 to the local routing for $[p_1]$ and obtain a local routing for N_1.

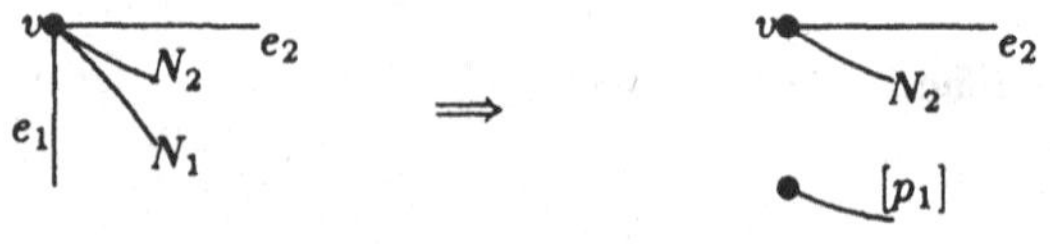

Fig. 6. The else-case of procedure Simplify1.

Lemma 3. *The problem P' defined above is good, i.e., the else-case of procedure* Simplify1 *maintains the invariant.*

Procedure Simplify1 leaves us with a reduced routing problem to which we apply procedure Simplify2, cf. Prog. 3.

---

procedure Simplify2
begin (* P is good and reduced *)
  let $e^* = (a, b)$ be the vertical edge incident to the left upper corner a;
  if $\exists$ saturated 1-bend cut through e^*
  then let X be the leftmost saturated 1-bend cut through e
    let $([p_1], [p_2])$ be the rightmost decomposition with respect to X.
    replace net $[p_1 p_2]$ by nets $[p_1]$ and $[p_2]$.

  else remove the four edges on the boundary of the trivial
    face to the right of e^*

  fi
  (* P is good *)
end

Prog. 3

We need some additional concepts. A vertex $a = (x, y)$ of the routing region R is called the *left upper corner* of R if there is no vertex (x', y') of R with $y' > y$ or with $y' = y$ and $x' < x$. We use b to denote the vertex $b = (x, y - 1)$ and $e^* = (a, b)$ to denote the vertical edge incident to a. We consider 1-bend cuts X which go through edge e^* and distinguish two cases: either there exists a saturated 1-bend cut through edge e^* (then-case) or there exists no such cut (else-case). In the latter case we remove the four edges on the boundary cycle of the trivial face to the right of e^* (cf. Figure 7).

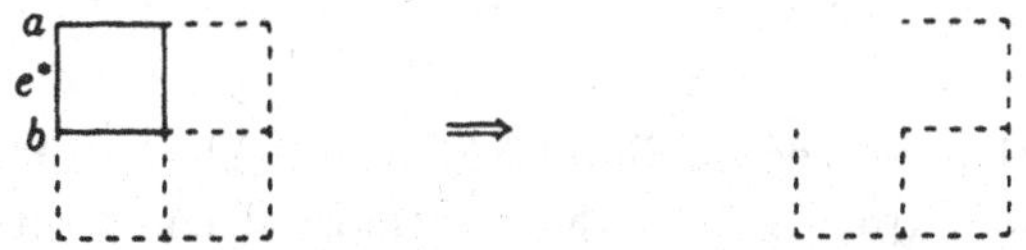

Fig. 7. The else-case of procedure Simplify2.

Lemma 4. *The else-case of procedure* Simplify2 *maintains the invariant.*

Let us consider the then-case next. We observe first that a saturated 1-bend cut through edge e^* must consist of two segments s_1 and s_2 and that the second segment runs downwards. This can be seen as follows: A horizontal cut through edge e^* cannot be saturated since each of the vertices of degree two in the top row are not terminal of any net and each of the l vertices of degree three is the terminal of exactly one net. Hence the capacity exceeds the density by at least two. A similar argument shows that s_2 cannot bend upwards. So s_2 must run downwards. Among the saturated 1-bend cuts through edge e^* we choose the one with the maximal segment s_1. We call this cut the *leftmost saturated 1-bend cut through edge* e^*.

Next consider any net N. A *decomposition of N with respect to vertex a* is a pair $([p_1], [p_2])$ where p_1 ends in vertex a, p_2 starts in vertex a and $N = [p_1 p_2]$. Let $([p_1], [p_2])$ be a decomposition of net N and let $([q_1], [q_2])$ be a decomposition of N' with respect to a. The decomposition $([p_1], [p_2])$ is *right-of* decomposition $([q_1], [q_2])$ if $[p_2]$ is *right-of* $[q_2]$.

We are now ready for the description of the then-case. Let X be the leftmost saturated 1-bend cut through edge e^*. Let $D = \{([q_1], [q_2]);\ ([q_1], [q_2])$ is the decomposition with respect to a of some net N where either $N \in \mathcal{N}$ or $N^{-1} \in \mathcal{N}$ and $cross([q_1 q_2], X) = cross([q_1], X) + cross([q_2], X)\}$ and let $([p_1], [p_2]) \in D$ be *right-of* every other element of D. We call $([p_1], [p_2])$ the *rightmost decomposition with respect to* X.

Remark: The set D is not-empty since the cut X is saturated. Let $N \in \mathcal{N}$ be a net which goes across X. We can write $N = [q_1 e^* q_2]^\epsilon$ with $\epsilon \in \{-1, +1\}$. Then $([q_1], [e^* q_2])$ is an element of D. ∎

In the then-case we replace the net $[p_1 p_2]$ (or $[p_1 p_2]^{-1}$, whichever is in $\mathcal{N}$) by the nets $[p_1]$ and $[p_2]$, cf. Figure 8. Call the modified problem P'. It is clear that a solution for the modified problem P' directly yields a solution for P. We also have

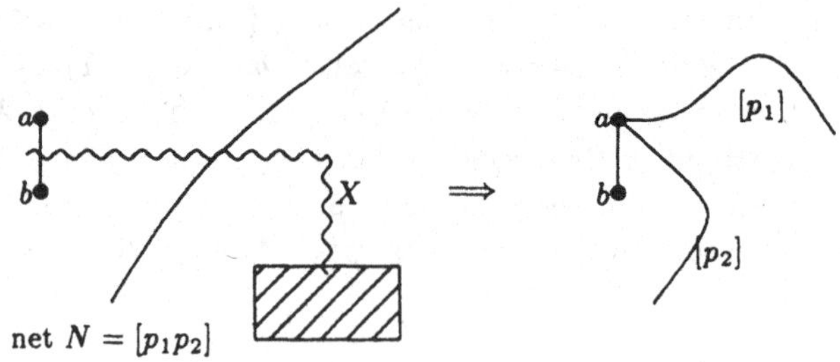

Fig. 8. The then-case of procedure Simplify2. X is the leftmost saturated 1-bend cut through edge e^* and $([p_1], [p_2])$ is the rightmost decomposition with respect to X.

Lemma 5. *The problem P' defined above is good, i.e., the then-case of procedure* Simplify2 *maintains the invariant.*

Theorem 2: Let P_0 be a solvable even local routing problem. Then our algorithm constructs a solution in $O(n)$ iterations of the main loop.

Proof: If P_0 is solvable then P_0 is good (with respect to P_0). We infer from lemmas 2 to 5 that all intermediate problems are good, and hence the final problem is good. The set of the edges in the final problem is empty and hence our algorithm finds a solution for the routing problem. The bound on the number of iterations follows from the remark made immediately before definition 2. ∎

Theorem 2 implies part a) of theorem 1. Clearly, if P_0 is solvable then the cut condition holds. Conversely, if the cut condition holds then the cut condition for 1-bend cuts holds and P_0 is good. Thus our algorithm constructs a solution.

III. Correctness, IV. Implementation

See full paper.

V. Conclusion

We showed that the local routing problem for two-terminal nets is solvable in quadratic time. There are three major open problems:

1) Allow more general routing regions than grid graphs. In particular, prove a similar result for arbitrary planar graphs.

2) Extend the result to nets with more than two terminals.

3) Improve the running time. This question is adressed in the first author's Ph.D. thesis where an alternative and considerably more complex implementation with running time $O(n \log n)$ will be described.

VI. References

[BB] M. Brady/D. Brown: "VLSI Routing: Four Layers Suffice", MIT VLSI Conference 1984

[BM] M. Becker/K. Mehlhorn: "Algorithms for Routing in Planar Graphs", Technical Report, FB 10, Universität des Saarlandes, August 1984

[CS] R. Cole/A. Siegel: "River Routing Every Which Way, but Loose", 25th FOCS, 65–73

[F] A. Frank: "Disjoint Paths in Rectilinear Grids", Combinatorica 2, 4 (1982), 361–371

[HS] C. van Hoesel/A. Schrijver: "Edge-disjoint Homotopic Paths in a Planar Graph with One Hole", Technical Report, Amsterdam 1986

[KM] M. Kaufmann/K. Mehlhorn: "Generalized Switchbox Routing", Technical Report, FB 10, Universität des Saarlandes, 1984

[KvL] M. E. Kramer/J. van Leeuwen: "Wire Routing is NP-complete", Technical Report RUU-CS-82-4, 1982, Utrecht

[L] U. Lauther: "The SIEMENS CALCOS System for Computer Aided Design of Cell Based IC Layout", Proc. 1st ICCC, 1980, pp 768–771

[LMM] Ch. Leiserson/F. Miller Maley: "Algorithms for Routing and Testing Routability of Planar VLSI Layouts", 17th STOC 85

[MNS] K. Matsumoto/T. Nishizeki/N. Saito: "An Efficient Algorithm for Finding Multicommodity Flows in Planar Networks", SICOMP, Vol 15:2 (1986), 495–510

[MP] K. Mehlhorn/F. Preparata: "Routing through a Rectangle", JACM 1986, Vol 33, 60–85

[NSS] T. Nishizeki/N. Saito/K. Suzuki: "A linear-time routing algorithm for convex grids", IEEE Transactions on Computer Aided Design, CAD-4, 68–76, 1985

[OS] H. Okamura/P. D. Seymour: "Multicommodity Flows in Planar Graphs", Journal of Combinatorial Theory 31, Series B, 1981, 75–81

[PL] F. Preparata/W. Lipski, Jr: "Three Layers are Enough", 23rd FOCS 1982, 350–357

[R] R. L. Rivest: "The "PI" (Placement and Interconnect) System", 19th Design Automation Conference, 475–481, 1982

GEOMETRIC RELATIONS AMONG VORONOI DIAGRAMS

Franz Aurenhammer
Institutes for Information Processing
Technical University of Graz and Austrian Computer Society
Schiesstattgasse 4a, A-8010 Graz, Austria

Hiroshi Imai
Department of Computer Science and Communication Engineering
Kyushu University, Hakozaki, Fukuota 812, Japan

Abstract: Two general classes of Voronoi diagrams are introduced and, along with their modifications to higher order, are shown to be geometrically related. This geometric background, on one hand, serves to analyze the size and the combinatorial structure, and on the other hand, implies general and efficient methods of construction, for various important types of Voronoi diagrams considered in the literature.

1. **Introduction**. Let G denote a finite subset of the d-dimensional Cartesian space R^d for $d \geq 1$, and let f be a function from $R^d \times G$ to R. The points in G (which are called *generators*, or also sources or sites) and (the *distance function*) f impose a subdivision on R^d in a very natural way: For $p, q \in G$, let

$$dom(p,q) = \{x \in R^d \mid f(x,p) < f(x,q)\}$$

be the *dominance* of p over q, and define

$$reg(p) = \bigcap_{q \in G-\{p\}} dom(p,q)$$

as the *region* of p among G (with respect to f). The set of all *reg*(p) for $p \in G$, along with the components that describe the

---

Research of the first author was supported by the Austrian Fond zur Foerderung der wissenschaftlichen Forschung.

boundary of *reg*(p) in an explicit manner, induce a diagram in R^d that is probably best known in the fields of discrete and computational geometry under the name *Voronoi diagram* of G and f (here V(G,f) for short).

Up to now, many different types of Voronoi diagrams have been investigated from both the geometric and the algorithmic point of view. The purpose of this paper is to point out that a particular type of Voronoi diagram is very general in the sense that it can be brought, geometrically, into connection with various other types. It is the diagram $V(\Gamma,\varphi)$, for $\Gamma \subsetneq R^d$ some set of generators, and for

$$\varphi(x,p) = (x-p)^2+\omega(p), \quad \omega(p)\in R$$

the *power function* (or the Laguerre distance). $V(\Gamma,\varphi)$ has appeared in the literature under the names *power diagram* [3] (the notion we will adopt and abbreviate by PD), Dirichlet cell complex [15], sectional Dirichlet tesselation [2], Laguerre-Voronoi diagram [12], and others. The generality inherent in the concept of PDs is already reflected by the following two phenomena: PDs (in R^d) are intimately related to such central concepts in discrete and computational geometry as convex hulls and hyperplane arrangements (in R^{d+1}), see [3]. Moreover, many cell complexes in R^d that, a priori, are not defined via the notion of Voronoi diagram (e.g. hyperplane arrangements, or simple complexes for $d\geqslant 3$) can be interpreted as PDs, see [4].

The linkage of PDs to various types of Voronoi diagrams is of particular interest. In the following sections, three general classes of Voronoi diagrams are introduced and shown to be geometrically related to PDs. For each class, several examples are given along with transforms that relate them to PDs. Due to the assertion below, PDs in R^d can be constructed efficiently, and there exist tight upper bounds on their size. This provides a general, dimension-independent construction method for Voronoi diagrams which has many practical applications in the low-dimensional case. The high-dimensional instances give rise to various problems in discrete geometry as well as in complexity theory.

Proposition 1: Let $size_d(n)$ denote the maximal number of faces of the convex hull CH of n points in R^d, and let $time_d(n)$ be the time complexity of constructing CH. The following holds:

[16] $size_d(n) = O(n^{\lfloor d/2 \rfloor})$.

[18,19] $time_d(n) = O(max\{size_d(n)),n\log n\})$ for d even, and $time_d(n) = O(n^2+size_d(n)\log n)$ for d odd.

[3,12] For $\Gamma \subsetneq R^d$ and $|\Gamma|=n$, a power diagram $V(\Gamma,\varphi)$ realizes at most $size_{d+1}(n)$ components and can be constructed in $O(time_{d+1}(n))$ time and optimal $O(size_{d+1}(n))$ space.

By construction of a diagram the computation of a data structure is meant which reflects the combinatorial structure realized by the individual components of the diagram. Since we here are mainly concerned with geometrical properties of diagrams, we refrain from any implementation details for which we refer e.g. to the above two papers.

2. **Affine Voronoi diagrams**. Let $V(G,f)$ be a Voronoi diagram in R^d. For two distinct generators $p,q \in G$ their *separator* is defined by

$$sep(p,q) = R^d-(dom(p,q) \cup dom(q,p)).$$

We will term $V(G,f)$ *affine* if $sep(p,q)$ is a hyperplane of R^d, for any distinct $p,q \in G$. Intuitively speaking, affine diagrams are just the Voronoi diagrams whose regions are convex polyhedra. Whether $V(G,f)$ is affine only depends on the properties of the distance function f. Moreover, if $V(G,f)$ is affine and F is a strictly monotone function on the range of f then $V(G,F \circ f)$ is affine, too. The following general assertion can be stated:

Theorem 1: For any affine Voronoi diagram $V(G,f)$ in R^d there exist a set Γ of generators and a power function φ such that

$$V(\Gamma,\varphi) = V(G,f).$$

The result follows from the property $sep(p,q) \cap sep(q,r) \subseteq sep(p,r)$, that trivially holds for any f and distinct $p,q,r \in G$, and that is necessary and sufficient for a set of hyperplanes of R^d to be defined by the power function [3]. The remainder of this section will show that Γ and φ can be calculated directly from G and f, in time $O(|\Gamma|)$, for any particular type of affine Voronoi diagram considered in the literature so far.

Let the *general quadratic-form distance* Q be defined by

$$Q(x,p) = (x-p)^T M(x-p)+w(p),$$

for $w(p)\in R$ and M a real and (w.l.o.g.) symmetric d×d-matrix. Unified treatments of the type V(G,Q) of diagram are proposed in [9] by means of arrangements and in [11] by exploiting a transform that maps V(G,Q) into a PD. The following approach is preferable because of its simplicity: Since for distinct $p,q\in G$, their separator

$$sep(p,q) = \{x\in R^d \mid 2(q-p)^T Mx=q^T Mq-p^T Mp+w(p)-w(q)\}$$

is a hyperplane, we deduce from Theorem 1 that V(G,Q) actually is a power diagram. In fact, it coincides with $V(\Gamma,\varphi)$, for

$$\Gamma = \{\pi \mid \pi=Mp,\ p\in G\},$$
$$\varphi(x,\pi) = (x-\pi)^2+\omega(\pi),$$
$$\omega(\pi) = -\pi^2+p^T Mp+w(p).$$

To keep this paper short, elementary analytic proofs are omitted throughout. Observe at this place that the power function φ depends only on the constants ω if Γ is fixed. Hence $V(\Gamma,\varphi)$ is determined if Γ and ω are. We may require that matrix M is non-singular. If M contains only d-i independent rows ($1\leq i\leq d-1$) then *sep*(p,q) is parallel to the same i coordinate axes for all $p,q\in g$, $p\neq q$. In this case, V(G,Q) essentially is the diagram in the lower-dimensional space R^{d-i}.

The two most prominent representants of diagrams definable in R^d via the general quadratic-form distance Q are the closest-point Euclidean Voronoi diagram [19] (M=I, the identity matrix; w(p)=0, $\forall p\in G$) and its furthest-point counterpart [19] (M=-I; w(p)=0, $\forall p\in G$). For M=I and arbitrary $w(p)\in R$, the power diagram [12,3] is obtained. In the light of Theorem 1, this leads us to the following conclusion:

Corollary 1: The class of diagrams definable by Q coincides with the class of power diagrams and thus with the class of affine Voronoi diagrams.

This means that PDs are the simplest type of diagrams

definable by Q that are universal in this class. PDs are straightforward generalizations of (the most fundamental) closest-point Euclidean Voronoi diagrams which themselves, however, are not universal in the above class. Though of minor importance, two additional types of diagrams in that class should be mentioned. For $M = \begin{pmatrix} 0 & 1 \\ 1 & 0 \end{pmatrix}$ and $w(p)=0$, $Q(x,p)$ describes the area of the axis-parallel rectangle with diagonal vertices p and x. $V(G,Q)$ now can be used to find the largest empty axis-parallel rectangle among G [8]. Somewhat a mixture of the Euclidean closest- and furthest-point Voronoi diagram in R^d is induced by the Jordan matrix $M = \text{diag}[\sigma_1,\ldots\sigma_d]$, for $\sigma_i \in \{-1,1\}$ and $w(p)=0$. This type is mentioned (but without applications) in [12,9].

From Corollary 1 it is obvious that the classes of diagrams created by Q and by the *affine distance*

$$A(x,p) = p^T x+w(p), \quad w(p)\in R,$$

respectively, are identical (see also [9]). Note that a power diagram $V(\Gamma,\varphi) = V(G,A)$ (whose existence follows from Corollary 1) is given by

$$\Gamma = \{\pi \mid \pi=-p/2,\ p\in G\}$$
$$\omega(\pi) = -\pi^2+w(p).$$

In [1,12], affine Voronoi diagrams of the form $V(G,Q)\cap h$, for a set G of generators and a particular hyperplane h in R^{d+1}, have received some attention. Let Γ and φ be such that the power diagram $V(\Gamma,\varphi)$ coincides with $V(G,Q)$, and let π' denote the orthogonal projection of $\pi\in\Gamma$ onto h (h may be arbitrary). If we choose

$$\Gamma' = \{\pi' \mid \pi\in\Gamma\} \text{ and}$$
$$\varphi' \text{ such that } \omega'(\pi') = \omega(\pi)-(\pi-\pi')^2$$

then $V(\Gamma',\varphi') = V(G,Q)\cap h$ holds.

This closes our considerations on affine Voronoi diagrams. As a conclusion, all types of diagrams discussed above realize the same number of polyhedra as power diagrams, and can be constructed within the same complexity bounds (cf. Proposition 1). This unifies several previously known results on affine diagrams.

3. **Affinely transformable Voronoi diagrams**. One is tempted to mean that affine diagrams are the only Voronoi diagrams that are geometrically related to power diagrams. It is the purpose of this section to characterize the type of diagrams V(G,f) that represent projected sections of PDs.

Let h_0 be the hyperplane $x_{d+1}=0$ of R^{d+1}. *proj*(S) denotes the vertical (i.e., parallel to the x_{d+1}-axis) projection of $S \subseteq R^{d+1}$ onto h_0 and *aff*(S) denotes the affine hull of S. For some strictly increasing function F: R→R and distinct generators p,q∈G, we define

$$cone_F(p) = \{(x, x_{d+1}) \mid x \in h_0, x_{d+1} = F(f(x,p))\}$$

$$\alpha_F(p,q) = aff(cone_F(p) \cap cone_F(q)).$$

A diagram V(G,f) in h_0 is termed *affinely transformable* if there exists an F such that $\alpha_F(p,q)$ is a hyperplane of R^{d+1}, for any distinct p,q∈G. Moreover, we say that V(G,f) can be *embedded* into a Voronoi diagram V in R^{d+1} if V realizes a region C for each p∈G such that $proj(C \cap cone_F(p)) = reg(p)$, for some F. By means of the terminology introduced, the following important connection can be established.

Theorem 2: A Voronoi diagram V(G,f) in h_0 is affinely transformable iff it can be embedded into a power diagram in R^{d+1}.

Proof: For $x \in h_0$ and p∈G, let x_p be the vertical projection of x onto $cone_F(p)$. By definition of *dom*(p,q), $x \in dom(p,q)$ is equivalent to f(x,p)<f(x,q) and, since F is strictly increasing, to F(f(x,p))<F(f(x,q)) which means that x_p is below (i.e., has smaller x_{d+1}-coordinate than) x_q. The definition of $\alpha_F(p,q)$ and the fact that it is a hyperplane of R^{d+1} now imply that $x_p \in hsp(p,q)$ iff $x \in dom(p,q)$, where *hsp*(p,q) is a fixed (open) halfspace of R^{d+1} bounded by $\alpha_F(p,q)$. Recall that $reg(p) = \bigcap_{p \neq q} dom(p,q)$ and consider the convex polyhedron $C = \bigcap_{p \neq q} hsp(p,q)$. Then $x \in reg(p)$ holds iff $x_p \in C$, that is, $reg(p) = proj(C \cap cone_F(p))$.

In particular, $x \in sep(p,q)$ is equivalent to x_p $(=x_q)$ $\in \alpha_F(p,q)$, for $x \in h_0$. From $sep(p,q) \cap sep(q,r) \subseteq sep(p,r)$ we now deduce $\alpha_F(p,q) \cap \alpha_F(q,r) \subseteq \alpha_F(p,r)$ which tells us that these hyperplanes are the separators for some power diagram V in R^{d+1} (cf. Theorem 1). Consequently, polyhedron C is one of the regions of V which proves that V(G,f) can be embedded into V □

Theorem 2 suggests that the regions of an affinely transformable diagram $V(G,f)$ can be obtained by projecting certain sections of the polyhedra of a power diagram $V(\Gamma,\varphi)$ in one dimension higher. (Note, however, that not all polyhedra may contribute to regions of $V(G,f)$.) Provided a suitable function F is known, $cone_F(p)$ is computationally simple (in the sense that its intersection with a polyhedron C can be computed in time proportional to the number of faces of C), and Γ and φ are available, the complexity of constructing $V(\Gamma,\varphi)$ is an upper bound for that of $V(G,f)$. All three conditions are met if f is one of the following distance functions.

Let $p,q \in G \subsetneq h_0$ and $x \in h_0$. The *additive Euclidean distance* a is given by

$$a(x,p) = |x-p|-w(p), \; w(p) \geq 0.$$

Its separators $sep(p,q)$ are hyperboloids in h_0 with rotation axes through p and q. If we choose $F(a)=a$ then $cone_F(p)$ is described by the equation $x_{d+1} = |x-p|-w(p)$, and thus is a cone with vertical rotation axis and apex $(p,-w(p))$. It is an easy analytic exercise to prove that $\sigma_F(p,q)$ is a hyperplane of R^{d+1} and that $V(G,a)$ can be embedded into the power diagram $V(\Gamma,\varphi)$, for

$$\Gamma = \{\pi=(p,w(p)) \mid p \in G\},$$
$$\omega(\pi) = -2w(p)^2.$$

The planar instances of $V(G,a)$ have been treated, for example, in [2] from the mathematical, and in [14,20,10] from the algorithmic standpoint. The above relationship between $V(G,a)$ and PDs yields the only known construction method in higher dimensions. It is particularly efficient in R^3, where $V(G,a)$ can be shown to contain $\Theta(|G|^2)$ components and is constructed in $O(|G|^2 \log|G|)$ time.

The second class of diagrams considered here is generated by the *multiplicative Euclidean distance* m, for

$$m(x,p) = |x-p|/w(p), \; w(p)>0,$$

which yields spheres in h_0 as separators. Setting $F(m)=2m^2$ yields the equation $x_{d+1} = 2|x-p|^2/w(p)^2$ for $cone_F(p)$, which describes a paraboloid with apex (p,o) and focus $(p,w(p)^2/4)$. As a matter of fact, $V(G,m)$ in h_0 can be embedded into the power diagram $V(\Gamma,\varphi)$ in R^{d+1}, if we take

$$\Gamma = \{\pi=(p,w(p)^2/2) \mid p\in G\},$$
$$\omega(\pi) = -w(p)^4/4.$$

Among others, [5], [2,7], and [3] consider the one-, two-, and higher-dimensional instances of diagrams of the type $V(G,m)$, respectively. The algorithmic results obtained there via different approaches all are achieved by our general construction method. In the most interesting cases of $G\subsetneq R^1$, $G\subsetneq R^2$ (and $G\subsetneq R^3$), the method can be shown to be optimal to within a constant factor (and the factor $log|G|$), respectively.

4. **Generalizing to higher order**. The well-known concept of modifying a Voronoi diagram $V(G,f)$ in R^d to higher order [19] involves generating its regions by subsets rather than by elements of G. For $S\subsetneq G$, its *region* is defined by

$$reg(S) = \bigcap_{p\in S,\, q\in G-S} dom(p,q).$$

The subdivision of R^d induced by $reg(S)$, for all $S\subsetneq G$ with $|S|=k$, is commonly called the *order k-Voronoi diagram* of G (with respect to f), for short $k\text{-}V(G,f)$. A very interesting and important fact is that the class of power diagrams in R^d is closed under order-k modification.

Theorem 3. For any order-k power diagram $k\text{-}V(G,f)$ in R^d there exist a set Γ_k of generators and a power function φ_k such that

$$V(\Gamma_k,\varphi_k) = k\text{-}V(G,f).$$

The existence of Γ_k and φ_k follows from a result in [4]. In the proof below (that is essentially distinct and shorter), Γ_k and φ_k actually are constructed.

Proof: We define Γ_k and φ_k as follows:

$$\Gamma_k = \{\pi_S = \sum_{p\in S} \mid S\subsetneq G,\ |S|=k\},$$

$$\omega_k(\pi_S) = \sum_{p\in S}(p^2+w(p))-\pi_S{}^2.$$

Let $T = (S-\{p\})\cup\{q\}$, for $p\in S$ and $q\in G-S$. *dom*(p,q) denotes the dominance of p over q in $V(G,f)$, and $dom_k(\pi_S,\pi_T)$ denotes the dominance of π_S over π_T in $V(\Gamma_k,\varphi_k)$. By simple analytic calculations, $dom(p,q) = dom_k(\pi_S,\pi_T)$ holds. From

$$reg(S) = \bigcap_{p\in S, q\in G-S} dom(p,q)$$

$$= \bigcap_{T=(S-\{p\})\cup\{q\}} dom(p,q)$$

we thus deduce

$$reg(S) = \bigcap_{T=(S-\{p\})\cup\{q\}} dom_k(\pi_S,\pi_T)$$

which is identical to

$$\bigcap_{T\subsetneq G, |T|=k} dom_k(\pi_S,\pi_T) = reg_k(\pi_S),$$

since only the former dominances contribute to the intersection. In other words, the region of S in k-$V(G,f)$ coincides with the region of π_S in $V(\Gamma_k,\varphi_k)$ for each $S\subsetneq G$ with $|S|=k$. This proves $k\text{-}V(G,f) = V(\Gamma_k,\varphi_k)$ □

Let us consider the consequences of Theorem 3. A serious shortcoming of the set $\Gamma_k\subsetneq R^d$ of generators constructed in its proof is that Γ_k may contain a large number (in fact, $\Theta(|G|^k)$) of *redundant* generators, i.e., generators which define an empty polyhedron in $V(\Gamma_k,\varphi_k) = k\text{-}V(G,f)$. Hence its algorithmic application becomes attractive only if we bypass the calculation of redundant generators in Γ_k. Assume that G contains no redundant generator. Then one possible approach (which is detailed, in a geometrically dual environment, for Euclidean closest-point Voronoi diagrams in [6]) relies on the following:

Observation 1: Let $\pi_S,\pi_T\in\Gamma_k$ be non-redundant. $\pi_{S\cup T}$ is non-redundant in Γ_{k+1} iff the intersection g of the closures of $reg_k(\pi_S)$ and $reg_k(\pi_T)$ has dimension d-1.

Proof: Observe first that g has dimension d-1 iff S is of the form $(T-\{p\})\cup\{q\}$, such that *aff* g is the hyperplane *sep*(p,q) of R^d. This is equivalent to the existence of a point $x\in g$ that satisfies

$$f(x,p)=f(x,q)<f(x,r)<f(x,t),$$

for all $r \in S \cap T$ and all $t \in G-(S \cap T)$. Because of $(S \cap T) \cup \{p,q\} = S \cup T$, the above can be rewritten to

$$\exists x \in R^d: f(x,r) < f(x,t),\ \forall r \in S \cup T,\ \forall t \in G-(S \cup T),$$

which just means that $x \in reg_{k+1}(S \cup T) \neq \emptyset$, such that $\pi_{S \cup T}$ is non-redundant in Γ_{k+1} □

Using Observation 1 and the formulas in Theorem 3, Γ_k and φ_k can be obtained in time proportional to the size of $V(\Gamma_{k-1},\varphi_{k-1})$ provided this diagram has been constructed. As easily verified, we may take the input data G and f for Γ_1 and φ_1, respectively. This implies an iterative method for calculating Γ_k and φ_k whose time complexity is the same as for constructing all diagrams $V(\Gamma_i,\varphi_i)$, for $i=1,\dots,k-1$. It is well known that the maximal size of an order-i Voronoi diagram for n generators (and thus the cardinality of Γ_i) is increasing with i. Hence if k is considered as a constant, (as done in many practical applications) the time needed for calculating Γ_k and φ_k is dominated by the time needed for constructing $V(\Gamma_k,\varphi_k) = k\text{-}V(G,f)$ from Γ_k and φ_k. In conjunction with Proposition 1, this leads to the following efficient result:

Corollary 2: Let $m=R(n,k,d)$ denote the maximal number of regions realized by an order-k power diagram of n generators in R^d. If G contains n non-redundant generators and k is a constant then $k\text{-}V(G,f)$ can be constructed in $O(time_{d+1}(m))$ time and $O(size_{d+1}(m))$ space.

Our investigations in Section 2 immediately imply that, under the above conditions, any affine order-k Voronoi diagram in R^d can be constructed within the bounds in Corollary 2. Note that they are valid for affine order-(n-k) diagrams, too, since these diagrams are order-k diagrams for the same set of generators and the matrix M in the quadratic-form distance changed to -M. In addition, results for affinely transformable order-k diagrams can be obtained. Modifying the notion of $cone_F(p)$ introduced in Section 3 to order k by defining

$$cone_F(S) = \{(x,x_{d+1}) \mid x \in h_0,\ x_{d+1} = \max_{p \in S} F(f(x,p))\},$$

for $S \subsetneq G$, $|S|=k$, yields the following order-k version of Theorem 2 (that can be proved in a similar matter).

Theorem 2': $V(G,f)$ in h_o is affinely transformable iff k-$V(G,f)$ can be embedded into an order-k power diagram k-$V(\Gamma,\varphi)$ in R^{d+1}.

Note that Γ can be chosen to contain no redundant generator iff G does (which we will assume now). Thus, if $cone_F(S)$ is 'computationally simple' and Γ and φ are available then k-$V(G,f)$ (and thus also $(n-k)$-$V(G,f)$) can be constructed in $O(time_{d+2}(R(n,k,d+1)))$ time by Corollary 2, for $|G|=n$ and k a constant.

This implies the only known method for constructing the order-k modifications of the diagrams $V(G,a)$ and $V(G,m)$ treated in Section 3. Its efficiency is difficult to analyze since not much is known on the size of order-k diagrams. While $R(n,k,d)$ is in $\Omega(n^{\lceil d/2 \rceil})$ and in $O(n^{d+1})$ [3,9], it can be shown that the size of k-$V(G,a)$ (k-$V(G,m)$) is in $\Omega(n)$ and $O(n^3)$ ($\Omega(n^2)$ and $O(n^3)$) for $h_o=R^2$ and in $\Omega(n^2)$ and $O(n^4)$ ($\Omega(n^2)$ and $O(n^4)$) for $h_o=R^3$.

5. **Concluding Remarks**. We have introduced the general classes of affine and affinely transformable Voronoi diagram and have shown that they, as well as their order-k modifications, are related to a class that, in some sense, is universal among Voronoi diagrams: power diagrams. Power diagrams have been thoroughly investigated, from both the mathematical and the algorithmic standpoint, in the past. Hence many results carry over to the above classes which include various important types of Voronoi diagrams.

Several questions are raised by our investigations. Which other types of Voronoi diagrams are, e.g., affinely transformable? Do the diagrams induced by the L_p-metric (see e.g. [13]) fit into this class? It can be shown that the diagrams induced by $f(x,p) = |x-p|/w_1(p)-w_2(p)$, $w_1(p),w_2(p),c>0$, (which is a "mixture" of the additive and multiplicative Euclidean distance) do not. Concerning order-k power diagrams, a fast method for (directly) calculating the non-redundant generators in Γ_k would considerably speed up the algorithms proposed for affine and affinely transformable order-k diagrams. In addition, only relatively weak upper and lower bounds on the size of order-k PDs are known for $2<k<n-2$ and $d>3$ (see e.g. [3,9]. However, as the efforts of many researchers have shown, establishing "good" bounds seems to be very complicated.

REFERENCES

[1] Ash, F.P., and Bolker, E.D. Recognizing Dirichlet tesselations. Geometriae Dedicata 19,2 (1985), 175-206.

[2] Ash, F.P., and Bolker, E.D. Generalized Dirichlet tesselations. Manuscript; submitted to Geometriae Dedicata.

[3] Aurenhammer, F. Power diagrams: properties, algorithms, and applications. SIAM J. Comput. 16,1 (1987).

[4] Aurenhammer, F. A criterion for the affine equivalence of cell complexes in R^d and convex polyhedra in R^{d+1}. To appear in Discrete & Computational Geometry.

[5] Aurenhammer, F. The one-dimensional weighted Voronoi diagram. IPL 22 (1986), 119-123.

[6] Aurenhammer, F. A new duality result concerning Voronoi diagrams. LNCS 226 (1986), 21-30.

[7] Aurenhammer, F., and Edelsbrunner, H. An optimal algorithm for constructing the weighted Voronoi diagram in the plane. Pattern Recognition 17,2 (1984), 251-257.

[8] Chazelle, B., Drysdale, R.L, III., and Lee, D.T. Computing the largest empty rectangle. SIAM J. Comput. 15,1 (1986), 300-315.

[9] Edelsbrunner, H., and Seidel, R. Voronoi diagrams and arrangements. Discrete & Computational Geometry 1,1 (1986), 25-44.

[10] Fortune, S. A sweepline algorithm for Voronoi diagrams. Proc.2nd ACM Symp. Computational Geometry, Yorktown Heights (1986).

[11] Imai, H. The Laguerre-Voronoi diagram and the Voronoi diagram for the general quadratic-form distance. Manuscript (1985).

[12] Imai, H., Iri, M., and Murota, K. Voronoi diagram in the Laguerre geometry and its applications. SIAM J. Comput. 14,1 (1985), 93-105.

[13] Lee, D.T. Two-dimensional Voronoi diagrams in the L_p-metric. J. ACM (1980), 604-618.

[14] Lee, D.T., and Drysdale, R.L, III. Generalized Voronoi diagrams in the plane. SIAM J. Comput. 10,1 (1981), 73-87.

[15] Linhart, J. Dirichletsche Zellenkomplexe mit maximaler Eckenanzahl. Geometriae Dedicata 11 (1981), 363-367.

[16] McMullen, P. The maximal number of faces of a convex

polytope. Mathematatika 17 (1970), 179-184.

[17] Seidel, R. A convex hull algorithm optimal for point sets in even dimensions. Rep. 81-14, Dept. of Computer Science, Univ. of BC, Vancouver B.C. (1981).

[18] Seidel, R. Constructing higher-dimensional convex hulls at logarithmic cost per face. Proc. 18th ACM Symp. STOC (1986).

[19] Shamos, M.I., and Hoey, D. Closest-point problems. Proc. 17th. IEEE Symp. FOCS (1975), 151-162.

[20] Yap, C.K. An O(nlogn) algorithm for the Voronoi diagram of a set of simple curve segments. Courant Institute of Math. Sciences NYU, New York; Manuscript (1984).

Finding the Largest Empty Rectangle on a Grated Surface

J. Dean Brock

Department of Computer Science
University of North Carolina at Chapel Hill
Chapel Hill, NC 27514 USA

Abstract

Suppose we are given a two-dimensional rectangular surface upon which is placed a grating of size n by m square elements. The $(n+1) \times (m+1)$ intersection points of this grid are either empty or occupied. We describe an $O(n \times m)$ algorithm for finding the largest, in area, empty subrectangle of the original rectangle. The algorithm was inspired by the dynamic programming [1] and plane-sweep [5] paradigms.

Previous algorithms have been given for the similar problem in which the occupied points are given as points within a two-dimensional continuum, *i. e.*, not restricted to grid crossings. One previous algorithm [4] for this problem has $O(F^2)$ worse case and $O(F \log^2 F)$ expected time, while another [3] has $O(F \log^3 F)$ time, where F is the number of occupied points. We compare this result to our own, with special consideration to intended application areas and to the situation where the number of occupied points is proportional to the area of the original rectangle.

Problem Statement

Let G be a two-dimensional array with indices chosen from the set $[0..n] \times [0..m]$. G corresponds to a regularly spaced grid placed on a rectangular surface A of size n by m units. The elements of G are the grating intersection points.

They are either *empty* or *occupied*. All other points of A are assumed to be empty. Our task is to find the largest sub-rectangle of A, with edges parallel to the edges of A, whose elements are all *empty*.

Let *RectEmpty* be a predicate such that $RectEmpty(x_{lo}, y_{lo}, x_{hi}, y_{hi})$ holds if and only if there is an empty rectangle whose lower left corner is located at point (x_{lo}, y_{lo}) and whose upper right corner is located at point (x_{hi}, y_{hi}). Or, more formally:

$$RectEmpty(x_{lo}, y_{lo}, x_{hi}, y_{hi}) \iff \forall x, y : x_{lo} < x < x_{hi} \;\&\; y_{lo} < y < y_{hi} \Rightarrow G[x, y] \text{ is } empty$$

Our problem is to find to find the co-ordinates of an empty rectangle as large as any other empty rectangle within G. The formal statement of our problem is:

Given: G, a $[0..n, 0..m]$ array of *empty* or *occupied* elements.

Find: x'_{lo}, y'_{lo}, x'_{hi} and y'_{hi} such that $RectEmpty(x'_{lo}, y'_{lo}, x'_{hi}, y'_{hi})$ and

$$\forall x_{lo}, y_{lo}, x_{hi}, y_{hi} : RectEmpty(x_{lo}, y_{lo}, x_{hi}, y_{hi}) \Rightarrow (x_{hi} - x_{lo}) \times (y_{hi} - y_{lo}) \leq (x'_{hi} - x'_{lo}) \times (y'_{hi} - y'_{lo})$$

We will do this with a five-pass algorithm that will examine each position of G once during each pass. Consequently, our algorithm executes in time $O(n \times m)$.

Algorithm

Our algorithm uses five n by m arrays in addition to G itself. One array is created on each of the first three passes, and two arrays are created on the fourth pass. On the fifth pass these arrays are examined to find the maximum empty rectangle. It is possible, in actual program implementation, to reduce both the number of arrays and passes. For clarity, we will not do so here.

Three of the arrays give, for each point (x, y), the co-ordinate of the row (or column) of the next occupied point one encounters moving directly left, right, and down from (x, y). Should no occupied point be encountered before the boundary is reached, the appropriate array element is set to the co-ordinate of the boundary. We will call these arrays *LineLeft*, *LineRight*, and *LineDown*. Thus:

$$LineLeft[x,y] = \{max(x') \mid x' = 0 \text{ or } x' < x \text{ and } G[x',y] \text{ is } occupied\}$$
$$LineRight[x,y] = \{min(x') \mid x' = n \text{ or } x < x' \text{ and } G[x',y] \text{ is } occupied\}$$
$$LineDown[x,y] = \{max(y') \mid y' = 0 \text{ or } y' < y \text{ and } G[x,y'] \text{ is } occupied\}$$

Each of the three arrays can easily be computed in one pass of G. For example, *LineLeft* can be computed in one left-to-right sweep of G. As we move to the right in each row, we need only keep track of the last *occupied* space traversed. The following lemma gives the rather trivial analysis for the first three passes of our algorithm.

Lemma 1

Arrays *LineLeft*, *LineRight*, and *LineDown* may be computed in $O(n \times m)$ time.

The fourth pass is by far the most complicated. It computes two arrays *RectLeft* and *RectRight*. For a given point (x, y) which is on neither the bottom, left, nor right boundaries, $RectLeft[x,y]$ and $RectRight[x,y]$ contain the left and right endpoints of the largest empty rectangle that: (1), lies totally within the bottom part of G from row y on down; and (2), completely contains the vertical *empty* segment of G beginning at (x, y) and going straight down to the bottom boundary or the next occupied point. Thus, $RectLeft[x,y]$ and $RectRight[x,y]$ give the left and right edges of the widest of the tallest empty rectangles containing (x, y) in their top edge. Clearly, this rectangle need not be the largest empty rectangle containing (x, y) in G from row y down. A graphical representation of *RectLeft* and *RectRight* is given in Figure 1.

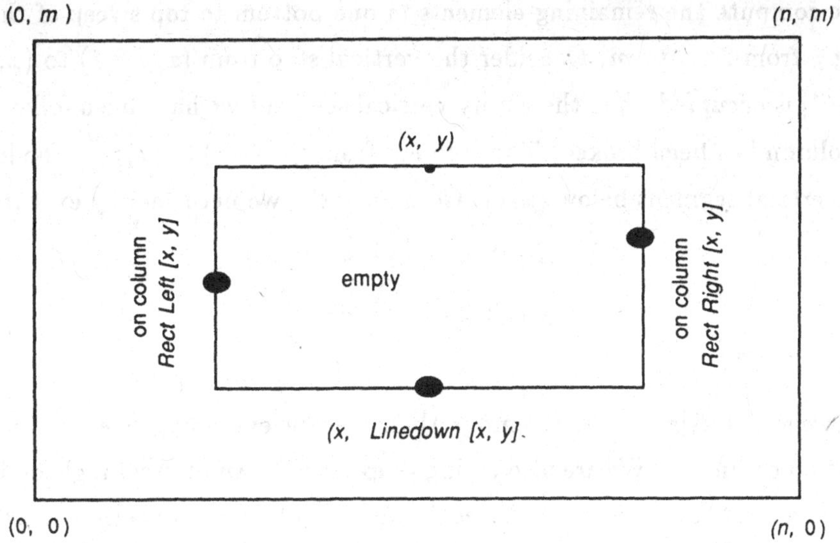

Figure 1. *RectLeft* and *RectRight*

We will let *TallMax* be the predicate that formally encodes the correctness of *RectLeft* and *RectRight*. $TallMax(x, y, x_{lo}, x_{hi})$ holds if and only if

1. $x_{lo} \leq x \leq x_{hi}$;
2. $RectEmpty(x_{lo}, LineDown[x, y], x_{hi}, y)$ holds, that is, the rectangle between columns x_{lo} and x_{hi} and rows $LineDown[x, y]$ and y is empty; and
3. if $RectEmpty(x'_{lo}, LineDown[x, y], x'_{hi}, y)$ and $x'_{lo} \leq x \leq x'_{hi}$, then $x_{lo} \leq x'_{lo}$ and $x'_{hi} \leq x_{hi}$, that is, x_{lo} and x_{hi} are the left and right ends of the largest rectangle satisfying the first and second point.

This definition is not very useful when applied to the the bottom row ($y = 0$) or left or right columns ($x = 0$ or $x = n$) and will never be used there.

In the fourth pass of our algorithm, we wish to compute *RectLeft* and *RectRight* such that, $TallMax(x, y, RectLeft[x, y], RectRight[x, y])$ is true for all grid points (x, y). This is easily done for the row immediately above the bottom boundary, we merely set $RectLeft[x, 1]$ to be 0, and set $RectRight[x, 1]$ to be n, for the area between rows 0 and 1 of G is without question empty.

We compute the remaining elements in one bottom to top sweep of the grid varying y from 2 up to m. Consider the vertical step from $(x, y-1)$ to (x, y). If $G[x, y-1]$ is *occupied*, then the empty vertical segment we have been following in the x column has been broken. The segment from $(x, y-1)$ to (x, y) is the longest empty vertical segment below (x, y). Consequently, we need merely execute:

$$RectLeft[x, y] \leftarrow 0$$
$$RectRight[x, y] \leftarrow n$$

to satisfy $TallMax$.

However, if $G[x, y-1]$ is empty then we are extending a empty vertical segment on column x. We are also trying to extend the empty rectangle delimited by columns $RectLeft[x, y-1]$ and $RectRight[x, y-1]$. Our concern is whether or not there is some point on row $y-1$ that falls inside this potential empty rectangle. Consulting *LineLeft* and *LineRight* gives an immediate answer to this question. If there is some point on row $y-1$ to the left of $(x, y-1)$ inside the rectangle we are trying to extend, then $LineLeft[x, y-1]$ will be greater than $RectLeft[x, y-1]$. In this case, we should set $RectLeft[x, y]$ to $LineLeft[x, y-1]$. Otherwise, the extension is possible and we should set $RectLeft[x, y]$ to $RectLeft[x, y-1]$.

By similar reasoning, one can see that $RectRight[x, y]$ should be set to the lesser of $RectRight[x, y-1]$ and $LineRight[x, y-1]$ as shown in Figure 2.

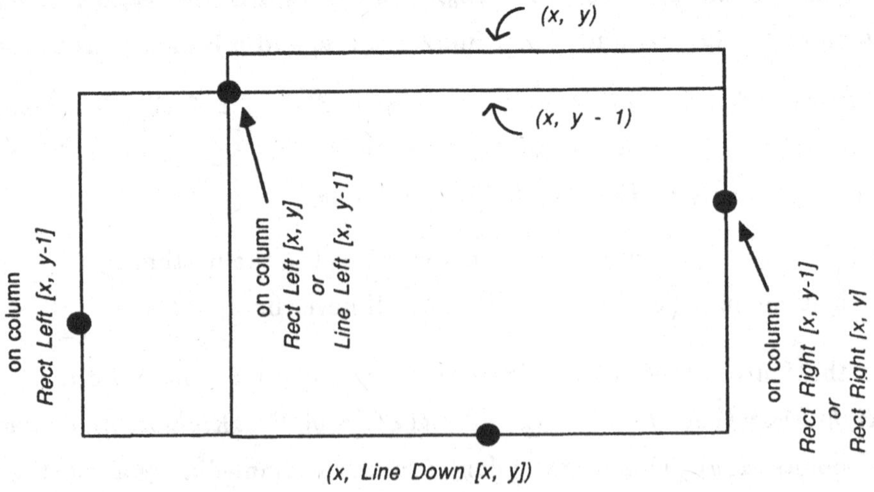

Figure 2. Computing new values of *RectLeft* and *RectRight*

These facts validate the next lemma:

Lemma 2

The arrays *RectRight* and *RectLeft* can be computed in $O(n \times m)$ time so that $TallMax(x, y, RectLeft[x, y], RectRight[x, y])$ holds by the following:

```
for x ← 1 to n − 1
    RectLeft[x, 1] ← 0
    RectRight[x, 1] ← n
for y ← 2 to m
    for x ← 1 to n − 1
        if G[x, y − 1] = occupied then
            RectLeft[x, y] ← 0
            RectRight[x, y] ← n
        else
            RectLeft[x, y] ← max(RectLeft[x, y − 1], LineLeft[x, y − 1])
            RectRight[x, y] ← min(RectRight[x, y − 1], LineRight[x, y − 1])
```

In the fifth step, we finally pick out the largest empty rectangle. To do this, we examine all points (x, y) to find the one which maximizes

$$(RectRight[x, y] - RectLeft[x, y]) \times (y - LineDown[x, y]).$$

Note that the above expression will always correspond to an empty rectangle of G. Let (x, y) be any point of G (except on the bottom, left, and right boundaries). By Lemma 2, we know that $TallMax(x, y, RectLeft[x, y], RectRight[x, y])$. Hence by the definition of $TallMax$, (x, y) is on the top row of an empty rectangle whose lower left corner is $(RectLeft[x, y], LineDown[x, y])$ and whose upper right corner is $(RectRight[x, y], y)$. The size of this empty rectangle is given by the above expression. [See Figure 1.] We must also consider the degenerate case then the largest empty rectangle is actually an empty column (of size n). However, it's trivial to add a test for this case, and we will ignore it in the remainder of our exposition.

In Lemma 2 we successfully argued that our algorithm will not be "fooled" into recognizing spurious empty rectangles. Now, we need only show that the maximization step finds the largest empty rectangles.

Suppose there is an empty rectangle with lower left corner (x_{lo}, y_{lo}) and upper right corner (x_{hi}, y_{hi}) which is as large in area as any empty rectangle in G. This rectangle is illustrated in Figure 3.

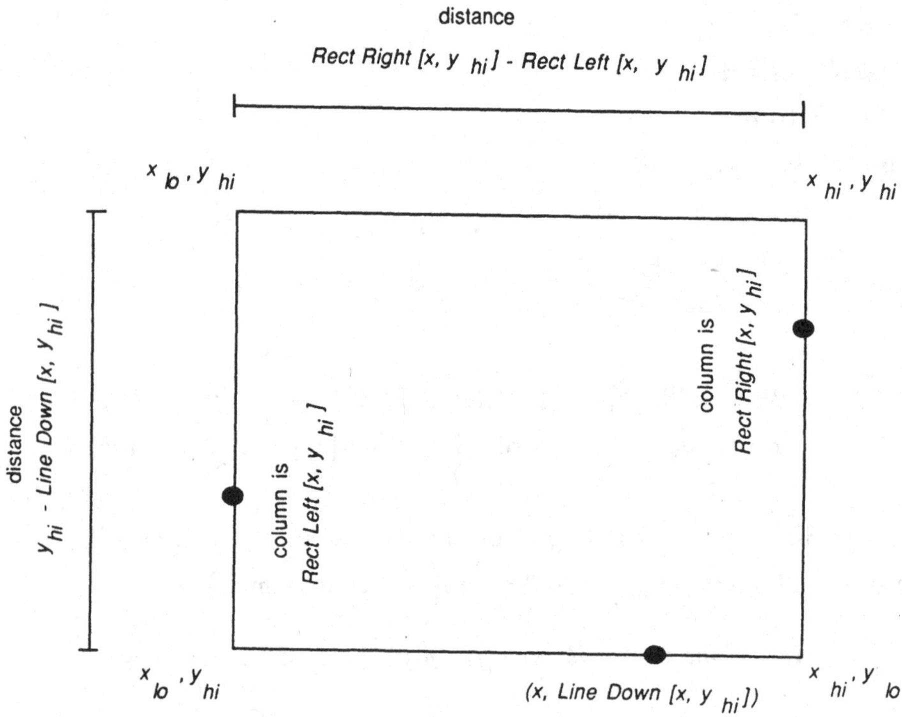

Figure 3. Uncovering the largest empty rectangle

Consider the grid points on its uppermost row: $(x_{lo}, y_{hi}) \ldots (x_{hi}, y_{hi})$. We know that there must be some x between x_{lo} and x_{hi} such that $LineDown[x, y_{hi}]$ is y_{lo} for, if this were not so, it would be possible to extend this empty rectangle downward at least one row to a larger one. Consequently, from Lemma 2 we may infer that $TallMax(x, y_{hi}, RectLeft[x, y_{hi}], RectRight[x, y_{hi}])$ holds implying, by the definition of $TallMax$, that $RectLeft[x, y_{hi}]$ and $RectRight[x, y_{hi}]$ are the left and right ends of the largest empty rectangle below row y_{hi} of G containing the column segment $G[x, y_{lo} \ldots y_{hi}]$. Consequently, $RectLeft[x, y_{hi}]$ must be x_{lo},

$RectRight[x, y_{hi}]$ must be x_{hi}, and our maximization algorithm will find this largest empty rectangle at point (x, y_{hi}).

Thus we have proven the correctness of the fifth step.

Lemma 3

Given the arrays *LineDown*, *RectRight*, and *RectLeft* computed as specified above. Let (x, y) be the point that maximizes the expression:

$$(RectRight[x,y] - RectLeft[x,y] + 1) \times (y - LineDown[x,y] + 1).$$

Then the rectangle with $(RectLeft[x,y], LineDown[x,y])$ as its lower left corner $(RectRight[x,y], y)$ as its upper right co-ordinate is empty, and there is no larger, in area, empty rectangle in G.

This of course leads to:

Theorem 4

The largest empty rectangle of G can be computed in time $O(n \times m)$.

Conclusion

The author is aware of two previously published algorithms for the more general largest empty rectangle problem in which occupied points were not restricted to grid point intersection points. The expected time of Naamad, Lee, and Hsu's [4] algorithm for this problem is $O(F \log^2 F)$, where F is the number of occupied points. Their worse-case time is $O(F^2)$. Chazelle, Drydale, and Lee [3] later presented an algorithm with worse-case time of $O(F \log^3 F)$.

Either of these algorithms could be used to find largest empty rectangles on our grated surfaces. If the occupied points are sparse, *i. e.* if F becomes insignificant relative to $n \times m$ as the size of the problem increases, then these algorithms would be asymptotically faster than ours. However, most of the potential applications for these algorithms involve situations in which the number of occupied points should be proportional to the area. For example, the number of defects within a piece of fabric or sheet metal should be proportional to its area. If $F \propto n \times m$, as it is in these common cases, then our algorithm is of time $O(F)$.

It is also quite easy to generalize our algorithm to related problems. For example, by changing the expression maximized on the fifth pass, we can look for the largest empty rectangle subject to restrictions on length, width, or even ratio of length to width without changing the required execution time $O(n \times m)$. We could also, after running another pass to generate arrays *RectUp* and *RectDown* similar to *RectLeft* and *RectRight*, answer in constant time questions such as: Do points P, Q, R, and S support an empty rectangle?

The obvious weakness of this algorithm is its insistence on the grating. Although there are some strong application-oriented properties that attenuate this shortcoming (for example, fabric is woven and sheet metal is sold in "standard" lengths and widths), it would be desirable to be able to address the more general problem. Obviously our algorithm could be used to *approximate* the largest empty rectangle. Grids have previously been used in approximation algorithms for other geometric problems, for example constructing convex hulls [2]. Given F points in the original rectangle, we could place a grid with $O(F)$ cells on the original rectangle and get a good approximate solution by bringing each occupied point to the nearest grid crossing and taking care not to allow maximal empty rectangles to form in areas outside of the original *real* rectangle. We could also use a finer grid of $O(F \log F)$ cells, which would produce even better results when F is extremely large, while still requiring only $O(F \log F)$ worse-case time.

Acknowledgments

I wish to thank Joan Curry for reading and commenting on drafts of this paper and Sailesh Chutani for animating the algorithm.

This work was supported in part by an IBM Faculty Development Award.

References

[1] Bellman, R. E., *Dynamic Programming*, Princeton University Press, 1957.

[2] Bentley, J. L., Faust, M. G., and Preparata, F. P., "Approximation algorithms for convex hulls," *Communications of the ACM 25*, 1(January 1982), 64-68.

[3] Chazelle, B., Drysdale, III, R. L., and Lee, D. T., "Computing the largest empty rectangle," *STACS 84: Symposium of Theoretical Aspects of Computer Science* (Fontet, M., and Mehlhorn, K., Eds.), *Lecture Notes in Computer Science 166*, April 1984, 43-54.

[4] Naamad, A., Lee, D. T., and Hsu, W.-L., "On the maximum empty rectangle problem," *Discrete Applied Mathematics 8*, 3(July 1984), 267-277.

[5] Nievergelt, J., and Preparata, F. P., "Plane-sweep algorithms for intersecting geometric figures," *Communications of the ACM 25*, 10(October 1982), 739-747.

EFFICIENT GRAPH ALGORITHMS USING LIMITED COMMUNICATION ON A FIXED-SIZE ARRAY OF PROCESSORS †

Kshitij Doshi   Peter Varman
Department of Electrical and Computer Engineering
Rice University
Houston, Texas 77001, U.S.A.

Abstract

Parallel algorithms for finding the minimum spanning tree of a weighted undirected graph and the bridge-connected and biconnected components of an undirected graph on a linear array of processors are presented. On an n-vertex graph, our algorithms perform in $O(n^2/p)$ time on an array of size p, for all p, $1 \leq p \leq n$, thus providing optimal speedup for dense graphs. The paper describes two approaches to limit the communication requirements for solving the problems. The first is a divide-and-conquer strategy applied to Sollin's algorithm for finding the minimum spanning tree of a graph. The second uses a novel data-reduction technique that constructs an auxiliary graph with no more than 2n-2 edges, whose bridges and articulation points are the bridges and articulation points of the original graph.

1. Introduction

In this paper we present parallel algorithms for a number of graph problems on a fixed-size network of processors. The processors are connected together in the form of a one-dimensional array so that any processor (except the two at the end) can directly communicate with only its left and right neighbors. Each processor in the array is a sequential random access machine [1] equipped with its own local random-access memory. Communication between adjacent processors in the array may be effected either by means of bidirectional communication links between them or through a common memory shared by two adjacent processors.

The problems that we consider in this paper are those of finding the *connected components*, the *minimum spanning tree* of a weighted graph, and the *bridge-connected* and *biconnected components* of an undirected graph. On a graph of n vertices represented by an $n \times n$ adjacency matrix, we solve all of the above mentioned problems in $O(n^2/p)$ time using a linear array of p processors, for all p, $1 \leq p \leq n$. Thus our algorithms achieve a speedup linear in the number of processors employed within the range 1 to n. In particular, with n processors, the algorithms require an optimal O(n) time. Informally, since $O(n^2)$ data items of the adjacency matrix must be examined by the algorithm, at least $O(n^2/p)$ time is needed, and, since computations on this model require O(p) time to communicate over the array diameter, $\Omega(n)$ can be shown to be a lower bound on the time complexity for this model. Our results compare favorably with previously described algorithms for these problems on fixed-size processor networks (see Section 1.2). In addition, the simplicity of the computational model makes it attractive from a practical viewpoint.

Our algorithm for finding the minimum spanning tree (MST), which obviously may also be used for determining the connected components, is based on a "divide-and-conquer" strategy applied to Sollin's [2] algorithm for the problem. Our algorithms for finding the bridges and the articulation points of a graph are quite new, in that they are not implementations of known sequential or parallel algorithms that, to our knowledge, have appeared in the literature. The algorithms for the latter two problems employ a novel method of data reduction to construct an auxiliary graph composed of at most 2n - 2 edges, whose articulation points (bridges) are also the articulation points (bridges) of the original graph.

In the next section we describe in more detail the computation model employed. In section 1.2, we review the known parallel algorithms for these problems and indicate briefly the difficulty in attempting to directly adapt

† This research was supported in part by an IBM Faculty Development Award.

these schemes to this model. In sections 2, 3 and 4 we present the algorithms for finding the minimum spanning tree, the bridges and the articulation points respectively. For convenience we have assumed that the input to our algorithms is a connected graph; the modifications required to accommodate disconnected graphs involve purely clerical details.

1.1. Computation Model

The computation model employed is a linear array of p processors. Each processor has an index from the set {0, ..., p-1}, and the processor j, $1 \le j \le p-2$, is connected by bidirectional communication links to the processors j-1 and j+1, which are referred to as the *left* and the *right* neighbors respectively of j. A processor may communicate only with its left or right neighbor in a unit time step.

Each processor in the array is a sequential random access machine (RAM) equipped with a sizable amount of local random-access memory. As in the uniform-cost sequential RAM model [1], each access by a processor to its local memory for either reading or writing requires unit time. Operands are limited to be of size $O(\log I)$ bits, where I is the size of the input. This restriction applies both to the number of bits that may be accessed from memory in one cycle and to the number of bits that may be communicated between neighbors in unit time.

Algorithm performance on this model can be compared with the sequential time complexities for the problem on the sequential uniform cost random access machines (See [1]).

1.2. Overview

Several sequential algorithms for computing the minimum spanning tree (forest) of an undirected graph are known; among them are those by Prim[3], Dijkstra[4], Kruskal[5], Sollin[2], and Cheriton and Tarjan[6]. Among the parallel algorithms proposed on fixed-connection networks of processors, are those proposed by Bentley[7], Bentley and Ottmann[8], Leighton[9], Nath, Maheshwari and Bhatt[10], Atallah and Kosaraju[11], and Huang[12]. Bentley [7] and Bentley and Ottmann [8] described algorithms for computing the MST on a set of n points on a binary tree and a linear array $n/\log n$ processors respectively in $O(n \log n)$ time. In the case that p, $p < n/\log n$, processors are available, the algorithm performs in time $O(n^2/p)$, thus achieving linear speedup for all p in the range $1 \le p \le n/\log n$. Leighton [9], Nath, Maheshwari and Bhatt [10] provided $O(\log^2 n)$ time solutions for the problem on a $n \times n$ mesh of trees network. Atallah and Kosaraju [11] presented an $O(n)$ time algorithm for this problem using an $n \times n$ mesh connected array of processors. Finally, Huang [12] described an algorithm that achieves a time complexity of $O(n^2/p)$ for all p, $1 \le p \le n^2/\log^2 n$, on a $\sqrt{p} \times \sqrt{p}$ mesh of trees network.

With the exception of the algorithms proposed in [7-9] the algorithms in the above list are not efficient for implementation on a network having a fixed number of processors. The algorithm presented in this paper requires time $O(n^2/p)$ using a linear array of p processors, for all p, $1 \le p \le n$. The challenge in designing the algorithm arises from the need to limit both the total amount of data communication required as well as the distance through which data has to be communicated. The peculiar problems arising in this context do not manifest themselves in the high bandwidth networks such as meshes of trees [9], which in addition to having several parallel data paths also possess a much smaller ($\log n$) communication diameter. On the other hand, previous algorithms [7,8], on limited bandwidth models like ours, yield linear speedup only up to $n/\log n$ processors.

Parallel algorithms on PRAM models for finding the biconnected components of a graph include those of Savage and Ja-Ja[13], Tsin and Chin[14] and Tarjan and Vishkin[15]. Huang's algorithm [12] for finding the biconnected components on a mesh of trees is based on the algorithm proposed in [14,15]. It is, however, difficult to efficiently employ the same technique on a linear array of processors. The difficulty arises from the amount of data communication the algorithm demands, and, the distance over which the data must be transmitted in every iteration of the algorithm. A simulation of this technique on a linear array, for example, requires time $O(n^2/p + (n\sqrt{p} + p)\log n)$. In this case linear speedup is achieved only for p less than $(n/\log n)^{2/3}$. In the above time-complexity expression, the term $n\sqrt{p}\log n$ arises from $\log n$ iterations, in each of which, some link in the array must, in the worst case, handle up to $O(n/\sqrt{p})$ amount of data from each of p processors. The last term, $p \log n$ arises from the consideration of the diameter over which the communication occurs. Clearly, a scheme that must perform efficiently on a linear array over a wider range of p must address the possibility of reducing the data, and the communication necessary to solve the problem.

Our optimal MST algorithm that achieves linear speedup for up to n processors employs a divide-and-conquer strategy. A factor that dominates the time complexity for large values of p ($p > n/\sqrt{\log n}$), is the need to transmit data over the entire length of the array for log n iterations. Our algorithm computes the MSFs over small contiguous segments of the array and then "merges" these MSFs to find the MSFs over larger segments. In the process of computing these local MSFs, a number of edges (those not in the computed MSFs) are eliminated from future consideration. This allows us to conduct the final computation on a smaller length of the array and limit the time necessary for communication.

We take a different approach for reducing the data when computing the articulation points of a graph. From the given graph G we construct an auxiliary graph, consisting of the union of an arbitrary spanning tree, T , on G and a minimum spanning forest (with suitably defined edge "weights") on G – T. In Theorem 4.1 we show that this auxiliary graph (with at most 2n-2 edges) has the same articulation points as the input graph. The algorithm for finding the bridges of an undirected graph uses a similar, though simpler, form of data reduction as that employed for finding the articulation points. Theorem 3.1 formally demonstrates that an auxiliary graph consisting of the union of an arbitrary spanning tree, T, on G and an arbitrary spanning forest on G–T has exactly the same bridges as does G.

2. Minimum Spanning Tree

In this section we present the algorithm for computing the minimum spanning tree of a weighted undirected graph, $G = \langle V, E \rangle$, $|V| = n$, represented by an $n \times n$ adjacency matrix, W of weights. Element $w_{ij} \in W$, $0 \le i, j \le n-1$ denotes the weight of the undirected edge (i j). If the vertices i and j are not connected, then $w_{ij} = \infty$. For convenience, we assume that G is connected; straight-forward modifications of the algorithms being proposed can handle the case when G is composed of several components.

Data Distribution

The adjacency matrix for the graph is distributed over the p processors as described below. W is partitioned into p, $1 \le p \le n$, square blocks where each block is an $n/\sqrt{p} \times n/\sqrt{p}$ submatrix of W. Each block is initially stored in the local memory of a processor according to the following *shuffled row and column* assignment scheme (see Figure 1). Each of the p blocks of W is defined by a row and a column index in a $\sqrt{p} \times \sqrt{p}$ square array of blocks. Let B_{ij} represent a block at row position i and column position j ($0 \le i, j < \sqrt{p}$). Let $b_k b_{k-1} b_{k-2} b_{k-3} \cdots b_1 b_0$ be the binary representation of an integer q, $0 \le q \le p-1$. Then, the processor indexed q is assigned the block B_{st} of the adjacency matrix, where s and t are integers whose binary representations are $b_k b_{k-2} \cdots b_3 b_1$ and $b_{k-1} b_{k-3} \cdots b_2 b_0$ respectively.

2.1. Linear Array Solution

Procedure Simple MST given below describes a scheme for computing an MST on G.

Procedure Simple MST

1. Partition the $n \times n$ adjacency matrix W as described in section 2, so that processor i, $0 \le i \le p-1$, receives an $n/\sqrt{p} \times n/\sqrt{p}$ block of W corresponding to a subgraph $G_i = \langle V_i, E_i \rangle$ of G.
2. Every processor i computes a minimum spanning forest *(MSF)* on the graph G_i in its local memory using the sequential Prim-Dijkstra [4] algorithm. Edges not in the MSF are discarded from further consideration. Let the total number of edges in the union of the p MSFs be denoted by s.
3. The p MSFs, one on each G_i, are merged to form the MST on G. This is accomplished by using the procedure Array Merge (n, s, p) to be described presently.

Comment :

Step 2 takes time $O(n^2/p)$. Observe that the number of edges left in any processor at the end of step 2 does not exceed $2n/\sqrt{p}$. Hence, step 3, as shown in the comments on the time complexity for algorithm ArrayMerge , takes $O(n + (n/\sqrt{p} + p)\log n)$ time.

Procedure Array Merge(v, e, m), used in step 3 of procedure Simple MST above, computes an MST on a connected graph of v vertices and e edges on an m processor linear array as follows. The e edges are distributed evenly among the processors -- e/m edges in each.[1] Like Sollin's algorithm, the procedure consists of log v iterations. Initially, each of the v vertices is a component consisting of the vertex itself. Components created in an iteration of the algorithm are merged along edges of minimum weight in the succeeding iteration.

Procedure Array Merge (v, e, m)

Repeat steps (1) through (3) for log v iterations

Comments :

Let the iteration number be k. Denote the number of distinct components in the kth iteration by $NumComp^{(k)}$.

1. Each processor determines from among its set of edges, the edges of minimum weight incident upon each of the $NumComp^{(k)}$ components. It does so by serially scanning the list of its edges, and initializing appropriately the $NumComp^{(k)}$ entries in an array LocalMin[1 .. v]. LocalMin [u] contains the weight and the endpoints of the minimum weighted edge incident upon component u. This is the edge whose weight is the smallest among all edges available in that processor and having one end point belonging to component u. (The entry for an isolated component that has no edge incident upon any vertex in it, may be initialized to a null edge of $+\infty$ weight.)
2. For each component u, compute Min[u] equal to the minimum of the LocalMin[u] computed in each processor. Processor 0 initiates the computation by transmitting to processor 1, the $NumComp^{(k)}$ entries in LocalMin[] that were identified in step 1 as the minimum weighted edges on each of the $NumComp^{(k)}$ components. Every processor i, i > 0, receives from processor i-1 a list of $NumComp^{(k)}$ edges that processors 0 through i-1 have determined to be the minimum weighted edges incident upon the $NumComp^{(k)}$ components. Processor i compares the list received from processor i-1 with its own array Local–Min[] and creates an updated list consisting of the edges of smaller weights. If i is not the rightmost processor then the updated list is in turn transmitted to processor i+1. This step is performed in a pipelined mode. Processor i receives a single edge from processor i-1, updates it and transmits the updated information to processor i+1 before receiving the next edge from processor i-1.
3. The updated list created by processor m-1 (the rightmost processor) consists of the set of edges that are added to the MST in this iteration. The new component numbers, for each of the components of the previous iteration, are also determined by the $m-1^{th}$ processor. This information (the selected MST edges and the new component numbers) is sent back, to processors m-2 through 0. Each processor marks the selected edges that it contains and updates the component identifiers for the vertices spanned by its edges.

End Repeat

Comments on the Time Complexity :

Step 1 requires $O(e/m)$ time in every iteration. Step 2 requires $O(NumComp^{(k)} + m)$ time for the kth iteration. Step 3, for the kth iteration, can be performed in $O(NumComp^{(k)} + e/m + m)$ time. Since $NumComp^{(k)}$ is no more than $v/2^k$, the overall time complexity of procedure Array Merge is $O(v + (e/m + m) \log v)$.

Lemma 2.1 :

Procedure Simple MST computes the MST of an n vertex graph in time $O(n^2/p)$ using a linear array of p

---

[1] Assume for simplicity that m divides e.

processors, $1 \le p \le n/\sqrt{\log n}$. The algorithm therefore achieves linear speedup using p, $1 \le p \le n/\sqrt{\log n}$, processors.

Proof : Each processor in step 1 of the procedure computes the MSF on a graph having at most $2n/\sqrt{p}$ vertices. This step requires $O(n^2/p)$ time. Procedure Array Merge computes the MST on an n vertex graph using p processors with at most $2n/\sqrt{p}$ edges per processor. This step therefore requires at most $O(n^2/p + n + (n/\sqrt{p} + p) \log n)$ time. The total time complexity of the algorithm which is the sum of these two quantities is readily seen to be $O(n^2/p)$, for all p, $1 \le p \le n/\sqrt{\log n}$.

2.2. An Optimal Linear Array Algorithm

In this section we describe a scheme for computing the MST that yields linear speedup on a linear array of size p for all p up to n. In examining the expression for the time complexity of procedure Array Merge, it can be seen that when p exceeds $n/\sqrt{\log n}$, the term $p \log n$ is the dominant term in the expression. This term reflects the fact that in each of the $\log n$ iterations of Sollin's method, data is communicated over the entire length (p) of the linear array. The new scheme avoids the inefficiency resulting from transmitting the data over the entire length of the linear array in every iteration. It accomplishes this by iteratively constructing the spanning tree; in each iteration it merges together the MSFs computed in physically contiguous subarrays.

The merging procedure is initiated after the computation of the local MSFs in each processor. It may be recalled that each processor handles a subgraph corresponding to the $n/\sqrt{p} \times n/\sqrt{p}$ portion of the adjacency matrix and that the adjacency matrix is so distributed that physically contiguous sets of 2^{2k}, $0 \le k \le ½ \log p$, processors handle an $n\,2^k/\sqrt{p} \times n\,2^k/\sqrt{p}$ portion of it. In every iteration of the merge, four of the MSFs computed in the previous iteration are merged together to produce an MSF on the graph corresponding to a larger block of the adjacency matrix. This scheme therefore requires $½ \log p$ iterations to find the final MST. The details for the kth $(1 \le k \le ½ \log p)$ iteration are explained below.

For the kth iteration, the linear array is divided into $p/2^{2k}$ groups, where each group consists of 2^{2k} adjacent processors. Each group is made up of four subgroups having $2^{2(k-1)}$ processors each. In the $k{-}1^{th}$ iteration the processors in each subgroup would have computed an MSF over an $n2^{(k-1)}/\sqrt{p} \times n2^{(k-1)}/\sqrt{p}$ sized block of the adjacency matrix W. In the kth iteration the processors in each group compute an MSF over the union of the four MSFs computed in their subgroup.

Let $v^{(k)}$ denote the number of vertices being handled by a group in the kth iteration. Let $e^{(k)}$ denote the total number of edges in the MSFs computed by the four subgroups in the $k{-}1^{th}$ iteration. It may be seen that :

$$\text{(i) } v^{(k)} \le 2^{k+1} n/\sqrt{p}$$
$$\text{(ii) } e^{(k)} \le 2v^{(k)},$$

Our objective is to complete the kth iteration in time $O(v^{(k)} + T^{(k)})$, where $T^{(k)}$ does not exceed $n^2/p \log p$. Two cases need to be considered in attempting to meet this time bound. The first situation occurs when k is small and hence the MSFs are being merged over a small number of processors. The second situation arises for values of k approaching $½ \log p$.

The first case :

Consider the merging of four MSFs in the kth iteration, where k satisfies $2^{2k} \le v^{(k)}/\log v^{(k)}$. At the beginning of the iteration the $e^{(k)}$ edges in the four subgroups being merged are redistributed among the 2^{2k} processors in the group so that no processor has more than $e^{(k)}/2^{2k}$ edges. Procedure Array Merge is then invoked to determine the MSF over this subgraph. The redistribution of the edges can be done in time $O(e^{(k)} + 2^{2k})$ and procedure Array Merge requires $O(v^{(k)} + (e^{(k)}/2^{2k} + 2^{2k}) \log v^{(k)})$ time. The time for the kth iteration for k satisfying $2^{2k} \le v^{(k)}/\log v^{(k)}$ is therefore given by $O(v^{(k)} + v^{(k)} \log v^{(k)}/2^{2k})$.

The second case :

Next, consider the case when k satisfies $2^{2k} > v^{(k)}/\log v^{(k)}$. If the approach used in the previous case were followed here the time complexity of the kth iteration would approach $n + p \log n$ (up to constant factors) as k approached $½ \log p$ and consequently result in less than linear speedup when p exceeds $n/\log n$. To ensure linear speedup for all p up to n the computations of the kth iteration $(2^{2k} > v^{(k)}/\log v^{(k)})$ are organized over a smaller number of processors than is available in the group. Specifically, for the kth iteration, the $e^{(k)}$ edges are concentrated in the leftmost $p' = v^{(k)}/\log v^{(k)}$ processors of the group. No processor will have more than $e^{(k)}/p'$ edges. The procedure Array Merge is invoked to compute the MSF on the p′ processors of each group. At the end of this computation the edges of the MSF are broadcast to all the processors in the group. The concentration of the edges and the broadcast of the newly computed MSF can be done in time $O(e^{(k)} + 2^{2k})$. Procedure Array Merge applied to the length p′ of the array requires time $O(v^{(k)} + (e^{(k)}/p' + p') \log v^{(k)})$. Noting that $e^{(k)} \leq 2v^{(k)}$, the time complexity of the kth iteration is then, $O(v^{(k)} + \log^2 v^{(k)})$.

The total time over all ½ log p iterations may be obtained by summing the times for each iteration in the two ranges of k. For the first case, summing over the values of k (satisfying $2^{2k} \leq v^{(k)}/\log v^{(k)}$) we obtain for the time complexity of this part of the algorithm :

$$\begin{aligned}
&\sum_k O(v^{(k)} + v^{(k)} \log v^{(k)}/2^{2k}) \\
&\leq c \sum_k v^{(k)} + c' \sum_k (v^{(k)} \log v^{(k)}/2^{2k}) \\
&\leq cn/\sqrt{p} \sum_k 2^{k+1} + c'n/\sqrt{p} \sum_k 2^{-k+1} (\log n/\sqrt{p} + k + 1) \\
&\leq cn/\sqrt{p}\, 2^{\frac{1}{2}\log p+2} + c'n/\sqrt{p} \log n/\sqrt{p} \\
&\leq 4cn + c'n/\sqrt{p} \log n/\sqrt{p}
\end{aligned}$$

which is $O(n + n/\sqrt{p} \log n/\sqrt{p})$. For the second part of the algorithm, summing the time complexity for values of k satisfying $2^{2k} > v^{(k)} \log^2 v^{(k)}$, we get $\sum_k O(v^{(k)} + \log^2 v^{(k)}) = O(n + \log^2 n \log p)$. Thus, all the ½ log p iterations are completed in time $O(n + n/\sqrt{p} \log (n/\sqrt{p}) + \log^2 n \log p)$, which is $O(n^2/p)$, for all p, $1 \leq p \leq n$.

3. Bridge Connected Components

Let $G = \langle V, E \rangle$ be an undirected graph with $|V| = n$. An edge $(u\ v) \in E$ is a bridge in G if and only if the graph $\langle V, E-(u\ v) \rangle$ has more components than G. Alternatively, it can be shown that an edge is a bridge edge if and only if it appears in every spanning forest on the graph.

For convenience we restrict our attention to connected graphs. The technique discussed here can be easily extended to graphs of several components.

One straight-forward scheme to identify the bridges of G uses the observation that any spanning tree on G contains every bridge edge of G. This scheme therefore constructs a spanning tree on G and then tests each tree edge to check whether or not it is a bridge of G. It does so, by examining for each tree edge (u v), whether the graph created by its removal from G, i.e. the graph $\langle V, E - (u\ v) \rangle$, has two components or one. Assuming that G is a dense graph in general, this scheme must find, for each of the n–1 tree edges, the connected components of a dense graph. This would result, given that we can find connected components in time $O(n^2/p)$, in a time complexity of $O(n^3/p)$.

Our algorithm follows the above scheme for bridge identification, but reduces the time required per tree edge by employing an interesting form of data reduction. The technique enables us to test whether or not a tree edge is a bridge by computing the connected components over a sparse graph having at most 2n – 2 edges. The basis of our algorithm is formalized in theorem 3.1 below.

Theorem 3.1 :

Let $T = \langle V, E_T \rangle$ be a spanning tree on $G = \langle V, E \rangle$ and let $F = \langle V, E_F \rangle$ be a spanning forest on the graph $\langle V, E - E_T \rangle$. Let $\hat{G}$ be the graph $\langle V, E_T \cup E_F \rangle$. Then, an edge in $\hat{G}$ is a bridge if and only if it is a bridge in G.

Proof : Every bridge edge of G appears in T and hence in $\hat{G}$. Consider therefore, if possible, a bridge edge (u v) of $\hat{G}$ that is not a bridge of G. Since T is a spanning tree also on $\hat{G}$, it follows that $(u\ v) \in E_T$. A path P_{uv} between vertices u and v and not containing the edge (u v) exists in G; otherwise (u v) would be a bridge in G. Let $P_{uv} = (u \cdots i\, j \cdots v)$, where (i j) represents any intermediate edge. Either $(i\ j) \in E_T$, or $(i\ j) \in E - E_T \Rightarrow$ there exists a path between i and j in a spanning forest on $\langle V, E - E_T \rangle$, i.e. in F. It follows that every such pair of vertices i and j has a path connecting them in $\hat{G}$, and none of these paths contain (u v). Vertices u and v are therefore connected in $\hat{G}$ by a path that excludes edge (u v). But this contradicts the assumption that (u v) is a bridge of $\hat{G}$.

We now give an outline of the procedure to find bridges of a graph:

Procedure: Identify Bridges

1. Construct a spanning tree T on G.
2. Delete all the edges of T from G and construct a spanning forest F on the remaining graph.
3. Discard all the edges of G that are not in T or F.
4. For each edge e in T do:

   If the graph formed by the deletion of e from $T \cup F$ has more than one component then mark e as a bridge edge.

   End For

The implementation of this procedure on a linear array is straight-forward. The tree T and the forest F can be constructed as described in section 4.2. In time $O(n+p)$, the edges of $T \cup F$ (at most $2n-2$ of them) are transmitted to all processors in the array. Each processor then executes n/p iterations of the loop in procedure Identify Bridges, to determine whether its set of n/p of the edges of T are bridges. Since $T \cup F$ has no more than $2n-2$ edges, each of the iterations can be performed sequentially in $O(n)$ time. Thus, all the bridges of G can be identified in time $O(n^2/p)$.

4. Articulation Points

Let $G = \langle V, E \rangle$ be a connected graph on n vertices. A vertex $a \in V$ is an articulation point (AP) of G if the removal of a, together with the edges incident upon it, disconnects the graph, i.e. splits G into two or more components. A vertex is an articulation point of a disconnected graph if it is an articulation point of a connected component of the graph.

A naive parallel algorithm for finding the articulation points of G consists of independently examining each vertex (on separate processors if available) and determining whether or not its removal disconnects G. A problem with this approach is that it is computationally wasteful, since it requires determining the connected components on n graphs each having almost as many edges as G.

The strategy that is employed to overcome this problem is similar in principle to that used in the bridge identification algorithm of the previous section. Starting from $G = \langle V, E \rangle$, we construct a sparse graph $\hat{G} = \langle V, \hat{E} \rangle$ having at most $2n-2$ edges such that G and $\hat{G}$ have the same articulation points. The computation is then completed by finding the articulation points of $\hat{G}$ either sequentially (by one processor) using the depth-first-search based algorithm [1] or in parallel by a direct application of the definition to each vertex of $\hat{G}$.

The algorithm for finding the articulation points of a graph based on the above strategy is presented in Procedure Articulation Points.

Procedure Articulation Points

Comments :

The input to the algorithm is a connected graph $G = \langle V, E \rangle$, and an arbitrarily chosen vertex $r \in V$.

1. Construct a spanning tree $T = \langle V, E_T \rangle$ on G with r as the root.
2. For each vertex $u \in V$ determine :

   (i) depth(u) equal to the distance in T between u and r.

   (ii) pre-order(u) equal to the numbering of u in a preorder traversal of T beginning at r.

3. For each pair of distinct vertices {u, v} of G, determine LCA(u, v), the lowest common ancestor of vertices u and v.
4. For each edge (u v) $\in E - E_T$, determine weight(u, v) = $\langle \alpha_{uv}, \beta_{uv}, \gamma_{uv} \rangle$, where :
   (i) α_{uv} = depth(LCA(u, v))
   (ii) β_{uv} = if LCA(u v) $\neq$ u, v then 0 else 1
   (iii) γ_{uv} = Max(pre-order(u), pre-order(v)).
5. Construct a minimum weight spanning forest F = $\langle V, E_F \rangle$ on the graph $\langle V, E - E_T \rangle$ where the weight of an edge (u v) is determined by the lexicographic ordering of the triple weight(u, v).
6. Construct the graph $\hat{G} = \langle V, E_T \cup E_F \rangle$.
7. Find the articulation points of $\hat{G}$ (by either the sequential algorithm of [1] or, in parallel, by checking for each vertex if it is an AP of $\hat{G}$).

In a series of lemmas culminating in theorem 4.1, we show that the graphs G and $\hat{G}$ constructed by procedure Articulation Points have the same articulation points. We briefly summarize some terminology from graph theory that we will be using. Given a rooted tree T = $\langle V, E_T \rangle$, a vertex u $\in$ V is an ancestor of a vertex v $\in$ V if u lies on the path from v to the root; also v is a descendant of u. A vertex is trivially an ancestor (descendant) of itself. A vertex u is a proper ancestor (proper descendant) of a vertex v if u is an ancestor (descendant) of v and u $\neq$ v. The lowest common ancestor of a pair of vertices x and y, denoted by LCA(x, y), is the vertex that is an ancestor of both x and y, and none of whose proper descendants is an ancestor of both x and y. Vertex u is a child of v if v is an ancestor of u and (u, v) $\in$ E. An interior vertex of T is a vertex that is neither the root nor a leaf in T. A path in a graph $\langle V, E \rangle$ refers to a simple path and is denoted by an ordered sequence of vertices $(i_0\ i_1\ \cdots\ i_m)$, where $i_k \in V$, $0 \le k \le m$, and edges $(i_k\ i_{k+1}) \in E$. An intermediate vertex on a path is a vertex on the path that is not one of the endpoints. In the lemmas below, the graphs T, G and $\hat{G}$ correspond to those defined in Procedure Articulation Points.

Lemma 4.1 :

Let u be a vertex of T that is not a leaf. Let (i j) $\in$ E be an edge such that in T vertices i and j are descendants of two different children of u. Then, i and j are connected in $\hat{G}$ by a path that does not have u as an intermediate vertex.

Proof : Observe that LCA(i, j) = u and that i, j $\neq$ u. The edge (i j) $\in E - E_T$ requiring that (i j) be connected by some path P_{ij} in F. If P_{ij} = (i j) the lemma holds. Else if P_{ij} does not contain u, again the lemma holds. Assume therefore that $P_{ij} = (i \cdots xuy \cdots j)$. If x were a descendant of u in T, then weight(i j) < weight(x u) since $\alpha_{xu} = \alpha_{ij}$ = depth(u) and β_{xu} (= 1) > β_{ij} (= 0); i.e. edge(x u) cannot be in the MSF F, if x is a descendant of u. Similarly no edge (y u) can be in F if y as a descendent of u. It follows that x and y are both non-descendants of u. Let P_{xy} be the path in T connecting x and y. Then the sequence of edges $(i \cdots x\ P_{xy}\ y \cdots j)$ constitutes a path in $\hat{G}$ between i and j that does not contain u.

Lemma 4.2 :

Let u be an interior vertex of T. Let (i j) $\in$ E be an edge such that in T vertex i is a descendant of some child of u and vertex j is not a descendant of u. Then, i and j are connected in $\hat{G}$ by a path that does not have u as an intermediate vertex.

Proof : Observe that (i j) $\in E - E_T$ and that LCA(i, j) is a proper ancestor of u. Therefore, there exists a path P_{ij} in F between i and j. If P_{ij} = (i j), the lemma holds. Else, the lemma also holds if P_{ij} does not contain u. Assume therefore that $P_{ij} = (i \cdots xuy \cdots j)$. Vertex x cannot be a descendant of u else weight (x u) > weight (i j) following the fact that α_{xu} (= depth(u)) > α_{ij} (= depth of a proper ancestor of u). Similarly, y cannot be a descendant of u. As in the previous lemma, the path in T between x and y, and the portions $(i \cdots x)$ and $(y \cdots j)$ of path P_{ij} together constitute an i-j path in $\hat{G}$ that does not contain u.

Theorem 4.1 :

A vertex in V is an articulation point of $\hat{G}$ if and only if it an articulation point of G.

Proof : The "if" part holds since $\hat{G}$ contains only a subset of edges of G. In proving the "only if" part, we need consider only non-leaf vertices in T since a leaf vertex of T is not an articulation point of either G or $\hat{G}$. Let $u \in V$ be an arbitrary interior vertex of T, which is not an articulation point of G. Between any two vertices i, $j \neq u$ that are in the same connected component of G, there exists a path P_{ij} $(i \cdots x\, y \cdots j)$ in G that does not contain u; we need to show that in $\hat{G}$, the same pair (i and j) is connected by some path without u as an intermediate vertex.

Clearly edge (x y) exists in G. Four possibilities exist concerning x, y and u in T:

(1) Both x and y are descendants of the same child of u.

(2) x and y are descendants of different children of u.

(3) One vertex of the pair (say x) is a proper descendant of u and the other is not.

(4) Neither x nor y is a descendant of u.

In cases (1) and (4), edges in T between x and LCA(x, y) and between y and LCA(x, y) together constitute a path between x and y that excludes u. Lemmas 4.1 and 4.2 demonstrate respectively that in cases (3) and (4), there exist paths in $\hat{G}$ between x and y that do not contain u. It follows therefore that all pairs of successive vertices on P_{ij} remain connected in $\hat{G}$ by paths that exclude u; i.e. i and j remain connected in $\hat{G}$ by some path that does not contain u.

4.1. Implementation on a Linear Array

In this section we describe the implementation of the procedure Articulation Points on a linear array of p processors ($p \leq n$). With respect to the procedure, listed in Section 4, we note that the construction of the spanning tree T and the minimum spanning forest F can be accomplished in time $O(n^2/p)$ using the algorithm of Section 3. The computation of depth(u) and pre–order(u) for vertices in T can be performed in O(n) time by one processor and the results distributed to all the processors in time $O(n+p)$. The computation of LCA(u, v) for each pair of distinct vertices u and v in $O(n^2/p)$ time is however not quite as straight-forward and is addressed in the discussion below.

Each processor in the array has an $n/\sqrt{p} \times n/\sqrt{p}$ block of the adjacency matrix of G. Each processor is also provided with a copy of the spanning tree T on G. Let **R** and **C** denote the sets of vertices corresponding to the rows and columns respectively, of the portion of the adjacency matrix being handled by one processor. We need to compute, in each processor, LCA(x, y) in T for each of the n^2/p pairs of vertices x, y, $x \in$ R and $y \in$ C.

Given the spanning tree, a processor can directly identify the LCAs over its block of the adjacency matrix in $n/\sqrt{p}$ traversals of the tree; but that takes $O(n^2/\sqrt{p})$ time. Alternatively, a processor can identify LCA's over an $n \times n/p$ section of the adjacency matrix by performing n/p traversals of the tree, in $O(n^2/p)$ time; but redistributing the LCA information to the processors can be shown to require $O(n^2/\sqrt{p})$ time. We therefore resort to a tree-compression strategy described by procedure DetermineLCAs. The procedure "compresses" the tree T into an auxiliary tree T′ having $O(n/\sqrt{p})$ vertices (including the $2n/\sqrt{p}$ vertices in $\mathbf{R} \cup \mathbf{C}$) so that the LCAs in T and T′ of a pair of vertices from **R** and **C** are the same. The last step of the algorithm involves finding the LCA of a pair of vertices by performing a binary search on an Euler tour around the tree as discussed in [15].

Lemmas 4.3, 4.4 and theorem 4.2 prove that the LCAs are identified correctly in $O(n^2/p)$ time.

Lemma 4.3 :

Let u, v and w be three vertices in an n-vertex rooted tree, such that pre-order(u) < pre-order(v) < pre-order(w). Then, either LCA(u, v) = LCA(u, w) or LCA(u, w) = LCA(v, w).

Proof : If depth(LCA(u, v)) < depth(LCA(v, w)), then LCA(u, w) = LCA(u, v) [see figure 2(a)].
If depth(LCA(u, v)) > depth(LCA(v, w)) then LCA(u, w) = LCA(v, w) [see figure 2(b)].
Finally, consider the case: depth(LCA(u, v)) = depth(LCA(v, w)). Then, LCA((u, v)) = LCA((v, w)). In this case, if depth(LCA(u, v)) > depth(LCA(u, w)) [figure 2(c)] then LCA(v, w) is a proper ancestor of LCA(u, v) which is a contradiction; furthermore, if depth(LCA(u, v)) < depth(LCA(u, w)) [figure 2(d)] then pre-order(v) cannot lie between pre-order(u) and pre-order(w). The only possibility in this case, therefore, is that depth(LCA(u, v)) = depth(LCA(u, w)), i.e. LCA(u, v) = LCA(u, w) = LCA(v, w).

Lemma 4.4 :

Let $\{v_1, v_2, \cdots, v_m\}$ be a set of marked vertices in an n-vertex rooted tree, with the v_i in an ascending order

---

Procedure Determine LCAs

Comments :

The outline given here is for one processor. Let **R** and **C** be the sets of vertices corresponding to the rows and of columns respectively, of the partition of adjacency matrix assigned to the processor. Let T be the rooted tree on the graph constructed by procedure Articulation Points, and distributed to all the processors in the array.

1. Construct E, an Euler tour around T.
2. Traverse E, to find the pre-order numbers of all the vertices and order the vertices in $\mathbf{R} \cup \mathbf{C}$ into the ordered set $X = x_1, x_2, \ldots, x_m$, $m=2n/\sqrt{p}$, such that the x_i are in ascending order of pre-order numbers.
3. For each pair $\{x_i\ x_{i+1}\}$ $(1 \le i \le m-1)$, of vertices of X, find LCA(x_i, x_{i+1}) by performing a binary search on E.
4. Mark as special the root of T, all vertices of X, and all the vertices that have been identified as LCAs in the previous step.
5. Construct an auxiliary tree T′ consisting only of special vertices. Two vertices in T′ are joined by an edge if and only if they are connected in T either by an edge or by a path in which all the intermediate vertices are not special.
6. For each vertex u in **R** do

   For all the vertices v in **C** determine the least common ancestors for the pairs {u, v} by performing a traversal of T′.

   End For

Comments :

In step 5, the tree T′ can be constructed by performing a depth first traversal of T, during which, all children of each non-special vertex are made the children of its father and the vertex is then removed from T.

---

of pre-order numbers. Let $L = \{\ \mathrm{LCA}(v_i, v_{i+1}) \mid 1 \le i \le m-1\ \}$. Then, LCA($v_i$, v_j) $\in$ L for all i, j, $1 \le i, j \le m$.

Proof : Consider any pair of marked vertices $\{v_i, v_j\}$, $i < j$, in the tree. If $j = i+1$ then LCA(v_i, v_j) is already in L. If $j = i+2$, then, by lemma 4.3, LCA(v_i, v_j) is one of LCA(v_i, v_{i+1}) or LCA(v_{i+1}, v_{i+2}), and hence is in L. For $j > i+2$, it can be easily seen, by successively invoking lemma 4.3 on the sequence of vertex pairs between i and j, that LCA(v_i, v_j) must be one of the vertices that is LCA(v_k, v_{k+1}), $i \le k \le j-1$. That is, LCA(v_i, v_j) $\in$ L.

Theorem 4.2 :

Procedure Determine LCAs correctly identifies LCA(u, v), $u \in \mathbf{R}$, $v \in \mathbf{C}$ in time $O(n^2/p)$.

Proof : From lemma 4.4, it follows that in the fourth step of procedure Determine LCAs all vertices LCA(u, v), $u \in \mathbf{R}$, $v \in \mathbf{C}$, would have been marked as special. The compressed tree $\hat{T}$ that is constructed in the fifth step of the algorithm preserves the LCA relationships in that a vertex which is an LCA of some pair of vertices in T′ is also the LCA of the same pair in T.

From lemma 4.4 it follows that at most $2n/\sqrt{p} - 1$ vertices will be identified as LCAs by the algorithm and hence there will be at most $4n/\sqrt{p}$ special vertices and this will be the number of vertices in T′.

The final step in the algorithm consists of $n/\sqrt{p}$ iterations (one iteration for each vertex in R) and each iteration involves a traversal of the tree $\hat{T}$ having $4n/\sqrt{p}$ vertices and edges. Thus, this step can be performed in time $O(n^2/p)$ by one processor. Step 3 takes $O(n/\sqrt{p}\log n)$ time. The other steps in the algorithm can be easily seen to require no more than O(n) time. Thus, the time complexity for the procedure is $O(n^2/p)$, $1 \leq p \leq n$.

5. Conclusion

In this paper we presented parallel algorithms for finding the minimum spanning tree, bridges, and articulation points of a graph on a fixed-size one-dimensional linear array of processors. On a graph of n vertices represented by an $n \times n$ adjacency matrix, our algorithms require time $O(n^2/p)$ time using a linear array of p processors, for all p, $1 \leq p \leq n$, thereby achieving a speedup linear in the number of processors employed. In particular, using n processors our algorithms match the lower bound of $\Omega(n)$ for the time complexity on this model. The paper also described a novel data reduction technique, for solving the problems of finding the bridge connected and biconnected components of a graph. Our results compare favorably with previously described algorithms for these problems on fixed-size processor networks.

Acknowledgement

We thank referees for their comments, especially for bringing reference [8] to our attention.

References

1. Aho, A. V., Hopcroft, J. E., and Ullman, J. D., "The Design and Analysis of Computer Algorithms," Addison-Wesley, Reading Mass. 1974.

2. Berge, C., and Ghouila-Hari, A., "Programming Games and Transportation Networks," Wiley, New York, 1965.

3. Prim, R. C., "Shortest Connection Networks and Some Generalizations," Bell Syst. Tech. Jl., 36, p.1389, 1957.

4. Dijkstra, E. W., "A Note on Two Problems in Connection with Graphs," Numerische Mathematik, 1, p. 269, 1959.

5. Kruskal, J. B. Jr., "On the Shortest Spanning Tree of a Graph and the Traveling Salesman Problem," Proc. American Mathematical Soc., 7, p.48, 1956.

6. Cheriton, D., and Tarjan, R. E., "Finding Minimum Spanning Trees," SIAM J. Comp., 5(1976), pp. 724-742.

7. Bentley, J. L., "A Parallel Algorithm for Constructing Minimum Spanning Trees," J. Algorithms, pp. 51-59, 1980.

8. Bentley, J. and Ottmann, T., "The Power of One Dimensional Vector of Processors," Universitat Karlsruhe, Bericht 89, April 1980.

9. Leighton, T., "Parallel Computation using Meshes of Trees," Proc. 1983 Int. Workshop on Graph Theoretic Concepts in Computer Science," 1983.

10. Nath, D., Maheshwari, S. N., and Bhatt, C. P., "Efficient VLSI Networks for Parallel Processing based on Orthogonal Trees," IEEE Trans. Comput., Vol. C-32, 6, pp. 569-581, 1983.

11. Atallah, M. J., and Kosaraju, S. R., "Graph Problems on a Mesh Connected Processor Array," Proc. 14th ACM Symp. Theory of Comp., pp. 345-353, 1982.

12. Huang, M. A., "Solving Some Graph Problems with Optimal or Near-Optimal Speedup on Mesh-of-Trees Networks," Proc. 26th Annual IEEE Symp. Foundations of Comput. Sci., pp. 232-240, 1985.

13. Savage, C. and Ja'Ja, J., "Fast Efficient Parallel Algorithms for some Graph Problems", SIAM J. Comp., 10, (1981), pp. 682-691.

14. Tsin, Y. and Chin, F., "Efficient Parallel Algorithms for a Class of Graph Theoretic Algorithms", SIAM J. Comp., 14, (1984), pp. 580-599.

15. Tarjan, R. E., and Vishkin, U., "Finding Biconnected Components and Computing Tree Functions in Logarithmic Time," 25th Ann. ACM Symp. on Theory of Computing, (1984), pp. 230-239.

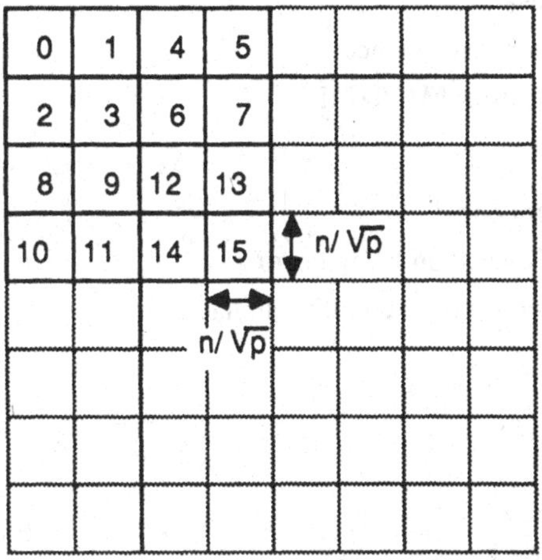

Figure 1. Adjacency Matrix Partitions

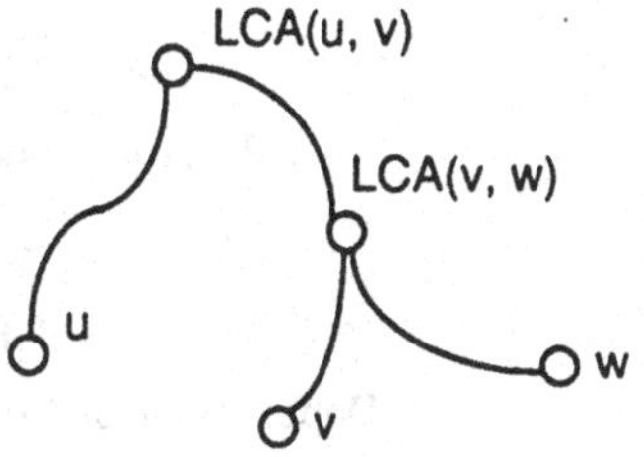

Figure 2(a)

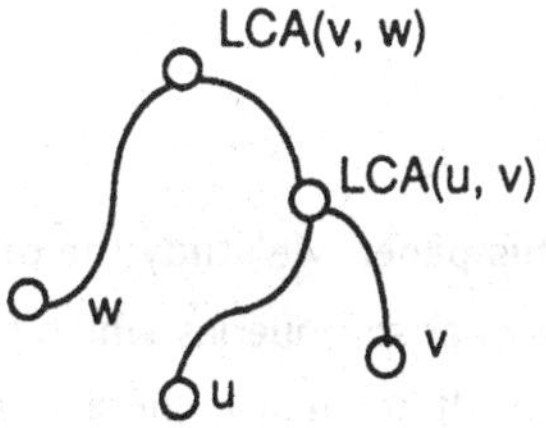

Figure 2(b)

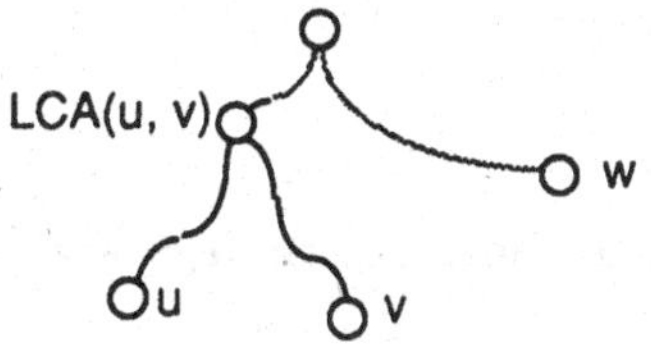

Figure 2(c)

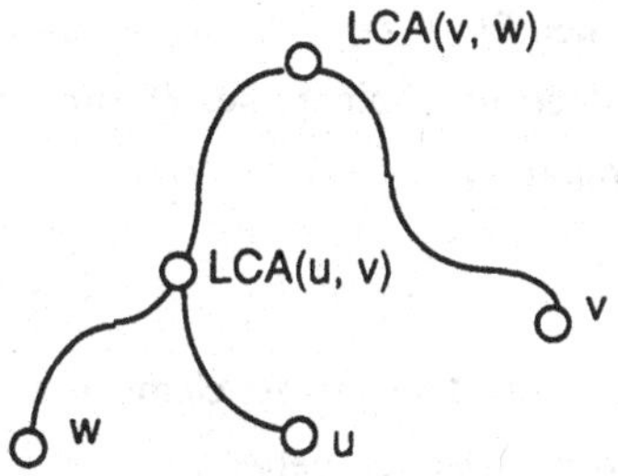

Figure 2(d)

ON SELECTING THE LARGEST ELEMENT IN SPITE OF ERRONEOUS INFORMATION

B. Ravikumar
Department of Computer Science
University of Minnesota, Minneapolis, MN 55455

K. Ganesan
Department of Computer Science
Boston University, Boston, MA 02215

and

K.B. Lakshmanan *
Department of Computer Science and Engineering
Indian Institute of Technology, Madras 600 036, India

Abstract

In this paper, we study the problem of finding the largest of a set of n distinct integers using comparison queries which receive "yes" or "no" answers, but some of which may be erroneous. If at most e queries can receive erroneous answers, we prove that $(e+1)n-1$ comparisons are necessary and sufficient to find the largest. If there is further restriction that errors are confined to "no" answers and that all "yes" answers are guaranteed to be correct, then $2n+2e-4$ comparisons are sufficient. This contrasts with earlier results relating to errors in binary search procedures where both versions of the problem have the same complexity.

Keywords: selection, largest element, comparisons, errors, lies, adversary strategy, analysis of algorithm, selection networks

---

* Presently visiting the Department of Electrical Engineering, McGill University, Montreal, P.Q. H3A 2A7, Canada, where this research was supported in part by an NSERC Operating Grant A0890.

1. Introduction

Consider a game between two players named A and B. Player A thinks of a set of n distinct integers $x_1, x_2, \ldots, x_n$, and player B has to find out the index, or the position of the largest element, by asking A a series of queries of the form "Is $x_i < x_j$?", for some $i, j \in \{1, 2, \ldots, n\}$. It is well known that $n-1$ queries are necessary and sufficient to accomplish the above task. To make the game more interesting, let us permit player A to lie. That is, in response to a query from B, player A can reply "yes" when, factually, he has to say "no", and vice versa. Let us also assume that player A can lie at most e times, and that n and e are known to both players at the beginning of the game. In this paper, we will show that there exists a strategy for player B that requires at most $(e+1)n-1$ queries for finding the largest. We will also show that this strategy is optimal in the worst case sense. For this, we will provide a strategy for the adversary player A, to answer as many as $(e+1)n-2$ queries in a way that the largest cannot be determined even at that stage. This proves that $(e+1)n-1$ queries are necessary. Observe that for $e=0$, i.e., for the no-lie case, our result reduces to the well-known bound on the number of comparison queries needed for finding the largest.

The above version of the problem may aptly be termed a full-lie case, in contrast to a half-lie version to be described below. Suppose that there is further restriction that the lies are confined to "no" answers and that every "yes" answer of player A is guaranteed to be correct. In this case, we will show that player B needs at most $e+1$ queries for $n=2$ and $e \geq 1$, and $2n+2e-4$ queries for $n \geq 3$ and $e \geq 1$, to find the largest. We will also show that the strategy for player B is optimal within two queries by demonstrating a corresponding adversary answering strategy for player A.

The problems of coping with erroneous information while searching, selecting and sorting are of sufficient interest due to several reasons, and have been suggested for study by a number of authors in the past [1,2,6,7]. Recently, Rivest et al. [5] have studied the problem of coping with errors in binary search procedures and have shown that the optimal algorithm for searching an unknown in the set $\{1, 2, \ldots, n\}$ requires $\log n + e \log\log n + O(e \log e)$ comparisons in the worst case, where all logarithms are to base 2. More importantly, they show that the worst-case complexity of the half-lie version is the same as that of the full-lie version. This contrasts with our result for the problem of finding the largest where the full-lie and half-lie versions have different complexities. In [3,4], we present some extensions to the results of Rivest et al. for the search problem.

The design of fault-tolerant networks for selecting is another problem of interest that is related to our result in this paper. A comparator, the basic unit in a selection network, is a two-input, two-output element that can compare and place the larger of the two inputs on a specified output port and the smaller on the other output port. Yao and Yao [9] assume that a faulty comparator is one which simply transmits the input values to the output ports without any processing, and show that $(e+1)(n-1)$ comparators are necessary and sufficient to build a fault-tolerant network for finding the largest, if at most e of the comparators can be faulty. Note that the optimal number of comparators in this result is e less than the optimal number of comparison queries for the full-lie case in our result. Moreover, the fault-tolerance capability of Yao and Yao 's network is crucially dependent on the fact that they assume a faulty comparator as one which simply transmits the inputs to the output ports without any processing, as if it is really non-existent. If we assume, on the other hand, that a faulty comparator is capable of switching the inputs, or delivering the inputs after comparison in wrong output ports, then a fault-tolerant network cannot really be built. This is because of the fact that a comparator network has no memory and that the comparators at the very end of the network could be the really faulty ones. So, Yao and Yao's results are meaningful only if, after fabricating a comparator network, the faulty ones are explicitly identified by testing, and then bypassed.

2. The Full–Lie Case

2.1 A strategy for finding the largest

In this section, we will provide a strategy for player B that requires at most $(e+1)n-1$ queries to reliably find out the position of the largest element. The strategy is much the same as in the no-lie case, except that it is necessary to repeat some of the queries, since the responses of player A cannot be taken as they are. Hence, at the start of the algorithm, player B will repeat the query "Is $x_1 < x_2$?" enough number of times, until $(e+1)$ "yes" or $(e+1)$ "no" answers are received. Since player A can lie at most e times a reply that has been confirmed $e+1$ times has to be necessarily true. Thus the larger of x_1 and x_2 can be reliably determined. Moreover, player B can even identify those previous responses, if any, of player A that are lies and determine the maximum number of times player A can lie in the future. Let this number be e_3. At this stage, the larger of x_1 and x_2 can be compared against x_3, again repeatedly until (e_3+1) "yes" or (e_3+1) "no" answers are received so that the largest of x_1, x_2, and x_3 can be reliably determined. Proceeding in this way player B can determine the largest of the n elements. The basic idea is simple. At a typical stage $j \geq 2$, at most e_j lies will be permitted with $e_j \leq e$ and $e_2 = e$. The largest of the elements $x_1, x_2, \ldots, x_{j-1}$ will be compared against a new element x_j, enough number of times to reliably determine the largest of $x_1, x_2, \ldots, x_j$. Since at most e_j lies are permitted, if player A lies t_j times during this stage, the number of queries needed will be $e_j + 1 + t_j$. Hence, the total number of queries Q required by player B during the entire computation is given by

$$Q = \sum_{j=2}^{n} (e_j + 1 + t_j) \le (e+1)(n-1) + \sum_{j=2}^{n} t_j.$$

But, since $\sum_{j=2}^{n} t_j$ denotes the total number of lies in the entire game, it is bounded above by e. Thus, player B will have to ask at most $(e+1)(n-1)+e = (e+1)n-1$ comparison queries in the worst case. It is easy to see that this worst case situation arises when player A saves his false replies to the last stage so that $t_j = 0$ for $j = 2, 3, \ldots, n-1$ and $t_n = e$. Since $e_2 = e$ and $e_{j+1} = e_j - t_j$, for $j = 2, 3, \ldots n-1$, in the worst case $e_j = e$, for $j = 2, 3, \ldots, n$. A similar analysis shows that the best case situation for player B arises when player A exhausts all his false replies at the beginning, i.e., when $t_2 = e$ and $t_j = 0$ for $j = 3, 4, \ldots, n$. In this best case, player B needs only $2e + n - 1$ queries. Observe that if player A uses his opportunity to lie at early stages, then to that extent uncertainity regarding answers given at later stages will get reduced. Thus player B will not have to repeat the queries too many times.

2.2 An adversary strategy for answering the queries

In this section we will provide a strategy for player A to answer as many as $(e+1)n-2$ queries in a way that the largest cannot be determined by player B even at that stage. Observe that to play such an adversary role, player A need not first think of a set of n distinct integers and than respond in accordance with it; he just has to keep track of the responses he has given in terms of which elements have not been excluded to be the largest. The idea is that if challenged at any stage, player A should be able to construct a set of integers for $x_1, x_2, \ldots, x_n$ and a true–false marking for the responses given so far, to demonstrate that he has been playing well within the rules of the game. Moreover, the adversary strategy for player A must be general enough, making no assumptions whatsoever about the querying strategy player B may adopt. The use of a similar adversary based argument in constructing a lower bound for the problem of searching an ordered table is illustrated in [8].

Before we explain the adversary strategy let us introduce a concept of a *negative vote* for an element of the set. If the query "Is $x_i < x_j$?" is answered "yes", we say that the element x_i has received a negative vote to be the largest. Similarly, if the query is answered "no" then the element x_j receives a negative vote. Observe that any element of the set that has received $e+1$ or more negative votes has to be excluded from being the largest.

While answering the queries, player A maintains a set L of elements which still qualify to be the largest. Initially, therefore, L contains all the n elements. Player A also keeps track of the number of negative votes received by each element. The exact query answering strategy depends on the stage in which the query process is in. The first stage consists of the first $(e+1)(n-1)-1 = (e+1)n-e-2$ queries. The second stage consists of the next e queries. During the first stage, player A answers without lying the queries as if he has a set of numbers that satisfy the inequalities $x_1 < x_2 < \ldots < x_n$. After answering every query, he updates the count of the number of negative votes received by the elements. Whenever the number of negative votes received by an element of the set exceeds e, it is removed from the set L. Observe that during this stage the element x_n will never receive a negative vote. Hence this element will remain in the set L. Moreover, all through and even at the end of the first stage, there will be at least one more element that has not received $e+1$ or more negative votes and hence remains in the set L. For continuing the adversary answering strategy, player A must identify a specific element x_m, other than x_n, remaining in L, at the end of the first stage. If there are only two elements left in L then there will be no choice. But if there is choice, player A can pick any element remaining in L other than x_n arbitrarily. Now, at the end of the first stage, player B cannot claim to know the largest element. If player B claims any element other than x_n to be the largest, player A can counter it by saying that x_n is indeed the largest since it has not received any negative vote and that all his responses are true. On the other hand, if player B claims x_n to be the largest, player A can claim that x_m is indeed the largest and that all those responses in which x_m received negative votes - less than or equal to e in number - are to be treated as lies.

The second stage of the adversary answering strategy consists of the next e queries. Player A will respond to the queries in a way that x_m receives no more negative votes. Thus, he will answer the queries, without lying, as if he has a set of n numbers that satisfy the inequalities $x_1 < x_2 < \ldots < x_{m-1} < x_{m+1} < \ldots < x_n < x_m$. Notice, however, that some of the responses in the second stage may be in direct contradiction to what has been said in the first stage. In particular, if the query involves x_m and x_j, for some $m+1 \leq j \leq n$, then such a contradiction can arise. Also notice that during this second stage x_m will not receive a negative vote, while x_n may receive some, but not more than e. Again, even at the end of the second stage, i.e., even after $(e+1)n-2$ queries, player B cannot claim to know the largest. If player B claims any element other than x_n to be the largest, player A can counter it by saying that x_n is indeed the largest and that all responses in the second stage for the queries involving x_m and x_j, for $m+1 \leq j \leq n$, which appear to make x_m the largest are in fact lies. On the other hand, if player B claims x_n to be the largest, player A can claim that x_m is indeed the largest and that all responses in the first stage in which x_m received negative votes and hence may appear to make it smaller than $x_{m+1}, \ldots, x_n$ are to be treated as lies. It is important to note that the number of responses claimed to be lies is not more than e in either case. Thus, the adversary answering strategy permits player A to respond to as many as $(e+1)n-2$ queries in a way that player B cannot be sure of the largest element. This completes the proof that $(e+1)n-1$ queries are necessary in the worst case to determine the largest.

3. The Half-Lie Case

3.1 A strategy for finding the largest

Recall that in the half-lie case all "yes" responses given by player A are guaranteed to be correct. It is the "no" responses that can be either true or false. Therefore, given two elements x_i and x_j, in order to determine reliably the largest of these two, the query "Is $x_i < x_j$?" has to be repeated enough number of times until $(e+1)$ "no" or a single "yes" response is received. If $e+1$ queries were, in fact, asked and all of them received "no" responses, then no lies have been exposed. On the other hand, if $t+1$ queries, $t \leq e$, were asked and all but the last received "no" responses, then t lies have been exposed, so that player A can lie at most $e-t$ times in the future. In any case, we require at most $e+1$ queries to determine the larger, if e is the maximum number of lies permitted. Thus, by a simple application of this query *repetition* technique for every one of the $n-1$ queries of the no-lie case, the largest of a set of n distinct integers can be determined with at most $(e+1)(n-1)$ comparison queries. But, for $n \geq 4$ and $e \geq 2$, there is a better algorithm which exploits the fact that "yes" responses cannot be false and this algorithm requires at most $2n+2e-4$ queries in the worst case.

A query *alteration* technique works as follows: If the response for the query "Is $x_i < x_j$?" is "no", the next query asked is "Is $x_j < x_i$?" If the response is "no" again, the next query asked is "Is $x_i < x_j$?", and so on. This technique forces player A to answer "yes" and thereby eliminate one of the two elements from being the largest or answer "no" and thereby contradict some of the previous responses. Since such contradictions will have to be finally explained away as lies, the alternation technique forces player A to use up his lies in early stages of the game and thereby reduce the uncertainity regarding the responses for player B. While comparing x_i and x_j, if e is the maximum number of lies permitted, the alternation technique will require at most $2e+1$ queries to be asked before the larger is reliably determined. If $2e+1$ queries were, in fact, asked then depending on the outcome, e of the responses can be clearly identified as false. In other words, player A has been forced to use all his lies, and that he cannot lie henceforth. But, in general, the queries may be alternated and an "yes" answer may be received at the $(2t+1)th$ or $(2t+2)th$ query, $t < e$. In either case, t of the previous responses can be identified as false, and player A can lie at most $e-t$ times in the future.

For finding the largest of a set of n distinct integers a combination of query alternation and repetition techniques can be used. The algorithm has $n-1$ stages corresponding to the $n-1$ queries of the no-lie case. At a typical stage $j, 2 \leq j \leq n$, the largest of the elements $x_1, x_2, \ldots, x_{j-1}$ will be compared against a new element x_j, enough number of times to reliably determine the largest of $x_1, x_2, \ldots, x_j$. As before, let e_j denote the maximum number of lies permitted at this stage. For choosing the queries, the query repetition technique will be used if $j = n$ or $e_j = 0$; Otherwise, the query alternation technique will be used. At the end of the stage, if t_j is the number of lies exposed, then the maximum number of lies permitted in the next stage is computed as $e_j - t_j$.

It is easy to observe that if $e = 0$ the algorithm requires exactly $n-1$ queries. Also,for $n = 2$ and $e \geq 1$ the algorithm uses only the repetition technique which requires $e+1$ queries. But, if $n \geq 3$ and $e \geq 1$, then a combination of alternation and repetition techniques will be used and this requires a careful analysis. Let t_j denote the number of lies exposed in the jth stage. Also, let $k, 2 \leq k \leq n$, be the smallest integer such that $t_k = e_k$, if there exists one. Then min $(k, n-1)$ gives the last stage for which the query alternation technique is used. The total number of queries Q required by player B during the entire computation can now be bounded as follows:

Case 1. $k \leq n-1$.

$$Q \leq \sum_{j=2}^{k-1}(2t_j + 2) + (2t_k + 1) + (n-k)$$

$$= n + k + \sum_{j=2}^{k} 2t_j - 3$$

$$\leq 2n + 2e - 4.$$

Case 2. $k = n$.

$$Q \leq \sum_{j=2}^{n-1}(2t_j + 2) + (t_n + 1)$$

$$= 2n + \sum_{j=2}^{n} 2t_j - t_n - 3$$

$$\leq 2n + 2e - 4.$$

Case 3. There exists no $k, 2 \leq k \leq n$, such that $t_k = e_k$.

$$
\begin{aligned}
Q &\leq \sum_{j=2}^{n-1} (2t_j + 2) + (e_n + 1) \\
&= 2n + 2e - e_n - 3 \\
&\leq 2n + 2e - 4.
\end{aligned}
$$

Thus, for $n \geq 3$ and $e \geq 1$, player B will have to ask at most $2n + 2e - 4$ queries in the worst case. Observe that for $n = 3$ and $e \geq 1$, player B could have merely used the query repetition technique, and yet the number of queries would have been no more than $2n + 2e - 4 = 2(e + 1)$. Similarly, for $e = 1$ also player B could have merely used the repetition technique and the number of queries needed would have been no more than $2n + 2e - 4 = 2(n - 1)$. Thus, only for $n \geq 4$ and $e \geq 2$ combining the two techniques yields a strictly better strategy.

3.2 An adversary strategy for answering the queries

In order to show that player B needs at least q queries to find out the largest, we must construct an adversary strategy to answer as many $q - 1$ queries in such a way that there exist at least two elements, either of which can be claimed as the largest by suitably marking the responses as true/false, ensuring, of course, that only "no" responses are marked as false, and that their number is less than or equal to e. In this section, by constructing such answering strategies, we will show that for $n = 2$ and $e \geq 1$ player B needs at least $e + 1$ queries. Similarly, we will show that for $n = 3$ and $e \geq 1$, player B needs at least $2(e + 1)$ queries. Also, for $n \geq 3$ and $e = 1$ we will show that player B needs at least $2(n - 1)$ queries. Hence we observe that the querying strategy provided in Section 3.1 for player B is optimal for these cases. However, for $n \geq 4$ and $e \geq 2$, we only show that player B needs at least $2n + 2e - 6$ queries implying that the querying strategy provided for player B is optimal within two queries, independent of n and e.

As in Section 2.2, to play such an adversary role player A need not first think of a set of n distinct integers and respond in accordance with it; he just has to keep track of the responses given in terms of which elements have not been excluded to be the largest. Again, as in Section 2.2, the concept of a negative vote will be needed here. If the query "Is $x_i < x_j$?" is answered "no", we say that the element x_j has received a negative vote to be the largest. Any element that receives $e + 1$ or more negative votes has to be excluded from being the largest. On the other hand, if the query is answered "yes", the element x_i receives a negative vote. It also has to be excluded from being the largest.

Consider the case $n = 2$ and $e \geq 1$. The adversary answering strategy is to simply say "no" for the first e queries. Clearly player B cannot claim to know the largest at this stage since each element would have received less than or equal to e negative votes and hence either one can be demonstrated by player A to be the largest by suitably marking some of the responses as false. Thus, player B needs at least $e + 1$ queries. For the case $n = 3$ and $e \geq 1$ also, the answering strategy is to respond with "no" for the first $2e + 1$ queries. Even at this stage player B cannot claim to know the largest. But suppose he claims $x_i, i \in \{1, 2, 3\}$ to be the largest. Then player A will be able to counter it by a constructing a set of three numbers such that either $x_j < x_i < x_k$ or $x_k < x_i < x_j$, for $i, j, k, \in \{1, 2, 3\}$ and $i \neq j \neq k \neq i$. This can be seen as follows. Let q_{ij} denote the number of times the query "Is $x_i < x_j$?" was answered "no". Then if the order $x_j < x_i < x_k$ is to be claimed as correct, the number of responses to be marked as false equals $q_k = q_{ji} + q_{jk} + q_{ik}$. On the other hand, if $x_k < x_i < x_j$ is to be claimed as the correct order, the number of responses to be marked as false equals $q_j = q_{ki} + q_{kj} + q_{ij}$. Since $q_k + q_j \leq 2e + 1$,either q_k or q_j must be less than or equal to e Therefore, by suitably marking some of the responses, less than or equal to e in number, as false, player A can counter the assertion that x_i is indeed the largest. Thus, player B needs at least $2(e + 1)$ queries.

For the case of $n \geq 3$ and $e = 1$, however, the adversary answering strategy is very different.' Here we need a concept of a *rank* of an element of the set $x_1, x_2, \ldots, x_n$. Initially all the elements are given the rank $n + 1$, but they are changed to unique ranks in the range 1 to n as the queries are answered. In fact, the first element to receive a negative vote is given the rank one. The next element to receive a negative vote is given rank two, and so on. After $n - 1$ ranks are assigned the remaining element is assigned the rank n. Player A has to keep track of the ranks assigned to different elements in order to play the adversary role.

The adversary answering strategy for the first $2n - 3$ queries is as follows. For the query "Is $x_i < x_j$?", player A will consult the rank associated with the elements x_i and x_j. If $rank(x_i) = rank(x_j) = n + 1$, then player A will answer "no", assign a negative vote and the next available rank to x_j. If $rank(x_i) < rank(x_j)$, then player A will answer "yes", assign a negative vote to x_i and immediately exclude it from being the largest. If $rank(x_i) > rank(x_j)$, then player A will answer "no", assign a negative vote to x_j and exclude it from being the largest, if it has already received $e + 1$ negative votes. Observe that all responses given are consistent as if the value associated with x_i is the same as its rank. Also observe that any element that has been excluded from being the largest would have received at least two negative votes. Thus, after answering $2n - 3$ queries in the above manner there will be at least two elements left, which have not been excluded from being the largest. Clearly, any one of these elements can be claimed as largest by player A, in the process having to mark at most one "no" response as false. Thus, player B needs at least $2n - 2$ queries to find out the largest.

For $n \geq 4$ and $e \geq 2$ also the adversary answering strategy will use the two concepts — negative vote and rank. The strategy for assigning negative votes and ranks will be just the same as described for the case $n \geq 3$ and $e = 1$, with the exception that the ranks $n-2, n-1$ and n will not be assigned to the elements of the set $x_1, x_2, \ldots, x_n$ when called for in the above strategy and will be maintained simply as $n + 1$ until $2(e - 1) + 1$ queries have been answered among these three elements themselves. The net effect will be to have a set of $2e - 1$ "no" responses among these three elements alone, with other responses being consistent as if the value of x_i is the same as its rank, no matter how the three ranks $n - 2$ to n are assigned to the three elements still having the rank $n + 1$. Besides, as in the case of $n = 3$ and $e \geq 1$, the $(2e - 1)$ "no" responses would still leave player B in doubt as to which one of these three is really the largest even among them. At the next query among these three elements, player A can fix the rank among these three elements in a way that at most $e - 1$ of the $2(e - 1) + 1$ "no" responses will have to be marked as false and then respond accordingly to the new query as if the value of x_i is the same as its rank for these elements also. Player A can also immediately exclude the elements with rank $n - 2$ and $n - 1$ from being the largest. But the element with rank n will continue to qualify for being the largest.

At this stage, if player A has already responded to $2n + 2e - 6$ queries, this completes our proof. On the other hand, if he has responded to less than $2n + 2e - 7$ queries he will continue to respond to further queries consistent with the rank assignment until $2n+2e-7$ queries have been responded. Even at this stage player B cannot claim to know the largest. Since at least $2e$ queries have been answered among the elements with rank $n - 2$ to n alone, and each of the other $n - 3$ elements must receive at least two negative votes before getting excluded from being the largest, there must remain at least one more element with just one negative vote. If player B claims the element with rank n to be the largest, player A can counter it by claiming any of these elements still not being excluded as the largest to be the real largest element, in the process marking one more query with "no" response as false. On the other hand, if player B claims any element other than the one with rank n to be the largest, player A can counter it by saying that the element with rank n is indeed the largest, in the process marking no more queries, other than the earlier $e - 1$, as false. Thus, player B needs at least $2n + 2e - 6$ queries to find out the largest.

4. Concluding Remarks

In this paper, we have shown that $(e+1)n-1$ comparisons are necessary and sufficient for finding the largest of a set of n distinct integers, when the outcome of as many as e of them can be erroneous. We have also shown that the half-lie version of the problem, where the possibility of errors is confined to one type of responses, has a lower complexity than the full-lie version. It is fairly easy to pursue the problems of coping with erroneous information while sorting or finding the median, and demonstrate asymptotically optimal algorithms [3]. But optimal algorithms for other selection problems such as finding the second largest, finding the largest and the smallest together, etc., are yet to be found in this context.

Acknowledgment

We thank Libbey Griffith for help in preparing the manuscript.

References

[1] R.A. DeMillo, D.P. Dopkin, and R.J. Lipton, Combinatorial Inference, in *Foundations of Secure Computation*, R.A. DeMillo, D.P. Dopkin, A.K. Jones and R.J. Lipton, Eds., Academic Press, New York, 1978, pp.27-37.

[2] G.O.H. Katona, Combinatorial Search Problems, in *A Survey of Combinatorial Theory*, J.N. Srivastava et al., Eds., North-Holland, Amsterdam, 1973, pp. 285-308.

[3] B. Ravikumar, Coping With Errors in Searching, Selecting and Sorting, M.S. Thesis, Indian Institute of Technology, Madras, India, August 1983.

[4] B. Ravikumar and K.B. Lakshmanan, Coping with Known Patterns of Lies in a Search Game, *Theoretical Computer Science*, Vol. 33, No.1, Sept. 1984, pp.85-94.

[5] R.L. Rivest, A.R. Meyer, D.J. Kleitman, K. Winklman and J. Spencer, Coping with Errors in Binary Search Procedures, *Journal of Computer and System Sciences*, Vol. 20, No. 3, June 1980, pp. 396-404.

[6] J.F. Traub, G.W. Wasilkowski and H. Wozniakowski, *Information, Uncertainty, Complexity*, Addison-Wesley, Reading, MA, 1983.

[7] S.M. Ulam, *Adventures of a Mathematician*, Scribner, New York, 1976.

[8] B. Weide, A Survey of Analysis Techniques for Discrete Algorithms, *Computing Surveys*, Vol.9, No.4, Dec. 1977, pp. 291-313.

[9] A.C. Yao and F.F. Yao, On Fault-Tolerant Networks for Sorting, *SIAM Journal of Computing*, Vol.14, No.1, Feb. 1985, pp. 120-128.

The Correlation Between the Complexities of the Non-Hierarchical and Hierarchical Versions of Graph Problems

T. Lengauer

Fachbereich 17
Universität-GH Paderborn
4790 Paderborn

K.W. Wagner

Institut für Mathematik
Universität Augsburg
8900 Augsburg

ABSTRACT

In [Le 82, Le 85, Le 86a, Le 86b] a hierarchical graph model is discussed that allows to exploit the hierarchical description of the graphs for the efficient solution of graph problems. The model is motivated by applications in CAD, and is based on a special form of a graph grammar. The above references contain polynomial time solutions for the hierarchical versions of many classical graph problems. However, there are also graph problems that cannot benefit from the succinctness of hierarchical description of the graphs.

In this paper we investigate whether the complexity of the hierarchical version of a graph problem can be predicted from the complexity of its non-hierarchical version. We find that the correlation between the complexities of the two versions of a graph problem is very loose, i.e., such a prediction is not possible in general. This is contrary to corresponding results about other models of succinct graph description [PY 86, Wa 86].

One specific result of the paper is that the threshold network flow problem, which asks whether the maximum flow in a (hierarchical) directed graph is larger than a given number, is log-space complete for PSPACE in its hierarchical version and log-space complete for P in its non-hierarchical version. The latter result affirms a conjecture by [GS 82].

Other typical results settle the complexities of the hierarchical version of the clique-, independent set-, and Hamiltonian circuit problem.

1. Introduction

In the past, several models for the succinct description of large graphs have been proposed [Ga 82, GW 83, Wa 84, Le 85]. Each graph model has been investigated w.r.t. how the succinctness of the graph description can be exploited to speed up the solution of graph problems. While the models of [GW 83, Wa 84] allow effective speedup for practically no interesting graph problem, many natural and important graph problems can benefit from the succinctness in the models of [Ga 82, Le 85]. For examples of hierarchical solutions of graph problems see also [Le 82, Le 86a, Le 86b]. On the other hand also in these models there are graph problems for which no significant speedup is possible.

This paper discusses the hierarchical graph model of [Le 85]. We investigate the question whether the knowledge of the complexity of the non-hierarchical version of a graph problem implies some knowledge of the complexity of its hierarchical version. In other words, is there some correlation between the non-hierarchical and hierarchical complexities of graph problems? The corresponding question can be answered affirmatively in the case of the small circuit model of [GW 83]. Indeed, [PY 86] show that if a graph problem Π is NP-hard in a certain strong sense (projection hardness as defined by [SV 81]), then the succinct version of Π in the small circuit model is NTIME(2^{Pol})-hard using the normal concept of polynomial reducibility. Since most of the reductions done to prove NP-hardness are projections in the sense of [SV 81] this establishes a strong correlation between the complexities of the classical and succinct versions of a graph problem.

We will show that the same is not true for the model of [Le 85]. Indeed, we find that the complexity of the non-hierarchical version of a graph problem says practically nothing about the complexity of its hierarchical version. The results of the paper are summarized in the following table.

HIER. \ NON-HIER.	L	NL	P	NP
L	VERTEX			
NL	EDGE	BFO-GAP		
P	LDP-BD-BFO-AGAP	GAP	BFO-AGAP	
NP	LD-CLIQUE LBW-BFO-CLIQUE	CGAP	BFO-ACGAP	CLIQUE
PSPACE	LDP-MCV	LBW-BFO-3COLOR LBW-BFO-IS	MCV NF	HC 3COLOR IS
NTIME (2^{Pol})				LAYOUT

The rows and columns in the table are labelled with the classes L (deterministic logarithmic space), NL (non-deterministic logarithmic space), P, NP, PSPACE, NTIME(2^{Pol}) (non-deterministic exponential time, *Pol* stands for any polynomial). A graph problem is put in the table entry (X,Y) if its non-hierarchical version is log-space complete for Y, and its hierarchical version is log-space complete for X. Note that the upper right corner of the table is forbidden, since the hierarchical graph model of [Le 85] properly contains the classical non-hierarchical graph model. Furthermore the lower left corner of the table is forbidden since the at most exponential data compression of the hierarchical model of [Le 85] allows an at most exponential blow-up of the complexities.

The fact that we can fill each of the remaining entries in the table is evidence for the absence of a strong correlation between the complexities of the non-hierarchical and hierarchical versions of a graph problem. Thus it is unlikely, that "generic" hierarchical graph algorithms exist that solve large classes of graph problems at once.

Some of the problems we use to fill the table are somewhat artificial and constructed specifically to fit into some table entry. But among the problems we consider are also such natural problems as the clique problem, the network flow problem, the circuit value problem, the 3-coloring problem, the independent set problem, the Hamiltonian circuit problem, and a natural graph layout problem previously discussed by [DT 81].

In all cases but one the non-hierarchical complexities have either been known before or their proof is a simple exercise. The exception is the network-flow problem that has not been known to be P-complete in its threshold version.

The paper is organized as follows:

In Section 2 we define the hierarchical graph model and the notation used to denote the graph problems discussed in the paper. The following sections discuss the graph problems. Here we divide the graph problems considered into natural groups. Section 3 discusses graph problems that are trivial non-hierarchically. Section 4 discusses reachability problems on graphs. Section 5 considers classical NP-complete graph problems. Section 6 discusses two special graph problems, namely the circuit value problem and the network flow problem. The circuit value problem is important for the simulation of large circuits (see [Le 86c]). The complexity of the network flow problem is proved using the results on the circuit value problem. In Section 7 we give conclusions.

2. Basic definitions

In this section we define the hierarchical graph model. For space reasons we will state some definitions informally. The formal definitions can be found in [Le 86a].

Definition 2.1: A *hierarchical graph* $\Gamma=(G_1,\ldots,G_k)$ consists of k subcells $G_i, 1\le i\le k$. Each subcell is a graph that contains three kinds of vertices called pins, inner vertices, and nonterminals. The pins are the vertices through which the subcell can be connected to from the outside. The inner vertices cannot be connected to from the outside. The nonterminals stand for previously defined subcells. Specifically, a nonterminal inside G_i has a name and a type. The name is a unique number or string, the type is a number from $1,\ldots,i-1$. A nonterminal v of type j stands for a copy of subcell G_j. The neighbours of v correspond 1-to-1 to pins of G_j via a mapping that is given as a part of Γ. A hierarchical graph Γ is expanded by expanding cell G_k recursively. To expand cell G_i we expand all of its subcells $G_1,\ldots,G_{i-1}$ recursively and replace each nonterminal v of type j with a copy of the expansion of subcell G_j. The result of the expansion is denoted with $E(\Gamma)$. Figures 1 and 2 show a hierarchical graph and its expansion. Here in Figure 1, squares denote pins and circles denote nonterminals. Inside a cycle the name and type of the corresponding nonterminal is given. The 1-to-1 correspondence between the neighbours of a nonterminal v of type j and the pins of G_j is given implicitly by their position in the figure. Furthermore we can structure $E(\Gamma)$ into a tree form, showing the structure of the hierarchical composition of $E(\Gamma)$ (see Figure 3). (Note that the number of pins in a subcell is *not* restricted.) Each vertex and edge in $E(\Gamma)$ *belongs* to a node in the hierarchy tree. An edge belongs to the node representing the copy of the subcell that contributes the edge. A vertex can be contributed by several copies. Here the convention is that the vertex belongs to the node that represents the subcell contributing the vertex as an inner vertex. Vertices and edges in $E(\Gamma)$ are identified by giving the names of the nodes on the path in the hierarchy tree that leads from the root to the node the vertex resp. the edge belongs to. Then the vertex resp. the edge is identified in the corresponding subcell. Thus the identification of a vertex/edge in $E(\Gamma)$ may be as long as $O(n)$.

Let n denote the length of an encoding of Γ. Here we assume graphs to be encoded by adjacency lists, and numbers to be encoded in binary.

Let N be the length of an encoding of $E(\Gamma)$. Clearly $N=2^{O(n)}$ must be the case, and there are cases, in which $N=2^{\Omega(n)}$ is the case.

Note that even though we assume that the G_i do not contain multiple edges, $E(\Gamma)$ may contain multiple edges.

If Π is a graph problem that asks a question about the graph G, we denote with Π_{HG} the problem that given a hierarchical graph Γ asks the same question about $E(\Gamma)$. Equivalently we can consider Π as the restriction of Π_{HG} to hierarchical graphs Γ with $k=1$. A natural way of answering Π_{HG} is to expand Γ and run a (non-hierarchical) solution algorithm for Π on $E(\Gamma)$. Because of the large size of N w.r.t. n this can be very inefficient. We are interested in whether there are more efficient ways of solving Π_{HG}.

[Le 82, Le 85, Le 86a, Le 86b] discuss several natural and important graph problems Π such that Π and Π_{HG} are both in P, i.e., the succinctness of the hierarchical description leads to large savings in computing space and time for solving Π.

The method employed for the hierarchical solution of all of these problems is the so-called bottom-up method, a table driven method that looks at each subcell only once, no matter how often it is replicated in $E(\Gamma)$.

In this paper we prove a number of completeness results that show that the hierarchical structure of a graph cannot always be exploited to gain efficiency in the solution of a graph problem. All completeness results we prove or cite from the literature will be w.r.t. log-space reductions.

We will consider several kinds of graph problems. Many problems will be on the class of all directed or undirected graphs. Sometimes we will consider subclasses of graphs, such as all graphs whose depth is logarithmic in their size, or all graphs whose bandwidth is logarithmic in their size. In this case, all graphs are problem instances, but we will only accept graphs that belong to the subclass. I.e., the test whether the problem instance belongs to the subclass considered is part of the problem. Some problems we consider are on ordered graphs. An ordered (non-hierarchical) directed graph is a graph whose vertices are ordered such that each edge leads from smaller vertex to the larger vertex. The ordering of the vertices is part of the problem instance. Thus an ordered graph is necessarily acyclic. In an ordered hierarchical graph Γ we consider the vertices inside the cells to be ordered. These orderings on the vertices of the subcells can induce an ordering on the vertices of the expansion $E(\Gamma)$ in two natural ways: Let $(i_1,\ldots,i_{m_1})$ and $(j_1,\ldots,j_{m_2})$ be the path names for two vertices in $E(\Gamma)$.

Breadth-first: $(i_1,\ldots,i_{m_1})<(j_1,\ldots,j_{m_2})$ exactly if $m_1<m_2$ or ($m_1=m_2$ and there is a $k\in 0,\ldots,m_1-1$ such that $i_r=j_r$ for $r=1,\ldots,k$ and $i_{k+1}<j_{k+1}$).

We call a hierarchical graph ***breadth-first ordered***, if $E(\Gamma)$ is an ordered graph with respect to this ordering.

Note that a hierarchical graph Γ is breadth-first ordered exactly if

- each cell G_i of Γ is ordered in the sense that each edge between two terminal vertices leads from the smaller to the larger vertex in G_i
- the pins of each subcell G_i of Γ have indegree 0, i.e., no edge in $E(\Gamma)$ is directed upwards in the hierarchy tree.

Depth-first: $(i_1,\ldots,i_{m_1})<(j_1,\ldots,j_{m_2})$ by the lexicographic ordering.

We call the hierarchical graph Γ ***depth-first ordered*** if $E(\Gamma)$ is an ordered graph with respect to the depth-first ordering.

Note that a hierarchical graph Γ is depth-first ordered exactly if

- each cell G_i of Γ is ordered in the sense that each edge between two terminal vertices leads from the smaller to the larger vertex in G_i.
- each pin of each subcell G_i in Γ has either indegree-0 or outdegree-0. Let v be a nonterminal of type G_i and w be a neighbour of v. If w corresponds to a pin with outdegree>0 (indegree>0) then $w<v$ ($v<w$).

Both kinds of numbering are of service to us. The breadth-first numbering preserves the locality in a sense that ensures that a graph problem does not become much harder when hierarchical graphs are considered. The depth-first ordering is consistent with threading techniques on trees that are essential for the reductions used in some completeness proofs.

We will use the following conventions to denote the graph problems. Each graph problem will be denoted by an acronym, preceded by one or more prefixes denoting a restriction of the general graph problem. Here is a list of the prefixes we use.

Prefix	Restricted class of graphs
BFO−	All ordered (hierarchical) graphs with breadth-first ordering
DFO−	All ordered (hierarchical) graphs with depth-first ordering
LDP−	All directed (hierarchical) graphs whose depth is at most $\log N$, where N is the number of vertices in the (expanded) graph
LD−	All undirected (hierarchical) graphs, where each vertex in the (expanded) graph has degree at most $\log N$, N as above.
LBW−	All undirected (hierarchical) graphs with a vertex numbering, such that the bandwidth of the (expanded) graph with this numbering is at most $\log N$. The numbering is classified by using the prefix *BFO−* or *DFO−*. (The vertex numbering is part of the input.)
BD−	All directed (hierarchical) graphs such that each vertex in the (expanded) graph has indegree and outdegree at most 2.

As an example of how we use this notation consider the graph accessibility problem.

GRAPH ACCESSIBILITY (*GAP*)

Given: A directed graph $G=(V,E)$. Two vertices $a,b \in V$.

Question: Is there a path between a and b in G?

The corresponding problem on ordered graphs is the following:

ORDERED GRAPH ACCESSIBILITY (*BFO−GAP*)

Given: A directed graph $G=(V,E)$ with an ordering on the vertex set V. Two vertices $a,b \in V$.

Question: Is G ordered, i.e., does every edge in G lead from the smaller to the larger vertex, and is b reachable from a?

The prefix *BFO−* here signifies, that the hierarchical version $BFO{-}GAP_{HG}$ uses the breadth-first ordering.

We are now ready to consider the first group of graph problems.

3. Vertices and edges

For a graph given by adjacency lists the question whether a given vertex or edge belongs to that graph is trivial. However, this is not so clear for hierarchical graphs.

VERTEX

Given: A graph $G=(V,E)$ and an element $a \in N$.

Question: Is $a \in V$?

EDGE

Given: A graph $G=(V,E)$ and $a,b \in V$.

Question: Is $(a,b) \in E$?

Proposition 3.1: *VERTEX,EDGE* ∈ L•

In hierarchical graphs vertices are identified by path names (see Definition 2.1). The pathname describes the path in the hierarchy tree leading to this vertex. Consequently,

Proposition 3.2: $VERTEX_{HG}$ ∈ L. •

However, it is harder to check whether a given edge belongs to a hierarchical graph.

Theorem 3.3: $EDGE_{HG}$ is NL-complete.

Proof: a) $EDGE_{HG} \in$ NL: A non-deterministic depth search on the hierarchy tree can find a subcell contributing the given edge in log-space, if it exists.

b) $EDGE_{HG}$ is NL-hard: We reduce the problem $BFO-GAP$ (Section 2) which is NP-complete [Su 73] to $EDGE_{HG}$. For the ordered graph $G=(\{1,\ldots,m\},E)$ we define the hierarchical graph $\Gamma=(G_{m-1},\ldots,G_2,G_1)$ as follows: $V_i = \{j:(i,j)\in E\} = \{j_1,\ldots,j_{r_i}\}$. The G_i look as shown in Figure 4. For $i=2,\ldots,m-1$ the vertices a und b are defined as pins. Obviously, there exists a path in G from 1 to m if and only if $(a,b)\in E(\Gamma)$. •

Remark 1: This proof shows also that the number of different paths leading from 1 to m coincides with the multiplicity of the edge (a,b) in $E(\Gamma)$. The problem, whether the number of different paths between two given vertices of an ordered graph exceeds a given k is #L-complete. Consequently, the problem of whether the multiplicity of a given edge in a hierarchical graph exceeds a given k is also #L-complete. However, the problem of whether a given hierarchical graph has a multiple edge is easily shown to be NL-complete (the reduction is similar to that in the above proof).

Remark 2: A slight modification of the above reduction shows that the problem of whether a hierarchical graph with a given breadth-first ordering of the vertices does not have logarithmic bandwidth is NL-complete.

4. Graph accessibility problems

The graph accessibility problem GAP (see Section 2) was the first problem which could be shown to be NL-complete [Sa 73]. This result could also be proved for the restricted problem $BFO-GAP$ [Su 73]. (Actually a slight modification of $BFO-GAP$ has been investigated in [Su 73].)

Theorem 4.1: ([SA 73, SU 73]): GAP and $BFO-GAP$ are NL-complete. •

Similar results have been proved for alternating graphs and P-completeness. An alternating graph [Im 79] is a directed graph whose vertices are labeled by $\vee$ and $\wedge$. The reachability in an alternating graph is defined as follows:

- each vertex is reachable from itself,
- a $\vee$-vertex a is reachable from a vertex b if there exists a successor of a which is reachable from b, and
- a $\wedge$-vertex a is reachable from a vertex b if all successors of a are reachable from b.

AGAP

Given: An alternating graph G and two vertices a,b of G.

Question: Is b reachable from a?

It has been shown in [Im 79] that $AGAP$ is P-complete. A minor modification of the proof yields the same result for $BFO-AGAP$.

Theorem 4.2: ([Im 79]): $AGAP$ and $BFO-AGAP$ are P-complete. •

For hierarchical graphs the unordered and the breadth-first ordered versions of graph accessibility problems have different complexities. Since in hierarchical graphs paths with breadth-first ordering of the vertices can lead only along paths from the root to a leaf in the hierarchy tree an instance of $BFO-GAP_{HG}$($BFO-AGAP_{HG}$) can be tested within logarithmic space by a non-deterministic (alternating) turing machine. Consequently, $BFO-GAP_{HG} \in NL$ ($BFO-AGAP_{HG} \in P$; for the relationship between alternating space and deterministic time see [CK 78]). Since the non-hierarchical problems are restrictions of the hierarchical problems Theorem 4.1 and Theorem 4.2 yield

Theorem 4.3: 1. $BFO-GAP_{HG}$ is NL-complete.
2. $BFO-AGAP_{HG}$ is P-complete. •

In contrast with this result we have

Theorem 4.4: 1. GAP_{HG} is P-complete.
2. $AGAP_{HG}$ is PSPACE-hard.
3. $AGAP_{HG}$ is in DTIME(2^{Pol}).

The proof will be given in a separate paper. We only mention that the P-hardness of GAP_{HG} is shown by reduction from $AGAP$ and that the PSPACE-hardness of $AGAP_{HG}$ is shown by reduction from the monotone circuit value problem (for the definition of this problem see Section 6).

Remark: Slight modifications of the proof of Theorem 4.4.1 yield that the hierarchical versions of the following problems are also P-complete: the accessibility problem for undirected graphs, the problem of whether a given directed graph has a cycle, and the problem of whether a given graph is bipartite.

In search for a ***deterministic*** log-space graph accessibility problem we consider the restriction $LDP-BD-BFO-AGAP$ of $BFO-AGAP$.

By a depth-first search algorithm one can easily show

Theorem 4.5: $LDP-BD-BFO-AGAP$ is in L. •

For the hierarchical version of this problem we show

Theorem 4.6: $LDP-BD-BFO-AGAP_{HG}$ is P-complete.

Proof: The membership in P follows from the fact that $BFO-AGAP_{HG}$ is in P (Theorem 4.2), and that the log-depth property can be tested in polynomial time. On the other hand, the P-complete problem $BFO-AGAP$ can be reduced to $LDP-BD-BFO-AGAP_{HG}$ by a simple padding argument. Let G be an alternating graph with vertices $v_1,\dots,v_m$. We construct a hierarchical graph Γ such that $E(\Gamma)$ includes G, and, in addition, 2^n isolated new vertices. Consequently, the indegree and outdegree of $E(\Gamma)$ are bounded by 2, the depth of $E(\Gamma)$ is at most n, i.e., $E(\Gamma)$ has logarithmic depth, $E(\Gamma)$ is breadth-first ordered if and only if G is ordered, and b is reachable from a in $E(\Gamma)$ if and only if it is so in G. •

At the end of this section we investigate two graph accessiblity problems whose hierarchical versions are NP-complete.

CHROMATIC GRAPH ACCESSIBILITY PROBLEM ($CGAP$)

Given: A directed graph $G=(V,E)$, natural numbers k,m, a coloring $\gamma : E \to \{1,\dots,m\}$ and $a,b \in V$.

Question: Is $k \le m \le \log|V|$, and do there exist k different colors $i_1,\dots,i_k \in \{1,\dots,m\}$ such that there exists a path from a to b in the graph $(V, E \cap \gamma^{-1}(i_1,\dots,i_k))$?

Analogously we define the chromatic accessibility problem on alternating graphs (*BFO−ACGAP*).

<u>Theorem 4.7:</u> *CGAP* is NL-complete.

<u>Proof:</u> *CGAP* is in NL because one can choose non-deterministically k colors and then test the *GAP* instance only using edges having a chosen color. On the other hand, the NL-complete problem *GAP* can be reduced to *CGAP* as follows: Let $G=(V,E)$ be a graph and let $a,b \in V$. Define $\gamma(e)=1$ for all $e \in E$. Then there exists a path in G from a to b if and only if there exists one color $i_1 \in 1$ such that there exists a path in $(V, E \cap \gamma^{-1}(i_1))(=G)$ from a to b. •

<u>Theorem 4.8:</u> *BFO−ACGAP* is P-complete.

<u>Proof:</u> Analogously to the preceeding proof, but the algorithm for *BFO−ACGAP* ∈ P tries successively all at most $2^m \le 2^{\log|V|} = |V|$ possibilities to choose k colors. •

In contrast to Theorem 4.7 and Theorem 4.8 we show

<u>Theorem 4.9:</u> $CGAP_{HG}$ and $BFO-ACGAP_{HG}$ are NP-complete.

<u>Proof:</u> $CGAP_{HG}$ is in NP. Given an instance (V,E,k,m,γ,a,b) of the $CGAP_{HG}$ problem where (V,E,γ) is described by a hierarchical graph of length n. Consequently, $|V| \le 2^n$. It can be checked in polynomial time whether $k \le m \le \log|V|$. Then k different colors $i_1,\dots,i_k \in \{1,\dots,m\}$ are chosen non-deterministically, and the GAP_{HG} problem is solved in polynomial time (see Theorem 4.4.1) only using edges colored by the colors $i_1,\dots,i_k$. $BFO-ACGAP_{HG}$ ∈ NP can be proved in the same manner.

$CGAP_{HG}$ is NP-hard. We reduce the NP-complete problem 3*SAT* to $CGAP_{HG}$. Let $H \equiv C_1 \mathrm{UND} C_2 \mathrm{UND} \cdots \mathrm{UND} C_m$ be a Boolean formula with $C_i \equiv (x_{i_1} \vee x_{i_2} \vee x_{i_3})$ for $i=1,2,\dots,m$ and $x_{i_j} \in \{z_1,\dots,z_r,\bar{z}_1,\dots,\bar{z}_r\}$ (the set of variables in H and their negations). Consider the edge-colored graph G shown in Figure 5.

There exist $2r$ colors where

$$a_{i_j} = \begin{cases} s & \text{if } x_{i_j} = z_s \\ r+s & \text{if } x_{i_j} = \bar{z}_s \end{cases}$$

Obviously, H ∈ 3*SAT* if and only if b can be reached from a using at most r colors. In order to achieve that $r \le \log$ (number of vertices of the graph) we use the padding argument from the proof of Theorem 4.6.

The graph constructed in this manner is breadth-first ordered and can also be considered as an alternating graph with only ∨-vertices. Hence, $BFO-ACGAP_{HG}$ is NP-hard. •

5. Some "classical" NP-complete problems

We start with the *CLIQUE* problem, and also consider its restrictions *LD−CLIQUE* and *LBW−BFO−CLIQUE*.

Observing that the vertices of a clique of a hierarchical graph already belong to one suitably chosen subcell and using the fact that hierarchical edge testing is in NL we obtain $CLIQUE_{HG}$ ∈ NP. Consequently, the complexities of the hierarchical and the non-hierarchical clique problem coincide.

<u>Theorem 5.1:</u> $CLIQUE_{HG}$ is NP-complete. •

Since the *LBW−BFO* property (Remark 2 after Theorem 3.3) and the *LD* property for hierarchical graphs can be tested in polynomial time we can conclude that also $LD\!-\!CLIQUE_{HG}$ and $LBW\!-\!BFO\!-\!CLIQUE_{HG}$ are both in NP. On the other hand, using the padding trick from the proof of Theorem 4.6, we can reduce *CLIQUE* to $LD\!-\!CLIQUE_{HG}$ and to $LBW\!-\!BFO\!-\!CLIQUE_{HG}$. Hence

Theorem 5.2: $LD\!-\!CLIQUE_{HG}$ and $LBW\!-\!BFO\!-\!CLIQUE_{HG}$ are NP-complete. •

It can readily be seen that the complexities of the non-hierarchical versions of these problems are very low.

Theorem 5.3: *LD−CLIQUE* and *LBW−BFO−CLIQUE* are in L. •

Now we consider three NP-complete problems whose hierarchical versions make a "medium complexity jump". The problems we consider are the Hamiltonian circuit problem (*HC*), the independent set problem (*IS*), and the 3-colorability problem (3*COLOR*) [GJ 79].

Theorem 5.4: ([Ka 72]): *HC*, *3COLOR*, and *IS* are NP-complete. •

Using a technique from [Wa 84], we can prove:

Theorem 5.5: HC_{HG}, $3COLOR_{HG}$, and IS_{HG} are PSPACE-complete. •

The reductions made in these proofs show even:

Theorem 5.6: $LBW\!-\!BFO\!-\!HC_{HG}$,$LBW\!-\!BFO\!-\!3COLOR_{HG}$ and $LBW\!-\!BFO\!-\!IS_{HG}$ are PSPACE-complete. •

Details of these proofs will be published in a separate paper.

Theorem 5.7: ([MS 72]): *LBW−BFO−*3*COLOR* and *LBW−BFO−IS* are NL-complete. •

Note, that for *LBW−BFO−HC* only NL-hardness is known.

We conclude this section with a NP-complete problem whose hierarchical version makes a "maximum complexity jump".

LAYOUT

Given: A graph G, natural numbers m_1,m_2.

Question: Can G be embedded in the square grid of width m_1 and height m_2 such that vertices of G are mapped into vertices of the grid, edges of G are mapped into paths on the grid, and different edges e_1,e_2 of G are mapped into non-crossing paths p_1,p_2 of the grid.

Theorem 5.8: ([DT 81]): LAYOUT is NP-complete. •

We reprove this result by a master reduction. This reduction has the advantage of being easily extended to a hierarchical construction that shows

Theorem 5.9: $LAYOUT_{HG}$ is NTIME(2^{Pol})-complete. •

Details will be published separately.

6. The circuit value and the network flow problem

In this section we discuss a graph problem that is the basis of practically all digital simulation methods on hierarchical circuits.

MONOTONE CIRCUIT VALUE (*MCV*)

Given: A directed acyclic graph C called a circuit with one distinguished vertex (output), the sources (inputs) labeled with symbols from $\{0,1\}$ and the interior vertices labeled with symbols from $\{\vee, \wedge\}$.

Question: Does the output of C yield a 1?

[Go 77] shows that *MCV* is log-space complete for P. We can show the following theorem.

Theorem 6.1: MCV_{HG} is log-space complete for PSPACE.

Proof Sketch: In order to show that $MCV_{HG} \in$ PSPACE we give a nondeterministic algorithm that guesses the intermediate results of the circuit and verifies them by a preorder traversal of the hierarchy tree.

In order to show that MCV_{HG} is PSPACE-complete we reduce the PSPACE-complete Quantified Boolean Formula Problem *QBF* [SM 73] to MCV_{HG}. This is done by converting the quantified Boolean formula $\Phi = Q_n x_n, \ldots, Q_1 x_1 F(x_1, \ldots, x_n)$, $Q_i \in \{\forall, \exists\}$ for $i=1,\ldots,n$ into a hierarchical circuit $\Gamma = (C_0, \ldots, C_n)$ that computes Φ. Here C_0 is a circuit representing $F(x_1, \ldots, x_n)$, and for $i>0$, C_i is a circuit representing the formula $\Phi_i = Q_i x_i, \ldots, Q_1 x_1 F(x_1, \ldots, x_n)$. C_i contains two copies of C_{i-1} and an $\wedge$-vertex ($\vee$-vertex) if $Q_i = \forall$ ($Q_i = \exists$). ▪

Since the hierarchical circuit Γ constructed in the proof of Theorem 6.1 has logarithmic depth, and since it can be tested in polynomial space whether the expansion of a hierarchical directed graph has logarithmic depth, we have the following corollary:

Corollary 6.2: $LDP-MCV_{HG}$ is PSPACE-complete.

Note that $LDP-MCV \in$ L.

The second natural graph problem we investigate in this section is the network flow problem.

NETWORK FLOW (*NF*)

Given: A directed edge-labeled graph G, two vertices $s,t \in V$, a number $k \in$ N.

Question: Is the maximum directed network flow from s to t in G at least as large as k?

While it was not known before whether *NF* is log-space complete for P, [GS 82] show that the slightly modified problem that asks whether the maximum network flow is odd is log-space complete for P.

We have the following results:

Theorem 6.3: a) *NF* is log-space complete for P.
b) NF_{HG} is PSPACE-complete.

Proof Sketch: a) First we note that *LMCV* is log-space complete for P. Here *LMCV* is the monotone circuit value problem restricted to layered circuits, i.e., circuits that have the following property:

- The set of vertices is subdivided into k levels numbered from 1 to k. The inputs form level 1. All edges ending in a vertex at level $i+1$ must start at a vertex in level i. The output vertex is on level k. All vertices of level i have the same outdegree $m (i=1,...,k-1)$.

Now we reduce *LMCV* to *NF* by transforming the circuit C into a dag G. We do this by replacing each vertex that is not an input of C by a "double-rail logic" graph construct as in Figure 6. The edges in the construct for a vertex on level i all have capacity $M_i=(2m)^{k-i}$. Then we add a source vertex s to G and connect it with edges to all vertices in G that represent input "literals" that are 1. All of these edges have capacity M_1. Finally we add an edge with capacity 1 from the vertex in G representing the output of C to the sink t of G. This edge is hatched in Figure 6b.

We can prove that the maximum flow in G is $n \cdot M_1$ if the output of C yields a 1, otherwise the maximum flow in G is $n \cdot M_1 - 1$. Here n is the number of inputs of C.

b) A similar argument as in Theorem 6.1 shows that $NF_{HG} \in$ PSPACE. For the PSPACE-hardness we reduce *QBF* to NF_{HG}. We use the same construction as in the proof of Theorem 6.1, except that now we substitute the constructs of Figure 6 for the interior vertices of the cells of Γ. •

The construction in the proof of Theorem 6.2 b) constructs only acyclic graphs with edge capacities up to $2^{POLY(n)}$. Furthermore edges with such a capacity can be defined hierarchically in space $POLY(n)$ using capacity-1 edges. Thus we have the following corollary:

Corollary 6.4: NF_{HG} is PSPACE-complete even if the graphs are restricted to be acyclic, and only edge capacity 1 is allowed.

7. Conclusions

We determined the complexity of the non-hierarchical and hierarchical versions of several graph problems in order to give evidence for the fact that there is no correlation between the complexities of these two versions of a graph problem. The reasons for this spread of complexities are manifold. Some problems, such as the clique problem or some problems on breadth-first ordered graphs (e.g. *BFO−GAP*) have a "local" flavor that only requires to search small regions of the hierarchy tree to solve the problem. For such problems the hierarchical version is not harder than the non-hierarchical version. For other problems, such as the circuit value, network flow or layout problems considered, the boundary description that is provided by the fact that all pins have to be explicitly identified for each copy of a cell is not enough to eliminate "interference" between a cell and its environment. E.g., in the circuit value problem, state information has to be maintained that can be very much different for different copies of the same cell. In the layout problem the question whether a cell can be packed tightly into its neighbourhood does not depend on its connections to the neighbourhood via edges, but rather on how the neighbourhood is laid out. In both cases a large amount of additional information has to be computed for each cell copy resulting in a high complexity of the hierarchical version of the problem.

Generic algorithms for transforming non-hierarchical graph algorithms into hierarchical graph algorithms will have to detect and use such problem characteristics. Thus a simple generic transformation that is applicable to a general class of graph problems is unlikely to exist.

Many proofs have only been sketched in this paper. Specifically proofs of the complexity results about the more natural graph problems contain some technical intricacies. These proofs will be detailed in a separate paper.

References

[CK 78] Chandra, A.K./Kozen, D./Stockmeyer, L.J.: Alternation. Research report RC 7489, IBM Thomas J. Watson Research Center 1978. See also: JACM 28 (1981), 114-133

[DT 81] Dolev, D./Trickey, H.: On linear area embedding of planar graphs. Tech. Rep. STAN-CS-81-876, Comp. Sci. Dept., Stanford University, Stanford CA 94305 (1981)

[Ga 82] Galperin, H.: Succinct Representations of Graphs. Ph.D. Thesis, Dept. of Elec. Eng. and Comp. Sci., Princeton University, Princeton (N.J.) (1982)

[GJ 79] Garey, M.R./Johnson, D.S.: Computers & Intractability. Freeman, San Francisco (1979)

[Go 77] Goldschlager, L.: The monotone and planar circuit value problems are log-space complete for P. SIGACT News 9,2 (1977), 25-29

[GS 82] Goldschlager, L.M./Shaw, R.A./Staples, J.: The maximum flow problem is log-space complete for P. Theor. Comp. Sci. 21 (1982), 105-111

[GW 83] Galperin, H./Wigderson, A.: Succinct representation of graphs. Information & Control 56 (1983), 183-198

[Im 79] Immerman, N.: Length of predicate calculus formulas as a new complexity measure. 20th IEEE-FOCS (1979), 337-347. See also: JCSS 22 (1981), 384-406

[Ka 72] Karp, R.M.: Reducibilities among combinatorial problems. Complexity of Computer Computations (R.E. Miller, J.W. Thatcher, eds.), Plenum Press, N.Y. (1972), 85-103

[Le 82] Lengauer, T.: The complexity of compacting hierarchically specified layouts of integrated circuits. 23rd IEEE-FOCS (1982), 358-368

[Le 85] Lengauer, T.: Efficient solution of connectivity problems on hierarchically defined graphs. "Theoretische Informatik" No. 24, FB 17, Universität-GH Paderborn, Paderborn, West-Germany (1985). Short version in: Proc. of WG '85 (H. Noltemeier, ed.), Trauner Verlag (1985), 201-216

[Le 86a] Lengauer, T.: Efficient algorithms for finding minimum spanning forests of hierarchically defined graphs. Proc. of STACS 86, Springer Lecture Notes in Computer Science No. 216 (1986), 153-170

[Le 86b] Lengauer, T.: Hierarchical planarity testing algorithms. Proc. of ICALP 86, Springer Lecture Notes in Computer Science No. 226 (1986), 215-225

[Le 86c] Lengauer, T.: Exploiting hierarchy in VLSI design. VLSI Algorithms and Architectures (F. Makedon et al., eds.), Springer Lecture Notes in Computer Science No. 227 (1986), 180-193

[MS 72] Meyer, A./Stockmeyer, L.J.: The equivalence problem for regular expressions with squaring requires exponential space. 13th IEEE-SWAT (1972), 125-129

[PY 86] Papadimitriou, C.H./Yannakakis, M.: A note on succinct representation of graphs. Manuscript (1986), to appear in Information & Control.

[Sa 73] Savitch, W.J.: Maze recognizing automata and nondeterministic tape complexity. JCSS 7 (1973), 389-403

[SM 73] Stockmeyer, L.J./Meyer, A.R.: Word problems requiring exponential time. 5th ACM-STOC (1973), 1-9

[Su 73] Sudborough, I.H.: On tape-bounded complexity classes and multihead finite automata. 14th IEEE-SWAT (1973), 138-144

[SV 81] Shyum, S./Valiant, L.G.: A complexity theory based on Boolean algebra. Proc. 22nd IEEE-FOCS (1981), 244-253

[Wa 84] Wagner, K.: The complexity of problems concerning graphs with regularities. Proc. of MFCS 84, Springer Lecture Notes in Computer Science No. 176 (1984), 544-552

[Wa 86] Wagner, K.: The complexity of combinatorial problems with succinct input representation. Acta Informatica 23 (1986), 325-356

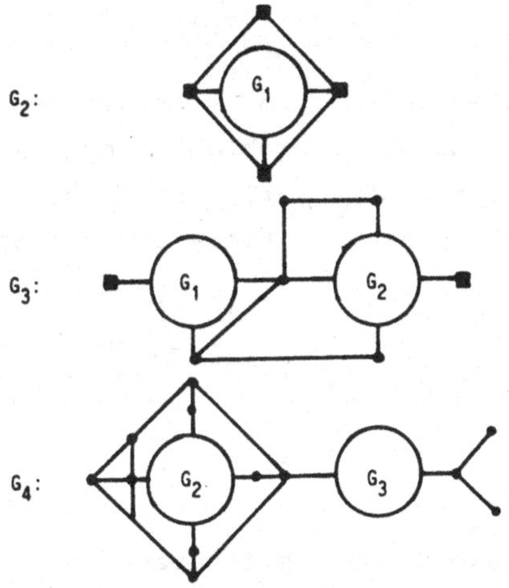

Figure 1: $\Gamma = (G_1, G_2, G_3, G_4)$

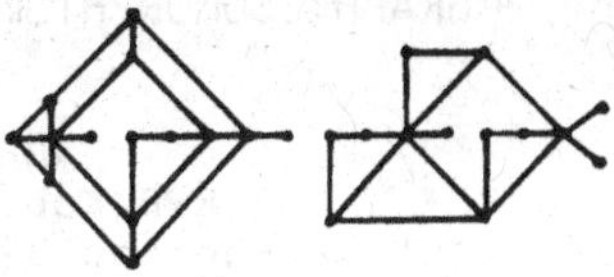

Figure 2: $E(\Gamma)$

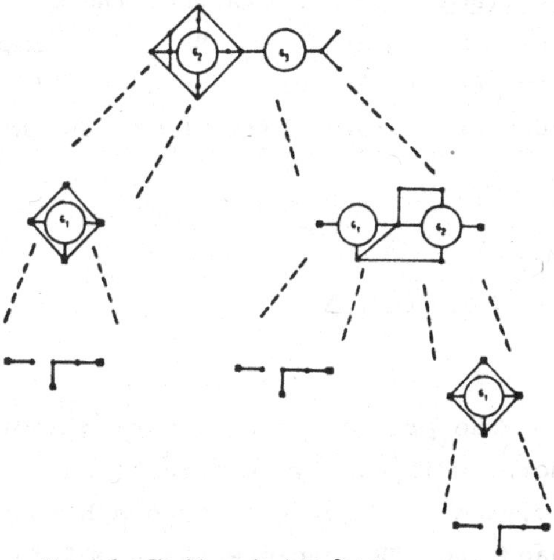

Figure 3: The hierarchy tree for Γ

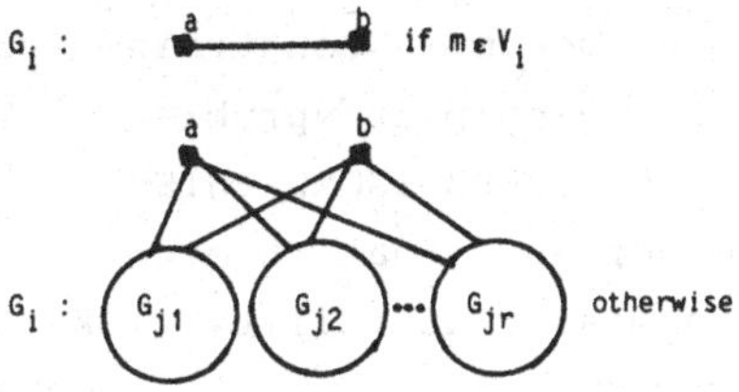

Figure 4: BFO-GAP $\leq_m^{\log}$ $EDGE_{HG}$

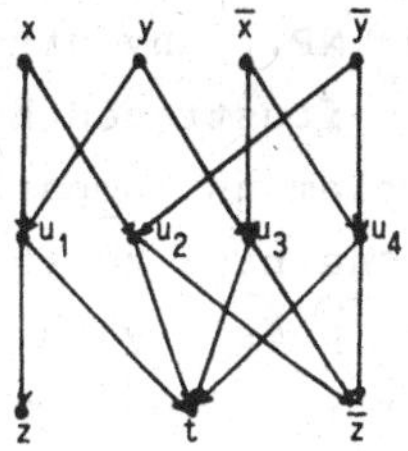

a) Construction for $z = x \wedge y$

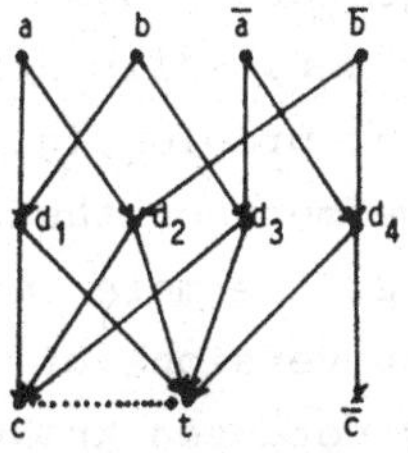

b) Construction for $c = a \vee b$

Figure 6: LMCV $\leq_m^{\log}$ NF

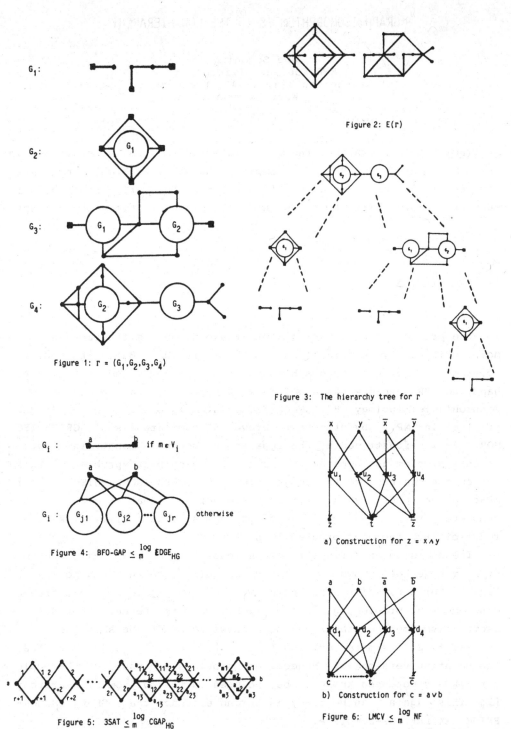

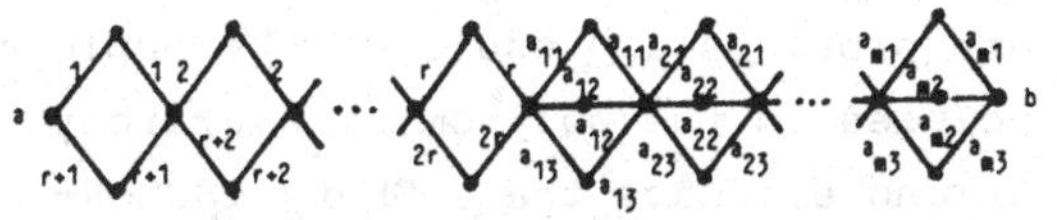

Figure 5: 3SAT $\leq_m^{\log}$ $CGAP_{HG}$

GRAPH ISOMORPHISM IS IN THE LOW HIERARCHY

Uwe Schöning
EWH Koblenz, Informatik
Rheinau 3-4, D-5400 Koblenz
West Germany

Abstract. It is shown that the graph isomorphism problem is located in the low hierarchy in NP. This implies that this problem is not NP-complete (not even under weaker forms of polynomial-time reducibilities, such as γ-reducibility) unless the polynomial-time hierarchy collapses.

1. INTRODUCTION

The problem of determining whether two given finite graphs are isomorphic is easily seen to belong to the class NP. But up to now, no polynomial algorithm for graph isomorphism is known. And on the other hand, no NP-completeness proof is known either. According to Garey and Johnson's terminology [8], GRAPH ISOMORPHISM is one of the few "open problems in NP. Any attempt to prove NP-completeness of GRAPH ISOMORPHISM was frustrated by the apparently much more constrained nature of this problem as compared to the usual NP-complete problems. This led on the one hand to the conjecture that GRAPH ISOMORPHISM is not NP-complete (possibly in P), on the other hand that it might be NP-complete w.r.t. some weaker kind of polynomial reducibility (like γ-reducibility, see open problem 1 in [1]).

Indeed, some (nontrivial) special cases of the graph isomorphism problem have been shown to be in P and also some in NP $\cap$ co-NP (cf. [12].) Further, unlike the known NP-complete problems, the corresponding counting problem (given two graphs, compute the number of different isomorphisms between them) has been shown to be of the same "degree" of complexity as the mere decision problem [17, see also 12]. Note that the counting versions of NP-complete problems are usually #P-complete, but #P is not even known to be included in the polynomial hierarchy [2]. This, again, can be taken as strong evidence that GRAPH ISOMORPHISM is not NP-complete.

Very recently, it has been shown that graph (non-) isomorphism can be "proved" in a certain probabilistic way in terms of so-called interactive proof systems [10]. More formally, the complement of GRAPH ISOMORPHISM is element of the class IP. Further, in [11] it is shown that the class IP equals the class AM that was introduced by Babai [3] in terms of certain "Arthur versus Merlin" games. Furthermore, it can be shown [6] that if a set whose complement is in AM were NP-complete, then the polynomial-time hierarchy of Stockmeyer [21] has only finitely many levels; more specifically, it "collapses" to Σ_2^p.

There is another approach to these questions which will be exploited here. In [18], this author introduced a low and a high hierarchy of classes within the class NP. The definition is analogous to the definition in recursive function theory (cf. [15]), and has been designed to possibly being able to classify those "intermediate" problems in NP. The two bottom levels of the low hierarchy turned out to be P and NP $\cap$ co-NP, and the two bottom levels of the high hierarchy turned out to be the NP-complete sets (under polynomial-time Turing reducibility and strong nondeterministic polynomial-time Turing reducibility, resp.) Strong nondeterministic reducibilities were introduced by Long [16] as a generalization of γ-reducibility [1, see also 8]. This author posed in [18] the open problem whether GRAPH ISOMPORPHISM is in L_2^p, the next level of the low hierarchy after L_1^p = NP $\cap$ co-NP. Exactly this is what will be shown in this paper.

There is still another view of the low and high hierarchies, because they give a uniform framework for understanding those polynomial hierarchy collapsing results, like the one mentioned above. It follows directly from the definitions of the low and high hierarchies that a set being located in the low hierarchy cannot also be in the high hierarchy unless the polynomial-time hierarchy collapses. Since the NP-complete sets (even under weak forms of polynomial reducibility) are all located in the high-hierarchy, such a "low" set like GRAPH ISOMORPHISM cannot be NP-complete (and e.g. not even γ-complete). This, in particular, answers Adleman and Manders open problem 1 in [1] whether GRAPH ISOMORPHISM is γ-complete negatively (assuming the polynomial hierarchy does not collapse to Σ_2^p).

To prepare our lowness result, we start with giving a direct proof of the fact that the complement of GRAPH ISOMORPHISM is in Babai's class AM without refering to the notion of interactive proof systems or games. Then it is shown that NP $\cap$ co-AM is included in L_2^p which finally yields GRAPH ISOMORPHISM $\in L_2^p$.

2. PRELIMINARIES

We assume the reader is familar with complexity theory based on the model of Turing machines, especially with the classes P and NP and the concept of NP-completeness (cf. [8]). Some more particular classes that we use are BPP (bounded error probabilistic polynomial time, see [9]), and the classes Σ_k^p and Π_k^p of the polynomial-time hierarchy [21].We will frequently use the alternating quantifier characterizations of these classes, and also their relativizations with respect to some oracle set.

We will consider finite graphs $G = (V,E)$ on the vertex set $V = \{1,...,n\}$. A permutation p on $\{1,...,n\}$ is an automorphism of graph G if $p(G) = G$. Here, $p(G)$ is the graph (V,E') where $(p(u),p(v)) \in E'$ iff $(u,v) \in E$. The set of automorphisms of G is denoted $Aut(G)$ (which actually is a group under the composition operation). A graph G' is isomorphic to G if $G' = p(G)$ for some permutation p. Note that the number of different isomorphic graphs to G is $n!/|Aut(G)|$ (see [12]).

The graph isomorphism problem is given as the set GRAPH ISOMORPHISM $= \{ (G_1,G_2) \mid G_1$ and G_2 are isomorphic$\}$ which is easily seen to be located in the class NP, but currently not known to be NP-complete nor to be in P.

3. GRAPH ISOMORPHISM IS IN CO-AM

The class AM was introduced by Babai [3] in terms of certain "Arthur versus Merlin" games. Recently it has been shown by Goldwasser and Sipser [11] that the class AM equals the class IP (which stands for Interactive Proof Systems). The relevance to the graph isomophism problem is that it has been shown by Goldreich, Micali and Widgerson [10] that GRAPH ISOMORPHISM (and in particular, its complement) is element of IP.

For the sake of self-containment of this paper, we will give a proof of the fact that the complement of the graph isomorphism problem is in AM (i.e. GRAPH ISOMORPHISM $\in$ co-AM) which follows already by combining the papers [10] and [11] mentioned above. For this purpose, we give a straightforward definition of Babai's class AM whithout mentioning proof systems or games in the following.

Definition 1. A set A is in the class AM if there is a set B in NP and a polynomial p such that for all x, $|x| = n$,

$$\text{Prob} [\ (x,y) \in B \ \text{ iff } \ x \in A\ ] \geq 3/4$$

where y is chosen uniformly at random from $\Sigma^{p(n)}$.

Note that the constant 3/4 is arbitrary, and could be substituted by any constant of the form $1/2 + \varepsilon$ whithout changing the defined class.

It is obvious that $NP \subseteq AM$ (by taking $B = A \times \Sigma^*$) and that $BPP \subseteq AM$ (by taking $B \in P$). Informally speaking, the definitional step from NP to AM is the same as from P to BPP, expressed by the "equation":

$$\frac{BPP}{P} = \frac{AM}{NP}$$

The set inclusion structure between these classes and some other classes of the polynomial-time hierarchy is as follows.

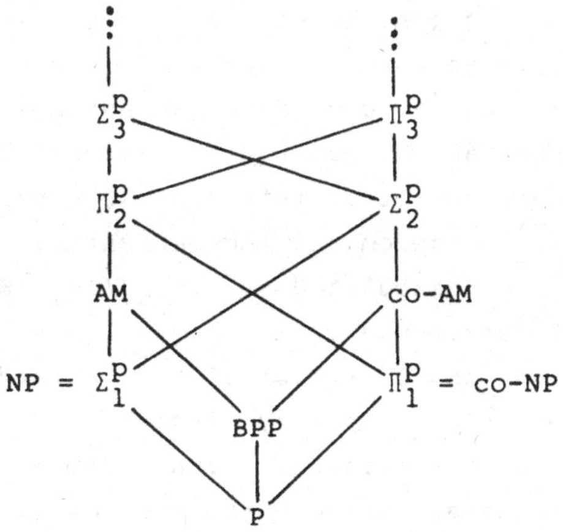

The inclusion $AM \subseteq \Pi_2^p$ can be seen by adapting Lautemann's proof [14] of $BPP \subseteq \Sigma_2^p$. Also in Zachos et al. [23,24] a different proof of this inclusion can be found.

Now we need the following combinatorial definition and lemma.

Definition 2. For two graphs with n vertices define $num(G_1,G_2)$ to be the number of different triples of the form (H,p,i) where H is an isomorphic graph to either G_1 or G_2, and p is an automorphism for G_i, $i \in \{1,2\}$.

Lemma. If G_1 and G_2 are isomorphic, then $num(G_1,G_2) = 2n!$, otherwise $num(G_1,G_2) \geq 4n!$.

Proof. If the graphs are isomorphic, then $|Aut(G_1)| = |Aut(G_2)|$, and the set of isomorphic versions of G_1 is the same as for G_2. Therefore, $num(G_1,G_2) = (n!/|Aut(G_1)|) * (|Aut(G_1)| + |Aut(G_2)|) = 2n!$. If the graphs are not isomorphic, then all $n!/|Aut(G_1)|$ isomorphic versions of G_1 are different from all $n!/|Aut(G_2)|$ isomorphic versions of G_2. Hence, $num(G_1,G_2) = (n!/|Aut(G_1)| + n!/|Aut(G_2)|) * (|Aut(G_1)| + |Aut(G_2)|) \geq 4n!$. #

Note that the objects (H,p,i) that are counted in $num(G_1,G_2)$ can be nondeterministically generated in polynomial time. (On input (G_1,G_2), guess permutations p,q and $i,j \in \{1,2\}$; and check whether $p \in Aut(G_i)$. If so, output $(q(G_j),p,i)$.) This observation will later become important.

In their recent paper, Boppana and Hastad [6] count the number of pairs (H,p) such that H is isomorphic to either G_1 or to G_2, and $p \in Aut(H)$. Then, the number of such pairs is n! for isomorphic graphs and 2n! for non-isomorphic graphs. This more elegant pair-counting trick can be used in the following just as well as our triples.

The following lemma appears in a similar form in Sipser [20] and also in Goldwasser and Sipser [11], and can be considered as an application of universal hashing due to Carter and Wegman [7]. A random hash function $H : \Sigma^t \to \Sigma^m$ is given by a Boolean (t,m)-matrix whose elements $h_{ij} \in \{0,1\}$ are picked uniformly at random and independently. Then the j:th bit of $H(a_1 \dots a_t) \in \Sigma^m$ is calculated by $(h_{1j} \wedge a_1) \oplus \dots \oplus (h_{tj} \wedge a_t)$, i.e. matrix multiplication modulo 2.

The lemma states that on every fixed "small" subset of Σ^t a randomly selected collection of hash functions $\{H_i\}$ is very likely to be collision-free. But on a too "big" subset a collision is unavoidable. Here, a "collision" means the existence of an x such that for every H_i there is a $y \neq x$ with $H_i(x) = H_i(y)$.

Hashing Lemma. (a) If $X \subseteq \Sigma^t$ has cardinality at most 2^{m-1} , then for randomly selected hash functions $H_1,\dots,H_{m+1} : \Sigma^t \to \Sigma^m$, with probability at most 1/4,

$$(\exists x \in X)\ (\forall i \leq m+1)\ (\exists y \in X)\ [\ y \neq x \text{ and } H_i(x) = H_i(y)\ ]. \quad (*)$$

(b) If X has more than $(m+1)2^m$ elements, then the probability for (*) is 1.

Proof. omitted. (a) is essentially the Coding Lemma of [20], and (b) follows from the Pidgeon Hole Principle (see also [22, Theorem 3.1]). #

We like to apply the Hashing Lemma to the set $X = \{ (H,p,i) \mid (H,p,i)$ as in Definition 2 $\}$. Then, for G_1, G_2 being isomorphic, we have $|X| = 2n!$, and for G_1, G_2 not being isomorphic, $|X| \geq 4n!$. But unfortunately, the bounds 2^{m-1} and $(m+1)2^m$ are too weak to distinguish between $2n!$ and $4n!$. But let us, instead, apply the Hashing Lemma to the set $Y = X^k$ (k depending on n). In this case, $|Y| = (2n!)^k$ for isomorphic graphs, and $|Y| \geq (4n!)^k$ for non-isomorphic graphs. Now the Hashing Lemma is applicable, if we choose, e.g., $k = n$ and $m = 1 + \lceil n * \log_2(2n!) \rceil$, and the following theorem can be established.

Theorem. There is a set B in NP and a polynomial p such that for every pair of graphs G_1, G_2 with n vertices,

$$\text{Prob}[\ (G_1,G_2,w) \in B\ ] \leq 1/4$$

if G_1, G_2 are isomorphic, and

$$\text{Prob}[\ (G_1,G_2,w) \in B\ ] = 1$$

if G_1, G_2 are non-isomorphic. Hereby, w is randomly chosen from $\Sigma^{p(n)}$ with uniform distribution. Hence, GRAPH ISOMORPHISM $\in$ co-AM.

Proof. The set B essentially is the collision predicate (*) with w being an encoding of the collection of random hash functions. The fact that $B \in NP$ follows from the observation that the elements in X (which now is Y as discussed above) can be nondeterministically generated, and that the universal quantifier in (*) has only polynomial range and can thus be eliminated. #

There are several comments be be made. First note that recently also other authors independently presented direct proofs of GRAPH ISOMORPHISM $\in$ co-AM [4,6]. Note also that the statement of the theorem is actually a little stronger than what is needed for the membership in co-AM because of the probability 1 on the one side. But actually, this non-symmetric situation can always be achieved for any problem in co-AM (or AM, resp.), see [23,24]. This is interesting since on the P-level it is not clear whether BPP = R.

Boppana and Hastad [6] show that $NP \subseteq$ co-AM implies $\bigcup_k \Sigma_k^p \subseteq$ co-AM. Then using the fact that $AM \subseteq \Pi_2^p$, it follows that GRAPH ISOMORPHISM cannot be NP-complete unless the polynomial-time hierarchy collapses to $\Pi_2^p = \Sigma_2^p$. In the following we will obtain the stronger result that not even weaker forms of NP-completeness (like γ-completeness) are possible for GRAPH ISOMORPHISM unless the polynomial-time collapses.

4. LOWNESS OF GRAPH ISOMORPHISM

A set A in NP is (polynomially) low$_k$ (in symbols: $A \in L_k^P$) if $\Sigma_k^P(A) \subseteq \Sigma_k^P$, and A is high$_k$ (in symbols: $A \in H_k^P$) if $\Sigma_{k+1}^P \subseteq \Sigma_k^P(A)$. This author [18] introduced this definition in the context of polynomial-time computations as a translation of a corresponding definition in recursive function theory (see e.g. [15]). Obviously, $L_0^P \subseteq L_1^P \subseteq \ldots$ and $H_0^P \subseteq H_1^P \subseteq \ldots$. It is easy to see that L_0^P is the class P, and H_0^P is the class of NP-complete sets w.r.t. $\leq_T^P$-reducibility. Further, it can be shown [18] that L_1^P = NP $\cap$ co-NP, and H_1^P equals the class of NP-complete sets w.r.t. $\leq_T^{sn}$-reducibility which was introduced and investigated by Long [16]. Note that the more familiar γ-reducibility [1, see also 8] is a special case of $\leq_T^{sn}$-reducibility, hence the γ-complete sets are included in H_1^P. Adleman and Manders [1] presented some examples of γ-complete sets not known to be NP-complete in the usual sense, and they conjectured that GRAPH ISOMORPHISM might also be γ-complete.

In a sense, the high hierarchy generalizes the notion of NP-completeness as shown by the following proposition.

Proposition. [18] There exists a set in NP being both low$_k$ and high$_k$ if and only if the polynomial-time hierarchy collapses to Σ_k^P, i.e. $\bigcup_n \Sigma_n^P = \Sigma_k^P$.

Observe that the case k=0 just means the well known fact that a NP-complete set is in P if and only if P = NP.

Other known results about the low and high hierarchies are that the sparse sets in NP, the classes R and NP $\cap$ BPP are included in L_2^P, and the sets in NP having polynomial-size circuits are in L_3^P [13,19].

The main result of this section will be that NP $\cap$ co-AM is included in L_2^P and thus giving GRAPH ISOMORPHISM $\in L_2^P$. We state our theorem in a little more general form.

Theorem. For any set C in AM $\cap$ co-AM, $\Sigma_2^P(C) = \Sigma_2^P$.

Proof. First we need to observe that , as in the case of the class BPP, a certain probability "amplification" property holds for AM (noted in Bennett and Gill [5], a rigorous proof can be found e.g. in [19]).

Claim 1. If a set A is in AM, then for every polynomial q there exists a set B in NP and a polynomial p such that for all x, $|x| = n$, if $w \in \Sigma^{p(n)}$ is chosen uniformly at random, then with probability at least $1-2^{-q(n)}$, $x \in A$ iff $(x,w) \in B$.

Proof. As first noted by Bennett and Gill [5], by a "majority vote" argument, the error probability can be exponentially decreased, as desired. More formally, the set B from Definition 1 has to be substituted by B' where $(x,w_1w_2...w_t) \in B'$ iff for more than $t/2$ many i's, $(x,w_i) \in B$. Hereby, t is a suitable polynomial in n (actually a linear function in $q(n)$). A detailed proof may be found, e.g., in [19, chapter 2]. #

Now let C be in $AM \cap co\text{-}AM$ and let $L \in \Sigma_2^p(C)$. Hence,

$$L = \{ x \mid (\exists y) \ (\forall z) \ (x,y,z) \in L(M,C) \},$$

where M is a deterministic, polynomial-time oracle machine, and the quantifiers range over strings up to some polynomial size (in $|x|$). By the fact that $C \in AM \cap co\text{-}AM$, and using Claim 1, it can be seen that for any polynomial r there are sets B_1, B_2 in NP such that for all n with probability at least $1-2^{-n}$,

$$C_{\leq r(n)} = \{x \mid (x,w) \in B_1 \}_{\leq r(n)} \quad \text{and}$$
$$\overline{C}_{\leq r(n)} = \{x \mid (x,w) \in B_2 \}_{\leq r(n)}, \qquad (**)$$

where w is chosen uniformly at random from $\Sigma^{p(n)}$ (p being a suitable polynomial, depending on r). Now call a w good (w.r.t. n) if it satisfies (**). The following claim essentially states that "goodness" can be expressed by an existential and a universal quantifier.

Claim 2. If $E \subseteq \Sigma^{p(n)}$ is some set of strings with $|E| \geq (1-2^{-n})2^{p(n)}$, then (a) and (b) hold.

(a) $(\exists u=(u_1,...,u_{p(n)})) \ (\forall v) \ [\text{for some } i \leq p(n),\ u_i \oplus v \in E]$,

(b) $(\forall u=(u_1,...,u_{p(n)})) \ (\exists v) \ [\text{for all } i \leq p(n),\ u_i \oplus v \in E]$.

Here $\oplus$ means bitwise addition modulo 2.

The Proof is a modification of Lautemann's proof [14] showing $BPP \subseteq \Sigma_2^p$ and can be found in [19, p. 74]. #

Now we apply Claim 2 with E being the set of all good w. Then we can get the following characterization of L:

$$L = \{ x \mid (\exists u)(\exists y)(\forall v)(\forall z) \ [\text{for some } i \leq p(n),\ (u_i \oplus v,x,y,z) \notin K]\}$$

Now, several points need clarification. First, choose the polynomial r such that on inputs of the form (x,y,z), M does not ask its oracle queries longer than $r(|x|)$. Given r, obtain sets $B_1, B_2 \in NP$ satisfying (**). Then the set K appearing in the above characterization of L is defined via the following nondeterministic, polynomial-time Turing machine (thus $K \in NP$):

On input (w,x,y,z):
run M on input (x,y,z) and reject if M accepts, and accept if M rejects. Oracle queries of M are handled as follows: if s is the query string, first guess nondeterministically whether $s \in C$ or $s \notin C$. In the first case, verify that $(s,w) \in B_1$, in the second case verify that $(s,w) \in B_2$. If the verification succeeds, continue with the answer "yes" ("no", resp.), otherwise reject.

To see that the above characterization of L is correct, observe that for all good w, $(w,x,y,z) \in K$ iff $(x,y,z) \notin L(M,C)$. Then, to verify the caracterization of L, use Claim 2 (a) for the forward direction, and Claim 2 (b) for the backward direction.

Note that all quantifiers in the above characterization of L are polynomially bounded, and by the fact that $K \in NP$, the expression in brackets is in co-NP, hence L has a Σ_2^P-characterization. This proves that $\Sigma_2^P(C) = \Sigma_2^P$. ##

From the theorem several corollaries can be obtained.

<u>Corollary</u>. [25] $\Sigma_2^P(BPP) = \Sigma_2^P$.

<u>Corollary</u>. [14] $BPP \subseteq \Sigma_2^P \cap \Pi_2^P$.

<u>Corollary</u>. $NP \cap$ co-AM is included in L_2^P.

<u>Corollary</u>. GRAPH ISOMORPHISM is low_2.

Hereby, open problem 3 in [18] is answered positively.

<u>Corollary</u>. GRAPH ISOMORPHISM cannot be in H_k^P unless the polynomial-time hierarchy collapses to $\Sigma_{max\{2,k\}}^P$.

A special case of the previous Corollary is the following

<u>Corollary</u>. GRAPH ISOMORPHISM cannot be NP-complete (under $\leq_m^P$, $\leq_T^P$,

$\leq_\gamma$, $\leq_R$, $\leq_T^{sn}$ - reducibility) unless the polynomial-time hierarchy collapses to Σ_2^p .

For the case of γ-completeness (i.e. NP-completeness under $\leq_\gamma$-reducibility) this answers open problem 1 in [1] negatively (assuming the polynomial hierarchy does not collapse to Σ_2^p).

One might argue that this lowness result for GRAPH ISOMORPHISM just shows once more that GRAPH ISOMORPHISM will most likely be in P. On the other hand, observe that in [13] it is shown that under the assumption that EXPTIME $\neq$ NEXPTIME, there exist sets in $L_2^p - L_0^p = L_2^p - P$. And under the stronger assumption that NEXPTIME is not closed under complementation, $L_2^p - L_1^p = L_2^p - (NP \cap \text{co-}NP)$ is not empty. Hence, GRAPH ISOMORPHISM might very well be located in such a difference class.

Acknowledgements

I like to thank Osamu Watanabe for many discussions on the subject of this paper, and for contributing some of the initial ideas. Kurt Mehlhorn and Klaus Wagner commented an earlier version of this paper so that the present version could be improved.

References

1. L. Adleman and K. Manders, Reducibility, randomness, and intractability, Proc. 9th STOC 1977, 151-163.

2. D. Angluin, On counting problems and the polynomial-time hierarchy, Theor. Comput. Sci. 12 (1980), 161-173.

3. L. Babai, Trading group theory for randomness, Proc. 17th STOC 1985, 421-429.

4. L. Babai, Arthur-Merlin games: a randomized proof system and a short hierarchy of complexity classes, manuscript, 1986.

5. C.H. Bennett and J. Gill, Relative to a random oracle A, $P^A \neq NP^A \neq$ co-NP^A with probability 1, SIAM J. Comput. 10 (1981), 96-113.

6. R.B. Boppana and J. Hastad, Does co-NP have short interactive proofs?, manuscript, 1986.

7. J.L. Carter and M.N. Wegman, Universal classes of hash functions, J. Comput. Syst. Sci. 18 (1979), 143-154.

8. M.R. Garey and D.S. Johnson, Computers and Intractability: A Guide to the Theory of NP-Completeness, Freeman, San Francisco, 1979.

9. J. Gill, Computational complexity of probabilistic Turing machines, SIAM J. Comput. 6 (1977), 675-695.

10. O. Goldreich, S. Micali and A. Widgerson, Proofs that release minimum knowledge, MFCS 84, Lecture Notes in Computer Science 233, Springer, 639-650.

11. S. Goldwasser and M. Sipser, Private coins versus public coins in interactive proof systems, 18th STOC 1986, 59-68.

12. C.M. Hoffmann, Group-Theoretic Algorithms and Graph Isomorphism, Lecture Notes in Computer Science 136, Springer, 1982.

13. K. Ko and U. Schöning, On circuit-size complexity and the low hierarchy in NP, SIAM J. Comput. 14 (1985), 41-51.

14. C. Lautemann, BPP and the polynomial hierarchy, Inform. Proc. Letters 17 (1983), 215-217.

15. M. Lerman, Degrees of Unsolvability, Omega-Series, Springer, 1983.

16. T.J. Long, Strong nondeterministic polynomial-time reducibilities, Theor. Comput. Sci. 21 (1982), 1-25.

17. R. Mathon, A note on the graph isomorphism counting problem, Inform. Proc. Letters 8 (1979), 131-132.

18. U. Schöning, A low and a high hierarchy within NP, Journ. Comput. Syst. Sci. 27 (1983), 14-28.

19. U. Schöning, Complexity and Structure, Lecture Notes in Computer Science 211, Springer, 1986.

20. M. Sipser, A complexity theoretic approach to randomness, Proc. 15th STOC 1983, 330-335.

21. L.J. Stockmeyer, The polynomial-time hierarchy, Theor. Comput. Sci. 3 (1977), 1-22.

22. L.J. Stockmeyer, On approximation algorithms for #P, SIAM J. Comput. 14 (1985), 849-861.

23. S. Zachos, Probabilistic quantifiers, adversaries, and complexity classes: an overview, Proc. Structure in Complexity Theory Conf., Lecture Notes in Computer Science 223, Springer, 1986, 383-400.

24. S. Zachos and M. Fürer, Probabilistic quantifiers vs. distrustful adversaries, manuscript, 1985.

25. S. Zachos and H. Heller, A decisive characterization of BPP, Information and Control 69 (1986), 125-135.

A HIERARCHY THEOREM FOR ALMOST EVERYWHERE COMPLEX SETS WITH APPLICATION TO POLYNOMIAL COMPLEXITY DEGREES [1]

John G. Geske
Computer Science Department
Iowa State University
Ames, Iowa 50011

Dung T. Huynh
Computer Science Department
University of Texas at Dallas
Richardson, Texas 75083-0688

Alan L. Selman
College of Computer Science
Northeastern University
Boston, Massachusetts 02115

1 Introduction

There are two parts to this paper. In the first part we prove a deterministic time hierarchy for almost everywhere (a.e.) complexity that is as tight as the well known Hartmanis-Stearns hierarchy theorem for infinitely often (i.o.) complexity. Recall that if a language $L \notin \mathrm{DTIME}(t(n))$ for some time function t, then for every deterministic Turing machine M that recognizes L there exist infinitely many inputs x for which the running time of M on x is slower than $t(|x|)$. This leaves open the possibility that there exists some other infinite set of inputs which M can recognize within the time bound t. In many applications one wants to know that $L \notin \mathrm{DTIME}(t(n))$ a.e., that is, for every deterministic Turing machine M that recognizes A, M runs for more than $t(|x|)$ steps for all but finitely many strings x [2] [16].

Gill and Blum [8] compared i.o. complexity to the stronger notion of a.e. complexity, and concluded that "it may be fundamentally more difficult to construct almost everywhere complex functions than infinitely often complex functions." Our theorem is contrary to that intuition. It is a significant improvement over the previously known hierarchy result for a.e. complex sets, as reported by Seiferas, Fischer and Meyer [19], and in fact, is a significant improvement over the hierarchy theorem for *immune sets* presented by Flajolet and Steyaert [6]. Also, our result is independent of the results of Paul [15] and Fürer [7], who present much tighter time hierarchies of i.o. complex sets than the Hartmanis-Stearns result by restricting the class of machines examined to a fixed number of worktapes. We place no such restriction on the machines examined. We obtain, as a corollary, the a.e. complex space hierarchy result of Meyer and McCreight [13].

[1]This work was supported in part by the National Science Foundation under grants DCR 84-02033, DCR 85-17277 and DCR 86-96082

The second part of this paper is motivated by nothing less than a reexamination of what it means for a set to be NP-complete. The early history of the theory of NP-complete sets was fraught with confusing attempts at notation and concepts. Several authors attempted to formulate NP-completeness without the use of polynomial time reducibilities. Sahni [17] and Sahni and Gonzales [18], for example, called a set $A \in$ NP *P-complete* if and only if $A \in$ P implied P = NP. It soon became clear that such a nonconstructive test did not properly capture the notion of NP-completeness. For, as was trivially observed in [3], if P $\neq$ NP then every set in NP − P obeys the criterion set forth by Sahni. Namely, by Ladner's result [11] that if P $\neq$ NP then there exist a multitude of sets in NP that are not polynomially equivalent it follows that P-complete is not the same as NP-complete.

Are there sets in NP that in a mathematically meaningful sense should be considered to be complete for NP, but that are not NP-complete in the usual sense that every set in NP is $\leq_m^P$-reducible to it? Here we define a nonconstructive binary relation that makes precise the notion that "the complexity of A is polynomially related to the complexity of B." This is the weakest mathematically meaningful notion that captures all other polynomial reducibilities, including polynomial time Turing reducibility. This new relation yields new completeness and hardness notions for complexity classes. We fall short of answering our question about completeness for NP. But, we do show that there are sets that are hard for NP that are not NP-hard in the usual sense, and we do show that there are sets that must be considered to be complete for the complexity class EXP that are not even $\leq_T^P$-complete for EXP.

In a certain way hardness and completeness with respect to the relation we shall define is related to a.e. complexity. Thus, the results we will obtain in this section depend extensively on the hierarchy theorem proved in the first part of this paper. Our results provide new insight into the structure of the "hard instances" of complete sets. We show that the hard instances of complete sets for EXP and TIME(2^{poly}) have fairly regular distribution. These results are in contrast to the *distributional view* of computational complexity that suggests the hard instances of an intractable problem are distributed in some very irregular manner, but feasable algorithms can only determine "smooth" distributions, and support the more recent view of *instance complexity* that is based on the intuitive feeling that individual instances of an intractable problem are inherently hard [10] [14].

2 The Hierarchy Theorem

A few words about notation: Let C be a complexity class. An infinite set A is *C-immune* if A contains no infinite subset in C [6]. An infinite, co-infinite set A is *C-bi-immune* if A and $\overline{A}$ are C-immune [1]. If C = DTIME($t(n)$) for some time function t, then A is *C-complex* if $A \notin$ DTIME($t(n)$) a.e., that is, for every deterministic Turing machine M that recognizes A, M runs for more than $t(|x|)$ steps for all but finitely many strings x [2] [16]. It is easy to see that a set A is DTIME($t(n)$)-complex if and only if it is DTIME($t(n)$)-bi-immune.

The following theorem essentially says that given any two well-behaved time functions t_1 and t_2 for which $\lim_{n\to\infty} \inf t_1(n) \log t_1(n)/t_2(n) = 0$ then DTIME($t_2(n)$) contains a DTIME($t_1(n)$)-complex set, *e.g.*, DTIME($n^2 2^n$) contains a DTIME(2^n)-complex set. The exact statement of the theorem is somewhat complicated for the following technical reason. The intuition behind the proof of this hierarchy theorem is that by "slowing down" the diagonalization process sufficiciently, it should be possible to ensure that the constructed set is not in DTIME($t_1(n)$) a.e. For many classes, it is possible to slow down this diagonalization by an arbitrarily small function — the function $f(n)$ given below.

Theorem 2.1 *If $t_2(n)$ is a monotone increasing fully time-constructable function such that*

$$\liminf_{n\to\infty} \frac{t_1(n) \log t_1(n)}{t_2(n)} = 0,$$

and there exists a fully time-constructable monotone increasing and unbounded function $f(n)$ such that

$$\liminf_{n\to\infty} \frac{f(n) t_1(n) \log t_1(n)}{t_2(n)} = 0,$$

then there exists a DTIME($t_1(n)$)*-complex set in* DTIME($t_2(n)$).

For most running times $t_1(n)$ and $t_2(n)$ such that $\lim_{n\to\infty} \inf t_1(n) \log t_1(n)/t_2(n) = 0$, one can find a suitable $f(n)$ such that the condition $\lim_{n\to\infty} \inf f(n) t_1(n) \log t_1(n)/t_2(n) = 0$ is satisfied. For example, if $t_1(n) = 2^n$, and $t_2(n) = n^2 2^n$, then by the Hartmanis-Stearns Hierarchy Theorem, DTIME(2^n) $\subset$ DTIME($n^2 2^n$). By Theorem 2.1, letting $f(n) = \log n$, there exists a DTIME(2^n)-complex set in DTIME($n^2 2^n$). The best previously known result [19] was that there existed DTIME(2^n)-complex sets in DTIME($(2+\epsilon)^n$), for any $\epsilon > 0$. As a further example, by Theorem 2.1, we now know that there exist P-complex sets in DTIME($n^{\log n}$).

The proof of Theorem 2.1 is presented in the Appendix. The finite-injury priority argument uses an elegant characterization of C-complex sets due to Balcázar and Schöning [1].

A tighter result is possible for deterministic space classes[13]; since we are allowed to reuse tape cells, it is not necessary to slow down the diagonalization as was necessary for the time case. One should also note here that, as with the time case, $s_2(n)$ must be monotone increasing to insure the cancellation of transducers diagonalized at previous stages.

Corollary 2.2 *If $s_2(n)$ is a fully space-constructable monotone increasing function, $s_1(n)$ and $s_2(n)$ are at least $\log_2 n$, and*

$$\liminf_{n\to\infty} \frac{s_1(n)}{s_2(n)} = 0,$$

then there is a DSPACE($s_1(n)$)*-complex set in* DSPACE($s_2(n)$).

These hierarchies are as tight as the hierarchies for the i.o. cases. By straightforward restrictions on our construction, it is possible to derive similar *immunity results* for sets that, for syntactic reasons, cannot be a.e. complex. Tally sets — languages over $\{1\}^*$— cannot be a.e. complex, but by a restricted version of Theorem 2.1 we can construct a P-immune tally set A in DTIME($n^{\log n}$). In fact stronger than this, we can construct A such that $\overline{A} \cap \{1\}^*$ is also P-immune.

Traditionally, translational lemmas have been used to derive even tighter results than allowable by the hierarchy theorems. For example, DTIME(2^n) $\subset$ DTIME($n\,2^n$) can only be obtained in this fashion. Unfortunately, the padding technique used in translation lemmas does not carry over for the a.e. complex case; padded strings allow for easily recognized subsets to exist. As padding plays a key role in Seiferas, Fischer and Meyer's [19] derivation of hierarchies for the nondeterministic classes, their results do not carry over for the a.e. complex case. The more recent results of Žák [20] also do not carry over in this case. It appears that new techniques will have to be developed for results of this nature to be achieved for the a.e. complex cases. Resolution of these difficulties remain open.

3 Polynomial Complexity Degrees

The importance of polynomial time-bounded Turing reducibility is the fact that, placing faith in an appropriate variant of Church's Thesis, it is the most general *constructive* relation which, when it holds between two sets A and B, $A \leq_T^P B$, asserts that the "complexity" of A is "polynomially related to" the "complexity" of B. We wish to make this statement precise.

For every recursive set A, M_A denotes a deterministic Turing machine that recognizes A, and T_{M_A} denotes the running time of M_A. Let A and B be recursive sets. When we assert that $A \leq_T^P B$ we are asserting the existence of a polynomial time-bounded oracle Turing machine that recognizes A using B as an oracle. Consider the following oracle Turing machine program given in Figure 1 that witnesses $A \leq_T^P B$, runs in polynomial time-bound $p(n)$, and in which queries to the oracle are replaced with executions of a Turing machine M_B that recognizes B. The reduction yields a Turing machine M_A which accepts A so that

$$\forall x \in \Sigma^* (\, T_{M_A}(x) \leq p(|x|) \max \{T_{M_B}(y) : |y| \leq p(|x|)\,\}), \tag{1}$$

where T_M denotes the running time of machine M.

We have seen that $A \leq_T^P B$ implies the existence of a polynomial p such that

$$\forall \mathrm{M}_B \exists \mathrm{M}_A \forall x \in \Sigma^* (\, T_{M_A}(x) \leq p(|x|) \max \{T_{M_B}(y) : |y| \leq p(|x|)\,\}). \tag{2}$$

We take (2) to be the mathematical definition of the phrase "the complexity of A is polynomially related to the complexity of B."

Definition 3.1 *A binary relation $\leq_C$ over the recursive sets is defined as follows. Given recursive sets A and B, $A \leq_C B$ if and only if there exists a polynomial p such that*

$$\forall \mathrm{M}_B \exists \mathrm{M}_A \forall x \, (T_{M_A}(x) \leq p(|x|) \max \{T_{M_B}(y) : |y| \leq p(|x|)\}).$$

```
begin
  input x;
   ⋮
  for up to p(|x|) steps do
  begin
     ⋮
    generate a query q to oracle B;
      input q to M_B;
        run M_B on q;
      return; (answer to query)
     ⋮
  end;
end.
```

Figure 1: Turing Reduction of A to B

Obviously $A \leq_T^P B$ implies $A \leq_C B$. $A \leq_C B$ is the weakest notion that captures all other polynomial time reducibilities and is even weaker than the reducibility defined by Even, Long and Yacobi [4]. It is easy to see that $\leq_C$ is a reflexive and transitive relation, and therefore $\leq_C \cap \leq_C^{-1}$ is an equivalence relation.

The equivalence classes of this equivalence relation are called ***polynomial complexity degrees.*** For each recursive set A, the equivalence class that contains A is denoted $C(A)$, for it represents a formal definition of the "polynomial complexity" of A. (The approach taken here to define the polynomial complexity of A is analogous to the approach taken by mathematicians in defining the cardinality of a set A.)

Now define a partial ordering $\leq$ over the polynomial complexity degrees as follows. Let $\mathbf{a}$ and $\mathbf{b}$ be arbitrary complexity degrees.

$$\mathbf{a} \leq \mathbf{b} \Leftrightarrow \exists A \exists B (A \in \mathbf{a} \wedge B \in \mathbf{b} \wedge A \leq_C B). \tag{3}$$

The $\leq$ relation is a well-defined partial ordering on the polynomial complexity degrees, and induces an upper semi-lattice with 0-element ($\mathbf{0} = P$) on the recursive sets. A set A is ***$\leq_C$-hard*** for a complexity class $\mathcal{C}$ if $L \in \mathcal{C}$ implies $C(L) \leq C(A)$, and A is ***$\leq_C$-complete*** for $\mathcal{C}$ if, in addition, $A \in \mathcal{C}$.

We are interested in complexity classes, such as EXP and TIME(2^{poly}), that cannot be characterized by DTIME($t(n)$) for some fixed function t. Though we will not give the definition here, the notion of $\mathcal{C}$-complex is extended to such complexity classes $\mathcal{C}$ in the obvious way, so that $\mathcal{C}$-complex and $\mathcal{C}$-bi-immune remain equivalent.

The following propositions follow from straightforward analyses of the definitions.

Proposition 3.2 *Every* C*-complex set is* $\leq_C$*-hard for* C.

Proposition 3.3 *If for some polynomial* p, A *is* DTIME$(2^{p(n)})$*-complex then* A *is* $\leq_C$*-hard for* TIME(2^{poly}).

It follows from these propositions that one way to obtain $\leq_C$-hard sets for DTIME$(t(n))$ is to use our Hierarchy Theorem in order to obtain DTIME$(t(n))$-complex sets.

Theorem 3.4 *For every recursive set* $A \in C - \mathrm{P}$ *there exists a sparse recursive set* B *such that* B *is* C*-complex and* $A \not\leq_T^{\mathrm{P}} B$.

The proof is an intricate finite-injury priority argument.

Corollary 3.5 *For every recursive set* $A \notin \mathrm{P}$ *there exists a sparse recursive set* B *such that* $C(A) \leq C(B)$ *and* $A \not\leq_T^{\mathrm{P}} B$.

Corollary 3.6 *For every set* A *in* NP − P *there exists a sparse recursive set* $B \in$ TIME(2^{poly}) *such that* $C(A) \leq C(B)$ *and* $A \not\leq_T^{\mathrm{P}} B$.

Proof. Let $A \in$ NP − P. By Theorem 3.4, there exists a sparse recursive set B that is DTIME$(2^{q(n)})$-complex for some polynomial q, and $A \not\leq_T^{\mathrm{P}} B$. Since NP $\subseteq$ TIME(2^{poly}), it follows immediately from Proposition 3.3 that $C(A) \leq C(B)$.□

Our first significant statement is easily obtained by letting A be the NP-complete set SAT.

Corollary 3.7 *There exists a sparse recursive set* B *in* TIME(2^{poly}) *that is* $\leq_C$*-hard for* NP *and is not* $\leq_T^{\mathrm{P}}$*-hard for* NP.

This result is in contrast to Karp and Lipton [9] where it was shown that there can be no sparse NP-hard sets unless the polynomial hierarchy collapses to Σ_2^P.

Now we will consider the class EXP = $\bigcup_c$ DTIME(2^{cn}).

Theorem 3.8 *For every* 2^n*-complex set* A *in* EXP *there exists a set* B *in* EXP *such that* $C(A) = C(B)$ *and* $A \not\leq_T^{\mathrm{P}} B$.

The set B is constructed so that $A \not\leq_T^{\mathrm{P}} B$ and so that B is DTIME(2^{2n})-complex. This is done by interleaving a diagonalization with the proof technique of the Hierarchy Theorem. Then, by Proposition 3.3, $C(A) = C(B)$ since both sets are $\leq_C$-hard for TIME(2^{poly}).

Our next significant result about $\leq_C$ *vs.* $\leq_T^{\mathrm{P}}$ can now be stated.

Corollary 3.9 $\leq_T^{\mathrm{P}}$*-complete and* $\leq_C$*-complete sets differ in* EXP.

Proof. The proof of Theorem 3.8 yields sets A and B in EXP that are DTIME(2^n)-complex and $A \not\leq_T^{\mathrm{P}} B$. Thus, B is not $\leq_T^{\mathrm{P}}$-complete for EXP, but by Proposition 3.3 B is $\leq_C$-complete for EXP.□

Even tighter constructions yield the following results.

Theorem 3.10 *There exist recursive sets A and B in* EXP *such that $C(A) = C(B)$ and $A \not\leq_T^P B$ and $B \not\leq_T^P A$.*

Theorem 3.11 *There exist recursive sets A and B in* DTIME$(n^2 2^n)$ *such that $A \not\leq_C B$ and $B \not\leq_C A$.*

Now we will use $\leq_C$ to analyze the structure of complete sets. First note that $\leq_C$-complete for a class $\mathcal{C}$ does not imply $\mathcal{C}$-complex for the class $\mathcal{C}$ because natural complete sets, such as SAT, are not a.e. complex.

The next theorem uses Lynch's notion of a complexity core [5] [12] [14] to show that sets that are very difficult to recognize are not necessarily $\leq_C$-hard.

Theorem 3.12 *There exists a recursive set A such that every infinite subset of A is a* TIME(2^{poly})-*core, and A is not $\leq_C$-hard for* TIME(2^{poly}).

The set A is constructed so that it is very difficult to recognize, but it has very large polynomially recognizable "gaps" between hard instances. Indeed, polynomial distribution of hard instances implies $\leq_C$-hardness for many complexity classes.

We make the following definitions.

Definition 3.13 *Given a Turing machine M and a function f on the natural numbers, the set of f-hard instances for M is*

$$H(M, f) = \{x \in \Sigma^* : T_M(x) > f(|x|)\}.$$

Definition 3.14 *A set A is polynomially distributed (p-distributed) if there exists a polynomial p such that*

$$\forall^\infty x \in A \exists y \in A(|x| < |y| \leq p(|x|)).$$

A function g is a *generator* for EXP if for every integer c there exists a polynomial p such that $g(p(n)) \geq 2^{cn}$. For example, $g(n) = 2^n$ is a generator for EXP.

Theorem 3.15 *A set A is $\leq_C$-hard for* EXP *if and only if for every Turing machine recognizer M_A of the set A and some generator f of* EXP, *$H(M_A, f)$ is p-distributed.*

Therefore since every $\leq_T^P$-complete set for EXP is $\leq_C$-complete, it follows that the "hard instances" for these sets must be at most a polynomial "distance" apart. A similar theorem can be stated for TIME(2^{poly}).

Further work, along these lines, relates polynomial distribution of hard instances with the structure of complexity cores, and this work is in the spirit of Orponen and Schöning [14].

References

[1] J.L. Balcázar and U. Schöning. Bi-immune sets for complexity classes. *Math. Sys. Theory*, 18(1):1–10, 1985.

[2] L. Berman. On the structure of complete sets: almost everywhere complexity and infinitely often speedup. In *Proc. 17th IEEE Symposium on Foundations of Computer Science*, pages 76–80, 1976.

[3] R. Book, C. Wrathall, A. Selman, and D. Dobkin. Inclusion complete tally languages and the Hartmanis-Berman conjecture. *Math. Syst. Theory*, 11:1–8, 1977.

[4] S. Even, T.J. Long, and Y. Yacobi. A note on deterministic versus nondeterministic complexity. *Information and Control*, 55:117–124, 1982.

[5] S. Even, A.L. Selman, and Y. Yacobi. Hard-core theorems for complexity classes. *J. Ass. Comp. Mach.*, 32:205–217, 1985.

[6] P. Flajolet and J.M. Steyaert. On sets having only hard subsets. In *Automata, Languages, and Programming, Lecture Notes in Computer Science vol. 14*, pages 446–457, Springer-Verlag, Berlin, 1974.

[7] M. Fürer. The tight deterministic time hierarchy. In *Proc. 14th Annual ACM Symp. on Theory of Computing*, pages 8–16, 1982.

[8] J. Gill and M. Blum. On almost everywhere complex recursive functions. *J. Ass. Comp. Mach.*, 21:425–435, 1974.

[9] R.M. Karp and R. Lipton. Some connections between nonuniform and uniform complexity classes. In *Proc. 12th ACM Symposium on Theory of Computing*, pages 302–309, 1980.

[10] K. Ko, P. Orponen, U. Schöning, and O. Watanabe. What is a hard instance of a computational problem? In *Structure in Complexity Theory, Lecture Notes in Computer Science vol. 223*, pages 197–217, Springer-Verlag, Berlin, 1986.

[11] R. Ladner. On the structure of polynomial time reducibility. *J. Ass. Comp. Mach.*, 22:155–171, 1975.

[12] N. Lynch. On reducibility to complex or sparse sets. *J. Ass. Comp. Mach.*, 22:341–345, 1975.

[13] A.R. Meyer and E.M. McCreight. Computationally complex and pseudo-random zero-one valued functions. In Kohavi and Paz, editors, *Theory of Machines and Computations*, pages 19–42, Academic Press, 1971.

[14] P. Orponen and U. Schöning. The structure of polynomial complexity cores. In *Automata, Languages, and Programming, Lecture Notes in Computer Science vol. 176*, pages 452–458, Springer-Verlag, Berlin, 1984.

[15] W.J. Paul. On time hierarchies. In *Proc. 9th Annual ACM Symp. on Theory of Computing*, pages 218–222, 1977.

[16] M.O. Rabin. *Degree of difficulty of computing a function and a partial ordering of recursive sets.* Tech. Report 2, Hebrew University, Jerusalem, Israel, 1960.

[17] S. Sahni. Computationally related problems. *SIAM J. Computing*, 3:262–279, 1974.

[18] S. Sahni and T. Gonzales. P-complete approximation problems. *J. Ass. Comp. Mach.*, 23:555–565, 1976.

[19] J.I. Seiferas, M.J. Fischer, and A.R. Meyer. Separating nondeterministic time complexity classes. *J. Ass. Comp. Mach.*, 25:146–167, 1978.

[20] S. Žák. A Turing machine time hierarchy. *Theor. Comput. Sci.*, 26:327–333, 1983.

Appendix

Here we present the proof of Theorem 2.1 for those interested in the technical details. We use the *multiple-tape off-line Turing transducer*, considering it both as an acceptor and as a computer of a function, as the model of computation. Let $\{M_i\}_{i\in\mathbf{N}}$ be an effective enumeration of deterministic Turing transducers so that for every recursive set A there exists some M_i such that $A = L(M_i)$; φ_i denotes the function computed by transducer T_i.

Let $\{f_i\}_{i\in\mathbf{N}}$ be a recursively indexed set of fully time-constructable unbounded functions such that if $f_{i_1}, f_{i_2} \in \{f_i\}$ and $i_1 < i_2$, then $f_{i_1}(n) < f_{i_2}(n)$ for almost all n. Let $L(i,n) = \{x : T_i$ accepts x in $f_n(|x|)$ steps $\}$ and define the deterministic time complexity class $C = \{L(i,n) : i,n \in \mathbf{N}\}$. $\mathcal{F}_C$ is the class of functions computable on deterministic transducers with the same enumeration of time bounds. By choosing an appropriate enumeration of functions, the classes P, EXP and TIME(2^{poly}) can be specified in this fashion. We may similarly define the deterministic space classes.

Given a set $A \subseteq \Sigma^*$, a function $f : \Sigma^* \rightarrow \Sigma^*$ is *finite-one* if for every $y \in \Sigma^*$, $f^{-1}(y)$ is finite.

Theorem 1 *(Balcázar, Schöning) A recursive set A is C-complex if and only if for every function $f \in \mathcal{F}_C$ such that $f(A) \cap f(\overline{A}) = \emptyset$, f is finite-one.*

Given functions $t_2(n)$ and $f(n)$, we construct a recursive a.e. complex set A inductively on the enumerated strings of Σ^*. We consider the following infinite enumeration of *restraining conditions*:

$$R_i : \varphi_i \text{ is not finite} - \text{one} \Rightarrow \varphi_i(A) \cap \varphi_i(\overline{A}) \neq \emptyset.$$

A condition R_j is *satisfiable* if its antecendent is true. A satisfiable condition R_j is *satisfied* if $\varphi_j(A) \cap \varphi_j(\overline{A}) \neq \emptyset$. At each stage we attempt to satisfy the least (smallest indexed) restraining condition that has not yet been satisfied. Such a construction is given in Figure 2. In the construction, S is a set of restraining conditions (transducer indices) to be considered.

Lemma 2 *$A \in$ DTIME$(t_2(n))$.*

```
stage i
  begin
    Let n := ⌊log i⌋;
    Let m := min(f(n), ⌊log n⌋);
    Let S := {1, ..., ⌊√m⌋};
    Let W := set of the first ⌊√m⌋ strings;
    Within time t_2(n) execute as many previous stages as
      possible, beginning with stage 1, removing trans-
      ducer indices out of S that have been diagonalized
      during previous stages;
    for each j ∈ S do
      Simulate M_j for ⌊t_2(n)/f(n)⌋ steps to determine
        whether there is a string w in W such that
        M_j(w) = M_j(w_i);
    if yes then begin
                Let ĵ be the least transducer index with
                  this property;
                Let w_î be the least string in W with this
                  property;
                {* Note that M_ĵ is diagonalized by the
                  following statement *}
                if w_î ∈ A then add w_i to Ā
                            else add w_i to A
               end
  end stage i
```

Figure 2: Inductive construction of an a.e. complex set.

Proof. We show that there exists a Turing machine that executes the algorithm given in Figure 2 in time $t_2(n)$. On an input x of length n, the time to cancel machines from previous stages requires time $t_2(n)$. At most $\lfloor\sqrt{f(n)}\rfloor$ transducers must be simulated on at most $\lfloor\sqrt{f(n)}\rfloor$ strings, so at most $f(n)$ simulations must be made. Each simulation is run within $\lfloor t_2(n)/f(n)\rfloor$ steps. (Note that for a machine to do this requires that both $t_2(n)$ and $f(n)$ be fully time-constructable.) Therefore the simulations require at most $t_2(n)$ steps, and the total time necessary to execute the algorithm is $O(t_2(n))$. By the conditions placed on $t_1(n)$ and $t_2(n)$, we have $\lim_{n\to\infty} \inf t_2(n)/n = \infty$ and so, by the Linear Speedup Theorem, we arrive at our desired result.□

Lemma 3 *For every $t_1(n)$ computable φ_j that is not finite-one, R_j is satisfied.*

Proof. Let T_l be a $t_1(n)$ time-bounded transducer such that φ_l is not finite-one and $\varphi_l(A)\cap\varphi_l(\overline{A}) = \emptyset$. Because of the conditions placed on $t_2(n)$ and $f(n)$, we can assume without loss of generality that at some stage i in the construction, for all indicies $j < l$, either $j \notin S$, *i.e.*, R_j has already been satisfied, or φ_j is finite-one. So, l is the smallest satisfiable index in S at stage i, and remains the smallest satisfiable index at all future stages until R_l is satisfied.

The time needed to simulate T_l on an input of length n is $c\,t_1(n)\log t_1(n)$, where c is a constant depending on T_l. Note that the Hennie-Stearns Theorem is needed here since we make no assumptions about the number of worktapes T_l may have. We are only allowed to simulate T_l for $\lfloor t_2(n)/f(n)\rfloor$ steps. However, since φ_l is not finite-one, and by the conditions placed on $t_2(n)$ and $f(n)$, there exist strings w_j, w_k such that $|w_j| < \left\lfloor\sqrt{\min(f(|w_k|), \lfloor\log|w_k|\rfloor)}\right\rfloor, \varphi_l(w_j) = \varphi_l(w_k)$, and w_k is a sufficiently large string such that $c\,t_1(|w_j|)\log t_1(|w_j|) + c\,t_1(|w_k|)\log t_1(|w_k|) < t_2(|w_k|)/f(|w_k|)$. Therefore there is enough time to complete the simulation and witness the fact that $\varphi_l(w_j) = \varphi_l(w_k)$. If $w_j \in A$ then $w_k \in \overline{A}$, otherwise $w_j \in \overline{A}$ and $w_k \in A$. In either case $\varphi_l(A) \cap \varphi_l(\overline{A}) \neq \emptyset$ and R_l is satisfied.□

Proof of Theorem 2.1. Follows directly from Lemmas 2 and 3 and the fact (easily verifiable) that if Lemma 3 holds then the conditions of Theorem 1 are satisfied.□

SELF-REDUCIBILITY

(Extended abstract, october 1986)

José L. Balcázar
Facultad de Informática U.P.C.
08028 Barcelona, SPAIN

1. Introduction.

The concept of self-reducible set has been used in complexity theory by several authors so far. We indicate here some references related to our work.

In [12] and [13], Schnorr uses two kinds of self-reducibility to study the relationship between the decisional and functional versions of NP-complete problems. We will generalize his results to all NP-complete sets, extending them later to the case of optimization problems.

A very recent work of Ko [7] relates certain forms of "helping" to self-reducible sets. He asks for structural characterizations of the classes studied. Here we show that the techniques used to strengthen the results of Schnorr rely on a clear property (which we name "self-computable witnesses") which characterizes exactly the "self-1-helpers" of [7].

The self-reducibility of some NP-complete sets plays a crucial role in the research on reductions to sparse sets and non-uniform classes. See [2], [4], and [8]. In [5] there are many results about the relationships between non-uniform and uniform complexity classes. These results are obtained by three seemingly different methods, one of which is called "self-reducibility method". Concerning polynomial advice classes, the results are:

1. <u>Theorem</u>.

(a) If PSPACE is included in P/poly then PSPACE = $\Sigma_2 \cap \Pi_2$.

(b) If EXPTIME is included in PSPACE/poly then EXPTIME = PSPACE.

(c) If NP is included in P/poly then $\forall i \geq 2$ $\Sigma_i = \Sigma_2$.

(d) If EXPTIME is included in P/poly then EXPTIME = $\Sigma_2 \cap \Pi_2$. Moreover, this implies P $\neq$ NP.

The same reference contains similar results regarding classes defined by logarithmic advice.

Some of these results (parts (a) and (c) above) have been reproved and generalized in [1]. Two of the techniques of [5] have been shown there to be forms of self-reducibility. More precisely, their "self-reducibility" method corresponds to the disjunctive self-reducibility, while their "recursive definition" method is the truth-table self-reducibility, both as defined in [6].

Parts (b) and (d) of theorem 1 are proven in the original reference by a third technique: the "round robin tournament" method. As expressed by S. Mahaney in [9], p. 106, "it is not clear whether it [the round robin tournament method] might be subsumed by the above method of recursive definition."

We are interested in studying the possibility of such a subsumption. In fact, we show that, for polynomial advice classes, the sets to which the round robin tournament method applies (or very similar ones) possess a generalized form of self-reducibility structure. This allows to obtain all the remaining results of theorem 1, together with other results, as corollaries of our main theorems. Thus, we partially answer Mahaney's question by presenting a partial subsumption of the round robin tournament method by a self-reducibility method.

2. Definitions and basic properties.

All our sets consist of words over the alphabet $\Gamma=\{0,1\}$. We denote by λ the empty word. Complexity classes are defined in the usual way: among them, P, NP, PSPACE, and the classes of the polynomial time hierarchy. Departing from the usual convention, our NP-complete sets are defined in the more general way, as complete under polynomial time Turing reductions. For definitions see [14].

EXPTIME is the class of sets decided in time 2^{n^k} for some k, as in [5]. It coincides with APSPACE (alternating polynomial space). See [3] for complexity classes defined by alternating machines. These machines will be used in section 4.

PF is the class of all functions computable in polynomial time. PF(A) is the relativization of PF to oracle A. SAT denotes the well-known NP-complete problem of deciding the satisfiability of boolean formulas, and QBF the PSPACE-complete problem of deciding the truth of quantified boolean formulas.

The notation C/F for non-uniform classes is used as in [5]. C/F denotes the class of sets decidable by machines as specified by C with the help of an advice function from F. We will use the classes in the polynomial time hierarchy and PSPACE in place of C, and the functions polynomially bounded in length in place of F.

In the following we define several notions of self-reducibility which have been used recently in the literature. We start with the definition given in [1], where it was used to prove theorem 21 below. In order to distinguish it from our other definitions of self-reducibility, we will call it here "ldq-self-reducibility". The prefix "ldq" stands for "length-decreasing queries". The definition is as follows:

2. Definition. A set A is polynomial time ldq-self-reducible if and only if there is a polynomial time deterministic oracle Turing machine such that A = L(M,A), and on each input of length n every word queried to the oracle has length less than n.

Our work relies on two generalizations of this concept. The first one is the definition of self-reducibility proposed in [11].

3. Definition. A set A is polynomial time self-reducible if and only if there is a polynomial time deterministic oracle Turing machine such that A = L(M,A), and on each input x every word queried to the oracle is smaller than x in a (fixed) partial order satisfying:

(a) If x is smaller than y then $|x| \leq p(|y|)$ for some polynomial p.
(b) It is decidable in polynomial time whether x is smaller than y.
(c) Every decreasing chain is bounded in length by a polynomial of the length of its maximum element.

We will omit the words "polynomial time", which are to be assumed in every use we make of any of these definitions 2 and 3.

It can be seen that this definition captures the essential properties of the self-reducible sets (mainly, the NP-complete, co-NP-complete, and PSPACE-complete sets). Note that definition 3 is required in order to make the concept invariant under polynomial time isomorphism.

Some well-known properties of these definitions are:

4. Proposition.

(a) If A is self-reducible then $A \in$ PSPACE.
(b) If M witnesses the self-reducibility of both A and B then A = B.

The proof of (a) consists of solving the queries recursively, and keeping track of the recursion in a polynomially high stack. A proof of (b) (for the length-decreasing queries case) can be found in [1].

Some additional properties of self-reducible sets can be shown if the self-reducibility structure has a particular form. We define here the only one we will use, the disjunctive self-reduciblity:

5. Definition. The set A is d-self-reducible if and only if it is self-reducible, and the oracle machine M witnessing this fact accepts its input whenever the oracle answers positively to any of the queries.

In [6] other forms of self-reducibility are presented (conjunctive, positive truth-table ...) and some of their properties are studied. The following easy property is argued in this reference:

6. Proposition. If A is d-self-reducible then $A \in NP$.

The second generalization we will study is, to our knowledge, new. It is a modification of the ldq-self-reducibility:

7. Definition. A set A is polynomial time wdq-self-reducible if and only if there is a polynomial time deterministic oracle Turing machine such that $A = L(M,A)$, and on each input x of length n every word queried to the oracle either has length less than n, or has length n and is lexicographically smaller than x.

The prefix "wdq" stands for "word-decreasing queries". Observe that this definition allows exponentially long decreasing chains, but keeps the running time of the self-reducing machine polynomially bounded. Part (b) of proposition 4 holds also for this definition, and part (a) is tanslated into:

8. Proposition. If A is wdq-self-reducible then $A \in EXPTIME$.

This definition encompasses many of the "games" used in [5]. A generalization combining definition 3 and definition 7 can be proposed in a straightforward way. Other generalizations can be obtained using different time or space bounds for the self-reducing machine, and other bounds on the length of the decreasing chains. For instance, a "fully exponential" version would be to allow exponentially long decreasing chains and a exponential time self-reducing machine.

The interest and usefulness of these concepts will be subject of further research. In particular, the applicability of these concepts to other classes studied in [5] (like the classes defined by logarithmic advice) will be studied in forthcoming work.

3. Functional and optimization versions of NP-complete problems.

Sets in NP are usually interpreted as decision problems. Functional versions of these problems are interesting too, and can be defined for every set in NP as follows. Consider any NP set A. By the quantifier characterization of NP, we know that there is a set B in P and a polynomial p such that

$$(\star) \qquad x \in A \text{ if and only if } \exists\, y\ |y| \leq p(|x|)\ \langle x,y\rangle \in B$$

In many particular cases, each such y is in some sense the "solution" of the problem A for input x. In a more general sense, the word y is said to be a "witness" of the fact that x is in A.

Thus, we can consider the functional version of this generic NP set A, consisting of, given input x, computing a solution y if such a solution exists; i.e. compute a y such that $\langle x,y\rangle \in B$. Observe, first, that this is not necessarily a single valued function, and second, that this problem depends on the set B in P from which we have defined A by existential quantification, and on the polynomial p. We also refer to this problem as "computing witnesses".

Fix a B in P and a polynomial p. Let A be the NP set for which $(\star)$ holds. We define the functional solutions of the set A as follows:

9.<u>Definition</u>. The set funct-sols(B,p) is the set

$$\{\ f\ /\ \forall x\ (\text{ if } \exists y\ |y| \leq p(|x|)\ \langle x,y\rangle \in B \text{ then } f(x) \text{ is defined, } |f(x)| \leq p(|x|), \text{ and } \langle x,f(x)\rangle \in B\ )\ \}$$

In [13] it is shown that for "self-transformable" problems (a weaker form of disjunctive self-reducibility) there is a functional solution that is "equally hard" to compute as the decisional form of the problem. This encompasses most of the known NP sets. However, we want to generalize it so that it includes all NP-complete sets, without the need of checking whether they are self-transformable. Note that it is not known whether all the NP-complete sets (even with respect to the stronger m-reducibility) are self-reducible.

To do this, we will apply a prefix searching technique as suggested in [16], as follows:

10. Definition. The set prefix-sols(B,p) is the set
{ ⟨x,z⟩ / ∃y |y| ≤ p(|x|) ⟨x,y⟩ ∈ B such that z is a prefix of y }

The interest of this set lies in the following observation, which is also stated in [15]:

11. Lemma. For every B ∈ P and polynomial p, prefix-sols(B,p) is d-self-reducible.

In [15] it is also shown that every d-self-reducible set is (conjunctively) Turing equivalent to a set of the form prefix-sols(B,p). Also, other applications of these notions are presented to p-separability and public key cryptosystems.

We can state the following theorem:

12. Theorem. Let A be any NP-complete set, and let B in P and p such that (*) holds. Then funct-sols(B,p) $\cap$ PF(A) ≠ ∅.

The interpretation of this result is that there is a functional solution of the NP-complete set A which is "no much harder to compute" than A itself, since this functional solution is Turing reducible to A in polynomial time.

Proof (sketch). By proposition 6 and lemma 11, since A is NP-complete, prefix-sols(B,p) is Turing reducible to A, say via machine M. Then a functional solution f for A can be computed by keeping a prefix of f(x) in a local variable, and extending it a bit at a time using the machine M and the oracle A to ensure that the extension is always a prefix of a solution. ∎

We can use the same principles to characterize self-1-helpers. We define the following concepts:

13. Definition. A set A is a self-1-helper if and only if there is an oracle machine M such that for every oracle X, L(M,X) = A, and such that M with oracle A works in polynomial time.

The definition of self-1-helpers is due to Ko [7]; motivation and insights about this notion can be found there.

14. Definition. A set A in NP has self-computable witnesses if and only if there is a set B in P and a polynomial p such that (*) holds, and for which funct-sols(B,p) $\bigcap$ PF(A) $\neq \emptyset$.

Thus, for such a set, solutions can be computed with an oracle for the set. To put it in another way, given the set A as an "untrustworthy" oracle, and given an input x which is answered positively by A, the oracle allows us to produce a polynomial time checkable proof that his answer was correct.

15. Theorem. A set A is a self-1-helper if and only if has self-computable witnesses.

Proof (sketch). If A is a self-1-helper via machine M, then the following set B shows that M has self-computable witnesses:

$$B = \{ \langle x,y \rangle \ / \ y \text{ encodes a polynomially long computation of } M \text{ accepting } x \}$$

The fact that for every oracle X, L(M,X) = A, must be used to show that B fulfills (*). To show the converse, consider a machine that, on input x, uses its oracle to try to construct a polynomially long witness, by simulating the machine which computes a solution, and then uses the polynomial time set B to check that the solution was correct. If it is not, then it decides whether x is in A by simulating an exponential time machine for A. ∎

For optimization problems, instead of computing one of a set of solutions, some solution has to be selected. We consider only minimization problems. The decisional version of these NP-complete problems is: given an input x, and an integer k, is there a solution with cost smaller than k?

The functional versions of these problems, as explained above, would consist of finding a solution with a cost smaller than k. However, the practical interest is not to compute a solution below a given cost, but finding the less expensive one. It is known that for some particular cases, a polynomial time algorithm for the decisional problem provides a polynomial time algorithm for the minimization problem (see, e.g., [10], pp. 185-188). We use self-reducibility to show that for all such NP-complete sets, finding this solution is again "no much harder than" (i.e. polynomial time Turing reducible to) deciding whether a solution exists.

We define minimization NP problems in the most intuitive way, as a set of pairs

$$\{ \langle x,k\rangle \ / \ \exists\, y \ |y| \ \leq p(|x|) \ \langle x,y\rangle \in B \text{ with } cost(y) \ \leq k \}$$

where "cost" is a polynomial time computable function from $\Gamma^{\star}$ to $\Gamma^{\star}$ measuring the cost of solution y. To this set we can associate the set of functions computing optimal solutions, which depends of B, the polynomial p, and the cost function.

16.<u>Definition</u>. The set opt-sols(B,p,cost) is the set

$$\{ f \ / \ f \in \text{funct-sols}(B,p), \text{ and } \forall\, g \in \text{funct-sols}(B,p),\ \forall\, x,\ cost(f(x)) \ \leq \ cost(g(x)) \}$$

In order to show that some optimal solution is computable in polynomial time with the oracle set A, we define two "prefix" sets:

17.<u>Definition</u>. The sets prefix-sols(B,p,cost) and prefix-opt(B,p,cost) are defined as follows:

$$\text{prefix-sols}(B,p,cost) = \{ \langle x,k,z\rangle \ / \ \exists y \ |y| \ \leq \ p(|x|) \ \langle x,y\rangle \in B \text{ such that } cost(y) \ \leq \ k \text{ and } z \text{ is a prefix of } y \}$$

$$\text{prefix-opt}(B,p,cost) = \{ \langle x,z\rangle \ / \ \exists y \ |y| \ \leq \ p(|x|) \ \langle x,y\rangle \in B \text{ such that } z \text{ is a prefix of } y, \text{ and } \forall w \ |w| \ \leq \ p(|x|) \ \langle x,w\rangle \in B,\ cost(y) \ \leq \ cost(w) \}$$

Again, we have the following result, whose proof is analogous to that of lemma 11:

18.<u>Lemma</u>. The set prefix-sols(B,p,cost) is d-self-reducible.

The next theorem formalizes the standard way to prove this result for particular problems. See [10].

19.<u>Theorem</u>. The set prefix-opt(B,p,cost) is Turing reducible in polynomial time to the set prefix-sols(B,p,cost).

<u>Proof</u> (sketch). We can identify the optimal cost k in polynomial time by querying prefix-sols(B,p,cost) by searching for the maximum k such that $\langle x,k,\lambda\rangle$ is in prefix-sols(B,p,cost). This can be done in polynomial time using binary search (logarithmic in the range of k, which in turn is exponential in $|x|$, since "cost" is computable in

polynomial time). Once the optimal value of k is known, use the fact that ⟨x,z⟩ is in prefix-opt(B,p,cost) if and only if ⟨x,k,z⟩ is in prefix-sols(B,p,cost). ∎

Now we are ready to state the main result about optimization problems.

20.<u>Theorem</u>. If A is a NP-complete minimization problem, defined by the set B in P, polynomial p, and cost function "cost", then

$$\text{opt-sols}(B,p,\text{cost}) \cap PF(A) \neq \emptyset.$$

<u>Proof</u> (sketch). A function in opt-sols giving optimal solutions can be obtained from prefix-opt by extending bitwise a prefix. By theorem 19, oracle queries to prefix-opt(B,p,cost) can be answered in polynomial time with an oracle for prefix-sols(B,p,cost), which by lemma 18 and proposition 6 is in NP. Since A is NP-complete, the reduction to A can be used for solving queries to prefix-sols(B,p,cost). This allows to construct an optimal solution in polynomial time with oracle A. ∎

<u>4. Non-uniform classes and self-reducibility</u>.

This section is devoted to obtain results from the definition of wdq-self-reducibility (definition 7). Our aim is to find a framework in which all parts of theorem 1 appear as natural consequences of more general facts about such a kind of self-reducible sets. In particular, we want to show that the results about EXPTIME do not depend on this particular class, but on the fact that wdq-self-reducible complete sets exist for the class. We show that this holds for many deterministic time classes.

We consider classes of the form C/poly, as in theorem 1. In [1], the following result is shown:

21.<u>Theorem</u>. If $A \in \Sigma_i$/poly and A is ldq-self-reducible then $\Sigma_2(A)$ is included in Σ_{i+2}. In particular, $A \in \Sigma_{i+2}$.

This property was very useful, allowing to prove parts (a) and (c) of theorem 1 using the ldq-self-reducibility of SAT and QBF, as well as some other results regarding the collapse of the relativized polynomial time hierarchy. Furthermore, this concept unifies two of the three methods of [5] as particular cases of ldq-self-reducibility.

We obtain in this section all the remaining facts of theorem 1. The key point is that theorem 21 carries over to wdq-self-reducible sets.

22.__Theorem__. If $A \in \Sigma_i$/poly and A is wdq-self-reducible then $\Sigma_2(A)$ is included in Σ_{i+2}. In particular, $A \in \Sigma_{i+2}$.

__Proof__ (sketch). Membership to A can be expressed as follows: "x is in A if and only if there is a polynomially long advice string y which is correct for A up to length $|x|$, and which leads B to accept x", where B is a Σ_i predicate. The fact that y is correct for A can be checked by an universal quantifier using the self-reducing machine M of A, by a predicate of the form "for each x, y leads B to accept x if and only if M accepts x using B and y to solve the oracle queries". Two quantifiers have been added. For any $\Sigma_2(A)$ predicate, the same argument can be rephrased using the additional quantifiers to check this $\Sigma_2(A)$ predicate. ∎

All ldq-self-reducible sets lie in PSPACE, as shown in proposition 4. However, for wdq-self-reducible sets, membership in PSPACE/poly is a meaningful condition.

23.__Theorem__. If $A \in$ PSPACE/poly and A is wdq-self-reducible then $A \in$ PSPACE.

The proof is similar to that of theorem 22.

Using these two theorems, we will obtain many results from the existence of wdq-self-reducible sets in some classes broader than PSPACE. The proof relies in the following lemma, which relates wdq-self-reducibility to computations of alternating Turing machines:

24.__Lemma__. Let f be a time-constructible function majorized by some polynomial. Consider the following set:

{ $\langle m,0^n,M,I\rangle$ / M is an alternating machine, I is a configuration of M, and M starting at I accepts in alternating time m and alternating space f(n) }

This set is in the class ASPACE(f), and is wdq-self-reducible.

__Proof__ (sketch). On input $\langle m,0^n,M,I\rangle$, if I is not final and m is not 0, compute the two branching configurations I_0, I_1 of M reachable from I, query the oracle about $\langle m-1,0^n,M,I_0\rangle$ and $\langle m-1,0^n,M,I_1\rangle$, and accept according to the answers and to the state (existential or universal) of I. The membership to ASPACE(f) is straightforward. ∎

The following theorem allows to apply theorems 22 and 23 to most of the deterministic time classes between PSPACE and EXPTIME:

25.<u>Theorem</u>. Let f be as in lemma 24, and assume that f grows faster than log n. Let F be a family of functions such that $2^f \in \Theta(F)$ and $F \subset O(2^{f^{O(1)}})$. Then:

(a) $DTIME(F) \subset \Sigma_i$/poly implies $DTIME(F) \subset \Sigma_{i+2}$.

(b) $DTIME(F) \subset$ PSPACE/poly implies $DTIME(F) \subset$ PSPACE.

<u>Proof</u> (sketch). Using results of [3], it can be shown that under these hypothesis the set defined in lemma 24 is complete for DTIME(F). Therefore, it must belong to the non-uniform class in the left hand side of each implication. Since it is wdq-self-reducible, by theorems 22 and 23 it belongs to the uniform class in the right hand side of each implication. The statements follow from the closure of the uniform classes under polynomial time reductions. ∎

We can state now as a corollary parts (b) and (d) of theorem 1:

26.<u>Corollary</u>.

(a) If EXPTIME $\subset$ P/poly then EXPTIME = $\Sigma_2 \cap \Pi_2$.

(b) If EXPTIME $\subset$ PSPACE/poly then EXPTIME = PSPACE.

<u>Proof</u>. Take f(n) = n. All hypothesis of theorem 25 hold for $F = \{ 2^{n^k} \}$. Therefore, both inclusions from left to right follow from theorem 25. Left to right inclusions are immediate. ∎

Observe that this proof is the same as given in [1], in the sense that ldq-self-reducibility is a particular case of wdq-self-reducibility. Hence, all four parts of theorem 1 follow from theorem 25.

Other classes to which theorem 25 applies are presented in the following corollary. The proof is now quite easy.

27.<u>Corollary</u>. Let F be any of the following three classes:

1. $\{ 2^{c \cdot n} \ / \ c > 0 \}$,
2. $\{ n^{c \cdot \log n} \ / \ c > 0 \}$,
3. $\{ n^{\log^k n} \ / \ k > 0 \}$.

Then:

(a) If DTIME(F) $\subset$ P/poly then DTIME(F) $\subset$ $\Sigma_2 \cap \Pi_2$.

(b) If DTIME(F) $\subset$ PSPACE/poly then DTIME(F) $\subset$ PSPACE.

To end, we show how to obtain the consequence P $\neq$ NP as in theorem 1, (d), from much weaker hypothesis.

28. Corollary. Let $\varepsilon(n)$ be a slowly growing, unbounded function such that $(\log n)\cdot\varepsilon(n)$ is time-constructible, and such that DTIME($n^{\varepsilon(n)}$) $\neq$ P (such functions can be obtained as in the time hierarchy theorem). If DTIME($n^{\varepsilon(n)}$) is included in P/poly, then P $\neq$ NP.

Proof. By theorem 25, under these hypothesis, DTIME($n^{\varepsilon(n)}$) is included in Σ_2. Therefore P $\neq$ Σ_2, which implies P $\neq$ NP. ∎

Note that $\varepsilon(n)$ is assumed to be as small as desired, given that DTIME($n^{\varepsilon(n)}$) $\neq$ P. Hence, the hypothesis "DTIME($n^{\varepsilon(n)}$) is included in P/poly" can be read as "a polynomially long advice saves any time at all". The corollary shows that if this is the case, then P $\neq$ NP.

References.

[1] J.L. Balcázar, R. Book, U. Schöning: "The polynomial time hierarchy and sparse oracles". J. ACM 33, 3 (1986), 603-617.

[2] P. Berman: "Relationship between density and deterministic complexity of NP-complete languages". ICALP 1978, Springer LNCS 62, 63-71.

[3] A. Chandra, D. Kozen, L. Stockmeyer: "Alternation". J. ACM 28, 1 (1981), 114-133.

[4] S. Fortune: "A note on sparse complete sets". SIAM J. Comp. 8, 3 (1979), 431-433.

[5] R. Karp, R. Lipton: "Some connections between non-uniform and uniform complexity classes". 12 ACM STOC, 1982, 302-309.

[6] Ker-I Ko: "On self-reducibility and weak p-selectivity". J. Comp. Sys. Sci. 26, 2 (1983), 209-221.

[7] Ker-I Ko: "On helping by robust oracle machines". Manuscript (1986).

[8] S. Mahaney: "Sparse complete sets for NP: solution of a conjecture by Berman and Hartmanis". J. Comp. Sys. Sci. 25 (1982), 130-143.

[9] S. Mahaney: "Sparse sets and reducibilities". In: Studies in complexity theory, ed. R. Book, Pitman 1986.

[10] K. Mehlhorn: Data structures and algorithms, vol. 2 "Graph algorithms and NP-completeness". EATCS Monographs, Springer 1984.

[11] A. Meyer, M. Paterson: "With what frequency are apparently intractable problems difficult?". M.I.T. Technical report TM-126 (1979).

[12] C.P. Schnorr: "Optimal algorithms for self-reducible problems". ICALP 1976, ed. S. Michaelson and R. Milner, Edinburgh Univ. Press, 322-337.

[13] C.P. Schnorr: "On self-transformable combinatorial problems". Symposium on Mathematische Optimierung, Oberwolfach 1979.

[14] U. Schöning: Complexity and structure. Springer LNCS 211, 1986.

[15] A. Selman: "Remarks about natural self-reducible sets in NP and complexity measures for public key cryptosystems". Manuscript (1984).

[16] L. Valiant: "The relative complexity of checking and evaluating". Inf. Proc. Letters 5 (1976), 20-23.

Probability One Separation of the Boolean Hierarchy

*Jin-yi Cai**
Computer Science Department
Cornell University
Ithaca, NY 14853

Abstract

As a natural extension of P and NP, the Boolean closure of NP has attracted much attention recently. Many interesting properties of the class BH were discussed in [CH86] and [Wag85].

In this paper, we show that a random oracle A separates the Boolean hierarchy into an infinite hierarchy, i.e.

$$P^A \neq NP^A \neq NP^A(2) \neq \cdots \neq NP^A(k) \neq \cdots \neq BH^A$$

with probability one.

The proof technique is a combination of the "sawing" argument introduced in [CH86] and the method of Bennet and Gill [BG81] to handle the base case.

1 Introduction

The Boolean hierarchy BH is defined to be the natural completion of the class NP under Boolean operations.

The first step in the this direction was taken by C. H. Papadimitriou and M. Yannakakis in 1982 [PY82] when they defined the class D^P. This is the class of languages that can be expressed as the intersection of a language in NP with another in $coNP$ (or, equivalently as the difference between two languages in NP, hence the name D^P).

*Research supported by a Sage Fellowship and NSF grant DCR-8301766.

The class D^P, which characterizes a wide variety of optimization problems, has been intensely studied [PW85] [CM86].

As a natural completion, the Boolean hierarchy was introduced independently in [CH86] and [Wag85].

Definition 1.1

$$NP(0) = P$$

$$NP(1) = NP$$

$$NP(2) = D^P = \{L_1 \cap \overline{L_2} | L_1, L_2 \in NP\}$$

$$NP(3) = \{(L_1 \cap \overline{L_2}) \cup L_3 | L_1, L_2, L_3 \in NP\}$$

$$NP(4) = \{L_1 \cap \overline{L_2}) \cup L_3) \cap \overline{L_4} | L_1, L_2, L_3, L_4 \in NP\}$$

$$\vdots$$

$$BH = \bigcup_i NP(i)$$

As characterizations of the class BH, we have the following theorems [CH86].

Theorem 1.2 *Any of the following classes is precisely $NP(n)$, where the L_i's are in NP.*

For n even, $\{(((L_1 \cap \overline{L_2}) \cup L_3) \cdots \cup L_{n-1}) \cap \overline{L_{n-1}}\}$,

and for n odd, $\{((L_1 \cap \overline{L_2}) \cup L_3) \cdots \cup L_n\}$.

For n even, $\{(L_1 - L_2) \cup \cdots \cup (L_{n-1} - L_n)\}$,

and for n odd, $\{(L_1 - L_2) \cup \cdots \cup (L_{n-2} - L_{n-1}) \cup L_n\}$.

$\{L_1 - (L_2 - (\cdots (L_{n-1} - L_n) \cdots))\}$.

Theorem 1.3 *The Boolean hierarchy BH is the closure of NP under Boolean operations.*

Theorem 1.4 *The Boolean hierarchy is the closure of NP under polynomial time bounded truth-table reductions: $BH = \{L | L \leq^P_{btt} SAT\}$.*

Many interesting properties of BH were studied in [CH86]. We showed that there were natural complete languages in each level of the Boolean hierarchy. We exhibited relativized worlds where the Boolean hierarchy was infinite, i.e. all levels of the hierarchy were separated. This result is intriguing, as oracles making the Polynomial-time hierarchy infinite took many years to discover [Yao85].

To prove our separation result, we introduced the "sawing" technique. It places successively more stringent requirements on the oracle extensions, while seeking to *force* a desired behavior.

The "sawing" argument turned out to be quite versatile; in fact, we showed many other results by modifying our "sawing" argument. For example, for each k, we have worlds where the Boolean hierarchy extends exactly k levels, with $PSPACE$ collapsing to the $k+1$ level. (Note that the analogous statement for the Polynomial-time hierarchy is still open.) Also the Boolean hierarchy has quite amazing conections with respect to immunity, sparse sets and Exponential-time classes E vs. NE, etc.

In this paper, we prove that with probability one, a random oracle A separates the Boolean hierarchy into an infinite hierarchy. Again, we note that the analogous statement for the Polynomial-time hierarchy is open [Cai86].

The study of separation by random oracles was initiated by Bennet and Gill.

Fix an alphabet $\Sigma = \{0, 1\}$. Intuitively, a random oracle set $A \subseteq \Sigma^*$ is generated as follows. For each string $x \in \Sigma^*$, we flip a fair coin, and depending on the outcome, we put x in A or not. Formally, we may represent each A by its characteristic function, and then map to a real number in binary expansion $\in [0, 1]$. Now we define the probability measure μ on the oracle space to be the Lebesque measure on $[0, 1]$. One may easily verify that the formal definition does represent our intuitive notion of a random set as described.

Theorem 1.5 *[BG81] With probability one, $NP^A \neq coNP^A$.*

This result is very appealing intuitively. In fact probability one separation was such a strong separation that the two authors went on to propose their *Random Oracle Hypothesis*, which asserted, roughly speaking, that everything happened with probability one about complexity classes did happen in the real world. Unfortunately the Random Oracle Hypothesis was proved to be false in its stated generality [Kur82]. Nonetheless, probability one separation remained a favorite topic. Recently, Ambos-Spies has provided a thread of positive evidence in the spirit of the Random Oracle Hypothesis [Amb86].

2 Probability One Separation of BH

In this section we prove the following:

Theorem 2.1 *A random oracle separates the Boolean hierarchy with probability one,*

$$P^A \neq NP^A \neq NP^A(2) \neq \cdots \neq NP^A(k) \neq \cdots \neq BH^A.$$

The proof idea is as follows. For every k fixed, we will define a $coNP^A(k)$ language L^A. Then we prove that for some constant $\epsilon > 0$, for any oracle NP machines $N_1, \ldots, N_k$,

$$\mu\{A|[[L(N_1^A) \cap \overline{L(N_2^A)}] \cup \cdots] \cup L(N_k^A) \neq L^A\} > \epsilon.$$

(Here ϵ may depend on k, but it is independent of the machines N_i.)

By a theorem of Bennet and Gill in [BG81] (their Lemma 1), this implies

$$\mu\{A|L^A \notin NP^A(k)\} = 1.$$

Hence $NP^A(k)$ is separated from $coNP^A(k)$ with probability one. Since there are only countably many levels in the Boolean hierarchy, these infinitely many separations occur simultaneously with probability one.

The proof of theorem 2.1 is a combination of the "sawing" argument with the techniques introduced in [BG81] to handle the NP vs. $coNP$ case.

To illustrate the flavor, let's assume a test language in $coNP^A(3)$ is given,

$$L^A = \{1^n|[(\nexists x P_1^A(x)) \vee (\exists y P_2^A(y))] \wedge (\nexists z P_3^A(z)), |x| = |y| = |z| = n\}$$

where P_1^A, P_2^A and P_3^A are some easy oracle dependent properties.

To show that an $NP^A(3)$ language $[L(N_1^A) \cap \overline{L(N_2^A)}] \cup L(N_3^A)$ differs from L^A on a "nontrivial" amount of A, we proceed as follows:

Take a large n. Consider the computation $N_3^A(1^n)$ in two cases:

- Case 1. N_3^A accepts 1^n with a "nontrivial" amount of A. Then *either* it includes a "nontrivial" amount of A with $\exists z P_3^A(z)$, in which case we are done; *or* it includes a "nontrivial" amount of A with $\nexists z P_3^A(z)$. Since N_3 is a nondeterministic polynomial time machine, a single accepting path does not query too many strings. Thus for many z one may alter A so that N_3^A still accepts 1^n but $P_3^A(z)$ holds for some z of length n, resulting a "nontrivial" amount of error.

- Case 2. N_3^A rejects 1^n for all but a "trivial" amount of A. Now we concentrate on those A with the property that $\nexists z P_3^A(z)$, and the previous argument is repeated—we have essentially reduced the case to that of $L(N_1^A) \cap \overline{L(N_2^A)}$ vs. a coD^P property $(\nexists x P_1^A(x)) \vee (\exists y P_2^A(y))$.

So let's consider the computation $N_2^A(1^n)$ in two cases:

- Case 1. N_2^A accepts 1^n with a "nontrivial" amount of A with $\nexists z P_3^A(z)$. Then *either* it includes many A with $\exists y P_2^A(y)$, in which case we are done, since for these A, $1^n \in L^A$ but the $NP^A(3)$ language said no; *or* it includes many A with $\nexists y P_2^A(y)$, in which case we can demonstrate as before a "nontrivial" amount of error.

- Case 2. N_2^A rejects 1^n for all but a "trivial" amount of A with $\nexists z P_3^A(z)$. Now we concentrate on those A with the property that $\nexists z P_3^A(z) \wedge \nexists y P_2^A(y)$; and in essence we are dealing with the case NP vs. $coNP$. Apply the argument once more and we are done.

Next we will give the formal proof.

Define the characteristic function

$$\chi^A(x) = \begin{cases} 1 & \text{if } x \in A \\ 0 & \text{otherwise} \end{cases}$$

Define $\chi_k^A(x) = \chi^A(x0101^k) \cdots \chi^A(x01^{|x|}01^k)$. We note that if $x01^i01^k = y01^j01^l$, then $k = l$, $i = j$ and $x = y$.

Thus for A random,

$$\{\chi_k^A(x) | k = 1, 2, 3, \ldots, x \in \Sigma^*\}$$

is a family of independent random variables, with the probability distribution

$$\forall k, x, Prob.(\chi_k^A(x) = z) = \frac{1}{2^{|x|}}$$

for all $z \in \Sigma^*$, $|z| = |x|$.

Fix any k and length n, we define

$$\begin{aligned} C_{k,n}^0 &= \{A | (\forall x)[\chi_k^A(x) \neq 1^n]\}, \\ C_{k,n}^1 &= \{A | (\exists x)[x \neq 1^n \wedge \chi_k^A(x) = 1^n \wedge (\forall y \neq x)[\chi_k^A(y) \neq 1^n]\}. \end{aligned}$$

We will abbreviate $C_{k,n}^0$ as C_k^0 or C^0 when context permits. Similarly we abbreviate $C_{k,n}^1$ as C_k^1 or C^1.

Let $m = 2^n$, we note that

$$\begin{aligned} \mu(C_{k,n}^0) &= \begin{pmatrix} m \\ 0 \end{pmatrix} \left(\frac{1}{m}\right)^0 \left(\frac{m-1}{m}\right)^m = \left(1 - \frac{1}{m}\right)^m, \\ \mu(C_{k,n}^1) &= \begin{pmatrix} m-1 \\ 1 \end{pmatrix} \left(\frac{1}{m}\right)^1 \left(\frac{m-1}{m}\right)^{m-1} = \left(1 - \frac{1}{m}\right)^m. \end{aligned}$$

Thus $\mu(C_{k,n}^0) = \mu(C_{k,n}^1) \to 1/e$, as $n \to \infty$.

We also define $Z = \{z | |z| = n \wedge z \neq 1^n\}$ for any fixed n, which we endow with the discrete measure ν: $\nu(\{z\}) = 1$ for any $z \in Z$.

Thus the Cartesian product $C^0 \times Z$ and $C^1 \times Z$ are equipped with the a product measure $\mu \times \nu$.

We define

$$\begin{aligned} \varphi : C^0 \times Z &\longrightarrow C^1 \times Z \\ (A, z) &\longmapsto (A_z, u) \end{aligned}$$

where $A_z = A \cup \{01^i01^k | 1 \leq i \leq |x|\}$ and $u = \chi_k^A(z)$.

Note that if $A \in C^0$, then $\forall z \in Z$, $A_z \in C^1$ with the unique z such that $\chi_k^A(z) = 1^n$, and $u = \chi_k^A(z) \neq 1^n$.

We show that φ is a measure isomorphism (one-to-one, onto and measure preserving).

Denote $C_k^0[z \to u] = \{A \in C_k^0 | \chi_k^A(z) = u\}$, and similarly $C_k^1[z \to 1^n] = \{A \in C_k^1 | \chi_k^A(z) = 1^n\}$. We have the following disjoint unions:

$$\begin{aligned} C^0 \times Z &= \bigcup_{z \in Z} (C^0 \times \{z\}) \\ &= \bigcup_{z \in Z} (\bigcup_{u \in Z} (C^0[z \to u] \times \{z\})) \\ C^1 \times Z &= \bigcup_{z \in Z} (C^1[z \to 1^n] \times Z) \\ &= \bigcup_{z \in Z} (\bigcup_{u \in Z} (C^1[z \to 1^n] \times \{u\})) \end{aligned}$$

Since the Lebesque measure is shift-invariant, φ maps $C_{k,n}^0[z \to u] \times \{z\}$ 1-1 onto $C_{k,n}^1[z \to 1^n] \times \{u\}$ preserving the measure $\mu \times \nu$. Thus φ is a measure isomorphism from $C^0 \times Z$ to $C^1 \times Z$.

Fix any oracle NP Turing machine N^A, its computation path can query at most polynomially many strings.

$$\begin{aligned} \text{Let} \quad C_{k,n}^{0,+} &= \{A \in C_{k,n}^0 | N^A(1^n) \text{ accepts } \} \\ C_{k,n}^{1,+} &= \{A \in C_{k,n}^1 | N^A(1^n) \text{ accepts } \} \end{aligned}$$

We have the following fact [BG81].

Lemma 2.2 *For some sequence $\varepsilon_n \to 0$,*

$$\mu(C_{k,n}^{1,+}) \geq (1 - \varepsilon_n) \cdot \mu(C_{k,n}^{0,+}).$$

Proof

$$\begin{aligned} \mu(C^{1,+}) &= \frac{\mu \times \nu(C^{1,+} \times Z)}{\nu(Z)} \\ &= \frac{1}{\nu(Z)} \cdot \int_{C^1 \times Z} \chi^{C^{1,+} \times Z} d(\mu \times \nu) \\ &= \frac{1}{\nu(Z)} \cdot \int_{C^0 \times Z} \chi^{C^{1,+} \times Z}(\varphi(A, z)) d(\mu \times \nu) \\ &\geq \frac{1}{\nu(Z)} \cdot \int_{C^{0,+} \times Z} \chi^{C^{1,+} \times Z}(\varphi(A, z)) d(\mu \times \nu) \\ &= \frac{1}{\nu(Z)} \cdot \int_{C^{0,+}} d\mu \int_Z \chi^{C^{1,+} \times Z}(\varphi(A, z)) d\nu \end{aligned}$$

where the third equality follows from φ being measure preserving, and the fifth equality is by *Fubini's Theorem*.

Since any accepting path of N^A can only be dependent on polynomially many strings of A, it follows that uniformly for all $A \in C_{k,n}^{0,+}$, for asymptotically all $z \in Z$, A_z given by $\varphi(A, z)$ does not alter the accepting computation, i.e. $A_z \in C_{k,n}^{1,+}$.

Thus for some $\epsilon_n \to 0$,

$$\forall A \in C^{0,+}, \int_Z \chi^{C^{1,+}\times Z}(\varphi(A, z))d\nu \geq (1 - \epsilon_n) \cdot \nu(Z).$$

(Here the ϵ_n is uniform for A.)

Hence, $\mu(C^{1,+}) \geq (1 - \epsilon_n) \cdot \mu(C^{0,+})$. **QED**

Since the family $\{\chi_k^A(x) | k = 1, 2, 3, \ldots, x \in \Sigma^*\}$ is independent, we have the following:

Corollary 2.3 *For any property P and any set of indices $\{i_1, \ldots, i_j\} \not\ni k$,*

$$\mu(C_{k,n}^{1,+}(P)) \geq (1 - \epsilon_n) \cdot \mu(C_{k,n}^{0,+}(P))$$

where for $C = C_{k,n}^{0,+}$ or $C_{k,n}^{1,+}$, $C(P) = \{A \in C | P(\chi_{i_1}^A, \ldots, \chi_{i_j}^A)\}$.

We are ready to prove Theorem 2.1. We will prove for every k, $NP^A(k) \neq coNP^A(k)$ with probability one. Thus

$$P^A \neq NP^A \neq NP^A(2) \neq \cdots \neq NP^A(k) \neq \cdots \neq BH^A$$

with probability one.

Fix any k. Without loss of generality, assume k is an odd number. (By our downward separation result in [CH86], $NP^A(k) \neq coNP^A(k) \Longrightarrow \forall l \leq k, NP^A(l) \neq coNP^A(l)$.) Let's define a test language

$$\begin{aligned} L^A &= \{1^n | \{\cdots\{(\nexists x_1)[\chi_1^A(x_1) = 1^n] \vee (\exists x_2)[\chi_2^A(x_2) = 1^n]\} \wedge \cdots\} \\ &\quad \wedge (\nexists x_k)[\chi_k^A(x_k) = 1^n]\}. \end{aligned}$$

Clearly $L^A \in coNP^A(k)$, for all A.

We prove that for any oracle NP machines $N_1, \ldots, N_k$,

$$\mu\{A | [[L(N_1^A) \cap \overline{L(N_2^A)}] \cup \cdots] \cup L(N_k^A) \neq L^A\} > \frac{1}{12^{k+1}}.$$

For the given machines, we choose a large n so that $\epsilon_n < 1/4$. Consider the following procedure.

$Res = \mathcal{P}(\Sigma^*)$, the power set of Σ^*

$s_0 = 0$

For $s = k$ to 1 do

Let $C^{0,+} = \{A \in C^0_{s,n} | N^A_s(1^n) \text{ accepts } \} \cap Res$

$C^{1,+} = \{A \in C^1_{s,n} | N^A_s(1^n) \text{ accepts } \} \cap Res$

If $\mu\{A \in Res | N^A_s(1^n) \text{ accepts } \} > \frac{1}{2^{2s}} \cdot \frac{1}{3^k}$

then $s_0 = s$

If $\mu(C^{0,+}) \leq \frac{1}{2^{2s+1}} \cdot \frac{1}{3^k}$

then quit

else $\mu(C^{1,+}) \geq (1-\epsilon_n) \cdot \mu(C^{0,+}) > \frac{3}{4} \cdot \frac{1}{2^{2s+1}} \cdot \frac{1}{3^k}$, quit

else $Res = Res \cap \{A | (\nexists x_s)[\chi^A_s(x_s) = 1^n]\}$

end. {For}

We Observe that when the procedure terminates, either $s_0 > 0$, indicating a breaking point, or $s_0 = 0$, the initial value.

Suppose $s_0 > 0$, then $Res = \{A | (\forall i > s_0)[(\nexists x_i)[\chi^A_i(x_i) = 1^n]]\}$. We have been assured that

$$\mu\{A \in Res | (\exists x_{s_0})[\chi^A_{s_0}(x_{s_0}) = 1^n] \wedge (N^A_{s_0}(1^n) \text{ accepts })\} > \frac{3}{4} \cdot \frac{1}{2^{2s_0+1}} \cdot \frac{1}{3^k},$$

while

$$\mu\{A \in Res | (\exists s > s_0)[N^A_s(1^n) \text{ accepts }]\} \leq \sum_{s>s_0} \frac{1}{2^{2s}} \cdot \frac{1}{3^k}.$$

A simple calculation shows that

$$\mu\{A \in Res | \mathcal{E}\} > \frac{1}{12^{k+1}},$$

where $\mathcal{E}$ stands for the event

$$(\exists x_{s_0})[\chi^A_{s_0}(x_{s_0}) = 1^n] \wedge (N^A_{s_0}(1^n) \text{ accepts }) \wedge (\nexists s > s_0)[N^A_s(1^n) \text{ accepts }].$$

But on those A, the $NP^A(k)$ machine differs from L^A.

Now let's assume $s_0 = 0$, then $Res = \{A|(\forall i, 1 \leq i \leq k)[(\nexists x_i)[\chi_i^A(x_i) = 1^n]]\}$, and we have

$$\mu(Res) \approx \left(\frac{1}{e}\right)^k,$$

$$\mu\{A \in Res|(\exists s, 1 \leq s \leq k)[N_s^A(1^n) \text{ accepts }]\} \leq \sum_{s=1}^{k} \frac{1}{2^{2s}} \cdot \frac{1}{3^k} < \frac{1}{3^k}.$$

Hence, the $NP^A(k)$ machine again differs from L^A for a set of A of measure greater than

$$\mu(Res) - \frac{1}{3^k} > \frac{1}{12^k}.$$

The proof is completed.

3 Conclusions

We have the following corollaries.

Corollary 3.1 *With probability one, there is no complete language for the whole Boolean hierarchy (under many-one p-reductions).*

Corollary 3.2 *The Boolean hierarchy BH is properly contained in Δ_2^P in almost all relativized worlds.*

We note that the analogous statement of our Theorem 2.1 for the Polynomial hierarchy is still open [Cai86].

Conjecture 3.3 *The Polynomial hierarchy PH extends infinitely in almost all relativized worlds.*

Regarding the Random Oracle Hypothesis, although the original *ROH* was disproved, the author believes a more careful formulation should be searched. We propose as an open problem to formulate a more sensible *ROH*.

Acknowledgement

The author is very thankful to Professor Juris Hartmanis and Lane Hemachandra for invaluable advice and discussions.

References

[Amb86] Klaus Ambos-Spies. Randomness, relativization, and polynomial reducibilities. In *Structure in Complexity Theory*, pages 23–34, Springer-Verlag *Lecture Notes in Computer Science #223*, 1986.

[BG81] C. Bennet and J. Gill. Relative to a random oracle A, $P^A \neq NP^A$ with probability 1. *SIAM J. on Computing*, 10:96–113, 1981.

[Cai86] J. Cai. With probability one, a random oracle separates $PSPACE$ from the polynomial-time hierarchy. In *STOC*, pages 21–29, 1986.

[CH86] J. Cai and Lane A. Hemachandra. The Boolean hierarchy: hardware over NP. In *Structure in Complexity Theory*, pages 105–124, Springer-Verlag *Lecture Notes in Computer Science #223*, 1986.

[CM86] J. Cai and G. Meyer. Graph minimal uncolorability is D^P-complete. *SIAM Journal on Computing*, 1986. To appear.

[Hel84] H. Heller. Relativized polynomial hierarchies extending two levels. *Mathematical Systems Theory*, 17:71–84, 1984.

[Kur82] S. A. Kurtz. On the random oracle hypothesis. In *STOC*, pages 224–230, 1982.

[PW85] C. H. Papadimitriou and D. Wolfe. The complexity of facets resolved. In *FOCS*, pages 74–78, 1985.

[PY82] C. H. Papadimitriou and M. Yannakakis. The complexity of facets (and some facets of complexity). In *STOC*, pages 255–260, 1982.

[Wag85] K. Wagner. On the boolean closure of NP. In *Proc. of the 1985 International Conference on Fundamentals of Computation Theory*, pages 485–493, Springer-Verlag *Lecture Notes in Computer Science* , 1985.

[Wag86] K. Wagner. More complicated questions about maxima and minima, and some closures of NP. In *Prod. of ICALP '86*, Springer-Verlag *Lecture Notes in Computer Science* , 1986.

[Wec85] G. Wechsung. *More about the Closure of NP*. Technical Report TR N/85/43, Friedrich-Schiller-Universität, December 1985.

[Yao85] A. Yao. Separating the polynomial-time hierarchy by oracles. In *FOCS*, pages 1–10, 1985.

[Yes83] Y. Yesha. On certain polynomial-time truth-table reducibilities of complete sets to sparse sets. *SIAM Journal on Computing*, 12(3):411–425, 1983.

REVERSAL COMPLEXITY OF MULTICOUNTER AND MULTIHEAD MACHINES

Juraj Hromkovič
Dept. of Theoretical Cybernetics and Mathematical Informatics
Comenius University, 842 15 Bratislava, Czechoslovakia

Abstract. It is proved that the family of languages recognized by one-way real-time nondeterministic multicounter machines with constant number of counter reversals is not closed under complementation.

The best known lower bound $\Omega(n^{1/3}/\log_2 n)$ on the complexity measure REVERSALS·SPACE·PARALLELISM of multihead alternating machines is improved to $\Omega(n^{1/2}/\log_2 n)$. Several strongest lower bounds for different complexity measures are direct consequences of this result.

1. INTRODUCTION

This paper consists of two independent parts. The first one devoted to the reversal complexity of multicounter machines is involved in Section 2, and the second one devoted to the reversal complexity of multihead machines is included in Section 3.

Unrestricted one-way deterministic two-counter machines accept all recursively enumerable sets [4]. So far various types of restricted multicounter machines have been considered to define proper subclasses (see, for example [1,2,5-8,11,13]). We shall consider one-way nondeterministic k-counter real-time machines - 1-kC-NTIME(id), and this same ones with constant [f(n), for a function f: $N \to N$] number of reversals - 1-kC-NTIME-REV(id,Const) [1-kC-NTIME-REV(id,f(n))]. On the other hand 1-kC-NREV(f(n)) denotes one-way nondeterministic k-counter machines with f(n) reversal number bound and no restriction on the time complexity. We use the notation of Wagner and Wechsung [13], where the formal definitions can be found. Let

$$\text{1-multiC-M} = \bigcup_{k \in N} \text{1-kC-M} ,$$

for $M \in$ {NTIME(id), NTIME-REV(id,Const), NTIME-REV(id,f(n)), NREV(f(n))}.

Let, for a machine type M, $\mathcal{L}$(M) denote the family of languages recognized by machines of type M. It is known [13] that $\mathcal{L}$(1-multiC-NTIME(id)) and $\mathcal{L}$(1-multiC-NTIME-REV(id,Const)) are AFLs.

The only stated open problem [13] concerning the closure properties of these language families is whether they are closed under complementation. We give the negative answer on this question for $\mathcal{L}$(1-multiC-NTIME-REV(id,Const)). In fact, we prove a more powerful result: $\mathcal{L}$(1-multiC-NTIME-REV(id,f(n))) is not closed under complementation for any function $1 \leq f(n) = o(n)$.

The second problem considered in this paper is devoted to proving nontrivial lower bound for a large family of universal computing models. We consider the multihead alternating machines, MAMs, introduced in [9] as parallel computing model. It consists of a separate input tape having arbitrary large (but fixed) number of heads and a number of internal configurations. Because no restriction is given on the organisation of the working space MAMs cover the alternating multihead multitape multidimensional Turing machines, alternating RAMs, etc..

We study the complexity measures REVERSALS, SPACE, and PARALELLISM as defined in [9]. Informally, for a multihead alternating machine A, the space complexity $S_A(n) = \log_2(C_A(n))$, where $C_A(n)$ is the number of all internal configurations of A used in all accepting computation trees of A on inputs of the length n. The reversal complexity $R_A(n)$ is the maximum of input head reversals used in all sequential subcomputations of the accepting computation trees of A on inputs of length n. The parallel complexity is the maximum of universal configurations (branchings) used in all accepting computation trees of A on inputs of the length n .

The lower bound REVERSALS·SPACE·PARALLELISM (RSP) $\in \Omega(n^{1/3}/\log_2 n)$ was established for MAMs recognizing the language $(L_R)^*$ (where L_R is the reversal language introduced in [12]) in [9]. We note that no tight upper bound for the recognition of $(L_R)^*$ is known, and we conjecture that no tight upper bound can be obtained. We shall prove RSP $\in \Omega(n^{1/2}/\log_2 n)$ and RSP $\in O(n^{1/2})$ for the recognition of another language S. The strongest lower bounds $\Omega(n^{1/2}/\log_2 n)$ on reversal (RP) complexity of two-way nondeterministic (alternating) multihead finite automata, and several further lower bounds for another computing models are direct consequences of this result.

2. MULTICOUNTER MACHINES

Let us consider the following languages:

$$L = \{a^{j_1}b^{j_1}a^{j_2}b^{j_2} \ldots a^{j_k}b^{j_k} \mid k \geq 1,\ j_i \in N \text{ for } i = 1,\ldots,k\},$$

$L_E = \{a^{i_1}ba^{i_2}ba^{i_3}b \ldots ba^{i_m}bba^r \mid m,r \in N,\ i_k \in N$ for $k = 1,\ldots,m$, and there are $z,l \in \{1,\ldots,m\}$ that $i_l + i_z = r\}$.

Clearly, $L^C = \{a^{i_1}b^{j_1}a^{i_2}b^{j_2} \ldots a^{i_k}b^{j_k} \mid k \in N,\ i_1, j_k \in N \cup \{0\},\ i_r, j_r \in N$ for $r = 1,\ldots,k$, and there is a $z \in \{1,\ldots,k\}$ such that $i_z \neq j_z\}$, $(L_E)^C = R_1 \cup L_1$, where $R_1 = ((a^+b)^+ba^+)^C$ and $L_1 = \{a^{i_1}ba^{i_2}b \ldots a^{i_m}bba^r \mid m,r \in N,\ i_k \in N$ for $k = 1,\ldots,m$, and for all $l,z \in \{1,\ldots,m\}$: $i_l + i_z \neq r\}$.

It can be easy seen that the following proposition holds.

Lemma 2.1 The languages L_E and L^C belong to $\mathcal{L}$(1-1C-NTIME-REV(id,Const)).

Now, let us show that L is too hard to be recognized by one-way nondeterministic multicounter machines with o(n) number of reversals.

One of the proof techniques used in this paper is the technique of cycles developed for one-way multicounter machines in [7]. It is based on the study of computations in which a multicounter machine reads a group of identical symbols whose number is greater than the number of states. Clearly, there has to be a state q which will be entered twice or more in different configurations in this part of computations. If no futher state q and no two equal states different from q occur in the part of computation from q to q then we say that this part of the computation is a cycle with state characteristic q, reading head characteristic - the number (positive or zero) of symbols over which the reading head moves to the right in this cycle, and counter characteristic, for each counter, which is the difference between the counter contents at the beginning and at the end of the cycle. Obviously, for a one-way multicounter machine A with s states and k counters, the number of cycles with different characteristics is bounded by $s \cdot s(2s+1)^k$.

Lemma 2.2 Let f be a function from N to N such that $f(n) = o(n)$. Then $L \notin \mathcal{L}$(1-multiC-NREV(f(n))) .

Sketch of the proof. We make the proof by contradiction. Let, for a $k \in N$, there be a 1-kC-NREV(f(n)) machine A recognizing L. Let A have s states, and $d = s^2(s+1)^k$. Let us consider the input word

$$x = (a^{s+1}b^{s+1})^{(s+1)(d+1)(k+1)f(n)}a^t b^t$$

of the length $n = (2s+2)(d+1)(s+1)(k+1)f(n) + 2t$. Since $f(n) = o(n)$, we can assume, for sufficiently large n, that such a word exists. Using a similar proof technique as in [8] it can be proved that there is a subword

$$y = (a^{s+1}b^{s+1})^{d+1}$$

of x such that the part C_y of the accepting computation on x fulfils the following conditions:

1, C_y involves no cycle with reading characteristic 0 ,

2, No counter is reversed in C_y ,

3, No counter is emptied in C_y .

There is at least one cycle in the part of computation C_y on each subword a^{s+1} of y. Since the number of cycles is bounded by d there are some cycles p_1 and p_2 in C_y with the same characteristics which are situated in two parts of C_y on two different groups of a's of y. Let the reading head characteristic of p_1 and p_2 be $m \geq 0$.

Choosing m symbols a from the first group of a's and pumping a^m to the second group of a's we obtain a word x' which does not belong to L. Using the properties 1, 2, and 3 of C_y an accepting computation on x' can be constructed in the same way as in 8 . □

So, we have a language L^C which can be recognized in real time with one counter using one reversal, and whose complement L cannot be recognized in arbitrary time with arbitrary large number of counters using at most o(n) reversals. One of the direct consequences of Lemmas 2.2 and 2.1 is the following negative answer on the open problem of Wagner and Wechsung [13].

Theorem 2.3 The families of languages $\mathcal{L}$(1-kC-NTIME-REV(id,Const)), for any $k \in N$, and $\mathcal{L}$(1-multiC-NTIME-REV(id,Const)) are not closed under complementation.

We note that we were not able to solve the second open problem [13] asking whether $\mathcal{L}$(1-multiC-NTIME(id)) is closed under complementation. But, we conjecture that the following proposition holds.

Proposition 2.4 $(L_E)^C \notin \mathcal{L}$(1-multiC-NTIME($n^c$)) for any $c \in N$.

3. MULTIHEAD ALTERNATING MACHINES

To prove the lower bound on the complexity measure REVERSALS·SPACE ·PARALLELISM (RSP) we shall consider the language S used to obtain lower bounds on TIME·SPACE·(PARALLELISM) in [3,9]. Let $\oplus : \{0,1\}^2 \to \{0,1\}$ denote the Boolean sum operator.

$$S = \{ x_1 2^m x_2 2^m \ldots 2^m x_r 2^z \mid x_i \in \{0,1\}^m , \sum_{i=1}^{r}\oplus x_i = 0^m , m \geq 1, r \geq 1, z \geq 1 \} ,$$

where $\sum_{i=1}^{r}\oplus = 0^m$ means that $x_{1j} \oplus x_{2j} \oplus \ldots \oplus x_{rj} = 0$ for $j = 1,\ldots,m$

and $x_i = x_{i1}x_{i2} \dots x_{im}$ for $i = 1,\dots,r$. To obtain tight lower and upper bounds we shall consider some special subsets of S defined in the following way. Let f and g be some functions from N to N such that $n - 2f(n)g(n) \geq 0$ for all $n \in N$. Then

$$S(f,g) = \{x_1 2^{g(n)} x_2 2^{g(n)} \dots 2^{g(n)} x_{f(n)} 2^{g(n)+z(n)} \mid n \in N,\ x_i \in \{0,1\}^{g(n)}$$

$$\text{for } i = 1,\dots,f(n),\ \sum_{i=1}^{f(n)}{}^{\oplus}\ x_i = 0^{g(n)},\ z(n) = n - 2f(n)g(n)\}.$$

Theorem 3.1 Let f and g be functions from N to N such that $f(n) = \lfloor n^{1/2} \rfloor$ and $g(n) = \lfloor n^{1/2}/2 \rfloor$. Let A be a MAM fulfilling $S(f,g) \subseteq L(A) \subseteq S$. Then

(a) $R_A(n) S_A(n) P_A(n) \in \Omega(n^{1/2}/\log_2 n)$

(b) If $S_A(n) \geq \log_2 n$ then $R_A(n) S_A(n) P_A(n) \in \Omega(n^{1/2})$.

Sketch of the proof. The proof is done by contadiction. Let, for a $k \in N$, A be a k-head alternating machine such that $S(f,g) \subseteq L(A) \subseteq S$ and $R_A(n) S_A(n) P_A(n) \notin \Omega(n^{1/2}/\log_2 n)$ [$\Omega(n^{1/2})$ in the case $S_A(n) \geq \log_2 n$]. We shall show that A accepts a word $y \notin S$ what proves Theorem 3.1 .

Since $R_A(n) S_A(n) P_A(n) \notin \Omega(n^{1/2}/\log_2 n)$ [$\Omega(n^{1/2})$ if $S_A(n) \geq \log_2 n$] there is a positive integer s with the following properties:

(i) $dk^3 P_A(s) R_A(s) + 1 < \lfloor s^{1/2} \rfloor = f(s)$

(ii) $(k\log_2(s+2) + S_A(s))4kdR_A(s)P_A(s) + 1 < \lfloor s^{1/2}/2 \rfloor = g(s)$,

where d is the maximal possible branching from a universal state of A.

Let us consider the accepting computation trees on the words

$$w = x_1 2^m x_2 2^m \dots 2^m x_r 2^{m+z} \in S_s(f,g) .$$

For any $i,j = 1,\dots,r$, $i < j$, and any accepting computation tree D on w, we shall say that x_i and x_j are compared in D iff there is a configuration in D in which one of the heads is positioned on x_i and another head is positioned on x_j . Using the property (i) of s we prove the following fact.

Fact 3.1.1 Let D be an accepting computation on a word $w \in S_s(f,g)$. Then there exist positive integers $i,j \in \{1,\dots,f(s)\}$ that x_i and x_j are not compared in D.

The proof of Fact 3.1.1 A pair of heads can compare at most $kf(s)$ pairs of subwords of w in any part of a sequential computation without reversals. So, k heads can compare at most

$$\binom{k}{2} kR_A(s)f(s) \leq k^3 R_A(s) f(s)$$

in any sequential computation from the root of D to a leaf of D. Since the number of leaves is bounded by $dP_A(s)$ we obtain that there are at most $dk^3R_A(s)P_A(s)f(s)$ pairs of subwords (x_h,x_v) compared in D. The property (ii) of s and the fact that the number of pairs (x_h,x_v) is

$$\binom{f(s)}{2} \leq f^2(s)/16$$

completes the proof of Fact 3.1.1 .

The proof of Theorem 3.1 continued. Let, for each $w \in S_s(f,g)$, D_w be a fixed accepting computation tree on w. The number of words in $S_s(f,g)$ is $2^{g(s)(f(s)-1)}$. Using Fact 3.1.1 we obtain that there exist positive integers a and b, $1 \leq a < b \leq f(s)$, such that the subwords x_a and x_b are not compared in at least

$$2^{g(s)(f(s)-1)}/f^2(s)$$

accepting computation trees on different words in $S_s(f,g)$.

Let, for any accepting computation tree D_w on $w \in S_s(f,g)$ a prominent configuration be the configuration in which one of the heads is positioned on the first or the last symbol of x_a (or x_b) after crossing the whole subword $2^{g(s)}$ or x_a (x_b) in the previous part of the computation. The pattern of the word w, for each word $w \in S_s(f,g)$, is the tree $\bar{D}_w$ with the following properties:

(I) The root of $\bar{D}_w$ is the root of D_w .

(II) The rest nodes of $\bar{D}_w$ are the nodes of D_w corresponding to the prominent configurations.

(III) The nodes u and v are connected by an edge in $\bar{D}_w$ iff D_w involves a path from u to v that involves no node labelled by a prominent configuration.

Now, the following proposition can be proved using similar considerations as in [9].

Fact 3.1.2 The number of all different patterns of the words in $S_s(f,g)$ is bounded by

$$e(s) = 2^{(k\log_2(s+2) + S_A(s))4kdR_A(s)P_A(s)} .$$

Using the property (ii) of s we can prove

$$e(s)f^2(s) < 2^{g(s)} - 1 .$$

So, for $m = g(s)$, we have two words

$$u = x_1 2^m \ldots 2^m x_{a-1} 2^m x_a 2^m x_{a+1} \ldots 2^m x_{b-1} 2^m x_b 2^m x_{b+1} \ldots 2^m x_{f\,s}\; 2^{m+z(s)}$$

$$\acute{u} = x_1 2^m \ldots 2^m x_{a-1} 2^m \acute{x}_a 2^m x_{a+1} \ldots 2^m x_{b-1} 2^m \acute{x}_b 2^m x_{b+1} \ldots 2^m x_{f\,s}\; 2^{m+z(s)}$$

with the following properties:

(1) u and $\acute{u}$ belong to $S_s(f,g)$

(2) $x_a \neq \acute{x}_a$ and $x_b \neq \acute{x}_b$

(3) u and $\acute{u}$ have the same pattern $\bar{D} = \bar{D}_{\acute{u}} = \bar{D}_u$

(4) the subwords x_a and x_b ($\acute{x}_a$ and $\acute{x}_b$) are not compared in

D_u $(D_{\acute{u}})$.

Now, using the properties (1), (3), and (4) of u and $\acute{u}$, and a similar technique as in [9,10] an accepting computation tree on the word

$$y = x_1 2^m x_2 \dots 2^m x_{a-1} 2^m x_a 2^m x_{a+1} \dots 2^m x_{b-1} 2^{m} \acute{x}_b 2^m x_{b+1} \dots 2^m x_{f(s)} 2^{m+z(s)}$$

can be constructed. Since (2) holds $y \notin S$. This completes the proof. □

Corollary 3.2 Let A be a multihead nondeterministic machine such that $S(\lfloor n^{1/2} \rfloor, \lfloor n^{1/2}/2 \rfloor) \subseteq L(A) \subseteq S$. Then

(a) $R_A(n) S_A(n) \in \Omega(n^{1/2}/\log_2 n)$

(b) If $S_A(n) \geq \log_2 n$ then $R_A(n) S_A(n) \in \Omega(n^{1/2})$.

Corollary 3.3 Let A be a two-way alternating multihead finite automaton such that $S(\lfloor n^{1/2} \rfloor, \lfloor n^{1/2}/2 \rfloor) \subseteq L(A) \subseteq S$. Then

$$R_A(n) P_A(n) \in \Omega(n^{1/2}/\log_2 n).$$

Corollary 3.4 Let A be a two-way nondeterministic multihead finite automaton such that $S(\lfloor n^{1/2} \rfloor, \lfloor n^{1/2}/2 \rfloor) \subseteq L(A) \subseteq S$. Then

$$R_A(n) \in \Omega(n^{1/2}/\log_2 n) .$$

Corollary 3.5 Let A be a one-way alternating multihead finite automaton such that $S(\lfloor n^{1/2} \rfloor, \lfloor n^{1/2}/2 \rfloor) \subseteq L(A) \subseteq S$. Then

$$P_A(n) \in \Omega(n^{1/2}/\log_2 n) .$$

It is no problem to show that there is an on-line deterministic multitape Turing machines recognizing $S(\lfloor n^{1/2} \rfloor, \lfloor n^{1/2}/2 \rfloor)$ in linear time and $O(n^{1/2})$ space, or two-way deterministic multihead finite automaton recognizing $S(\lfloor n^{1/2} \rfloor, \lfloor n^{1/2}/2 \rfloor)$ with $O(n^{1/2})$ number of heads reversals. So, one can see that using these tight upper bounds several hierarchy results for the complexity measures of different computing devices can be established. Because of the many possibilities to prove tight upper bound, and of the very large number of following hierarchy results we omit the formulation of them.

Dymond and Cook [14] state the extended parallel computation thesis claiming that space and the number of reversals of sequential computations (deterministic multitape Turing machines) are simultaneously polynomially related to the requirements on time and hardware of parallel computing models (for example, of parallel RAM's). Using this theses we can formulate the following result.

Theorem 3.6 For any parallel machine class fulfilling the extended parallel computation thesis, there is a constant b such that

$$\text{PARALLEL TIME} \cdot \text{HARDWARE} \in \Omega(n^b)$$

for the recognition of the language S .

Concluding this Section we give a stronger lower bound on RSP of the MAMs using n^c $(0 < c < 1)$ space .

Theorem 3.7 Let, for a $c: 0 < c < 1$, f_c and g_c be functions from N to N such that $f_c(n) = \lfloor n^{(1-c)/2} \rfloor$ and $g_c(n) = \lfloor n^{(1+c)/2} \rfloor$. Let A be a MAM fulfilling $S(f_c, g_c) \subseteq L(A) \subseteq S$ and $S_A(n) \geq n^c$. Then

$$R_A(n) S_A(n) P_A(n) \in \Omega(n^{(1+c)/2}) .$$

Sketch of the proof. We prove this result by contradiction. Let, for a $k \in N$, A be a k-head alternating machine such that $S(f_c, g_c) \subseteq L(A)$, and $R_A(n) S_A(n) P_A(n) \notin \Omega(n^{(1+c)/2})$, $S_A(n) \geq n^c$. Following the proof of Theorem 3.1 we shall show that A accepts a word $y \notin S$.

Since $R_A(n) S_A(n) P_A(n) \notin \Omega(n^{(1+c)/2})$ there is a positive integer s such that

(iii) $64k^3 d S_A(s) R_A(s) P_A(s) + 1 < \lfloor s^{(1+c)/2}/2 \rfloor = g_c(s)$

(iv) $s^c \geq k \log_2(s+2)$

hold (the constant d is the maximal number of branches following from a universal state of A) . Since $S_A(s) \geq s^c$ the inequality (iii) implies

(v) $32k^3 d R_A(s) P_A(s) < \lfloor s^{(1+c)/2}/s^c \rfloor = \lfloor s^{(1-c)/2} \rfloor = f_c(s)$.

Using (v) we obtain that Fact 3.1.1 holds in this proof too. Following (iv) and the proof technique in [9,10] one can prove that the number of all different patterns (we consider that the notions - prominent configuration and pattern are defined in the same way as in the sketch of the proof of Theorem 3.1) of the words in $S_s(f_c, g_c)$ is bounded by

$$e(s) = 2^{8kd S_A(s) R_A(s) P_A(s)} .$$

Using (iii) one can simply prove

$$e(s) f^2(s) < 2^{g_c(s)} - 1 .$$

Now, the proof can be completed in the same way as in Theorem 3.1 . □

Corollary 3.8 Let A be a nondeterministic multihead machine fulfilling $S(f_c, g_c) \subseteq L(A) \subseteq S$ and $S_A(n) \geq n^c$ [$S_A(n) \in \Omega(n^c)$ and $S_A(n) \in O(n^c)$]. Then

$$R_A(n) S_A(n) \in \Omega(n^{(1+c)/2}) \quad [R_A(n) \in \Omega(n^{(1-c)/2})].$$

Noting that the lower bound established in Theorem 3.7 and Corollary 3.8 are optimal, and that several hierarchy results follows from this fact we conclude the paper.

ACKNOWLEDGEMENT

Using this oportunity I would like to express my deep complement and thanks to Professor Wagner and to Professor Wechsung for writing the excellent monograph "Computational Complexity" that is the best information source covering the computational complexity of uniform computing models that I know.

REFERENCES

1, Chan, T.: Reversal complexity of counter machines. Proc. IEEE STOC 1981, IEEE, New York, pp.146-157.

2, Ďuriš, P. - Galil, Z.: On reversal bounded counter machines and on pushdown automata with a bound on the size of the pushdown store. Inform. Control 54, 3, 1982, 217-227.

3, Ďuriš, P. - Galil, Z.: A time-space tradeoff for language recognition. Math. Systems Theory 17, 1984, 3-12.

4, Ginsburg, S.: Algebraic and Automata - Theoretic Properties of Formal Languages. North-Holland Publ. Comp., Amsterdam 1975.

5, Greibach, S.A.: Remarks on blind and partially blind one-way multicounter machines. Theoret. Comput. Sci. 7, 1978, 311-324.

6, Hack, M.: Petri Net Languages, Computation Structures. Group Memo 124, Project MAC, MIT, 1975.

7, Hromkovič, J.: Hierarchy of reversal and zerotesting bounded multicounter machines. Proc. 11th MFCS'84 (M.P.Chytil, V.Koubek eds.), Lect. Notes in Comp. Science 176, Springer-Verlag 1984, 312-321.

8, Hromkovič, J.: Hierarchy of reversal bounded one-way multicounter machines. Kybernetika 22, 2, 1986, 200-206.

9, Hromkovič, J.: Tradeoffs for language recognition on parallel computing models. Proc. 13th ICALP'86 (L.Kott ed.) , Lect. Notes in Comp. Science 226, Springer-Verlag 1986, pp. 157-166.

10, Hromkovič, J.: On the power of alternation in automata theory. J. Comput. System Sciences 31, 1, 1985, 28-39.

11, Ibarra, O.H.: Reversal-bounded multicounter machines and their decision problems. J. of ACM 25, 1978, 116-133.

12, Rosenberg, A.L.: On multihead finite automata. IBM J. R. and D. 10, 1966, 388-394.

13, Wagner, K. - Wechsung, G.: Computational Complexity. Mathematische Monographien, Band 19, VEB Deutscher Verlag der Wissenschaften,

Berlin 1986.

14, Dymond, P.W. - Cook, S.A.: Hardware complexity and parallel computations. Proc. 21th Annual IEEE FOCS 1980, pp. 360-372.

COMPUTING THE COUNTING FUNCTION OF CONTEXT-FREE LANGUAGES

A. Bertoni - M. Goldwurm - N. Sabadini
Dipartimento di Scienze dell'Informazione
Università di Milano

Abstract

Given a language $L \subseteq \Sigma^*$, we consider the problem of computing the function $F_L : \{1\}^* \rightarrow \mathbb{N}$, where $F_L(1^n)$ is the number of strings of length n in L. The complexity of computing F_L is studied in the case of context-free languages. It is shown that, if L is unambiguous context-free, then F_L can be computed in NC^2, hence admitting a fast parallel algorithm.

On the contrary, an inherent ambiguous context-free language L is exhibited such that, if F_L were computable in polynomial time, then there would not exist any sparse sets in NP-P.

1. Introduction and preliminary definitions

For a given language $L \subseteq \Sigma^*$, let us consider the function $F_L : \{1\}^* \rightarrow \mathbb{N}$, defined by

$$F_L(1^n) = \#\{ x \,/\, x \in L, |x|=n \},$$

where $|x|$ denotes the length of the string x.

The study of F_L is particularly interesting when L is context-free for at least two main reasons. First of all, it is known from [Chomsky-Schuetzenberger 63] and [Salomaa-Soittola 78] that, if L is unambiguous context-free, then the analytic function $f(z) = \sum_n F_L(1^n) z^n$ is algebraic. This fact is successfully used by [Flajolet 85] for proving

---

This research has been supported by Ministero della Pubblica Istruzione in the frame of the Project 40% "Progetto e analisi di algoritmi".

structural properties (i.e. inherent ambiguity) of some context-free languages, avoiding direct involved proofs.

In the second place, Schuetzenberger's technique for solving combinatorial counting problems by reducing them to counting problems on languages (through isomorphisms that preserve the sizes), is successfully resumed by [Delest-Viennot 84] and applied to enumeration problems on polyominoes.

In this work the computational complexity of F_L is studied in a systematic way. In order to do that, we define the problem NUMSEQ(L) for each language L in the following way :

INSTANCE: $\{1^n\}$ for integer n.

QUESTION: compute the binary representation of $F_L(1^n)$.

In section 2 we prove that, if L is an unambiguous context-free language, there exists a fast parallel algorithm for computing F_L; in particular we show that NUMSEQ(L) belongs to NC^2 which is the second level of the hierarchy $\{NC^k\}$ introduced by [Ruzzo 81] and [Cook 85].

In section 3 we show that, if L is recognizable by a Deterministic Turing Machine (DTM) in polynomial time, then there is a context-free language L' with ambiguity degree 2, such that NUMSEQ(L) is polynomially reducible to NUMSEQ(L').

In section 4 it is studied the relationship between NUMSEQ(L), for $L \in P$, and the classes EXPTIME, NEXPTIME and #EXPTIME.

Section 5 gives evidence of the computational difficulty of NUMSEQ(L) for inherent ambiguous context-free languages L. In particular, we exhibit a language L of ambiguity degree 2 such that, if F_L were solvable in polynomial time, then EXPTIME = NEXPTIME. From a result on the classes P and NP due to [Hartmanis-Immerman-Sewelson 85], this fact would imply that there are no sparse sets in NP-P.

2. NUMSEQ(L) and unambiguous context-free languages

Each sequence $\{F_L(n)\}$ can be represented by the corresponding analytic function which, in some cases, is an elegant tool for determining general properties of the language.

Def. 2.1 The generating function of a language L is the function

$$f_L(z) = \sum_{n=0,\infty} F_L(1^n)\, z^n \ .$$

For every language L, $f_L(z)$ can be seen as a complex variable function analytic in a neighbourhood of zero; in fact, if r denotes the convergence ratio of the power series, then $1/|\Sigma| \le r \le 1$.

Here we are interested in the analytic functions that are algebraic. We recall that a function f(z) is said algebraic if there exists a finite sequence of polynomials $q_0(x), q_1(x), \ldots, q_d(x)$, such that, for every z,

$$\sum_{k=0,d} q_k(z)\, f^k(z) = 0 .$$

The degree of the algebraic function is the least integer d such that the above relation holds.

The following theorem (see [Chomsky-Shueztenberger 63]) states the main property of the generating functions of unambiguous context-free languages.

Theorem 2.1 If L is an unambiguous context-free language then $f_L(z)$ is algebraic.

Such a result is used by [Flajolet 85] for proving the inherent ambiguity of some context-free languages.

In the following we use theorem 2.1 and the properties of algebraic functions for designing a fast parallel algorithm which solves NUMSEQ(L) when L is unambiguous context-free. In particular we use the following result due to [Comptet 64].

Theorem 2.2 Given an algebraic function $f(z) = \sum_{n=0,\infty} y(n)\, z^n$ of degree d, there exists an integer n° and a finite sequence of polynomials $p_0(x), p_1(x), \ldots, p_q(x)$ such that:

1) $p_j(x) \neq 0$ for every j;

2) the degree of $p_j(x)$ is less than d;

3) for every $n \ge n°$, $p_0(n) \cdot y(n) + p_1(n) \cdot y(n-1) + \ldots + p_q(x) \cdot y(n-q) = 0$.

In order to classify the problem NUMSEQ(L), when L is unambiguous context-free, with respect to parallel complexity, we recall the definition of the hierarchy (NC^k).

Def. 2.2 For every integer k, NC^k is the set of problems solvable by a family of uniform boolean cicuits of depth $O(\log^k n)$ and size $n^{O(1)}$.

Uniform boolean circuits are considered a standard model of parallel computation and are widely studied in the literature ([Borodin 77],[Ruzzo 81],[Cook 85]). Informally, we recall that the families of uniform boolean circuits are sets of combinational circuits satisfying a suitable condition of uniformity which allows a DTM (or other abstract machine) to generate "easily" a description of each circuit ([Ruzzo 81]). (For our purposes, here we are not interested in distinguishing the different uniformity conditions presented in literature.) Size and depth of a circuit are respectively the number of nodes and the length of the longest path from an input to an output node; these measures correspond respectively to hardware and time costs in parallel computations.

The class $NC = \bigcup_k NC^k$ has been proposed as the representative class of problems which admit fast parallel algorithms. NC is robust with respect to other formalisms: for instance, it can be defined as the class of problems solvable on parallel RAM in polylog time with a polynomial number of processors ([Pippenger 79]). Clearly, all the problems in NC can be solved in polynomial time on DTM.

The main result of this section is stated by the following proposition.

Theorem 2.3 For every unambiguous context-free language L NUMSEQ(L) belongs to NC^2.

Proof (outline). Let us consider an unambiguous context-free language L. By theorem 2.1, its generating function $f(z) = \sum_{n=0,\infty} y(n)\, z^n$ is algebraic. So we can determine the integer $n°$ and the polynomials $p_0(x), p_1(x), \ldots, p_q(x)$ which satysfies condition 3) of theorem 2.2. By such a relation we can state that, for every $n \geq n°$

$$y(n) = r_1(n) \cdot y(n-1) + \ldots + r_q(n) \cdot y(n-q) \qquad (*)$$

where, for every j, $r_j(x) = -p_j(x)/p_0(x)$ is a suitable rational function. Now let us define the sequence of column vectors $\{\underline{z}(n)\}$, where

$$\underline{z}(n) = (\, y(n-1), y(n-2), \ldots, y(n-q)\,)_T .$$

So, by relation (*), it is easily shown that, for every $n \geq n°$,

$$\underline{z}(n+1) = A[n] \cdot \underline{z}(n)$$

where A[n] is the following qxq matrix :

$$\begin{matrix} r_1(n) & r_2(n) & r_3(n) & \ldots & r_{q-1}(n) & r_q(n) \\ 1 & 0 & 0 & \ldots & 0 & 0 \\ 0 & 1 & 0 & \ldots & 0 & 0 \\ \ldots & \ldots & \ldots & \ldots & \ldots & \ldots \\ 0 & 0 & 0 & \ldots & 1 & 0 \end{matrix}$$

Therefore, solving NUMSEQ(L) on input $\{1^n\}$ is reduced to computing the first component of

$$\underline{z}(n+1) = \prod_{j=n°,n} A[j] \cdot \underline{z}(n°) \quad .$$

We can write A[n] in the form $B[n]/p_0(n)$, being $p_0(n)$ an integer coefficient polynomial and B[n] a qxq matrix, the components of which are integer coefficient polynomials. Then

$$\underline{z}(n+1) = a_n / b_n ,$$

where $a_n = \prod_{j=n°,n} B[j]\cdot\underline{z}(n°)$, and $b_n = \prod_{j=n°,n} p_0(j)$.

We can now summarize the algorithm in the following steps:

(1) compute in parallel $B[n°], \ldots , B[n], p_0(n°), \ldots , p_0(n)$.

Since we evaluate polynomials on O(log n)-bits integers, such a calculus can be made in NC^1, recalling that the sum and product of two n-bits integers are in NC^1 ([Cook 85]).

(2) Compute $\prod_{j=n°,n} p_0(j)$ and $\prod_{j=n°,n} B[j]\cdot\underline{z}(n°)$.

Using a logarithmic sum technique, we can realize a family of uniform boolean circuits of polynomial size for calculating $\prod_{j=n°,n} p_0(j)$. Let $|p_0(j)|$ be the number of bits of $p_0(j)$; then the depth of these circuits is less than

$$\Sigma_{j=1,\lceil \log n \rceil} O(\log(2^j \cdot \log n)) = O(\log^2 n) .$$

By an analogous reasoning, it is easily shown that also $\prod_{j=n°,n} B[j]\cdot\underline{z}(n°)$ can be computed by a family of uniform boolean circuits of depth $O(\log^2 n)$ and polynomial size.

(3) Compute a_n / b_n .

We recall that integer division of two n-bits numbers can be realized by a family of circuits of depth O(log n loglog n) ([Reif 83], [Cook 85].) Since the size of both a_n and b_n is bounded by O(n log n), our last operation can be implemented on a family of circuits of depth O(log n loglog n).

All the families of boolean circuits we have considered are uniform, have depth $O(\log^2 n)$ and polynomial size. So we conclude that NUMSEQ(L) belongs to NC^2.□

3. NUMSEQ(L) for languages in P

In the previous section we have proved that NUMSEQ(L) is "efficiently parallelizable" if L is unambiguous context-free. In this section we analyze the complexity of the same problem for ambiguous context-free languages or, more generally, for languages decidable in polynomial time. More precisely, we consider the following classes:

- NA of unambiguous context-free languages;

- A_k of ambiguous context-free languages with ambiguity degree k. We recall that a language L is in A_k if there exists a grammar G which generates L such that every string admits at most k different leftmost derivations in G [Chomsky-Shuetzenberger 63];
- P of languages decidable in polynomial time on DTM.

Our first result is that the problem NUMSEQ(L) for languages L in A_2 is as difficult as NUMSEQ(L) for languages L in P. In order to prove this statement, we need some preliminary lemmas; in the following we consider a standard model of DTM with a single one way tape that is infinite on the right [Hopcroft-Ullman 69].

By simulating a counter and using a standard padding technique, we can obtain the following lemma.

Lemma 3.1 Let L be a language in P. Then there exists a polynomial p and a DTM $M = \langle \Sigma, \Gamma, K, q_0, F, \delta \rangle$ such that :

1) M accepts L;
2) the sequence of instantaneous descriptions which represents the computation of the machine M on input $x \in \Sigma^*$ is codified by a word on $(\Gamma \cup \{m\} \cup K)^*$ of length $p(|x|)$, where m is a special symbol, $m \notin \Gamma$, $m \notin K$.

For a detailed definition of sequence of instantaneous descriptions we refer to [Hartmanis 67], where a relation between DTM's computations and context-free languages has been stated by means of the following languages.

Def. 3.1 Let M be a deterministic Turing machine. Then :

1) $L_0(M) = m\,\{y_k\, m\, y_j^T\, m \,/\, y_k \vdash_M y_j\}^*\, m$
2) $L_1(M) = m\, S\, m\, \{y_j^T\, m\, y_k\, m \,/\, y_j \vdash_M y_k\}^*\, H^T\, m\, m$

where:
- S is the set of all the start possible instantaneous descriptions (ID);
- H consists of all accepting ID's of M;
- m is not a tape or state symbol of M.

(Here, for every string z, z^T denotes the transposed string of z; moreover, $\vdash_M$ denotes the one step transition between ID's of M.)

The following lemma summarizes some properties of L_0 and L_1.

Lemma 3.2 For every DTM M :

1) $L_0(M)$ and $L_1(M)$ are unambiguous context-free languages;

2) $L_0(M) \cap L_1(M)$ is the set of all accepting computations of M.

Proof. Proposition 1) is proved in [Hartmanis 67].
Proposition 2) is immediate from the definitions.□

The following proposition easily follows from lemma 3.1 and lemma 3.2.

Lemma 3.3 Given a language $L \in P$, there are a polynomial p, a DTM M which accepts L, and two languages $L_0(M)$, $L_1(M)$ belonging to NA such that :

1) if $x \in L$ and I_x is the accepting sequence of instantaneous descriptions of M on x, then $|I_x| = p(|x|)$;

2) $x \in L$ if and only if $I_x \in L_0(M) \cap L_1(M)$.

We can now state the main result of this section.

Theorem 3.1 The following sentences are equivalent :

a) for every language $L \in P$, NUMSEQ(L) is solvable in polynomial time;

b) for every language $L' \in A_2$, NUMSEQ(L') is solvable in polynomial time;

Proof. The implication a) ⇒ b) is immediate since $A_2 \subset P$.

As for b) ⇒ a), given a language $L \in P$, accepted by a DTM M, we consider the languages $L_0=L_0(M)$, $L_1= L_1(M)$ as in lemma 3.2. Then, we have :

1) $L_0 \cup L_1 \in A_2$;

2) $F_{L0 \cup L1} = F_{L0} + F_{L1} - F_{L0 \cap L1}$.

By theorem 2.3, being L_0 and L_1 unambiguous, if $F_{L0 \cup L1}$ is computable in polynomial time, so is $F_{L0 \cap L1}$.

Furthemore, by lemma 3.3, we have that $x \in L$ iff $I_x \in L_0 \cap L_1$ and $|I_x|=p(|x|)$ for a suitable polynomial p ; observing that $x \neq x'$ implies $I_x \neq I_{x'}$, we can conclude that $F_L(1^n) = F_{L0 \cap L1}(1^{p(n)})$.

Hence, a polynomial algorithm for F_L can be derived from a polynomial algorithm for $F_{L0 \cup L1}$.□

4. NUMSEQ(L) for languages in P and the class #EXPTIME

In this section we are interested in the characterization of NUMSEQ(L) for languages in P, with respect to complexity classes of counting problems.

Some different computational models for counting problems have been proposed in the literature: for example Counting Turing Machines [Valiant 79] and Threshold Machines [Simon 75].

We briefly recall some definitions:

Def.4.1 A Counting Turing Machine (CTM) is a standard nondeterministic Turing Machine with an auxiliary output device that (magically) prints on a special tape the number of accepting computations induced by the input.

Def.4.2 A CTM M has time complexity T(n) if the longest accepting computation induced by the set of all inputs of size n take T(n) steps, when the CTM is regarded as a standard nondeterministic Turing Machine with no auxiliary device.

The class #P of functions that can be computed by polynomial time Counting Turing Machines has been introduced and extensively studied in [Valiant 79]; furthermore, the class #PSPACE of functions computed by polynomial space Counting Turing Machines was studied in [Bertoni-Mauri-Sabadini 81].

Here we are interested in the class #EXPTIME, that is the class of functions computed by exponential time bounded Counting Turing Machines. We recall that the classes EXPTIME and NEXPTIME can be defined as follows:

$$\text{EXPTIME} = \bigcup_{c \geq 1} \text{TIME}(2^{cn})$$

$$\text{NEXPTIME} = \bigcup_{c \geq 1} \text{NTIME}(2^{cn})$$

In order to obtain a more precise comparison between NUMSEQ(L) for $L \in P$ and complexity classes of counting problems, we slightly modify the definition of F_L. We consider the alphabet {0,1} and we consider the bijective function $R : \mathbb{N} \to \{ 1 \cdot \{0,1\}^* \cup \{0\} \}$ where, for every integer n, R(n) is the binary representation of n. (Here the symbol denotes concatenation between strings.)

Given a language $L \subseteq \Sigma^*$ we define the function $F_L^{@} : \{0,1\}^* \to \mathbb{N}$ as follows:

$$F_L^{@}(x) = \#\{ z \mid |z| = n,\ z \in L \text{ and } R(n) = 1 \cdot x \}.$$

Now, the following theorems allows us to characterize the class of counting problems associated to NUMSEQ(L), defined in terms of $F_L^{@}$, for languages in P:

Theorem 4.1 If L is a language in P, then $F_L^@ \in$ #EXPTIME.

Proof (outline): Given a Deterministic Turing Machine M that accepts L in polynomial time, we construct a Nondeterministic Turing Machine M' s.t., on input $x \in \{0,1\}^*$, the machine M' interprets $1 \cdot x$ as the binary representation of an integer n and generates, non deterministically, all the strings of length n in Σ^*. Then M', having a given string $y \in \Sigma^*$ of length n on its tape, simulates the machine M on input y. It is easy to verify that the machine M' works in exponential time and the number of computation sequences accepted by M' is $F_L^@(x)$.□

Theorem.4.2 Let $f: \{0,1\}^* \to \mathbb{N}$ be a function in #EXPTIME. There exist a language $L \in P$ and a polynomial p such that:

$f(x) = \# \{z \mid z \in L, |z| = p(n) \text{ and } R(n) = 1 \cdot x\}$.

Proof (outline). Since $f \in$ #EXPTIME, there exists a Nondeteministic Turing Machine M such that, on input $x \in \{0,1\}^*$, all the computation sequences of M (seen as words on $(\Gamma \cup \{m\} \cup K)^*$) have length $\leq 2^{c|x|}$; moreover, there are exactly f(x) accepting computation sequences. We can define a Nondeterministic Turing Machine M' which modifies the computation sequences of M on input x by prolonging them up to a length n^{c^*}, where $1 \cdot x$ is the binary representation of n and c^* is a suitable constant such that $n^{c^*} > 2^{c|x|}$; moreover, simulating M, M' has exactly f(x) accepting computations.

Let L be the language defined as follows:

L = { l | l is an accepting computation sequence of the machine M' on input of the form $\{0,1\}^*$ }.

It holds: a) $L \in P$;

b) $f(x) = \# \{z \mid z \in L, |z| = p(n) \text{ and } R(n) = 1 \cdot x\}$, where p is a suitable polynomial. □

5. NUMSEQ(L) for ambiguous context-free languages

In the previous section we have proved that NUMSEQ(L) for languages in P admits a polynomial algorithm on Deterministic Turing Machine if and only if that holds also for languages in A_2. Unfortunately, it is possible to exhibit a language L^* in A_2 such that a polynomial time algorithm on DTM for L^* would imply that EXPTIME = NEXPTIME.

As far as the classes P and NP are concerned, this is equivalent to the non existence of sparse sets in NP-P. We recall that a set S is said to be sparse if S contains only polynomially many elements up to size n, i.e. $|S\cap(\varepsilon\cup\Sigma)^n| \le n^k + k$. For a discussion on sparse sets the reader is referred to [Hartmanis-Immerman-Sewelson 85].

Theorem 5.1 There is a language $L \in A_2$ such that if F_L is computable in polynomial time then EXPTIME = NEXPTIME.

Proof (outline) Let A be a problem complete in NEXPTIME with respect to polynomial time reducibility. By theorem 4.2, there exists a language $L_A \in$ P and a polynomial p such that:

a) $x \in A$ iff $\#\{z \mid z \in L_A, |z| = p(n) \text{ and } R(n)=1\cdot x\} > 0$.

Furthermore, by lemma 3.3, we can find two unambiguous languages L_0, L_1 and a polynomial q such that:

b) for every n, $\#\{z \mid z \in L_A, |z| = n\} = \#\{z' \mid z' \in L_0 \cap L_1, |z'| = q(n)\}$.

Considering the language $L = L_0 \cup L_1$, we can observe that:

1) $L = L_0 \cup L_1 \in A_2$;

2) if $F_{L_0 \cup L_1}$ is computable in polynomial time, then also $F_{L_0 \cap L_1}$ is computable in polynomial time. In fact $F_{L_0 \cap L_1} = F_{L_0} + F_{L_1} - F_{L_0 \cup L_1}$, and F_{L_0}, F_{L_1} are in NC^2 by theorem 2.3.

Then $F_{L_0 \cup L_1}$ computable in polynomial time implies $A \in$ EXPTIME, because conditions a) and b) give us a deterministic exponential algorithm for recognizing A; being A complete in NEXPTIME by hypothesis, we would have immediately that EXPTIME = NEXPTIME.□

As a direct consequence of this theorem and a result of [Hartmanis-Immerman-Sewelson 85], we can conclude that the following theorem holds.

Theorem 5.2 There is a language $L \in A^2$ such that, if F_L is computable in polynomial time, then there are no sparse sets in NP-P.

References

[Bertoni-Mauri-Sabadini 81] A. Bertoni, G. Mauri, N. Sabadini, *A characterization of the class of functions computable in polynomial time by Random Access Machine*, Proc. 13th ACM STOC, 168-176, 1981.

[Borodin 77] A. Borodin, *On relating time and space to size and depth*, SIAM J. Comput. 6, 733-744, 1977.

[Comptet 64] L. Comptet, *Calcul pratique des coefficients de Taylor d'une fonction algebrique*, L'Enseignement Mathematique X, 267-270, 1964.

[Cook 85] S.A. Cook, *A taxonomy of problems with fast parallel algorithms*, Information and Control, 64, 2-22, 1985.

[Chomsky-Shuetzenberger 63] N. Chomsky, M.P. Schuetzenberger, *The algebraic theory of context free languages*, Comp. Prog. and Formal Systems, North-Holland, 118-161, 1963.

[Delest-Viennot 84] M.P. Delest, G. Viennot, *Algebraic languages and polyominoes enumeration*, Theoretical Computer Science 34, North-Holland, 169-206, 1984.

[Flajolet 85] P. Flajolet, *Ambiguity and trascendence*, Proc. ICALP '86 Conf., Nafplion, 1985.

[Hartmanis 67] J. Hartmanis, *Context-free languages and Turing machine computations*, Proc. of the Symposium on Applied Mathematics 19, 42-51, 1967.

[Hartmanis-Immerman-Sewelson 85] J. Hartmanis, N. Immerman, V. Sewelson, *Sparse sets in NP-P: EXPTIME versus NEXPTIME*, Information and Control 65, 158-181, 1985.

[Hopcroft-Ullman 69] J.E. Hopcroft, J.D. Ullman, *Formal languages and their relation to automata*, Add. Wesley, Reading, Mass.,1969.

[Pippenger 79] N. Pippenger, *On simultaneous resource bounds (preliminary version)*, Proc. 20th IEEE FOCS, 307-311, 1979.

[Salomaa-Soittola 78] A.Salomaa, M.Soittola, *Automata theoretic aspects of formal power series*, Springer Verlag, New York 1978.

[Simon 75] J. Simon, *On some central problems in Computational Complexity*, Doctoral Thesis, Dept. Computer Sci., Cornel University, Ithaca, 1975.

[Ruzzo 81] W.L. Ruzzo, *On uniform circuit complexity*, JCSS 22, 385-383, 1981.

[Reif 83] J.H. Reif, *Logarithmic depth ciruits for algebraic functions*, 24th IEEE FOCS, 138-145, 1983.

[Valiant 79] L.G. Valiant, *The complexity of computing the permanent*, Theoretical Computer Science 8, North-Holland, 189-202, 1979.

ON THE k-FREENESS OF MORPHISMS ON FREE MONOIDS

Veikko Keränen
Department of Mathematics, University of Oulu
Linnanmaa, SF-90570 Oulu, Finland

Abstract. Let an integer $k \geq 2$ be fixed. A word is called k-repetition free, or shortly k-free, if it does not contain any non-empty subword of the form R^k. A morphism $h: X^* \to Y^*$ is called k-free if the word $h(w)$ is k-free for every k-free word w in X^*. We investigate the general structure of k-free morphisms and give outlines for the proof of the following result: if a non-trivial morphism $h: X^* \to Y^*$, where $\mathrm{card}(X) \geq 2$ and $\mathrm{card}(Y) \geq 2$, is k-free for some integer $k \geq 2$, then, except a certain possibility concerning one infrequent situation in the case $k = 3$, h is a primitive ps-code. Moreover, an effective characterization is provided for all k-free morphisms $h: X^* \to Y^*$ in the case $k \geq q_h + 1$, and for a wide class of morphisms in the case $2 \leq k \leq q_h$, where $q_h = \max\{|h(a)| \mid a \in X\}$.

1. Introduction

The systematic investigation of k-free words, as well as words on the whole, seems to have been started by Axel Thue [12,13] at the beginning of this century. One of his results in [12] was that over a three letter alphabet there exist infinitely long square-free words, i.e. words that contain no repetitions at all. (The terms square-free and cube-free are often used instead of 2-free and 3-free.) Thue also showed that there exist infinitely long cube-free words over a binary alphabet. Later, results concerning k-free words have been applied in various areas of mathematics, for example in group theory, in symbolic dynamics and in connection with unending games and non-counting languages. In recent years this basic combinatorial structure of words has been a subject of an active investigation and plenty of new results have been obtained in this field. For a general survey of these results we refer to Berstel [2].

Most examples of infinitely long k-free words constructed in literature are obtained by iterating a morphism. This means that the theory of repetitions is closely related to the theory of L systems (for L systems see [11]). Moreover, this leads us to the questions concerning the k-freeness of morphisms. In [1] Bean, Ehrenfeucht and McNulty gave certain sufficient conditions for a morphism to be k-free. However, their results do not exhaustively characterize k-free morphisms. Many effective characterizations for square-free morphisms have been presented later. The most precise of them are found in Crochemore [3], where it is proved, for example, that a morphism

$h: X^* \to Y^*$, with X containing three letters, is square-free if and only if $h(w)$ is square-free whenever w in X^* of length ≤ 5 is square-free. A result due to Leconte [8] says that a morphism $h: X^* \to Y^*$ is power-free (i.e. n-free for every integer $n \geq 2$) if and only if h is square-free and $h(aa)$ is cube-free for every letter a in X. In [9] Leconte obtains results which resemble some of our results in this article. Lastly, we mention one of our earlier results proved in [5] (see also [6]): Let $h: \{a,b\}^* \to Y^*$ be a non-trivial length-uniform morphism and $k_0 \geq 3$ a fixed integer. Then h is k_0-free if and only if $h(a)$, $h(b)$, $h(ab)$ are primitive and $h(w)$ is k_0-free whenever w in $\{a,b\}^*$ of length ≤ 4 is so. Moreover, if h is k_0-free, then it is k-free for every integer $k \geq k_0$.

In this article we investigate the structure of k-free morphisms in the general case. Theorem 6 shows that out of non-trivial morphisms only primitive ps-codes (see Section 2 for definitions) can be k-free for some integer $k \geq 2$, $k \neq 3$. For the case $k = 3$ it is easy to see that every non-trivial cube-free morphism is a ps-code, but it is an open question whether there exists any non-trivial morphism that is both cube-free and imprimitive. However, non-trivial morphisms of a certain type, including length-uniform morphisms and morphisms over a binary alphabet, can be cube-free only if they are primitive. Theorem 1 shows that it is decidable whether an effectively given bifix code is primitive. This means that it is decidable whether an effectively given morphism is a primitive ps-code. In the general case this problem may be quite hard to solve. Sometimes, however, it becomes almost trivial. For example, a length-uniform morphism $h: \{a,b\}^* \to Y^*$ is a primitive ps-code if and only if the words $h(a)$, $h(b)$ and $h(ab)$ are primitive; see Theorem 3.

Let a morphism $h: X^* \to Y^*$ be (effectively) given and let $q_h = \max\{|h(a)| \mid a \in X\}$. For a given integer $k \geq q_h + 1$ it will be decidable whether h is k-free; see Theorems 11, 6 and 1 below. Moreover, Corollary 12 shows that in the case $q_h \geq 2$, h is k-free for every integer $k \geq 2q_h - 1$ if and only if h is a primitive ps-code. For deciding whether h is k-free for a given k with $2 \leq k \leq q_h$ one may find Theorem 13 very useful.

2. Preliminaries

The number of elements in a finite set A is denoted by card(A). For a real number r we denote by $\lceil r \rceil$ the least integer no less than r. For integers m, n and q we write $m \equiv n \pmod{q}$ if there exists an integer i such that $m - n = iq$.

Alphabets, which are assumed to contain two or more letters, are denoted by X and Y. The free monoid [the free semigroup] generated by X is denoted by X^* [X^+]. For the length of a word w in X^* we use the notation $|w|$, and by λ we mean the empty word. The notation w^i, where w is a word and $i \in \mathbb{N}$, is defined so that $w^0 = \lambda$ and $w^{i+1} = w^i w$. We stress the fact that in this study only integer powers of words are considered.

A word u is called a <u>subword</u> [an <u>inner subword</u>] of a word w if $w = vuv'$ for some words [non-empty words] v and v'. The notation $SW(w)$ $[ISW(w)]$ stands for the set of all subwords [inner subwords] of w. If $v = \lambda$ $[v' = \lambda]$, then u is called a <u>prefix</u> [a <u>suffix</u>] of w. By $PREF(w)$ $[SUFF(w)]$ we mean the set of all prefixes [suffixes] of w. For a language L we write $Q(L)$, where Q is SW, ISW, PREF of SUFF, to denote the set $\cup_{w \in L} Q(w)$.

A word w is called <u>primitive</u> if $w \neq u^n$ for all words u and all integers $n \geq 2$, i.e. if $w \neq \lambda$ and w is not a power of a word $\neq w$. If w is not primitive, then it is called <u>imprimitive</u>.

Let $k \geq 2$ be a given integer. A <u>k-repetition</u> is a non-empty word of the form R^k (only integer powers are considered). Instead of 2-repetitions [3-repetitions] we often speak of <u>squares</u> [<u>cubes</u>]. A word is called <u>k-repetition free</u>, or shortly <u>k-free</u>, if it does not contain any k-repetition as a subword. A word sequence or a set is k-free if all words in it are k-free.

A <u>morphism</u> h is a mapping between free monoids X^* and Y^* with $h(uv) = h(u)h(v)$ for every u and v in X^*. Especially, $h(\lambda) = \lambda$. A morphism $h: X^* \to Y^*$ is uniquely defined by giving the value $h(a) \in Y^*$ for each a in X.

A morphism $h: X^* \to Y^*$ is <u>trivial</u> if $h(X) = \{\lambda\}$ and <u>λ-free</u> if $\lambda \notin h(X)$. Let $card(X) \geq 2$. A <u>bifix code</u> $h: X^* \to Y^*$ is a morphism such that, for every a, b in X with $a \neq b$, $h(a)$ is neither a prefix nor a suffix of $h(b)$. Note that a bifix code over X is always λ-free. A <u>ps-code</u> $h: X^* \to Y^*$ is a morphism for which the situation

$$h(a) = ps \quad \text{and} \quad h(b) = ps', \; h(c) = p's$$

with a,b,c in X (possibly $c=b$), p,s,s',p' in Y^*, always implies $b = a$ or $c = a$. Obviously every ps-code over X is also a bifix code. We say that a morphism h over X is <u>length-uniform</u> if $|h(a)| = |h(b)|$ for every a and b in X. If h is length-uniform and $|h(a)| \geq 2$ for every a in X, then h is termed <u>uniformly growing</u>. For a given morphism $h: X^* \to Y^*$ we define $q_h = \max\{|h(a)| \mid a \in X\}$.

A morphism $h: X^* \to Y^*$ is called <u>primitive</u> if $h(w)$ is primitive for every primitive word w in X^*; otherwise h is <u>imprimitive</u>. For a given integer $k \geq 2$, h is called <u>k-free</u> if $h(w)$ is k-free for every k-free w in X^*.

Next we define the notions of a <u>cut</u> and a <u>block</u>, which are both important and very convenient in our presentation. The notion of a cut comes from Karhumäki [4]. Let $H = \{u_1,\dots,u_m\}$ be a set of words over Y, and let $w = w_1 \cdots w_n$ with w_i in H^*. Then we say that the positions of w determined by the prefixes $w_1 \cdots w_j$, $j = 1,\dots,n$, are H-cuts, or just cuts if H is clear. The occurrences of the subwords $w_i \cdots w_j$, $1 \leq i \leq j \leq n$, which start and end with a cut, are called H-blocks or blocks. Note that also λ can occur as a block. We denote blocks as $[w_i \cdots w_j]$ and write $w = [w_1][w_2]\cdots[w_n]$ to indicate certain cuts of w. For us H will be the set $h(X)$ where h is a bifix code. Thus, the H-cuts of w will be unique, since for every

$u \in h(X^*)$ there will be only one word $x \in X^*$ such that $h(x) = u$.

3. Primitiveness

The results of this section are important for the characterization of k-free morphisms, because, as we shall see in Theorem 6 below, in almost every case a morphism has to be a primitive ps-code in order that it could be k-free for some integer $k \geq 2$.

Theorem 1. It is decidable whether an effectively given bifix code $h: X^* \to Y^*$ is primitive.

In the proof of Theorem 1, found in [7], we give an upper bound for the lengths of primitive words w in X^+ for which it is sufficient to test the primitiveness of $h(w)$ in order to decide whether a given bifix code $h: X^* \to Y^*$ is primitive. This upper bound can be very large in the general case. Sometimes, however, the testing is easy to carry out. For example, in the case of morphisms over a binary alphabet the following result is known.

Theorem 2 (Lentin and Schützenberger [10]). An injective morphism $h: \{a,b\}^* \to Y^*$ is primitive if and only if $h(w)$ is primitive for all words $w \in a^*b \cup ab^*$ such that $|h(w)| < 3|h(ab)|$.

Moreover, Theorem 3 below shows that if a morphism $h: \{a,b\}^* \to Y^*$ is length-uniform, it is almost trivial to check whether h is primitive. Theorem 3 is an easy consequence of Theorem 2 (in [7] we have proven it also without the aid of Theorem 2).

Theorem 3. A length-uniform morphism $h: \{a,b\}^* \to Y^*$ is primitive if and only if the words $h(a)$, $h(b)$ and $h(ab)$ are primitive.

4. k-freeness

We give necessary conditions which a non-trivial morphism $h: X^* \to Y^*$ has to satisfy in order to be k-free for some integer $k \geq 2$. Moreover, an effective characterization is provided for all k-free morphisms in the case $k \geq q_h + 1$, and for a wide class of k-free morphisms in the case $2 \leq k \leq q_h$ (recall that $q_h = \max\{|h(a)| \mid a \in X\}$).

Our first necessary condition for k-free morphisms is given by the following easily provable lemma. Also, it is easy to check whether a given morphism satisfies this condition.

Lemma 4. If a non-trivial morphism $h: X^* \to Y^*$ is k-free for some integer $k \geq 2$, then h is a ps-code.

Proof. Assume that h is neither trivial nor a ps-code. Then there is a letter $a \in X$ such that $h(a) = ps$ and $h(b) = ps'$, $h(c) = p's$ for some letters $b,c \in X-\{a\}$. If $h(a) = \lambda$, then $h(x) \neq \lambda$ for some letter x (h is not trivial). In this case $h(xax^{k-1}) = (h(x))^k \neq \lambda$ is not k-free although xax^{k-1} is so. On the other hand, if $h(a) = ps \neq \lambda$, then $h(ca^{k-1}b) = p's(ps)^{k-1}ps' = p'(sp)^k s'$, meaning that h cannot be k-free for any $k \geq 2$. This proves Lemma 4. □

In the case concerning cube-freeness we restrict our considerations to morphisms $h: X^* \to Y^*$ satisfying

$$h(a^3) \neq \alpha h(w^3)\beta, \tag{1}$$

whenever $a \in X$, $w \in X^+$; $|h(a)| < |h(w^3)| < 9|h(a)|/7$; $5|h(a)|/7 < |\alpha|,|\beta| < |h(a)|$ and $\alpha \in SUFF(h(u))$, $\beta \in PREF(h(v))$ for some $u,v \in X^*$. Condition (1) is not very restrictive, quite on the contrary, there remains plenty of free scope for choosing a morphism that satisfies it. For example, every length-uniform morphism trivially satisfies this condition. Moreover, the following result holds for morphisms over a binary alphabet.

<u>Lemma 5</u>. Let $X = \{a,b\}$. Then every non-trivial cube-free morphism $h: X^* \to Y^*$ satisfies condition (1).

Proof. Assume that $h: \{a,b\}^* \to Y^*$ is a non-trivial cube-free morphism. By Lemma 4, h is a ps-code. Thus $h(a)$ and $h(b)$ are non-empty. Arguing indirectly, assume that $h(x^3) = \alpha h(w^3)\beta$ for some $x \in \{a,b\}$, $w \in \{a,b\}^+$, α and β, where $|h(x)| < |h(w^3)| < 9|h(x)|/7$, $h(w^3) \notin SW(h(xx))$ and $\alpha \in SUFF(h(u))$, $\beta \in PREF(h(v))$ for some words $u,v \in \{a,b\}^*$. Obviously we must have $w = y$ with $y \in \{a,b\}$, $y \neq x$ (note especially $h(ww) \in SW(h(xx))$). Moreover, because α and β are of length $> 5|h(x)|/7$, $|h(y)| = |h(w)| < 3|h(x)|/7$ and $h(y^3) \notin SW(h(xx))$, we may assume that $u = v = x$ in our antithesis. Thus $h(x) = \alpha s = p\alpha$ with $1 \leq |s| = |p| = |h(x)| - |\alpha| < 2|h(x)|/7$, implying $p^2 \in PREF(\alpha)$. Then, however, $p^3 \in PREF(h(x))$, a contradiction since h is cube-free. □

The following theorem is one of our main results.

<u>Theorem 6</u>. Let an integer $k \geq 2$ be arbitrary but fixed and let $h: X^* \to Y^*$ be a non-trivial k-free morphism that in the case $k = 3$, $card(X) \geq 3$ satisfies condition (1). Then h is a primitive ps-code.

Contrary to the case of Lemma 4, we do not know any quick method of proving Theorem 6. The proof, found in [7], can be described shortly as follows: Let the assumptions of Theorem 6 hold. By Lemma 4 h is a ps-code. Arguing indirectly, assume that h is imprimitive. Let w be one of the shortest primitive words in X^+ such that $h(w)$ is imprimitive, i.e. $h(w) = R^n$ for some non-empty word R and integer $n \geq 2$. Then we can show that the word $u = w^{k-1}$ is k-free. However, $h(u) = R^k R^{k'}$ with $k' \geq 0$, a contradiction with the assumption that h is k-free.

We do not know whether the restriction concerning (1) is really needed in Theorem 6. So the question, whether there exists a non-trivial morphism that is both imprimitive and cube-free, remains open.

In order to present also sufficient conditions concerning k-free morphisms we need the following lemmas.

Lemma 7. Let $h: X^* \to Y^*$ be a ps-code and $k \geq 2$ a fixed integer. Let w be a k-free word in X^* and suppose that $h(w) = \alpha R^k \beta$ for some α, β and R. Then

$$h(w) = \alpha R^k \beta \neq [\alpha R^m s][h(u)][pR^n \beta], \tag{2}$$

whenever $u \in SW(w)$, $m + n = k - 1$ and $ps = h(a)$ for some letter a in X. Moreover, for any pair (p_1,p_2) of prefixes of w such that $|\alpha| \leq |h(p_1)|,|h(p_2)| \leq |\alpha R^k|$ one has $|h(p_2)| \neq |h(p_1)| + |R|$.

Proof. For convenience denote $R^k = R_1 \cdots R_k$, $R_i = R$. Suppose that in some case one could replace "$\neq$" with "=" in (2). Then $R_{m+1} = s[h(u)]p$ with $ps = h(a)$. Let $m > 0$, the case $n > 0$ being symmetrical. Because h is a ps-code, we have $[\alpha R^m s] = [\alpha R^{m-1} sh(u)ps] = [\alpha R^{m-1} s][h(ua)]$. So clearly $[\alpha R^m s] = [\alpha s][(h(ua))^m] = [\alpha s][h((ua)^m)]$ and, analogously, $[pR^n \beta] = [h((au)^n)][p\beta]$. Thus $h(w) = \alpha R^k \beta = [\alpha s][h((ua)^m)][h(u)][h((au)^n)][p\beta] = [\alpha s][h((ua)^m u(au)^n)][p\beta] = [\alpha s][h((ua)^{k-1}u)][p\beta]$. Now either $\alpha s = h(va)$ or $p\beta = h(av)$ for some v (h is a ps-code). Hence $h((au)^k)$ or $h((ua)^k)$ is a block of $h(w)$. Then, however, $(au)^k$ or $(ua)^k$ is a subword of w, contradicting the k-freeness of w. Thus "$\neq$" in (2) is established.

To prove the second claim of Lemma 7, assume that $p_2 = p_1 x$ and $w = p_2 y$ for some words p_1,p_2,x,y such that $x \neq \lambda$, $|\alpha| \leq |h(p_1)|,|h(p_2)| \leq |\alpha R^k|$ and $|h(x)| = |R|$. Then

$$h(w) = h(p_1 xy) = \alpha R^k \beta = \underbrace{\alpha R^t R'}_{h(p_1)} \; \underbrace{R''R'}_{h(x)} \; \underbrace{R''R^{t'} \beta}_{h(y)} \tag{3}$$

for some integers t,t', with $t+t' = k-2$, and words R',R'' with $R'R'' = R$. Now we have $x = zbz'$ for some letter b and words z,z' with $h(z)p = R''$, $sh(z') = R'$, where $ps = h(b)$. Because $R' = sh(z')$ and h is a ps-code, z' is a suffix of p_1. Thus, see (3), $h(w) = \alpha R^k \beta = [\alpha R^t s][h(z')][h(z)][pR'R''R^{t'} \beta] = [\alpha R^t s][h(z'z)][pR^{t'+1} \beta]$, a contradiction with (2). This proves Lemma 7. □

Corollary 8. Let $h: X^* \to Y^*$ be a length-uniform ps-code and $k \geq 2$ a fixed integer. If w is a k-free word in X^*, then $h(w)$ has no subword of the form R^k with $0 < |R| \equiv 0 (\mathrm{mod}\ q_h)$.

Proof. Suppose that Corollary 8 is not true but, for some k-free w, $h(w) = \alpha R^k \beta$ with $0 < |R| \equiv 0(\mathrm{mod}\ q_h)$. Then $h(w) = \alpha R^k \beta = [\alpha s][h(u)][pR^{k-1}\beta] = [\alpha s][h(u)][psh(u)pR^{k-2}\beta]$ for some u in $SW(w)$ and p,s with $|ps| = q_h$. Consequently, $ps = h(a)$ for some a in X. This gives a contradiction with Lemma 7 (consider there the case $m = 0$, $n = k - 1$). □

Using the following lemma (we omit its proof) we can now show, for example, that every primitive ps-code $h: X^* \to Y^*$, with $q_h \geq 2$, is k-free for all $k \geq 2q_h - 1$; see Theorem 11 and Corollary 12.

Lemma 9. Let $h: X^* \to Y^*$ be a primitive ps-code, $k \geq 2$ a fixed integer and w a k-free word in X^*. Let $R^k \neq \lambda$ occur in $h(w)$ in such a way that $h(w) = \alpha R^k \beta = [\alpha\alpha'][h(u)][\beta'\beta]$. Then $|u| < |R|$.

In the proof of Theorem 11 (the case $q_h = k_0 = 2$ there) we can apply the following theorem proved by Leconte in [8]. For more characterizations of square-free morphisms the reader is referred for example to Crochemore [3].

Theorem 10 (Leconte [8]). Let $h: X^* \to Y^*$ be a morphism such that $h(w)$ is square-free for every square-free $w \in X^*$ of length ≤ 3. Then

(i) h is k-free for all integers $k \geq 4$;

(ii) h is cube-free if $h(a^2)$ is cube-free for every letter $a \in X$;

(iii) h is square-free if $h(w)$ is square-free for every square-free $w \in X^*$ of length $\leq e(h) + 2$, where $e(h) = \max\{|u| \mid h(u)$ is a proper subword of $h(a)$ for some $a \in X\}$.

Inspired by the above theorem, we prove a result concerning also morphisms that do not satisfy the square-freeness condition of Theorem 10.

Theorem 11. Let $h: X^* \to Y^*$ be a morphism such that $q_h \geq 2$. Choose integers r and k_0 such that $1 \leq r \leq \max\{1, q_h - 2\}$ and $k_0 \geq q_h + \lceil (q_h - 2)/r \rceil$. Then h is k-free for every integer $k \geq k_0$ if and only if

(i) h is a primitive ps-code; and

(ii) $R^{k_0} \notin SW\{h(w) \mid w \in X^*, |w| = |R| + 1 \ (w \neq a^2$ if $k_0 = 2)\}$ whenever $|R| = 1,\dots,r$.

Proof. Consider the "only if" part of Theorem 11. Let h be k-free for every $k \geq k_0$. Then (i) holds by Theorem 6. Moreover, (ii) holds since h and w are k_0-free. Observe that in (ii) $|R|+1 \leq r+1 \leq q_h-1 < k_0$ if $q_h > 2$, and $|R|+1 = r+1 = 2 \leq k_0$ $(w \neq a^2$ if $k_0 = 2)$ if $q_h = 2$.

In proving the "if" part assume that (i) and (ii) are satisfied. Firstly, let $q_h = k_0 = 2$. Assume that u is a square-free word in X^* of length ≤ 3. Then $h(u)$ is square-free, otherwise R^2 is in $SW(h(u))$ for $|R| = 1, 2$ or 3, a contradiction with condition (ii) or with the fact that h is a ps-code or with the fact that h is primitive. Moreover, because h is a ps-code with $q_h = 2$, $e(h) = 0$ concerning part (iii) of Theorem 10. So h is square-free. Obviously $h(a^2)$ is here cube-free for each letter a in X. Hence, by Theorem 10, h is power-free, that is, h is k-free for every $k \geq 2 = k_0$.

Let $q_h \geq 2$ and $k_0 \geq 3$. Assume that $h(u) = \alpha R^k \beta$ for some $R \neq \lambda$ and k-free u, where $k \geq k_0$ is arbitrary but fixed. Here $k_0 > q_h$. So condition (ii) and Lemma 9 imply $|R| > r$ (recall that every w in (ii) is k-free). Then, however, $|R^k| \geq q_h|R| + q_h - 1$, since $|R^k| \geq k_0|R| \geq (q_h + \lceil (q_h-2)/r \rceil)|R| \geq q_h|R| + (q_h-2)|R|/r > q_h|R|+q_h-2$. So we have $h(u) = \alpha R^k \beta = [\alpha\alpha'][h(v)][\beta'\beta]$ with $|v| \geq |R|$. This contradiction with Lemma 9 now proves Theorem 11. □

<u>Corollary 12</u>. Let $h: X^* \to Y^*$ be a morphism with $q_h \geq 2$. Then h is k-free for every integer $k \geq 2q_h - 1$ if and only if it is a primitive ps-code.

Proof. Choose $r = 1$ and $k_0 = 2q_h-1$ in Theorem 11 and observe that there is no a in X such that $a^{k_0} \in SW\{h(w) \mid |w| = 2\}$ if h(b) is primitive for every b in X. □

Using Corollary 12 and Theorem 3 we now see that a uniformly growing morphism $h: \{a,b\}^* \to Y^*$ is k-free for every integer $k \geq 2q_h - 1$ if and only if the words h(a), h(b) and h(ab) are primitive.

Let a morphism $h: X^* \to Y^*$ and an integer $k \geq 2$ be (effectively) given. If $k \geq q_h + 1$, it is decidable whether h is k-free; see Theorems 11, 6 and 1. For the case $2 \leq k \leq q_h$ Theorem 13 below may be very useful (its proof is found in [7]). Theorem 13 is interesting also in connection with Theorem 11.

For a morphism $h: X^* \to Y^*$ and a word γ in Y^* we mean by $D_h(\gamma)$ and $D_h'(\gamma)$ the following:

$$D_h(\gamma) = \{(s,u,p) \mid s \in SUFF(h(X)) - h(X),\ u \in X^*,\ p \in PREF(h(X)) - h(X) \text{ and } \gamma = sh(u)p\}$$

and

$$D_h'(\gamma) = \{(p,s) \mid h(a) = p\gamma s \text{ for some letter } a \in X \text{ and non-empty words } p,s\}.$$

<u>Theorem 13</u>. Let $h: X^* \to Y^*$ be a non-trivial morphism and $r \geq 1$ a fixed integer. Let

$$k_0 = k_0(h,r) = \max\{card(D_h(\gamma)) + card(D_h'(\gamma)) \mid \gamma \in SW_r(h(X^*))\}$$

and k a given integer $> k_0$. Moreover, assume that $k \neq 3$ or card(X) = 2 or h satisfies the subword property (1) or h is primitive. Then h is k-free if and only if h is a primitive ps-code and every subword of h(w) of length $\leq k(r-1)/(k-k_0)$ is k-free whenever w in X^* is k-free.

As an example of the use of Theorem 13 one can show that the endomorphism $g: \{a,b\}^* \to \{a,b\}^*$ defined by

$$g(a) = ab, \qquad g(b) = baabaabbabba$$

is k-free for every integer $k \geq 3$ (choosing $r = 5$ one gets $k_0 = k_0(g,r) = k_0(g,5) = 2$).

Naturally it is of interest to know how exhaustively Theorem 13 characterizes k-free morphisms, i.e. how k_0 decreases as r gets greater. We answer this question only in the case of length-uniform morphisms $h: \{a,b\}^* \to Y^*$ for which h(a), h(b) and h(ab) are primitive. Choose r so that $r \geq 3|h(a)|$. Then one can verify that $k_0 \leq 2$.

Acknowledgement

I want to thank Professor Paavo Turakainen for his guidance during my research work.

References

[1] Bean, D.R., A. Ehrenfeucht, and G.F. McNulty: Avoidable patterns in strings of symbols. - Pacific J. Math. 85, 1979, 261-294.

[2] Berstel, J.: Some recent results on squarefree words. - Lecture Notes in Comput. Sci. 166. Springer, Berlin - Heidelberg - New York - Tokyo, 1984, 14-25.

[3] Crochemore, M.: Sharp characterizations of squarefree morphisms. - Theoret. Comput. Sci. 18, 1982, 221-226.

[4] Karhumäki, J.: On cube-free ω-words generated by binary morphisms. - Discrete Appl. Math. 5, 1983, 279-297.

[5] Keränen, V.: On k-repetition free words generated by length uniform morphisms over a binary alphabet. - Preprint series in mathematics, Univ. Oulu, 1984.

[6] Keränen, V.: On k-repetition free words generated by length uniform morphisms over a binary alphabet. - Lecture Notes in Comput. Sci. 194. Springer, Berlin - Heidelberg - New York - Tokyo, 1985, 338-347.

[7] Keränen, V.: On the k-freeness of morphisms on free monoids. - Ann. Acad. Sci. Fenn. Ser. A I Math. Dissertationes 61, 1986.

[8] Leconte, M.: A characterization of power-free morphisms. - Theoret. Comput. Sci. 38, 1985, 117-122.

[9] Leconte, M.: Kth power-free codes. - Lecture Notes in Comput. Sci. 192. Springer, Berlin - Heidelberg - New York - Tokyo, 1985, 172-187.

[10] Lentin, A., and M.P. Schützenberger: A combinatorial problem in the theory of free monoids. - R.C. Bose, and T.E. Dowling (eds.): Combinatorial mathematics and its applications. North Carolina Press, Chapel Hill, N.C., 1969, 128-144.

[11] Rozenberg, G., and A. Salomaa: The mathematical theory of L systems. - Academic Press, London, 1980.

[12] Thue, A.: Über unendliche Zeichenreihen. - Norske Vid. Selsk. Skr., I. Mat. Nat. Kl., Christiania, 7, 1906, 1-22.

[13] Thue, A.: Über die gegenseitige Lage gleicher Teile gewisser Zeichenreihen. - Norske Vid. Selsk. Skr., I. Mat. Nat. Kl., Christiania, 1, 1912, 1-67.

AVOIDABLE PATTERNS ON 2 LETTERS*

Ursula SCHMIDT

Institut für Angewandte Informatik
und Formale Beschreibungsverfahren
Universität Karlsruhe
Postfach 6980
7500 KARLSRUHE
West-Germany

ABSTRACT

We examine avoidable patterns, unavoidable in the sense of Bean, Ehrenfeucht, McNulty. We prove that each pattern on two letters of length at least 13 is avoidable on an alphabet with two letter. The proof is based essentially on two facts: First, each pattern containing an overlapping factor is avoidable by the infinite word of Thue-Morse; secondly, each pattern without overlapping factor is avoidable by the infinite word of Fibonacci.

1. INTRODUCTION

During the last years, several papers considered combinatorial properties of words, in connection with the occurrence of subwords of a special form. For example, some papers were devoted to the study of the generation of square-free or overlap-free words (Berstel [2,4], Lothaire [6]), others to their determination and factorization (Crochemore [5], Main, Lorentz [7], Restivo, Salemi [8]). We are interested in a more general problem introduced in 1979 by Bean, Ehrenfeucht, McNulty [1], namely the study of so-called avoidable patterns.

It is possible to formulate the problem of unavoidable patterns as follows: We say that a word w divides a word u if there exists a non-erasing morphism h such that $h(w)$ is a subword of u. The word w is avoidable (resp. avoidable on an alphabet A with m ietters) if there exists an infinite word on a finite alphabet (resp. on an alphabet A with m letters) which is not divisible by w.

Bean, Ehrenfeucht, McNulty proved that each word w on an alphabet E with n letters of length at least 2^n is avoidable; in fact, they showed that w is avoidable on an alphabet A with m letters where m is exponential in n. In this article, we study the minimal alphabet A on which words on an alphabet E with 2 letters are avoidable.

---

* This article was done while the author stayed at LITP, Université Pierre et Marie Curie, Paris

We show that in the case of words on a 2 letter alphabet E we have $m = 2$ for nearly all words. More precisely, we prove that each word on E of length at least 13 is avoidable on a 2 letter alphabet A. The proof is based essentially on two results: First, each pattern containing an overlapping factor is avoidable by the infinite word of Thue-Morse; secondly, each pattern without overlapping factor is avoidable by the infinite word of Fibonacci.

We present the main theorems in section 3, which follows the definition section. Section 4 contains the ideas of the proofs of some theorems. The complete proofs as well as some remarks on words on a 3 letter alphabet are presented in Schmidt [9].

2. PRELIMINARIES

We denote by A^* (resp. A^+) the free monoid (resp. semi-group) generated by the alphabet A. The elements of A^* and A^+ are called *words*. The cardinality of the alphabet A is denoted by $|A|$.

We say that w is a *subword* of the word u, if there are words w_1 and w_2 such that $u = w_1 w w_2$. If $w = a_1 a_2 \cdots a_n$ with $a_i \in A$, for all $i = 1, \ldots, n$, then $\tilde{w} = a_n \cdots a_1$ is the reversal of w. The length of a word w is denoted by $|w|$.

Let A and E be alphabets. A homomorphism $h : E^* \to A^*$ is *non-erasing*, if $|h(e)| \geq 1$ for each $e \in E$.

Let $p \in E$, $u \in A$. The word p *divides* u (or: u is *divisible* by p) if there exists a non-erasing homomorphism $h : E^* \to A^*$ such that $h(p)$ is a subword of u.

Examples with $E = \{x, y\}$, $A = \{a, b, c\}$:

- *ababaab* is an instance of $xxyx$, so $xxyx$ divides *aababaabab*.
- x^2 doesn't divide *abcacbabcab*.

If p doesn't divide u, we say also that u *avoids* p. Clearly, if u avoids p, then each subword of u also avoids p.

If u avoids x^2 (resp. x^3), we say that u is *square-free* (resp. *cube-free*).

Let A be an alphabet with m letters. The word p is *avoidable on the m letter alphabet* or *m-avoidable* if there exists an infinite set F of words on A which avoid p. We say that p is *avoidable* provided there exists a finite alphabet A such that p is avoidable on A. Otherwise p is called *unavoidable*. In other words, p is unavoidable if each infinite set of words on a finite alphabet contains a word which is divisible by p.

An *infinite word* on A is a mapping $\mathbf{x} : \mathbf{N} \to A$, denoted by $\mathbf{x} = x_1 x_2 \cdots x_n \cdots$, where $x_n = x(n)$. So we can conclude that p is avoidable if and only if there exists an infinite word $\mathbf{x}$ on a finite alphabet such that $\mathbf{x}$ avoids p.

Examples with $E = \{a, b\}$:

1) *aba* is unavoidable
2) a^2 is not avoidable on $A = \{a, b\}$, since the only square-free words on A are a, b, ab, ba, aba and bab; but Thue [11] found an infinite square-free word on a three letter alphabet, so a^2 is avoidable.

Clearly, if p is m-avoidable, then it is k-avoidable for all $k > m$.

Since the composition of two non-erasing morphisms is also a non-erasing morphism, the division is a transitive relation (it is also reflexive, but not symmetrical). This gives us the following property:

Property 1:

Let p and u be words on finite alphabets. If p divides u and p is m-avoidable, then u is also m-avoidable.

In particular, all words containing a square are 3-avoidable. So we can state the

Lemma 1:

Let $E = \{a, b\}$. If $|p| \geq 4$, then p is avoidable.

Bean, Ehrenfeucht, McNulty [1] showed that a doubled word is avoidable; a doubled word is defined as a word where each letter occurring in it occurs at least twice. One can affirm by induction on n that every word of length at least 2^n on a n letter alphabet contains a doubled word of length at most 2^n as a subword. Therefore we have the following general version of lemma 1:

Theorem 2 (Bean, Ehrenfeucht, McNulty [1]):

Let $p \in E^*, |E| = n$. If $|p| \geq 2^n$, then p is avoidable.

Two other properties of avoidable words are easily verified:

Property 2:

A pattern $p \in E^*$ is avoidable, if and only if $\sigma(p)$ is avoidable, where $\sigma : E \to E$ is an arbitrary permutation of the letter of E.

Property 3:

A pattern p is avoidable if and only if its reversal $p^{\sim}$ is also avoidable.

Therefore we may consider avoidable or unavoidable patterns up to permutations and reversal.

We note $s : E^* \to \mathbf{N}$ the function defined by

$$s : E^* \to \mathbf{N}, \quad s(p) = \min\{\, m \mid p \text{ is } m\text{-avoidable} \,\}.$$

For p unavoidable we set $s(p) = \infty$. Clearly, no word is 1-avoidable, so $s(p) \geq 2$ for all p and all E.

Examples: $s(aba) = \infty, \quad s(a^2) = 3.$

Now lemma 1 can be restated in the following manner, in view of function s and by taking example 2 into account:

Proposition 3:

Let $E = \{a, b\}$. *If* $p \in E^+$ *is avoidable, then* $s(p) \leq 3$.

3. RESULTS

Our aim is to investigate the patterns on the 2 letter alphabet $E = \{a, b\}$. In particular, we wish to know which of them are 2-avoidable, i.e. we are looking for patterns $p \in E$ with $s(p) = 2$.

We start this section with our main theorem which gives a very precise answer to this question. The rest of this section is composed of two parts: First, we give some results which allow to establish that "nearly all" words on E are 2-avoidable (Theorem 9); then we set out some other theorems such that the main theorem will be a consequence of them.

Let us state our main theorem:

Theorem 1:

All words $p \in E^+, E = \{a, b\}$, *of length at least 13 are* 2*-avoidable.*

We pursue with some notations and results by Thue [11,12]. Let $A = \{a, b\}$. The homomorphism $\mu : A^+ \to A^+$ is defined by

$$\mu(a) = ab, \quad \mu(b) = ba.$$

When iterating this homomorphism, we get two sequences of words:

$$u_n = \mu^n(a), \qquad v_n = \mu^n(b).$$

These words are called *words of Thue-Morse*. They are related by the formulas

$$u_{n+1} = u_n v_n, \qquad v_{n+1} = v_n u_n \qquad (n \geq 0).$$

The first elements of the sequences are

$$\begin{array}{ll} u_0 = a & v_0 = b \\ u_1 = ab & v_1 = ba \\ u_2 = abba & v_2 = baab \\ u_3 = abbabaab & v_3 = baababba \\ u_4 = abbabaabbaababba & v_4 = baababbaabbabaab \end{array}$$

By further iteration, μ generates an infinite word $\mu^\omega(a)$ which is called the *infinite word of Thue-Morse* and is denoted by m:

$$\mathrm{m} = \mu^\omega(a) = abbabaabbaababbabaababba\cdots.$$

Theorem 2 (Thue [11, 12]):

The word m *avoids* a^3 *and* $ababa$.

Words avoiding the pattern *ababa* are called *overlap-free*. So we can deduce the following

Corollary 3:

Each word which contains an overlapping factor or a cube is 2-avoidable.

Now it remains to examine overlap-free words. Restivo, Salemi [8] found a very precise factorization, for which we need some further notations.

Let $a_n = \{a_n, b_n\}$ be a pair of words on A^+ inductively defined by

$$a_0 = a \qquad b_0 = b$$
$$a_{n+1} = a_n b_n b_n a_n \qquad b_{n+1} = b_n a_n a_n b_n \quad (n \geq 0).$$

For example, we have

$$a_1 = abba \qquad b_1 = baab$$
$$a_2 = abbabaabbaababba \qquad b_2 = baababbaabbabaab$$

The elements of A_n are related to the words of Thue-Morse by the formulas

$$a_n = u_{2n}, \qquad b_n = v_{2n} \quad (n \geq 0)$$

For $n \geq 0$, we define G_n (resp. D_n) as the set of left (resp. right) borders of order n:

$G_n = \{ 1,\ a_n,\ b_n,\ a_nb_n,\ b_na_n,\ a_na_n,\ b_nb_n,\ a_na_nb_n,\ a_nb_na_n,\ b_na_nb_n,$
$b_nb_na_n,\ a_na_nb_na_n,\ a_nb_na_nb_n,\ b_na_nb_na_n,\ b_nb_na_nb_n \}$

$D_n = G_n^{\sim} = \{ w^{\sim} \mid w \in G_n \}$.

We note $\quad A_n^i = \{ w = w_1 \cdots w_i | w_k \in A_n, 1 \leq k \leq i \}$.

Now we can give the result of Restivo, Salemi [8]:

Theorem 4:

Let $w \in E^*$ be an overlap-free word. There exists an integer $k \geq 0$ such that w can be factorized as follows:

$$w = g_0 g_1 \cdots g_{k-1} u d_{k-1} \cdots d_1 d_0,$$

where $g_i \in G_i, d_i \in D_i, 0 \leq i \leq k-1$ and $u \in \bigcup_{i=2}^{11} A_k^i$, and this factorization is unique.

This theorem states that the "central part" u of a finite overlap-free word is a subword of the infinite word $\mathbf{m}$ of Thue-Morse, whereas the "borders" have a different structure.

Since the words $g_j, d_j, 0 \leq j \leq k-1$, and u have bounded length, we may state the following corollary, using the word u_i of Thue-Morse:

Corollary 5:

For all $i \in \mathbf{N}$, there exists $c_i \in \mathbf{N}$ such that each overlap-free word on E of length at least c_i contains u_i as a subword.

Remind that $u_{2i} = a_i$ and that $u_{2i+1} = a_i b_i$.

Now, if we find i such that u_i is 2-avoidable, then we can deduce that "nearly all" overlap-free words are 2-avoidable.

Clearly, $i \geq 1$. As each word on E of length 11 contains an instance of $abba$, the pattern u_2 is not 2-avoidable, either.

We continue with u_3, and we are able to establish the following

Theorem 6:

The word $u_3 = abbabaab$ is 2-avoidable.

In fact, this is a corollary of

Theorem 7:

The infinite word $\mathbf{f}$ of Fibonacci avoids $abbabaab$.

We use the following characterization of $\mathbf{f}$: Let $A = \{a, b\}$. The *infinite word* $\mathbf{f}$ *of Fibonacci* is generated by the homomorphism

$\phi : A^+ \to A^+$

$\phi(a) = ab, \quad \phi(b) = a;$

so,

$$\mathbf{f} = \phi^\omega(a).$$

As a consequence of Corollary 5 and Theorem 6, we have the

Corollary 8:

Each overlap-free word $p \in E^+$ of length at least c_3 is 2-avoidable.

We put the corollaries 3 and 8 together to give

Theorem 9:

For $|E| = 2$, each word on E^+ which is "long enough" is 2-avoidable.

Now, in the second part of this section, we will precise what is "long enough", vaguely called c_3 in corollary 8. Since $|g_i| = |d_i| \leq 4^{i+1}$ and $2 \cdot 4^k \leq 11 \cdot 4^k$, we could state without further reflections, that

$$c_3 = \max\{\ |g_0| + |g_1| + |d_0| + |d_1| \ \mid\ g_i \in G_i, d_i \in D_i, i = 1,2 \text{ and } u \in \bigcup_{i=2}^{11} A_3^i\ \}$$

that is $c_3 = 216$.

This is a very large bound. So one should reason about the structure of the g_i, d_i and u for to obtain a smaller number.

We found it more interesting to consider the proof of Theorem 7 and to apply its methods to another subword of the infinite word of Thue-Morse. We are able to establish the following result:

Theorem 10:

The infinite word **f** *of Fibonacci avoids abbaabba.*

This word *abbaabba* is a subword of the fourth word v_4 of Thue-Morse. We state as a consequence

Corollary 11:

The pattern abbaabba is 2-avoidable.

Let $X = \{ a^3, ababa, abbabaab, (abba)^2 \} \subset E^+$.
The set X is a set of 2-avoidable words, and we know that each word on E which is "long enough" is divisible by an $x \in X$. So we may look for $l \in \mathrm{N}$ minimal such that all words on E with length l are divisible by an $x \in X$. We are able to state

Theorem 12:

For all words $p \in E^+$ of length at least 13 there exists $x \in X$ such that p is divisible by x.

Now Theorem 1 is a consequence of Theorem 12.

Remark: It is not known whether this bound is optimal, i.e. whether there exists $l \in \mathrm{N}$, $l < 13$, such that each $w \in E^+$ with $|w| \geq l$ is 2-avoidable. At any rate, $l > 5$, because *aabaa* is not 2-avoidable.

4. SKETCH OF THE PROOFS

The interesting results are the theorems 7, 10 and 12. We start this section with recalling some properties of the subwords of the infinite word **f** of Fibonacci.

Let $F(\mathbf{f})$ be the set of all subwords of **f**; let $A = \{a, b\}$; let $\phi : A^+ \to A^+$ be the homomorphism generating **f**.

Proposition 1 (Séebold [10]):

The words b^2, a^3, babab, aabaabaa are not subwords of **f**.

A word $w \in A^*$ is a *conjugate* of a word $w' \in A^*$, if there exist $u, v \in A^*$ such that $w = uv$ and $w' = vu$.

Proposition 2 (Séebold [10]):

If $u^2 \in F(\mathbf{f})$, then there exists $u' \in A^+$ such that u is a conjugate of u' and there exists $n \in \mathrm{N}$ such that $u' = \phi^n(a)$.

Proposition 3 (Berstel [3]):

If $u \in F(\mathbf{f})$, then $\tilde{u} \in F(\mathbf{f})$.

Now we will give a sketch of the proof of theorem 7, making use of propositions 1 to 3:

Proof of Theorem 7:

We will show the

Claim: The infinite word $\mathbf{f}$ doesn't contain a word of the form

$$w = uvvuvuuv_1$$

where v_1 equals the word v without its last letter.

This claim implies that $\mathbf{f}$ doesn't contain a word of the form $uvvuvuuv$; that means $\mathbf{f}$ avoids $abbabaab$.

Proof of the claim:

Suppose that $\mathbf{f}$ contains a word of the form $uvvuvuuv_1$. Hence, u^2, v^2 and $(uv)^2$ are supposed to be subwords of $\mathbf{f}$. Property 2 implies that

$$|u| = |\phi^r(a)|, \quad |v| = |\phi^s(a)|, \quad |vu| = |\phi^t(a)|,$$

hence $t = r + s$ and $s = r + 1$ or $s = r - 1$.

Without loss of generality, let $|u| = |\phi^r(a)|, |v| = |\phi^{r-1}(a)|$. Now, the proof is made by induction on r. As the basis of induction, one shows that the claim is true for $r = 2, 3$.

Then suppose $w = uvvuvuuv_1 \in F(\mathbf{f})$, where $|u| = |\phi^{r+1}(a)|, |v| = |\phi^r(a)|$.

We distinguish four cases depending on whether the first letter of u resp. v is a or b.

1) If the first letter of u and v is a, we may decompose w to form $\phi^{-1}(w)$ before the letter a: Let $u = au'$, $v = av'$, $v_1 = av_1'$. Then

$$w = au'av'av'au'av'au'au'av_1'.$$

Let $x = \phi^{-1}(u)$, $y = \phi^{-1}(v)$, $y' = \phi^{-1}(v_1)$. Hence,

$$\phi^{-1}(w) = xyyxyxxy'.$$

Since $|u| = |\phi^{r+1}(a)|$ and $|v| = |\phi^r(a)|$, we have $|x| = |\phi^r(a)|$ and $|y| = |\phi^{r-1}(a)|$. It remains to show that the prefix y_1 of y' of length $|y| - 1$ is a prefix of y and that $\phi^{-1}(w) \in F(\mathbf{f})$. It follows a contradiction to the hypothesis of induction.

— The word v doesn't end with a^2, since $a^3 \notin F(\mathbf{f})$.

— If v ends with ba, then y ends with ab and v_1 ends with b. Hence, $y' = \phi^{-1}(v_1) \in F(\mathbf{f})$ and $\phi^{-1}(w) \in F(\mathbf{f})$. Since y' ends with a, so y' is equal to y without its last letter; $y_1 = y'$.

— If v ends with ab, then y and v_1 end with a. The last letter of y' has no importance; it is sufficient to consider the length of the words: We have $|y| = |y'|$, and the prefix of y of length $|y|-1$ equals the prefix y_1 of y' of length $|y|-1$. Hence, $y_1 = \phi^{-1}(\bar{v}) \in F(\mathbf{f})$, where $v = \bar{v}ab$, and so $\phi^{-1}(w) \in F(\mathbf{f})$.

2) If the first letter of u is a and the first letter of v is b, then we get a contradiction to the hypothesis of induction by using proposition 3 for $\phi^{-1}(w)$.

3), 4) If the first letter of u is b, then we shift the form $uvvuvuuv_1$ one letter to the left. Doing this yields $\bar{w} = \bar{u}\bar{v}\bar{v}\bar{u}\bar{v}\bar{u}\bar{u}\bar{v}_1$, where $\bar{u}$, $\bar{v}$ and $\bar{v}_1$ begin with the letter a. So we reduced these cases to case 1). □

The proof of theorem 10 is made with nearly the same arguments; but the basis of the induction is more general, because there doesn't exist a relation between $|u| = |\phi^r(a)|$ and $|v| = |\phi^s(a)|$. □

Proof of theorem 12

Given the set X, one has to examine all words on $E = \{a, b\}$ of length k, for $k = 1, 2, \ldots, l$, if they are divisible by an $x \in X$.

Suppose that we found all words on E of length k which avoid all $x \in X$, and that there exists at least one such word. Accordingly to property 1) (section 1), it is sufficient to extend those words to words of length $k+1$ avoiding all $x \in X$. Furthermore, accordingly to properties 2) and 3) (section 1), it is sufficient to extend the words of length k at the right with one letter to obtain the words of length $k+1$ which have to been examined.

In doing this, and beginning with the word a, we find that the set of words w of length 13 such that w avoids each $x \in X$ is empty. □

REFERENCES

[1] Bean D. R., Ehrenfeucht A., McNulty G. F.: Avoidable Patterns in Strings of Symbols. Pacific J. Math. 85, 261-294 (1979)

[2] Berstel J.: Sur les mots sans carré définis par un morphisme. Proc. of the Intern. Coll. on Automata, Languages and Programming, Lecture Notes in Computer Science, Vol. 71, pp. 16-25, Springer 1979

[3] Berstel J.: Mots de Fibonacci. Séminaire d'Informatique Théorique 1980-81, Rapport LITP, Paris

[4] Berstel J.: Some recent results on square-free words. STACS 84, Lecture Notes in Computer Science, Vol. 166, pp. 14-25, Berlin-Heidelberg-New York: Springer 1984

[5] Crochemore M.: Régularités évitables. Thèse d'Etat, Rapport LITP 83-43, Paris, 1983

[6] Lothaire: Combinatorics on Words. Addison-Wesley 1984

[7] Main M. G., Lorentz R. J.: An $O(n \log n)$ Algorithm for Finding All Repetitions in a String. J. Algorithms 5, 422-432 (1984)

[8] Restivo A., Salemi S.: On Weakly Square-free Words. Bull. EATCS 21, 49-56 (1983)

[9] Schmidt U.: Motifs inévitables dans les mots. Thèse de l'Université Pierre et Marie Curie (Paris 6), Rapport LITP, Paris, 1986

[10] Séebold P.: Propriétés combinatoires des mots infinis engendrés par certains morphismes.

[11] Thue A.: Über unendliche Zeichenreihen. Norske Vid. Selsk. Skr., I. Mat. Nat. Kl., Christiania, 7, 1-22 (1906)

[12] Thue A. Über die gegenseitige Lage gleicher Teile gewisser Zeichenreihen. Norske Vid. Selsk. Skr., I. Mat. Nat. Kl., Christiania, 1, 1-67 (1912)

POLYNOMIAL OPERATIONS ON RATIONAL LANGUAGES

Mustapha ARFI

Laboratoire d'Informatique Theorique et Programmation
Université Paris VI - 4, Place Jussieu
75252 Paris Cedex 05 - FRANCE

ABSTRACT : Given a class $\mathcal{C}$ of languages, let Pol($\mathcal{C}$) be the polynomial closure of $\mathcal{C}$, that is, the smallest class of languages containing $\mathcal{C}$ and closed under the operations union and marked product L a L', where a is a letter. We determine the polynomial closure of various classes of rational languages and we study the properties of polynomial closures. For instance, if $\mathcal{C}$ is closed under quotients (resp. quotients and inverse morphism) then Pol($\mathcal{C}$) has the same property. Our main result shows that if $\mathcal{C}$ is a boolean algebra closed under quotients then Pol($\mathcal{C}$) is closed under intersection. As an application, we refine the concatenation hierarchy introduced by Straubing and we show that the levels $\frac{1}{2}$ and $\frac{3}{2}$ of this hierarchy are decidable.

INTRODUCTION

The famous Kleene's theorem (1954) states that a language on a finite alphabet is accepted by a finite automaton if and only if it can be expressed from the letters by means of the three operations union, product and star.

These three operations are, together with the other boolean operations (intersection and complement), the most important operations on rational languages and, in spite of thirty years of research, their study is far to be completed. The star operation leads to the still open problems of star height. The product and the boolean operations lead to concatenation hierarchies of Brzozowski and Straubing. Other interesting problems can be found in the papers of Brzozowski [1] and Hashiguchi [3,4,5].

The aim of this article is to study more closely the "polynomial" operations, that is the union and the product. In fact, as for the case of the concatenation hierarchies, it is more suitable to substitute to the usual concatenation product LL' a "marked" product L a L', where a is a letter. The polynomial closure Pol($\mathcal{C}$) of a class of languages $\mathcal{C}$ has been defined by Schützenberger [14] : Pol($\mathcal{C}$) is the smallest class containing $\mathcal{C}$ and closed under finite union and marked product. We first describe the polynomial closure of various classes of languages, and then we study the properties preserved by polynomial operations. For instance, we show that if $\mathcal{C}$ is closed under quotients (residuals) then Pol($\mathcal{C}$) is closed under quotients and product. If, furthemore, $\mathcal{C}$ is closed under inverse morphism, then so is Pol($\mathcal{C}$). Our main result shows that if $\mathcal{C}$ is a boolean algebra closed under residuals, then Pol($\mathcal{C}$) is closed under intersection.

This result allows us to refine the concatenation hierarchy proposed by Straubing in the following way:

- Level 0 consits of the two languages $\emptyset$ and A^*
- Level $n + \frac{1}{2}$ is the polynomial closure of level n
- Level $n + 1$ is the boolean closure of level $n + \frac{1}{2}$.

Thomas [19] has emphazised the connection between the levels n of this hierarchy and the hierarchies of the first order logic. Perrin and Pin [7] have extended this result to the levels $n + \frac{1}{2}$ but they have defined the level $n + \frac{1}{2}$ as the closure of the level n under polynomial operations and intersection. Our main result shows that it is unnecessary to consider the intersection and therefore our definition and theirs coincide.

It is well-known that decidability problems concerning concatenation hierarchies are difficult to solve. For instance, for Straubing's hierarchy, we know only that levels 0 and 1 are decidable. Straubing has recently shown that if L is a language on a two-letter alphabet, then one can decide whether L belongs to level 2. Up to date, all the other cases remain open prblems.

We first establish the decidability of level $\frac{1}{2}$ by using a remarkable syntactic property of its languages. Then, starting from a deep result of Hashiguchi [5] , we show that level $\frac{3}{2}$ is also decidable whatever is the size of the alphabet.

More precisely, our study breaks up into three main sections. In the first one, we give the basic definitions and concepts, illustrated by some examples, and we state a first result that will play an important role on decidability questions. In the second part, we establish the connection between recongizable operations (quotients, inverse morphism and intersection) and the two polynomial operations defined above. Throughout the third and last section are presented the decidability problems together with their consequences on Straubing's hierarchy.

I. POLYNOMIAL OPERATIONS

The reader may refer to [2,8,9] for all undefined terms. The following definition is adapted from Eilenberg [2] :

A class of languages is a correspondence $\mathcal{C}$ that assigns, to each finite alphabet A, a set $A^*\mathcal{C}$ of recongnizable languages on A^*.

Let then $\mathcal{C}$ be a class of languages. To each finite alphabet A, we associate a set, $\mathrm{Pol}(A^*\mathcal{C})$, of languages on A^*, which is the smallest family containing $A^*\mathcal{C}$, closed under possibly empty finite union and the operation "marked product" expressed as follows : $(L, L') \mapsto LaL'$, where a is a letter. We define by this process a new class of languages, $A \mapsto \mathrm{Pol}(A^*\mathcal{C})$, denoted by $\mathrm{Pol}(\mathcal{C})$. It will be called the polynomial closure of $\mathcal{C}$.

A "$\mathcal{C}$-elementary language on A^*" is a language of the form $L_0 a_1 L_1 \dots a_n L_n$, where $n \geqslant 0$, $L_i \in A^*\mathcal{C}$ for $i \in \{0,\dots,n\}$ and $a_i \in A$ for $i \in \{1,\dots,n\}$. With this definition, one can see that a language L belongs to $\mathrm{Pol}(A^*\mathcal{C})$ if and only if L is a possibly empty finite union of $\mathcal{C}$-elementary languages on A^*.

Example 1 :

Consider the class $\mathcal{C}$ defined by :

$$A^*\mathcal{C} = \{\emptyset, A^*\} \text{ (or simply } \{A^*\}\text{)}.$$

Then $\mathrm{Pol}(A^*\mathcal{C})$ is the set of finite unions of languages of the form $A^* a_1 A^* \dots a_n A^*$, where $n \geqslant 0$ and $a_i \in A$ for $1 \leqslant i \leqslant n$.

We also have :

$$\mathrm{Pol}(A^*\mathcal{C}) = \{L \sqcup\!\sqcup A^* \ ; \ L \subset A^*\},$$

where $\sqcup\!\sqcup$ denotes the shuffle product. See [6] .

Example 2 :

Let $\mathcal{F}$ be the class of languages defined as follows :

$$A^*\mathcal{F} = \{B^* \ ; \ B \subset A\}.$$

One can easily verify that $\mathrm{Pol}(A^*\mathcal{F})$ consists of the finite unions of languages of the form $A_0^* a_1 A_1^* \dots a_n A_n^*$; $n \geqslant 0$, $A_i \subset A$ for $i \in \{0,\dots, n\}$ and $a_i \in A$ for $i \in \{1,\dots, n\}$.

We shall later see, in the study of concatenation hierarchies, the importance of these two examples together with the following theorem.

Consider the varieties of monoids defined by :

$\underline{J}_1$: idempotent and commutative monoids

$\underline{J}$: $\mathcal{J}$-trivial monoids

$\underline{R}$: $\mathcal{R}$-trivial monoids

$\underline{R}^r$: $\mathcal{L}$-trivial monoids

$\underline{DA}$: monoids, the regular $\mathcal{D}$-classes of which are aperiodic semigroups.

We shall denote respectively by $\mathcal{J}_1$, $\mathcal{J}$, $\mathcal{R}$, $\mathcal{R}^r$ and $\mathcal{D}a$ the corresponding varieties of languages. Consider again the class $\mathcal{F}$ of the second example. Recall that it is defined by : $A^*\mathcal{F} = \{B^* ; B \subset A\}$.

Theorem 1.1 : The following equalities hold :

$$\mathrm{Pol}(\mathcal{J}_1) = \mathrm{Pol}(\mathcal{J}) = \mathrm{Pol}(\mathcal{R}) = \mathrm{Pol}(\mathcal{R}^r) = \mathrm{Pol}(\mathcal{D}a) = \mathrm{Pol}(\mathcal{F}).\ //$$

2) POLYNOMIAL OPERATIONS AND RECOGNIZABLE OPERATIONS

The polynomial operations are the union and the marked product defined above. In this section, our purpose is to study the connections between these two operations and some recognizable ones like quotients, inverse morphism and intersection.

a) Closure under quotients and (classical)product

Let $\mathcal{C}$ be a class of languages. $\mathcal{C}$ is said to be closed under quotients (resp. left quotients, resp. right quotients) if, for each finite alphabet A, each element $a \in A$ and each language $L \in A^*\mathcal{C}$, $a^{-1}L$ and $La^{-1} \in A^*\mathcal{C}$ (resp. $a^{-1}L \in A^*\mathcal{C}$, resp. $La^{-1} \in A^*\mathcal{C}$).

$\mathcal{C}$ is said to be closed under product if, for each finite alphabet A and for all languages $L, L' \in A^*\mathcal{C}$, the product $L.L'$ belongs to $A^*\mathcal{C}$.

Proposition 2.1 : Let $\mathcal{C}$ be a class of languages closed under quotients (resp. left quotients, resp. right quotients), then $\mathrm{Pol}(\mathcal{C})$ has the same property. Furthemore, $\mathrm{Pol}(\mathcal{C})$ is closed under product. //

Corollary 2.2 : The polynomial closure of a viariety of languages is closed under quotients and concatenation product. //

b) Closure under inverse morphism

Let $\mathcal{C}$ be a class of languages. We shall say that $\mathcal{C}$ is closed under inverse morphism if, for each morphism $\varphi : A^* \longrightarrow B^*$, $L \in B^*\mathcal{C}$ implies $L\varphi^{-1} \in A^*\mathcal{C}$. We then have :

Proposition 2.3 : Let $\mathcal{C}$ be a class of languages closed under quotients and inverse morphism. Then Pol($\mathcal{C}$) is closed under inverse morphism.//

Corollary 2.4 : If $\mathcal{V}$ is a variety of languages, then Pol($\mathcal{V}$) is closed under inverse morphism. //

It is an immediate consequence of proposition 2.3.

c) Closure under intersection

We shall end this section by giving sufficient conditions for a polynomial closure to be closed under finite intersection.

Let $\mathcal{C}$ be a class of languages. $\mathcal{C}$ is said to be closed under union (resp. intersection, resp. difference) if, for each finite alphabet A, $L, L' \in A^*\mathcal{C}$ implies $L \cup L' \in A^*\mathcal{C}$ (resp. $L \cap L' \in A^*\mathcal{C}$, resp. $L \setminus L' \in A^*\mathcal{C}$).

We can state now the fundamental theorem of this section.

Theorem 2.5 : Let $\mathcal{C}$ be a class of languages closed under union, intersection, difference and quotients. Then Pol($\mathcal{C}$) is closed under intersection. //

If $\mathcal{C}$ is a class of languages, we say that $\mathcal{C}$ is a boolean algebra if, for each finite alphabet A, $A^*\mathcal{C}$ is a boolean algebra.

As an immediate consequence, we obtain the corollary below.

Corollary 2.6 : Let $\mathcal{C}$ be a boolean algebra closed under quotients (which is the case of a variety of languages). Then Pol($\mathcal{C}$) is closed under intersection. //

Note : The proof of theorem 2.5 is rather long and requires a preliminary lemma using automata theory. In fact, the proof provides an algorithm in order to decompose an intersection of languages belonging to the polynomial closure of a class $\mathcal{C}$ into the union of $\mathcal{C}$-elementary languages. The following example gives an illustration.

Example : Consider the class $\mathcal{C}$ of the first example (first section) defined by $A^*\mathcal{C} = \{ \emptyset , A^* \}$. This class is the trivial variety. Recall that Pol($A^*\mathcal{C}$) consists of the finite unions of languages of the form $A^* a_1 A^* \dots a_n A^*$, $n \geqslant 0$ and $a_i \in A$ for $i \in \{1,.., n\}$. According to the previous corollary, Pol($\mathcal{C}$) is closed under intersection. Let's take the alphabet $A = \{a,b\}$ and the two following languages of Pol($A^*\mathcal{C}$) : $K = A^* a A^*$ and $K' = A^* b A^*$. We obtain the decomposition of $K \cap K'$ in $\mathcal{C}$-elementary languages :

$$K \cap K' = A^* a A^* b A^* \cup A^* b A^* a A^* .$$

3) CONCATENATION HIERARCHIES AND DECIDABILITY PROBLEMS

Consider the concatenation hierarchy defined as follows :

$$A^*\mathcal{V}_0 = \{ \emptyset , A^* \}$$

$$A^*\mathcal{V}_{n+\frac{1}{2}} = \mathrm{Pol}(A^*\mathcal{V}_n)$$

$$A^*\mathcal{V}_{n+1} = \mathrm{Bool}\ (A^*\mathcal{V}_{n+\frac{1}{2}})$$

where the symbol "Bool" means "boolean closure". We construct this way a hierarchy of classes of languages :

$$\mathcal{V}_i : A \longmapsto A^*\mathcal{V}_i \ ; \ i = 0, \tfrac{1}{2}, 1, \tfrac{3}{2}, 2, \ldots$$

For the levels indexed by integers, this hierarchy coincide with Straubing's hierarchy [18] . Therefore, levels ($\mathcal{V}_n$, $n \in \mathbb{N}$) are varieties of languages.

The connection between the levels n of our hierarchy and the hierarchies of the first order logic has been established by Thomas [19] . The generalization to levels $n + \frac{1}{2}$ has been made by Perrin and Pin [7] . However, they have defined the level $n + \frac{1}{2}$ as the closure of the level n under the polynomial operations together with the intersection. Now, theorem 2.5 shows that their definition is unaltered if we remove the intersection. Thus, our definition and theirs coincide.

We say that a class $\mathcal{C}$ of languages is decidable if, for each alphabet A, there exists an algorithm to decide whether or not a given rational language L belongs to $A^*\mathcal{C}$.

It is easy to see that $\mathcal{V}_0$ is decidable. The decidability of $\mathcal{V}_{\frac{1}{2}}$ results immediately from the following statement.

Theorem 3.1 : Let $L \subset A^*$ be a rational language and $\eta : A^* \longrightarrow M$ be the syntactic morphism of L. Set $P = L\eta$. Then

$L \in A^*\mathcal{V}_{\frac{1}{2}}$ if and only if :

$$\forall\, r,s,t \in M, \quad rt \in P \Longrightarrow rst \in P. //$$

The decidability of $\mathcal{V}_1$ has been proved by I. Simon [16] .

Theorem 3.2 : A rational language L belongs to $A^*\mathcal{V}_1$ if and only if its syntactic monoid is $\mathcal{J}$-trivial.//

We shall now state the most important result of this last section.

Theoreme 3.3 : $\mathcal{V}_{\frac{3}{2}}$ is decidable.//

The proof lays upon a great result of Hashiguchi [5] . Let A be a finite alphabet and $A^*\mathcal{S}$ a finite family of rational languages on A^*. Let Ω be a subset of $\{\cup, ., *\}$. We shall denote by $\mathcal{C}^{\Omega}(A^*\mathcal{S})$ the smallest family of languages on A^* containing $A^*\mathcal{S}$ and closed under the operations of Ω .

Theoreme 3.4 : $\mathcal{C}^{\Omega}(A^*\mathcal{S})$ is decidable.//

We use this theorem to prove the following proposition.

Proposition 3.5 : Let $\mathcal{C}$ be a class of languages. Assume that :

(i) Pol($\mathcal{C}$) is closed under product.

(ii) For each finite alphabet A, $A^*\mathcal{C}$ is a finite family and $\{1\} \in$ Pol($A^*\mathcal{C}$).

Then Pol($\mathcal{C}$) is decidable.//

Consider now the class $\mathcal{F}$ introduced at the first section :

$$A^*\mathcal{F} = \{B^* \ ; \ B \subset A\} .$$

Recall that Pol($A^*\mathcal{F}$) consists of the finite unions of $\mathcal{F}$-elementary languages :

$$A_0^* a_1 A_1^* \dots a_n A_n^* \quad ; n \geqslant 0, A_i \subset A \text{ for } i \in \{0,.., n\} \text{ and } a_i \in A \text{ for } i \in \{1,..,n\} .$$

As a consequence of Proposition 3.5, we have :

Corollary 3.6 : Pol($\mathcal{F}$) is decidable. //

Theorem 3.3 follows from theorem 1.1,corollary 2.2 and Corollary 3-6

So far, only the decidability of levels 0 and 1 was known. We have just established the decidability for levels $\frac{1}{2}$ and $\frac{3}{2}$. Straubing has recently shown that if L is a language over a two-letter alphabet , then one can decide whether L belongs to level 2. The case of the second level for arbitrary finite alphabet and the case of the upper levels still remain open.

ACKNOWLEDGEMENTS

I wish to thank especially Jean-Eric PIN for many helpful suggestions and encouragements.

REFERENCES

[1] J.A. Brzozowski, open problems about regular languages. Formal language theory, perspective and open problems (R.V. Book editor) Academic Press (1980) 23-47.

[2] S. Eilenberg, Automata, Languages and Machines. Academic Press, vol.A(1974), vol.B(1976).

[3] K. Hashiguchi, Regular languages of star height one. Information and Control 53(1982) 199-210.

[4] K. Hashiguchi, Limitedness theorem on finite Automaton with distance functions. JCSS 24 (1982) 233-244.

[5] K. Hashiguchi, Representations theorems on regular languages. JCSS 27 (1983) 101-115.

[6] M. Lothaire, Combinatorics on words. Addison-Wesley 1983.

[7] D. Perrin, J-E. Pin, First Order Logic and Star Free Sets, JCSS 32 (1986) 393-406.

[8] J-E. Pin, Varieties of formal languages. North Oxford (London) Plenum (New York) 1986.

[9] J-E. Pin, Variétés de langages et variétés de semigroupes. Thèse d'Etat, Paris (1981).

[10] J-E. Pin, Hiérarchies de Concaténation, RAIRO Theoretical Informatics 18 (1984) 23-46.

[11] J-E. Pin, Langages rationnels et reconnaissables. Cours Université de Naples, 1984

[12] J-E. Pin, H. Straubing, Monoids of upper-triangular matrices Proceedings of the conference "semigroups-Structure theory and Universal algebraic problems". Szeged August 1981.

[13] M-P. Schützenberger, Sur le produit de concaténation non ambigu. Semigroup Forum 18 (1979) 331-340.

[14] M-P. Schützenberger, sur certaines opérations de fermeture dans les langages rationnels. Istituto Nazionale di Alta Mathematica. Symposia Mathematica. Vol XV (1975) 245-253.

[15] I. Simon, Hierarchies of Events with do-depth one. Thesis, University of Waterloo, 1972.

[16] I. Simon, Piecewise Testable Events. Lecture Notes in Computer Science 33. Springer Verlag (1975) 214-222.

[17] H. Straubing, Aperiodic homomorphisms and the concatenation product of recognizable sets. J.Pure and Applied Algebra 15(1979) 319-327.

[18] H. Straubing, Finite semigroup varieties of the forme $\underline{V} * \underline{D}$ J. Pure and applied Algebra 36 (1985) 53-94.

[19] W. Thomas, Classifying regular events in Symbolic Logic. JCSS 25 (1982) 360-376.

SOME STRUCTURAL ASPECTS OF HYPERGRAPH LANGUAGES GENERATED BY HYPEREDGE REPLACEMENT

Annegret Habel & Hans-Jörg Kreowski
Universität Bremen, Fachbereich Mathematik/Informatik
Postfach 33 04 40, D-2800 Bremen 33

ABSTRACT

Hyperedge replacement systems are introduced as a device for generating hypergraph languages including graph languages and string languages (where the strings are uniquely represented as certain graphs). Our concept combines a context-free type of rewriting with a comparatively large generative power. The former is indicated, for example, by a pumping lemma, the latter by the examples (among them you find the refinement of Petri nets, the analysis of flow diagrams, the structural description of molecules and some typical non-context-free string languages).

1. INTRODUCTION

Graph grammars and graph languages have been studied since the late sixties and have been motivated by various application areas such as pattern recognition, semantics of programming languages, compiler description, data base systems, specification of data types, developmental biology, etc. (see /CER 79/,/ENR 83/ for a survey). Unfortunately, the general approaches (see e.g., Ehrig /Eh 79/ and Nagl /Na 79/) cover lots of potential applications while only the more specific approaches (for the special case of node rewriting see, e.g., Janssens and Rozenberg /JR 80/ and for the case of edge replacement see our approach in /Kr 77+79, HK 83+85/) promise a rich mathematical outcome. In this paper, we propose a kind of compromise by introducing hyperedge replacement systems reviving some ideas from the early seventies which can be found in Feder's /Fe 71/ and Pavlidis' /Pa 72/ work. On one hand, Petri nets, functional expressions, program flow diagrams, molecule structures and many other complex data and information structures can be interpreted in a natural way as hypergraphs (the hyperedges of which may have many "tentacles" to grip at their source and target nodes rather than two "arms" as the edges of ordinary graphs). On the other hand, the replacement of hyperedges provides a type of context-free rewriting on the level of hypergraphs saving many of the fundamental properties of context-free rewriting on strings and on ordinary graphs. Hence we are confident that our new framework combines the theoretical attractivity of a class of context-free grammars and languages with the prospects for nice applications.

To be more matter of fact, our paper is organized as follows: The notion of hyperedge replacement systems (context-free hypergraph grammars), their derivation process and their generated hypergraph languages are introduced in Section 2. In Section 3, we state a pumping lemma which generalizes those pumping lemmas known for context-free string and graph languages. It says roughly that each sufficiently large hypergraph in a context-free hypergraph language decomposes into FIRST$\otimes$LINK$\otimes$LAST such that FIRST$\otimes$LINK^i$\otimes$LAST for $i \geq 0$ belongs to the given language. The crucial part is to find the proper composition $\otimes$ for hypergraphs. Finally, in Section 4, we apply the pumping lemma to various languages proving that they cannot be generated by context-free hypergraph grammars. In particular, we can show that the generative power of our grammars depends strongly on the so-called order, this is an upper bound for the number of "tentacles" a non-terminal hyperedge may have (for gripping at their source and target nodes). In other words, the order induces an infinite hierarchy of classes of hypergraph languages, which remains infinite even if one considers graph or string languages only. The string (graph) languages include certain non-context-free languages, and the graph languages of order 2 are just those which can be generated by edge replacement.

In the present version of this paper all lengthy proofs are omitted; they will be found in a forthcoming technical report. To make the paper self-contained the necessary notions of hypergraphs are recalled in the Appendix. It may be of interest that Bauderon's and Courcelle's framework of graph expressions /BC 85/ describe graphs and classes of graphs similar to the hypergraph languages studied in this paper.

2. HYPEREDGE REPLACEMENT SYSTEMS AND RELATED CONCEPTS

In this section we introduce hyperedge replacement systems generalizing edge replacement systems as introduced in /Kr 77+79/ and context-free string grammars. They can be seen as a hypergraph-manipulating and hypergraph-language generating device and turn out to be closely related to other concepts in computer science.

Based on hyperedge replacement, one can derive multi-pointed hypergraphs from multi-pointed hypergraphs by applying productions of a simple form.

2.1 DEFINITION (productions)

A (context-free) hypergraph production over $N \subseteq C$ is an ordered pair $p=(A,R)$ with $A \in N$ and $R \in \mathcal{H}$. In this case lhs(p) refers to the left-hand side A and rhs(p) to the right-hand side R. The type of p, denoted by type(p), is given by the type of R.

2.2 DEFINITION (derivations)

Let P be a fixed set of productions (over N).

1. Let $G \in \mathcal{H}$ and $B \subseteq E_G$. A mapping prod:B—> P is called a G-assignment provided that type(prod(e))=type(e) and lhs(prod(e))=l_G(e) for all e∈B.
2. Let $G,H \in \mathcal{H}$, let prod:B—>P be a G-assignment. Then G directly derives H through prod if H≅RES(G,repl) where repl:B→$\mathcal{H}$ is defined by repl(e)=rhs(prod(e)) for all e∈B. We write $G \underset{prod}{\Longrightarrow} H$ and say that $G \Longrightarrow H$ is a direct derivation from G to H (through prod).
3. A sequence of direct derivations

$$H_0 \underset{prod_1}{\Longrightarrow} H_1 \underset{prod_2}{\Longrightarrow} \cdots \underset{prod_k}{\Longrightarrow} H_k$$

is called a derivation from H_0 to H_k. This is abbreviated by $H_0 \overset{*}{\Longrightarrow} H_k$ or $H_0 \overset{*}{\underset{P}{\Longrightarrow}} H_k$ provided that the set P of productions is of interest.

REMARKS: 1. The application of a production p=(A,R) of type (k,l) to a multi-pointed hypergraph G requires the following two steps only:
- Choose a hyperedge e of type (k,l) with l_G(e)=A.
- Replace the hyperedge e in G by the multi-pointed hypergraph R.

In particular, there is no additional application condition employed.

2. The direct derivations have some significant properties, which will turn out to be quite frequently used in the next sections: The definition of a direct derivation includes the case that no hyperedge is replaced. This dummy step derives a hypergraph isomorphic to the deriving one. Moreover, whenever two hyperedges can be replaced in parallel, they can be replaced one after the other leading to the same derived hypergraph.

Using the introduced concepts of productions and derivations context-free hypergraph grammars and languages can be introduced in a straightforward way.

2.3 DEFINITION (hyperedge replacement systems)

1. A (context-free) hypergraph grammar is a system HG=(N,T,P,Z) where $N \subseteq C$ is a set of nonterminals, $T \subseteq C$ is a set of terminals, P is a finite set of (context-free) hypergraph productions over N and $Z \in \mathcal{H}$ is a multi-pointed hypergraph, called initial hypergraph.

2. The hypergraph language L(HG) generated by HG consists of all terminal labeled multi-pointed hypergraphs derivable from Z:

$$L(HG) = \{H \in \mathcal{H} \mid Z \overset{*}{\underset{P}{\Longrightarrow}} H \text{ and } l_H(e) \in T \text{ for all } e \in E_H\}.$$

3. A hypergraph language L, i.e. $L \subseteq \mathcal{H}$, is called context-free if there is a context-free hypergraph grammar HG with L(HG)=L.

REMARKS: 1. Hypergraph grammars as introduced above are based on the replacement of hyperedges. To emphasize this aspect they are sometimes called hyperedge replacement systems. Hyperedge replacement works absolutely local without any effect to the context of the hyperedges replaced.

2. Given a context-free hypergraph grammar the type of the initial hypergraph plays an essential role: it determines the type of all generated hypergraphs. In particular, a language which contains hypergraphs of different types cannot be generated by the grammars introduced above.

2.4 RELATED CONCEPTS: Hyperedge replacement systems are closely related to other concepts in computer science. Because of the limited space, these relationships can be only sketched roughly.

(a) Feder /Fe 71/ studies plex grammars and plex languages. His notion of an n attaching-point entity is essentially a handle in our sense where begin (or alternatively end) is the empty string. Hence the interconnections of such entities, forming plex structures, can be regarded as special hypergraphs so that Feder's context-free plex grammars and languages fit in our framework. In particular, his plex generation of natural rubber molecules provides an example for a hyperedge replacement system. Similarly, Pavlidis' mth order graph grammars based on so-called mth order structures (see /Pa 72/) may be interpreted as a special case of our hypergraph grammars.

(b) Farrow, Kennedy and Zucconi /FKZ 76/ consider a so-called "semi-structured flow graph" grammar which turns out to be a special context-free hypergraph grammar. In particular, the control flow graphs of semi-structured programs which are used for data flow analysis can be generated by a context-free hypergraph grammar. Similarly, the transformation system for structure recognition purposes given by Lichtblau /Li 85/ can be described by hypergraph productions. Finally, there is a close relationship between the flow graph grammars considered by Schmeck /Sc 73/ and our hypergraph grammars.

(c) Batini and D'Atri /BD 81/ present a formalism based on hypergraphs and hypergraph grammars to investigate the advantages of a top down design of a relational data base model. Grammars, whose underlying structures are arbitrary relational structures are investigated e.g. in /Ra 75/,/EKMRW 81/,/EHR 86/. Because relational structures can be regarded as hypergraphs, one may think about our approach as the subclass of context-free structure manipulating systems.

(d) Valette /Va 79/ as well as Suzuki and Murata /SM 80/ investigate stepwise refinements and analysis of Petri nets. Since Petri nets can be defined as hypergraphs, their methods for refining Petri nets through step-by-step transformations of transitions can be described by the application of context-free hypergraph productions.

(e) Castellani and Montanari /CM 83/ define grammars for distributed systems. The productions of such a grammar represent the possible standalone evaluations of system components. They correspond to our context-free hypergraph productions.

(f) Edge-replacement systems as investigated in /Kr 77+79/ and /HK 83+85/ are special context-free hypergraph grammars. On the other hand context-free hypergraph grammars can be transformed into graph grammars which are based on the algebraic approach of graph grammars (cf. e.g. /Eh 79/). Hence all results known in this general approach apply to our grammars.

3. A PUMPING LEMMA FOR CONTEXT-FREE HYPERGRAPH LANGUAGES

The main result presented in this paper is a pumping lemma for context-free hypergraph languages. Roughly speaking, it says that each sufficiently large hypergraph belonging to a context-free hypergraph language can be decomposed into three hypergraphs FIRST, LINK and LAST, so that a suitable composition of FIRST, LAST and n copies of LINK for each natural number n yields also a member of the language. This theorem generalizes the pumping lemma for context-free graph grammars (given in /Kr 79/) as well as the well-known pumping lemma for context-free string grammars (cf. e.g. /HU 69/, Theorem 4.7.).

For a precise formulation of the pumping lemma we use an operation which allows to compose hypergraphs in a suitable way. We use the notion of a location to determine where a multi-pointed hypergraph may be inserted into another one. Insertion of a handle is explicitly constructed, arbitrary insertion is defined as a special case of hyperedge replacement.

3.1 DEFINITION (insertion of a hypergraph)

1. Let $G,H\in\mathcal{H}$ and $loc:\{\underline{begin}_H,\underline{end}_H\}\longrightarrow V_G^*$ a mapping satisfying $|loc(\underline{begin}_H)|=|\underline{begin}_H|$ and $|loc(\underline{end}_H)|=|\underline{end}_H|$. Then loc is called a location for H in G.

2. Let $G\in\mathcal{H}$, H be a multi-pointed handle with the hyperedge b and loc be a location for H in G. Then the result of the insertion of H in G at loc is the multi-pointed hypergraph X with $E_X=E_G+\{b\}$, $V_X=V_G$, $s_X(e)=s_G(e)$, $t_X(e)=t_G(e)$, $l_X(e)=l_G(e)$ for all $e\in E_G$ and $s_X(b)=loc(\underline{begin}_H)$, $t_X(b)=loc(\underline{end}_H)$, $l_X(b)=l_H(b)$. X is denoted by $G\,{}_{loc}^{\oplus}H$.

3. Let $G,H\in\mathcal{H}$ and loc be a location for H in G. Moreover, let $Hb\in\mathcal{H}$ be a multi-pointed handle with hyperedge b and $\underline{type}(Hb)=\underline{type}(H)$ and locb be the location for Hb in G with $locb(\underline{begin}_{Hb})=loc(\underline{begin}_H)$ and $locb(\underline{end}_{Hb})=loc(\underline{end}_H)$. Then the result X of the insertion of H in G at loc is defined to be the result of the replacement of {b} in $G\,{}_{locb}^{\oplus}Hb$ through $\underline{repl}:\{b\}\longrightarrow\mathcal{H}$ with $\underline{repl}(b)=H$. X is denoted by $G\,{}_{loc}^{\oplus}H$.

REMARKS: 1. The insertion of a multi-pointed handle Hb (with the hyperedge b and the label $l_{Hb}(b)=A$) and of a multi-pointed hypergraph H in the multi-pointed hypergraph G can be depicted by

2. Let X be the result of the insertion of H in G at loc. Then G is a subhypergraph of X. Moreover, H can be embedded into X in a natural way. We need only the mapping $in:V_H\longrightarrow V_X$ induced by the insertion of H in G at loc which is defined by $in(v)=v$ for all $v\in V_H-EXT_H$, $in(\underline{begin}_{H,i})=loc(\underline{begin}_H)_i$, $in(\underline{end}_{H,j})=loc(\underline{end}_H)_j$ for $\underline{begin}_{H,i}$, $\underline{end}_{H,j}\in EXT_H$. (Note that all nodes occurring in $\underline{begin}_H$ and $\underline{end}_H$ are different, i.e. in becomes a mapping).

3.2 DEFINITION

Let $H\in\mathcal{H}$ and $loc:\{\underline{begin}_H,\underline{end}_H\}\longrightarrow V_H^*$ be a location for H in H. Moreover, let EMPTY be a empty (k,1)-hypergraph with $\underline{type}$(EMPTY)=$\underline{type}$(H). For each $n\in\mathbb{N}$, the multi-pointed hypergraph H^n with location $loc^n:\{\underline{begin}_H,\underline{end}_H\}\longrightarrow V^*_{H^n}$ for H in H^n is recursively defined as follows:

(1) $H^0 = EMPTY$, $loc^0(\underline{begin}_H) = \underline{begin}_{EMPTY}$, $loc^0(\underline{end}_H) = \underline{end}_{EMPTY}$,

(2) $H^{i+1} = H^i \oplus_{loc^i} H$, $loc^{i+1}(\underline{begin}_H) = (in^{i+1})^*(loc(\underline{begin}_H))$,

$loc^{i+1}(\underline{end}_H) = (in^{i+1})^*(loc(\underline{end}_H))$

where $in^{i+1}:V_H\longrightarrow V_{H^{i+1}}$ denotes the mapping induced by the insertion of H in H^i.

REMARKS: 1. H^1=H and loc^1=loc (up to isomorphism).

2. Intuitively, the multi-pointed hypergraph H^n is created from n copies of the hypergraph H which are inserted into each other. This can be depicted as follows

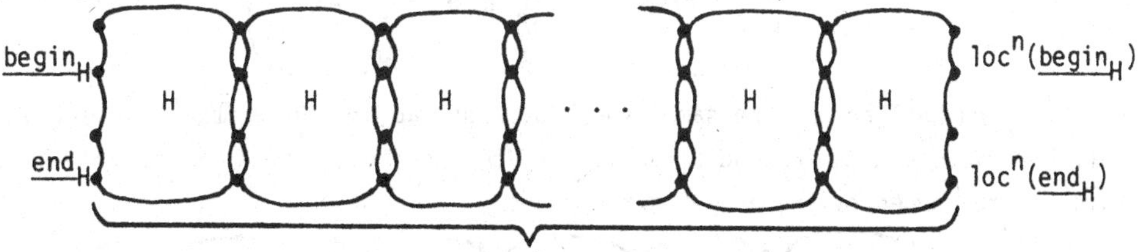

One more prerequisite is required for our pumping lemma. Context-free hypergraph grammars can be classified according to the upper bounds of the numbers of external nodes in the right-hand sides of their productions which will be called orders. Actually, we are going to formulate a pumping lemma for each order. The resulting classification of context-free hypergraph languages will be subject of a more detailed study in the next section.

3.3 DEFINITION (order)

1. A context-free hypergraph grammar HG=(N,T,P,Z) is said to be $\underline{\text{of order}}$ r (for some $r\in\mathbb{N}$) if for every production (A,R) in P $|\underline{begin}_R|+|\underline{end}_R|\leq r$.

2. A context-free hypergraph language L is $\underline{\text{of order}}$ r if there is a context-free hypergraph grammar HG of order r with L(HG)=L.

3. The class of all context-free hypergraph grammars of order r is denoted by $\underline{CFHG}_r$. The class of all context-free hypergraph languages of order r is denoted by $L(\underline{CFHG}_r)$.

REMARK: Obviously, we have $L(\underline{CFHG}_0)\subsetneq L(\underline{CFHG}_1)\subseteq L(\underline{CFHG}_2)\subseteq \ldots$. It will be shown in the next section that all the inclusions are proper.

3.4 THEOREM (pumping lemma)

Let L be a context-free hypergraph language of order r. Then there exist constants p and q depending only on L, such that the following is true: If there is a multi-pointed hypergraph H in L with $\underline{size}$(H)>p, then there are multi-pointed hypergraphs FIRST,LINK and LAST and locations floc for LINK in FIRST, lloc for LAST in LINK with

$H = FIRST \underset{floc}{\oplus} (LINK \underset{lloc}{\oplus} LAST)$,

$\underline{type}(LINK)=\underline{type}(LAST), \underline{size}(LINK \underset{lloc}{\oplus} LAST) \leq q$,

$LINK \neq EMPTY$ and $|\underline{begin}_{LINK}|+|\underline{end}_{LINK}| \leq r$

such that for each integer $i \geq 0$, $FIRST \underset{floc}{\oplus} (LINK^i \underset{lloc^i}{\oplus} LAST)$ is in L.

REMARKS: 1. The location $floc: \{\underline{begin}_{LINK}, \underline{end}_{LINK}\} \to V_F^*$ for LINK in FIRST induces tions for $LINK^i \underset{lloc^i}{\oplus} LAST$ in FIRST ($i \geq 0$). All these locations are, somewhat ambiguously, denoted by floc.

2. The multi-pointed hypergraph H in the pumping lemma is composed of hypergraphs FIRST, LINK and LAST. This can be depicted by

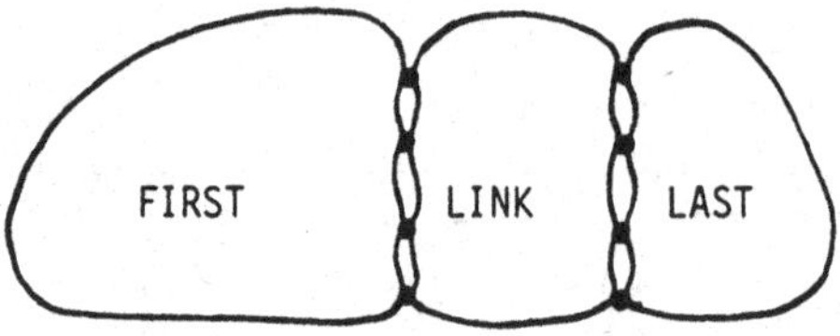

Since LINK and LAST are of the same type LAST- instead of LINK - may be inserted in FIRST. Moreover, LINK - instead of LAST - may be inserted in LINK. Hence pumping is possible. The pumped hypergraphs have the shape

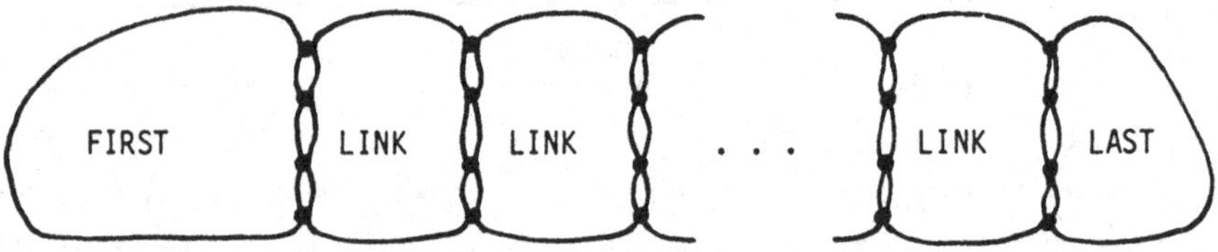

3. The requirement $LINK \neq EMPTY$ guarantees that the pumped hypergraphs are different from the given one and from each other.

4. Note that the number of external nodes of the LINK-component is bounded by r. This requirement restricts the number of possible decompositions of H.

5. In some sense the pictures above are over-intuitive, because they suggest that FIRST, LINK and LAST are connected hypergraphs - but they are not in general.

6. The pumping property is a necessary condition for a hypergraph language to be a context-free language. One of the main uses of the pumping lemma is to prove that specific hypergraph languages are not context-free (see Section 4).

We close this section by the discussion of some examples for context-free hypergraph languages.

3.5 EXAMPLE (context-sensitive string language)

The string graph language $SL_3=\{(a^nb^nc^n)^{\S} | n \geq 1\}$ can be generated by a context-free hypergraph grammar of order 4. (Note that the corresponding string language is not context-free.) The generating productions are the following:

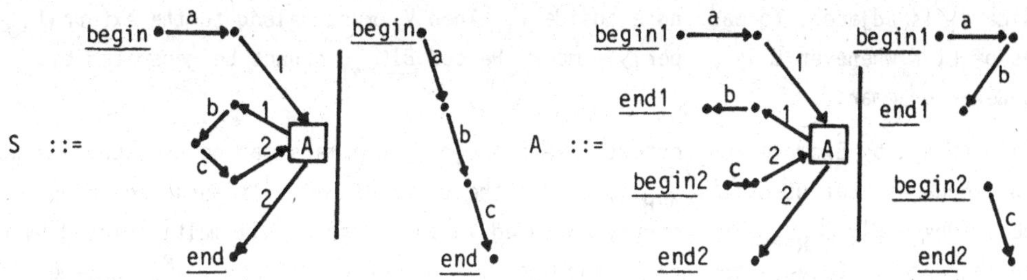

3.6 EXAMPLE (bipartite graphs)

A graph is said to be bipartite if its node set V can be partitioned into two non-empty sets V_1 and V_2 such that no two nodes in the same set are adjacent (cf. Berge /Be 73/). The set of all bipartite graphs with $|V_1|=r$ is denoted by $\underline{BIP}_r$.

The set $\underline{BIP}_r$ ($r\geqslant 1$) can be generated by a context-free hypergraph grammar $\underline{bip}_r$ of order r so that the bipartite graphs in $\underline{BIP}_r$ can be pumped according to the pumping lemma. The productions of $\underline{bip}_r$ are as follows:

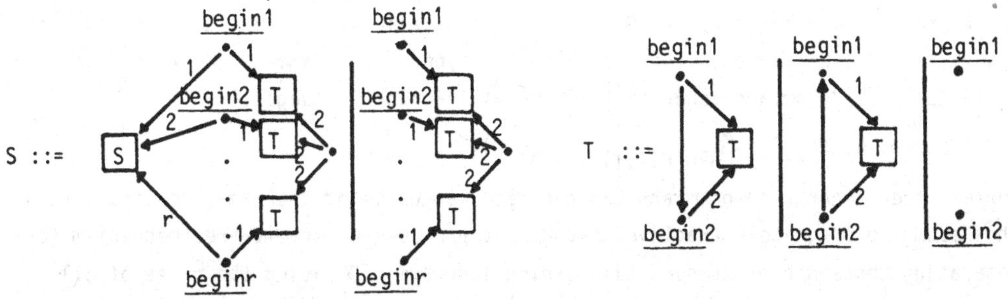

S and T are nonterminals. And there is meant to be only one terminal label. (Hence terminal edges are sufficiently represented by unlabeled ones.) Finally, the (r,0)-handle induced by S is used as initial hypergraph of $\underline{bip}_r$.

Other graph languages characterized by certain graphtheoretic properties can be generated by context-free hypergraph grammars. Hence our new framework may be of some interest even from a graphtheoretic point of view.

4. GENERATIVE POWER OF CONTEXT FREE HYPERGRAPH GRAMMARS

This section is devoted to a subtler view on the order of context-free hypergraph grammars and the resulting generative power.

Using the pumping lemma for context-free hypergraph languages, we are in the position to show that the class of order-r languages, $r\geqslant 0$, form a proper hierarchy.

4.1 THEOREM: For each $r\geqslant 0$: $L(\underline{CFHG}_r) \subsetneq L(\underline{CFHG}_{r+1})$.

REMARK: Theorem 4.1 means in particular that the number of external nodes in the right-hand sides of productions cannot be bounded without reducing the generative power.

SKETCH OF PROOF: According to 3.6, $\underline{BIP}_{r+1} \in L(\underline{CFHG}_{r+1})$ ($r\geqslant 0$). Using the pumping lemma, one can show that $\underline{BIP}_{r+1} \notin L(\underline{CFHG}_r)$. This can be seen as follows: Let V_1 denote the fixed set of r+1 nodes in each element of $\underline{BIP}_{r+1}$. Let G be a "complete" element where each node outside V_1 is adjacent to each node inside V_1. Then V_1 must belong to the external nodes of LINK whenever G is properly pumped. Hence, $\underline{BIP}_{r+1}$ cannot be generated by an order-r grammar.

As illustrated by Example 3.6 context-free hypergraph grammars can be used to generate graph languages. Let us use $\mathcal{L}_{GRAPH}$ to denote the class of all multi-pointed graph languages. (Obviously, $\mathcal{L}_{GRAPH}$ is properly included in the class of all multi-pointed hypergraph languages.) Because the graph languages $\underline{BIP}_{r+1}$ for $r \geq 0$ belong to $\mathcal{L}_{GRAPH}$, we get the following result as corollary of the theorem above.

4.2 <u>COROLLARY</u>: For each $r \geq 0$:

$$L(\underline{CFHG}_r) \cap \mathcal{L}_{GRAPH} \subsetneqq L(\underline{CFHG}_{r+1}) \cap \mathcal{L}_{GRAPH}.$$

Context-free graph grammars as considered in /HK 83+85/ can be seen as specific context-free hypergraph grammars: A context-free hypergraph grammar HG=(N,T,P,Z) is a context-free graph grammar, if the right-hand sides of the productions as well as Z are (1,1)-graphs. Now the class of all graph languages generated by a context-free graph grammar is denoted by L(CFGG); the class of all (1,1)-graph languages is denoted by $\mathcal{L}_{GRAPH(1,1)}$. We can show that context-free hypergraph grammars of order 2 and context-free graph grammars generate the same (1,1)-graph languages.

4.3 <u>THEOREM</u>: $L(\underline{CFHG}_2) \cap \mathcal{L}_{GRAPH(1,1)} = L(\underline{CFGG})$.

Context-free hypergraph grammars can generate languages of "string-like structures". This seems to be quite attractive, because it provides a context-free mechanism for generating certain context-sensitive string languages. Denoting the class of all string graph languages by $\mathcal{L}_{STRING}$ we get again an infinite hierarchy. The power of hypergraph replacement systems in generating languages from $\mathcal{L}_{STRING}$ increases whenever the considered order increases by more than 1. Somewhat amazing, the grammars of order 2r and 2r+1 for $r \geq 0$ generate the same subclass of $\mathcal{L}_{STRING}$.

4.4 <u>THEOREM</u>: For each $r \geq 0$:

$$L(\underline{CFHG}_{2r}) \cap \mathcal{L}_{STRING} = L(\underline{CFHG}_{2r+1}) \cap \mathcal{L}_{STRING},$$

$$L(\underline{CFHG}_{2r}) \cap \mathcal{L}_{STRING} \subsetneqq L(\underline{CFHG}_{2r+2}) \cap \mathcal{L}_{STRING}.$$

<u>REMARK</u>: Let $A=\{a_1,\ldots,a_r\}$ for $r \geq 1$ be an alphabet, and let SL_r denote the string graph language $\{(a_1^n a_2^n \ldots a_r^n)^{\S} \mid n \geq 1\}$. Then it is possible to show that SL_{2r+1} and SL_{2r+2} both can be generated by context-free hypergraph grammars of order 2r+2. The grammars are similar to the one given in Example 3.5.

It has been shown that context-free hypergraph grammars are more powerful than context-free graph grammars and string grammars. It remains the question: How powerful context-free hypergraph grammars are? One of the main uses of results like the pumping lemma discussed in Section 3 is to prove that specific hypergraph languages are not context-free languages - a task which in general is rather difficult. We derive now a corollary from the pumping lemma which applies very nicely to show that specific hypergraph languages are not context-free.

4.5 COROLLARY (sublinear growing)
Let L be an infinite context-free hypergraph language. Then there exist an infinite sequence of multi-pointed hypergraphs in L, H0,H1,H2,..., and constants $c,d \in \mathbb{N}$ with $c+d>0$ such that for all $i \geq 0$

$$|V_{Hi}| + c = |V_{H(i+1)}| \text{ and}$$
$$|E_{Hi}| + d = |E_{H(i+1)}|.$$

PROOF: The desired sequence of hypergraphs can be obtained by pumping of a sufficiently large hypergraph H0 in L. The constant c can be chosen to be the number of internal nodes of LINK and the constant d can be chosen as the number of hyperedges of LINK. Because LINK $\neq$ EMPTY we get $c \neq 0$ or $d \neq 0$.

REMARK: Corollary 4.5 is an immediate consequence of the Pumping Lemma. A more general statement would be possible yielding a full version of Parikh's Theorem for context-free hypergraph languages. But this would require a separate proof.

4.6 EXAMPLE (complete graphs)
The set of all complete graphs cannot be generated by a context-free hypergraph grammar because their growing with respect to the number of hyperedges is not sublinear as required by Corollary 4.5.

4.7 EXAMPLE (square grids)
The set of all square grids of the form

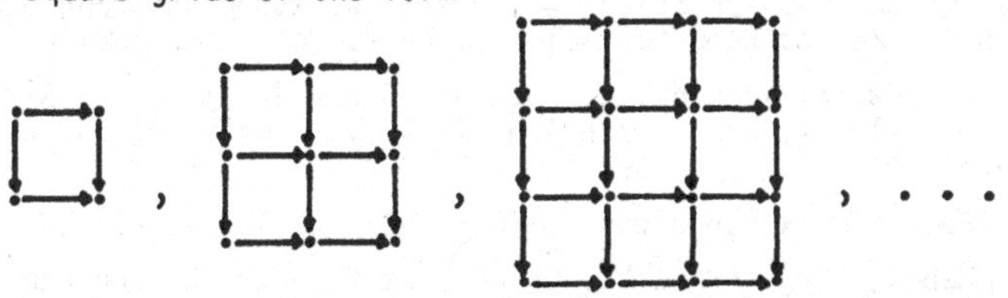

cannot be generated by a context-free hypergraph grammar because they grow too fast.

CONCLUSION

In this paper, we try a very first step towards a systematic investigation of context-free hypergraph grammars and languages. Nevertheless the framework proves to be promising in two resprects: Firstly, it covers examples interesting from the point of view of applications, of graph theory and of the formal (string and graph) language theory. Secondly, it promotes a sound mathematical theory with the prospect of rich results. But more work is necessary to get a clearer picture. Let us point out some of the questions which require answers:
(1) Context-free hypergraph grammars generalize context-free string and graph grammars. Besides the more difficult technicalities, there is definitely a price one has to pay for this more in generative power. But which?
(2) How can graph theory be employed to get a deeper insight into the structure and behavior of context-free hypergraph grammars?
(3) Besides the relationships pointed out so far, how may the theory of context-free hypergraph grammars be applied to the analysis and synthesis of Petri nets, flow diagrams, chemical structures, etc.?

(4) Can the class of string (graph) languages generated by context-free hypergraph grammars - remember that the class contains all context-free languages and certain context-sensitive ones - be characterized?

ACKNOWLEDGEMENT

We would like to thank our referees for their valuable comments on the considerations of this paper and Karin Limberg for her excellent typing.

REFERENCES

/BC 85/ M. Bauderon, B. Courcelle: Graph Expressions and Graph Rewriting, Comp. Sci. Research Report no. 8525, University of Bordeaux (1985)

/BD 81/ C. Batini, A. D'Atri: Schema Hypergraphs: A Formalism to Investigate Logical Data Base Design, Lect. Not. Comp. Sci. 100, 177-194 (1981)

/Be 73/ C. Berge: Graphs and Hypergraphs, North-Holland (1973)

/CM 83/ I. Castellani, U. Montanari: Graph Grammars for Distributed Systems, Lect. Not. Comp. Sci. 153 (1983), 20-38

/CER 79/ V. Claus, H. Ehrig, G. Rozenberg (eds.): Graph-Grammars and Their Application to Computer Science and Biology, Lect. Not. Comp. Sci. 73 (1979)

/Eh 79/ H. Ehrig: Introduction to the Algebraic Theory of Graph Grammars, Lect. Not. Comp. Sci. 73, 1-19 (1979)

/EHR 86/ H. Ehrig, A. Habel, B.K. Rosen: Concurrent Transformations of Relational Structures, Fundamenta Informaticae IX 13-50 (1986)

/EKMRW 81/ H. Ehrig, H.-J. Kreowski, A. Maggiolo-Schettini, B.K. Rosen, and J. Winkowski: Transformations of Structures: An Algebraic Approach, Math. Syst. Theory 14, 305-334(1981)

/ENR 83/ H. Ehrig, M. Nagl, G. Rozenberg (eds.): Graph-Grammars and Their Application to Computer Science, 2nd Int. Workshop on Graph Grammars and Their Application to Computer Science, Lect. Not. Comp. Sci. 153 (1983)

/FKZ 76/ R. Farrow, K. Kennedy, L. Zucconi: Graph Grammars and Global Program Data Flow Analysis, Proc. 17th Ann. IEEE Symp. on Found. of Comp. Sci., Houston Texas, Oct. 1976, 42-56

/Fe 71/ J. Feder: Plex Languages, Inform. Sci. 3 (1971), 225-241

/HK 83/ A. Habel, H.-J. Kreowski: On Context-Free Graph Languages Generated by Edge Replacement, LNCS 153, 143-158 (1983)

/HK 85/ --: Characteristics of Graph Languages Generated by Edge Replacement, University of Bremen, Comp. Sci. Report No. 3/85 (1985), to appear in Theor. Comp. Sci.

/HU 69/ J.E. Hopcroft, J.D. Ullman: Formal Languages and Their Relation to Automata, Addison-Wesley 1969

/JR 80/ D. Janssens, G. Rozenberg: On the Structure of Node-Label-Controlled Graph Grammars, Information Science 20, 191-216 (1980)

/Kr 77/ H.-J. Kreowski: Manipulationen von Graphmanipulationen, Ph. D. Thesis, Techn. Univ. Berlin, Comp. Sci. Dept., 1977

/Kr 79/ --: A Pumping Lemma for Context-Free Graph Languages, LNCS 73, 270-283 (1979)

/Li 85/ U. Lichtblau: Decompilation of Control Structures by Means of Graph Transformations, LNCS 185, 284-297 (1985)

/Na 79/ M. Nagl: A Tutorial and Bibliographical Survey on Graph Grammars, LNCS 73, 70-126 (1979)

/Pa 72/ T. Pavlidis: Linear and Context-Free Graph Grammars, Journ. ACM 19, 1, 11-23 (1972)

/Ra 75/ V. Rajlich: Dynamics of Discrete Systems and Pattern Reproduction, Journ. Comp. Syst. Sci. 11, 186-202 (1975)

/Sc 73/ H. Schmeck: Flow Graph Grammars and Flow Graph Languages, in M. Nagl, J. Perl (eds.): Graphtheoretic Concepts in Computer Science, Proc. of the WG' 83, 319-329 (1983)

/SM 80/ I. Suzuki, T. Murata: Stepwise Refinements of Transitions and Places, Informatik-Fachberichte 52, Springer, 136-141 (1980)

/Va 79/ R. Valette: Analysis of Petri Nets by Stepwise Refinements, Journ. Comp. Syst. Sci. 18, 35-46 (1979)

APPENDIX

This appendix provides all necessary notational prerequisites concerning hypergraphs, generalizing the notion of graphs (cf. e.g. Berge /Be 73/), and hyperedge replacement.

1. Let C be an arbitrary, but fixed alphabet, called a set of labels (or colors).

2. A (directed, hyperedge-labeled) hypergraph over C is a system (E,V,s,t,l) where E is a finite set of hyperedges, V is a finite set of nodes (or vertices), $s:E \longrightarrow V^*$ and $t:E \longrightarrow V^*$ [1] are two mappings, assigning (a string of) source nodes and (a string of) target nodes to each hyperedge, and $l:E \longrightarrow C$ is a mapping, called hyperedge-labeling.

3. A multi-pointed hypergraph over C is a system $H=(E_H,V_H,s_H,t_H,l_H,begin_H,end_H)$ where (E_H,V_H,s_H,t_H,l_H) is a hypergraph over C and $begin_H, end_H \in V_H^*$ are strings of nodes distinguishing pairwise different nodes of V_H. The set of all multi-pointed hypergraphs over C is denoted by $\mathcal{H}$.

4. Given $H \in \mathcal{H}$, a hyperedge $e \in E_H$ is called a hyperedge of type (k,l), a (k,l)-edge for short, if $|s(e)|=k$ and $|t(e)|=l$. [2] The pair (k,l) will be denoted by type(e).

5. A multi-pointed hypergraph $H \in \mathcal{H}$ is called a hypergraph of type (k,l), a (k,l)-hypergraph for short, if $|begin_H|=k$ and $|end_H|=l$. The pair (k,l) will be denoted by type(H). The nodes occurring in $begin_H$ or end_H are called the external nodes of H. The set of external nodes of H is denoted by EXT_H. All other nodes of H are called internal.

6. For $H \in \mathcal{H}$, size(H) denotes the number of hyperedges and nodes of H.

7. In drawings of hypergraphs, a dot (•) represents a node, and a graphical structure of the form

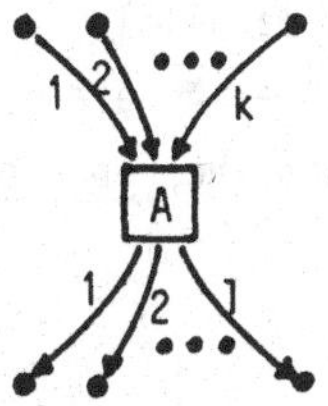

---

1) V* denotes the set of all strings over V, including the empty string.

2) Let w be string. The |w| denotes the length of w.

depicts a hyperedge with source and target where the label is inscribed in the box, the i-th arrow incoming into the box starts at the i-th source ($i=1,\ldots,k$) and the j-the arrow outgoing from the box reaches the j-th target ($j=1,\ldots,l$). In other words, our graphical representation makes use of the ont-to-one correspondence between hypergraphs and bipartite graphs.

8. Edge-labeled graphs and string graphs (representing strings in a unique way) are considered as special case of hypergraphs: A multi-pointed graph is a multi-pointed hypergraph in which all hyperedges are (1,1)-edges, this means hyperedges with exactly one source and one target node. In drawings, a (1,1)-edge is drawn as  instead of . A string graph is a (1,1)-hypergraph of the form $H=(\{e_1,\ldots,e_n\},\{v_0,\ldots,v_n\},s_H,t_H,l_H,v_0,v_n)$ where $s_H(e_i)=v_{i-1}$, $t_H(e_i)=v_i$ for $i=1,\ldots,n$. If $w=l_H(e_1)\ldots l_H(e_n)$, then H is called the string graph induced by w and is denoted by $w^{\S}$.

9. Corresponding to labels and natural numbers $k,l\in\mathbb{N}$ we get special multi-pointed hypergraphs, called "handles": A handle is a multi-pointed hypergraph of the form $H=(\{e\},V_H,s_H,t_H,l_H,\underline{begin}_H,\underline{end}_H)$ where $V_H=EXT_H, s_H(e)=\underline{begin}_H)$ and $t_H(e)=\underline{end}_H$. If e is a (k,l)-edge and $l_H(e)=A$, then H is called a handle induced by A and is denoted by $A(k,l)^{\S}$.

10. A (k,l)-hypergraph of the form $H=(\emptyset,V_H,s_H,t_H,l_H,\underline{begin}_H,\underline{end}_H)$ is said to be empty if $V_H-EXT_H=\emptyset$.

11. Let $H1,H2\in\mathfrak{H}$. Then H1 is called a (multi-pointed) subhypergraph of H2, denoted by $H1\subseteq H2$, if $E_{H1}\subseteq E_{H2}$, $V_{H1}\subseteq V_{H2}$, $s_{H1}(e)=s_{H2}(e)$, $t_{H1}(e)=t_{H2}(e)$, $l_{H1}(e)=l_{H2}(e)$ for all $e\in E_{H1}$ and $\underline{begin}_{H1}=\underline{begin}_{H2}$, $\underline{end}_{H1}=\underline{end}_{H2}$.

12. Let $H1,H2\in\mathfrak{H}$. Then H1 and H2 are isomorphic, denoted by $H1\cong H2$, if there are bijective mappings $f_E:E_{H1}\longrightarrow E_{H2}$, $f_V:V_{H1}\longrightarrow V_{H2}$ such that $f_V^*(s_{H1}(e))=s_{H2}(f_E(e))$[3], $f_V^*(t_{H1}(e))=t_{H2}(f_E(e))$, $l_{H1}(e)=l_{H2}(f_E(e))$ for $e\in E_{H1}$, $f_V^*(\underline{begin}_{H1})=\underline{begin}_{H2}$, $f_V^*(\underline{end}_{H1})=\underline{end}_{H2}$.

13. The key construction in this paper is the replacement of some hyperedges in a multi-pointed hypergraph by multi-pointed hypergraphs. For each hyperedge the replacing hypergraph must be of the same type. Then the result of the replacement of a (k,l)-edge b by a (k,l)-hypergraph repl(b) may be obtained by removing b and adding repl(b) in such a way that the external nodes of repl(b) are identified with the corresponding source and target nodes of b. The following formal definition allows to replace an arbitrary collection of hyperedges in parallel.

Let $G\in\mathfrak{H}$ and $B\subseteq E_G$. Moreover, let $\underline{repl}:B\longrightarrow\mathfrak{H}$ be a mapping satisfying the condition: type(repl(b))=type(b) for all $b\in B$. Then the replacement of B in G through repl yields the multi-pointed hypergraph H with

3) Let A and B be sets and $f:A\longrightarrow B$ be a mapping. Then $f^*:A^*\longrightarrow B^*$ denotes the mapping defined by $f^*(a_1\ldots a_n)=f(a_1)\ldots f(a_n)$ for $a_1\ldots a_n\in A^*$.

- $E_H=(E_G-B)+\sum_{b\in B} E_{\underline{repl}(b)}$,[4]
- $V_H=V_G+\sum_{b\in B}(V_{\underline{repl}(b)}-EXT_{\underline{repl}(b)})$,
- $s_H:E_H \longrightarrow V_H^*$, $t_H:E_H \longrightarrow V_H^*$ and $l_H:E_H \longrightarrow C$ defined by

  $s_H(e)=s_G(e)$, $t_H(e)=t_G(e)$ and $l_H(e)=l_G(e)$ for all $e\in E_G-B$,

  $s_H(e)=\underline{im}_b^*(s_{\underline{repl}(b)}(e))$, $t_H(e)=\underline{im}_b^*(t_{\underline{repl}(b)}(e))$ and $l_H(e)=l_{\underline{repl}(b)}(e)$

  for all $b\in B$ and $e\in E_{\underline{repl}(b)}$

  where $\underline{im}_b:V_{\underline{repl}(b)} \longrightarrow V_H$ is defined by $\underline{im}_b(v)=v$ for

  $v\in V_{\underline{repl}(b)}-EXT_{\underline{repl}(b)}$, $\underline{im}_b(\underline{begin}_{\underline{repl}(b),i})=s_G(e)_i$ and $\underline{im}_b(\underline{end}_{\underline{repl}(b),j})=t_G(e)_j$,
- $\underline{begin}_H=\underline{begin}_G$ and $\underline{end}_H=\underline{end}_G$.

The resulting multi-pointed hypergraph H is denoted by RES(G,repl).

14. By assumption all distinguished nodes of repl(b) are pairwise different so that $\underline{im}_b$ becomes a mapping. On the other side it is not required that all source and target nodes of a hyperedge b are different. Hence $\underline{im}_b$ may idenify some external nodes of repl(b). Up to this aspect, the replacement of some hyperedges means that they are blown up into subhypergraphs:

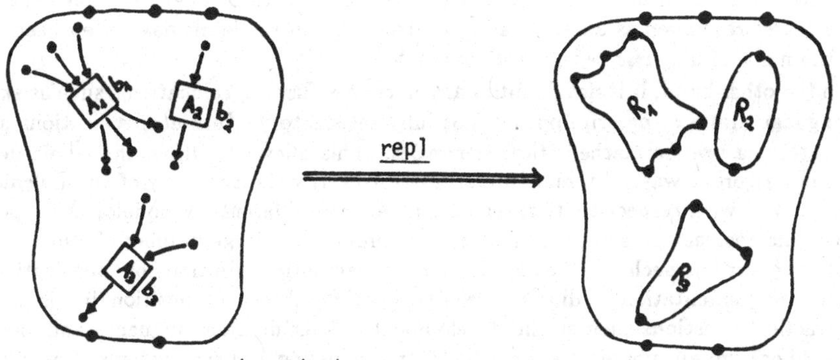

($\underline{repl}(b_i)$ = R_i for i=1,2,3).

4) Let A,B be sets. Then A+B denotes their disjoint union and A-B the set $\{a\in A | a\notin B\}$. For a finite set I, $\sum_{i\in I} A_i$ denotes the disjoint union of sets A_i.

Specification and Implementation of Concurrently Accessed Data Structures: An Abstract Data Type Approach

Stéphane Kaplan[1,2] & Amir Pnueli[1]

Introduction

The significance of the specification step in the process of software development has been widely recognized. A specification must be at the same time loose and abstract: several possible implementations should be possible, though requirement and decision details must be hidden at this very stage. In order to allow the definition of large real-size systems, a flexible *hierarchical* methodology supporting modular treatment should be applicable to all the development steps. It must be possible to divide a problem into simpler sub-problems (identified with modules), to deal with them separately, and to finally put the different modules together. The treatment of a submodule will allow further subdivisions as well as development steps (from the specification to the implementation phases) independently from other modules. Lastly, the process from specification to implementation is usually gradual. When considered in a top-down scheme, each partial implementation decision circumscribes a smaller class of possible implementations, and may be therefore viewed as a specification in itself. All these claims have often been advocated, under the name of *stepwise refinement* approach.

On the other hand, it is not doubtful anymore that fuzzy specifications, such as sketchy, natural language drafts or descriptions are not fully satisfactory. *Formal* specifications are needed, that relate to a precise mathematical semantics. This allows to direct the whole development process in a rigorous way, and, more importantly, to verify the adequacy of an implementation of a given module with respect to its specification. Among different methodologies proposed so far, the algebraic abstract data type formalism has stimulated a large number of studies considering theoretical questions such as: the syntactical and semantic definitions of specifications and the relation of implementation holding between them, hierarchical compositionality issue, as well as more practical questions such as the development of specification languages and environments, automated or semi-automated proof methods, and modeling real-size systems. Roughly speaking, an algebraic specification (synonymous with "abstract data type") provides a functional description of a system by identifying the operations that may take place and introducing algebraic laws between these operations.

However, an essential constraint on this methodology is that it implicitly applies to non-concurrent, strictly sequential systems. Due to the generalized development of *concurrent* systems, this has become too drastic a limitation. The purpose of this paper is to propose an extension of the classical framework of abstract data types in order to take concurrency issues into account. More precisely, we intend to describe data, and programs handling them, that are *shared* by several concurrent processes.

[1] Dept. of Applied Mathematics, The Weizmann Institute of Science, Rehovot 76100, Israel.

[2] LRI. Bât. 490. Faculté des Sciences, 91405 Orsay Cedex, France.

The work of the second author has been partially supported by the INRIA and by the Esprit project METEOR.

In the sequential case, programs and procedures are adequately represented by *operations* which are an integral part of algebraic specifications. This is because the algebra of operation composition and definition by equations is an adequate sequential (functional) programming language. However, once concurrency is introduced, the data operations are not sufficient to describe concurrency between processes. Consequently, the specifications we consider in this paper are partitioned into two components: the *data* component, and the *processes* component. The data component is identical to the specifications which are used in the sequential case. It consists of domains and operations that construct and extract objects from these domains and equations between the operations define their meaning. The processes component consists of some atomic processes whose effect when applied to data elements is defined using the data operations, and composite processes which are defined by sequential and concurrent compositional of simpler processes. Fortunately, there are developed algebraic theories for both data specifications [14, 16, 17, 20] and process specifications ([6, 7, 21, 22]), which so far have been studied separately. One of the contributions of this paper is the study of combined specifications which contain both a data and a processes components.

Typically, in a development process proceeding through several specification levels, the specifications at the higher levels of description will be functional and their process part consist almost completely of atomic processes simply defined as the application of an operation. At a lower level concurrency will become more visible and the processes component contain many composite processes defined by concurrent composition.

The central questions addressed in this paper are then:

- how to design data and process specifications in a modular, hierarchical way, according to the methodological constraints described so far?
- what does it mean for a high level, combined data and process specification, to be implemented by a lower level combined specification, and how to prove this?
- how do we relate a process that has been defined as atomic on the higher level, to an implementation defined as non-atomic and guarantee that the non-atomic implementation behaves as specified in spite of possible interference?

Our approach to the processes component of the specification has been inspired by the "process algebra" approach [6, 7, 8, 25], that has provided algebraic description of concurrency issues, and investigated the semantics of several primitives for concurrency. We consider here processes as functional entities acting on shared data structures. Sequential composition of processes corresponds to functional composition, and concurrency is modelled by interleaving of the different processes. Proving that a process specification implements a higher level process requires proving first that the functional properties of the specification hold in the implementation, and secondly that the granularity of the implementation is consistent with the granularity of the specification. This means that if increased concurrency occurs in the implementation, the corresponding interleavings should be "observationally equivalent" to the action described by the specification.

The questions of correct behavior under interference and the refinement of actions considered atomic on a higher level, have been extensively studied in non-algebraic frameworks ([19, 23]). The treatment there used logic as the specification language, and the main device suggested is the design of appropriate invariants, which capture intermediate steps in the performance of a non-atomic operation, and are immune to interference.

For our treatment of the data component of the combined specification we draw heavily on the theory developed and presented in [14, 15, 16, 24]. Extensions of this formalism that consider concurrency issues were presented in [2, 11]. For the interaction between processes and data, and definitions based on this interaction, we use many ideas suggested in Backus' FP language ([4, 5, 26]) and some data-flow languages [1, 13]).

The paper is organized as follows. Section 1 is dedicated to the analysis of a simple working example of a specification and its suggested implementation. Most of the problems addressed in the rest of the paper are illustrated on this example. Section 2 defines the notion of combined specifications and of implementations. Section 3 identifies the properties that must be checked in order to prove that an implementation satisfies its specification. A proof method for this purpose is introduced. In Section 4, the validity of the example of Section 1, and of a more complex implementation is proven according to the method of Section 3. Lastly, Section 5 extends the previous definitions and proof method to generalized concurrent specifications. An example of such an implementation is given, with the proof of its correctness.

It should be noted that, in order to improve readability, several technical parts have been deferred to appendices at the end of the paper.

1. Analysis of a Specification and of Two Possible Implementations

In this section, we develop an example of a "high-level" specification for stacks. Then, two possible implementations are successively presented and discussed. The main purpose of this part is to illustrate the formal notions that are introduced in the next sections, and to provide insight on how we intend to treat the questions addressed in this paper.

Our specification of stacks is as follows:

```
process specif PSTACK =                    -- processes acting on stacks
    data specif : STACK
    atomic processes:
        pop :                  → atomic
        add : elem             → atomic
        empty :                → atomic
        equations for atomic processes         ∀e ∈ elem, ∀s ∈ stack
         pop :: ⊙              = ∅
         pop :: push(e,s)      = s
         add(e) :: s           =push(e,s)
         empty :: s            = ⊙
end specif PSTACK.
                               With:
data specif STACK =
    used specifs : ELEM
    new sort : stack
    constructors:
        ⊙:                     → stack
        push: elem×stack       → stack
end specif STACK.
```

We now provide some informal explanations about this specification, the corresponding formal concepts being introduced in Section 2. PSTACK is a "*process* specification" of processes acting on stacks. As any *process* specification, it consists of two parts:

- A *data* specification STACK, that defines the concrete, static objects on which the processes of PSTACK will act. It is a classical algebraic specification, that introduces a new domain of values (a "sort" is the usual vocabulary) called *stack*. These values are synthesized by the two "constructors" '⊙' and 'push', and are thus of the form:

$$\odot, \quad \text{push}(e_1, \odot), \quad \text{push}(e_2, \text{push}(e_1, \odot)), \ldots$$

  STACK is actually a parameterized specification; the only constraint about its formal parameter ELEMENT is that it must have a sort called *elem*.

- PSTACK then defines processes acting on *stack*. Its processes are formed by various combination of its declared atomic processes. For instance, $p =$ (empty; add(e_1) $\|$ add(e_2);pop) is a process, where ';' and '$\|$' stand respectively for sequential and parallel composition. The atomic processes pop, add(e), empty are defined by their behaviour, i.e., how their application effects the environment (in this case, an element of *stack*). This is done in the "equations for atomic processes" part.
  The '::' operator is similar to Backus' FP application operator. $p :: s$ stands for the result of the action of the process p on the stack s. Its explicit declaration is missing: it belongs, such as ';', '$\|$', to the machinery of process application, composition, etc... that is common to all process specification, and therefore understated (cf. Section 2).

Popping the empty stack '$\odot$' yields an immediately deadlocking computation; it returns the special "no-result" value '$\emptyset$' (cf. Section 2). For a discussion on the debated issue of the algebraic specification of error handling mechanisms in the sequential case, we refer e.g. to [9,10].

PSTACK may be considered as a high-level specification since details that are irrelevant at this detail of specification are absent: nothing is said about actual implementation choices.

In order to illustrate the other end of the design process, we proceed to describe a possible lower-level implementation PAP of PSTACK. PAP is a *process* specification:

- its *data* part AP[1] implements the *data* part STACK of PSTACK. We choose to implement a stack by a pair consisting of an array, that stores the values pushed on the stack, and a pointer (a natural number) to the first free location in the array;
- each atomic process of PSTACK is implemented by a process of PAP. Here, empty and pop are implemented by the atomic processes $\overline{empty}$ and $\overline{pop}$. On the other hand, add is implemented by the non-atomic process $\overline{add}$, sequential composition of the atomic processes 'inc' (that increments the pointer), and 'ass' (that assigns the element at the previous location of the pointer):

$\overline{add}(x)$:

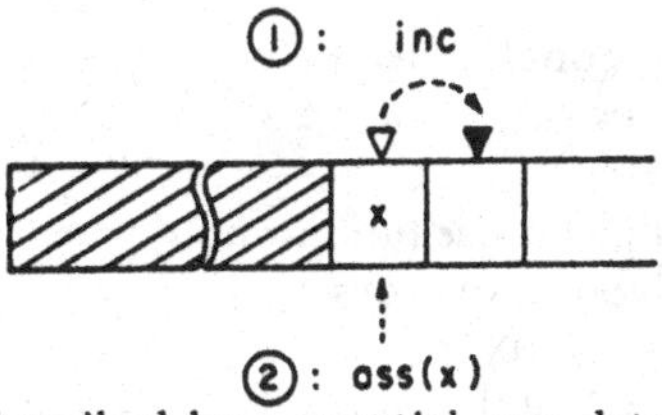

Non-atomic actions will be described by sequential, non-deterministic and parallel composition of smaller, atomic or non-atomic actions.

The implementation is as follows: [cf. figure 1 next page]

[1] "AP" stands for array with pointers.

data specif: AP

atomic processes: $\overline{empty}, \overline{pop}$, inc : $\to atomic$

ass : $elem \to atomic$

non-atomic processes: $\overline{add}$: $elem \to process$

equations for atomic processes:

$$\overline{empty} :: \langle a,n\rangle = \langle ea,0\rangle$$
$$\overline{pop} :: \langle a,n\rangle = if\ n=0\ then\ \emptyset\ else\ \langle a[pred(n)] := \perp, pred(n)\rangle$$
$$inc :: \langle a,n\rangle = \langle a,n+1\rangle$$
$$ass(e) :: \langle a,n\rangle = \langle a[pred(n)] := e, n\rangle$$

equations for non-atomic processes

$$\overline{add}(e) = inc;\ ass(e)$$

end specif PAP.

where

data specif AP = -- arrays with pointer

used-specifs : ELEMENT, NATURAL

new-sorts : *array, ap*

constructors

$ea :\ \to array$

$(\_[\_] := \_) : array \times natural \times elem \to array$

$\langle \_,\_ \rangle : array \times natural \to ap$

derived operators

$\overline{\odot} :\ \to ap$

$\overline{push} : elem \to ap$

equations between constructors :

$$(ea[i] := \perp) = \text{ea}$$
$$((a[i] := e)[i'] := e') = if\ i=i'\ then\ a[i'] := e\ else\ (a[i'] := e')[i] := e$$

equations for derived operators

$$\overline{\odot} = \langle ea,0\rangle$$
$$\overline{push}(e,\langle a,n\rangle) = \langle a[n] := e, n+1\rangle$$

endspecif AP

Figure 1: The PAP process specification

Comments

- We freely use so-called "dist-fix" syntax for the operators of the specification. The symbol "_" is a place-holder for the arguments. For instance, $a[i] := e$ stands for $(\_[\_] := \_)\ (a,i,e)$.
- '$\perp$' must be a particular constant of sort *elem* (representing the undefined value).
- As explained before, the behaviour of the atomic actions $\overline{empty}$, $\overline{pop}$, inc and ass(e) is described via their action on the environment, i.e. an array with pointer. This is achieved by interpreting $f :: \langle a,n\rangle$ for $f \in \{\overline{empty}, \overline{pop}, inc, ass(e)\}$. On the other hand, $\overline{add}(e)$ being non-atomic, is expressed by the sequential composition of two atomic actions. Of course, more complex formation of processes is allowed in what follows.

Now, to say that PAP is a correct implementation of the specification PSTACK essentially means two things:

(α) The properties of STACK, after a convenient translation, are satisfied by the models of PAP. This leads to prove, for instance, that $\overline{pop} :: \overline{add}(e,\langle a,n\rangle) = \langle a,n\rangle$, i.e.:

$$\langle (a[n] := e)[pred(n+1)] := \perp,\ pred(n+1)\rangle = \langle a,n\rangle \qquad (*)$$

holds for the elements of PAP that "represent elements" of STACK. Since such elements of PAP satisfy $a[n] = \perp$, property (*) is verified. It turns out that this is very similar to the proofs usually carried out in the field of abstract data types;

(β) It should be checked also that, when several processes of PAP act *concurrently* on a shared stack, they interact gracefully. Consider for instance the process $p = \overline{add}(e_1) \parallel \overline{add}(e_2)$ which stands for the parallel composition of $\overline{add}(e_1)$ and $\overline{add}(e_2)$. We shall see that:

$$p = \overline{add}(e_1); \overline{add}(e_2) + \overline{add}(e_2); \overline{add}(e_1) + inc; inc; ass(e_1); ass(e_2) + inc; inc; ass(e_2); ass(e_1)$$

where '+' is the nondeterministic choice operator. Now, whereas the processes $\overline{add}(e_1)$; $\overline{add}(e_2)$ or $\overline{add}(e_2); \overline{add}(e_1)$ do behave in a fine way when applied to a stack, the processes $inc; inc; ass(e_1); ass(e_2)$ or $inc; inc; ass(e_2); ass(e_1)$ will clearly yield erratic results, such as: $inc; inc; ass(e_1); ass(e_2)$:

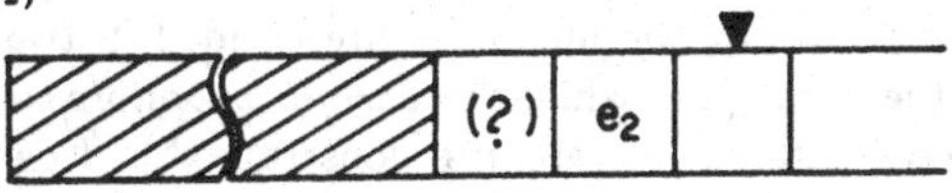

that is a couple ⟨array,pointer⟩ not corresponding any longer to the representation of any expected result. Hence, PAP *cannot be considered as an acceptable implementation of* STACK.

It is however easy to modify PAP in order to obtain a correct implementation of STACK. In the new specification PAP$^+$, a *semaphore* is set by inc and released by ass. Actually, we need not define too precisely what a semaphore exactly is; what we utilize, in such a synchronizing device, will be expressed easily and without unnecessary details, by some equations. In PAP$^+$, the environment is built by a constructor:

$$\langle \_,\_,\_ \rangle : array \times nat \times bool \rightarrow aps \quad \text{-- array with pointer and semaphore}$$

where the third argument stands for the semaphore.

The interesting fragment of the new process specification PAP$^+$ is now:

equations for atomic actions

$\overline{empty} :: \langle a, n, True \rangle = \langle ea, 0, True \rangle$

$\overline{empty} :: \langle a, n, False \rangle = \emptyset$

$\overline{pop} :: \langle a, n, b \rangle = if\ n = 0\ then\ \emptyset\ else\ \langle a[pred(n)] := \perp, pred(n), b \rangle$

$inc :: \langle a, n, True \rangle = \langle a, n+1, False \rangle$

$inc :: \langle a, n, False \rangle = \emptyset$

$ass(e) :: \langle a, n, b \rangle = \langle a[pred(n)] := e, n, True \rangle$

equations for non-atomic actions

$\overline{add}(e) = inc; ass(e)$

endspecif PAP$^+$.

Here, $\emptyset$ is a constant of sort *aps*, corresponding to erroneous, immediately deadlocking computations. It is clear that a process $inc; inc; ass(e_1); ass(e_2)$ applied to a good environment[2] will produce $\emptyset$. Now, it is the case that PAP$^+$ is an actual implementation of STACK, which is proven in full details in section 5. Note that it is not compulsory to clean up $\langle a, n, b \rangle$ during the application of $\overline{pop}$; the equation

$$\overline{pop} :: \langle a, n, b \rangle = if\ n = 0\ then\ \emptyset\ else\ \langle a, pred(n), b \rangle$$

defines an implementation that is not correct in our approach, but that would be correct with a slightly improved notion of implementation between *data* specifications. Again, we use in this article a very simple notion of implementation between *data* specifications in order to concentrate on *process* specifications.

---

[2] i.e. of the form $\overline{push}(d_1, \ldots, \overline{push}(d_n, \odot) \ldots)$.

2. The Formal Concepts

In this section, we introduce the formal background for our approach. We assume that the reader has some knowledge about classical abstract data types. For instance, since *data* specifications are exactly hierarchical abstract data types, they will not be fully discussed here; the missing definitions and notations are given in Appendix A. On the other hand, *process* specifications, that constitute the topic of this article, are discussed in full details hereafter.

Thus, a *data* specification is simply an abstract data type (also called an algebraic specification) with hierarchical constraints. Briefly (again, cf. Appendix A for formal definitions), a *data* specification consists of domain identifiers (called *sorts*), typed *operators* on the domains, and of *equations*. Usually, a *data* specification SPEC will be built over a more basic *data* specification PREDEF. It is assumed that SPEC preserves the meaning of PREDEF, which roughly means that SPEC does not modify the properties, nor the elements, of PREDEF ("hierarchical constraints of modularity"). Lastly, the operators are divided in two groups: the *constructors* synthesize the values of the data type, while the *derived operators* correspond to computations performed on these values ("internal hierarchical constraints"). Now, the semantics of such a *data* specification is usually described as its initial model.

We now proceed to describe our key-concept of *process* specification. A *process* specification formally consists of two parts:

- A *data* specification DATA, corresponding to the data structures that may be accessed concurrently. We suppose that DATA has a distinguished sort identifier s (often called its sort of interest). For instance, in the DATA part AP of the process specification PAP, we have s = ap.
- A new part that specifies the *processes* that act on the elements of sort s. It consists of
  - new sorts *atomic* and *process* standing respectively for atomic and compound processes. It is assumed that both act on items of sort s;
  - two sets of new operators names, standing for atomic and non-atomic process declarations, of respective domains *atomic* and *process*. Each of these operators is defined by a set of equations; constraints on the equations are given later.

The link between these two parts is via the application operator '::', similar to Backus' FP application operator. Notice that processes apply to one single value, representing the overall environment. However, this single value ranges over the sort s, which can be arbitrarily complex.

A schematic representation of the entities and relations involved in a process specification is presented in Fig. 2.

We now define the semantics of such a specification. The following operators are introduced:

- $\cup : s \times s \to s$ and $\emptyset : \to s$ standing respectively for nondeterministic choice and error (deadlock) in the items of DATA^s;
- $\_$: *atomic* $\to$ *process*, that is a "coercion" (empty-syntax operator) allowing to consider each atomic process as a process;
- $+$, ; , $\|$: *process* $\times$ *process* $\to$ *process*, standing respectively for nondeterministic choice, sequential composition and parallel composition of processes. An auxiliary operator $⫽$: *process*$\times$*process* $\to$ *process* (parallel composition with first action committed to come from the first argument) is used. $\delta : \to$ *atomic*, the deadlocking process, and **id**:$\to$ *process*, the identity process, are regarded as atomic actions.
- $\_::\_$: *process* $\times$ $s \to s$, representing the application of a process to an item of s.

The semantic of these operators is defined by the following set of axioms:

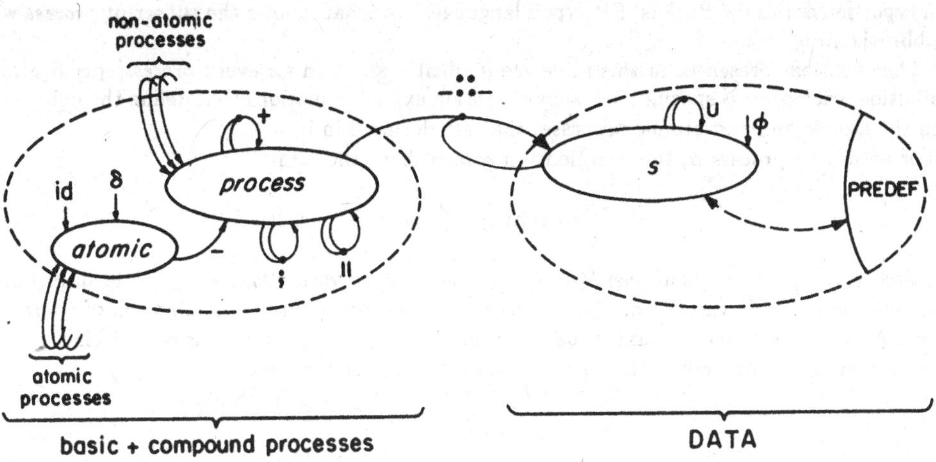

Figure 2: Organization of a process specification

$\forall x,y,z \in X^s,\ \forall \alpha \in X^{atomic},\ \forall p,q,n \in X^\pi$	
① $(x \cup y) \cup z = x \cup (y \cup z)$	② $(p+q)+r = p+(q+r)$
$x \cup y = y \cup x$	$p+q = q+p$
$x \cup x = x$	$p+p = p$
$x \cup \emptyset = x$	$p+\delta = p$
③ $(p+q) :: x = (p :: x) \cup (q :: x)$	④ $(p;q);r = p;(q;r)$
$p;q :: x = q :: (p :: x)$	$\delta;p = \delta$
$\delta :: x = \emptyset$	$id;p = p$
$id :: x = x$	$p;id = p$
⑤ $p \parallel q = p \mathbin{\lfloor\!\lfloor} q + q \mathbin{\lfloor\!\lfloor} p$	
$(p+q) \mathbin{\lfloor\!\lfloor} r = p \mathbin{\lfloor\!\lfloor} r + q \mathbin{\lfloor\!\lfloor} r$	
$(\alpha;p) \mathbin{\lfloor\!\lfloor} q = \alpha;(p \parallel q)$	
$\delta \mathbin{\lfloor\!\lfloor} q = \delta$	
$id \mathbin{\lfloor\!\lfloor} q = q$	

Notes: $\parallel$ and $\lfloor\!\lfloor$ have precedence over +, and + over ::. These axioms are inspired in part by the ACP framework (cf. e.g. [6,7], where it is also shown that several other primitives for process composition may be defined in such an axiomatic manner)[3] and by the paper [12] on an abstract

[3] For instance, we define and use a critical section operator $\ll\_\gg$ in section 4.

data types semantics for Backus' FP typed languages. In what follows the subscript *process* will be abbreviated by 'π'.

The equations presented in this table are implicitly assumed for every *process* specification. In addition, each *process* specification should contain explicit equations that define the behaviour of all the atomic and non-atomic processes that are declared in it.

- For an *atomic* process α, the equations on α must have the form

$$⑥ : \alpha(\vec{x}) :: \xi = t(\xi, \vec{x}),$$

where $\vec{x} = (x_1, \ldots, x_p)$ is an instantiation of the vector of variables of α, and ξ is an instantiation of the generic variable of s. The "context" t is formed with a combination of operators of DATA. For instance, the axiom $ass(e) :: \langle a, n\rangle = \langle a[pred(n)] := e, n\rangle$ is of this kind;
- for a *non-atomic* process ν, the equations on ν must have the form

$$⑦ : \nu(\vec{x}) = t(\vec{x}, \vec{\omega})$$

where $\vec{x} = (x_1, \ldots, x_p)$ is, as before, an instantiation of the vector of variables of ν, and $\vec{\omega} = (\omega_1(\vec{x}), \ldots, \omega_n(\vec{x}))$ is a vector of atomic processes. The "context" t is formed by combination of the operators +, ;, $\mathbin{⫫}$ and $\|$ (and possibly in a richer way if richer combinators *à la ACP* are used). For instance, the axiom $\overline{add}(e) = inc; ass(e)$ is of this kind.

<u>Definition</u> 2.1

The semantics $[\![\mathcal{P}]\!]$ of a *process* specification $\mathcal{P}$ is the terminal hierarchical model of the following algebraic specification.

specification $\Delta_{\mathcal{P}}$ =
  used specifs : DATA$^+$
  new sorts : *atomic, processes*
  constructors :
    id, δ, $\alpha_1, \ldots, \alpha_p$ -- for *atomic*
    +, ;, – --for *process*
  derived operators :
    :: -- into *s*
    $\mathbin{⫫}$, $\|$, $\gamma_1, \ldots, \gamma_q$ -- into *process*
  equations between constructors :②④
  equations for :: :③, $⑥_{\alpha_1}, \ldots, ⑥_{\alpha_p}$
  equations for $\|$, $\mathbin{⫫}$:⑤
  equations for $\nu_1, \ldots, \nu_q$:$⑦_{\nu_1}, \ldots, ⑦_{\nu_q}$
end specif $\Delta_{\mathcal{P}}$

With :

specification DATA$^+$ =
  used specif : DATA
  constructors : $\emptyset, \cup$
  equations between constructors :①
endspecif DATA$^+$

$[\![\mathcal{P}]\!]$ is characterized, among the models of $\Delta_{\mathcal{P}}$ by its congruence $\equiv_{\mathcal{P}}$. The restriction of $\equiv_{\mathcal{P}}$ to DATA$^+$ coincides with the *initial* congruence $\equiv$ of DATA$^+$, and the restriction of $\equiv_{\mathcal{P}}$ to *process* is defined (cf. Appendix A) by:

$$p \equiv_{\mathcal{P}} p' \Leftrightarrow \forall d \in \mathcal{P}^{DATA}, \quad \forall K \in \mathcal{P}^{\pi}[X],$$
$$K[p] :: d \equiv K[p'] :: d$$

$\mathcal{P}^{\pi}[X]$ is the set of all the *contexts* of sort *process*. For instance, $K[X] = (p_1 \| X \| p_2)$ is a context. This characterization means that two processes are equal modulo $\equiv_{\mathcal{P}}$ iff there is no experiment that can discriminate between them; such processes are said to be *observationally* equivalent. Note that, in practice, p and p' are "programs" that will probably differ syntactically (i.e. in the *initial* mode of $\Delta_{\mathcal{P}}$); but we are interested in abstracting away from this, in order to identify a process with the class of its different behaviours.

It can be checked that equations ①,②,③,④,⑤ automatically satisfy their hierarchical constraints. Thus, possible violations of these constraints may only result from ⑥ or ⑦:

- incompleteness or contradictions in ⑥ will violate the "modularity" hierarchical constraints of the specification, generating respectively "junk" or "confusion" in s.
- similarly, incompleteness or contradiction in ⑦ will violate "internal" constraints, generating "junk" or "confusion" in *action* and *process* (w.r.t. their set of constructors).

As a conclusion, it is the responsibility of the writer of *process* specifications to guarantee the completeness and the non-contradiction of the axioms for *atomic* (⑥) and *non-atomic* (⑦) actions; on the other hand, this is all the specifier has to do, since the whole machinery for processes is implicit (syntactically), and satisfies automatically its own constraints.

We now define our notion of implementation. Let $\mathcal{P}$ and $\mathcal{P}'$ be two *process* specifications. A *signature morphism* φ from $\mathcal{P}$ to $\mathcal{P}'$ is a mapping that maps each sort and each operator of $\mathcal{P}$ into sorts and operators of $\mathcal{P}'$. Some reasonable properties of φ are assumed: the image by φ of the *data* part of $\mathcal{P}$ is contained in the data part of $\mathcal{P}'$, $::_{\mathcal{P}}$ is transformed into $::_{\mathcal{P}'}$ (and identically for $+$, $;$, $\|$, etc.). A precise definition is given in Appendix B. It is also shown that it is enough to describe the action of φ on the sorts and and the constructors of the *data* part of $\mathcal{P}$ and *on the atomic actions* of $\mathcal{P}$. For instance, a natural φ: PSTACK $\rightarrow$ PAP^+ is described by:

$$\varphi(stack) = aps,$$
$$\varphi(\odot) = \overline{\odot}, \quad \varphi(push) = \overline{push}$$
$$\varphi(\mathrm{pop}) = \overline{\mathrm{pop}}, \quad \varphi(empty) = \overline{empty}, \quad \varphi(add) = \overline{add}$$

Definition 2.2

We say that a *process* specification $\mathcal{P}$ is implemented by a *process* specification $\mathcal{P}'$ via a signature morphism φ *iff* the *algebraic* specification $\Delta_{\mathcal{P}}/\equiv_{\mathcal{P}}$ is implemented by the *algebraic* specification $\Delta_{\mathcal{P}'}/\equiv_{\mathcal{P}'}$ via φ.

By convention, $\Delta_{\mathcal{P}}/\equiv_{\mathcal{P}}$ stands for the specification $\Delta_{\mathcal{P}}$ augmented with the equations of $\equiv_{\mathcal{P}}$. Definition 2.2 uses the notion of implementation between abstract data types given in Appendix A. Note that the only finitely generated model of $\Delta_{\mathcal{P}}/\equiv_{\mathcal{P}}$ is $[\![\mathcal{P}]\!]$ itself. In the next section, we examine how to check that a *process* specification is implemented by another. In what follows, "the specification" will often stand for the specification to be implemented, and "the implementation" for the implementing specification.

Lastly, we remark that our notion of implementation is compositional, which means that the relation "is an implementation of" is reflexive and transitive.

3. How to Prove Implementations

According to definition 2.1, proving an implementation requires to check that some equalities are satisfied in the implementation. We examine now what are exactly the properties that need be proven, and how to prove them. In this section, we restrict our attention to the particular case where *each action of the specification is implemented by a sequential composition of atomic actions*; this holds for instance with our working example PAP$^+$. The general case is treated in section 5.

A first group of properties that must be proven is concerned with the validity in $\mathcal{P}'$ of the "static" properties of $\mathcal{P}$. This amounts to show that:

- $\mathrm{DATA}_{\mathcal{P}}$, of the *data* part of $\mathcal{P}$, is implemented by $\mathrm{DATA}_{\mathcal{P}}$;
- For any atomic process a of $\mathcal{P}$, for any data d belonging to the sort of interest of $\mathcal{P}$ (i.e., the sort to which a applies), then

$$\varphi(a ::_{\mathcal{P}} d) \equiv_{\mathcal{P}'} \varphi(a) ::_{\mathcal{P}'} \varphi(d).$$

These properties are proven exactly in the same way as one proves implementations for classical abstract data types. Well-known methods for this have been investigated, and we shall not delve into this question. It is left as an exercise to the reader to show that these properties hold when we implement PSTACK by PAP or by PAP$^+$. Note that these properties are exactly the properties of type (α) presented in section 1. Lastly, the same will hold for declared non-atomic processes under our assumption (Appendix B) that declared non-atomic processes are translated by φ in a homomorphic way.

In order to introduce the second group of properties, and to guarantee that we prove all that must be proven, we consider the process specification $\mathcal{P}$ as a two-layer hierarchical specification:

- a subspecification $\mathcal{P}_{basic}$ of the *basic* processes, i.e., the processes built with the atomic and non-atomic actions, and composed by + and ; , and their respective axioms ②, ③, ④, ⑥, ⑦.
- $\mathcal{P}$ itself built over $\mathcal{P}_{basic}$ by the introduction of $⫫$ and $\|$ and the axioms ⑤.

$\mathcal{P}$ satisfies its hierarchical constraints w.r.t. $\mathcal{P}_{basic}$ because ⑤ is a hierarchically complete and consistent definition of $\|$ and $⫫$. Now, φ is a morphism from the algebra $T_{\mathcal{P}}$ of the terms of $\mathcal{P}$ (cf. Appendix A) into $T_{\mathcal{P}'}$; moreover, if the previous constraints of type (α) are satisfied, φ also defines a morphism from $\mathcal{P}_{basic}$ into $\mathcal{P}'_{basic}$. This important fact means that, as long as no concurrency is involved, "static" properties of the previous type (α) are enough to ensure the correctness of an implementation. Slightly anticipating, we can say that the real problems start with concurrency. The question is then under what condition may φ be factorized further from $\mathcal{P}$ into $\mathcal{P}'$?

To answer this, we notice that for any process p of $T_{\mathcal{P}}$ (without variables), there exists a unique[4] $p_0 \in T_{\mathcal{P}_{basic}}$ such that $p \equiv_{\mathcal{P}} p_0$. We say that p_0 is a *normal form* of p. Hence, we define a mapping $\varphi_0 \colon \mathcal{P}^{\pi} \to \mathcal{P}'^{\pi}$ by $\varphi_0(p) = \varphi(p_0)$. The restriction of φ_0 to $\mathcal{P}_{basic}$ coincides with φ. It is easy to check that $\varphi_0(p+q) \equiv_{\mathcal{P}'} \varphi_0(p) + \varphi_0(q)$, $\varphi_0(p;q) \equiv_{\mathcal{P}'} \varphi_0(p); \varphi_0(q)$. Thus, in order to check that $\mathcal{P}$ is implemented by $\mathcal{P}'$, it is sufficient to prove that $\varphi_0(p ⫫ q) \overset{f_0}{\equiv}_{\mathcal{P}'} \varphi_0(p) ⫫ \varphi_0(q)$ and $\varphi_0(p \| q) \overset{f_0}{\equiv}_{\mathcal{P}'} \varphi_0(p) \| \varphi_0(q)$, where:

$$p' \overset{f_0}{\equiv} q' \;\Leftrightarrow\; \forall d \in \mathcal{P}^{s},\ \forall K \in \mathcal{P}^{\pi}[X],\ \varphi(K)[p'] :: \varphi(d) \equiv \varphi(K)[q'] :: \varphi(d)$$

It is this last condition that was not satisfied while trying to implement PSTACK by PAP. Actually, let p and q be in $\mathcal{P}_{basic}$. There exists a $\psi \in \mathcal{P}'_{basic}$ such that $\varphi_0(p) \| \varphi_0(q) = \varphi_0(p \| q) + \psi$, and ψ comes from the interleavings of $\varphi_0(p)$ and $\varphi_0(q)$ that are not images by φ_0 of interleavings of p and q. For instance, with PSTACK implemented by PAP or PAP$^+$, $p = add(e_1)$ and $q = add(e_2)$, we have $\psi = inc; inc; ass(e_1); ass(e_2) + inc; inc; ass(e_2); ass(e_2)$. Moreover:

- In PAP$^+$, $\psi \overset{f_0}{\equiv} \delta$ and thus $\varphi_0(p) \| \varphi_0(q) \overset{f_0}{\equiv} \varphi_0(p \| q)$
- In PAP, $\varphi_0(p) \| \varphi_0(q) \overset{f_0}{\not\equiv} \varphi_0(p \| q)$

In general, we have $\varphi_0(p \| q) \leq \varphi_0(p) \| \varphi_0(q)$, where the relation $\beta \leq \alpha$ (β is *less non-deterministic* than α) is defined by $\beta \leq \alpha$ *iff* there exists a ψ such that $\alpha \overset{f_0}{\equiv} \beta + \psi$. Let $\sum_{i=1}^{n} \alpha_i$,

[4] modulo ② ··· ④

$\sum_{j=1}^{p} \beta_j$ be normal forms of respectively $\varphi_0(p \parallel q)$ and $\varphi_0(p) \parallel \varphi_0(q)$.[5] In order to ensure that $\varphi_0(p \parallel q) \overset{f_0}{\equiv} \varphi_0(p) \parallel \varphi(q)$, we only need to guarantee that $\beta_j \leq \varphi_0(p \parallel q)$, $\forall j \in [1 \ldots p]$. This is difficult to do in general, and we shall strengthen this condition in the following definition:

Definition 3.1

$\mathcal{P}'$ is a *strong implementation* of $\mathcal{P}$ *iff*

(α) DATA$_{\mathcal{P}}$ is implemented by DATA$_{\mathcal{P}'}$ via φ and $\forall a \in \mathcal{P}^{atomic}$, $\forall d \in \mathcal{P}^{s}$, $\varphi(a :: d) = \varphi(a) :: \varphi(d)$

(β) for any processes p, q of $\mathcal{P}$, and the normal forms $\sum_{i=1}^{n} \alpha_i$, $\sum_{j=1}^{p} \beta_j$ of $\varphi_0(p \parallel q)$ and $\varphi_0(p) \parallel \varphi_0(q)$ respectively:

$$\forall j \in [1 \ldots p], \quad \beta_j \overset{f_0}{\equiv} \delta \text{ or } \exists i \in [1 \ldots n] \text{ s.t. } \beta_j \overset{f_0}{\equiv} \alpha_i$$

Note: It is easy to prove that strong implementations are implementations. The converse is false in general.

3.1 A Proof Method for Strong Implementations

Let β_j appear in the normal form of $\varphi_0(p) \parallel \varphi_0(q)$ and not in the normal form of $\varphi_0(p \parallel q)$. There are two cases to consider:

- Either $\beta_j \overset{f_0}{\equiv} \delta$, as with $p = \overline{add}(e_1)$ and $q = \overline{add}(e_2)$ in PAP$^+$
- Or there exists an $i \in [1 \ldots n]$ such that $\beta_j \overset{f_0}{\equiv} \alpha_i$. For instance, with $p = \text{add}(e)$, $q = \text{pop}$, we have $\varphi_0(p) \parallel \varphi_0(q) = \varphi_0(p \parallel q) + \beta$; with $\beta = inc; \overline{pop}; ass(e)$. In PAP$^+$, $\beta \overset{f_0}{\equiv} \overline{pop}; inc; ass(e) \overset{f_0}{\equiv} \overline{pop}; \overline{add}(e)$. For instance, if:

$$x = \langle ea([0] := e_0, \ldots, [n] := e_n), n+1 \rangle, \quad \text{then:}$$

$$\beta :: x = inc; \overline{pop}; ass(e) :: x = \langle ea([0] := e_0, \ldots, [n-1] := e_{n-1}[n] := e), n+1 \rangle).$$

Similarly, with $p = \overline{add}(e_1); \overline{add}(e_2)$, $q = \overline{pop}; \overline{pop}; \overline{pop}$ and $\beta = inc; \overline{pop}; ass(e_1); \overline{pop}; inc; \overline{pop}; ass(e_2)$, we would show that $\beta \overset{f_0}{\equiv} \overline{pop}; \overline{add}(e_1); \overline{pop}; \overline{pop}; \overline{add}(e_2)$ by successive groupings. This suggests a general proof method.

To this effect, we shall denote by $At_{\mathcal{P}}$ the atomic actions of a process specification $\mathcal{P}$. $At^*_{\mathcal{P}}$ stands for the sequences of such actions (combined by the associative ';' with **id** as the neutral element). $\overline{A}$ stands for the implementation of an $A \in At_{\mathcal{P}}$. Recall that by hypothesis in this section, $\overline{A}$ is of the form $a_1; \ldots; a_n$ with $a_i \in At_{\mathcal{P}'}$. For $s_1, \ldots, s_n$ in $At^*_{\mathcal{P}}$, merge$(s_1, \ldots, s_n)$ stands for the set of all possible merges of $s_1, \ldots, s_n$. Lastly, let p, $p' \in At^*_{\mathcal{P}}$. We say that p is a *substring* of p', and we write $p \lhd p'$, *iff* there exist $q_1, q_2 \in At^*_{\mathcal{P}}$ such that $p' = q_1; p; q_2$.

Definition 3.2

Let $A \in At_{\mathcal{P}}$ such that $\overline{A} = a_1; \ldots; a_n$ with $\forall i \in [1 \ldots n], a_i \in At_{\mathcal{P}'}$. $\overline{A}$ is *regroupable* iff:
for any $B_1, \ldots, B_m \in At_{\mathcal{P}}$,
for any $p_0, \ldots, p_n \in At^*_{\mathcal{P}'}$ s.t. $p_0; \ldots; p_n \in \text{merge}(\overline{B}_1, \ldots, \overline{B}_m)$,
if $p = p_0; a_1; p_2; a_2; \ldots; p_{n-1}; a_n; p_n$ and $p \overset{f_0}{\not\equiv} \delta$, **then** there exist $q_1, q_2 \in At^*_{\mathcal{P}'}$ s.t.

(i) $p \overset{f_0}{\equiv} q_1; \overline{A}; q_2$

(ii) $q_1; q_2 \in \text{merge}(\overline{B}_1, \ldots, \overline{B}_m)$

[5] from now on, $\sum_{i=1}^{n} \alpha_i$ stands for $\alpha_1 + \cdots + \alpha_n$

(iii) *if* $\overline{B}_i \lhd p_k$ for some $k = 0, 1, \ldots$ *then* $\overline{B}_i \lhd q_j$ for some $j = 1, 2$.

The meaning of this definition is as follows: p is the generic form of a merge of $\overline{A}$ and $\overline{B}_1, \ldots, \overline{B}_m$. Then (i) says that either it is observationally equivalent to δ or to a merge $q_1; \overline{A}; q_2$ of $\overline{A}$ and $\overline{B}_1, \ldots, B_m$ (according to (ii)) where the atomic actions that form $\overline{A}$ may be grouped together. Moreover, this grouping should note separate actions, forming a $\overline{B}_i$, that were already grouped (according to (iii)). We now have the central result:

THEOREM 3.1

Let $\mathcal{P}$ and $\mathcal{P}'$ as in definition 3.1, such that (α) holds. Then (β) holds, i.e., $\mathcal{P}'$ is a strong implementation of $\mathcal{P}$, *iff* for each $A \in At_{\mathcal{P}}$, $\overline{A}$ is regroupable.

This is the theoretical point allowing for the proofs of implementations that follow in this paper.

Proof of Theorem 3.1:

- Suppose that $\mathcal{P}'$ is a strong implementation of $\mathcal{P}(\mathcal{D})$, then $p = p_0; a_1; \ldots; p_{n-1}; a_n; p_n$ belongs to merge($\overline{B}_1, \ldots, \overline{B}_m, \overline{A}$). Thus, there must exist a permutation τ of $[1 \ldots m]$ and an index $j \in [1 \ldots m]$ such that
  $p \stackrel{f_0}{\equiv} \overline{B}_{\tau(1)}; \ldots; \overline{B}_{\tau(j-1)}; \overline{A}; \overline{B}_{\tau(j)}; \ldots; \overline{B}_{\tau(m)}$.[6]
  The conditions of definition 3.2 are satisfied with $q_1 = \overline{B}_{\tau(1)}; \ldots; \overline{B}_{\tau(j-1)}$ and $q_2 = \overline{B}_{\tau(j)}; \ldots; \overline{B}_{\tau(m)}$
- Conversely, suppose that every $\overline{A}$ is regroupable. Let $p \in$ merge($\overline{B}_1, \ldots, \overline{B}_m$), $p \stackrel{f_0}{\not\equiv} \delta$. We show by induction on m that there exists a permutation τ of $[1 \ldots m]$ such that $p \stackrel{f_0}{\equiv} \overline{B}_{\tau(1)} \ldots \overline{B}_{\tau(m)}$. If $m = 1$, the result is trivial. Suppose that it is true for a certain value of m and let $p \in$ merge($\overline{B}_1, \ldots, \overline{B}_{m+1}$). Since $\overline{B}_{m+1}$ is regroupable, there exist q_1 and q_2 such that $p \stackrel{f_0}{\equiv} q_1; \overline{B}_{m+1}; q_2$ and $q_1; q_2 \in$ merge($\overline{B}_1, \ldots, \overline{B}_m$). $q_1; q_2 \stackrel{f_0}{\not\equiv} \delta$ since otherwise we would have $p \stackrel{f_0}{\equiv} \delta$. By the induction hypothesis, there exists a permutation τ of $[1 \ldots m]$ such that $q_1; q_2 = \overline{B}_{\tau(1)}; \ldots; \overline{B}_{\tau(m)}$. There exists a $j \in [1 \ldots m]$ and two string $B^{\ominus}$ and $B^{\oplus}$ such that $\overline{B}_{\tau(j)} = B^{\ominus}; B^{\oplus}$, $q_1 = \overline{B}_{\tau(1)}; \ldots; \overline{B}_{\tau(j-1)}; B^{\ominus}$ and $q_2 = B^{\oplus}; \overline{B}_{\tau(j+1)}; \ldots; \overline{B}_{\tau(m)}$. Then $p \stackrel{f_0}{\equiv} \overline{B}_{\tau(1)}; \ldots; \overline{B}_{\tau(j-1)}; B^{\ominus}; \overline{B}_{m+1}; B^{\oplus}; \overline{B}_{\tau(j+1)}; \ldots; \overline{B}_{\tau(m)}$. Using the fact that $\overline{B}_{\tau(j)}$ is regroupable immediately leads to the conclusion. ∎.

4. Examples of Specification Proofs

Using Theorem 3.1, we are going to prove in this section the correctness of two implementations of STACK.

4.1 Proof of the Correctness of PAP$^+$

We prove that the process specification PAP$^+$ described in section 1 is a correct implementation of the data specification STACK. Since $\overline{pop}$, $\overline{empty}$ are atomic, they are regroupable. We need only prove that $\overline{add}(x) = inc$; ass(x) is regroupable. To show this, let $p = \Gamma; inc; \gamma_1; \ldots; \gamma_\ell; ass(x); \Gamma'$ with $\Gamma, \Gamma' \in (At_{PAP^+})^*$ and $(\gamma_i) \in At_{PAP^+}$ such that $\Gamma; \gamma_1; \ldots; \gamma_\ell; \Gamma' \in$ *merge*($\overline{B}_1, \ldots, \overline{B}_m$). In this representation, the explicitly displayed *inc* and *ass* are corresponding components in the decomposition of some $\overline{add}$. Let us also assume that $p \stackrel{f_0}{\not\equiv} \delta$ and that *inc* is the first occurrence of this symbol in p. Then:

[6] The particular cases $j = 1$ and $j = m+1$ corresponding respectively to $\overline{A}; \overline{B}_{\tau(1)}; \ldots; \overline{B}_{\tau(m)}$ and $\overline{B}_{\tau(1)}; \ldots; \overline{B}_{\tau(m)}$

- no γ_i is equal to '*inc*'. Else, let γ_{i_0} be the first one. $\gamma_1;\ldots;\gamma_{i_0-1}$ contains no occurrence of '*ass*' since there is no possible matching '*inc*' in p before γ_{i_0}. Then the semaphore is still false at γ_{i_0} (this means that for any y, finitely generated by STACK, there exist a and n such that $(\Gamma;\gamma_1;\ldots;\gamma_{i_0-1}) :: y = \langle a, n, False\rangle$) and thus $p \overset{f_0}{\equiv} \delta$.
- no γ_i is equal to '*ass*' since there should be a matching *inc* before it.
- no γ_i is equal to $\overline{empty}$. Else, let γ_{i_0} be the first one. We have $\gamma_1 = \ldots = \gamma_{i_0-1} = \overline{pop}$. Thus $(\Gamma;\gamma_1;\ldots;\gamma_{i_0-1}) :: x = \langle a, n, False\rangle$ and $p \overset{f_0}{\equiv} \delta$.
- So $\gamma_1 = \ldots = \gamma_\ell = \overline{pop}$. One checks easily the lemma:

$$inc;\ \text{pop}^\ell;\ ass(x) \overset{f_0}{\equiv} \text{pop}^\ell;\ inc;\ ass(x)$$

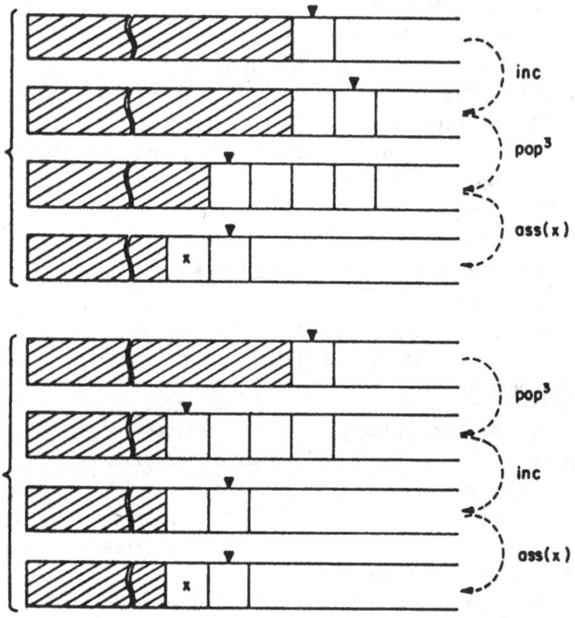

Note that both expressions applied to '$\overline{\odot}$' yield '$\emptyset$'.

So $p \overset{f_0}{\equiv} \Gamma;\ \gamma_1;\ldots;\gamma_\ell;\ \overline{add}(x);\ \Gamma'$, which satisfies the conditions of the definition.

Consider now the case that *inc* was not the first occurrence of the '*inc*' symbol in p. We may assume by induction that in Γ, each *inc* appears immediately followed by its matching $ass(x)$. Then the previous case analysis applies: each γ_i must be equal to $\overline{pop}$ and the same conclusion is reached. ∎

4.2 Another implementation of STACK

We consider here a more complex process implementation PAP2 of the STACK specification. In this implementation stacks are represented by *two* arrays with pointers, storing respectively the first and second "halves" of the data that are successively pushed and popped. Thus, the specification ELEM must have a constructor $(\_,\_): item \times item \to elem$ and two operators 1st and 2nd: $elem \to item$ such that $1^{st}[(i_1, i_2)] = i_1$ and $2^{nd}[(i_1, i_2)] = i_2$. A stack generated by the expression $\text{push}((a,b), \text{push}((c,d), \odot))$ will be represented by:

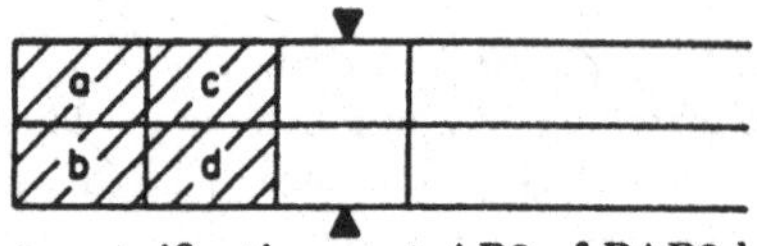

A data element of the new data specification part AP2 of PAP2 has the form

$$\langle array_1, pointer_1, array_2, pointer_2, semaphore\rangle.$$

Pointer$_i$ is incremented by inc_i. The operations ass_i, pop_i and $\overline{empty}$ have their intuitive meaning. The cooperation of the different processes that may share a data of AP2 is ensured via a semaphore on inc_1, and a critical section around ass_1 and ass_2. The specification is as follows:

process specif PAP2 =   - -processes on AP2

    data specif: AP2   **where**

        data specif AP2 =

            used-specif: ELEM, NATURAL

            new sorts: *ap2*

            constructor:

            $\langle \_,\_,\_,\_,\_\rangle$: $array \times natural \times array \times natural \times boolean \rightarrow ap2$

            derived operators

            $\overline{\odot} :\rightarrow ap2$

            $\overline{push}$: $elem \times ap2 \rightarrow ap2$

            equation for derived operators

            $\overline{\odot} = \langle ea, 0, ea, 0, T\rangle$

            $\overline{push}(e, \langle a_1, n_1, a_2, n_2, b\rangle) =$

                $\langle a_1[pred(n_1)] := 1^{st}(e), n_1 + 1, a_2[pred(n_2)] := 2^{nd}(e), n_2 + 1, b\rangle$

        endspecif AP2.

    atomic actions

        $\overline{empty}$, inc_1, inc_2, pop_1, pop_2: $\rightarrow atomic$

        ass_1, ass_2: $item \rightarrow atomic$

    non atomic actions:

        $\overline{pop}$: $\rightarrow process$

        $\overline{add}$: $elem \rightarrow process$

    equations for atomic actions

$\overline{empty} :: \langle a_1, n_1, a_2, n_2, b\rangle = if\ \neg b\ then\ \emptyset\ else\ \langle ea, 0, ea, 0, T\rangle$

$inc_1 :: \langle a_1, n_1, a_2, n_2, b\rangle = if\ \neg b\ then\ \emptyset\ else\ \langle a_1, n_1 + 1, a_2, n_2, F\rangle$

$inc_2 :: \langle a_1, n_1, a_2, n_2, b\rangle = \langle a_1, n_1, a_2, n_2 + 1, F\rangle$

$pop_1 :: \langle a_1, n_1, a_2, n_2, b\rangle = if\ n_1 = 0\ then\ \emptyset\ else\ \langle a_1[pred(n_1)] := \emptyset, pred(n_1), a_2, n_2, b\rangle$

$pop_2 :: \langle a_1, n_1, a_2, n_2, b\rangle = if\ n_1 \geq n_2\ then\ \emptyset\ else\ \langle a_1, n_1, a_2[pred(n_2)] := \perp, pred(n_2), b\rangle$

$ass_1(i) :: \langle a_1, n_1, a_2, n_2, b\rangle = if\ n_1 \neq n_2 \vee n_1 = 0\ then\ \emptyset\ else \langle a_1[pred(n_1)] := i, n_1, a_2, n_2, b\rangle$

$ass_2(i) : \langle a_1, n_1, a_2, n_2, b\rangle = \langle a_1, n_1, a_2[pred(n_2)] := i, n_2, T\rangle$

    equations for non-atomic actions

        $\overline{pop} = pop_1; pop_2$

        $\overline{add}(e) = inc_1; inc_2; \ll ass_1[1^{st}(e)]; ass_2[2^{nd}(e)] \gg$

end specif PAP2.

Comments:

- We have used a new constructor $\ll\_\gg$:*process* $\rightarrow$ *atomic* defining ***critical sections***. A critical section is considered, algebraically, as an atomic action. We add the following axiom: $\ll p \gg :: x = p :: x$ $(\forall x \in X^s, \forall p \in X^\pi)$. The previous axioms about atomic actions still apply. For instance:
  $(\ll p \gg; p') ⫾ p'' = \ll p \gg; (p' \parallel p'')$.
- Cooperation between several processes is controlled in three different ways:

- via the semaphore raised by inc_1, released by ass_2 and consulted by $\overline{empty}$. Note that the meaning of 'raising', 'releasing' and 'consulting' is conveyed by the axioms that we wrote. This illustrates the advantages of 'high-level' (i.e. algebraic) descriptions of low-level processes
- via the control over n_1 and n_2 performed by inc_1 and inc_2
- via the critical region $\ll ass_1; ass_2 \gg$.

These control mechanisms are easy to handle at such a level of description of processes.

As before, proving the correctness of PAP2 requires to check that (α) and (β) are satisfied. The (α) part is strictly similar to the PAP$^+$ case; we shall thus concentrate on the (β) part, successively establishing that $\overline{add}$ and $\overline{pop}$ are regroupable.

Proof that $\overline{add}$ is regroupable:

Let

$$p = \Gamma_1;\ inc_1;\ \Gamma_2;\ inc_2;\ \Gamma_3;\ ass_1(x_1);\ \Gamma_4;\ ass_2(x_2);\ \Gamma_5$$

with $\Gamma_k \in At^*(k \in [1\ldots 4])$. We assume that $p \overset{f_0}{\not\equiv} \delta$. Then necessarily $\Gamma_4 = \epsilon$, since $\langle\langle ass_1; ass_2 \rangle\rangle$ is a critical region. Consider first the case that the displayed inc_1 is the first occurrence of inc_1 in p. Thus $\Gamma_1 \in \{\overline{empty}, pop_2, \overline{pop_2}\}^*$, which implies that $\Gamma_1 = \epsilon$ or $\Gamma_1 = \overline{empty}$.

Let $\gamma \in \Gamma_2; \Gamma_3$ be the first operation in $\Gamma_2; \Gamma_3$ which is one of: *empty*, inc_1, inc_2, ass_1 and ass_2. It cannot be an *empty* or an inc_1 because these operations are enabled only when the sempahore is true. Since the semaphore has been set to false by the inc_1 preceding Γ_2, and there is no later ass_2 which could reset the sempahore prior to γ, γ can be neither *empty* nor inc_1. Neither can γ be one of inc_2, ass_1, or ass_2. This is because any of these operations requires a preceding corresponding inc_1. By assumption, Γ_1 contains no *inc*, the explicitly displayed inc_1, in front of Γ_2 already corresponds to the explicitly displayed inc_2, ass_1 and ass_2, and γ is the first of its kind in $\Gamma_2; \Gamma_3$. Consequently γ cannot be any of these five operations. We conclude that $\Gamma_2; \Gamma_3 \in \{pop_1, pop_2\}^*$.

Let $E^0 \in ap2$ such that $p :: E^0 \not\equiv \emptyset$. We denote by E^1 the value $\Gamma_1 :: E_0$ and we let $n_1(E^1) = n_1^1$ and $n_2(E^1) = n_2^1$ where $n_i(.)$ is the projection of $ap2$ along the counter i. We suppose that $\Gamma_2; \Gamma_3$ decrements n_1 by k_1 and n_2 by k_2. There are two cases:

α) $n_1^1 + 1 - k_1 > 0$ and $n_2^1 + 1 - k_2 > 0$. Then $(\Gamma_1; inc_2; \Gamma_2; inc_2; \Gamma_3) :: E^0 \equiv E^2$, where E^2 is such that $n_1(E^2) = n_1^1 + 1 - k_1$ and $n_2(E^2) = n_2^1 + 1 - k_2$. But then $E^2 \equiv (\Gamma_1; \Gamma_2; \Gamma_3; inc_1; inc_2) :: E^0$.

β) $n_1^1 + 1 - k_2 \leq 0$ or $n_2^1 + 1 - k_2 \leq 0$. Then $(\Gamma_1; inc_1; \Gamma_2; inc_2; \Gamma_3; \langle\langle ass_1; ass_2 \rangle\rangle) :: E_0 \equiv \emptyset$, which is contradictory. Thus, $p \overset{f_0}{\equiv} \Gamma_1; \Gamma_2; \Gamma_3;\ \overline{add}(x); \Gamma_4; \Gamma_5$ and $\overline{add}$ is regroupable.

In the more general case that Γ_1 may contain previous inc_1, we may assume by induction that the corresponding *add* operations have already been regrouped. This means that all of the $\{inc_2, ass_1, ass_2\}$ sequences corresponding to inc_1's contained in Γ_1 are also in Γ_1. It follows again that $\Gamma_2; \Gamma_3$ cannot contain any of these operations and consists purely of $\{pop_1, pop_2\}^*$, which can be permuted with the displayed inc_1,inc_2 similarly to the previous case. ∎

Proof that $\overline{pop}$ is regroupable:

Let $p \in At^*$ such that the possible $\overline{add}$'s occuring in p are regrouped. $p \in \{\overline{add}, \overline{empty}$ $pop_1, pop_2\}^*$. We assume that $p \overset{f_0}{\not\equiv} \delta$ and we show that the pop_2, pop_2 may be regrouped in p.

- We can write $p = \alpha_1; \overline{empty}; \alpha_2; \ldots; \overline{empty}; \alpha_n$ with $\alpha_i \in \{\overline{add}, pop_2, pop_2\}^*$, under the convention that possibly $\alpha_1 = \epsilon$, or $\alpha_2 = \epsilon$, or $p = \alpha_0$ (the last case is if p contains no $\overline{empty}$). Let us first prove that for any i, the number of occurrences of pop_2 in α_i, called $\omega_1(\alpha_i)$, is equal to $\omega_2(\alpha_i)$.
  - α) if $\omega_1(\alpha_i) < \omega_2(\alpha_i)$, then just before performing the last pop_2 in α_i, we have $n_2 \leq n_2$, which contradicts $p \overset{f_0}{\not\equiv} \delta$.

β) if $\omega_1(\alpha_i) > \omega_2(\alpha_i)$ for some given i, then there exists a j such that $\omega_1(\alpha_j) < \omega_2(\alpha_j)$: this is because $\sum_{i=1}^{n} \omega_1(\alpha_i) = \sum_{i=1}^{n} \omega_2(\alpha_i)$. We then derive a contradiction as shown above.

- For a given i we can write $\alpha_i = \beta_1; \overline{add}(x_2)\beta_2; \ldots; \overline{add}(x_m); \beta_n$ with $\beta_j \in \{pop_1, pop_2\}^*$, under the same conventions as above. Again, denoting by $\omega_k(\beta_j)$ the number of occurrences of pop_k ($k = 1, 2$) in β_j, we show that $\omega_1(\beta_j) = \omega_2(\beta_j)$ for each β_j appearing within an α_i. Since $\overline{add}$ checks that $n_2 = n_2$, we only need to verify that $\omega_2(\beta_n) = \omega_1(\beta_n)$ for the segment β_n appearing last in α_i. Since we already established that $\omega_1(\alpha_i) = \omega_2(\alpha_i)$, and for all $j < n$, $\omega_1(\beta_j) = \omega_2(\beta_j)$, the equality $\omega_1(\beta_n) = \omega_2(\beta_n)$ must also hold.
- Now, the $\overline{pop}$'s are clearly regroupable in each β_j, appearing in any α_i, and thus finally in p. ∎

From the two previous results, we deduce that PAP2 is a correct (strong) implementation of STACK.

5. Implementations — The General Case

Until now, we have considered only implementations in which an (atomic) action of $\mathcal{P}$ is implemented by a sequence of atomic actions of $\mathcal{P}'$: $\overline{A} = \alpha_1; \alpha_2; \ldots; \alpha_k$. In general, $\overline{A}$ may be an expression involving atomic actions, composed by the operators $+$, ; or $\|$. In any case, $\overline{A}$ has a normal form:

$$\overline{A} = \sum_{j=1}^{m(A)} \Pi_{i=1}^{n(j,A)} \alpha_{i,j}^{A}, \qquad \text{with } \alpha_{i,j}^{A} \in At_{\mathcal{P}'}.$$

For instance, if $\overline{A} = \alpha_1 \parallel (\alpha_2; \alpha_3)$, then $\overline{B} = \alpha_1; \alpha_2; \alpha_3 + \alpha_2; \alpha_1; \alpha_3 + \alpha_2; \alpha_3; \alpha_1$. We shall denote by $\Pi_{\mathcal{P}'}$ the set of the components $(\Pi_{i=1}^{n(j,A)} \alpha_{i,j}^{A})_{j \in [1 \ldots m(A)]}$ for all $A \in At_{\mathcal{P}}$. The previous definitions become, in the general case:

Definition 5.1

- $\mathcal{P}'$ is a *strong implementation* of $\mathcal{P}$ *iff*
  - (α) (as in definition 3.1)
  - (β): for any $\pi_i \in \Pi_{\mathcal{P}'}$, for any

    $p \in merge(\pi_1, \ldots, \pi_m)$, such that $p \overset{f_0}{\not\equiv} \delta$, there exists a permutation τ of $[1 \ldots m]$ such that $p \overset{f_0}{\equiv} \pi_{\tau(1)}; \ldots; \pi_{\tau(m)}$.
- Let $\pi \in \Pi_{\mathcal{P}'}$, with $\pi = \alpha_1; \ldots; \alpha_n$. π is *regroupable* iff
  for any $\beta_1, \ldots \beta_m \in \Pi_{\mathcal{P}'}$,
  for any $p_0, \ldots, p_n \in At_{\mathcal{P}'}^{*}$ s.t. $p_0; \ldots; p_n \in merge(\beta_1, \ldots \beta_m)$
  if $p = p_0; \alpha_1; p_1; \ldots; p_{n-1}; \alpha_n; p_n$ and $p \overset{f_0}{\not\equiv} \delta$, then there exist $q_1, q_2 \in At_{\mathcal{P}'}^{*}$ such that:
  - (i) $p \overset{f_0}{\equiv} q_1; \pi; q_2$
  - (ii) $q_1; q_2 \in merge(\beta_1, \ldots, \beta_m)$
  - (iii) $\forall i \in [1 \ldots m]$, *if* $\beta_i \triangleleft p_k$ for some $k = 0, 1, \ldots$ *then* $\beta_i \triangleleft q_j$ for some $j = 1, 2$.

This is compatible with the definitions of section 3: if every action is implemented by a sequence of atomic action, we recover these definitions with $\Pi_{\mathcal{P}'} = \{\overline{A}, A \in \mathcal{P}(\mathcal{D})\}$, $\overline{B}_i = \beta_i$ and $\overline{A} = \pi$. As before, we have the following result:

Theorem 5.1:
$\mathcal{P}'$ is a strong implementation of $\mathcal{P}$ *iff* (α) holds and every $\pi \in \Pi_{\mathcal{P}'}$ is regroupable.

Example:
In this example, a stack is implemented by *two parallel stacks* holding, as before, the first and second "halves" of the *elements* that are successively pushed. The atomic action $\text{push}_1(e)$ pushes

the *item* $1^{st}(e)$ on the first stack, and similarly for $\text{push}_2(e)$. We now let $\overline{add}(e) = \text{push}_1(e) \parallel \text{push}_2(e)$. Consider the possible executions of $p = \overline{add}[(i,j)] \parallel \overline{add}[(i,k)]$. The item i is pushed on the first stack and, in the most general protocol, three actions are possible:

- pushing j or k on the second stack
- pushing i again on the first stack. This requires to remember that either j and k have to be eventually pushed at the parallel locations of the second stack.

We will forbid the latter possibility, by deciding that if a $\text{push}_1[(i,j)]$ (for instance) has taken place, then a $\text{push}_2[(i',k)]$ must take place with $i = i'$. If $k \neq j$, this leaves pending a $\text{push}_2[(i,j)]$ and a $\text{push}_1[(i,k)]$, which is sound. We use a device d taking values 0,1 or 2. If $d = 0$, a $\text{push}_1(e)$ or $\text{push}_2(e)$ can indifferently take place. If $d = 1$, a $\text{push}_1(e)$ just happened and a $\text{push}_2(e')$ must occur, with $1^{st}(e) = 1^{st}(e')$ (and conversely if $d = 2$).

The specification is:

process specif PDS// =   -- processes on DS
    data specif: DS   **where**
        data specif DS =
            used specif : ELEM, ITEM, STACK-OF-ITEM[7], 3-VALUE
            new sort : *ds*
            constructor :
            $\langle \_,\_,\_ \rangle$: *stack-of-item*$\times$ *stack-of-item* $\times$ *3-val*$\rightarrow$ *ds*
            derived operators:
            $\overline{\odot} : \rightarrow ds$
            $\overline{push} : elem \times ds \rightarrow ds$
            equations for derived operators:
            $\overline{\odot} = \langle \odot, \odot, 0 \rangle$
            $\overline{push}(e, \langle s_1, s_2, d \rangle) = \langle push_1, (1^{st}(e), s_1), push_2(2^{nd}(e), s_2), d \rangle$

        end specif DS
    atomic actions
        $\overline{empty}, \overline{pop}$ $\rightarrow$ *atomic*
        $\text{push}_1,\text{push}_2$: *element* $\rightarrow$ *atomic*
    non atomic actions
        $\overline{add}$: element $\rightarrow$ process
    equations for atomic actions

$\overline{empty} :: \langle s_1, s_2, d \rangle = if\ d \neq 0\ then\ \emptyset\ else\ \langle \odot, \odot, 0 \rangle$
$\overline{pop} :: \langle s_1, s_2, d, \rangle = if\ d \neq \emptyset \wedge s_1 \neq \odot \wedge s_2 \neq \odot\ then\ \emptyset\ else\ \langle \text{pop}(s_1), \text{pop}(s_2), 0 \rangle$
$\text{push}_1(e) :: \langle s_1, s_2, d \rangle =$
    $if\ d = 0\ then\ \langle \text{push}[1^{st}(e), s_1], s_2, 1 \rangle$
    $elseif\ d = 2 \wedge 2^{nd}(e) = top(s_2)\ then\ \langle \text{push}[1^{st}(e), s_1], s_2, 0 \rangle$
    $else\ \emptyset$
$\text{push}_2(e) :: \langle s_1, s_2, d \rangle =$
    $if\ d = 0\ then\ \langle s_1, \text{push}[2^{nd}(e), s_2], 2 \rangle$
    $else\ if\ d = 1 \wedge 1^{st}(e) = top(s_1)\ then\ \langle s_1, \text{push}[2^{nd}(e), s_2], 0 \rangle$
    $else\ \emptyset$
    equations for non-atomic actions
        $\overline{add}(e) = \text{push}_1(e) \parallel \text{push}_2(e)$
    endspecif PDS //.

Comments:

- The 3-VALUE specification is defined by a new sort *3-val* and three constants $0, 1, 2 : \rightarrow$ *3-val*.

[7] STACK-OF-ITEM is enriched by an operation top: *stack-of-item*$\rightarrow$*item* such that $top(push(i, s)) = i$, $top(\odot) = \perp$.

- There should be no confusion about the fact that in the specification STACK, the sort *stack* stands for stacks of *elements*, where as in the data part DS of the implementation, stacks of *items* are used.

The proof of PDS// involves the verification of (α) (which is identical to the previous ones), and the proof that each $\beta \in B_{PDS//}$ is regroupable. Here we have:

$$B_{PDS//} = \{\overline{empty}, \overline{pop}, \text{push}_1(e); \text{push}_2(e), \text{push}_2(e); \text{push}_1(e)\}$$

since the normal form of $\overline{add}(e)$ is $\text{push}_1(e); \text{push}_2(e) + \text{push}_2(e); \text{push}_1(e)$. We only need to prove that $\text{push}_1(e)$; $\text{push}_2(e)$ is regroupable (the case $\text{push}_2(e); \text{push}_1(e)$ being symmetric).

Proof that $\text{push}_1(e); \text{push}_2(e)$ is regroupable

We suppose that $p = \Gamma_1; \text{push}_1(e); \Gamma_2; \text{push}_2(e); \Gamma_3$ with $\Gamma_i \in At^*$ ($\forall i \in [1 \ldots 3]$), where the displayed push_1,push_2 correspond to the splitting of a given $\overline{push}$. We suppose that $p \not\equiv_{fo} \delta$. We must be in one of the two cases.

- $\text{push}_1(e)$ is immediately preceded by a $\text{push}_2(e')$, with $2^{nd}(e) = 2^{nd}(e')$. Then, we can write: $\Gamma_1 = \Gamma_1'$; $\text{push}_2(e')$ and $p = \Gamma_1'$; $\overline{add}(e)$; Γ_2; $\text{push}_2(e)$; Γ_3.
- $\text{push}_1(e)$ is immediately followed by a $\text{push}_2(e')$, with $1^{st}(e) = 1^{st}(e')$. Then, we can write: $\Gamma_2 = \text{push}_2(e')$; Γ_2' and $p = \Gamma_1$; $\overline{add}(e')$; Γ_2'; $\text{push}_2(e)$; Γ_3.

This means that in p, each occurrence of a push_1 or a push_2 may be considered as being grouped with one of its neighbors to form an $\overline{add}$. Now, the multiset of the items that are $\overline{add}$-ed this way in p is exactly the multiset of the items involved in the process of which p is an interleaving. This terminates the proof.

6. Conclusion

In this paper, we extended abstract data types methods to the question of the specification and the implementation of data structures accessed concurrently by several processes. Our approach provides the underlying theory for modularity and development by a stepwise refinement strategy of such systems.

We have identified the properties that must be checked in order to prove that an implementation is correct. They consist of two groups: the first one is similar to the properties usually required when proving the implementation of a classical, non-concurrent algebraic specification; they are dealt with in the usual fashion. The second group states that no new, undesirable interleavings occur in the implementation; we have designed a proof method for this.

One direction of future research, is to investigate the introduction of more sophisticated primitives for the construction of non-atomic processes (conditionals, guarded choice,...). Several new questions then arise; in particular, our notion of *strong* implementation should be refined, and our proof methods extended accordingly.

References

[1] W.B. Ackerman
Data Flow Languages *IEEE Computer*, 15/12, February 1982.

[2] E. Astesiano, G.F Mascari, G. Reggio, M. Wirsing
On the Parameterized Algebraic Specification of Concurrent Systems, Proc. of the CAAP'85 Conference, LNCS 185 (Springer Verlag), 1985.

[4] J.W. Backus
Can Programming be Liberated from the Von Neumann Style?, *Communications of the ACM*, August 1978.

[5] J.W. Backus
The Algebra of Functional Programs, Proc. of the International Colloquium on Formalization of Programming Concepts, LNCS 107 (Springer Verlag), 1981.

[6] J.C.M. Baeten, J.A. Bergstra, J.W. Klop
Algebra of Communicating Processes - Part II, Technical Note of the Esprit METEOR Project, 1985.

[7] J.A. Bergstra, J.W. Klop
Process Algebra for Synchronous Communication, *Information and Control*, **60**, 1984.

[8] J.A. Bergstra, J.V. Tucker
Top-Down Design and the Algebra of Communicating Processes, *Science of Computer Programming*, **5**, 1985.

[9] G. Bernot
Une Sémantique Algébrique pour une Spécification Différenciée des Exceptions et des Erreurs, Thèse de 3ème cycle, Université d'Orsay (France), 1985.

[10] G. Bernot, M. Bidoit, C. Choppy
Abstract Implementations and Corrections Proofs, Proc. of the STACS'86 conference, LNCS 210 (Springer Verlag), 1986.

[11] M. Broy
Specification and Top Down Design of Distributed Systems, Proc. of the TAPSOFT'85 Conference, LNCS 185 (Springer Verlag), 1985.

[12] C. Choppy, G. Guiho, S. Kaplan
A LISP compiler for FP languages and its proof via algebraic semantics. Proc. of the TAPSOFT'85 Conference, LNCS 185 (Springer Verlag), 1985.

[13] J.B. Dennis
First Version of a Data Flow Procedure Language, Proc. of the Colloque sur la Programmation, LNCS 19 (Springer Verlag), 1974.

[14] M.C. Gaudel
Génération et Preuve de Compilateurs Basées sur une Semantique Formelle des Languages de Programmation, Thèse d'Etat, Nancy, 1980.

[15] M.C. Gaudel, S. Kaplan
How to Write Meaningful Structured Specifications, Technical Note of the Esprit METEOR project, 1986.

[16] J.A. Goguen, J.W. Thatcher, E.G. Wagner (ADJ)
An Initial Algebra Approach to the Specification, Correctness and Implementation of Abstract Data Types, Current Trends in Programming Methodology (Prentice Hall - New Jersey), 1978.

[17] J.V. Guttag
The Specification and Application to Programming, Ph.D. Thesis, University of Toronto, 1975.

[18] S. Kamin
Final Data Type Specifications: a New Data Type Specification Method, ACM Transaction on Programming Languages and Systems, 511, 1983.

[19] L. Lamport
Specifying Concurrent Program Modules, *ACM Transactions on Programming Languages and Systems*, **512**, April 1983.

[20] B. Liskov, S. Zilles
Specification Techniques for Data Abstraction, *IEEE Transactions on Software Engineering*, March 1975.

[21] R. Milner
A Calculus of Communicating Systems, LNCS 92 (Springer Verlag), 1980.

[22] R. Milner

Lectures on a Calculus of Communicating Systems, Proc. of the Seminar on Concurrency, LNCS 197 (Springer Verlag), 1984.

[23] S.S. Owicki
Specifications and Proofs for Abstract Data Types in Concurrent Programs, Program Construction, LNCS 69 (Springer Verlag), 1979.

[24] D.T. Sanella, M. Wirsing
A Kernel Language for Algebraic Specification and Implementation, Proc. of the International Conference on Foundations of Computation Theory, LNCS 158 (Springer Verlag), 1983.

[25] F.W. Vaandrager
Verification of two Communication Protocols by means of Process Algebra, Report CS-R8608, CWI (Amsterdam), 1986.

[26] J.H. Williams
On the Development of the Algebra of Functional Programs, ACM Transaction on Programming Languages and Systems, 4/4, October 1982.

[28] W. Weihl
Data Dependent Concurrency Control and Recovery, ACM Operating Systems Review, 19/1, 1985.

[28] W. Weihl, B. Liskov
Implementation of Resilient, Atomic Data Types, ACM Transaction on Programming Languages and Systems, 7/2, 1985.

Appendix A

Classical Abstract Data Types — Basic Notions

In this appendix, we briefly review basic definitions and concepts that are classical in the field of abstract data types. We refer for instance to [14, 16, 17, 18, 24] for more advanced information.

- A *signature* consists of a family S of domain names (called sorts), and of a family Σ of operator names together with an arity function ar from Σ into S^+. We usually write $f : s_1 \times \ldots \times s_n \rightarrow s_{n+1}$ when $ar(f) = s_1 \ldots s_n s_{n+1}$.
- Let (S, Σ) be a signature. An S, Σ*-algebra* (or S, Σ-model) consists of a family of sets $(A_s)_{s \in S}$ and a family of operators $(f^A)_{f \in \Sigma}$ such that, if $f: s_1 \times \ldots \times s_n \rightarrow s_{n+1}$, then f^A is an application from $A_{s_1} \times \ldots \times A_{s_n}$ into $A_{s_{n+1}}$.
- A S, Σ*-morphism* h from an S, Σ-algebra A to an S, Σ-algebra B is a family $(h_s)_{s \in S}$ of applications $h_s: A_s \rightarrow B_s$ such that, for any $f: s_1 \times \ldots \times s_n \rightarrow s_{n+1}$, for any $t_i \in As_i$, $h_s[f^A(t_1, \ldots, t_n)] = f^B(h_{s_1}(t_1), \ldots, h_{s_n}(t_n))$. S, Σ-algebras with S, Σ-morphism form a category, $Alg_{S,\Sigma}$.
- $T_{S,\Sigma}$ denotes the *algebra of the terms* that are well-formed on the signature S, Σ. X shall stand for a family $(X_S)_{s \in S}$ of an infinite number of typed variables. $T_{S,\Sigma}(X)$ is the *algebra of the terms with variables*. $(T_{S,\Sigma})^s$ will represent the terms of sort s, and similarly for $(T_{S,\Sigma}(X))^s$.
- There exists a unique morphism, $eval_A$, from $T_{S,\Sigma}$ to a given S, Σ-algebra A. The class $Gen_{S,\Sigma}$ of the S, Σ-algebras A such that $eval_A$ is surjective is called the class of the finitely generated algebras.
- A *substitution* is an application σ from X to an S, Σ-algebra A. σ may be extended in a unique way into a morphism $\overline{\sigma}: T_{S,\Sigma}(X) \rightarrow A$. We generally assimilate σ and $\overline{\sigma}$ and write $t\sigma$ instead of $\sigma(t)$.
- An *equation* is a pair (M, N) of terms of $T_{S,\Sigma}(X)$ of the same sort s, usually denoted by $M = N$. For a set of equations E, we say that an S, Σ-algebra A *satisfies* E *iff* for any equation $M = N$

of E, for any substitution $\sigma: X \rightarrow T_{S,\Sigma}$, then $eval^A(M\sigma) = eval^A(N\sigma)$. We write $A \models E$. The class of all such algebras is denoted by $Alg_{S,\Sigma,E}$. Similarly, $Gen_{S,\Sigma,E}$ denotes the class of the finitely generated algebras satisfying E.

- A *congruence* $\equiv$ on an S,Σ-algebra A is a family $(\equiv_s)_{s\in S}$ of equivalence relations $\equiv_s$ on A_s such that if $f: s_1 \times j \ldots \times s_n \rightarrow s_{n+1}$, if $t_i, t'_i \in A_{s_i}$ and $t_i \equiv_{s_i} t'_i$, then $f^A(t_1,\ldots,t_n) \equiv_{s_{n+1}} f^A(t'_1,\ldots,t'_n)$ for a set of equations E and an S,Σ-algebra A, there exists a smallest congruence $\equiv^A_E$ on A that contains all the pairs $\{eval^A(M\sigma),\ eval^A(N\sigma)\}$ with the previous notations. We write $\equiv_E$ for $\equiv^{T_{S,\Sigma}}_E$.
- An *algebraic specification* is a triple $SPEC = \langle S,\Sigma,E\rangle$, where S,Σ is a signature and E a set of equations on S,Σ. We let Sig($SPEC$)$= S,\Sigma$. The corresponding classes Alg_{SPEC} and Gen_{SPEC} both admit $Init(SPEC) = T_{S,\Sigma}/\equiv_E$ as initial model, and $Term(SPEC) = Triv_{S,\Sigma}$ (the trivial model where each $(Triv_{S,\Sigma})^s$ is reduced to a point) as terminal model.[8] Once ordered by the relation $A < B$ iff there is a morphism from A to B, $Alg_{S,\Sigma E}$ and $Gen_{S,\Sigma E}$ are lattices.
- A *signature morphism* is an application $\varphi: S,\Sigma \rightarrow S',\Sigma'$ such that if $f: s_1 \times \ldots \times s_n \rightarrow s_{n+1}$, then $\varphi(f): \varphi(s_1) \times \ldots \times \varphi(s_n) \rightarrow \varphi(s_{n+1})$. In this case each S',Σ'-algebra A' may be regarded as a S,Σ-algebra by letting $(A'|_\varphi)^s = (A')^{\varphi(s)}$ for $s \in \Sigma$ and $f^{A'|_\varphi} = \varphi(f)^{A'}$ for $f \in \Sigma$. If $SPEC_0 = \langle S_0,\Sigma_0,E_0\rangle$ is a subspecification of $SPEC = \langle S,\Sigma,E\rangle$, which means that $S_0 \subseteq S$ and $\Sigma \subseteq \Sigma_0$, then there exists a canonical, injective signature morphism $i: S_0,\Sigma_0 \rightarrow S,\Sigma$. For an S,Σ-algebra A', we shall usually write $A'|_{SPEC_0}$ instead of $A'|_i$. $A'|_{SPEC_0}$ is simply the algebra A' where all the information about $SPEC$ deprived of $SPEC_0$ is "forgotten".

  If $\varphi: S,\Sigma \rightarrow S',\Sigma'$ is a signature morphism, it defines a S,Σ-morphism from $T_{S,\Sigma}$ into $T_{S',\Sigma'}|_\varphi$ (identified with $T_{S'\Sigma'}$) by $\varphi[f(t_1,\_,t_n)] = \varphi(f)[\varphi(t_1),\_,\varphi(t_n)]$.

We now consider the notion of *hierarchical* models and specifications (cf. eg. [15, 22]). From now on, $PREDEF = \langle S_{PREDEF}, \Sigma_{PREDEF}, E_{PREDEF}\rangle$ stands for a given predefined specification. It is understated that $PREDEF$ is rich enough to allow discriminations within the specification that "use" it. Typically, $PREDEF$ contains the boolean integers, etc. Then, let $SPEC = PREDEF \cup \langle S,\Sigma,E\rangle$ be a specification.

<u>Definition</u>

(i) $SPEC$ is *hierarchically consistent* (w.r.t. $PREDEF$)
iff $\forall t, t' \in (T_{SPEC})^s$, with $s \in S_{PREDEF}$,

$$t \equiv_{E_{PREDEF}\cup E} t' \quad\Leftrightarrow\quad t \equiv_{E_{PREDEF}} t'$$

(ii) $SPEC$ is *hierarchically complete* (w.r.t. $PREDEF$)
iff $\forall t \in (T_{SPEC})^s$, with $s \in S_{PREDEF}$,

$$\exists t_0 \in (T_{PREDEF}) \text{ such that } t \equiv_{E_{PREDEF}\cup E} t.$$

(iii) $SPEC$ is a *hierarchical extension* of $PREDEF$ iff
it is hierarchically consistent and complete w.r.t. $PREDEF$.
We write $SPEC \triangleright PREDEF$.

Condition (i) means that no "confusion" (i.e. no new relations) has been introduced in the predefined sorts, and condition (ii) means that no "junk" (i.e. no new values) has been generated in the predefined sorts. From now on, we always suppose that $SPEC \triangleright PREDEF$. We define

---

[8] Provided that every sort of the signature is *reachable* in the sense of [17].

the class Alg^h_{SPEC} of the hierarchical models of *SPEC* (w.r.t. *PREDEF*) as the class of models $A \in Alg_{SPEC}$ such that:

$$A|_{PREDEF} \approx_{PREDEF} Init(PREDEF)$$

Let A be in Alg^h_{SPEC}. We define the *observational congruence* $\stackrel{\circ}{\equiv}_A$ on A in the following way.

- for $s_0 \in S_{PREDEF}$, $t, t' \in A_{s_0}$,
  $t \stackrel{\circ}{\equiv}_A t'$ *iff* $t \equiv_A t'$
- for $s \in S \mid S_{PREDEF}$, $t, t' \in A_s$,
  $t \stackrel{\circ}{\equiv}_A t'$ *iff* $\forall s_0 \in S_{PREDEF}, \forall K \in [T_{SPEC}(X_s)]^{s_0}$
  $K^A[t] = K^A[t']$

The observational congruence on *Init*(*SPEC*)is simply denoted $\stackrel{\circ}{\equiv}$. Thus, two terms t and t' of A^s, s being a "new sort", are observationally equivalent *iff* any "experiment" (producing result in an "old" sort) yield the same result when applied on t or on t'. We then have:

THEOREM (cf. [18])

Alg^h_{SPEC} is a sublattice of Alg_{SPEC}.

(i) Its initial model is *Init*(*SPEC*).

(ii) Its terminal model is isomorphic to $A/\stackrel{\circ}{\equiv}_A$, for any $A \in Alg^h_{SPEC}$.

We shall denote by *Term*(*SPEC*) the terminal (hierarchical) model of Alg^h_{SPEC}. We shall for instance choose $Term^h(SPEC) = Init(SPEC)/\stackrel{\circ}{\equiv}$.

We are now able to provide semantics for the "data specifications". Let:

data specif D =
  used specif: $D_1, \ldots, D_n$
  new sorts: $s_1, \ldots, s_m$
  constructors: $c_1, \ldots, c_p$
  derived operators: $d_1, \ldots, d_q$
  equation between constructors: E_c
  equations for d_1: $E_{d_1}, \ldots,$ **equations for** $d_q = E_{d_q}$.
end specif D.

The semantics of D is as follows. Let $[\![D]\!]$ stand for the specification:

$$D_1 \cup \cdots \cup D_n \cup$$
$$\langle S = \{s_1, \ldots, s_m\}, \Sigma = \{c_1, \ldots c_p, d_1, \ldots, d_q\}, E = E_c \cup E_{d_2} \cup \cdots \cup E_{d_q} \rangle.$$

We say that D *satisfies its hierarchical constraints iff*:

(i) $D_1, \ldots, D_n$ satisfy their respective hierarchical constraints.

(ii) $[\![\underset{\sim}{D}]\!] = D_1 \cup \cdots \cup D_n \cup \langle S, \{c_1, \ldots, c_p\}, E_c \rangle$ is a hierarchical extension of $D_1, \ldots, D_n$.

(iii) $[\![D]\!]$ is a hierarchical extension of $[\![\underset{\sim}{D}]\!]$.

Condition (i) must be satisfied recursively. Conditions (ii) and (iii) respectively express that D behaves gracefully with respect to $D_1, \ldots, D_n$ and that the derived operators of D are well-defined with respect to the constructors of D. Now, if D satisfies its hierarchical constraints, its semantics is by definition $[\![D]\!]$; otherwise, it is not defined. From now on, we shall assimilate the presentation of D[9] of a "data specification" with its semantics $[\![D]\!]$; we shall also say that a specification is *correct* when it meets its hierarchical constraints.

[9] provided it satisfies its hierarchical constraints.

We now turn to the notion of implementation of one *data* specification by another *data* specification. As stated in this introduction to this section, *data* specifications are abstract data types in the classical sense. The implementation question has been debated very harshly (cf. e.g. [9]). Since it is not the purpose of this paper to contribute to the question in its generality but to concentrate on the concurrency aspect, and for sake of clarity, we shall use an elementary notion of implementation.

Definition

Let $SPEC, SPEC' \triangleright PREDEF$ be two data specifications, and let $\varphi = Sig(SPEC) \to Sig(SPEC')$ be a signature morphism leaving *PREDEF* invariant. We say that *SPEC* is implemented by *SPEC'* *iff* for every axiom $M = N$ of *SPEC*, we have:

$$Init(SPEC') \models \varphi(M)\sigma = \varphi(N)\sigma, \quad \forall\sigma: X_{\varphi(S)} \to T_{\varphi(S),\varphi(\Sigma)}$$

We explain the intuitive meaning of this definition on our working example of section 1. Suppose that AP is "enriched" into a new data specification $\overline{\text{AP}}$, via the addition of the fragment:

derived operators	:	$\overline{pop} : ap \to ap$
equation for $\overline{pop}$	:	$\overline{pop}(\langle a,n\rangle) = \langle a[pred(n)] := \perp, pred(n)\rangle$

Let $\varphi: Sig(STACK) \to Sig(\overline{\text{AP}})$ be the signature morphism defined by $\{stack \to ap, \odot \to \overline{\odot}, \text{push} \to \overline{\text{push}}, \text{pop} \to \overline{\text{pop}}\}$ and leaving ELEM invariant. The initial model of $\overline{\text{AP}}$ certainly does not satisfy $\varphi(\text{pop}(\text{push}(e,s))) = \varphi(s)$, i.e. $\overline{\text{pop}}(\overline{\text{push}}(e,ap)) = ap$, which is in turn equivalent to $\langle a[n] := \perp, n\rangle = \langle a,n\rangle$. This is false for $a[n] \neq \perp$. However, this is verified for any $x = \langle a,n\rangle$ that is in $T_{\varphi(S),\varphi(\Sigma)}$, i.e. that is a finite combination of $\overline{\odot}, \overline{\text{push}}, \overline{\text{pop}}$. This shows that $\overline{AP}$ is a correct implementation of STACK.

Appendix B

Process Specification: Formal Definitions

- Let $\mathcal{P}$ be a *process* specification, based on the *data* specification $\mathcal{D}$. We suppose that the "sort of interest" of $\mathcal{D}$ (i.e. the sort on which the processes of $\mathcal{P}$ act) is s.[10] Another *process* specification $\mathcal{P}'$ with $\mathcal{D}'$, s' and *process'* is given.

A ***signature morphism*** between the process specification $\mathcal{P}$ and $\mathcal{P}'$ is a classical signature morphism $\varphi: Sig(\mathcal{P}) \to Sig(\mathcal{P}')$ [cf. Appendix A] such that:
- $\varphi(\mathcal{D}) \subseteq \mathcal{D}'$ and $\varphi(s) = s'$
- $\varphi(process) = process'$
- $\varphi(\epsilon) = \epsilon'$ for $(\epsilon,\epsilon') \in \{\ (\emptyset_{\mathcal{D}},\emptyset_{\mathcal{D}'}), (\cup_{\mathcal{D}},\cup_{\mathcal{D}'}), (::_{\mathcal{P}},::_{\mathcal{P}'}), (id_{\mathcal{P}},id_{\mathcal{P}'}),$ $(\delta_{\mathcal{P}},\delta_{\mathcal{P}'}), (+_{\mathcal{P}},+_{\mathcal{P}'}), (;_{\mathcal{P}},;_{\mathcal{P}'}), (\|_{\mathcal{P}},\|_{\mathcal{P}'}), (\llcorner\!\llcorner_{\mathcal{P}},\llcorner\!\llcorner_{\mathcal{P}'})\ \}$

Now, we say that $\mathcal{P}$ ***is implemented by*** $\mathcal{P}'$ ***via*** the signature morphism of *process* specification φ *if* the *data* specification $[\![\mathcal{P}]\!]$ is implemented by the specification $[\![\mathcal{P}']\!]$ via φ (which is canonically considered as a signature morphism from $[\![\mathcal{P}]\!]$ to $[\![\mathcal{P}']\!]$).

- As a last point, if $\mathcal{P}$ is implemented by $\mathcal{P}'$ via a signature morphism φ, we notice that φ need only be defined by its restriction to $\mathcal{D}$, to the atomic actions and to the non-atomic actions of $\mathcal{P}$. Actually, there is not much choice in order to define φ on the non-atomic actions: let ν be a non-atomic such that: $\nu(\vec{x}) = t_{\mathcal{P}}(\vec{x},\vec{\omega})$ with the notations of section 2. 't' is a context made of

[10] the processes of $\mathcal{P}$ belong to sort *process*.

the operators $+_P$, $;_P$, $\llfloor_P$ and $\|_P$, $\vec{x}$ is the vector of variables of ν and $\vec{\omega} = (\omega_1(\vec{x}), \ldots, \omega_n(\vec{x}))$. Let $\vec{x}'$ stand for the vector of variables, and $\vec{\omega}'$ stand for $(\varphi(\omega_1)(\vec{x}'), \ldots, j\varphi(\omega_n)(\vec{x}'))$. Then it must be the case that: $\varphi(\nu)(\vec{x}') = t_{P'}(\vec{x}', \vec{\omega}')$.

Now $\varphi(\nu) = \nu'$ has in P' a definition $\nu'(\vec{x}) = t''_{P'}(\vec{x}', \vec{\omega}'')$. In the paper, we have supposed for sake of clarity that $t_{P'} = t''_{P'}$ and $\vec{\omega}' = \vec{\omega}''$, *syntactically*, i.e., that the definition of ν and ν' are "isomorphic" via φ. If it is not the case, we simply need to prove the additive property: $t'_P(\vec{x}', \vec{\omega}'') \stackrel{f_0}{\equiv} t_{P'}(\vec{x}', \vec{\omega}')$.

On implementations of loose abstract data type specifications and their vertical composition

Christoph Beierle
TK LILOG, IBM Deutschland GmbH
Postfach 80 08 80, D-7000 Stuttgart 1
EARN: BEIERLE at DSØLILOG

Angelika Voß
GMD, Forschungsgruppe Expertensysteme
Postfach 12 40, D-5205 St. Augustin 1
USENET: AVOSS%GMDXPS at GMDZI

Abstract: In an approach for the implementation of loose abstract data type specifications that completely distinguishes between the syntactical level of specifications and the semantical level of models, vertical implementation composition is defined compatibly on both levels. Implementations have signatures, models, and sentences where the latter also include hidden components, which allows for useful normal form results. We illustrate the stepwise development of implementations as well as their composition by some examples and describe the incorporation of the concept into an integrated software development and verification system.

1. Introduction

In the early days of abstract data types merely fixed ADT specifications with only isomorphic models were studied. Later on, so-called loose approaches were suggested where one considers not only the initial or terminal model of a specification but all models. As one of its main advantages a loose approach is better suited to capture the process of software development: One can start with a small and still vague specification with many different models, and then refine such a specification gradually by adding new axioms, sorts, and operations, thereby restricting the class of admissible models. During this process, lower level constructive definition techniques may be used to refine the higher level axiomatic definitions so that one finally arrives at a concrete problem solution, which could be a program or a functional prototype.

An implementation relation between loose specifications should reflect this refinement scenario: among the many different models of the source and target specifications one should be able to develop those of interest by gradually refining the implementation so that the set of models is restricted accordingly. Our implementation concept introduced in [BV 85a] generalizes the concept for implementations of loose specifications proposed by Sannella and Wirsing in [SW 82], which in turn generalizes the fixed case (e.g. [GTW 78], [Ehc 82], [EKMP 82], [Ga 83]). By using the notion of institution ([GB 83]) our approach abstracts from the types of sentences used in the underlying ADT specification method.

One of the central problems when dealing with implementations is their composability. In our concept of implementation specifications the composition of implementations can be defined both on the syntactical level of specifications and on the semantical level of models. Both levels are closed under their composition operations which are associative. In particular, by using a strong normal result we show that syntactical and semantical compositions are compatible with each other.

In Section 2 we summarize the basic idea of our implementation concept as given in [BV 85a], elaborate the requirements a composition operation should fulfill, and briefly state the assumptions about the underlying loose ADT specifications. In Section 3 we introduce the institution of implementation specifications without hidden components, and in Section 4 we extend this institution by introducing hidden parts. Section 5 contains our normal form theorem, and in Section 6 we develop syntactical and semantical composition operations and show their compatibility. Section 7 describes the incorporation of our concept into an integrated software development and verification system, and Section 8 contains a summary and a comparison.

Acknowledgements: We would like to thank Martin Wirsing and Jörg Siekmann for some valuable discussions and suggestions. This work was performed at the Universität Kaiserslautern and was supported in part by the Bundesministerium für Forschung and Technologie (IT 8302363) and the Deutsche Forschungsgemeinschaft (SFB 314).

2. Implementation specifications: Basic idea and requirements for their composition

As compared to fixed specifications, in the loose case we still have specifications, signatures, signature morphisms, etc, the essential difference lying in the number of models being considered. Therefore, an implementation for loose specifications should at least consist of an abstract specification, a concrete specification, and a signature morphism translating the abstract signature to the (possibly extended) concrete signature. Since a concrete specification can always be extended before giving the implementation, we will choose the technically simpler approach and omit any extension of the concrete specification as part of the implementation.

In [SW 82] Sannella and Wirsing require for every concrete model some abstract model and an abstraction function connecting them. If such a complete set of triples exists, the concrete specification is said to implement the abstract one, otherwise it does not. This is an implicit, non-constructive approach which gives no room for a notion of refinement between implementations since there is no way to characterize and restrict the set of triples - e.g. by constraints on the concrete or abstract models - any further.
Since the idea of loose specifications is to consider at first an arbitrary large set of models and to restrict this set stepwise by refining the specification, we think the adequate idea of implementations between loose specifications is to accept all meaningful combinations of an abstract model, a concrete model, and an abstraction function and to restrict them stepwise by refining the implementation.

To realize these ideas we introduce the notion of implementation models: A simple implementation $<SPa,\sigma,SPc>$ consisting of an abstract specification SPa, a concrete one SPc, and a signature translation σ between them denotes the set of all triples consisting of an abstract model Aa, a concrete one Ac, and an abstraction function α from the concrete to the abstract model. Such a tripel $<Ac,\alpha,Aa>$ is called an implementation model. As in the fixed case, the abstraction function may be partially defined and it must be surjective and homomorphic. (Note that in both cases the first component contains the source and the third component the target of the function in the middle component.)

A refinement between implementations should restrict the set of implementation models which can be done componentwise by restricting the sets of abstract models, of concrete models, and of abstraction functions. In the framework of loose specifications sets of models - like the abstract and the concrete ones - are restricted by adding sentences to the respective specification. To apply this technique to implementations we view abstraction functions, which operate on both concrete and abstract carriers, as algebra operations from concrete to abstract sorts. These operations can be restricted as usually by adding sentences over both the concrete and the abstract signatures extended by the abstraction operation names. Thus we admit arbitrary sentences over the abstract and the concrete signatures extended by the abstraction operation names, - later on we will extend this vocabulary by arbitrary hidden sorts and operations. These sentences will be called implementation sentences.

Adding a set IE of implementation sentences to a simple implementation $I\Sigma = <SPa,\sigma,SPc>$ we obtain an implementation specification $ISP = <I\Sigma, IE>$ that denotes all implementation models of $I\Sigma$ which satisfy IE. Analogously to specifications which consist of a signature in the simplest case, a simple implementation like $I\Sigma$ will also be called an implementation signature.

An implementation should be refinable by adding more implementation sentences to it and thus reducing the class of implementation models. This idea is extended analogously to loose ADT specifications by admitting a change of signature: There, a specification morphism is a signature morphism such that the translated sentences of the refined specification hold in the refining specification. Thus an implementation morphism or a refinement between two implementations is an implementation signature morphism such that the translated sentences of the refined implementation hold in the refining one.

Since an implementation signature contains two specifications, an implementation morphism is a pair $\tau = \langle \rho a, \rho c \rangle: I\Sigma_1 \rightarrow I\Sigma_2$ for $I\Sigma_j = \langle SPa_j, \sigma_j, SPc_j \rangle$ consisting of an abstract specification morphism ρa: $SPa_1 \rightarrow SPa_2$ and a concrete specification morphism ρc: $SPc_1 \rightarrow SPc_2$. Viewing ρa and ρc as signature morphisms τ constitutes a diagram

$$\begin{array}{ccc} SPa_1 & \xrightarrow{\sigma_1} & SPc_1 \\ \rho a \downarrow & & \downarrow \rho c \\ SPa_2 & \xrightarrow{\sigma_2} & SPc_2 \end{array}$$

that should commute as the following example suggests: Assume we have an implementation from sets over arbitrary elements to extended lists over arbitrary elements, and another i-signature from sets over natural numbers to extended lists over natural numbers. Then it should not matter whether we first represent sets over arbitrary elements by lists over arbitrary elements and then refine to lists over natural numbers, or if we first refine the sets over arbitrary elements to sets over natural numbers and then represent them as lists over natural numbers.

When implementing an abstract specification by a more concrete one which in turn is implemented by a third specification it is desirable to get automatically an implementation of the first by the third specification by composing the two individual implementations. Moreover, the sequence of compositions should be irrelevant, i.e. one would like to have an associative implementation composition operator.

In the most elaborated implementation concept for the fixed case given in [EKMP 82], proof theoretical and semantical conditions are given that guarantee composability. In the loose approach of [SW 82], full composability is given by the very definition of implementation: every concrete algebra must be associated to an abstract algebra. Further approaches studying such compositions of implementations are the approaches of [Hup 81], [GM 82], [Ga 83], [Li 83], and [SW 83].

In our concept of implementation specifications the question of composability arises on different levels: Simple implementations, implementation specifications, and implementation models should all be composable and closed under composition.

When composing simple implementations it is natural to require that the concrete specification of the first implementation is identical to the abstract one of the second implementation. In this case the composed implementation is obtained by taking the abstract specification of the first implementation and the concrete specification of the second one together with the composition of the two signature translations. A similar argument holds for the composition of implementation models. In particular one must ensure that the abstraction functions are composable and closed under composition. With the compositions of simple implementations and of implementation models we can constrain the composition of implementation specifications by the following compatibility condition: The set of models of a composed implementation specification should be identical to the set of models obtained by composing the sets of models of the individual implementation specifications. If this condition is fulfilled we say that the composition of implementation specifications is compatible with the composition of their implementation models.

Summarizing we require our implementation concept to offer composition operations for simple implementations (i.e. implementation signatures), implementation specifications, and implementation models such that all of them are closed under composition, and such that composition is associative and compatible w.r.t. implementation specifications and implementation models.

W.r.t. the underlying institution of loose specifications we only assume that the loose specifications have equational signatures with error constants, denote strict algebras, and are formally defined as the theories of an institution ([GB 83]). In particular, we do not make any assumptions about the types of sentences:

Assumption: SPEC-institution := <SIG, EAlg, ESen, $|\!\stackrel{s}{=}$ > is an institution where

- SIG is a category of equational signatures with an error constant error-s for each sort s.
- EAlg is a coproduct preserving model functor mapping a signature Σ to all strict Σ-algebras, which have flat cpos as carriers, strict operations, and the error constants denoting the bottom element.
- ESen is a sentence functor mapping a signature Σ to a set of Σ-sentences.
- $|\!\stackrel{s}{=}$ is the strict satisfaction relation.

SPEC denotes the category of theories in the SPEC-institution which will be called (loose) specifications, and Sig: SPEC $\rightarrow$ SIG is the functor forgetting specifications to their signatures.

3. Implementation specifications without hidden components

In this section we develop an institution of implementation specifications without hidden components along the ideas in Section 2.

3.1 Implementation signatures

Implementation signatures and morphisms constitute a category. In fact, it is the comma category induced by the functor Sig forgetting specifications to their signatures.

Definition 3.1 [ISIG, i-signature]
Given the forgetful functor Sig: SPEC $\rightarrow$ SIG, the comma category ISIG = (Sig$\downarrow$Sig) is the category of implementation signatures (i-signatures).

Since the category SIG is cocomplete and the functor Sig preserves all colimits, ISIG is cocomplete, too, by a general property of comma categories.

Fact 3.2 [colimits] ISIG is cocomplete.

3.2 Implementation models

We want to introduce abstraction operations as ordinary operations which are interpreted by abstraction functions and which can be restricted by ordinary sentences. Since in the framework of the SPEC-institution the algebra operations must be totally defined, we will also require that the abstraction operations are totally defined. This is no limitation because the algebras are cpos and there is an error constant for each sort denoting the minimum element. Thus $\alpha(x)$ is mapped to error whenever $\alpha(x)$ is meant to be undefined. Doing so we must only suitably restrict the homomorphism requirement

$$\alpha(\sigma(op)(x)) = op(\alpha(x))$$

which under these circumstances needs to hold only if $\alpha(x)$ is non-error.

Definition 3.3 [Σ-p-homomorphism]
Let A, B $\in$ EAlg(Σ) with Σ = <S,Op> $\in$ SIG. An S-sorted family of functions

$$h = \{h_s\colon A_s \rightarrow B_s \mid s \in S\}$$

is a partially-homomorphic Σ-homomorphism (or just Σ-p-homomorphism) iff

$$\forall\, op: s_1 \ldots s_n \to s \in \Sigma\ .$$
$$\quad \forall\, x_1 \in A_{s1}\ .\ \ldots\ \forall\, x_n \in A_{sn}\ .$$
$$\qquad h_{s1}(x_1) \neq \text{error-}s_{1B}\ \&\ \ldots\ \&\ h_{sn}(x_n) \neq \text{error-}s_{nB}$$
$$\qquad\quad \Rightarrow h_s(op_A(x_1,\ldots,x_n)) = op_B(h_{s1}(x_1),\ldots,h_{sn}(x_n))$$

Fact 3.4 [p-homomorphisms are closed under composition]

Let $\Sigma = \langle S, Op\rangle \in SIG$ and $f: A \to B$, $g: B \to C$ be Σ-p-homomorphisms. Then their composition $g \circ f := \{g_s \circ f_s \mid s \in S\}: A \to C$ is a Σ-p-homomorphism.

Definition 3.5 [PEAlg]

The functor PEAlg: SIG $\to$ CAT^{op} maps a signature Σ to the category of strict Σ-algebras with Σ-p-homomorphisms, and it maps a signature morphism σ to the forgetful functor PEAlg(σ) which is defined analogously to EAlg(σ).

Fact 3.6 [Partial]

The family of inclusion functors Partial_Σ: EAlg(Σ) $\to$ PEAlg(Σ) with $\Sigma \in SIG$ defines a natural transformation Partial: EAlg ==> PEAlg.

With PEAlg formalizing the property "partially homomorphic" we can define a preliminary model functor mapping an i-signature IΣ to the category of all tripels TA = $\langle Ac, \alpha, Aa\rangle$ where α is p-homomorphic but not necessarily surjective. Analogously to i-signature morphisms the morphisms in this category are pairs of homomorphisms

$\langle hc, ha\rangle : \langle Ac, \alpha, Aa\rangle \to \langle Bc, \beta, Ba\rangle$

that are compatible with the abstraction functions, i.e. it does not matter whether we first abstract Ac-elements with α to Aa-elements and then map them with hc to Bc-elements, or whether we first map the Ac-elements with hc to Bc-elements and then abstract them with β to Ba. As in the fixed case, the forgetful functor EAlg(σ) is applied to the source of the abstraction functions so that the compatability condition for the model morphisms is the commutativity of the diagram

$$\begin{array}{ccc}
\text{EAlg}(\sigma)(Ac) & \xrightarrow{\quad\alpha\quad} & Aa \\
{\scriptstyle \text{EAlg}(\sigma)(hc)}\downarrow & & \downarrow{\scriptstyle ha} \\
\text{EAlg}(\sigma)(Bc) & \xrightarrow[\quad\beta\quad]{} & Ba
\end{array}$$

in PEAlg(Σa). Similar to i-signatures, this situation can be expressed neatly as a comma category.

Definition 3.7 [Tripel(IΣ)]

Let IΣ = $\langle SPa, \sigma, SPc\rangle$ be an i-signature with Sig(SPa) = Σa and Sig(SPc) = Σc. The comma category

$$\text{Tripel}(I\Sigma) := (\text{Partial}_{\Sigma a} \circ \text{EAlg}(\sigma)|_{\text{EAlg}(SPc)} \downarrow \text{Partial}_{\Sigma a}|_{\text{EAlg}(SPa)})$$

is called the category of IΣ-tripels.

As with ordinary signatures, every i-signature morphism induces a forgetful functor between the respective model categories in the reverse direction. It is defined componentwise.

Fact 3.8 [Tripel(τ)]

Let $\tau = \langle \rho a, \rho c\rangle: I\Sigma_1 \to I\Sigma_2 \in ISIG$.

Tripel(τ): Tripel(IΣ_2) $\to$ Tripel(IΣ_1)

defined on objects by

$$\text{Tripel}(\tau)(\langle Ac, \alpha, Aa\rangle) := \langle \text{EAlg}(\rho c)(Ac), \text{PEAlg}(\rho a)(\alpha), \text{EAlg}(\rho a)(Aa)\rangle$$

and on morphisms by

$$\text{Tripel}(\tau)(\langle hc, ha\rangle) := \langle \text{EAlg}(\rho c)(hc), \text{EAlg}(\rho a)(ha)\rangle$$

is a functor.

The observations above yield a prelimininary model functor Tripel: ISIG $\to$ CAT^{op}. Tripel still allows e.g. a tripel where both Ac and Aa are given by the natural numbers and where α sends n to 2*n. Because the odd numbers on the abstract side are not represented by any objects on the concrete side we exclude such cases by restricting Tripel to consider only tripels with surjective abstraction functions.

Definition 3.9 [IMod(IΣ)]

For every IΣ ε ISIG the category of IΣ-implementation models (or just IΣ-i-models)

IMod(IΣ)

is the full subcategory of Tripel(IΣ) generated by all tripels with surjective abstraction function.

Fact 3.10 [IMod(τ), IMod]

For every τ: $I\Sigma_1 \to I\Sigma_2$ the restriction and corestriction of Tripel(τ) to $IMod(I\Sigma_2)$ and $IMod(I\Sigma_1)$ exists. It is denoted by

$IMod(\tau): IMod(I\Sigma_2) \to IMod(I\Sigma_1)$

and

IMod: ISIG $\to$ CAT^{op}

is called the modelling functor for implementation signatures.

3.3 Relating implementation signatures to specifications

Implementation sentences over an i-signature IΣ shall be expressed over the abstract signature Σa, the concrete signature Σc, and so-called abstraction operations to be interpreted as abstraction functions. In a first approach, we take all ordinary sentences over this vocabulary as implementation sentences. For reasons of convenience we use standard names for the abstraction operations:

Definition 3.11 [abs-operations]

For IΣ = <<Σa,Ea>,σ,<Σc,Ec>> ε ISIG and τ = <ρa,ρc>: IΣ $\to$ IΣ´ ε /ISIG/ we define:

abs-operations(IΣ) := $\{abs\text{-}s_{I\Sigma}: \sigma(s) \to s \mid s \in \Sigma a\}$

abs-operations(τ) := $\{(abs\text{-}s_{I\Sigma}, abs\text{-}\rho a(s)_{I\Sigma'}) \mid s \in \Sigma a\}$.

Fact 3.12 [ψ]

ψ: ISIG $\to$ SIG

defined on objects by ψ(IΣ) := Σa ⊍ Σc ⊍ abs-operations(IΣ)

and on morphisms by ψ(τ) := ρa ⊍ ρc ⊍ abs-operations(τ)

is a colimit preserving functor.

Defining an IΣ-implementation sentence to be an ordinary ψ(IΣ)-sentence p we must determine whether an IΣ-i-model MA = <Ac,α,Aa> satisfies p. Since the abstract symbols in ψ(IΣ) shall be interpreted by the abstract algebra Aa, the concrete symbols by the concrete algebra Ac, and the abstraction operations by the abstraction function α, we can take the disjoint union of Aa, Ac, and α to obtain a ψ(IΣ)-algebra interpreting ψ(IΣ); joining also IΣ-i-model morphisms yields a functor from IΣ-i-models to ψ(IΣ)-algebras.

Definition 3.13 [$join_{I\Sigma}(MA)$]

For an i-signature IΣ = <SPa,σ,SPc> and an IΣ-i-model MA = <Ac,α,Aa>

$join_{I\Sigma}(MA)$:= Aa ⊍ Ac ⊍ α

is the ψ(IΣ)-algebra A defined by

- for s ε Sig(SPa): $A_s := Aa_s$
- for s ε Sig(SPc): $A_s := Ac_s$
- for op ε Sig(SPa): $op_A := op_{Aa}$
- for op ε Sig(SPc): $op_A := op_{Ac}$
- for abs-s ε abs-operations(IΣ): abs-sA := αs.

Fact 3.14 [$join_{I\Sigma}$, join]

Defining $join_{I\Sigma}$ on IΣ-i-model morphisms g = <hc,ha> by

$$join_{I\Sigma}(g) := \{ha_s \mid s \in Sig(SPa)\} \cup \{hc_s \mid s \in Sig(SPc)\}$$

yields a functor

$$join_{I\Sigma}: IMod(I\Sigma) \rightarrow EAlg(\psi(I\Sigma))$$

and generalizing over all i-signatures yields a natural transformation

$$join: IMod \Longrightarrow EAlg \circ \psi$$

3.4 Implementation sentences without hidden components

We define the set of IΣ-implementation sentences without hidden components or just IΣ-i-sentences to be the set of all ordinary ψ(IΣ)-sentences. Such an IΣ-i-sentence p is satisfied by an IΣ-i-model MA exactly if MA viewed as the ψ(IΣ)-algebra $join_{I\Sigma}(MA)$ satisfies p.

Definition 3.15 [ISen1]

The implementation sentence functor without hidden components is given by

$$ISen1 := Sen \circ \psi: ISIG \rightarrow SET.$$

Definition 3.16 [$\models^i$]

Let IΣ ε ISIG, MA ε IMod(IΣ) and p ε ISen1(IΣ). MA satisfies p, written $MA \models^i_{I\Sigma} p$, iff $join_{I\Sigma}(MA) \models^e_{\psi(I\Sigma)} p$.

Fact 3.17 [satisfaction condition]

$$\forall \tau: I\Sigma_1 \rightarrow I\Sigma_2 \in ISIG \,.\, \forall MA \in IMod(I\Sigma_2) \,.\, \forall p \in ISen1(I\Sigma_1) \,.$$
$$MA \models^i_{I\Sigma 2} ISen1(\tau)(p) \iff IMod(\tau)(MA) \models^i_{I\Sigma 1} p.$$

3.5 The institution

Since the satisfaction condition holds the notions defined above constitute an institution. Like specifications are defined as the theories of the SPEC-institution, implementation specifications will be defined as the theories of this new institution.

Definition 3.18 [IMP1-institution]

IMP1-institution := <ISIG, ISen1, IMod, $\models^i$ >

is the institution of implementation specifications without hidden components.

IMP1 is its category of theories and it is called the category of implementation specifications without hidden components.

Since ISIG is cocomplete, general institution properties tell us that IMP1 is cocomplete as well.

Fact 3.19 [colimits] IMP1 is cocomplete.

3.6 Examples: Implementing sets by lists and lists by array-pointer pairs

In our examples we assume that the error constants are implicitly declared. As sentences we choose first order formulas where the bound variables are not interpreted as bottom elements. Besides we need some constraint mechanism to exclude unreachable elements (e.g. initial [HKR 80], data [BG 80], hierarchy [SW 82], or algorithmic constraints [BV 85b]). Note that our concept of implementation specifications does not restrict our choice since it completely abstracts from the types of sentences. However, since we allow the same types of sentences for implementation specifications as for the underlying ADT specifications, one general remark can be made: implementation verification tasks like proving an i-signature morphism to be an implementation refinement can be reduced to verification tasks of ADT specifications like proving a signature morphism to be a specification refinement. These in turn can be solved in any appropriate proof theory for the SPEC-institution (c.f. Section 7 and [BV 85b]).

We show how several well known implementations of sets by lists can be developed stepwise and hand in hand with the implementing specification. Presentations of the specifications are given in Figure 3.20(a); the sentences parts are not elaborated since they are standard.

On the abstract side we have the specification SET of sets with the empty set as constant, and operations to insert an element, to determine or remove the minimum element in a set, and to test for the empty set or for the membership of an element. Beside standard sets, there may be bags or unreachable elements of sort set. The set elements are described in the specification LIN-ORD which introduces a sort elem with an equality operation and an arbitrary reflexive linear ordering. The subspecification BOOL of LIN-ORD specifies the booleans with the usual operations true, false, not, and, or.

On the concrete side the specification LIST extends LIN-ORD to standard lists with the constant nil, the operations cons, car, and cdr, and a test nil? for the empty list. All lists must be generated from the elements by nil and cons. LIST is extended to LIST-S by introducing names for the set simulating operations, but without restricting these operations in order to obtain a variety of different models.

We can give a first simple i-specification I:SET/LIST-S from SET to LIST-S:

<u>ispec</u> I:SET/LIST-S =
<u>isig</u> $\sigma_{S/LS}$: SET → LIST-S

with the signature morphism translating sort set to list and translating the set operations to their simulating list operations (namely empty to nil, empty? to nil?, insert to l-insert, in? to l-in?, min to l-min, and remove-min to l-remove-min) without renaming the signatures of the common subspecifications LIN-ORD and BOOL. Since I:SET/LIST-S contains no i-sentences, its i-models comprise all possible representations of sets by lists.

I:SET/LIST-S can be refined in various ways by adding i-sentences restricting the abstraction operations of sort set, such that e.g.

- <u>a</u>ll lists represent sets (IA:SET/LIST-S),
- only lists with <u>u</u>nique entries may represent sets (IU:SET/LIST-S),
- only <u>s</u>orted lists may represent sets (IS:SET/LIST-S), or
- only <u>s</u>orted lists with <u>u</u>nique entries may represent sets (ISU:SET/LIST-S).

The last i-specification refines not only I:SET/LIST-S, but also IU:SET/LIST-S and IS:SET/LIST-S. The i-specifications are given in Figure 3.21 where we use abs-s: $\sigma_{S/LS}(s) \to s$ as the abstraction operation name of sort s.

Corresponding to the four alternative refinements of I:SET/LIST-S we could now specify alternative refinements of the concrete LIST-S specification by adding sentences fixing the set simulating operations. The resulting LIST-S refinements could in turn be used to refine the respective i-specifications by replacing LIST-S by the corresponding LIST-S refinement.

Here, however, we want to carry out the development in another direction by implementing the lists by array-pointer pairs. For this purpose we consider the three specifications listed in Figure 3.20(b): PAIR introduces standard arrays and pairs of an array with a natural number. PAIR-L fixes the new LIST simulating operations such that p-nil yields the new array with pointer zero, p-nil? checks whether the pointer is zero, p-cons puts an element in the field indicated by the pointer and increments the pointer by one, p-car gets the element in the field indicated by the pointer minus one, and p-cdr decrements the pointer by one. In contrast, the new operations in PAIR-LS are unrestricted in order to allow for a variety of i-models differing in their SET simulating operations.

```
spec LIN-ORD = BOOL u                                   (a)
   sorts elem
   ops   eq, le: elem elem → bool
   sentences ... < specifying eq as equality and
     le as an arbitrary reflexive linear ordering >

spec SET = LIN-ORD u
   sorts set
   ops   empty: → set
         insert: elem set → set
         min: set → elem
         remove-min: set → set
         empty?: set → bool
         in?: elem set → bool
   sentences ... < specifying the set operations
      with their usual meaning, but not
      necessarily excluding non-standard sets >

spec LIST = LIN-ORD u
   sorts list
   ops   nil: → list
         cons: elem list → list
         car: list → elem
         cdr: list → list
         nil?: list → bool
   sentences ... < specifying standard lists
      over elem generated by nil and cons >

spec LIST-S = LIST u
   ops   l-insert: elem list → list
         l-min: list → elem
         l-remove-min: list → list
         l-in?: elem list → bool
```

```
spec PAIR = LIN-ORD u NAT u                             (b)
   sorts array, pairs
   ops   new: → array
         put: array nat elem → array
         get: array nat → elem
         pair: array nat → pairs
         pa: pairs → array
         pn: pairs → nat
   sentences ...<specifying standard
         arrays and pairs of an array
         with a natural number>

spec PAIR-L = PAIR u
   ops p-nil: → pairs
       p-nil?: pairs → bool
       p-cons: elem pairs → pairs
       p-car: pairs → elem
       p-cdr: pairs → pairs
   sentences ...<specifying the
       LIST-simulating such that
       p-cons puts an elementinto
       the array and increments the
       pointer by one, p-cdr
       decrements the pointer by one,
       etc.>

spec PAIR-LS = PAIR-L
   ops p-insert: elem pairs → pairs
       p-in?: elem pairs → bool
       p-min: pairs → elem
       p-remove-min: pairs → pairs
```

Figure 3.20 The ADT specifications in the implementations of sets by lists (a) and of lists by array-pointer pairs (b)

```
ispec IA:SET/LIST-S = I:SET/LIST-S u
    isentences
        (∀ x: list . ∀ e: elem .
             abs-set(cons(e,x)) = insert(abs-elem(e),abs-set(x)))

ispec IS:SET/LIST-S = I:SET/LIST-S u
    isentences
        (∀ e, e1, e2:elem . ∀ x: list .
             abs-set(cons(e,nil)) = insert(abs-elem(e),empty) &
             le(e1,e2) = true & eq(e1,e2) = false =>
                abs-set(cons(e1,cons(e2,x))) =
                    insert(abs-elem(e1),abs-set(cons(e2,x)))  &
             le(e2,e1) = true & eq(e1,e2) = false =>
                abs-set(cons(e1,cons(e2,x))) = error-set        )

ispec IU:SET/LIST-S = I:SET/LIST-S u
    isentences
        (∀ e, e1, e2: elem . ∀ x: list .
             abs-set(cons(e,nil)) = insert(abs-elem(e),empty) &
             (in?(e,abs-set(x)) = true =>
                  abs-set(cons(e,x)) = error-set)                )

ispec ISU:SET/LIST-S = IU:SET/LIST-S u IS:SET/LIST-S
```

Figure 3.21 Some i-specifications implementing sets by lists

With the signature morphism $\sigma_{L/PL}$: Sig(LIST) → Sig(PAIR-L) mapping sort list to pairs, mapping operation op ε {nil, nil?, cons, car, cdr} to its simulating operation p-op, and leaving the rest unchanged, the i-specification implementing LIST by PAIR-L given by

```
i-spec  I:LIST/PAIR-L  =
     isig  σL/LP: LIST → PAIR-L
     isentences
           ∀ p: pairs .
                (p-nil?(p) = true  => abs-list(p) = nil)                    &
                (p-nil?(p) = false =>
                   abs-list(p) = cons(abs-elem(p-car(p)),abs-list(p-cdr(p))) )
```

fixes the abstraction operation abs-list. This i-specification can be extended to an i-specification implementing LIST-S by PAIR-LS with the signature morphism $\sigma_{LS/PLS}$: Sig(LIST-S) → Sig(PAIR-LS) mapping all operations l-op for op ε {insert ,in? ,min ,remove-min} to their simulating operation p-op and leaving the rest unchanged:

```
ispec  I:LIST-S/PAIR-LS  =  I:LIST/PAIR-L  u
    isig  σLS/PLS: LIST-S → PAIR-LS
```

comprises all i-models with fixed LIST simulating operations but with varying SET simulating operations. Figure 3.22 shows the relations between the specifications and i-specifications developed so far.

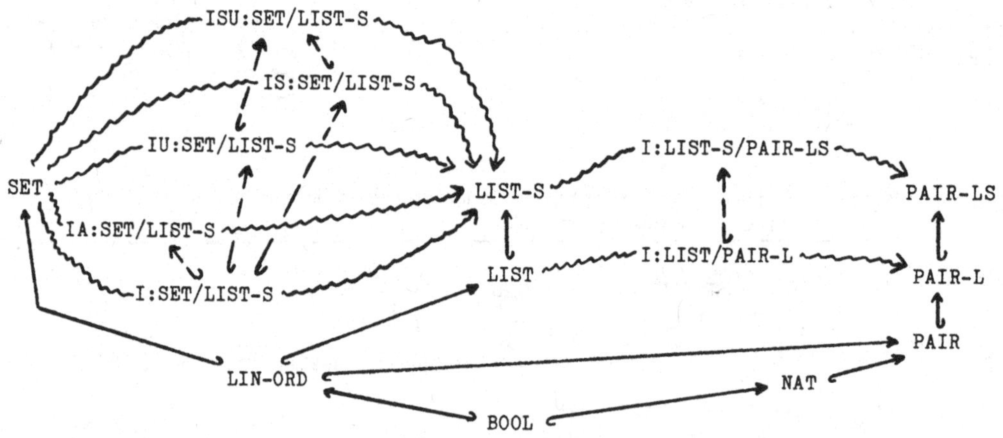

Figure 3.22: The relation between the specifications and i-specifications

4. Implementation specifications with hidden components

The inclusion of hidden specification parts into an ADT specification technique usually extends its expressive power ([TWW 82], [BBTW 81]), and when describing the composition of algebraic implementations hidden components are needed for the intermediate specification part ([EKMP 82]). We extend the IMP1-institution by so-called hidden specification sentences which are comparable to an algebraic specification mechanism called functor image restriction in [Ehg 81], reflections in [EWT 82] and derive ... from ... by-construct in [SW 83].

While so far an implementation sentence over an i-signature IΣ is an ordinary sentence over the vocabulary ψ(IΣ), we now extend ψ(IΣ) by arbitrary hidden sorts and operation symbols from an ordinary ADT specification SPh via some signature morphism δ: ψ(IΣ) → Sig(SPh).

Definition 4.1 [hidden specification sentence, HSen]

Let SPh ε SPEC, δ ε /SIG/ and τ ε /ISIG/. An $I\Sigma_2$-hidden specification sentence is a triple

$$sh = \langle SPh,\ \delta: \psi(I\Sigma_1) \to Sig(SPh),\ \tau: I\Sigma_1 \to I\Sigma_2 \rangle$$

and $HSen(I\Sigma_2)$ denotes the set of all $I\Sigma_2$-hidden specification sentences.

The translation of sh by $\tau': I\Sigma_2 \to I\Sigma'$ is the $I\Sigma'$-hidden specification sentence given by $HSen(\tau')(sh) := \langle SPh, \delta, \tau' \circ \tau \rangle$

Note that the third component τ of a hidden specification sentence allows for the translation of such sentences by arbitrary (i-signature) morphisms, thus serving the same function as the second component of the data constraints in [GB 83].

Writing sh for an $I\Sigma_2$-i-specification we are interested only in those $I\Sigma_2$-i-models MA that can be 'extended' to SPh models: MA satisfies sh iff MA forgotten along τ and viewed as a $\psi(I\Sigma)$-algebra is identical to some SPh-algebra A where the hidden part of A is forgotten along δ. This situation is illustrated in Figure 4.2 and made precise in Definition 4.3.

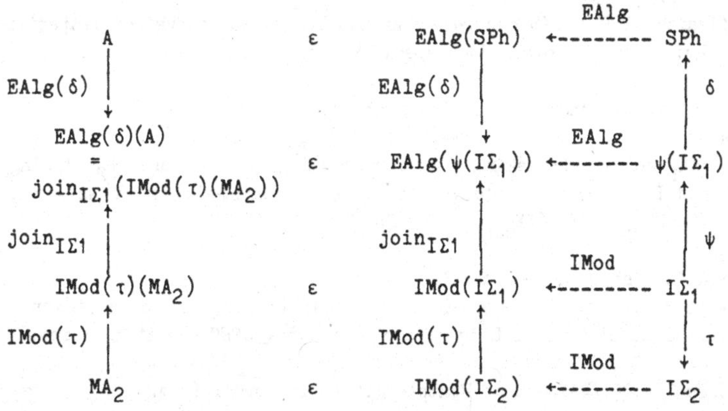

Figure 4.2 Satisfaction of a hidden specification sentence $\langle SPh,\ \delta: \psi(I\Sigma_1) \to SPh,\ \tau: I\Sigma_1 \to I\Sigma_2 \rangle$

Definition 4.3 [satisfaction $\models^i$ of a hidden specification sentence]

$\forall$ MA ε $IMod(I\Sigma_2)$.

$$MA_2 \models^i \langle SPh, \delta, \tau \rangle \iff \exists A \in EAlg(SPh)\ .\ EAlg(\delta)(A) = join_{I\Sigma 1}(IMod(\tau)(MA))$$

Example 4.4 [implementing sets via lists by array-pointer pairs]

An i-specification describing the composition of ISU:SET/LIST-S and I:LIST-S/PAIR-LS is

<u>ispec</u> ISU:SET/PAIR-LS
 <u>isig</u> $\sigma_{LS/PLS} \circ \sigma_{S/LS}$: SET → PAIR-LS
 <u>hidden-spec-sentences</u> <S-LS-PLS, δ, id>

with the hidden specification

<u>spec</u> S-LS-PLS = SET u LIST-S u PAIR-LS u
 <u>ops</u> $abs\text{-}set_{S/LS}$: list → set
 $abs\text{-}list_{LS/PLS}$: pairs → list
 $abs\text{-}set_{S/PLS}$: pairs → set
 <u>sentences</u>
 i-sentences(ISU:SET/LIST-S) u
 i-sentences(I:LIST-S/PAIR-LS) u
 $(\forall$ p: pairs . $abs\text{-}set_{S/PLS}(p) = abs\text{-}set_{S/LS}(abs\text{-}list_{LS/PLS}(p)))$

where the abstraction operations of the individual implementations are indexed correspondingly and where δ maps abs-set to $abs\text{-}set_{S/PLS}$. Note that for every denoted i-model $\langle A_{PAIR\text{-}LS}, \alpha, A_{SET} \rangle$ there must exist a LIST-S model $A_{LIST\text{-}S}$ and abstraction functions α_1 and α_2 such that $\langle A_{LIST\text{-}S}, \alpha_1, A_{SET} \rangle$ is an i-model of ISU:SET/LIST-S, $\langle A_{PAIR\text{-}LS}, \alpha_2, A_{LIST\text{-}S} \rangle$ is an i-model of I:LIST-S/PAIR-LS, and α is the composition of α_1 and α_2.

Fact 4.5 [satisfaction condition for hidden specification sentences]

$\forall\ \tau': I\Sigma_2 \to I\Sigma' \in ISIG\ .\ \forall\ MA \in IMod(I\Sigma')\ .\ \forall\ sh \in HSen(I\Sigma_2)\ .$

$$MA \models^{i}_{I\Sigma'} HSen(\tau')(sh) \iff IMod(\tau')(MA) \models^{i}_{I\Sigma 2} sh.$$

Definition 4.6 [IMP-institution, IMP]

$$\text{IMP-institution} := \langle ISIG, ISen, IMod, \models^{i} \rangle$$

is the institution extending the IMP1-institution by $ISen(I\Sigma) := ISen1(I\Sigma) \cup HSen(I\Sigma)$. IMP is the category of theories of this institution and called the category of implementation specifications (with hidden components).

5. Normal forms

The introduction of hidden specification sentences allows us to derive a very useful normal form result:

Fact 5.1 [normal form]

Any i-specification ISP $\in$ IMP can be transformed into an equivalent i-specification ISP′ in normal form having exactly one hidden specification sentence.

Proof: (idea) Given two hidden specification sentences

$$sh_j = \langle SP_j,\ \rho_j: \psi(I\Sigma_j) \to Sig(SP_j),\ \tau_j: I\Sigma_j \to I\Sigma \rangle$$

we can merge sh_1 and sh_2 by taking the coproduct SP_{cop} of SP_1 and SP_2, taking the coproduct $I\Sigma_{cop}$ of $I\Sigma_1$ and $I\Sigma_2$, and the uniquely determined morphisms ρ' and τ' as given in

$$sh = \langle SP_{cop},\ \rho': \psi(I\Sigma_{cop}) \to Sig(Sp_{cop}),\ \tau': I\Sigma_{cop} \to I\Sigma \rangle$$

To show that

$$IMod(I\Sigma, \{sh_1, sh_2\}) = IMod(I\Sigma, \{sh\})$$

and the generalization of this statement to (possibly infinite) sets of sentences relies on the fact that the model functor EAlg of the underlying SPEC-institution respects coproducts.

The i-specification ISU:SET/PAIR-LS of Example 4.4 is in normal form.

6. Composition

We now carry out the ideas from Section 2 about compositions.

6.1 Composition of implementation signatures

The composition of i-signatures is given by the composition of their signature translations. Obviously, this composition operation is associative.

Definition 6.1

For $I\Sigma_j = \langle SPa_j, \sigma_j, SPc_j \rangle$ with $j \in \{1,2\}$ and $SPc_2 = SPa_1$ the composition of $I\Sigma_1$ and $I\Sigma_2$ is given by

$$I\Sigma_1 \bullet I\Sigma_2 := \langle SPa_1,\ \sigma_2 \circ \sigma_1,\ SPc_2 \rangle$$

6.2 Composition of implementation models

The composition of an $I\Sigma_2$-i-model $MA_2 = \langle Ac_2, \alpha_2, Aa_2 \rangle$ with an $I\Sigma_1$-i-model $MA_1 = \langle Ac_1, \alpha_1, Aa_1 \rangle$ where $Aa_2 = Ac_1$ should yield an $I\Sigma_1 \bullet I\Sigma_2$-i-model resulting from the composition of their abstraction functions. In order to be able to compose the abstraction functions we must first apply the forgetful functor $PEAlg(\sigma_1)$ to α_2:

Fact 6.2 [composition of implementation models]

(1) The composition of MA_2 and MA_1 as given by $MA_2 \bullet MA_1 := \langle Ac_2,\ \alpha_1 \circ PEAlg(\rho_1)(\alpha_2),\ Aa_1 \rangle$ is an $I\Sigma_1 \bullet I\Sigma_2$-i-model.

(2) The composition operation on i-models is associative.

Given two i-specifications ISP_1 and ISP_2 with composable i-signatures, we can now compose all their respective i-models and obtain a subcategory of $IMod(I\Sigma_1 \bullet I\Sigma_2)$.

Definition 6.3 [composition of i-specification model categories]
$IMod(ISP_2 \bullet IMod(ISP_1)$
is the full subcategory of $IMod(I\Sigma_1 \bullet I\Sigma_2)$ generated by all $MA_2 \bullet MA_1$ with $MA_j \in IMod(ISP_j)$.

Fact 6.4 The composition operation on i-model categories is associative.

6.3 Composition of implementation specifications

The compositions of i-specifications and their i-model categories shall be compatible. With the notions introduced above we can formalize the compatibility condition by requiring

$$IMod(ISP_1 \bullet ISP_2) = IMod(ISP_2) \bullet IMod(ISP_1)$$

At least two questions arise immediately: Does there exist an i-specification ISP = $ISP_1 \bullet ISP_2$ describing the composition of ISP_1 and ISP_2 such that the compatibility condition is satisfied? And secondly, is there a constructive way to generate ISP for given ISP_1 and ISP_2? The following fact answers both questions in the affirmative.

Fact 6.5 [composition of i-specifications]
For any two i-specifications ISP_1 and ISP_2 with composable i-signatures there exists an i-specification $ISP_1 \bullet ISP_2$ such that the compatibility condition is satisfied.

Proof: (idea) In order to generalize the construction carried out in Example 4.4 we construct normal form presentations $ISPn_1$ and $ISPn_2$ which exist according to Fact 5.1, and perform the following steps:

(1) Combine the hidden specifications SPh_1 and SPh_2 of $ISPn_1$ such that the middle specification $SPa_2 = SPc_1$ is identified in this combination.
(2) Add the abstraction operations of $I\Sigma_1$, $I\Sigma_2$, and $I\Sigma_1 \bullet I\Sigma_2$, and add the corresponding composition axioms.

Steps (1) and (2) yield a hidden specification SPh describing a normal form representation of $ISP_1 \bullet ISP_2$.

As an illustration of Fact 6.5 consider again the composed i-specification ISU:SET/PAIR-LS from Example 4.4 which was constructed correspondingly yielding ISU:SET/LIST-S • I:LIST-S/PAIR-LS: The intermediate LIST-S specification is contained in the hidden specification, and the i-models denoted by the composed implementation are exactly those models that can be composed from the models of the two individual implementations. Similarly, we could compose I:LIST-S/PAIR-LS with any of the other four set-by-list implementations (c.f. Figure 3.22), yielding four different implementations of sets by array-pointer pairs.

Fact 6.6 The composition operation on i-specifications is associative.

Proof: By Fact 6.4 since the compatability condition holds.

7. Implementation specifications in a system integrating software development and verification

As already pointed out in Sections 1 and 2, there is a close correspondence between loose specifications and i-specifications w.r.t. their role in software development. Loose specifications provide a means for a formalized stepwise refinement scenario and the same is true for our implementation concept. The addition of new constraints to a loose specification corresponds to making further design decisions; likewise, the addition of i-sentences to an i-specification corresponds to further design decisions influencing e.g. the efficiency of certain operations (c.f. the set-by-list example in Section 3.6). Care must be taken because the process of refinement may yield an inconsistent specification having no models any more, and the same may happen to i-specifications. For both situations the same techniques can be used to cope with this problem, e.g. suitably restricting the class of admissible sentences or providing a constructively defined model. Such a model may be the program obtained gradually during the development process.

The latter approach is supported in the specification development language ASPIK within the Integrated Software Development and Verification (ISDV) system ([BV85b], [BOV 86]). ASPIK provides a uniform integration of high level axiomatic and lower level constructive specification techniques. An essential part of specification development in ASPIK is the gradual refinement of axiomatic parts by constructively defined models. That means an initially completely axiomatic specification is guaranteed to be consistent if its refinement process can be carried through to a completely constructive specification. This approach provides also a means for coping with the consistency problem of composed i-specifications: In general a composed i-specification may have no models although its component i-specifications have models. This cannot happen if the intermediate specification is refined to a model that lies in both classes of i-models. The arising verification tasks for i-specifications and their refinements are translated to verification tasks over ordinary specifications and their refinements (c.f. Section 3.6) and are passed over to automatic theorem proving systems connected to the ISDV system.

Beside consistency, the SW-property of i-specifications is another model theoretically defined notion: According to the approach of Sannella and Wirsing in [SW 82] we call an i-specification ISP = <IΣ, IE> with IΣ = <SPa, σ, SPc> an SW-implementation if IE is empty and if for every SPc-model Ac there exists an IΣ-i-model <Ac, α, Aa>. This definition shows that in the approach of [SW 82] syntax and semantics of implementations are not clearly distinguished. Based on the work of [SW 82], Urbassek [Urb 85] has developed syntactic criteria for i-specifications in ASPIK that guarantee the SW-property. While these criteria can also be used to guarantee the consistency of composed i-specifications, less restrictive syntactic criteria should be developed that relax the SW-property so that not every concrete model must implement an abstract one.

8. Conclusions

Our implementation concept for loose abstract data type specifications completely distinguishes between the syntactical level of specifications and the semantical level of models by introducing the notions of implementation signatures, - models, and - specifications. It provides the notion of implementation refinement which is not present in other approaches. Concepts like those of [GM 82] and [Sch 82] are based on behavioural abstraction and have been proposed for modules, and [Hup 80] considers implementations between canon specifications. The implementation concept for the kernel language ASL of [SW 83] merely requires that the abstract specification is included in the concrete one. This simple notion is based on the fact that, as a semantical language, ASL has very powerful specification building operations which however may not be present in a language for ADT specifications.

In e.g. [GM 82], [SW 82], [SW 83] and in the initial approach of [EKMP 82] implementation composition is defined and is explicitly shown to be associative. Whereas in the former composition is a totally defined operation this is true in [EKMP 82] for so-called weak implementations and for a particular class of strong implementations. Of the cited approaches only [EKMP 82] distinguishes completely between syntactical and semantical levels which is a prerequisite for studying the compatability problem of a composition operation. However, this problem is not addressed explicitly since every specification denotes a unique algebra and no explicit definition of a semantical composition operation is given.

Whereas the composition discussed in this paper is usually called vertical there is also a horizontal composition arising in the context of parameterized specifications (see e.g. [EK 82], [GM 82], [SW 82]). For the implementation concept proposed here we show in [BV 85b] that horizontal composition and instantiation of parameterized implementations are compatible with vertical composition, allowing to combine implementation specifications interchangeably in different directions with the same result.

References

[BBTW 81] Bergstra, J.A., Broy, M., Tucker, J.V., Wirsing, M.: On the power of algebraic specifications. Proc. 10th MFCS, LNCS Vol. 118, pp. 193-204, 1981.

[BG 80] Burstall, R.M., Goguen, J.A.: The semantics of Clear, a specification language. Proc. of Advanced Course on Abstract Software Specifications, LNCS Vol.86, pp. 292-332.

[BOV 86] Beierle,C., Olthoff, W., Voß, A.: Towards a formalization of the software development process. Proc. Software Engineering '86, Southampton, 1986.

[BV 85a] Beierle, C., Voß, A.: Implementation specifications. In: H.-J. Kreowski (ed): Recent Trends in Data Type specifications. Informatik Fachberichte 116, Springer, 1985.

[BV 85b] Beierle, C., Voß, A.: Algebraic specifications and implementations in an integrated software development and verfication system. Memo SEKI-85-12, FB Informatik, Univ. Kaiserslautern (joint SEKI-Memo containing the Ph.D. thesis by Ch. Beierle and the Ph.D. thesis by A. Voß), Dec. 1985.

[Ehc 82] Ehrich, H.-D.: On the theory of specification, Implementation and Parametrization of Abstract Data Types. JACM Vol. 29, No. 1, Jan. 1982, pp. 206-227.

[Ehg 81] Ehrig, H.: Algebraic Theory of Parameterized Specifications with Requirements. Proc. 6th Colloquium on Trees in Algebra and Programming (E. Astesiano, C. Böhm, eds.), LNCS 112, pp. 1-24, 1981.

[EKMP 82] Ehrig, H., Kreowski, H.-J., Mahr, B., Padawitz, P.: Algebraic Implementation of Abstract Data Types. Theor. Computer Science Vol. 20, 1982, pp. 209-254.

[EWT 82] Ehrig, H., Wagner, E., Thatcher, J.: Algebraic Constraints for specifications and canonical form results. Draft version, TU Berlin, June 1982.

[Ga 83] Ganzinger, H.: Parameterized Specifications: Parameter Passing and Implementation with respect to Observability. ACM TOPLAS Vol. 5, No.3, July 1983, pp. 318-354.

[GB 83] Goguen, J.A., Burstall, R.M.: Institutions: Abstract Model Theory for Program Specification. SRI International and University of Edinburgh, 1983, revised 1985.

[GM 82] Goguen, J.A., Meseguer, J.: Universal Realization, Persistent Interconnection and Implementation of Abstract Modules. Proc. 9th ICALP, LNCS 140, 1982, pp. 265-281.

[GTW 78] Goguen, J.A., Thatcher, J.W., Wagner, E.G.: An initial algebra approach to the specification, correctness, and implementation of abstract data types, in: Current Trends in Programming Methodology, Vol.4, Data Structuring (ed. R. Yeh), Prentice-Hall, 1978, pp. 80-144.

[Hup 80] Hupbach, U.L.: Abstract implementation of abstract data types. Proc. 9th MFLS, Rydzyna, Poland. LNCS, Vol. 88, pp. 291-304, 1980.

[HKR 80] Hupbach, U.L., Kaphengst, H., Reichel, H.: Initial algebraic specifications of data types, parameterized data types, and algorithms. VEB Robotron, Zentrum für Forschung und Technik, Dresden, 1980.

[Li 83] Lipeck, U.: Ein algebraischer Kalkül für einen strukturierten Entwurf von Datenabstraktionen. Dissertation. Bericht Nr. 148, Universität Dortmund, 1983.

[Sch 82] Schoett, O.: A theory of program modules, their specification and implementation. Draft report, Univ. of Edinburgh, 1982.

[SW 82] Sannella, D.T., Wirsing, M.: Implementation of parameterized specifications, Proc. 9th ICALP 1982, LNCS Vol. 140, pp 473 - 488.

[SW 83] Sannella, D., Wirsing, M.: A kernel language for algebraic specification and implementation. Proc. FCT, LNCS Vol. 158, 1983.

[TWW 82] Thatcher, J.W., Wagner, E.G., Wright, J.B.: Data Type Specification: Parameterization and the Power of Specification Techniques. ACM TOPLAS Vol. 4, No. 4, Oct. 1982, pp. 711-732.

[Urb 85] Urbassek, C.: Ein Implementierungskonzept für ASPIK-Spezifikationen und Korrektheitskriterien. Diploma thesis, Univ. Kaiserslautern, 1985.

Are Homomorphisms Sufficient for Behavioural Implementations of Deterministic and Nondeterministic Data Types?

Tobias Nipkow
Department of Computer Science
The University of Manchester

1 Introduction

The literature on abstract data types offers a wide variety of notions of implementation, many of them based on various kinds of homomorphism. This paper studies the model theoretic justification for using homomorphisms as implementation criteria for a number of distinct notions of behavioural correctness.

Our approach is strictly *semantic*, i.e. *specifications* and *implementations* are just regarded as algebras. This is appropriate for specification techniques which determine single representatives, like initial or final models, or *abstract model specifications* (also called "specification by example") as in VDM [J 80] or Alphard [WLS 76]. Most of the correctness criteria for implementations are based on the approach of [H 72] who uses homomorphisms from the implementing algebra back to the specification.

The implementation concept we study is that of *behavioural correctness* as in [GGM 76], [R 85], and [S 85]. The latter paper gives a complete model-theoretic characterization of behavioural implementations using relational generalizations of homomorphisms. This seems at odds with the more restrictive approaches based on functions. Indeed, it is easy to construct examples where an implementation can only be related back to the specification via a relation. Proponents of the homomorphism school will usually argue that this is due to a lack of abstraction in the specification. In [J 80] this is called "implementation bias". The real question is therefore: Given a specification A, is there always an equivalent specification A' (i.e. A and A' have the same set of implementations) such that from any implementation there is a *function* back to A'? In that case we call A' *fully abstract*. The main objective of this paper is to determine whether particular implementation concepts admit fully abstract models.

This is not purely of theoretical but also of practical interest because functions are usually easier to handle than relations. This is particularly true for verification support systems which often cannot deal gracefully with relations, e.g. systems based on term rewriting techniques.

The paper is devided into two parts. Section 2 studies model classes of partial algebras, section 3 deals with multi-algebras, the nondeterministic generalization of algebras. Due to partiality and nondeterminism there are a number of different implementation notions which are studied separately.

Some of the results on partial algebras are strongly reminiscent of results in [BW 82] and [BPW 84]. The difference is that they consider classes of algebras which satisfy sets of sentences whereas we use a single "reference" model. Still we are greatly indebted to the concepts and techniques developed in those papers. The classification of correctness notions is taken from [B 85]. The work on nondeterministic data types is based on [N 86] and [N 87] which contain a more comprehensive treatment.

2 Deterministic Data Types

Most of the following terminology is very basic and can be found in e.g. [BW 82]. Signatures are triples $\Sigma = (S,V,F)$ such that S is a set of *sorts*, $V \subseteq S$ a subset of *visible* sorts, and F a set of function symbols with associated arity of type $S^* \times S$, depicted as $f\colon w \longrightarrow s$. $T(\Sigma)$ is the term algebra over a signature Σ. A partial Σ-algebra A is an S-sorted set of carriers A_s, $s \in S$, plus a partial function f^A from A_w to A_s for every operation $f\colon w \longrightarrow s$ in F. Notice that the carrier of an algebra A is called A (in *italics*!). In the sequel all algebras are potentially partial. For some Σ-algebra A and some term $t \in T(\Sigma)$ the evaluation of t in A is denoted by t^A. We use two kinds of equalities: the existential equality $t =_e t'$ which asserts that t and t' are both defined and equal, and the strong equality $t = t'$ which asserts that t and t' are either both undefined or both defined and equal. The equation $t =_e t$ which just asserts the definedness of t is abbreviated to $D(t)$.

The following names are chosen to correspond to the notions *partial*, *robust*, and *total correctness* as outlined in [B 85]. To soften the confusion, correspondence with existing terminology is provided.

<u>2.1 Definition</u> Let C,A be two algebras. A relation $\sqsubseteq\, \subseteq C \times A$ such that $\sqsubseteq_V$ is 1 to 1 is called a

partial simulation iff for $f\colon w \longrightarrow s$, and $c \sqsubseteq_w a$: $D(f^C(c)) \Rightarrow (D(f^A(a)) \wedge f^C(c) \sqsubseteq_s f^A(a))$,
robust simulation iff $\sqsubseteq^{-1}$ is a partial simulation, and
bisimulation iff it is both a partial and a robust simulation.

In [S 85] partial simulations are called *semicorrespondences*, bisimulations are called *correspondences*. We often use the symmetry of partial and robust simulations to consider only one case.

<u>2.2 Fact</u> If there are partial simulations C $\sqsubseteq_1$ A and A $\sqsubseteq_2$ C then the relation $\sqsubseteq_1 \cap \sqsubseteq_2^{-1}$ is a bisimulation.

Homomorphisms can now be defined as special cases of simulations.

<u>2.3 Definition</u> Given two algebras C and A, a (possibly partial) function $h\colon C \longrightarrow A$ is called a

partial homomorphism iff h is a partial simulation and total on C,
robust homomorphism iff h is a robust simulation,
total homomorphism iff h is a partial and a robust homomorphism.

In [BW 82] we have *weak*, *total*, and *strong* instead of robust, partial and total respectively. In [Bu 86] robust homomorphisms are just homomorphisms, and total homomorphisms are called *closed*.

2.4 Definition Let A,B be two Σ-algebras such that $B \subseteq A$. B is called a *partial/total subalgebra* iff the inclusion from B to A is a partial/total homomorphism respectively. By $[\![A]\!]$ we denote the smallest total subalgebra of A. If $A = [\![A]\!]$, A is called *finitely generated* (*f.g.* in the sequel).

2.5 Fact If h: A ⟶ $[\![B]\!]$ is a partial/total homomorphism, then h: A ⟶ B is a partial/total homomorphism too.

As in [BPW 84] the main tool for the study of algebras are congruences on the term algebra. Whereas in [BPW 84] partial algebras are reduced to total algebras, we use partial term algebras. Although we are not just interested in f.g. algebras it is possible to study them in isolation and generalize the results to arbitrary algebras in a subsequent step.

2.6 Definition A congruence on an algebra A is an equivalence on A which is also a bisimulation between A and A. The restriction of a congruence ~ to its visible part $\sim_V$ is often denoted by ≃. Corresponding to every congruence ~ a quotient A/~ is defined in the ususal way.

Every Σ-algebra A induces a congruence $\sim_A$ on a partial subalgebra of T(Σ):

$$s \sim_A t \Leftrightarrow s^A =_e t^A$$

Obviously $T(\Sigma) \cap dom(\sim_A)$ is a partial subalgebra of T(Σ) and $\sim_A$ is a congruence on it. Thus there is an exact correspondence between the isomorphism classes of f.g. Σ-algebras and the congruences on the partial subalgebras of T(Σ). In the sequel the study of the former is replaced by that of the latter which we call *subcongruences* of T(Σ). (N.B.: subcongruences on T(Σ) are not restricted to be 1 to 1 on $T(\Sigma)_V$)

2.7 Definition Let A and C be two Σ-algebras. C is called *behaviourally weaker* than A iff

$\forall s,t \in T(\Sigma)_V$: $s^C =_e t^C \Rightarrow s^A =_e t^A$ and

$\forall t \in T(\Sigma)$: $D(t^C) \Rightarrow D(t^A)$

In this case we write C ⋖ A and we also call C a *partial implementation* of A and A a *robust implementation* of C. If both C ⋖ A and C ⋗ A hold, C is called *behaviourally equivalent* to A and we write C ≡ A. Notice that the partial subalgebra relationship is a special case of ⋖.

The relations ⋖ and ≡ apply to algebras just as well as to the induced congruences. Denoting the restriction of some relation ~ to some set S, i.e. $\sim \cap S^2$, by $\sim|S$ we get:

$$\sim_C \lessdot \sim_A \Leftrightarrow C \lessdot A \Leftrightarrow (\simeq_C = \simeq_A|dom(\simeq_C) \wedge dom(\sim_C) \subseteq dom(\sim_A))$$
$$\sim_C \equiv \sim_A \Leftrightarrow C \equiv A \Leftrightarrow (\simeq_C = \simeq_A \wedge dom(\sim_C) = dom(\sim_A))$$

Corresponding to these notions there are three classes of implementations of a given algebra A:

$Eq(A) \triangleq \{ C \mid A \equiv C \}$

$PImpl(A) \triangleq \{ C \mid C \lessdot A \}$

$RImpl(A) \triangleq \{ C \mid A \lessdot C \}$

In the sequel we study the lattice theoretic properties of these three classes and their consequences for implementation correctness proofs by model theoretic means. Building on the work of [S 85] there are simple characterizations of these three classes which are based on simulations.

2.8 Theorem For two Σ-algebras C and A, $C \lessdot A$ holds iff there is a partial simulation between C and A. From fact 2.2 it follows that $C \equiv A$ holds iff there is a bisimulation between C and A.

Thus simulations constitute a sound and complete proof technique for implementation correctness. In the sequel we investigate under which conditions it is possible to substitute simulations by weaker techniques, in particular homomorphisms.

2.1 Behavioural Equivalence

The structure of $Eq(A)$ (for some fixed A) can be studied via properties of congruences.

2.1.1 Lemma The set of all congruences on a Σ-algebra is a complete lattice ordered by $\subseteq$. Infimum is intersection and supremum equivalence-theoretic supremum.

2.1.2 Lemma Let A be some algebra, $B \subseteq A$, and let $\sim$ be an equivalence on B. Then the set of all congruences $\cong$ on A with $\cong|B = \sim$ forms a complete sublattice of all congruences on A.

Now define the containment ordering for behaviourally equivalent congruences:

$$\sim_1 \sqsubseteq \sim_2 \;\triangleq\; \sim_1 \equiv \sim_2 \wedge \sim_1 \subseteq \sim_2$$

From lemmas 2.1.1 and 2.1.2 we get the following corollary:

2.1.3 Corollary The set of congruences $\sim$ with $\sim \equiv \sim_A$ forms a complete lattice with ordering $\sqsubseteq$. The least element is $id(T(\Sigma)) \cup \cong_A$.

To connect the lattice of congruences back to algebras and homomorphisms, observe the following fact:

2.1.4 Fact For any two algebras A and B there is a total homomorphism from $[\![A]\!]$ to B iff

$\sim_A \subseteq \sim_B$ holds.

Therefore any algebra A induces a category of all f.g. algebras B ϵ *Eq*(A) and all total homomorphisms between them. Each category has an initial and final element denoted by I_A and Z_A. Because of fact 2.5, I_A is even initial in the complete category *Eq*(A). In general I_A and Z_A are identified with the respective quotients of T(Σ). In the terminology of [BW 82], I_A and Z_A are strongly initial and strongly terminal.

Therefore we know that for any algebra A there is a most concrete version I_A such that A ≡ B holds iff there is a total homomorphism from I_A to B. Although I_A could thus serve as a "universal model", this is not appropriate for practical purposes. Even for finite algebras A, I_A is in general infinite.

In contrast the terminal models are the smallest and have the following alternative characterization:

<u>2.1.5 Lemma</u> The largest element in the lattice of subcongruences ~ with $\sim \equiv \sim_A$ is

$$\sim_{max} = \{ (s,t) \mid D(s^A) \wedge \forall C \in T(\Sigma \cup \{x\})_V: C[s/x]^A = C[t/x]^A \}.$$

Thus the terminal models are exactly the fully abstract ones in the sense of [M 77].

Now we have a constructive definition of Z_A and we know that for any f.g. B, B ≡ A holds iff there is a total homomorphism from B to Z_A. This is a justification for notions of implementations based on homomorphisms from the concrete to the abstract space, e.g. as introduced in [H 72], although Hoare does not use total homomorphisms in our sense.

What about algebras with unreachable elements? One alternative is to allow for a separate "restrict" step in an equivalence proof. This is used e.g. in [EK 82]. In [J 80] this is covered by the concept of a "data type invariant". Alternatively the restriction and homomorphism can be merged, calling for a generalization such that there is a generalized total homomoprphisms from A to B iff there is a total homomorphism from ⟦A⟧ to B. It turns out that if we do not require total homomorphisms to be total functions, i.e. define them to be functional bisimulations, they have exactly that property:

<u>2.1.6 Fact</u> There is a functional bisimulation from A to B iff there is a total homomorphism from ⟦A⟧ to B.

This means that functional bisimulations with target Z_A exactly characterize all elements in *Eq*(A). Hence we know that this particular breed of homomorphisms can be used as a universal correctness criterion for behavioural equivalence if we guarantee that our reference model is fully abstract.

It should be noted that some of the results are already contained in section 8 and 9 of [BW 82]. The main difference is that they talk about algebras satisfying a set of sentences. Even if the existence of initial and terminal models is guaranteed, it is only in the class of all models. In particular not every homomorphic image of the initial model has to be a model too. Because we are interested in using homomorphisms as necessary and sufficient conditions for implementation, their results are only partially applicable.

2.2 Robust Implementations

Often behavioural equivalence is too strong because undefinedness in the specification is a shorthand for saying that any behaviour in the implementation is acceptable. This is the concept of robust correctness which is used e.g. in [H 72] or [J 80]. Because the partial subalgebra relationship is a special case of $\blacktriangleleft$, we have the following characterization of $\blacktriangleleft$:

<u>2.2.1 Lemma</u> A $\blacktriangleleft$ B holds iff I_A is a partial subalgebra of I_B.

For a given algebra A the set of all algebras B such that A is a partial subalgebra of B is a complete lower semilattice ordered by $\subseteq$ (less defined) with least element A. Therefore *RImpl*(A) forms a complete lower semilattice of classes of behaviourally equivalent algebras with *Eq*(A) as the least (defined) element. The corresponding relation between congruences is

$$\sim_1 \prec \sim_2 \;\triangleq\; \sim_1 \blacktriangleleft \sim_2 \wedge \sim_1 \subseteq \sim_2$$

<u>2.2.2 Fact</u> For any two algebras A and B there is a partial homomorphism from $[\![A]\!]$ to B iff $\sim_A \prec \sim_B$ holds.

<u>2.2.3 Lemma</u> The set of all congruences $\sim$ with $\sim_A \blacktriangleleft \sim$ forms a complete lower semilattice under the ordering $\prec$. Least element is $\sim_{IA}$, infimum is intersection.

Hence the category of all f.g. algebras B $\in$ *RImpl*(A) with partial homomorphisms between them has I_A as the initial object. From facts 2.5 and 2.2.2 it follows that B $\in$ *RImpl*(A) holds iff there is a homomorphism from I_A to B. Hence any robust implementation of an algebra A can be shown correct via a homomorphism from I_A.

Again this is not totally satisfactory because initial models are in general intractable. To get the corresponding result for terminal models, robust homomorphisms are necessary. The corresponding ordering on congruences is

$$\sim_1 \sqsubset \sim_2 \;\triangleq\; \sim_1 \blacktriangleright \sim_2 \wedge \sim_1 |dom(\sim_2) \subseteq \sim_2$$

<u>2.2.4 Fact</u> For any two algebras A and B there is a robust homomorphism from A to B iff $\sim_A \sqsubset \sim_B$.

This ordering induces the following structure on *RIimpl*(A):

<u>2.2.5 Lemma</u> The set of all subcongruences $\sim$ on T(Σ) with $\sim_A \blacktriangleleft \sim$ forms a complete upper semilattice under the ordering $\sqsubset$. The largest element is $\sim_{ZA}$, the supremum of a set of congruences *M* is the equivalence theoretic supremum of the restriction of all congruences in *M* to their common domain.

Hence we know that Z_A is the fully abstract model for all robust implementations of A and every robust implementation can be related back to Z_A via a robust homomorphism. If one analyzes the proof rules for implementations in [H 72] and [J 80] it turns out that they both use robust homomorphisms from the implementation back to the specification. Our results can be seen as a belated justification of the soundness and completeness of that method - if it were not for the fact that both authors allow nondeterministic data types. In that case the existence of fully abstract models cannot be guaranteed anymore as we shall see in section 3.

2.3 Partial Implementations

We are not concerned with a justification of the usefulness of particular implementation concepts. In the case of partial implementations such a rational can be found in [KA 84]. Suffice it to say that partial implementations are useful in contexts where the full capability of the specification is not required. In fact most implementations are partial because they run on a finite machine although the specification may require infinite carriers.

Although robust and partial implementations are complementary, the structures they induce are not fully symmetric. By lemma 2.2.1 we know that *PImpl*(A) is a complete lattice of classes of behaviourally equivalent algebras ordered by the partial subalgebra relationship between their initial elements. The greatest class is *Eq*(A), the least *Eq*(O) where O is the totally undefined algebra.

2.3.1 Lemma The set of all subcongruences $\sim$ on $T(\Sigma)$ with $\sim \lessdot \sim_A$ forms a complete lattice under the ordering $\sqsubset$. The least element is $\sim_{IA}$, the largest one is $\{\}$.

As usual this implies that *PImpl*(A) with partial homomorphisms is has an initial and a terminal element I_A and O respectively. Hence some B is a partial implementation of A iff there is a partial homomorphism from I_A to B. However the terminal element O does not enjoy the same property. Although O is the partial homomorphic image of every B ϵ *PImpl*(A), the reverse is not true. In fact, from every algebra C there is a partial homomorphism to O. Obviously O is not a sound reference model for partial implementations.

If we turn to the ordering $\lessdot$, we find the following situation:

2.3.2 Lemma The set of all subcongruences $\sim$ on $T(\Sigma)$ with $\sim \lessdot \sim_A$ forms a complete lower semilattice under the ordering $\lessdot$. The least element is $\{\}$. Infimum is intersection.

Now O is the initial object in *PImpl*(A) with partial homomorphisms. But again every Σ-algebra C is the partial homomorphic image of the empty Σ-algebra O. Hence lemma 2.3.2 does not help in our quest for suitable homomorphisms. Yet [KA 84] use partial homomorphisms as the basis for their implementation definition. This is certainly valid because $\lessdot$ implies $\lessdot$. But it is too strong in general. Not only does $\lessdot$ not always imply $\lessdot$. For most algebras A there is no equivalent fully abstract model. In other words: *PImpl*(A) does not always have a final element w.r.t. partial homomorphisms. Therefore lemma 2.3.2 cannot be strengthened. The reason is very simple: partial implementations can be less defined and can therefore collapse elements which are distinguishable in the specification. Take the following example:

2.3.3 Example Let $\Sigma = (\{H,I\}, \{I\}, \{\ 0,1: \longrightarrow I,\ c_0,c_1: \longrightarrow H,\ f: H \longrightarrow I\ \})$ and let A such that $\sim_A = id(T(\Sigma))$ which corresponds to the initial model. The subcongruence $\sim$ is given by $\{\ (0,0), (1,1), (c_0,c_0), (c_0,c_1), (c_1,c_1), (c_1,c_0)\ \}$. This means that c_0 and c_1 are collapsed and f is undefined on both of them. There is no congruence $\sim_B$ such that $\sim\ \lessdot \sim_B \equiv \sim_A$ holds because $\sim_B \equiv \sim_A$ requires $f(c_0)$ and $f(c_1)$ to be distinct whereas $\sim\ \lessdot \sim_B$ forces them to collapse.

The moral of this example is that although partial homomorphisms are certainly a sufficient condition for partial implementations, they can be too strict. Hence in general partial simulations are necessary.

3 Nondeterministic Data Types

The work in this section is based on the approach in [N 86] and [N 87]. For our current purposes it is sufficient to model nondeterministic data types by multi-algebras as e.g. in [Ha 80]. This means that nondeterministic functions are modelled by relations which can also be interpreted as set-valued functions. The interpretation of a function $f\colon w \longrightarrow s$ in a multi-algebra A can be any arbitrary subset of $A_w \times A_s$.

The principle problem with this approach is that the "behaviour" of a multi-algebra can not be captured in the behaviour of the term algebra. In [N 86] there is a series of examples which show that two multi-algebras may have the same behaviour w.r.t. to term evaluation in the term algebra but can be distinguished if the operations are combined with programming language constructs like assignment. Hence it is not possible to give a definition of behavioural equivalence based on term evaluation like in definition 2.7. Likewise it is not possible to study multi-algebras via congruences on the term algebra. Instead we use a purely algebraic definition of implementation based on the generalization of the simulation concepts. A justification of this approach in terms of the induced behaviour of programs over the nondeterministic types is the subject of [N 86] and [N 87]. In the worst case this can be taken as a study of various algebraic relationships which may or may not be relevant for implementations between data types.

The main thrust of this section will be to show that for most of the correctness notions fully abstract models do in general not exist, i.e. that correctness proofs need to be based on relations rather than functions.

We start with the definition of a number of variations of simulations for multi-algebras. It is obvious that they generalize the corresponding definitions on algebras. In the sequel not all the concepts will be defined fully formally but can easily be deduced from their deterministic counterparts.

3.1 Definition A relation $\sqsubseteq\, \subseteq C \times A$ between two multi-algebras C and A such that $\sqsubseteq_V$ is 1 to 1 is called a

partial simulation iff for all $f\colon w \longrightarrow s$ and all $c \sqsubseteq_w a$: $c' \in f^C(c) \Rightarrow \exists a' \in f^A(a)\colon c' \sqsubseteq_s a'$

robust simulation iff for all $f\colon w \longrightarrow s$ and all $c \sqsubseteq_w a$ with $f^A(a) \neq \{\}$:

$f^C(c) \neq \{\} \wedge (c' \in f^C(c) \Rightarrow \exists a' \in f^A(a)\colon c' \sqsubseteq_s a')$

simulation iff it is both partial and robust, and

bisimulation iff both $\sqsubseteq$ and $\sqsubseteq^{-1}$ are simulations.

3.1 Bisimulation Equivalence

The strongest correctness notion is that of bisimulation equivalence which is used in the CCS literature. The following simple algebraic results all have their equivalent in [C 85] where bisimulations and homomorphisms are discussed in the context of concurrent systems.

Let *total homomorphisms* be the restriction of bisimulations to total functions. Similarly let *congruences* be equivalences which are also bisimulations between the same multi-algebra. Congruences induce quotients in the obvious way.

3.1.1 Lemma Every bisimulation $\sim$ between two multi-algebras A and B induces two congruences $\sim_A \triangleq (\sim;\sim^{-1})^*$ and $\sim_B \triangleq (\sim^{-1};\sim)^*$ such that $[\![A]\!]/\sim_A$ and $[\![B]\!]/\sim_B$ are isomorphic. (Note: ";" is relational composition and "*" the transitive and reflexive closure).

3.1.2 Lemma The set of all congruences on a multi-algebra is a complete lattice ordered by $\subseteq$. Infimum is intersection and supremum equivalence-theoretic supremum.

3.1.3 Lemma Let A be some algebra, $B \subseteq A$, and let $\sim$ be an equivalence on B. Then the set of all congruences $\cong$ on A with $\cong|B = \sim$ forms a complete sublattice of all congruences on A.

3.1.4 Corollary On any multi-algebra A there exists a largest congruence $\sim$ such that $\simeq$ is the identity on A_V.

3.1.5 Corollary There is a bisimulation between two multi-algebras A and B iff there is a total homomorphism from $[\![B]\!]$ to $[\![A]\!]/\sim$, where $\sim$ is defined as in corollary 3.1.4.

Hence we know that bisimulation equivalence can be replaced by total homomorphism, provided our reference model is fully abstract. The problem with non-f.g. multi-algebras is solved in the usual way by making total homomorphisms partial as in section 2.1.

3.2 Behavioural Equivalence

Although bisimulations enjoy very pleasant properties, they are too strong a criterion for behavioural equivalence. In [N 86] it is shown that simulations between multi-algebras imply the *loose implementation* relationship between programs using them. Loose implementation means simply subset of outputs. Hence it follows that the existence of a simulation in each direction implies *total correctness*, i.e. equivalence of outputs. In contrast to fact 2.2 there are multi-algebras A and B and simulations between A and B in either direction, yet there is no bisimulation between them.

3.2.1 Example Let $\Sigma = (\{H,V\}, \{V\}, \{\, c: \longrightarrow H,\ f: H \longrightarrow H,\ g: H \longrightarrow V\,\})$.

A: $A_H = \{a_0, a_1\}$, $A_V = \{0,1\}$

$c^A = \{\, a_0 \,\}$, $f^A = \{\, (a_0,a_0), (a_0,a_1), (a_1,a_1) \,\}$, $g^A = \{\, (a_0,0), (a_1,1) \,\}$

C: $C_H = \{c_0, b, c_1\}$, $A_V = \{0,1\}$

$c^C = \{\, c_0, b \,\}$, $f^C = \{\, (c_0,c_0), (c_0,c_1), (c_1,c_1), (b,c_1) \,\}$, $g^C = \{\, (c_0,0), (c_1,1), (b,0) \,\}$

There are the two simulations $\sqsubseteq_1 = \{\, (c_0,a_0), (c_1,a_1), (b,a_0) \,\}$ and $\sqsubseteq_2 = \{\, (a_0,c_0), (a_1,c_1) \,\}$. But there is no bisimulation $\sim$ because operation c forces $b \sim a_1$ which in turn would force $c_1 \sim a_0$ and hence $0 \sim 1$ which cannot be because bisimulation must be 1 to 1 on V.

It is not difficult to show that the only total homomorphisms starting from C or A are in fact isomorphisms. But because C and A are not isomorphic, there is no common homomorphic image of C and A. This tells us two things. From lemma 3.1.1 we conclude that there is no bisimulation between C and A. Hence bisimulation equivalence is truely stronger than behavioural equivalence. In addition we know that behavioural equivalence does not admit final models w.r.t. to total homomorphisms. Hence simulations are in general necessary to show behavioural equivalence.

3.3 Loose, Robust and Partial Implementations

The results for the above three categories are equally negative when it comes to the existence of fully abstract specifications. For partial implementations this is already true for the deterministic case (see section 2.3). For loose and robust implementations this can be shown simultaneously because, for total multi-algebras, the two concepts coincide. We simply give an example of a multi-algebra which does not have a fully abstract equivalent.

3.3.1 Example

$\Sigma = (\{H1,H2,V\}, \{V\}, \{a: \longrightarrow H1,\ b: \longrightarrow H2,\ i1: H1 \longrightarrow H1,\ i2: H2 \longrightarrow H2,\ f: H1 \times H2 \longrightarrow V\})$

A: $A_{H1} = \{a_1,a_2\},\ A_{H2} = \{b_1,b_2\},\ A_V = \{0,1,2,3\}$

$a^A = \{a_1, a_2\}\quad b^A = \{b_1, b_2\}$

$i1^A = \{(a_1,a_2),(a_2,a_1)\}\quad i2^A = \{(b_1,b_2),(b_2,b_1)\}$

$f^A = \{((a_1,b_1),0),\ ((a_1,b_1),1),\ ((a_1,b_2),1),\ ((a_1,b_2),2),$
$((a_2,b_2),2),\ ((a_2,b_2),3),\ ((a_2,b_1),3),\ ((a_2,b_1),0)\}$

This specification has the property that one can either collapse *H1* or *H2* but not both of them.

The implementations C and D collapse *H1* and *H2* respectively.

C: $C_{H1} = \{c\},\ C_{H2} = \{c_1,c_2\},\ C_V = A_V$

$a^C = \{c\}\quad b^C = \{c_1, c_2\}$

$i1^C = \{(c,c)\}\quad i2^C = \{(c_1,c_2),(c_2,c_1)\}$

$f^C = \{((c,c_1),0),((c,c_2),2)\}$

C simulates A via $\sqsubseteq_C\ \triangleq \{(c,a_1),(c,a_2),(c_1,b_1),(c_2,b_2)\} \cup id(A_V)$.

D: $D_{H1} = \{d_1,d_2\},\ D_{H2} = \{d\},\ D_V = A_V$

$a^D = \{d_1, d_2\},\ b^D = \{d\}$

$i1^D = \{(d_1,d_2),(d_2,d_1)\},\ i2^D = \{(d,d)\}$

$f^D = \{((d_1,d),1),((d_2,d),3)\}$

D simulates A via $\sqsubseteq_D\ \triangleq \{(d_1,a_1),(d_2,a_2),(d,b_1),(d,b_2)\} \cup id(A_V)$.

All operations are total.

Now assume there is a to A equivalent multi-algebra P (in particular there must be a simulation P $\sqsubseteq_P$ A) such that C and D simulate P functionally (via g: C $\longrightarrow$ P and h: D $\longrightarrow$ P). First we show that $g(c) \sqsubseteq_P a_i$ for $i=1,2$:

$c \in a^C \Rightarrow g(c) \in a^P \Rightarrow (g(c) \sqsubseteq_P a_1 \vee g(c) \sqsubseteq_P a_2)$

$(c,c) \in i1^C \Rightarrow (g(c),g(c)) \in i1^P \Rightarrow (g(c) \sqsubseteq_P a_1 \Rightarrow g(c) \sqsubseteq_P a_2) \wedge (g(c) \sqsubseteq_P a_2 \Rightarrow g(c) \sqsubseteq_P a_1)$

In exactly the same way (but using *b* and *i2*) one can show that $h(d) \sqsubseteq_P b_1$ and $h(d) \sqsubseteq_P b_2$ hold. Since $g(c) \sqsubseteq_P a_i$, and $h(d) \sqsubseteq_P b_j$, $f^A(a_i,b_j) \neq \{\}$ implies $f^P(g(c),h(d)) \neq \{\}$. Because $\sqsubseteq_P$ must be 1 to 1 on V, $k \in f^{\mathrm{P}}(g(c),h(d))$ implies $k \in f^{\mathrm{A}}(a_i,b_j)$ for all $i,j \in \{1,2\}$. It follows from the definition of f^{A} that no such k exists, which is a contradiction. Therefore the required P does not exist.

The moral of this example is: in a nondeterministic context "relations are strictly more general than functions". The consequence for [H 72] and [J 80] is that their proof rules are incomplete when applied in a nondeterministic context and that this incompleteness can not be cured by abstracting and subsetting, as in the deterministic case. This is due to the lack of fully abstract specifications.

A word of caution w.r.t. robust implementations in a nondeterministic and nonsequential (c.f. [V 73]) context: the fact that an undefined term in the specification may return an arbitrary result in a robust implementation is justified only if the outcome of a program with an undefined subterm is either independent of that subterm (e.g. because it is guarded) or may be undefined too. This is not the case anymore with program constructs like angelic choice. Let ∇ be a nondeterministic choice construct such that $s \nabla t$ is defined iff s or t are defined. Let t be a term that is undefined in A and that may return 1 in some robust implementation C. Then the program $t \nabla 0$ is always defined but under A it only ever returns 0, whereas under C it can return both 1 and 0. Obviously robust correctness can lead to invalid implementations in a nonsequential environment.

4 Conclusion

For deterministic data types it has been shown that total and robust correctness admit fully abstract models and partial correctness does not. For nondeterministic data types only bisimulation equivalence gives rise to fully abstract models, total, loose, robust, and partial correctness do not. In the cases where fully abstract models do not exist, it is in general necessary to use simulations instead of homomorphisms for proof of correctness of data type implementations.

5 References

[B 85] M. Broy: *Extensional Behaviour of Concurrent, Nondeterministic Communicating Systems*, in: *Control Flow and Data Flow: Concepts of Distributed Programming* (M. Broy, ed.), Springer Verlag, 1985

[BW 82] M. Broy, M. Wirsing: *Partial Abstract Types*, Acta Informatica 18, 1, 1982

[BPW 84] M. Broy, J.C. Pair, M. Wirsing: *A Systematic Study of Models of Abstract Data Types*, Theoretical Computer Science, 1984

[Bu 86] P. Burmeister: *A Model Theoretic Oriented Approach to Partial Algebras*, Akademie-Verlag Berlin, 1986

[C 85] I. Castellani: *Bisimulations and Abstraction Homomorphisms*, in: Proc. CAAP'85, LNCS 185, 1985

[EK 82] H. Ehrig, H.-J. Kreowski: *Parameter Passing Commutes with Implementation of Parametrized Data Types*, in Proc. ICALP'82, LNCS 140, 1982

[GGM 76] V. Giarratana, F. Gimona, U. Montanari: *Observability Concepts in Abstract Data Types*, in: Proc. MFCS'76, LNCS 45, 1976

[Ha 80] G. Hansoul: *Systemes Relationelles Et Algebres Multiformes*, Ph.D. Thesis, Universite de Liege, 1980

[H 72] C.A.R. Hoare: *Proof of Correctness of Data Representation*, Acta Informatica 1, 1972

[J 80] C.B. Jones: *Software Development: A Rigorous Approach*, Prentice/Hall International, 1980

[KA 84] S. Kamin, M. Archer: *Partial Implementations of Abstract Data Types: A Dissenting View on Errors*, in: *Semantics of Data Types*, LNCS 173, 1984

[M 77] R. Milner: *Fully Abstract Models of Typed λ-Calculi*, Theoretical Computer Science 4, 1977

[N 86] T. Nipkow: *Nondeterministic Data Types: Models and Implementations*, Acta Informatica 22, 1986

[N 87] T. Nipkow: *Behavioural Implementations of Nondeterministic Data Types*, Ph.D. Thesis, University of Manchester, forthcoming

[R 85] H. Reichel: *Initial Restrictions of Behaviour*, in: *The Role of Abstract Models in Information Processing*, (E.J. Neuhold, G. Chroust, eds.), North-Holland, 1985

[S 85] O. Schoett: *Behavioural Correctness of Data Representations*, University of Edinburgh, Dept. of Computer Science, Internal Report CSR-185-85, 1985

[V 73] J. Vuillemin: *Correct and Optimal Implementation of Recursion in a Simple Programming Language*, in: Proc. 5th ACM Symposium on Theory of Computing, 1973

[WLS 76] W.A. Wulf, R.L. London, M. Shaw: *An Introduction to the Construction and Verification of Alphard Programs*, IEEE Trans. on Software Engineering 2, 4, 1976

SOME REMARKS ON PRESENTATIONS BY FINITE CHURCH-ROSSER THUE SYSTEMS

Volker Diekert
Institut für Informatik, Technische Universität München
Arcisstr. 21, D - 8000 München 2

Abstract: An infinite cancellative monoid where the classes of the syntactical congruence of its center form a finite group has no presentation by a finite Church-Rosser Thue System unless the monoid is isomorphic to $\mathbb{Z}$ or $\mathbb{N}$. This generalizes a result of Avenhaus et al. [1] on commutative monoids.

An infinite group with an abelian subgroup of finite index admits a finite Church-Rosser Thue presentation if and only if the group is isomorphic to $\mathbb{Z}$ or isomorphic to the free product $\mathbb{Z}/2\mathbb{Z} * \mathbb{Z}/2\mathbb{Z}$.

A group having a finite Church-Rosser Thue presentation is proved to be context-free.

Introduction: Rewriting techniques form an important tool for several areas in computer science. Of particular interest are finite rewriting systems which are noetherian and confluent, mainly because they allow an effective procedure for solving the word problem. However, in order to get reasonably efficient decision algorithms one has to put further restriction on the rewriting systems. Particular efficient algorithms are possible if all rules are length-decreasing. Thus, one is interested in monoids having a finite Church-Rosser Thue presentation. Here we investigate some of their algebraic properties.

The first aim of this paper is to extend a result of Avenhaus, Book, and Squier [1] to some non-commutative cases: We shall see that an infinite cancellative monoid where the syntactical monoid of its center is a finite group has a finite Church-Rosser Thue presentation if and only if it is the free cyclic group or the free cyclic monoid. We shall give an example how one can use this generalization. If the syntactical monoid of the center is not finite or not a group then the assertion does not hold any more. In fact, free (non-commutative) groups or monoids provide such examples.

In the second part of the paper we investigate groups with abelian subgroups of finite index. If such a group has a finite Church-Rosser presentation, then we prove that any abelian subgroup is finite or isomorphic to $\mathbb{Z}$. Using this, some group theoretical considerations give us the following: An infinite group has an abelian subgroup of finite index and a finite Church-Rosser Thue presentation if and only if the group is isomorphic to $\mathbb{Z}$ or isomorphic to the free product $\mathbb{Z}/2\mathbb{Z} * \mathbb{Z}/2\mathbb{Z}$.

The groups $\mathbb{Z}$ and $\mathbb{Z}/2\mathbb{Z} * \mathbb{Z}/2\mathbb{Z}$ are both context-free. A conjecture of Gilman [3, sect.3] says that free products of free or finite groups are the only context-free groups which have a presentation by finite confluent monadic semi-Thue systems. This conjecture has been proved in [2], [9] for so-called two-monadic systems. Our result implies the conjecture in the further case, where there is an abelian subgroup of finite index.

In the final part of the paper we show that if a group has a finite Church-Rosser Thue presentation then the group is context-free. Since there are context-free groups without such a presentation we have a proper inclusion between these classes of groups.

<u>Notations:</u> Throughout this paper X denotes a finite alphabet and X^* is the free monoid over X. By $|w|$ we mean the length of a word $w \in X^*$. A word $w \in X^*$ is called <u>primitive</u> if w is no proper power of any other word. Any non-empty word $w \in X^+$ has a <u>primitive root</u> $\rho(w)$, it is the unique primitive word such that $w = \rho(w)^t$ for some $t \geq 1$.

Semi-Thue systems are subsets $P \subset X^* \times X^*$, here they always will be finite. We write X^*/P for the quotient monoid and we use bars to denote images in X^*/P. A semi-Thue system P is called length-decreasing (monadic resp.) iff for all $(l,r) \in P$ it holds $|l| > |r|$ ($|l| > 1 \geq |r|$ resp.). By Irr(P) we mean the set of irreducible words, i.e. the complement of Irr(P) is the ideal in X^* generated by the left-hand sides of P. Capital letters M or G denote finitely generated monoids or groups. The center of a monoid M is the set $Z(M) := \{z \in M \mid zx = xz \text{ for all } x \in M\}$. The center defines a congruence on M in the following way: $x \equiv y$ iff there are $a,b \in Z(M)$ such that $xa = yb$ in M. The quotient by this congruence is the collapsing monoid M/Z(M). By Synt(Z(M)) we denote the syntactical monoid of the center. It is uniquely determined by its universal property: For any surjective homomorphisms
$p : M \to M'$ with $p^{-1}p(Z(M)) = Z(M)$ there is a unique homomorphism
$\overline{p} : M' \to \text{Synt}(Z(M))$ such that $\overline{p}p : M \to \text{Synt}(Z(M))$ is the canonical map-mapping.

Recall that Z(M) is recognizable in M if and only if Synt(Z(M)) is finite.
Finally, let $\mathbb{Z}$ and $\mathbb{N}$ denote the integers and non-negative integers respectively.

Part I

Definition: We say that a monoid M has a finite Church-Rosser Thue presentation iff there exists a finite confluent length-decreasing semi-Thue system $P \subset X^* \times X$ such that M and X^*/P are isomorphic.

Theorem 1: Let $P \subset X^* \times X^*$ be a finite confluent length-decreasing semi-Thue system, and let $M = X^*/P$. Assume that for all $x \in M$ there exists a $t \geq 1$ such that x^t is in the center of M. Then we find effectively primitive words $u_1, \ldots, u_m, v_1, \ldots, v_n \in X^*$ for some $m,n \geq 0$

and positive integers t(1), ..., t(n) such that the set of irreducible words Irr(P) is disjoint union:

$$Irr(P) = \{\lambda\} \cup \bigcup_{i=1}^{m} u_i^{+} \cup \bigcup_{j=1}^{n} (v_j^1 + v_j^2 + \dots + v_j^{t(j)}).$$

In addition M/Z(M) is a finite group.

Proof: The set Irr(P) is regular and closed under taking subwords. The assertion clearly holds for Irr(P) finite. For infinite Irr(P) the pumping lemma gives us an $n_0 \geq 1$ such that any $r \in Irr(P)$ with $|r| \geq n_0$ has a factorization $r = uvw$, $n_0 \geq |v| \geq 1$, and $uv^*w \subset Irr(P)$. Some power v^t, $t \geq 1$ becomes central in M, hence the words $v^t uvw$, $uvv^t w$, and $uvwv^t$ have the same image in $M = X^*/P$. By elementary properties of X^*, c.f. [4, sect. 1.3] the words uv and v have the same primitive root $\hat{u} = \rho(uv) = \rho(v^t) = \rho(v)$. Further, if $w \neq 1$ then $\rho(w) = \hat{u}$, too. In any case we conclude $r \in \hat{u}^* \subset Irr(P)$. The result on Irr(P) follows since $n_0 \geq |\hat{u}|$, hence only finitely many words $\hat{u}$ appear.

We also see that M/Z(M) is a finite union of finite cyclic groups, hence M/Z(M) is a finite group. □

We give a non-commutative example for Theorem 1.

Example 1: Let the alphabet X have at least two letters, let 0, a be two new symbols and $r \geq 2$. Define on $Y := X \cup \{0,a\}$ the following confluent monadic system P:

$$w \to 0, \text{ for all } w \in X^*, |w| = r + 1,$$
$$0x, x0 \to 0,$$
$$ax, xa \to a, \text{ for all } x \in X \cup \{0\}.$$

According to Theorem 1 we have:

$$Irr(P) = a^* \cup \{0\} \cup \bigcup_{j=1}^{n} (v_j^1 + v_j^2 + \dots + v_j^{t(j)}),$$

where $\{v_1, \dots, v_n\} = \{\rho(v) \mid v \in X^+, |v| \leq r\}$ and $r - |v_j| < |v_j^{t(j)}| \leq r$. for $j = 1, \dots, n$.

The monoid $M = Y^*/P$ has a recognizable center, given by $\{v \in X^* \mid |v| = r\} \cup a^* \cup \{0\}$. The collapsing monoid $M/Z(M)$ is the trivial group.

If the torsion condition in Theorem 1 is violated then the assertion needs not to hold.

Example 2: Let $Y = X \cup \{0,a\}$ as in Example 1 and let P' be the following confluent subsystem of P:

$$0x,\ x0 \to 0,$$

$$ax,\ xa \to a, \text{ for all } x \in X \cup \{0\}.$$

Again, the center $M' = Y^*/P'$ is recognizable and given by $a^* \cup \{0\}$. Also, $M'/Z(M')$ is the trivial group. However, we have $Irr(P) = a^* \cup \{0\} \cup X^+$. This is not of the form as Theorem 1 predicts.

Remark: Example 2 shows that we cannot replace the torsion condition by simply saying that $M/Z(M)$ has to be a finite group. However, in some cases it is possible:

Lemma 1: Let $\pi : M \to \mathrm{Synt}\ (Z(M))$ denote the canonical homomorphism.
a) If M is cancellative then it holds $\pi^{-1}(1) = Z(M)$
b) If if holds $\pi^{-1}(1) = Z(M)$ and if M has a finite Church-Rosser presentation then the following three assertions are equivalent:
i) For all $x \in M$ there is a $t \geq 1$ such that $x^t \in Z(M)$.
ii) The collapsing monoid $M/Z(M)$ is a finite group.
iii) The center $Z(M)$ is recognizable and $\mathrm{Synt}(Z(M))$ is a group.

Proof: Easy, left to the reader. □

From now on, we consider cancellative monoids only. Obviously, any finite monoid has finite Church-Rosser Thue presentation by its multiplicative table. So, we restrict ourselves to infinite cases. The following is an extension of a Theorem of Avenhaus et al. [1] on commutative monoids.

Theorem 2: Let M be an infinite cancellative monoid such that the syntactical monoid of its center is a finite group. If M has a finite Church-Rosser Thue presentation then M is isomorphic to $\mathbb{Z}$ or $\mathbb{N}$.

Before we prove this theorem, we show that none of the assumptions can be omitted:

1) The cancellativity is necessary by an example of [1]. Another example is provided by Example 1 above.
2) Take any group. Of course, it is cancellative, and the syntactical monoid of any subset is a group, too. There are non-cyclic groups with finite Church-Rosser Thue presentation, e.g. free non-commutative groups.
3) Empty semi-Thue-systems define finite Church-Rosser Thue presentations of free monoids. A free monoid is cancellative and the syntactical monoid of its center is always finite.

Proof of Theorem 2: We may assume that we have $M = X^*/P$ where $P \subset X^* \times X^*$ is a finite confluent length-reducing semi-Thue system. By the results so far we know that

$$\mathrm{Irr}(P) = \bigcup_{i=1}^{m} u_i^* \cup \bigcup_{j=1}^{n} (v_j^1 + v_j^2 + \ldots + v_j^{t(j)})$$

for some primitive words $u_1 \ldots u_m$, $v_1 \ldots v_n$. Note, it holds $m \geq 1$ since M is infinite. We prove that M is the group or monoid generated by $u := \rho(u_1) = u_1$: Let $w \in X^*$ be an arbitrary word. Let $w_0 := w$ and for $i \geq 1$ define $w_i \in \mathrm{Irr}(P)$ by the equation $\overline{uw_{i-1}} = \overline{w}_i$, recall that bars denote images in M. The sequence $(w_n)_{n \geq 1}$ forms an infinite subset of Irr(P). Thus, for some $j > i$, $s(k) > r(k)$, $k \in \{1, \ldots, m\}$ it holds $w_j = u_k^{r(k)}$ and $w_i = u_k^{s(k)}$. We see that

$$\overline{u}_k^{s(k)} = \overline{u}^{(j-i)}\ \overline{w}_i = \overline{u}^{(j-i)}\ \overline{u}_k^{r(k)} \quad \text{and} \quad \overline{u}_k^{s(k)-r(k)} = \overline{u}^{(j-i)}.$$

Now, u_k^* and $u^* = u_1^*$ are irreducible, hence we have $u_k \in \rho(u_1)^* = u_1^*$.

But then we have $\bar{u}^i\ \bar{w} = \bar{u}^t$ for some $t \geq 0$. It follows $\bar{w} = \bar{u}^{(t-i)}$ in M. This proves the Theorem. □

We give an example how one can use Theorem 2.

<u>Example 3:</u> Let $X = \{x,a\}$ and let $M = X^*/P$, where P is the following semi-Thue system:

$$ax \to x^2 a,$$
$$x^3 \to 1 .$$

The system P is noetherian and confluent, hence it is complete. It has one length-increasing rule. If we change the sides of this rule, we obtain a length-decreasing system $P' = \{x^2 a \to ax,\ x^3 \to 1\}$. But this new system is not confluent any more: Consider $x^3 a \overset{*}{\underset{P'}{\Rightarrow}} a$ and $x^3 a \overset{*}{\underset{P'}{\Rightarrow}} xax$. One might hope that one could come to some finite Church-Rosser presentation by some completion procedure. This is not possible. In fact, applying Theorem 2 we can say something more:

<u>Claim:</u> The monoid $M = X^*/P$ with $P = \{ax \to x^2 a,\ x^3 \to 1\}$ has no finite Church-Rosser Thue presentation.

<u>Part II</u>

We now investigate the situation where the cancellative monoid is already a group. For groups Theorem 2 may be read in the following way:

<u>Theorem 2':</u> An infinite group with a center of finite index has a finite Church-Rosser Thue presentation if and only if it is free cyclic.

<u>Example 4:</u> Let $X = \{x,a,b\}$ and let $P \subset X^* \times X^*$ be the following noetherian confluent semi-Thue system:

$$ax \to x^2 a,$$
$$bx \to x^2 b,$$
$$ab,\ ba,\ x^3 \to 1$$

Then $G = X^*/P$ is a central extension of $\mathbb{Z}$ by the symmetric group on three letters. (It is also the group associated to the monoid M in Example 3.) By Theorem 2' the context-free group G has no finite Church-Rosser Thue presentation.

It is a very strong assumption that the center has to be of finite index. We shall weaken this condition. We only ask for a recognizable commutative submonoid, which need not be central. Since the recognizable subsets of a group are the cosets of subgroups of finite index, we therefore ask for an abelian subgroup of finite index.

<u>Theorem 3:</u> Let G be a group which has a finite Church-Rosser Thue presentation. If G has an abelian subgroup of finite index then every abelian subgroup is finite or isomorphic to $\mathbb{Z}$.

<u>Proof:</u> If G is finite there is nothing to prove. So, we assume G to be infinite. We further assume that $G = X^*/P$ and $P \subset X^* \times X^*$ is finite confluent and length-decreasing. Let A be abelian and of finite index in G. Since Irr(P) is an infinite regular set which is closed under taking subwords, we find a word $a \in \mathrm{Irr}(P)$ such that $a^* \in \mathrm{Irr}(P)$ and $\bar{a} \in A$. Let $u = \rho(a)$ be the primitive root of a; we first prove that A lies in the subgroup generated by $\bar{u}$. Let $w \in \mathrm{Irr}(P)$ with $\bar{w} \in A$. Quite similar to the proof of Theorem 2 we set $w_o = w$ and for $i \geq 1$ we define $w_i \in \mathrm{Irr}(P)$ by the equation $\bar{a}\,\bar{w}_{i-1} = \bar{w}_i$ in A.

<u>Claim:</u> For some $n \geq 1$ we have $aw_n = w_n a$ in X^*.

<u>Proof of the Claim:</u> Assume we would have $aw_n \neq w_n a$ for all $n \geq 1$. Since the rules are length-decreasing, it holds $|w_n| \leq |a| - 1 + |w_{n-1}|$ for all $n \geq 1$. Hence, by induction: $|w_n| \leq n(|a| - 1) + |w|$ for all $n \geq 1$. Let $w' \in \mathrm{Irr}(P)$ such that $ww' = 1$ in G. By the confluence of P we have $a^n ww' \overset{*}{\underset{P}{\Rightarrow}} w_n w' \overset{*}{\underset{P}{\Rightarrow}} a^n$. This implies:
$n|a| \leq |w_n| + |w'| \leq n(|a| -1) + |w| + |w'|$ for all $n \geq 1$.

Since this is impossible, the claim results.

We therefore may assume $aw_n = w_n a$ for some $n \geq 1$. This means either $\rho(w_n) = \rho(a) = u$ or $w_n = 1$. In either case we see that w lies in the subgroup generated by u. In particular A must be isomorphic to $\mathbb{Z}$. Now, let $B \subset G$ any other infinite abelian subgroup. Since A is of finite index, we must have $A \cap B \neq \{1\}$. Hence B is of finite index in G, too. It follows $B \simeq \mathbb{Z}$. □

Corollary 1: The Jantzen monoid $G_1 = \{a,b\}^* / abba = 1$ has no finite Church-Rosser Thue presentation.

Proof: It is known [5] that G_1 is isomorphic to the non-trivial semidirect product $\mathbb{Z} \rtimes \mathbb{Z}$. This group has a free abelian subgroup of rank 2 which is of index two. □

Note, it is not possible to deduce Corollary 1 from Theorem 2':
The center of G_1 has infinite index.

Example 5: Let G be the free product $G = \mathbb{Z}/2\mathbb{Z} * \mathbb{Z}/2\mathbb{Z}$. Then G has a trivial center, but its commutator subgroup is cyclic and of index four. Clearly, G has a finite Church-Rosser Thue presentation. Therefore Theorem 3 applies to it. In fact, any non-trivial abelian subgroup is isomorphic to $\mathbb{Z}/2\mathbb{Z}$ or $\mathbb{Z}$.

The example 5 has not been taken by chance. In fact, we have a very precise algebraic characterisation of the situation as it is described in Theorem 3.

Theorem 4: Let G be an infinite group with an abelian subgroup of finite index. Then G has a finite Church-Rosser Thue presentation if and only if G is isomorphic to $\mathbb{Z}$ or isomorphic to the free product $\mathbb{Z}/2\mathbb{Z} * \mathbb{Z}/2\mathbb{Z}$.

Proof: By Theorem 3 it is enough to prove the following group theoretical fact:

Proposition: Let G be an infinite group with an abelian subgroup of finite index. If any abelian subgroup of G is finite or isomorphic to $\mathbb{Z}$ then G is isomorphic to $\mathbb{Z}$ or G is isomorphic to the free product $\mathbb{Z}/2\mathbb{Z} * \mathbb{Z}/2\mathbb{Z}$.

Proof of the proposition: Any subgroup of finite index contains a normal subgroup of G which has finite index, too. Hence we may assume that G is a group extension of $\mathbb{Z}$ by a finite group T. We then have short exact sequence:

$$1 \to \mathbb{Z} \xrightarrow{f} G \xrightarrow{g} T \to 1.$$

This extension makes $\mathbb{Z}$ into a T-module, the operation is given by a homomorphism $\sigma: T \to \mathrm{Aut}(\mathbb{Z}) = \{\pm 1\}$. Let $T' = \ker(\sigma)$ be the kernel of σ, and let $G' := g^{-1}(T')$.

We obtain a central extension

$$1 \to \mathbb{Z} \to G' \to T' \to 1.$$

The group G' is torsion free because otherwise there would be a non-cyclic infinite abelian subgroup. By [6, Prop 7.13] we see that G' is free abelian. It follows $G' \simeq \mathbb{Z}$. If G' is equal to G, we are through. Thus we assume $T/T' \simeq \mathbb{Z}/2\mathbb{Z}$. The group G' then becomes a $\mathbb{Z}/2\mathbb{Z}$-module with a non-trivial operation. We write $\mathbb{Z}(1)$ for this $\mathbb{Z}/2\mathbb{Z}$-module G'. We have following exact sequence:

$$1 \to \mathbb{Z}(1) \to G \to \mathbb{Z}/2\mathbb{Z} \to 1.$$

Let $g \in G$ such that the image of g generates $\mathbb{Z}/2\mathbb{Z}$. Clearly, g^2 is an element of $\mathbb{Z}(1)$ which is fixed under the operation of $\mathbb{Z}/2\mathbb{Z}$. Hence $g^2 = 1$ because there are no other fixed elements. The group extension therefore splits. (We also could simply observe that $H^2(\mathbb{Z}/2\mathbb{Z}, \mathbb{Z}(1))$ vanishes by cohomology of finite cyclic groups [8, Satz 6.1].) Since we have a split extension, G is isomorphic to the non-trivial semi-direct product of $\mathbb{Z}$ by $\mathbb{Z}/2\mathbb{Z}$. This group is presented by group-generators x and g with defining relations $gxg^{-1} = x^{-1}$, $g^2 = 1$. A Tietze-transformation $h := xg$ gives us the defining relations $h^2 = 1$, $g^2 = 1$, hence the result. □

Remark: Theorem 4 is related to a conjecture about context-free groups of Gilman [3, sect 3] The conjecture states: A group has a finite confluent monadic presentation if and only if it is a free product of free or finite groups.

It is known [2], [9] that the conjecture holds for so-called two-monadic systems. Here we get the conjecture in the following case. By Theorem 4 the conjecture of Gilman holds for groups which have an abelian subgroup of finite index. In fact, we have proven

Theorem 4': Let G be an infinite group with an abelian subgroup of finite index. Then the following assertions are equivalent:

i) G has a finite Church-Rosser Thue presentation.

ii) G has a finite confluent monadic presentation.

iii) G is a free product of free or finite groups.

iv) G is isomorphic to $\mathbb{Z}$ or isomorphic to $\mathbb{Z}/2\mathbb{Z} * \mathbb{Z}/2\mathbb{Z}$.

Part III

In this section we prove that groups which have a finite Church-Rosser Thue presentation are always context-free. (A group is called context-free if the kernel $L = p^{-1}(1)$ of any surjective homomorphism p of a free monoid onto G is a context-free language.) It is a remarkable fact that a group is context-free if and only if it has a free subgroup of finite index.

Theorem 5: Let G be a group with a finite Church-Rosser Thue presentation, then G is a context-free group.

Proof: Let $G = X^*/P$ where P is a finite confluent length-decreasing semi-Thue system. For $w \in X^*$ we write $\hat{w}$ for its irreducible descendant and

w^{-1} for the irreducible word such that ww^{-1} reduces to the empty word. Let us fix two integers: $k := 1 + \max\{|x^{-1}| ; x \in X\}$ and $m := \max\{|l| ; (l,r) \in P\}$. We have the following

<u>Lemma:</u> For all $g \in Irr(P)$ and $x \in X$ it holds $gx \in Irr(P)$ <u>or</u> there are $g', v, w \in X^*$ with $|w| \leq |v| \leq m\cdot k$, $g = g'v$, $g'w = \widehat{gx} \in Irr(P)$, and $vx \overset{*}{\underset{P}{\rightarrow}} w$.

<u>Proof of Lemma:</u> Assume that $g_1 := gx \notin Irr(P)$. Since $\hat{g}_1 x^{-1}$ reduces to $g \in Irr(P)$ and P is length-reducing we have $|\hat{g}_1| + k > |\hat{g}_1| + |x^{-1}| \geq |g|$. Therefore $|\hat{g}_1| > |g| - k$ holds. Hence at most k reduction steps from gx to $\hat{g}_1$ are possible which therefore involve the last mk letters of gx only. The claim follows.

<u>Proof of Theorem 5 continued:</u> We now describe a deterministic push down automaton which accepts the language $L = \{w \in X^* \mid \hat{w} = 1\}$. The states are the irreducible words of length at most $m\cdot k$. We use square brackets to denote states, thus we write $[z] = [z_1 \dots z_n]$ for states where $z = z_1 \dots z_n \in Irr(P)$, $z_i \in X$, $i = 1, \dots, n$, $n \leq mk$. The sign \$ denotes the bottom element of the stack. If the stack contains \$, $v_1, \dots, v_r$ in a state $[z]$ and $w_1, \dots, w_s$ is on the input tape we write $\$ v_1 \dots v_r [z] w_1 \dots w_s$ for the resulting configuration. The transition map is given by the following rules where $x, y, z_i \in X$, $i = 1, \dots, n$, $0 \leq n \leq mk$, and $z = z_1 \dots z_n$:

$\$[z]y$	$\rightarrow$	$\$[z']$	if $z' = \widehat{zy}$ and $|z'| \leq m\cdot k$,
$\$[z_1 \dots z_n]y$	$\rightarrow$	$\$z_1[z_2 \dots z_n y]$	if $z_1 \dots z_n y \in Irr(P)$ and $n = m\cdot k$,
$x[z]$	$\rightarrow$	$[z']$	if $z' = \widehat{xz}$ and $|z'| \leq m\cdot k$,
$x[z]y$	$\rightarrow$	$x[z']$	if $xz \in Irr(P)$, $|z| = mk$ and $z' = \widehat{zy} \neq zy$,
$x[z_1 \dots z_n]y$	$\rightarrow$	$xz_1[z_2 \dots z_n y]$	if $xz_1 \dots z_n y \in Irr(P)$ and $n = m\cdot k$.

We have $w \in L$ (this means $\hat{w} = 1$) if and only if we come from the configuration $\$[1]w$ to the configuration $\$[1]$. In fact, any configuration reachable from $[1]w for $w \in X^*$ has the form

$\$v_1 \ldots v_r [z_1 \ldots z_n] w_1 \ldots w_s$ where $v_1 \ldots v_r z_1 \ldots z_n \in Irr(P)$, $n \le mk$ and w reduces to $v_1 \ldots v_r z_1 \ldots z_n w_1 \ldots w_s$, further $n = mk$ if $r \ge 1$. The result follows by the Lemma. □

Corollary 1: Groups having a finite Church-Rosser Thue presentation form a proper subclass of the context-free groups.

Proof: $\mathbb{Z} \times \mathbb{Z}/2\mathbb{Z}$ is context-free without a finite Church-Rosser Thue presentation by the above. A non-commutative group for this situation is given in Example 4 above. □

As another consequence from the Theorem we obtain

Corollary 2: If $G = X^*/P$ is a finite Church-Rosser Thue presentation of a group then it is decidable whether G is free.

Proof: By [7] a context-free group is free if and only if it is torsion-free. Now, G is torsion-free if and only if the words $v \in X^*$ of length at most $\max\{|l| \; ; \; (l,r) \in P\}$ are torsion-free elements in G. A fixed word $v \in X^*$ is torsion free in G if and only if the context-free language $v^+ \cap \{w \in X^* \mid \hat{w} = 1\}$ is empty. □

Remark: By Theorem 5 we may view Corollary 2 as a special case of the following Theorem which we announce here only.

Theorem: If G is a context-free group, say specified by a context-free grammar for the kernel, then we can decide whether G is free.

Remark: When communicating Theorem 5 to Friedrich Otto I learned that he and K. Madlener jointly obtained the same result almost at the same time (yet unpublished).

References

[1] Avenhaus, J., Book, R., Squier, C., On expressing commutativity by Church-Rosser presentations: a note on commutative monoids, R.A.I.R.O. Informatique Théorique 18 (1984), 47 - 52

[2] Avenhaus, J., Madlener, K., On Groups Defined by Monadic Thue Systems, Colloquium on Algebra, Combinatorics, and Logic in Computer Science, Györ, Hungary, Sept. 1983

[3] Gilman, R.H., Computations with Rational Subsets of Confluent Groups, Proc. EUROSAM 1984, LNCS 174, (1984), 207 - 212

[4] Harrison, M.A., Introduction to Formal Language Theory, Addison-Wesley publishing company 1978

[5] Jantzen, M., Thue systems and the Church-Rosser property, MFCS Prag 1984, LNCS 176, 80 - 95 (1984)

[6] Lyndon, R.E., Schupp, P.E., Combinatorial group theory, Springer-Verlag 1977

[7] Muller, D.E., Schupp, P.E., Groups, the theory of ends and context-free languages, J. of Comp. and Syst. Sciences 26, 295 - 310 (1983)

[8] Neukirch, J., Klassenkörpertheorie, Biblio. Inst. Mannheim, Wien, Zürich 1969

[9] Otto, F., Decision problems and their complexity for monadic Church-Rosser Thue systems, Habilitationsschrift, Univ. Kaiserslautern 1985

Acknowledgement: I would like to thank Petra Leeb for her typing and Professor W. Brauer for his encouragement and support.

Ground Term Confluence in Parametric Conditional Equational Specifications†

Harald Ganzinger

Fachbereich Informatik
Universität Dortmund
D-4600 Dortmund 50, W. Germany
uucp, bitnet: hg@unido

ABSTRACT

We consider the problem of Knuth-Bendix-like completion for specifications with conditional equations for the particular case of achieving ground confluence. Inductive theorems of the given specification will be used for proving the convergence of critical pairs. The theorems may have the form of arbitrary first-order formulas, allowing for expressing properties of the theory that could otherwise not be specified equationally. A completion procedure will be given and demonstrated to be useful on examples which previous approaches fail to handle. Finally, an application of these ideas to parameterized specifications will be indicated.

1. Introduction

One of the principal concepts for the formal specification of software is that of abstract data types. Often such specifications are restricted to the equational or conditional equational type. The main motivation for this is on the semantic side the existence of initial models and on the operational side the ability to use term rewrite techniques for computing, theorem proving and program synthesis. The purpose of this paper is to consider the problem of Knuth-Bendix-like completion for conditional equational specifications. Knuth-Bendix completion in the equational case transforms a given specification, if it succeeds, into an executable one in which equality can be decided by reducing terms to normal forms. The various applications of the Knuth-Bendix completion procedure to problems in rewriting, theorem proving, program synthesis etc. are described in [Der83].

Our starting point has been the approach taken by Kaplan in [Kap84b]. We have been trying to apply his completion procedure to a number of examples that arise in practice. The conclusion gained from this experience was that although the general ideas appeared to be attractive, the completion procedure itself needed to be more refined in order to become useful in practice. Kaplan's concept is an interesting generalization of the concept of hierarchical conditional rewrite systems in which the conditions of a rule are restricted to equations over a lower-level signature as investigated in [PEE82], [Dro83], [RZ84], [ZR85], among others. Here a much weaker restriction to *fair* (or *simplifying*) rewrite rules (cf. below) suffices. Quite recently, Jouannaud and Waldmann [JW86] have improved the results of Kaplan in two ways: The class of rewrite rules that can be handled has been enlarged to the class of so-called *reductive rules*. The completion procedure of Kaplan has been modified to take care of the possible nontermination when trying to prove the unsatisfiability of conditions via narrowing.

In this paper we will concentrate on the more restricted problem of achieving ground confluence. There exist many interesting examples for specifications for which general confluence cannot be achieved. On the other hand, ground confluence already provides an operational model for functional programming. Function calls can be evaluated by reducing these to normal form. Moreover, ground confluence is sufficient to allow for many of the other classical applications of the completion procedure such as proving inductive theorems by completion [Fri86].

Our second goal has been to extend the completion technique to the case of parameterized specifications. Large specifications, to be comprehensible, must in any case be constructed from small pieces. Knuth-Bendix

† This work is partially supported by the ESPRIT-project PROSPECTRA, ref#390.

completion for large specifications can become unfeasable because of the at least quadratic number of possible overlaps between rules. Therefore, we investigate the requirements under which a parameterized specification can be completed independently of its actual parameters such that the combination of the completed procedure with any completed actual parameter yields an already complete instantiation.

In the paper we will refine Kaplan's completion procedure to deal with the restricted property of ground term confluence which is more often found to be present in practical examples. A major modification will be the consideration of parameter constraints in parameterized specifications. As parameter constraints arbitrary first-order formulas will be allowed. Hence one can more exactly characterize the class of admissible actual parameters compared to what is possible in the purely equational case. Actual specification parameters will be required to satisfy these constraints in their *inductive* theory. For the important case of persistent parameterized specifications, we will in fact be able to prove that parameterized specifications and actual parameters can be completed independently and then combined into a confluent system, if some further restrictions are obeyed.

The results presented in this paper are of more practical than theoretic nature. Our completion procedure will be based on a notion of term rewriting in contexts. The applicability of a rule, i.e. the satisfaction of the conditions of the rule, may here be inferred from the context. Convergence proofs for critical pairs will make use of well-coverings expressed as disjunctions of equations. Together, the notion of rewriting in contexts and the use of well-coverings make our approach to be related to the concept of contextual rewriting of Remy and Zhang [RZ84], [ZR85], without, however, needing to place hierarchy constraints on the conditions of rules.

2. Basic Notations

In this paper we consider terms over many-sorted signatures. A signature $\Sigma=(S,\Omega)$ consists of a set of sorts S and a family Ω of sets of sorted operator symbols with arity in S^*. T_Σ denotes the set of all Σ-terms, $(T_\Sigma)_s$ is the set of terms of sort $s\in S$. With X we denote a fixed set of sorted variables containing denumerably infinitely many variables for each sort. $T_\Sigma(X)$ is the set of all terms that may contain variables from X. Given a term or formula t, $var(t)$ denotes the set of variables occurring in t. Substitutions are denoted by σ, σ', etc. and their application to a term t by $t\sigma$. If u is an occurrence of a subterm in t, then t/u denotes that subterm at u and $t[u\leftarrow t']$ denotes the result of subterm replacement at u using t'.

A conditional equation over Σ is a formula of form

$$t_1=t'_1\wedge\cdots\wedge t_n=t'_n \Rightarrow t_0=t'_0$$

where $n\geq 0$ and $t_i,t'_i\in T_\Sigma(X)_{s_i}$. A conditional equation in which the order of terms in the conclusion is relevant is called a conditional rewrite rule. In other words, any conditional equation will also be considered a conditional rewrite rule by assuming the conclusion $t_0=t'_0$ to be oriented from left to right. For rewrite rules, an additional requirement is $var(t'_0)\subset var(t_0)$ and, for $i>0$, $var(t_i)\subset var(t_0)$ and $var(t'_i)\subset var(t_0)$, i.e. each variable that occurs in the rule must already occur in the left side of the conclusion.

Given a set of (conditional) equations E over Σ, $Th_{\Sigma,E}$ denotes the theory specified by it, i.e. the set of formulas in F_Σ which are valid in any model of E. Here F_Σ denotes the set of quantifier-free first-order formulas with equality, empty set of predicate symbols and function symbols from Σ. The inductive theory $ITh_{\Sigma,E}$ is the set of such formulas which is valid in the initial model of E. Of course, an equation, conditional or unconditional, that consists of ground terms only is in the inductive theory of E iff it is in the theory of E.

A specification is given as a pair (Σ,E) consisting of a signature and a (finite) set of equations over this signature. A hierarchical specification consists of a base level specification (Σ,E) and an enrichment (Σ',E') containing the base level specification as a subspecification.

Next we repeat Kaplan's notion of conditional rewriting. Given a set E of rules, $\rightarrow_E$ denotes the smallest precongruence (and $\xrightarrow{*}_E$ its reflexive and transitive closure) such that $t\rightarrow_E t'$ iff there exist a rule

$$t_1=t'_1\wedge\cdots\wedge t_n=t'_n \Rightarrow \lambda\rightarrow\rho$$

in E, an occurrence u in t and a substitution $\sigma:X\rightarrow T_\Sigma(X)$ such that $t/u=\lambda\sigma$, $t'=t[u\leftarrow\rho\sigma]$, and such that there exist terms s_i for which $t_i\sigma\xrightarrow{*}_E s_i$ and $t'_i\sigma\xrightarrow{*}_E s_i$. (For the latter situation we will subsequently write $t_i\sigma\downarrow_E t'_i\sigma$.) $\rightarrow_E$ is constructed as the limit

$$\rightarrow_E = \bigcup_{i=1}^{\infty}\theta^i(\emptyset),$$

where θ maps any precongruence $\rightarrow_1$ to the smallest precongruence $\rightarrow_2$ such that $\rightarrow_1 \subset \rightarrow_2$ and if, for a rule $t_1=t'_1 \wedge \cdots \wedge t_n=t'_n \Rightarrow \lambda \rightarrow \rho$, it is true that $t_i\sigma \downarrow_1 t'_i\sigma$ for all i, then $\lambda\sigma \rightarrow_2 \rho\sigma$. With this, the following theorem holds:

Theorem [Kap84a]
If $\rightarrow_E$ is confluent, then $\equiv_E = (\rightarrow_E \cup \rightarrow_E^{-1})^* = \downarrow_E$, where $\equiv_E$ is the smallest congruence generated by E. If $\rightarrow_E$ is confluent and noetherian, then $t \downarrow_E t'$ iff the normal forms of t and t' under $\rightarrow_E$ coincide.

A rewrite rule may be applied if each equation in its condition converges. We will later also consider the case where convergence can be inferred from given convergence assumptions. For that reason we will now introduce a notion of rewriting in the context of convergence assumptions. *Convergence assumptions* are sets C of unconditional equations $C=\{c_1=c'_1, \cdots, c_k=c'_k\}$. By $C\downarrow$ we denote the closure of C w.r.t the following axioms: $C \subset C\downarrow$ and $t=t \in C\downarrow$, for any term t. If $t=t' \in C\downarrow$, then $t'=t \in C\downarrow$. If $t=t' \in C\downarrow$ and K is a term, then $K[u \leftarrow t]=K[u \leftarrow t'] \in C\downarrow$. These axioms are obviously correct in the following sense:

Proposition 0
If $t=t' \in C\downarrow$ then, for any substitution $\sigma: X \rightarrow T_\Sigma(X)$ for which $c_i\sigma \downarrow_E c'_i\sigma$ for each convergence assumption $c_i=c'_i$ in C, it is $t\sigma \downarrow_E t'\sigma$.

Clearly, $C\downarrow$ is decidable for finite C.

Definition
Let $C=\{c_1=c'_1, \cdots, c_k=c'_k\}$ be a set of unconditional Σ-equations, E a set of Σ-rules and $t, t' \in T_\Sigma(X)$. t rewrites in context C under E to t', written $t \rightarrow_{C,E} t'$, if there exists a rule

$$t_1=t'_1 \wedge \cdots \wedge t_n=t'_n \Rightarrow \lambda \rightarrow \rho$$

in E, an occurrence u in t, a substitution $\sigma: X \rightarrow T_\Sigma(X)$ such that $t/u=\lambda\sigma$, $t'=t[u \leftarrow \rho\sigma]$, and for each $i \le n$ terms s_i, s'_i such that $t_i\sigma \xrightarrow{*}_{C,E} s_i$, $t'_i\sigma \xrightarrow{*}_{C,E} s'_i$ and $s_i=s'_i \in C\downarrow$. (We will subsequently write $t_i\sigma \downarrow_{C,E} t'_i\sigma$ to denote this converging of t_i and t'_i to a convergence assumption in C.)

For $C=\emptyset$, $\rightarrow_{C,E}$ coincides with $\rightarrow_E$. $\xrightarrow{*}_{C,E}$ denotes the respective reflexive and transitive closure. The construction of $\rightarrow_{C,E}$ as least fixpoint of a functional θ_C on precongruences is analogous to $\rightarrow_E$. Furthermore, an immediate consequence of proposition 0 is the following:

Proposition 1
Let $C=\{c_1=c'_1, \cdots, c_k=c'_k\}$ be a set of unconditional Σ-equations and $\sigma: X \rightarrow T_\Sigma(X)$ such that $c_i\sigma \downarrow_E c'_i\sigma$ for each equation in C. Let furthermore $t, t' \in T_\Sigma(X)$. Then $t \rightarrow_{C,E} t'$ implies $t\sigma \rightarrow_E t'\sigma$.

Of course, the applicability condition for a rewrite rule in $\rightarrow_E$ or $\rightarrow_{C,E}$ is not decidable. Kaplan [Kap84a] has investigated the subclass of *fair* or *simplifying* conditional rewrite systems, in which the right side of any rule as well as each term in the condition of the rule must be smaller (according to a given simplification ordering) than its left side. His results also apply to $\rightarrow_{C,E}$, i.e. to conditional rewriting in contexts. For fair systems, the applicability of a rule for $\rightarrow_{C,E}$ can then be decided by recursively reducing the instances of equations in conditions to normal form. The recursion is guaranteed to terminate as the terms in conditions become successively smaller. In the case of confluency, the above theorem yields a decision procedure for $\equiv_E$. The same properties hold in the restricted case of deciding the congruence of ground terms in case the TRS is reductive and confluent on ground terms.

Jouannaud and Waldmann [JW86] have extended Kaplan's results to the case in which the given termination ordering is just a reduction ordering in which subterms need not be smaller than the whole term. A rewrite system is called *reductive* if, according to a given reduction ordering, in any rule the right side as well as any term in the condition is smaller than the left side. In what follows, we will mainly restrict ourselves to reductive rewrite systems.

3. An Example

We will demonstrate some of the problems with conditional rewriting and confluence using the examples of natural numbers with maximum function and ordered lists.

sorts Bool Int List
ops

tt :	→ Bool
ff :	→ Bool
0 :	→ Int

s :	Int	$\rightarrow$ Int	
max :	Int Int	$\rightarrow$ Int	
_≤_ :	Int Int	$\rightarrow$ Bool	
[] :		$\rightarrow$ List	-- empty list
[_|_] :	Int List	$\rightarrow$ List	-- cons operation in C-Prolog notation
insert :	List Int	$\rightarrow$ List	-- insertion according to ≤
ordered :	List	$\rightarrow$ Bool	

Eqs

(1)		$0 \leq n = tt$
(2)		$s\,n \leq 0 = ff$
(3)		$s\,n \leq s\,m = n \leq m$
(4)	$x \leq y = tt \Rightarrow$	$max(x,y) = y$
(5)	$x \leq y = ff \Rightarrow$	$max(x,y) = x$
(6)		$x \leq max(x,y) = tt$
(7)		$y \leq max(x,y) = tt$
(8)		$ordered([]) = tt$
(9)		$ordered([x]) = tt$
(10)	$x \leq y = tt \Rightarrow$	$ordered([x,y\|zs]) = ordered([y\|zs])$ †
(11)	$x \leq y = ff \Rightarrow$	$ordered([x,y\|zs]) = ff$
(12)		$insert([],x) = [x]$
(13)	$x \leq y = tt \Rightarrow$	$insert([y\|ys],x) = [x,y\|ys]$
(14)	$x \leq y = ff \Rightarrow$	$insert([y\|ys],x) = [y\|insert(ys,x)]$
(15)		$ordered(insert(xs,x)) = ordered(xs)$.

It is obvious that the above system is simplifying, if one considers the equations to be oriented from left to right. The kind of path ordering proposed by Kapur et. al. [KNS85] is sufficient to prove this.

A central notion in proofs of confluence is that of a critical pair. In the case of conditional equations a generalization to *contextual critical pairs* is required.

Definition.
Let two conditional rules $C \Rightarrow M \rightarrow N$ and $D \Rightarrow G \rightarrow H$ be given and assume that their variables have been renamed such that they do not have any common variables. Assume moreover that u is an occurrence in M which is not a variable such that M/u and G can be unified with a mgu σ. Then, $(C \wedge D)\sigma \Rightarrow M[u \leftarrow H]\sigma = N\sigma$ is a *contextual critical pair*.

In the example, overlapping rules (5) and (7) yields the contextual critical pair

$$x \leq y = ff \Rightarrow y \leq x = tt \tag{16}$$

which is one formulation of the fact that ≤ is a total order. This equation is not reductive such that termination of rewriting cannot be further guaranteed. Even worse, overlapping rules (4) and (7) produces

$$x \leq y = tt \Rightarrow y \leq y = tt \tag{17}$$

which is the reflexivity of ≤ formulated such that the condition has more variables than the conclusion. Rules of this kind would require the guessing of solutions during rewriting and are therefore not allowed.

Overlapping the rules (14) and (15) yields

$$x \leq y = ff \Rightarrow ordered([y \mid insert(ys, x)]) = ordered([y \mid ys]) \tag{18}$$

The terms in the conclusion do not contain any redex. Hence they are already in contextual normal form in the sense of [RZ84] and [ZR85]. Therefore, their procedure as given in [ZR85] would return the answer "not confluent". However there is an experimental completion procedure in the current version of REVEUR4 (a system on top of REVE [Les83]) which seems to be able to handle examples of this kind.

† $[x, \cdots, y \mid zs]$ is an abbreviation for $[x \mid \cdots \mid [y \mid zs] \cdots]$.

We will propose some kind of combination of the approaches of Kaplan/Jouannaud/Waldmann and Remy/Zhang. From the former we adopt the notion of fairness (or reductivity), the definition of the conditional term rewriting relation $\rightarrow_E$ and the basic structure of the completion procedure. Hence we do not need to restrict ourselves to the case of hierarchical conditional equations. From the latter we adopt the restriction to considering confluence of ground terms and the use of covering predicates in convergence proofs. Before we will go into the technical details, we will briefly illustrate our ideas.

If one wants to prove confluence on ground terms one has to show for any contextual critical pair $C \Rightarrow N=M$ and for any ground substitution $\sigma: var(N=M) \rightarrow T_\Sigma$ for which $c_i\sigma \downarrow_E c'_i\sigma$, for each equation in C, that $N\sigma$ and $M\sigma$ can both be reduced to a single common term. This infinite set of ground substitutions must somehow be finitely approximated. In the following we will be using two kinds of inductive theorems to serve this purpose.

a) Negative assertions: Inductive theorems of the form

$$\neg(t_1=t'_1 \wedge \cdots \wedge t_n=t'_n)$$

assert that for no ground substitution σ the equalities $t_i\sigma=t'_i\sigma$ can be simultaneously valid. In the example, $\leq$ is a consistent enrichment of the booleans, i.e.

$$\neg\,(tt=ff) \tag{19}$$

is true in the initial algebra. Moreover, $\leq$ is a total order, i.e.

$$\neg(y \leq x = ff \wedge x \leq y = ff) \tag{20}$$

and

$$\neg(y \leq z = ff \wedge y \leq x = tt \wedge x \leq z = tt)\,. \tag{21}$$

Negative assertions may imply the unsatisfiability of the condition of a critical pair, allowing to discard it. Some of these assertions cannot be expressed by positive Horn clauses (e.g. (19)). Others, e.g. (20) and (21) can, but would violate the fairness constraints, and can therefore not be used for rewriting. The specific syntactic form of the negative assertions seems to simplify unsatisfiability proofs for conditions in many practical examples.

b) Covering assertions: Inductive theorems of the form

$$t_1=t'_1 \vee \cdots \vee t_n=t'_n$$

allow to conduct a case analysis on critical pairs. In the example we have

$$x \leq y = tt \vee x \leq y = ff\,. \tag{22}$$

This formula is valid in the initial model of the specification saying that $\leq$ is a total Boolean function which introduces no junk on Booleans. Because of the latter, the critical pair (16) is in the inductive theory equivalent to the two equations

$$y \leq x = ff \wedge x \leq y = ff \Rightarrow y \leq x = tt \tag{23}$$

$$y \leq x = tt \wedge x \leq y = ff \Rightarrow y \leq x = tt. \tag{24}$$

The convergence proofs for these two subcases of (16) are simple. (24) converges for any ground substitution as the conclusion occurs among the premisses, cf. Def. of $\rightarrow_E$. (23) converges as the condition contradicts the negative assertion (20) and hence cannot be satified.

This case analysis for critical pairs according to known covering properties deserves some further attention as it is somewhat more complicated than it may seem to be. Despite of the logical equivalence of (16) with $\{(23),(24)\}$ we are, when proving confluence, in general not allowed to simply replace (16) by $\{(23),(24)\}$. The problem is that the rewrite relation $\rightarrow_E$ is defined such that a rule may be applied only if any of its conditions $M\sigma=N\sigma$ not only is satisfied, but can in fact be *proved* valid by both reducing $M\sigma$ and $N\sigma$ to the same term. However, the validity of a covering property such $x \leq y = tt \vee y \leq x = tt$ in the inductive theory does in general not imply its *operational validity*, i.e. that $x\sigma \leq y\sigma \downarrow tt$ or $x\sigma \leq y\sigma \downarrow ff$, for each ground substitution σ. This motivates the following definition of the operational theory of a specification.

Definition
Given (Σ,E), $OTh_{\Sigma,E}$ denotes the set of all formulas in F_Σ that are operationally valid. Hereby, the equality "=" is

interpreted as "$\downarrow$", i.e. $t=t'$ is operationally valid if for any ground substitution $\sigma:X\rightarrow T_\Sigma$, $t\sigma\downarrow_E t'\sigma$. For the logical connectives the standard meaning is assumed.

Note that any negation of an equation $\neg(t=t')\in ITh_{\Sigma,E}$ is always also operationally valid whereas operationally valid equations are in particular inductive theorems.

In the example, (19)-(22) are operationally valid. A hierarchy argument can be used for inferring operational validity. The membership of a covering property such as $x\le y=tt \vee x\le y=ff$ in an inductive theory $ITh_{\Sigma,E}$ does imply that $x\sigma\le y\sigma\downarrow tt$ or $x\sigma\le y\sigma\downarrow ff$, for each ground substitution σ, if the covering property already holds in the inductive theory $ITh_{\Sigma',E'}$ of a ground-confluent *subspecification* (Σ',E') of (Σ,E), provided the enrichment (Σ,E) is sufficiently complete (cf. below) with respect to the base (Σ',E'). In our example, the subspecification for the Booleans and the natural numbers with 0, s and $\le$ is confluent and by itself also satisfies (22) in its initial model. The complete specification is a sufficiently complete enrichment of this base. This completes the convergence proof for (16).

In the following we will be using covering properties of lower levels of the specification hierarchy to split, where appropriate, a critical pair into a nesting of subcases for which the convergence proofs are simpler. This process closely corresponds to the notion of contextual rewriting of Zhang and Remy. Note, that we do not put a general hierarchy constraint on the conditions of equations. Only the splitting of critical pairs is based on covering properties of lower levels in the specification hierarchy.

Let us take a look at one more example. Overlapping (18) and (13) results in a critical pair

$$x\le y1=ff \wedge x\le y=tt \Rightarrow ordered([y1,x,y\mid ys])=ordered([y1,y\mid ys]) \tag{25}$$

If we split this equation using the covering property $y1\le x=ff \vee y1\le x=tt$, cf. (22), we obtain the two subcases

$$y1\le x=ff \wedge x\le y1=ff \wedge x\le y=tt \Rightarrow ordered([y1,x,y\mid ys])=ordered([y1,y\mid ys])$$

and

$$y1\le x=tt \wedge x\le y1=ff \wedge x\le y=tt \Rightarrow ordered([y1,x,y\mid ys])=ordered([y1,y\mid ys]).$$

The first of these is trivial, as the condition is in contradiction to (20). The second can by use of $y1\le y=ff \vee y1\le y=tt$, cf. (22), be further split into

$$y1\le y=ff \wedge y1\le x=tt \wedge x\le y1=ff \wedge x\le y=tt \Rightarrow ordered([y1,x,y\mid ys])=ordered([y1,y\mid ys]) \tag{26}$$

and

$$y1\le y=tt \wedge y1\le x=tt \wedge x\le y1=ff \wedge x\le y=tt \Rightarrow ordered([y1,x,y\mid ys])=ordered([y1,y\mid ys]).$$

The condition of the first contradicts the transitivity (21). The convergence of the last critical pair can be proved by rewriting in the context represented by its condition. In context $y1\le x=tt \wedge x\le y=tt$, $ordered([y1,x,y\mid ys])$ rewrites to $ordered([y\mid ys])$, as does $ordered([y1,y\mid ys])$ in context $y1\le y=tt$, cf. rule (10). This concludes the convergence proof for (25).

At this point some remarks about proving the unsatifiability of conditions seem to be in order. Kaplan [Kap84b] has suggested to use narrowing for this purpose. In cases such as the condition of (26) this will not succeed, as narrowing in its basic form [Fay79], [Hul80], produces an infinite set of solution substitutions for each single equation of the condition. Probably the extensions to narrowing as proposed by Rety et. al. [Ret85] would suffice to handle this particular case. This possibility of nontermination requires a technique of bounded narrowing [JW86]. In the context of parameterized specifications even if one can prove that for a positive formula ϕ no substitution σ exists such that $\phi\sigma$ can be derived from the equations of the formal parameter, the situation may be different for any actual parameter which is later passed to the specification. An actual parameters is usually allowed to have more equations than an equationally specified formal parameter, and hence may cause the existence of a σ solving ϕ.

To summarize what has been indicated above, our completion procedure will make use of additionally given inductive theorems. These additional inductive assertions will fall into two categories. The first kind is that of *covering assertions*, expressed by finite disjunctions of (unconditional) equations. The second kind is that of *negative assertions* expressed by the negation of a finite conjunction of unconditional equations. The former will be used to split critical pairs into equations which admit simpler convergence proofs, the latter to prove the unsatisfiablity of conditions.

The completion procedure to be given below will therefore have the type

$$KB : Equations \times Assertions \rightarrow Rules$$

If it does terminate on inputs E and A, it will have produced a set of rules R. $\rightarrow_R$ will then be ground confluent and noetherian, and it will generate the same inductive theory (the same initial model) as E, provided that the formulas in A are inductive theorems about E (and R) and that the covering assertions among them are, furthermore, also operationally valid wrt. R. This completion procedure will succeed more often than Kaplan's. It will however, upon termination, give a weaker result. First, only confluence on ground terms will be achieved. Secondly, only the inductive theory is preserved. Finally, the confluence is relative to the operational validity of the assumed assertions. The relativized confluence may appear unsatisfactory for the case of unstructured specifications, yet we do not believe that it can be avoided. In the context of parameterized specifications, any confluence proof is necessarily relative to the assertions in the specification of the formal parameter which characterizes the class of admissible actual parameters.

4. Convergence Proofs for Critical Pairs

We begin this section by repeating two theorems given in [Kap84b] and [JW86] about convergence of critical pairs and confluence of $\rightarrow_E$.

Theorem [Kap84b,JW86]
Given a reductive conditional term rewrite system E, $\rightarrow_E$ is locally confluent, and thus confluent, on T_Σ, iff for any contextual critical pair $C \Rightarrow t=t'$ between any two rules in E and for any substitution $\sigma:X \rightarrow T_\Sigma$ such that $C\sigma \in Th_{\Sigma,E}$, $t\sigma \downarrow_E t'\sigma$.

We call a critical pair $C \Rightarrow t=t'$ *convergent* (on T_Σ), if it satifies this property. The following is an obvious variation of this theorem also proved in [JW86]:

Proposition 2
Given a reductive conditional term rewrite system E, then $\rightarrow_E$ is locally confluent, and thus confluent, on T_Σ iff for any contextual critical pair $C \Rightarrow t=t'$ between any two rules in E it holds $t\sigma \downarrow_E t'\sigma$, for each substitution $\sigma:X \rightarrow T_\Sigma$ for which $N\sigma \downarrow_E M\sigma$, for each $N=M \in C$.

If a critical pair satisfies this weaker property we will call it *weakly (E-) convergent* (on T_Σ). Next we introduce the notion of *relative convergence*, which will be the basis of our further developments.

Definition
Let a signature Σ and a set E of Σ-rules be given. Furthermore, let $A \subset F_\Sigma$ be a set of assertions over Σ and γ be a conditional Σ-equation of form $C \Rightarrow U=V$. Assume that variables have been renamed such that no two distinct formulas in $A \cup \{\gamma\}$ share a common variable. γ is called *(E-) convergent (on T_Σ) relative to A*, if one of the following holds:

a) $U \downarrow_{C,E} V$

b) $(A\sigma \Rightarrow \neg C) \in Th_{\Sigma,E}$, for some substitution $\sigma:X \rightarrow T_\Sigma(var(\gamma))$

c) There exists a *covering assertion* $\alpha \equiv (e_1 \vee \cdots \vee e_k) \in A$ and a substitution $\sigma:X \rightarrow T_\Sigma(var(\gamma))$ such that each $C \wedge e_i\sigma \Rightarrow U=V$, $1 \leq i \leq k$, is E-convergent on T_Σ relative to A.

It is clear that this relative convergence property is in general undecidable. For the completion procedure below, however, any correct approximation of it is acceptable. Condition a) is, as mentioned above, decidable for reductive systems. Case b) requires $\neg C$ to follow from an instance $A\sigma$ of the (implicitly universally quantified) assumptions A. This is, of course, undecidable. In practice, however, even a simple-minded implication calculus seems to work out quite well. More powerful refutation proof techniques based on Knuth-Bendix completion as proposed by Hsiang and Dershowitz [HS83] can be used here. For case c) one has to decide upon when to terminate the recursion.

Proposition 3
Let (Σ',E') be an enrichment of a base specification (Σ,E). Let $A \subset ITh_{\Sigma',E'}$ such that each covering assertion in A is also operationally valid, i.e. member of $OTh_{\Sigma',E'}$. Then, a conditional equation γ over Σ is weakly E'-convergent on $T_{\Sigma'}$ if it is E-convergent on T_Σ relative to A.

Proof. By induction over the recursion level for case c). Suppose that there exists a substitution $\sigma':X \rightarrow T_{\Sigma'}$ such that $M\sigma' \downarrow_{E'} N\sigma'$, for each equation $N=M \in C$. We must show that $U\sigma' \downarrow_{E'} V\sigma'$. In the case of a) this follows immediately from propositions 0 and 1, respectively. Case b) is not applicable as this would contradict the assumption about the validity of $C\sigma'$. (Note that the initial model of (Σ',E') is a particular model of (Σ,E) in which any $A\sigma\sigma'$ is true and, thus, $C\sigma'$ false, if b) applies.) In case c) we note that α and therefore $\alpha\sigma$ is a covering assertion in $OTh_{\Sigma',E'}$. Thus, there exists an i such that $L_i\sigma\sigma'\downarrow_{E'}R_i\sigma\sigma'$, if $e_i \equiv L_i = R_i$. According to the induction hypothesis, $C \wedge e_i\sigma \Rightarrow U=V$ is weakly convergent. Hence, $U\sigma'\downarrow_{E'}V\sigma'$, which was to be shown. ♦

This proposition says that relative convergence implies weak convergence in any enrichment of the specification for which the assertions in A are operationally valid. Unfortunately, this additional requirement about operational validity of covering assertions cannot be dropped. $\equiv_E$ and $\downarrow_E$ must coincide on the equations $e_i\sigma\sigma'$. In the case of a hierarchical specification (Σ',E') over a base specification (Σ,E) there may be situations, where congruence and convergence are known to be the same. Let us consider the case of sufficiently complete enrichments:

Definition

A hierarchical specification is sufficiently complete, if for each term $t' \in T_{\Sigma'}$ of base sort there exists a base signature term $t \in T_\Sigma$ such that $t' \overset{*}{\rightarrow}_{(E'-E)} t$.

Proposition 4

Let a hierarchical, sufficiently complete specification be given such that $\equiv_E$ and $\downarrow_E$ coincide on T_Σ. Then, $(e_1 \vee \cdots \vee e_k) \in ITh_{\Sigma,E}$ implies $(e_1 \vee \cdots \vee e_k) \in OTh_{\Sigma',E'}$.

Proof. Let $\sigma':X \rightarrow T_{\Sigma'}$ be given. Because of the sufficient completeness there exists a $\sigma:X \rightarrow T_\Sigma$ such that for any term $t \in T_\Sigma(X)$ of an S-sort, $t\sigma' \overset{*}{\rightarrow}_{(E'-E)} t\sigma$. Clearly, $e_i\sigma \in ITh_{\Sigma,E}$, for some i. The E-convergence of $e_i\sigma$ then implies the E'-convergence† of $e_i\sigma'$. ♦

This says in particular that if we require confluency of the base specification and sufficient-completeness of the enrichment, the requirement in proposition 3 about the operational validity of any covering assertion follows from its (semantic and operational) validity in the base.

5. Outlines of a completion procedure

With the propositions in the preceeding section, we can now formulate our completion procedure. As basis we give a simple version (adapted from [Der83]) which can be made more efficient by using the techniques of [Hue81].

Completion Procedure

Input:

1. A set E_0 of conditional equations
2. A reduction ordering $<$ on $T_\Sigma(X)$
3. A set of assertions $A \subset F_\Sigma$

Output (if it terminates successfully):

A set R of reductive conditional rewrite rules such that each contextual critical pair between rules in R is convergent on T_Σ relative to A. Moreover, R generates the same inductive theory as E.

Algorithm

Initially, R is empty and $E=E_0$.

Repeat as long as equations are left in E. If none remain, terminate successfully.

1. Remove an equation $C \Rightarrow M=N$ or $C \Rightarrow N=M$ from E such that $M>N$ and such that each term in C is smaller that M. If none exists, abort.
2. Add the rule $C \Rightarrow M \rightarrow N$ to R.
3. Use R to reduce the right hand sides and conditions of existing rules (cf. 5.1).
4. Compute the set CP of all contextual critical pairs formed using the new rule.
5. Simplify and split critical pairs, yielding the set CP', cf. below.
6. Add CP' to E.

† The restriction to $(E'-E)$-rewriting of terms into base terms is not needed at this point, but will become necessary later.

7. Remove all the old rules $C' \Rightarrow M' \to N'$ from R if their left side M' can be reduced under $\to_{C',\{C \Rightarrow M \to N\}}$.
8. Remove any old equation $C' \Rightarrow M' = N'$ from E, if $M' \downarrow_{C',R} N'$.

End

In step 5, the propositions of the last section can be applied in the following way.

Repeat the following steps until the set of critical pairs does not change any further:

5.1. Normalize any equation $N=M$ in a condition C of a critical pair according to $\to_{C-\{N=M\},R}$ and their conclusions according to $\to_{C,R}$.

5.2. Remove any critical pair, for which any of the cases a) or b) in the definition of relative convergence applies.

5.3. Replace any critical pair $C \Rightarrow t=t'$ by $s_i\sigma = s'_i\sigma \wedge C \Rightarrow t=t'$, $1 \le i \le k$, if there exists a covering assertion $(s_1=s'_1 \vee \cdots \vee s_k=s'_k) \in A$ and a substitution $\sigma: X \to T_\Sigma(var(C \Rightarrow t=t'))$ such that each of the new critical pairs will be simpler than the given one after the next 5.1-step, or subject to elimination according to 5.2.. Do not split $C \Rightarrow t=t'$ if any of the resulting nontrivial equations violates the constraint that conditions must not have more variables than the conclusion.

If we run the above algorithm (and compute a simplification ordering according to [KNS85]) on input E as the set of axioms (1) - (15), $A=\{(19)-(22)\}$, it will successfully terminate. The resulting set of rules will be the oriented versions of (1) - (15), together with the critical pair (18). Therefore, (1) - (15), (18) is confluent on ground terms. It is not confluent on variable terms.

The proof of correctness of the above completion procedure is a nontrivial extension of Huet's for the equational case [Hue81] and will be the subject of a forthcoming paper. In the conditional case not only the sequence of rules is nonmonotonic but in addition the domain of applicability of even unchanged rules may change due to changes performed on other rules. Hence there are two different ways in which the rewriting relation may change during completion. This problem may have been overlooked by the authors of previous completion procedures [Kap84b], [JW86] when they claim that the correctness of their algorithms can be proved as in [Hue81].

6. Application to parameterized specifications

The completion procedure of the previous section produces relativized answers to confluence, depending on the validity of initially given inductive properties. In this section we show that such an approach may be useful for parameterized specifications. Parameterized specifications have been introduced as a means to build large specifications from small building blocks. Large specifications are incomprehensible if they are not composed of smaller pieces that can be more easily understood. When it comes to applying Knuth-Bendix-like completion to a large specification, very large running times must be accepted. One reason for this is that the number of possible overlappings between rules is at least quadratic in the number of rules. So, from a practical point of view, it would be nice, if the completion procedure could take advantage of the structure of a specification. In particular if a parametric specification needed to be inspected only once and independent of the various actual parameters that may be passed to it, much computational overhead might be avoided.

The conditional equational case here too adds serious difficulties. The question is what happens to confluence when one combines two confluent systems of rules as it is done when passing an actual parameter to a parameteric specification. In the unconditional case a system $(\Sigma+\Sigma 1, E+E1)$ is confluent on $T_{\Sigma+\Sigma 1}(X+X1)$ provided (Σ, E) and $(\Sigma 1, E1)$ are confluent on $T_\Sigma(X)$ and $T_{\Sigma 1}(X1)$, respectively, and that rules in E do not overlap with rules in $E1$. In our case complications arise from two sources. First, we are considering ground term confluence. Therefore, confluence properties are in general not even preserved under enrichment of the signature alone (without adding any new rules). Secondly, the application of a rewrite rule depends in the conditional case on the convergence of the equations in the condition. Rules that are not applicable at a given subterm may become applicable in the enriched system and vice versa.

The completion procedure which we have given in the last section has been designed to deal with these difficulties:

1. It does not abandon any equation $C \Rightarrow M=N$ for the reason that there exists no substitution $\sigma: X \to T_\Sigma(X)$ such that $C\sigma \in Th_{\Sigma,E}$. (This is in contrast to Kaplan's procedure.) If one passes an actual parameter to a specification, the actual parameter usually has more equations than the formal parameter. Therefore, C may be unsatisfiable in the parametric specification but nevertheless satisfiable for an actual parameter.

2. The procedure allows to also consider properties of the initial model that cannot or should not be expressed as conditional equations. In particular negations of equalities such as $\neg(tt = ff)$ which one might want to specify as constraints about the admissible actual parameters form the basis for proving unsatisfiability of conditions in contextual critical pairs.

Therefore, we envisage the following concept of parameterized specifications. A parameterized specification is a hierarchical specification (Σ', E') in which the base level specifies the (formal) parameter. As axioms in the parameter part we allow, apart from conditional equations, covering assertions and negative assertions. To emphasize this fact we will call them *parameter constraints.* (Concepts of parameterized specifications with (none-quational) constraints have been studied elsewhere in the literature, [EWT83] among others.) The axioms in the body $E'-E$ are restricted to conditional equations. A conditional equational specification $(\Sigma 1, E1)$ is called an admissible actual parameter if its signature is an enrichment of the formal parameter signature Σ † and if the formal parameter constraints are *inductive* theorems of the actual parameter. (This variant of admissibility has also been considered in [Ehr81].)

Example

spec Lists
parameter
sorts Elem Bool
ops

tt :		→ Bool
ff :		→ Bool
_≤_ :	Elem Elem	→ Bool

constraints
$x \le y = tt \vee x \le y = ff$
$\neg(tt = ff)$
$\neg(y \le x = ff \wedge x \le y = ff)$
$\neg(y \le y1 = ff \wedge y \le x = tt \wedge x \le y1 = tt)$
body
ops

[] :		→ List
[_|_] :	Elem List	→ List
insert :	List Elem	→ List
ordered :	List	→ Bool

Eqs

	ordered([]) = tt
	ordered([x]) = tt
$x \le y = tt \Rightarrow$	ordered([x,y|zs]) = ordered([y|zs])
$x \le y = ff \Rightarrow$	ordered([x,y|zs]) = ff
	insert([],x) = [x]
$x \le y = tt \Rightarrow$	insert([y|ys],x) = [x,y|ys]
$x \le y = ff \Rightarrow$	insert([y|ys],x) = [y|insert(ys,x)]
	ordered(insert(xs,x)) = ordered(xs)

If one starts the completion algorithm on this specification, taking A to consist of the 4 constraints, the algorithm terminates after adding the critical pair (18).

The specification that results from passing an actual parameter to a parametric specification is obtained by replacing the formal parameter part of the parameteric specification by the actual parameter. Let us formulate what has been said above in a number of definitions.

† Here one usually only requires the existence of a signature morphism from formal to actual parameters. In this paper, in order to simplify the technical presentation, we consider this restricted case. In the examples we allow for injective renaming of sorts and operators. We expect that our results can be extended to the full case.

Definition
A parameterized specification is a pair *SPEC* (*PAR*) of specifications $PAR = (\Sigma Par, CPar)$ and $SPEC = (\Sigma, E)$. *CPar* is the set of parameter constraints consisting of arbitrary formulas in $F_{\Sigma Par}$. *SPEC* is an enrichment of *PAR* such that the axioms in the *body* $E - CPar$ of the parameterized specifications are conditional equations over Σ.

Definition
Given a parameterized specification *SPEC* (*PAR*), a (nonparameterized) specification $SPEC1 = (\Sigma 1, E1)$ is called an *admissible actual parameter*, if $\Sigma 1 \supset \Sigma$ and if $CPar \subset ITh_{\Sigma 1, E1}$. The result of passing an admissible actual parameter *SPEC* 1, called the *SPEC* 1-*instance* of *SPEC* (*PAR*), is the (nonparameterized) specification $SPECI = (\Sigma 1 + (\Sigma - \Sigma Par), E1 + (E - CPar))$, where + means renaming those operators in the body of the parameterized specification that already occur in the actual parameter.

Definition
A parameterized specification *SPEC* (*PAR*) is called *consistent*, if it does not introduce "confusion" on any admissible actual parameter *SPEC* 1, i.e. if $t = t'$ is a ground equation in actual parameter terms, then $t = t' \in ITh_{SPEC1}$ iff $t = t' \in ITh_{SPECI}$.

Definition
A parameterized specification is called *sufficiently complete*, if any of its instances *SPECI* is a sufficiently complete enrichment of the actual parameter *SPEC* 1 with which the instance has been generated.

The following theorem about parameter passing and confluence holds:

Proposition 5
Let *SPEC* (*PAR*) be a parameterized specification. Assume that any contextual critical pair between any two body rules is convergent relative to *CPar*. Furthermore assume that *SPEC* (*PAR*) is consistent and sufficiently complete. Let *SPEC* 1 be an admissible actual parameter for *SPEC* (*PAR*) which is reductive and confluent on $T_{\Sigma 1}$. Then any critical pair formed from overlapping either two actual parameter rules or two body rules is (weakly) convergent on $T_{\Sigma I}$, i.e. on the ground terms of the instantiation.

Proof. First note that any parameter constraint in *CPar* is in the inductive theory of *SPECI*. This is a consequence of the consistency and sufficient-completeness requirements. Moreover, the confluence property of the actual parameter allows to apply proposition 4 to conclude the operational validity of the covering assertions in *CPar*. If the critical pair is formed from two body rules, its convergence follows from the propositions 3 and 4. Suppose now that $\cdots M = N \cdots \Rightarrow U = V$ is a critical pair between two rules of the actual parameter. From proposition 2 we know that for each $\sigma 1 : X \to T_{\Sigma 1}$ for which $\cdots M\sigma 1 \downarrow_{E1} N\sigma 1 \cdots$ we also have $U\sigma 1 \downarrow_{E1} V\sigma 1$. Let now $\sigma I : X \to T_{\Sigma I}$ be given. The sufficient-completeness of the parametric specification implies the existence of a $\sigma 1 : X \to T_{\Sigma 1}$ such that $t\sigma I \overset{*}{\to}_{(E-CPar)} t\sigma 1$, for any $t \in T_{\Sigma 1}(X)$. From this we infer $\cdots, M\sigma 1 \equiv_{SPECI} N\sigma 1, \cdots$ and, according to the consistency of the enrichment, $\cdots, M\sigma 1 \equiv_{SPEC1} N\sigma 1, \cdots$. Confluence and reductivity of the actual parameter imply then $\cdots M\sigma 1 \downarrow_{E1} N\sigma 1 \cdots$. As $E1 \subset EI$, we may now conclude that $\cdots U\sigma 1 \downarrow_{EI} V\sigma 1 \cdots$, which proves the convergence of this critical pair on $T_{\Sigma I}$. Other critical pairs cannot exist. ♦

As an immediate corollary we obtain the following proposition.

Proposition 6
Assume the requirements for proposition 5 and, furthermore:

1. The rules *E* 1 of the actual parameter do not overlap with the rules of the body of *SPEC* (*PAR*).
2. The rules of the body of *SPEC* (*PAR*) as well as the rules of the actual parameter *SPEC* 1 are redfuctive according to two reduction orderings that can be combined into one single reduction ordering on $T_{\Sigma I}(X)$.

Then the *SPEC* 1-instance of *SPEC* (*PAR*) is reductive and locally confluent (and thus confluent) on $T_{\Sigma I}$.

The last requirement can easily be checked in cases where the ordering is generated by precedences on operators, as is the case for the path ordering of [KNS85] which we use. Requirement 1 is fulfilled in many practical cases. In the above example there is no occurrence of a formal parameter operator in the left side of a rule of the parametric specification, which trivially implies 1. for any actual parameter. Proposition 5 says that when completing an instantiation only critical pairs between the body and the actual parameter must be considered further, whereas the convergence of any other critical pair is preserved. This considerably reduces the complexity of the completion procedure in practice. Requirement 2 of proposition 6 is, however, in any case necessary to obtain reductivity of the instantiation. If in addition requirement 1 is satisfied too, no other critical pairs can occur such that the instantiation needs not be further processed.

The hard part is to check the consistency and sufficient-completeness of the completed parameterized specification *SPEC*(*PAR*). Sufficient-completeness is not only needed for justifying the splitting of critical pairs according to covering properties. It is, together with consistency, also required for proving that critical pairs between actual parameter rules remain convergent after parameter passing. For unconditional equational actual parameter specifications which are confluent in the general case of terms with variables, proposition 5 holds also in the case of inconsistent parameterized specifications. Keep in mind that for purely equational specifications our completion algorithm, if successful, achieves confluence on terms with variables.

7. Conclusion

We have introduced a completion procedure for conditional equational specifications. Conditions are not restricted to lower-level operators in a specification hierarchy. Rather, the much weaker restriction to reductive conditional rewrite rules is made. In practice, confluence on terms with variables can be achieved only in very few cases. Therefore, we have considered the case of ground term confluence. Fair rewrite systems which are confluent on ground terms still provide a decision procedure for ground term equivalence and thus an operational model for term evaluation.

We believe to have refined Kaplan's procedure [Kap84b] to become successful on many examples that arise in practice. In this paper we have illustrated that it can handle the data type "ordered lists" together with max on natural numbers. The procedure terminates on more examples because it only gives a relativized answer. Completed specifications are confluent only if they satisfy those additional inductive and operational properties of the system that have been assumed during completion. Especial use is made of covering properties (finite disjunctions of equations) and of negative properties (finite disjunctions of negations of equations). The former serve to split critical pairs into simpler variants while the latter allow to infer the unsatifiability of conditions. This use of covering properties is related to the notion of well-coveredness in rewrite rule systems which is central to the results about contextual rewriting of Zhang and Remy [ZR85].

We have argued that such a technique is particularly useful for parametric specifications where one wants to infer the confluence of any actual instantiation from the confluence of the parametric specification relative to the parameter constraints and from the admissibility and confluence of the actual parameter. We have therefore considered a concept of parameterization where the formal parameter constraints may be arbitrary first-order formulas (w/o quantifiers). This allows to express covering assertions and negative assertions as needed for the confluence proof. For the important subcase of persistent specifications we have shown that relative confluence implies the confluence of any instantiation with an admissible actual parameter which is itself confluent, provided the simplification orderings can be combined. Even in case a rule of the body of the parametric specification overlaps with a rule of the actual parameter, only these critical pairs need to be considered further, whereas the critical pairs between any two actual parameter rules or between any two body rules are guaranteed to be convergent. This considerably decreases the effort required for completing large specifications, provided they are built from instantiating relatively small parametric specifications.

Acknowledgements. We are grateful to Peter Padawitz and Jean-Luc Remy for their detailed comments on a previous version of this paper.

8. References

[Der83] Dershowitz, N.: Applications of the Knuth-Bendix completion procedure. Aerospace Report ATR-83(8478)-2, The Aerospace Corp., El Segundo, Calif., USA, 1983.

[Dro83] Drosten, K.: Towards executable specifications using conditional axioms. Report 83-01, T.U. Braunschweig, 1983.

[Ehr81] Ehrig, H., Kreowski, H.-J., Thatcher, J.W., Wagner, E.G., and Wright, J.B.: Parameter passing in algebraic specification languages. LNCS 134, Springer 1981.

[EWT83] Ehrig, H., Wagner, E.G., Thatcher, J.W.: Algebraic specifications with generating constraints. Proc. ICALP 83, LNCS 154, 1983, 188-202.

[Fay79] Fay, M.: First-order unification in equational theories. 4th Workshop on Automated Deduction, Austin, 1979, 161-167.

[Fri86] Fribourg, L.: A strong restriction of the inductive completion procedure. Proc. ICALP 86, LNCS, 105-115.

[HD83] Hsiang, J. and Dershowitz, N.: A term rewriting theorem prover. Proc. 10th ICALP, 1983, 331-346.

[Hue81] Huet, G.: A complete proof of the correctness of the Knuth-Bendix completion algorithm. JCSS 23 (1981), 11-21.

[Hul80] Hullot, J.M.: Canonical forms and unification. 5th Workshop on Automated Deduction, Les Arcs, 1980, 318-334.

[JW86] Jouannaud, J.P., and Waldmann, B.: Reductive conditional term rewriting systems. Proc. 3rd TC2 Working Conference on the Formal Description of Prog. Concepts, Ebberup, Denmark, Aug. 1986, North-Holland, to appear.

[Kap84a] Kaplan, St.: Conditional rewrite rules. TCS 33 (1984), 175-193.

[Kap84b] Kaplan, St.: Fair conditional term rewrite systems: unification, termination and confluence. Report 194, U. de Paris-Sud, Centre d'Orsay, Nov. 1984.

[KNS85] Kapur, D., Narendran, P., and Sivakumar, G.: A path ordering for proving termination of term rewrite systems. LNCS 186, 1985, 173-187.

[Les83] Lescanne, P.: Computer experiments with the REVE term rewriting system generator. Proc. 10th ACM Symp. on POPL, Austin, Texas, 1983.

[PEE82] Pletat, U., Engels, G., and Ehrich, H.-D.: Operational semantics of algebraic specifications with conditional equations. Proc. 7th CAAP, LNCS, 1982.

[Ret85] Rety, P., Kirchner, C., Kirchner, H., and Lescanne, P.: NARROWER, a new algorithm for unification and its application to logic programming. Conf. on Rewriting Techniques and Applications, Dijon 1985, LNCS 202, 141-157.

[RZ84] Remy, J.L. and Zhang, H.: REVEUR 4: A system for validating conditional algebraic specifications of abstract data types. Proc. 6th ECAI, Pisa 1984, 563-572.

[ZR85] Zhang, H. and Remy, J.L.: Contextual rewriting. Conf. on Rewriting Techniques and Applications, Dijon 1985, LNCS 202,

Describing Semantic Domains with Sprouts

Gunther Schmidt
Rudolf Berghammer
Hans Zierer

Technische Universität München
Institut für Informatik
Postfach 20 24 20
D-8000 München 2

ABSTRACT: In denotational semantics the meaning of a construct of a programming language is modelled by an element of a (semantic) domain. Domains are essentially ordered sets, in which every element may be approximated by a directed set of compact elements.

We propose a new approach to domain construction using directed systems of certain finite subsets of a domain called sprouts. Every element of the domain can be considered as growing out from the sprouts, i.e. it can be uniquely approximated by an element of any given sprout. Sprouts consist only of compact elements and every compact element is contained in some of the sprouts.

The directed system of sprouts fits neatly to the usual domain constructions, so we are able to describe the approximations of an element of a composed domain by the corresponding approximations in the component domains very exactly. Furthermore, we get a constructive and less abstract description of profinite domains than given by C. Gunter with one added feature: Given a domain functional τ, the inverse limit of the retraction sequence $\mathbf{1}$, $\tau[\mathbf{1}]$, $\tau^2[\mathbf{1}]$, ... is indeed the least of a certain subset of fixed points of τ, namely of those being the vertex of a cone that is "definable" in some sense.

1. Introduction

In domain theory usually "countably algebraic complete partial orderings" are considered as domains. They are ordered sets in which every directed subset has a least upper bound, in which the subset of compact (or finite) elements is countable, and in which every element may be approximated by compact elements. This category of domains, however, is not closed w.r.t. the construction of function domains (cf. [Smyth 83]). Therefore, domains are frequently restricted to "consistently complete countably algebraic cpos" in which additionally every subset with an upper bound also has a least upper bound (cf. [Larsen Winskel 84]).

We propose a new approach to domain construction trying to base all constructive steps on finite sets. For the first time this approach was elaborated in [Schmidt 85] and presented in [Schmidt Berghammer Zierer 86a]. A full version of this paper with all proofs appeared as the technical report [Schmidt Berghammer Zierer 86b].

The main feature of our approach is considering certain finite subsets (of orderings) consisting only of compact elements. We call these finite subsets *sprouts*, because they are at the very beginning of our constructive approach to domain theory. All domains of practical interest (i.e., all domains that can be constructively generated) grow out of these finite sets. Given any sprout, every element of the domain can be uniquely approximated by an element of the sprout. Moving to a larger sprout improves the approximation. This leads to the definition of a domain as a pair consisting of an ordered set and a directed system of sprouts such that the least upper bound of all the approximations of an element from these sprouts and the element itself coincide. It turns out that this definition of a domain is closed w.r.t. the common generic constructions and w.r.t. the construction of an inverse limit.

Starting with so-called *explicit domains*, which are basically unordered finite sets, we define further domains step by step using generic means. The construction principles are described in a language of *domain expressions*. The definition of recursive domains by domain equations is included in this scheme. In particular, every domain turns out to be isomorphic to the inverse limit of the *retraction system* of its *sprout domains*.

The definition of domains by means of sprouts is similar to the *information systems* approach in [Scott 82]. Scott also considers finite subsets (the so-called *consistent sets*). But in contrast to the elements of "Con" sprouts are not necessarily consistent. Moreover, we can use the ordinary ("categorical") product, sum, and function domains with their canonical ordering relations. The connection between information systems and domains is established in [Larsen Winskel 84]. They abandon the *least informative* element (cf. [Scott 82], p.579) in the definition of information systems. We also use ordered sets which do not necessarily have a least element.

The domains defined in this paper exactly correspond to the *profinite domains*, which have been defined in [Gunter 85] with rather different means. In contrast to the descriptive method of Gunter our approach is more constructive and less abstract. In particular, we begin with finite subsets of the carrier set and, thus, obtain an intuitive basis for the description of *deflations* (cf. [Gunter 85]). By means of sprouts it is also easily possible to determine the deflations of a composed domain from the deflations of its components. Moreover, the retraction system of finite cpos which is necessary for profinite domains can be concretely specified as the system of sprouts.

As a new result we are able to give a universal characterization of the inverse limit of a retraction sequence resulting from a functional iteration. It may not be smaller than an arbitrary fixed point of the domain functional which is used in the iteration. However, among all those fixed points which are vertices of "definable" cones it is the least.

2. Sprouts and Domains

We recall some properties of orderings starting with an ordered set $(D, \sqsubseteq)$. A subset $X \subseteq D$ is called **directed,** if every finite subset of X has an upper bound in X. D is **inductively ordered** (or a **cpo**), if every directed subset $X \subseteq D$ has a least upper bound. An element $x \in D$ is called **compact** (sometimes also finite), if for every directed set $X \subseteq D$ with $x \sqsubseteq \sup X$ there is an element $x_0 \in X$ such that $x \sqsubseteq x_0$. Non-compact elements may sometimes be represented as least upper bounds of infinite directed sets. Therefore, they are called **limit points**. An isotone function $f : D \to D'$ between inductive orderings D and D' is **continuous**, if f preserves least upper bounds of directed sets.

Now, we define sprouts as certain finite subsets of inductively ordered sets.

2.1 Definition A subset K of an inductively ordered set $(D, \sqsubseteq)$ is called a **sprout** of D, if

- K is finite,
- every element $a \in K$ is compact,
- for every element $x \in D$ the set $\{a \in K \mid a \sqsubseteq x\}$ has a greatest element. We refer to this uniquely determined greatest element as being the **approximation of x from the sprout** K: $app_K(x) = \sup\{a \in K \mid a \sqsubseteq x\}$.

In the following theorem we give a sufficient condition for the existence of $app_K(x)$ for a certain sprout K and all $x \in D$. This condition is quite similar to the notion "consistently complete" and is more easily verified than Definition 2.1.

2.2 Theorem Let $(D, \sqsubseteq)$ be an inductive ordering and let $M \subseteq D$ be a finite subset fulfilling two conditions:

- If $a, b \in M$ have an upper bound, they have a least upper bound z belonging to M.
- For every $x \in D$ there exists an $a \in M$ such that $a \sqsubseteq x$.

Then for all $x \in D$ the set $\{c \in M \mid c \sqsubseteq x\}$ possesses a greatest element. □

Now we derive properties of the approximation of an element from a sprout.

2.3 Theorem Let $(D, \sqsubseteq)$ be an inductive ordering.

i) If $K \subseteq D$ is a sprout, then $app_K : D \to D$ is a function with the following properties

$app_K(a) = a$ for all $a \in K$,

$app_K(app_K(x)) = app_K(x)$ for all $x \in D$,

$x \sqsubseteq x' \Rightarrow app_K(x) \sqsubseteq app_K(x')$ for all $x, x' \in D$.

ii) If $K, L \subseteq D$ are sprouts such that $K \subseteq L$, then for every $x \in D$

$app_K(x) \sqsubseteq app_L(x)$,

$app_K(app_L(x)) = app_K(x)$,

$x \in K \Rightarrow app_K(x) = app_L(x)$.

iii) If $K, L \subseteq D$ are arbitrary sprouts, then $K \cap L$ is also a sprout. Furthermore,

$app_{K \cap L}(x) \sqsubseteq app_K(app_L(x))$.

Proof: i) The proof of $app_K(a) = a$ for all $a \in K$ is trivial, since $a \in \{x \in K \mid x \sqsubseteq a\}$. As $app_K(x) \in K$ we immediately obtain $app_K(app_K(x)) = app_K(x)$, i.e., the idempotency of app_K. The implication follows from the set inclusion $\{a \in K \mid a \sqsubseteq x\} \subseteq \{a \in K \mid a \sqsubseteq x'\}$ since the least upper bound operator sup is isotone w.r.t. set inclusion.
ii) The first property again holds, because the operator sup is isotone and $\{a \in K \mid a \sqsubseteq x\} \subseteq \{a \in L \mid a \sqsubseteq x\}$. From $app_L(x) \sqsubseteq x$ we obtain $app_K(app_L(x)) \sqsubseteq app_K(x)$, since app_K is isotone. This together with the properties proved so far implies $app_K(x) = app_K(app_K(x)) \sqsubseteq app_K(app_L(x))$. Thus, $app_K(x) = app_K(app_L(x))$. Finally, the third property follows from the first equation in i), because $x \in K$ and $x \in L$: $app_K(x) = x = app_L(x)$.
iii) If K and L are sprouts, then $K \cap L$ is also a finite set of compact elements. Now assume $x \in D$. Then the chain $a_1 \sqsupseteq a_2 \sqsupseteq \cdots$, where $a_1 = app_K(x)$ and for $i \geq 1$

$$a_{2i} = app_L(a_{2i-1}) \in L \qquad a_{2i+1} = app_K(a_{2i}) \in K,$$

has a least element $a_n \in K \cap L$, because K and L are finite. The resulting a_n is the greatest element of $\{a \in K \cap L \mid a \sqsubseteq x\}$: If $b \in K \cap L$ such that $b \sqsubseteq x$, then $b \sqsubseteq a_1$ and from monotonicity and idempotency of app_K and app_L we get $b \sqsubseteq a_i$ for every $i \geq 1$. Hence, $b \sqsubseteq a_n$. The rest of the proof is trivial. We use $K \cap L \subseteq K$, $K \cap L \subseteq L$, and ii):

$$app_{K \cap L}(x) = app_{K \cap L}(app_L(x)) \sqsubseteq app_K(app_L(x)).$$ □

2.4 Theorem Let an inductive ordering $(D, \sqsubseteq)$ and a sprout $K \subseteq D$ be given. If $\nu : K \to W$ is an isotone (and therefore continuous) function from K into an inductive ordering $(W, \sqsubseteq)$, then this function can be extended to a *continuous* function $\lambda : D \to W$ by $\lambda = app_K\, \nu$, i.e., by $\lambda(x) = \nu(app_K(x))$ for all $x \in D$.

Proof: Composition of isotone functions results in an isotone function. In order to show continuity of λ, we consider a directed set X. Clearly, $\sup \lambda(X) \sqsubseteq \lambda(\sup X)$, as λ is isotone. Define $a = app_K(\sup X)$. As a is compact and $a \sqsubseteq \sup X$, there exists $x_0 \in X$ such that $a \sqsubseteq x_0$, i.e., $\lambda(\sup X) = \nu(a) = \nu(app_K(a)) = \lambda(a) \sqsubseteq \lambda(x_0) \sqsubseteq \sup \lambda(X)$ as $app_K(a) = a$ and λ is isotone. Altogether, $\sup \lambda(X) = \lambda(\sup X)$. □

In particular, for every sprout $K \subseteq D$ the function $app_K : D \to D$ is continuous, because it is the extension of the embedding function $emb_K : K \to D$, $emb_K(a) = a$, which certainly is isotone. As $app_K(x) \sqsubseteq x$ and app_K is idempotent, app_K is a finite "deflation" [Gunter 85].

In general, the union of sprouts is not a sprout. Later on, we will approximate elements by their approximations from sprouts belonging to a directed set of sprouts and, thus, the following definition will prove useful.

2.5 Definition A **directed system of sprouts** in the inductive ordering $(D, \sqsubseteq)$ is a set $\mathcal{K}$ of sprouts of D directed w.r.t. set inclusion.

There is an interesting correlation between the two kinds of directed sets involved here.

2.6 Theorem If $\mathcal{K}$ is a directed system of sprouts in $(D, \sqsubseteq)$ and $x \in D$ an arbitrary element, then $\{app_K(x) \mid K \in \mathcal{K}\} \subseteq D$ is a *directed* set*).

Proof: Assume M to be a finite subset of $\{app_K(x) \mid K \in \mathcal{K}\}$. Then M may be written as $M = \{app_{K_i}(x) \mid K_i \in \mathcal{K}, 1 \leq i \leq n\}$. As $\mathcal{K}$ is directed, there exists an upper bound $\bar{K} \in \mathcal{K}$ such that $K_i \subseteq \bar{K}$, $1 \leq i \leq n$. From Theorem 2.3 ii) we derive $app_{K_i}(x) \sqsubseteq app_{\bar{K}}(x)$. Therefore, $app_{\bar{K}}(x)$ is an upper bound of M and is contained in the set $\{app_K(x) \mid K \in \mathcal{K}\}$. □

Due to Theorem 2.6 the least upper bound of all approximations of an element from the sprouts K of a directed system $\mathcal{K}$ of sprouts exists. Now we define domains by requiring that this least upper bound coincides with the original element.

2.7 Definition A **domain** is a triple $(D, \sqsubseteq, \mathcal{K})$ such that

- $(D, \sqsubseteq)$ is an inductive ordering,
- $\mathcal{K}$ is a directed system of sprouts in $(D, \sqsubseteq)$,
- for all $x \in D$ the equation $x = \sup\{app_K(x) \mid K \in \mathcal{K}\}$ holds.

In a domain, every element can be approximated by the compact elements of the sprouts. On the other hand, for every compact element there is a sprout which contains this element. This is an immediate consequence of the approximation equation $x = \sup\{app_K(x) \mid K \in \mathcal{K}\}$: From $x \sqsubseteq \sup\{app_K(x) \mid K \in \mathcal{K}\}$ we get $x \sqsubseteq app_{K_0}(x)$ where $K_0 \in \mathcal{K}$. However, $app_{K_0}(x) \sqsubseteq x$ and, thus, $x = app_{K_0}(x) \in K_0$.

Frequently, we will consider domains which are constructed in a specific way. For these **constructively generated domains** more properties hold than for arbitrary domains. The additional properties are then proved by induction on the construction. Confer Chapter 4 for more details.

Now we are going to define homomorphisms, i.e., functions preserving the structure of domains.

2.8 Definition Let two domains $(A, \sqsubseteq, \mathcal{K})$ and $(B, \sqsubseteq, \mathcal{L})$ and a function $\phi : A \to B$ be given. ϕ is called **sprout-faithful**, if for all sprouts $K \in \mathcal{K}$ there exists a sprout $L \in \mathcal{L}$ such that $\phi(K) \subseteq L$. ϕ is a **domain homomorphism**, if ϕ is continuous and sprout-faithful. A bijective domain homomorphism ϕ is called a **domain isomorphism**, if ϕ^{-1} is a domain homomorphism as well.

If we have finite domains which are trivially ordered, then every function between these domains is continuous and sprout-faithful. However, as soon as we consider domains with non-trivial ordering relations these conditions are rather incisive. E.g. a limit point cannot be assigned to a compact element by a sprout-faithful function. Note that $\phi(K)$ is contained in a sprout but need not necessarily be a sprout itself, nor need it be contained as an element in $\mathcal{L}$.

2.9 Theorem If $\phi : A \to B$ is a domain homomorphism and K, L are sprouts such that $\phi(K) \subseteq L$, then for all $x \in A$ the estimation $\phi(app_K(x)) \sqsubseteq app_L(\phi(x))$ holds.

Proof: Since $app_K(x) \sqsubseteq x$ and ϕ is isotone, we obtain $\phi(app_K(x)) \sqsubseteq \phi(x)$. app_L being isotone yields $app_L(\phi(app_K(x))) \sqsubseteq app_L(\phi(x))$. However, $\phi(app_K(x)) \in L$, since $\phi(K) \subseteq L$. Thus, $app_L(\phi(app_K(x))) = \phi(app_K(x))$ (cf. Theorem 2.3 i)). □

---

*) Having introduced the ordering relation on function domains in 3.5, it is easy to see that the subset $\{app_K \mid K \in \mathcal{K}\}$ of the domain of continuous functions from D to D is directed, too.

3. Construction of Domains

To interpret constructs occuring in programming languages, we need certain semantic domains. Starting from "primitive" domains, more complicated domains are constructed step by step. In this paper we admit the following constructions:

- Natural extension of a domain (to describe partial functions and non-strictness)
- Direct product and direct sum (co-product) of domains (to describe tuples, functions with more than one argument, conditionals etc.)
- Domain of (total, continuous) functions between two domains (to deal with recursion, declarations, variables etc.)
- Inverse limit of domains (to describe recursive data structures like lists, trees etc.)

Further constructive steps are conceivable, but not considered in this paper:

- Powerdomain of a domain (to describe nondeterminism)
- Restriction of a domain by a predicate (to describe subsorts)
- Quotient domain modulo a congruence relation (for data types, which are not freely generated, e.g. sets)
- Parallel composition of two domains (to describe parallel and concurrent programs)

We lay a safe foundation for these constructions by starting with finite sets, where we do not admit different degrees of information about an object, i.e., we have unordered (or trivially ordered) finite sets. The system of sprouts becomes trivial consisting of just one sprout made up of the entire set.

3.1 Explicit domains The carrier set of an **explicit domain** is a finite set A. Explicitly writing down all the representations of these elements is an integral constituent of the definition of an explicit domain.
We consider the identical relation as the ordering relation $\sqsubseteq$ on A.
The directed system of subsets is given by $\mathcal{K} = \{A\}$.

3.2 Natural extension of a domain If a domain $D = (A, \sqsubseteq, \mathcal{K})$ is given, we define the carrier set A^+ of the **natural extension** D^+ of D to be the set of all partially defined functions from $\{1\}$ to A. There are two kinds of such functions: First, one function f such that $f(1)$ is undefined. This function is represented as $\perp$. Then, the functions g with defined values $g(1)$, which can be represented by means of this value.
As ordering relation $\sqsubseteq$ on A^+ we choose

$$f \sqsubseteq g \ :\Leftrightarrow \ \begin{cases} f(1) \sqsubseteq g(1) & : \ f(1) \text{ and } g(1) \text{ are both defined} \\ f = \perp & : \ \text{otherwise.} \end{cases}$$

Obviously, $(A^+, \sqsubseteq)$ is an ordering and the undefined function $\perp$ is its least element.
The system of subsets $\mathcal{K}^+$ is defined by $\mathcal{K}^+ = \{K^+ \mid K \in \mathcal{K}\} \cup \{\{\perp\}\}$, where the set $K^+ = \{\perp\} \cup \{f \in A^+ \mid f(1) \in K\}$ is called the natural extension of the sprout K.

3.3 Direct product of domains If domains $D_1 = (A, \sqsubseteq, \mathcal{K})$ and $D_2 = (B, \sqsubseteq, \mathcal{L})$ are given, we define their **product domain** $D_1 \otimes D_2$ as follows:
The carrier set is the direct product $A{\times}B$ of the sets A and B. In addition, we have the two projections $\pi : A{\times}B \to A$ and $\rho : A{\times}B \to B$.
As ordering relation $\sqsubseteq$ on $A{\times}B$ we choose the product ordering established by $p \sqsubseteq q \ :\Leftrightarrow \ \pi(p) \sqsubseteq \pi(q)$ and $\rho(p) \sqsubseteq \rho(q)$.
The system of subsets $\mathcal{K}{\times}\mathcal{L}$ is defined by $\mathcal{K}{\times}\mathcal{L} = \{K{\times}L \mid K \in \mathcal{K}, L \in \mathcal{L}\}$.

3.4 Direct sum of domains If domains $D_1 = (A, \sqsubseteq, \mathcal{K})$ and $D_2 = (B, \sqsubseteq, \mathcal{L})$ are given, we define their **sum domain** $D_1 \oplus D_2$ as follows:
The carrier set is the direct sum $A{+}B$ of the sets A and B. In addition, we have the injective functions $\iota : A \to A{+}B$ and $\kappa : B \to A{+}B$.
As ordering relation $\sqsubseteq$ on $A{+}B$ we choose the sum ordering established by

$$c \sqsubseteq d \;:\Leftrightarrow\; \begin{cases} \exists\, a, a' : c = \iota(a) \text{ and } d = \iota(a') \text{ and } a \sqsubseteq a' & \textbf{or} \\ \exists\, b, b' : c = \kappa(b) \text{ and } d = \kappa(b') \text{ and } b \sqsubseteq b'. \end{cases}$$

This means that there is no (ordering) relation between elements of $\iota(A)$ and $\kappa(B)$. These two different parts are ordered exactly like A and B, respectively.
The system of subsets $\mathcal{K}+\mathcal{L}$ is defined by $\mathcal{K}+\mathcal{L} = \{\iota(K) \cup \kappa(L) \mid K \in \mathcal{K},\, L \in \mathcal{L}\}$.

3.5 Function domains If domains $D_1 = (A, \sqsubseteq, \mathcal{K})$ and $D_2 = (B, \sqsubseteq, \mathcal{L})$ are given, we define their **function domain** $D_1 \Rightarrow D_2$ as follows:
The carrier set is the set $[A \to B] = \{f \mid f \text{ continuous}\} \subseteq B^A$.
As ordering relation $\sqsubseteq$ on the domain of continuous functions we choose the function ordering established by $f \sqsubseteq g \;:\Leftrightarrow$ for all $x \in A \;:\; f(x) \sqsubseteq g(x)$.
The system of subsets $\mathcal{K} \vdash\!\!- \mathcal{L}$ is defined by

$$\mathcal{K} \vdash\!\!- \mathcal{L} = \{K \vdash\!\!- L \mid K \in \mathcal{K},\, L \in \mathcal{L}\} \text{ where } K \vdash\!\!- L = \{app_K f \mid f : K \to L \subseteq B \text{ isotone}\}.$$

In addition it is possible to define domains as limits. For that purpose the mathematical standard construction of an inverse limit is needed. Now, to describe the connections between domains we need not only domain homomorphisms but pairs of domain homomorphisms which interact in a special way. This leads to the following

3.6 Definition. Let two domains $D_1 = (A, \sqsubseteq, K)$ and $D_2 = (B, \sqsubseteq, \mathcal{L})$, a domain homomorphism $\phi : B \to A$, and an isotone function $\psi : A \to B$ be given. Then ϕ, ψ is called an **adjoint pair** of domain homomorphisms from D_2 to D_1, if the following conditions are fulfilled:

- $\phi(\psi(a)) = a$ for all $a \in A$
- $\psi(\phi(b)) \sqsubseteq b$ for all $b \in B$

ϕ is also called **upper adjoint** or **projection** and ψ **lower adjoint** or **embedding**. In [Gunter 85] more properties of adjoint pairs can be found, in particular connections with "deflations".

It is somewhat astonishing that the lower adjoint ψ is postulated only to be isotone. However, ψ is a domain homomorphism as well.

3.7 Theorem If ϕ, ψ is an adjoint pair from D_2 to D_1, then ψ is continuous and sprout-faithful.

Proof: In [Gunter 85], p. 36, it is proved that an isotone lower adjoint is always continuous and sends compact elements to compact elements. Thus, $\psi(x)$ is contained in a sprout L_x and $\psi(K)$ in $\bar{L}$ where $\bar{L}$ is an upper bound of the finite set $\{L_x \mid x \in K\}$ of sprouts. This shows that ψ is sprout-faithful. □

In the preceding proof we have also shown that a function ϕ which sends compact elements to compact elements is sprout-faithful. The converse of this statement is also true: If ϕ is sprout-faithful and x is compact, then x is contained in some sprout K. Hence, $\phi(x)$ is contained in a sprout L enclosing $\phi(K)$, i.e. $\phi(x)$ is also compact.

As a further consequence of Theorem 3.7 we get that two continuous functions which are inverse to each other (i.e. they are bijective), are both sprout-faithful and, thus, domain isomorphisms.

In the case of inductive orderings, directed subsets and their least upper bounds are considered. Analogously, in the class of domains directed families of domains are used to obtain limits. The relationships between two members of a family are determined by adjoint pairs.

3.8 Definition Let I be a directed index set. A family of domains $(D_i)_{i \in I} = (A_i, \sqsubseteq, \mathcal{K}_i)_{i \in I}$ is called a **directed retraction system** (or **inverse system**) of domains, if $j \leq k$ always implies the existence of an adjoint pair $\phi_j^k : A_k \to A_j$, $\psi_j^k : A_j \to A_k$ of domain homomorphisms with the following properties:

- $\phi_i^i = \psi_i^i = id_{A_i}$ (identity on A_i)
- $j \leq k \leq l$ implies $\phi_j^l = \phi_k^l \phi_j^k$ and $\psi_j^l = \psi_j^k \psi_k^l$

As the limit of a directed retraction system we define the inverse limit domain.

3.9 Inverse limit domain If $(D_i)_{i\in I} = (A_i, \sqsubseteq, K_i)_{i\in I}$ is a directed retraction system, we define the **inverse limit domain** $D^\infty = \textbf{lim}\ D_i = (A^\infty, \sqsubseteq, K^\infty)$ as follows:

The carrier set A^∞ is the set of the families $(s_i)_{i\in I}$ with $s_i \in A_i$ such that for all $j \leq k$: $\phi_j^k(s_k) = s_j$.

The ordering relation $\sqsubseteq$ on A^∞ is given by a component-wise definition:

$$(s_i)_{i\in I} \sqsubseteq (s'_i)_{i\in I} \;:\Leftrightarrow\; \forall i \in I : s_i \sqsubseteq s'_i$$

The system of subsets K^∞ originates from "throwing together" all sprouts of the single domains that are comparable by the embeddings ψ_i^k, $i \leq k$:

$$K^\infty = \{K_{i,K} \mid i\in I,\ K \in K_i\} \text{ where } K_{i,K} = \{(s_m)_{m\in I} \in A^\infty \mid s_i \in K,\ k \geq i \text{ implies } s_k = \psi_i^k(s_i)\}$$

Up to now only the definitions of naturally extended domains, product, sum, function, and limit domains have been given. In the following theorem we convince ourselves that we have really introduced domains.

3.10 Theorem: The triples we have defined in 3.1 through 3.5 and in 3.9 are domains according to Definition 2.7.

Proof: Clearly, all carrier-sets form cpos. It remains to show that

- every element of the system of subsets is a sprout
- the system is directed w.r.t. set inclusion and
- the approximation-equation $\sup\{app_K(x) \mid K \in K\} = x$ is fulfilled.

The details of the proof can be found in [Schmidt Berghammer Zierer 86b]. □

The class of domains together with the domain homomorphisms constitutes a category. Using categorical terminology the construction of product, sum, and function domain are the product, co-product, and exponentiation functors. As the category of domains has the initial object $\mathbf{0} = (\emptyset, \emptyset, \{\emptyset\})$ and the terminal object $\mathbf{1} = (\{\bot\}, =, \{\{\bot\}\})$, it is **bicartesian**.

For the natural extension of a domain and for product, sum, function, and inverse limit domains the following properties hold:

- $app_{K^+}(\bot) = \bot$ and for all $f \neq \bot$, $f \in A^+$: $app_{K^+}(f) = f\ app_K$
- The natural projections $\pi : A\times B \to A$ and $\rho : A\times B \to B$ are domain homomorphisms. Furthermore, the approximation functions are related in the following way:
  $app_{K\times L}(x, y) = (app_K(x), app_L(y))$
- The natural injections $\iota : A \to A+B$ and $\kappa : B \to A+B$ are domain homomorphisms. Furthermore, the approximation functions are related in the following way:
  $app_{K+L}(\iota(x)) = \iota(app_K(x))$ $\quad$ $app_{K+L}(\kappa(x)) = \kappa(app_L(x))$
- The approximation of a continuous function f from a sprout $K \vdash L$ is given by $app_{K\vdash L}(f) = app_K\ f\ app_L$.
  An element f of a function domain is compact, precisely when it fulfills $f = app_K\, f\, app_L$ for some sprouts K and L, i.e. all values of the function range over a finite set of compact elements and there is a sprout K such that $f = app_K\, f$.
- The approximation of an element $s = (s_i)_{i\in I}$ of the inverse limit domain $(A^\infty, \sqsubseteq, K^\infty)$ from a sprout $K_{i,K} \in K^\infty$ is given for each component by
  $(app_{K_{i,K}}(s))_i = app_K(s_i)$
  $(app_{K_{i,K}}(s))_j = \phi_j^k(\psi_i^k(app_K(s_i)))$ $\quad$ ($k\in I$ an upper bound of $i,j\in I$)
  Note that the first equation is only a special case of the second, more general one.

New domains may not only be obtained by the previously mentioned constructions. Also restricting a domain to a sprout of its directed system of sprouts yields a new (finite, but nontrivially ordered) domain. Together with the new domain we obtain an adjoint pair by which the sprout is embedded into the original domain.

3.11 Definition and Theorem If. $(A, \sqsubseteq, \mathcal{K})$ is a domain, $K \in \mathcal{K}$ and $\mathcal{K}_K = \{L \in \mathcal{K} \mid L \subseteq K\}$, then $(K, \sqsubseteq, \mathcal{K}_K)$ is also a domain (a so-called **sprout domain**), and the injective function $emb_K : K \to A$, $emb_K(a) = a$ together with the approximation $app_K : A \to K$ constitutes an adjoint pair of domain homomorphisms from $(A, \sqsubseteq, \mathcal{K})$ to $(K, \sqsubseteq, \mathcal{K}_K)$.

Proof: Every $L \in \mathcal{K}_K$ is a sprout and contained in $K \in \mathcal{K}_K$. Thus, $\mathcal{K}_K$ is directed w.r.t. set inclusion and for every $a \in K$ we get the approximation-equation

$$\sup\{app_L(a) \mid L \in \mathcal{K}_K\} = app_K(a) = a,$$

i.e., $(K, \sqsubseteq, \mathcal{K}_K)$ is a domain. The rest of the proof follows from Theorem 2.4 (continuity of app_K) and Theorem 2.3. □

As the system of sprouts of a domain is *directed*, we can find a directed retraction system for every domain $(A, \sqsubseteq, \mathcal{K})$. We choose $\mathcal{K}$ as an index set and consider the family $(K, \sqsubseteq, \mathcal{K}_K)_{K \in \mathcal{K}}$. The projections ϕ are the approximations from the smaller sprout, the embeddings ψ are the injections into the enclosing sprout. The remaining conditions for a directed retraction system are fulfilled as well (cf. Theorem 2.3).

3.12 Theorem Let $(A, \sqsubseteq, \mathcal{K})$ be a domain. The inverse limit domain of the directed retraction system $(K, \sqsubseteq, \mathcal{K}_K)_{K \in \mathcal{K}}$ of sprout domains is isomorphic to $(A, \sqsubseteq, \mathcal{K})$.

Proof: The inverse limit domain of the domains $(K, \sqsubseteq, \mathcal{K}_K)_{K \in \mathcal{K}}$ is given by the carrier set

$$K^\infty = \{(s_K)_{K \in \mathcal{K}} \mid s_K \in K \text{ and } \forall L, M \in \mathcal{K} : L \subseteq M \text{ implies } s_L = app_L(s_M)\},$$

the component-wise ordering on it, and the directed set

$$\mathcal{K}^\infty = \{K_{K,L} \mid K \in \mathcal{K}, L \in \mathcal{K}_K\} = \{K_{K,L} \mid K, L \in \mathcal{K}, L \subseteq K\}$$

where $K_{K,L} = \{(s_N)_{N \in \mathcal{K}} \in K^\infty \mid s_K \in L$ and $s_M = s_K$ for every $K \subseteq M \in \mathcal{K}\}$.

Now, we define the functions

$$\Phi : A \to K^\infty, \qquad \Phi(x) = (app_K(x))_{K \in \mathcal{K}}$$

$$\Psi : K^\infty \to A, \qquad \Psi((x_K)_{K \in \mathcal{K}}) = \sup\{x_K \mid K \in \mathcal{K}\}.$$

In [Schmidt Berghammer Zierer 86b] we prove that Φ and Ψ are continuous and inverse to each other (and thus also bijective and sprout-faithful). □

In [Gunter 85] a "profinite domain" is defined as a cpo which is isomorphic to the limit of a retraction system of finite cpos in the category of cpos with continuous projections as morphisms. As a result of Theorem 3.12 every domain is profinite, because the sprouts (i.e., the carrier sets of the sprout domains) are finite cpos. An equivalent and less abstract description of the profinite domains is given in Theorem 3.2.1 of [Gunter 85]: A cpo is a profinite domain if and only if there exists a directed set of finite deflations (i.e., continuous, idempotent, and contracting functions with finite range) such that the least upper bound of this set is the identity function. This characterization immediately shows that our domains *exactly* correspond to profinite domains.

3.13 Theorem

i) If $(D, \sqsubseteq, \mathcal{K})$ is a domain, then $M = \{app_K \mid K \in \mathcal{K}\}$ is a directed set of finite deflations such that $\sup M = id$. Thus, $(D, \sqsubseteq)$ is a profinite domain.

ii) If $(D, \sqsubseteq)$ is a profinite domain and M a directed set of finite deflations such that $\sup M = id$, then $(D, \sqsubseteq, \{f(D) \mid f \in M\})$ is a domain according to Definition 2.7. In particular, $f(D)$ is a sprout, and the equation $app_{f(D)} = f$ holds.

Proof: i) is trivial.
ii) First we show that $f(D)$ is a sprout. By assumption $f(D)$ is finite. If $a \in f(D)$, then $f(a) = a$ as f is idempotent. Therefore, given a directed set X with $a \sqsubseteq \sup X$ we get $a = f(a) \sqsubseteq f(\sup X) = \sup f(X) = f(x_0) \sqsubseteq x_0 \in X$, as the finite directed set $f(X)$ possesses a greatest element $f(x_0)$. This shows that every element of $f(D)$ is compact. Finally, if $x \in D$ then $f(x)$ is the greatest element of $\{a \in f(D) \mid a \sqsubseteq x\}$.
Assume $f_1, \ldots, f_n \in M$. As M is directed, there exists $\bar{f} \in M$ such that $f_i \sqsubseteq \bar{f}$ $(1 \leq i \leq n)$. Since f_i is idempotent and $\bar{f}$ is contracting, we get $a = f_i(a) \sqsubseteq \bar{f}(a) \sqsubseteq a$ for every $a \in f_i(D)$. Hence, $a = \bar{f}(a)$, i.e., $a \in \bar{f}(D)$ and $\bar{f}(D)$ is an upper bound of $f_i(D)$ w.r.t. set inclusion.
The approximation-equation follows immediately from $\sup M = id$. □

4. Constructively Generated Domains

The domains defined in Chapter 3 make up a rather big category — bigger than necessary for describing the semantics of programming languages. For this purpose domains should be constructed in a finite number of steps starting with "primitive" domains. We design a language of domain expressions to describe this restricted class of domains.

4.1 Definition Let a set E of symbols for explicit domains and a set V of domain variables be given. The set A of **domain expressions** over E and V is inductively defined by:

- $E \subseteq A$
- $V \subseteq A$
- For all $t \in A$: $t^+ \in A$
- For all $t_1, t_2 \in A$: $(t_1 \times t_2)$, $(t_1 + t_2)$ and $(t_1 \rightarrow t_2) \in A$
- For all $X \in V$ and $t \in A$: $(\mathbf{rec}\ X.t^+) \in A$, if at most X occurs freely in t^+, i.e., all other variables $Y \in V$ occuring in t^+ are already bound by **rec**.

Now we want to give an interpretation for **closed domain expressions** (i.e., domain expressions, in which every variable is bound by **rec**) such that a domain (according to Definition 2.7) may be assigned to every $t \in A$. We start the construction attaching an explicit domain D_e to each symbol $e \in E$ as its interpretation.

A domain is called **constructively generated**, if a closed domain expression exists such that the domain is the interpretation of this expression. As recursively defined domains are admitted, we will also give an interpretation for domain expressions which are not closed. An arbitrary domain expression t is interpreted as a **domain functional** τ_t, which maps a domain D into the domain $\tau_t[D]$.*) τ_t is determined inductively by defining for a domain D:

- $\tau_X[D] = D$ for $X \in V$

and by treating all the other cases according to the Definitions 3.1 through 3.5:

- $\tau_e[D] = D_e$
- $\tau_{t_1^+}[D] = (\tau_{t_1}[D])^+$
- $\tau_{t_1 \times t_2}[D] = \tau_{t_1}[D] \otimes \tau_{t_2}[D]$
- $\tau_{t_1 + t_2}[D] = \tau_{t_1}[D] \oplus \tau_{t_2}[D]$
- $\tau_{t_1 \rightarrow t_2}[D] = \tau_{t_1}[D] \Rightarrow \tau_{t_2}[D]$

Additionally, the case $t = \mathbf{rec}\ Y.t_1^+$ will be considered. The usual technique is to define the interpretation of $t = \mathbf{rec}\ Y.t_1^+$ as a fixed point of the domain functional $\tau_{t_1^+}$. To ensure the existence of a fixed point, we state in the following Theorem 4.4 that a domain functional τ_t is

*) In the expression $\mathbf{rec}\ X.t^+$ at most X occurs free. Therefore, it is sufficient to consider unary domain functionals. Systems of recursive domain equations can be treated analogously (cf. [Smyth Plotkin 82]), if domain functionals mapping tuples of domains into tuples of domains are used.

isotone and continuous w.r.t. the quasi ordering on domains (or ordering on the equivalence classes) defined by

$$D_1 \lesssim D_2 \ :\Leftrightarrow \ \text{there is an adjoint pair of domain homomorphisms from } D_2 \text{ to } D_1.$$

For technical reasons we need a property for adjoint pairs stronger than sprout-faithfulness.

4.2 Definition An adjoint pair $\phi : B \to A$, $\psi : A \to B$ of domain homomorphisms **commutes with the approximations** if for every sprout $L \in \mathcal{L}$ there exists a sprout $K \in \mathcal{K}$ such that $\phi(L) \subseteq K$ and $\psi\, app_L = app_K\, \psi$.

In this definition, it is assumed that $\mathcal{K}$ and $\mathcal{L}$ are the systems of sprouts in A and B, respectively. The justification of the wording "commutes with the approximations" is given by the following

4.3 Lemma. Let $\phi : B \to A$, $\psi : A \to B$ be an adjoint pair commuting with the approximations. If $L \in \mathcal{L}$ is an arbitrary sprout and $K \in \mathcal{K}$ a sprout such that $\phi(L) \subseteq K$ and $\psi\, app_L = app_K\, \psi$, then the equation $\phi\, app_K = app_L\, \phi$ holds, too.

Proof: Since $\phi(L) \subseteq K$, we obtain $app_L\, \phi = app_L\, \phi\, app_K$. Hence,

$$\phi\, app_K = \phi\, app_K\, \psi\, \phi = \phi\, \psi\, app_L\, \phi \sqsubseteq app_L\, \phi = app_L\, \phi\, app_K \sqsubseteq \phi\, app_K.$$ □

Now we can prove that a domain functional τ_t is continuous if the adjoint pairs of the directed retraction system under consideration commute with the approximations.

4.4 Theorem

i) Let $D_1 = (A, \sqsubseteq, \mathcal{K})$ and $D_2 = (B, \sqsubseteq, \mathcal{L})$ be domains and let τ_t be a domain functional such that $\tau_t[D_2] = (\bar{B}, \sqsubseteq, \bar{\mathcal{L}})$ and $\tau_t[D_1] = (\bar{A}, \sqsubseteq, \bar{\mathcal{K}})$. Then every adjoint pair of domain homomorphisms

$$\phi : B \to A, \qquad \psi : A \to B$$

commuting with the approximations induces an adjoint pair

$$\Phi : \bar{B} \to \bar{A}, \qquad \Psi : \bar{A} \to \bar{B}$$

of domain homomorphisms from $\tau_t[D_2]$ to $\tau_t[D_1]$ which also commutes with the approximations.

ii) Let $(D_i)_{i \in I}$ be a directed retraction system such that every adjoint pair commutes with the approximations and let τ_t be a domain functional. Then $\tau_t[\mathbf{lim}\ D_i]$ and $\mathbf{lim}\ \tau_t[D_i]$ are isomorphic.

Proof: The proofs are performed by induction on the structure of t (see [Schmidt Berghammer Zierer 86b]). □

The fixed point theorem for categories (applied to the category of domains) states that given a continuous domain functional τ and a domain D_0 which is expanded by τ (i.e., $D_0 \lesssim \tau[D_0]$) there exists a domain D such that $D_0 \lesssim D$ and $\tau[D]$ and D are isomorphic. This domain D is obtained as the inverse limit domain $\mathbf{lim}\ \tau^i[D_0]$. We begin the iteration by choosing the one-element domain $\mathbf{1} = (\{\bot_0\}, =, \{\{\bot_0\}\})$. Now, this domain must be expanded by τ_t (i.e., an adjoint pair from $\tau_t[\mathbf{1}]$ to $\mathbf{1}$ must exist). For that purpose it is necessary that the carrier set of $\tau_t[\mathbf{1}]$ have a least element. We enforce this by admitting domain expressions of the form $\mathbf{rec}\ Y.t_\bot^*$ only. Of course, less restrictive syntactic conditions could also be given.

The adjoint pair of domain homomorphisms from $\tau_{t_\bot^*}[\mathbf{1}]$ to $\mathbf{1}$

$$\phi_0^1 : A_1 \to A_0 \qquad \psi_0^1 : A_0 \to A_1,$$

is defined as follows: ϕ_0^1 maps all elements of the carrier set A_1 of the domain $\tau_{t_\bot^*}[\mathbf{1}]$ onto the element $\bot_0$ (the only element of the carrier set A_0 of $\mathbf{1}$). This element $\bot_0$ is mapped onto the least element $\bot_1$ of A_1 by ψ_0^1. Clearly, the adjoint pair (ϕ_0^1, ψ_0^1) commutes with the approximations. According to Theorem 4.4 i), thus, ϕ_0^1, ψ_0^1 give rise to the retraction sequence $(A_i, \sqsubseteq, K_i) = \tau_{t_i^+}^{i}[\mathbb{1}]$, $i \in \mathbb{N}_0$, where every adjoint pair (ϕ_i^j, ψ_i^j) also commutes with the approximations.

$$\mathbb{1} \;\underset{\phi_0^1}{\overset{\psi_0^1}{\rightleftarrows}}\; \tau_{t_i^+}[\mathbb{1}] \;\underset{\phi_1^2}{\overset{\psi_1^2}{\rightleftarrows}}\; \tau_{t_i^+}^{2}[\mathbb{1}] \;\underset{\phi_2^3}{\overset{\psi_2^3}{\rightleftarrows}}\; \cdots$$

As the domain functional $\tau_{t_i^+}$ is continuous (this follows from Theorem 4.4 ii)) and $\mathbb{1}$ is expanded (by $\tau_{t_i^+}$), we obtain the following

4.5 Theorem. $\mathbf{lim}\ \tau_{t_i^+}^{i}[\mathbb{1}]$ is a fixed point of the domain functional $\tau_{t_i^+}$, i.e.,

$\tau_{t_i^+}[\mathbf{lim}\ \tau_{t_i^+}^{i}[\mathbb{1}]]$ and $\mathbf{lim}\ \tau_{t_i^+}^{i}[\mathbb{1}]$ are isomorphic. □

We choose this fixed point $\mathbf{lim}\ \tau_{t_i^+}^{i}[\mathbb{1}]$ as the interpretation of the domain expression **rec** $Y.t_i^+$. The inverse limit $\mathbf{lim}\ \tau_{t_i^+}^{i}[\mathbb{1}]$ is again a domain because of Theorem 3.10. Thus, we have given an interpretation for all closed domain expressions.

In addition, $\mathbf{lim}\ \tau_{t_i^+}^{i}[\mathbb{1}] = \mathbf{lim}\ (A_i, \sqsubseteq, K_i) = (A^\infty, \sqsubseteq, K^\infty)$ is an upper bound of the sequence $(A_i, \sqsubseteq, K_i)$. We denote the projections by $\phi_i^\infty : A^\infty \to A_i$ and define the corresponding lower adjoints $\psi_i^\infty : A_i \to A^\infty$ component-wise by $(\psi_i^\infty(x))_j = \sup\{\phi_j^m(\psi_i^m(x)) \mid i,j \leq m\}$. In this case we have a linear ordering. Therefore, the definition could be simplified: If $j<i$, then $(\psi_i^\infty(x))_j = \phi_j^i(x)$, otherwise $(\psi_i^\infty(x))_j = \psi_i^j(x)$.

According to the usual procedure we will now investigate to which extent $\mathbf{lim}\ \tau_{t_i^+}^{i}[\mathbb{1}]$ admits a universal characterization as some sort of least fixed point.

We need the notion of a **cone**: If $(B_i, \sqsubseteq, L_i)_{i \in I}$ is an inverse system, then a cone of it is a domain $(B, \sqsubseteq, L)$ together with a family of adjoint pairs $p_i : B \to B_i$, $q_i : B_i \to B$, $i \in I$, such that for $j \geq i$ $p_i = p_j \phi_i^j$ and $q_i = \psi_i^j q_j$. B is called the **vertex** of the cone.

Clearly, $(A^\infty, \sqsubseteq, K^\infty)$ together with the adjoint pairs $(\phi_i^\infty, \psi_i^\infty)$ constitutes a cone of the retraction sequence $(A_i, \sqsubseteq, K_i)_{i \in \mathbb{N}_0}$. We are interested not in cones in general, but only in those which are in a certain sense "definable". After some time, the values $p_i(x)$ should "remain constant" for every compact x.

4.6 Definition Assume the notation introduced above. The cone $(B, \sqsubseteq, L)$ is **sprout-bounded**, if for every $L \in L$ there exists an index $i \in I$ such that $app_L\, p_j = app_L\, p_i \psi_i^j$ for every $j \geq i$.

By the following theorem we are justified in choosing $(A^\infty, \sqsubseteq, K^\infty)$ as the interpretation of the domain expression **rec** $Y.t_i^+$ in as far as it is the least among all the fixed points which are vertices of "definable" cones.

4.7 Theorem

i) $(A^\infty, \sqsubseteq, K^\infty)$ together with the adjoint pairs $(\phi_i^\infty, \psi_i^\infty)$ is a sprout-bounded cone of $(A_i, \sqsubseteq, K_i)_{i \in \mathbb{N}_0}$.

ii) If $(B, \sqsubseteq, L)$ is a sprout-bounded cone of $(A_i, \sqsubseteq, K_i)_{i \in \mathbb{N}_0}$, then there exists an adjoint pair of domain homomorphisms (Φ, Ψ) from B to A^∞ such that for every $i \in \mathbb{N}_0$ the equations $p_i = \Phi \phi_i^\infty$ and $q_i = \psi_i^\infty \Psi$ hold.

Proof: i) follows immediately from the definition of the sprout-system K^∞.
The proof of ii) can be found in [Schmidt Berghammer Zierer 86b]. □

The retraction sequence starting with **1** is of a rather special kind. For example, the following properties hold (using the same symbols as above and $i,j \in \mathbb{N}_0$, $i \leq j$, $K \in K_i$, $L \in K_j$):

- $\phi_i^j(L) \in K_i$ $\qquad\qquad$ $\psi_i^j(K) \in K_j$
- $\psi_i^j(\phi_i^j(K) \subseteq K$
- $app_L \, \phi_i^j = \phi_i^j app_{\phi_i^j(L)}$ $\qquad\qquad$ $app_K \, \psi_i^j = \psi_i^j app_{\psi_i^j(K)}$
- $\phi_i^j app_K = app_{\psi_i^j(K)} \phi_i^j$ $\qquad\qquad$ $\psi_i^j app_L = app_{\phi_i^j(L)} \psi_i^j$

Using these formulas it can be shown that some assertions are valid for the constructively generated domains which are not valid for arbitrary domains in general.

4.8 Theorem Let $(A, \sqsubseteq, K)$ be a constructively generated domain. Then:

i) The system K is closed w.r.t. intersection, i.e., $K, L \in K$ implies $K \cap L \in K$.

ii) $app_{K \cap L} = app_K \, app_L$ for all $K, L \in K$.

Proof: We prove i) and ii) in parallel by induction on the structure of t (cf. [Schmidt Berghammer Zierer 86b]). □

As an immediate consequence of Theorem 4.8 i) and ii) we obtain that the system of sprouts K is closed w.r.t. the approximation of a sprout from a sprout, i.e., $K, L \in K$ implies $app_K(L) = K \cap L \in K$.

Acknowledgement: We gratefully accepted detailed comments of the unknown referees.

References

[Gunter 85]
Gunter C.A.: Profinite Solutions for Recursive Domain Equations. CMU-CS-85-107, Carnegie-Mellon University, Pittsburgh, Pa. (1985)

[Schmidt 85]
Schmidt G.: Semantik der Programmiersprachen. Vorlesungsskriptum, Wintersemester 1985/86

[Schmidt Berghammer Zierer 86a]
Schmidt G., Berghammer R., Zierer H.: Beschreibung semantischer Bereiche mit Keimen. In: Radermacher F.J., Wirsing M. (eds.): Berichte aus den Informatikinstituten, 9. Jahrestagung der österreichischen Gesellschaft für Informatik, 27./28. Februar 1986. Conference Report MIP-8604, Universität Passau (1986), 199-216

[Schmidt Berghammer Zierer 86b]
Schmidt G., Berghammer R., Zierer H.: Describing Semantic Domains with Sprouts. Technical Report TUM-I8611, Institut für Informatik, Technische Universität München (1986)

[Scott 82]
Scott D.S.: Domains for Denotational Semantics. In: Nielsen M., Schmidt E.M. (eds.): *9th Int. Coll. on Automata, Languages and Programming*. Lecture Notes in Computer Science **140**, Springer (1982), 577-613

[Smyth 83]
Smyth M.B.: The Largest Cartesian Closed Category of Domains. *Theoretical Computer Science* **27** (1983), 109-119

[Smyth Plotkin 82]
Smyth M.B., Plotkin G.D.: The Category-Theoretic Solution of Recursive Domain Equations. *SIAM Journal on Computing* **11** (1982), 761-783

[Winskel Larsen 84]
Winskel G., Larsen K.G.: Using Information Systems to Solve Recursive Domain Equations Effectively. In: Kahn G., MacQueen D.B., Plotkin G. (eds.): *Semantics of Data Types*. Lecture Notes in Computer Science **173**, Springer (1984), 109-130

Comparing direct and continuation semantics styles for concurrent languages

- Revisiting an old problem from a new viewpoint - *

Egidio Astesiano - Gianna Reggio
Dipartimento di Matematica - Universita' di Genova (Italy)

MOTIVATIONS AND CONTENT

Recently the emphasis on the specification of large concurrent systems has raised much interest in combining operational techniques, like those embodied in CCS and based on a view of processes as labelled transition systems, with algebraic abstract data type techniques (see, e.g. [BW1], [AR2] and [AMRW]). Moreover recent complex languages with concurrent constructs like Ada® pose not only the problem of building large specifications of concurrent systems but also, because of the strict interference between sequential and concurrent features, require new techniques for keeping, as much as possible, a denotational (syntax-directed) style, which is now well understood and accepted. Most of the mentioned problems have been brought to light and confirmed in practice by some early attempts to formalize the semantics of Ada (e.g. by DDC [BO]).
In this context, and motivated by a concrete large project (see*), we have developed in [AR1] a syntax-directed formal method for giving a semantics to concurrent languages with high interference of sequential and concurrent features. Our method is in two steps. First, using a typical denotational style, a homomorphic translation into an intermediate language, making explicit the (possibly hidden) concurrent operators, is performed; second a semantics for the intermediate language is provided by algebraic techniques, formalizing processes as algebraic transition systems and defining a concurrent algebra as a terminal algebra determinated by a set of observational constraints on such transition systems. Hence our approach (called SMoLCS) brings together in a unique framework denotational, algebraic and operational techniques; in particular we emphasize that it allows the combination of an operational concrete viewpoint of concurrency (transition systems) with the possibility of modularity and abstraction (abstract data types), keeping an overall denotational style. The principles and foundations of that approach are presented in [AR1] and [ARW].
When applying our method to practice, we have been stimulated, also because of a cooperation with VDM users, to investigate and compare the use of the two main denotational styles, continuation and direct semantics, developed respectively by the Oxford (see [S], [G]) and the VDM (see [BJ]) groups.
In [AR1] a continuation style has been adopted. Here, with the help of a similar running example, we explain how our approach can be extended to use the direct style and investigate in which sense the two styles are semantically equivalent. Essentially it will be shown that in our framework the two styles are slight variants of a unifying viewpoint, since continuations are processes algebraically defined and direct semantics constructs, like the well known "trap exit mechanism", are just special operators on processes, with the appropriate characterizing semantic axioms.
The plan of the paper is the following. In a first section we recall, for helping the reader, the main features of the two styles for the sequential case. Then in the second we illustrate on a small example language how to handle concurrent features in a direct style; for completeness and for comparing the two styles we report in appendices the semantics of the same language following a continuation style, but we refer to [AR1] for motivations and technical comments. Finally, in the third section we study the relationship of the two styles proving that the two semantics are equivalent in a very deep sense. It is indeed shown that the two semantics of a statement, which are now two processes, are strongly equivalent in the sense of Milner and Park (strong bisimulation). It is important to note that the proof technique is rather general and can be used to deal with languages of any complexity. The proofs are only hinted to here, but have been carried out in full and can be found in a separate report.
The algebraic technical framework is that of partial algebras as developed in [BW2] and used in [ARW]. We assume some familiarity with the concepts of denotational semantics as in [S] and [BJ] and our previous paper [AR1].
It would be interesting to compare our approach to the natural semantics approach of [KCDDH], but we have not enough room for that here.

* Work partly funded and developed in connection with the work of the CRAI - Genoa group (E. Astesiano, A. Giovini, F. Mazzanti, G. Reggio, E. Zucca) for the EEC project "The draft formal definition of ANSI/MIL-STD 1815A Ada"(DDC-CRAI-IEI-Universities of Genoa, Pisa and Lyngby).
Also partly supported by a project MPI(40%).

® Ada is a registered trademark of the U.S. Government, Ada Joint Program Office.

1 CLASSICAL DIRECT AND CONTINUATION SEMANTICS

According to denotational semantics ([S], [G]) the meaning of a statement of a sequential imperative programming language is a transformation of the state (roughly a storage) and the semantic function for statements has functionality:

S: STAT $\to$ (*ENV* $\to$ (*STATE* $\to$ *STATE*));

while the one for expressions has functionality

E: EXP $\to$ (*ENV* $\to$ (*STATE* $\to$ *VAL*)).

For simplicity of notation, we assume that the notation ($D \to D'$) indicates the cpo of continuous functions between the cpo's D and D', whenever it is needed; otherwise it will denote simply the set of functions from D into D'.

In simple cases it is possible to give a nice denotational semantics following a direct style: i.e. where every construct has a straightforward meaning and this is associated directly to the various constructs. Problems arise when defining constructs that change the normal flow of the execution, for example exception mechanisms, subprogram returns, goto's and so on.

To handle them two methods have been developed:

- use of continuations by the Oxford school (Strachey and Wadsworth, see e.g. [S], [G]),
- use of an exit-trap mechanism by the VDM group (Bjørner and Jones [BJ]).

In the Oxford style the semantic function for statements takes another argument, the so called continuation, which represents the meaning of what follows a statement and is a state transformation.

S: STAT $\to$ (*ENV* $\to$ (*CONT* $\to$ *CONT*)),

where *CONT* = (*STATE* $\to$ *STATE*).

Thus the meaning of a statement is given indirectly depending on what follows it.

Now, for example, we can see how to handle exceptions: in the environment a denotation is associated to each exception identifier and exception denotations are just continuations; so we have

$S[\underline{\text{raise}}\ e]\rho\theta = \rho(e)$,

where $\rho(e)$ is the continuation which gives the semantics of what to do when the exception e is raised.

Of course, now we have the problem of associating the proper denotation to each exception; that is done when giving the semantics of a block:

$S[\underline{\text{begin}}\ st\ \underline{\text{when}}\ e_1\ \underline{\text{do}}\ st_1 \ldots \underline{\text{when}}\ e_n\ \underline{\text{do}}\ st_n\ \underline{\text{end}}]\rho\theta = S[st]\rho[S[st_1]\rho\theta/e_1,\ldots,S[st_n]\rho\theta/e_n]\theta$

The VDM style tries instead to keep a direct style changing the meaning of a statement, which clearly cannot be a state transformation anymore. The basic idea is to have

S: STAT $\to$(*ENV* $\to$ *ST-MEANING*)

where *ST-MEANING* = (*STATE* $\to$ (*STATE* $\times$ *FOLLOW*)) and *FOLLOW* = EID $\cup$ {next}.

If $S[st]\rho\sigma = \langle\sigma',f\rangle$, then f indicates the next point in the execution flow after the execution of st; precisely we have f = next when the execution follows the normal flow and f = e when the exception e is raised.

For readability reasons the VDM group has defined some operators on *ST-MEANING* :

- $\underline{\text{exit}}$ e corresponding to $\lambda\sigma. \langle\sigma,e\rangle$;
- st-meaning$_1$; st-meaning$_2$ corresponding to
  $\lambda\sigma.\ \underline{\text{let}}\ \langle\sigma',f\rangle$ = st-meaning$_1(\sigma)$ $\underline{\text{in}}$
  $\underline{\text{if}}$ f = next $\underline{\text{then}}$ st-meaning$_2(\sigma')$ $\underline{\text{else}}$ $\langle\sigma',f\rangle$;
- $\underline{\text{trap}}$ emap $\underline{\text{in}}$ st-meaning, where emap is a map from exceptions into statement meanings, corresponding to
  $\lambda\sigma.\ \underline{\text{let}}\ \langle\sigma',f\rangle$ = st-meaning(σ) $\underline{\text{in}}$
  $\underline{\text{if}}$ f $\in$ dom(emap) $\underline{\text{then}}$ emap(f) σ' $\underline{\text{else}}$ $\langle\sigma',f\rangle$.

Now exceptions can be handled as follows:

$S[\underline{\text{raise}}\ e]\rho = \underline{\text{exit}}\ e$

$S[\underline{\text{begin}}\ st\ \underline{\text{when}}\ e_1\ \underline{\text{do}}\ st_1 \ldots \underline{\text{when}}\ e_n\ \underline{\text{do}}\ st_n\ \underline{\text{end}}]\rho = \underline{\text{trap}}\ [e_1 \to S[st_1]\rho,\ldots,e_n \to S[st_n]\rho]\ \underline{\text{in}}\ S[st]\rho$.

Similarly we can handle the semantics of expressions and declarations, whenever they have side effects. In order to show the basic idea, let us briefly illustrate the case of the expressions.

In the Oxford style also the semantics of expressions is handled by using a class of continuations, precisely the expression continuations, that represent the meaning of what follows an expression; formally they are functions which, given the value of that expression, produce some state transformations (i.e. statement continuations):

ECONT = (*VAL* $\to$ *CONT*).

Consequently the semantic function for expressions has now functionality

E : EXP $\to$ (*ENV* $\to$ (*ECONT* $\to$ *CONT*)).

Following VDM the meaning of an expression is an element of (*STATE* $\to$ (*VAL* $\times$ *STATE*)), and, for readability purposes, some special operators are defined for handling these expression meanings. Let us now recall some of these operators.

Let f $\in$ (*STATE* $\to$ (*STATE* $\times$ *VAL*)), g $\in$ (*VAL* $\to$ (*STATE* $\to$ *STATE*)),

$\underline{\text{def}}$ f; g corresponds to $\lambda\sigma.\ \underline{\text{let}}\ \langle\sigma',v\rangle = f(\sigma)\ \underline{\text{in}}\ (g(v))(\sigma')$;

return v, where $v \in VALUE$, corresponds to $\lambda\sigma. <\sigma,v>$.
In this framework we have

$E: EXP \to (ENV \to (STATE \to (VAL \times STATE)))$.

2 DIRECT SEMANTICS STYLE FOR CONCURRENT LANGUAGES

We introduce briefly our methodology, called SMoLCS, for a "denotational" semantics of concurrent languages. This approach has been presented in [AR1] following a continuation style; here we show that also a direct semantics style can be followed. In order to be concrete, we will consider a simple language EL1, similar to the one used in [AR1], as a running example on which to show our approach and compare the two styles. The syntax and an informal explanation of EL1 are given in subsection 2.0; then in subsections 2.1 and 2.2 we define the semantic domains and functions and the concurrent algebra following a direct semantics style. Moreover we report in the appendices the corresponding semantics of EL1 given following a continuation style; for comments and explanations see [AR1].

2.0 The example language EL1

We give the abstract syntax in the usual BNF style, with referenced comments.

1 PROG ::= **program** BLOCK
2 BLOCK ::= DECS **begin** STAT **when** EID **do** STAT { **when** EID **do** STAT} **end**
3 DECS ::= **var** VID | DECS DECS
4 STAT ::= VID:= EXP | STAT; STAT | BLOCK | **if** EXP **then** STAT **else** STAT |
5 **while** EXP **do** STAT | **raise** EID |
6 **send**(CHID,EXP) | **rec** (CHID,VID) | **create process** BLOCK
7 EXP ::= CONST | EXP BOP EXP | VID.

Identifiers of variables (VID), exceptions (EID), channels (CHID), symbols of constants (CONST) and binary operators (BOP) are not further specified. A program is a block (1); and blocks can be nested (4); moreover we have the usual sequential statements (4,5) and an exception mechanism (2,5). When an exception e is raised in a block, by a raise statement, the block execution is abandoned, and if for some statement st, **when** e **do** st appears in the block, then st is executed, otherwise the exception is propagated outside the block.
The concurrent structure is generated by the creation of processes (6) (which are blocks); and processes can be executed in parallel. The variables declared in a block (2) are shared by the block itself and the processes created within the block. Note that also the program block can be considered a process. Together with shared variables, there is also a provision for handshaking communication via channels (6).

2.1 Semantic domains and functions

Following the paradigm of denotational semantics, semantics is given as a many-sorted homomorphism from (abstract) syntax into a semantic algebra.
The semantic functions, i.e. the functions constituting the homomorphism, are

$P: PROG \to ANSWER$ $\qquad$ $S: STAT \to (ENV \to BH)$
$E: EXP \to (ENV \to VAL\text{-}BH)$ $\qquad$ $D: DECS \to (ENV \to ENV\text{-}BH)$.

The semantic domains above are defined as follows.
We indicate by CALG the concurrent algebra, which will be defined in the following section; if srt is a sort of CALG, then $CALG_{srt}$ indicates the carrier of sort srt in CALG.
From the definition of CALG it will follow that a program has as value an element in $CALG_{state}$ representing the observational semantics of the program, i.e. an equivalence class of programs s.t. two programs are equivalent iff they produce the same observational results. Thus we define

$$ANSWER = CALG_{state}.$$

Using the direct semantics style, the semantic values of statements will be elements of sort behaviour in CALG, i.e. equivalence classes of behaviours, which are syntactic objects representing processes. Indeed, due to the presence of concurrency in EL1, statements are now modelled by processes:

$$BH = CALG_{behaviour}.$$

This definition of the statement values (*BH*) is truly the key of our approach as it will be better understood when explaining the clauses.
The values of expressions and declarations are still behaviours, but particular behaviours; the elements of *VAL-BH* are indeed behaviours representing processes whose activities terminate producing a value, while the elements of *ENV-BH* terminate producing an environment.

$$VAL\text{-}BH = CALG_{val\text{-}behaviour} \qquad ENV\text{-}BH = CALG_{env\text{-}behaviour}$$

VAL = $CALG_{val}$ *ENV* = $CALG_{env}$

In this case the environment is defined as a subalgebra of CALG, because now there are behaviours which terminate producing environments.

The semantic functions and domains for the continuation style are reported in Appendix 1. The semantic functions and domains and also the concurrent algebra related to the definition following the continuation style are distinguished by the subscript $_C$ (e.g. S_C, E_C).

In both styles there is a correspondence between the semantic domains used for sequential languages and those used for concurrent languages: the domain used in the sequential case (*STATE* $\rightarrow$ *STATE*) corresponds to behaviours, while domains having form (*STATE* $\rightarrow$ (*STATE* $\times$ *AB*)) correspond to behaviours which terminate producing elements of *AB*.

Note that using the direct semantics style in our approach we need to define, within the concurrent algebra, also the behaviours which terminate producing values, environments and so on; while using the continuation style it is sufficient to define simple behaviours. This is in complete agreement with what happens in the sequential case.

2.2 Semantic clauses

The definition of the semantic functions is by structural induction on the syntactic structure. It is important to note that we consider statically correct programs; moreover for simplicity we do not make provision for run time error checks, i.e. error messages are just values in the appropriate domains. The full clauses for the direct semantics style are given in fig.1; here we give referenced comments, which should be read in parallel. The clauses in the continuation style are in Appendix 2.

Clause 1 defines the semantics of a program consisting of a block bl as the value in the concurrent algebra CALG of the term $<S[bl]\rho_0,sh_0>$, that is the syntactic representation of a state of a labelled transition system SYST (defined later as an algebraic specification) representing the executions of the EL1 programs. Formally $<S[bl]\rho_0,sh_0>$ will be a term of sort state in a specification STATE, subspecification of SYST; its semantic value, as already said, is an equivalence class corresponding to an observational semantics on SYST (algebra CALG). For ease of notation here and in the following we will simply indicate by t the semantic value t^A of a term t in an algebra A. Note that $S[bl]\rho_0$ defines, inductively, a behaviour; intuitively a behaviour represents a process and formally is a term of sort behaviour in a specification of behaviours BEHAVIOUR, defined as a subspecification of STATE. A state of SYST has two components: the first is a multiset of behaviours while the second represents some information global to all behaviours (the state of the shared store).

In clause 2 ρ is a generic element in *ENV*. The behaviour associated by E to an expression has in some way the possibility of returning a value, while the behaviour operator $\mathbf{def}_{VAL}$... **in**... composes a behaviour producing a value with a behaviour waiting for a value returning another behaviour. The behaviour waiting for a value is defined by the term **λ**v.UPDATE(ρ(x),v) Δ **nil**. This term represents a function from values to behaviours and is a term of sort funct(val,behaviours) in a specification FUNCT(VAL,BEHAVIOUR), where v is a term of sort val-var in the same specification. The sort val-var is a subsort of val, i.e. there exists an injective total operation i: val-var $\rightarrow$ val and we use the syntactic convention that every term i(vvar) is simply written vvar. Without this convention the above term has to be written **λ** v . UPDATE(ρ(x),i(v)) Δ **nil**.

Note the difference between ordinary λ and bold **λ** : while λ is used in the metalanguage for denoting usual functions, **λ** . : val-var × behaviour $\rightarrow$ funct(val,behaviour) is an operation of the specification FUNCT(VAL,BEHAVIOUR) (subspecification of STATE) representing the purely algebraic counterpart of a space of functions (as it was done, more or less, in [BW3], when defining algebraically the semantics of a functional language).

The term UPDATE(ρ(x),v) Δ **nil** represents a behaviour, whose first action is to write v in the location of the shared memory ρ(x), and then becomes **nil** (the null behaviour); the symbol Δ has the same role as the dot in the CCS behaviour α.be. Behaviour actions will always be indicated by strings of capital letters.

Clause 3 significantly looks the same as in the purely sequential case, as clauses 5 and 15.

Note in clause 5 that ; is an operation on behaviours and in clauses 3 and 4 that also **if**...**then**...**else**... is an operation on behaviours and most importantly in clause 4 how fixpoints are handled. The actions of the behaviour **fix λ** bh.... will be defined in the algebraic specification BH-SYST (subspecification of SYST) correspondingly to the usual rewriting rule for the operational semantics of fixpoint operators (see [M1, M2]).

Clauses 6 and 7 explain how exceptions are handled. Thus also the handling of exceptions in our approach is similar to the one in the classical VDM denotational semantics, but now instead of elements of *ST-MEANING* we use processes which are behaviours, i.e. elements of *BH* .

The term $[e_1 \rightarrow S[st_1]\rho',...,e_n \rightarrow S[st_n]\rho']$ represents a map from exception identifiers into *BH* (a term of sort map(eid,behaviour) in a specification MAP(EID,BEHAVIOUR) subspecification of STATE), **trap**...**in**... and **exit**... are operators on behaviours. These operators will be formally defined in the specification BH-SYST.

Clause 13 makes explicit some hidden concurrency related to the evaluation of a variable. The idea behind the definition of the behaviour $\underset{VAL}{+}$ **λ** v . READ(r(x),v) Δ $\mathbf{return}_{VAL}$ v , where ρ(x) is a location, is that the content of the location ρ(x)

Fig. 1 Semantic clauses (direct semantics style)

1 $P[\underline{program}\ bl] = \langle S[bl]\rho_0, sh_0 \rangle$

ρ_0 and sh_0 indicate respectively the initial environment and the initial state of the shared store.

2 $S[x := e]\rho = def_{VAL}\ E[e]\rho \text{ in } \lambda v\ .\ UPDATE(\rho(x),v)\ \Delta\ nil$

nil represents the null behaviour.

3 $S[\underline{if}\ be\ \underline{then}\ st_1\ \underline{else}\ st_2]\rho = def_{VAL}\ E[be]\rho \text{ in } \lambda bv\ .\ \text{if } bv \text{ then } S[st_1]\rho \text{ else } S[st_2]\rho$

4 $S[\underline{while}\ be\ \underline{do}\ st]\rho = \text{fix } \lambda bh\ .\ def_{VAL}\ E[be]\rho \text{ in } \lambda bv\ .\ \text{if } bv \text{ then } (S[st]\rho;\ bh) \text{ else nil}$

5 $S[st_1; st_2]\rho = S[st_1]\rho;\ S[st_2]\rho$

6 $S[\underline{raise}(e)]\rho = TAU\ \Delta\ \text{exit } e$

7 $S[decs\ \underline{begin}\ st\ \underline{when}\ e_1\ \underline{do}\ st_1 \dots \underline{when}\ e_n\ \underline{do}\ st_n\ \underline{end}]\rho =$
$def_{ENV}\ D[decs]\rho \text{ in } \lambda \rho'\ .\ trap\ [e_1 \rightarrow S[st_1]\rho', \dots, e_n \rightarrow S[st_n]\rho'] \text{ in } S[st]\rho'$

8 $S[\underline{send}(chid,e)]\rho = def_{VAL}\ E[e]\rho \text{ in } \lambda v\ .\ SEND(chid,v)\ \Delta\ nil$

9 $S[\underline{rec}(chid,x)]\rho = \underset{VAL}{+}\ \lambda v\ .\ REC(chid,v)\ \Delta\ UPDATE(\rho(x),v)\ \Delta\ nil$

10 $S[\underline{create\ process}\ bl]\rho = CREATE(S[bl]\rho)\ \Delta\ nil$

11 $E[c]\rho = TAU\ \Delta\ return_{VAL}\ C[c]$

12 $E[e_1\ bop\ e_2]\rho = def_{VAL}\ E[e_1]\rho \text{ in } \lambda v_1\ .\ def_{VAL}\ E[e_2]\rho \text{ in }$
$\lambda v_2\ .\ TAU\ \Delta\ return_{VAL}\ Bop[bop](v_1,v_2)$

$C: CONST \rightarrow VAL,\quad Bop: BOP \rightarrow ((VAL \times VAL) \rightarrow VAL)$

are the semantic functions for constants and binary operators, which are not given here in full.

13 $E[x]\rho = \underset{VAL}{+}\ \lambda v\ .\ READ(\rho(x),v)\ \Delta\ return_{VAL}\ v$

14 $D[\underline{var}\ x]\rho = \underset{LOC}{+}\ \lambda l\ .\ ALLOC(l)\ \Delta\ return_{ENV}\ \rho[l/x]$

15 $D[decs_1\ decs_2]\rho = def_{ENV}\ D[decs_1]\rho \text{ in } \lambda \rho'.\ D[decs_2]\rho'$

End Fig. 1

will depend on the moment when the process, within which the evaluation of x is performed, gets access to the shared store; if v_0 is the value in $\rho(x)$ at that moment, then the action $READ(\rho(x),v_0)$ will be performed and the value v_0 will be returned.

$\lambda v\ .READ(\rho(x),v)\ \Delta\ return_{VAL} v$ represents a function from values to behaviours and is a term of sort funct(val,behaviour) in a specification FUNCT(VAL,BEHAVIOUR).

The term $\underset{VAL}{+}\ \lambda v.READ(\rho(x),v)\ \Delta\ return_{VAL}\ v$ represents a process which is the infinite sum, for v ranging in VAL, of the processes $READ(\rho(x),v)\ \Delta\ return_{VAL}$; in Milner's notation (see [M2]) it would be $\sum_{v \in VAL} READ(\rho(x),v)\ \Delta\ return_{VAL}\ v$; we prefer for technical reasons to consider $\underset{VAL}{+}$ as an operator of functionality funct(val,behaviour)$\rightarrow$ behaviour, as it is formally defined in the specification of BH-SYST.

Clauses 9 and 14 have to be interpreted analogously.

Clause 11 (and 12) shows a typical situation: it would be as in the purely sequential case, but in the concurrent case an action is performed, consisting in evaluating the constant; this action is internal, i.e. does not involve other processes, and hence it is indicated by TAU following Milner's notation. Representing explicitly that internal action is not necessary whenever the final observational semantics, represented by CALG, takes only care of the results of the actions and not of

their ordering.
Clauses 8,9 and 10 are usual clauses for concurrent statements; only recall the comment to clause 15 for interpreting the operation $\underset{VAL}{+}$ in 9 and note that the results of the action capabilities REC, SEND will be defined later in the definition of the concurrent systems SYST.
The denotational clauses of Fig. 1 can be seen as a translation into an intermediate language, a language of behaviours; in [AR1] a worked example of how the translation works can be found.

2.3 Concurrent algebra and semantics

In this section we briefly outline the definition of the concurrent algebra CALG, providing some semantic domains used in section 2.2, and show that denotational clauses define indeed a denotational semantics and lay the basis for the equivalence results of the following section.
The definition of CALG is done in two steps: the first specifies algebraically a concurrent system SYST, following a SMoLCS paradigm; the second specifies the observations we want to make about SYST and defines CALG as the terminal algebras satisfying such observational constraints.
The specification of SYST is an instantiation of a schema shown elsewhere [AR2, AMRW]. The concurrent system SYST consists in the algebraic specification of a labelled transition system, whose states correspond to the execution stages of EL1 programs.
The algebraic specification of a transition system consists of the specification of the states of the system, of the flags (labels) and of the transitions, which are defined using a boolean operation

$$\longrightarrow: state \times flag \times state \to bool.$$

In our notation $s \xrightarrow{f} s'$ will stand for $\longrightarrow(s,f,s') = true$.
The system SYST is specified in four steps, each one consisting of the specification of an algebraic transition system: BH-SYST, S-SYST, P-SYST, and finally SYST.
BH-SYST (behaviour system) is a labelled transition systems in which the states are terms of sort behaviour, used to represent states of EL1 processes; the transitions correspond to basic capabilities of actions of single processes, like reading, writing, sending, receiving messages and so on.
The states of S-SYST (S stands for synchronization) are parallel compositions of behaviours (multisets of), plus some global information (states of the shared store). The transitions are the results of synchronized cooperations among processes. Note that, for technical convenience, single process transitions are embedded into the new ones; moreover creation of a new process is seen as synchronization of the creating process with a **nil** process evolving into the created one.
The transitions of P-SYST (P stands for parallelism) correspond to contemporaneous (parallel) executions of several synchronous actions. Here the states are the same as for S-SYST and we take care of the mutually exclusive access to the shared store.
In the general SMoLCS schema SYST corresponds to the monitoring step, where the states are the same of P-SYST. Here, in the simple case of EL1, the global constraints imposed by the monitoring say only that a duration of a process action can be any.
$CALG_C$, the concurrent algebra for the continuation style, is defined analogously, giving a concurrent system $SYST_C$ and an observational semantics on it.
A most important fact is that SYST and $SYST_C$ differ only for the definition of the first step (the behaviour system). Here we give the complete definitions of SYST. For completeness in Appendix 3 we report from [AR1] the definitions of $BH\text{-}SYST_C$; $S\text{-}SYST_C$, $P\text{-}SYST_C$ and $SYST_C$ are defined in the same way of S-SYST, P-SYST and SYST.
In what follows VAL, EID, LOC and CHID are algebraic specifications which are not further specified (VAL includes also the boolean values) and MAP, PROD, MSET are the parametric algebraic specifications of maps, cartesian products and finite multisets (for a complete definition see e.g. [AMRW]). The notation SPEC[srt1/srt2] means that in the specification SPEC the sort srt1 is renamed as srt2.
For giving a semantics following the direct style, we need a **def... in...** operator for composing behaviours producing environments, elements of sort env-behaviour, with behaviours waiting for environments, defined by the specification FUNCT(ENV,BEHAVIOUR); so for defining BEHAVIOUR first we need to define the environments.

```
ENV =MAP(VID,LOC)[env/map(vid,loc)]
ACT  =   enrich VAL + LOC + CHID + BEHAVIOUR by
           sorts act
           opns   TAU:                                  → act
                  ALLOC: loc                            → act
                  UPDATE,READ: loc × val                → act
                  SEND,REC: chid × val                  → act
                  CREATE,BEING-CREATED:behaviour        → act
```

BEHAVIOUR =
enrich ACT +FUNCT(VAL,BEHAVIOUR) + FUNCT(LOC,BEHAVIOUR) +
FUNCT(ENV,BEHAVIOUR) + FUNCT(BEHAVIOUR,BEHAVIOUR) + MAP(EID,BEHAVIOUR) **by**

sorts behaviour, val-behaviour, env-behaviour

opns **nil** : → behaviour
if □ **then** □ **else** □: val × behaviour × behaviour → behaviour
□**;** □: behaviour × behaviour → behaviour
fix □: funct(behaviour, behaviour) → behaviour
trap □ **in** □: map(eid,behaviour) × behaviour → behaviour
exit □: eid → behaviour
{ □ Δ □: act × bh-srt → bh-srt
{ $\underset{T}{+}$ □: funct(t,bh-srt) → bh-srt |T =VAL,LOC}
{ **def**$_T$ □ **in** □: t-behaviour × funct(t,bh-srt) → bh-srt
return$_T$□: t → t-behaviour
|T =VAL,ENV}
| bh-srt = behaviour, val-behaviour, env-behaviour}

Note that BEHAVIOUR is defined in a recursive way. Indicating by **BH** the transformation implicitly defined by the right hand side of the definition, we can write BEHAVIOUR = **BH**(BEHAVIOUR). It is easy to check that, defining BEHAVIOUR^0 as the specification with just the sort behaviour and no operations nor axioms and BEHAVIOUR^n = **BH**(BEHAVIOUR^{n-1}), for n=3 we get the fixpoint specification BEHAVIOUR.
The transitions of BH-SYST are labelled by elements of sort act of the specification ACT.
The transition relation of BH-SYST is indicated by —>; —val> and —env> represent the transition relations for the behaviours returning values and environments .

BH-SYST =
enrich BEHAVIOUR + ACT + BOOL **by**

opns —>: behaviour × act × behaviour → bool
{ —t>: t-behaviour × act × t-behaviour → bool | T = VAL, ENV }

axioms
nil $\xrightarrow{\text{BEING CREATED(bh)}}$ bh
if true **then** bh_1 **else** bh_2 = bh_1 **if** false **then** bh_1 **else** bh_2 = bh_2

(bh_1 **;** bh_2)**;** bh_3 = bh_1 **;** (bh_2 **;** bh_3)
nil ; bh = bh bh **; nil** = bh
exit e **;** bh = **exit** e
$bh_1 \xrightarrow{a} bh_1' \supset (bh_1 ;\ bh_2) \xrightarrow{a} (bh_1' ;\ bh_2)$

fix bhfunct = bhfunct(**fix** bhfunct)

e ∈ dom(emap) = true ⊃ **trap** emap **in exit** e = emap(e)
e ∈ dom(emap) = false ⊃ **trap** emap **in exit** e = **exit** e
trap emap **in nil** = **nil**
bh $\xrightarrow{a}$ bh' ⊃ **trap** emap **in** bh $\xrightarrow{a}$ **trap** emap **in** bh'

{ a Δ bh —a—>> bh
{ tfunct(t) —a—>> bh' ⊃ $\underset{T}{+}$ tfunct —a—>> bh' | T = VAL, LOC }

{ bh —a—>> bh' ⊃ **def**$_T$ bh **in** tfunct —a—>> **def**$_T$ bh' **in** tfunct
def$_T$ **return**$_T$ t **in** tfunct = tfunct(t) | T = VAL, ENV }
| —>> = —>, —val>, —env>}.

The states of S-SYST are defined by the following specification.
STATE = **enrich** PROD(MSET(BEHAVIOUR),STORE)[state/prod(mset(behaviour),store)] **by**
axioms **nil** | bms = bms
STORE = MAP(LOC,VAL)[store/map(loc,val)].

(Note that | indicates multiset union and that the singleton multiset {e} is simply written e).
The added axiom **nil**|bms=bms permits to handle dynamic creation and termination of behaviours.
As flags of the synchronous actions we simply choose the same flags of the behaviour system (elements of sort act).
The transition relation of S-SYST is indicated by ———>.
S-SYST=
<u>**enrich**</u> BH-SYST + STATE <u>**by**</u>
<u>**opns**</u> ———>: state × act × state → bool

<u>**axioms**</u>

$bh \xrightarrow{TAU} bh' \supset \langle bh,sh\rangle \text{—TAU—>} \langle bh',sh\rangle$

$bh \xrightarrow{ALLOC(l)} bh' \wedge l \in dom(sh) = false \supset \langle bh,sh\rangle \text{—WRITE(l,undef)—>} \langle bh',sh[undef/l]\rangle$

$bh \xrightarrow{READ(l,v)} bh' \wedge sh(l) = v \supset \langle bh,sh\rangle \text{—TAU—>} \langle bh',sh\rangle$

$bh \xrightarrow{WRITE(l,v)} bh' \supset \langle bh,sh\rangle \text{—WRITE(l,v)—>} \langle bh',sh[v/l]\rangle$

$bh_1 \xrightarrow{SEND(cid,v)} bh_1' \wedge bh_2 \xrightarrow{REC(cid,v)} bh_2' \supset \langle bh_1|bh_2,sh\rangle \text{—TAU—>} \langle bh_1'|bh_2',sh\rangle$

$bh \xrightarrow{CREATE(bh_1)} bh' \wedge nil \xrightarrow{BEING\text{-}CREATED(bh_1)} bh_1 \supset \langle bh|\mathbf{nil},sh\rangle \text{—TAU—>} \langle bh'|bh_1, sh\rangle$.

The flags of P-SYST are defined by the following specification.
PFLAG = <u>**enrich**</u> ACT <u>**by**</u>
<u>**opns**</u> // : act × act → act
isupdating: loc × act → bool
<u>**axioms**</u> $a_1 /\!/ a_2 = a_2 /\!/ a_1$ $(a_1 /\!/ a_2) /\!/ a_3 = a_1 /\!/ (a_2 /\!/ a_3)$
isupdating(l,TAU) = false
$isupdating(l_1,WRITE(l_2,v)) = equal(l_1,l_2)$
$isupdating(l,a_1 /\!/ a_2) = isupdating(l,a_1) \vee isupdating(l,a_2)$.

The operation // defines the flags of the parallel actions corresponding to the contemporaneous executions of several synchronous actions; isupdating(l,a) is true iff a is the flag of a parallel action in which the content of the location l is updated. (Note that there are no synchronous actions labelled by READ(l,v) or ALLOC(l)). The transition relation of P-SYST is an extension of the one of S-SYST.
P-SYST =
<u>**enrich**</u> S-SYST + PFLAG <u>**by**</u>
<u>**axioms**</u>

$\langle bms_1,sh\rangle \text{—a—>} \langle bms_1',sh'\rangle \wedge \langle bms_2,sh\rangle \text{—TAU—>} \langle bms_2',sh\rangle \supset$
$\langle bms_1|bms_2,sh\rangle \text{—a//TAU—>} \langle bms_1'|bms_2',sh'\rangle$

$\langle bms_1,sh\rangle \text{—a—>} \langle bms_1',sh'\rangle \wedge$
$\langle bms_2,sh\rangle \text{—WRITE(l,v)—>} \langle bms_2',sh[v/l]\rangle \wedge isupdating(l,a) = false \supset$
$\langle bms_1|bms_2,sh\rangle \text{—a//WRITE(l,v)—>} \langle bms_1'|bms_2',sh'[v/l]\rangle$.

The only restriction on the use of shared variables is that two contemporaneous updatings of a single location are not allowed and that is formalized by the two axioms above. Note that the final state of the shared memory does not depend on the order in which the synchronous actions are composed.

As the whole system is closed, i.e. there are no interactions with the external world, the flags of the system SYST are simply defined by FLAG = <u>**sorts**</u> flag <u>**opns**</u> TAU:→ flag.
The transition relation of SYST is indicated by =====>.

SYST = <u>**enrich**</u> P-SYST + FLAG <u>**by**</u>
<u>**opns**</u> ===>: state × flag × state → bool
<u>**axioms**</u> $\langle bms,sh\rangle \text{—a—>} \langle bms',sh'\rangle \supset \langle bms|bms_1,sh\rangle \text{==TAU==>} \langle bms'|bms_1,sh'\rangle$.

The axiom says that any group of processes (bms_1) can always wait, formalizing that the duration of the behaviour actions can be any, and moreover that any action allowed in P-SYST (the premise of the axiom) is allowed to happen in an overall transition.
The paradigm under which an observational semantics is defined for a concurrent system (here applied to SYST) consists essentially of:
- a specification, defining the observations on the system (here SYST-PLUS), by means of boolean relations stating that

some observation values (here elements of the shared store) are true of some observed objects (here the states of SYST);
- a definition of a class of observationally equivalent algebras, each one containing the objects to be observed together with the relations and moreover preserving, as a subtype, a fixed model of the observed values;
- the definition of the observational semantics as the minimally defined and term generated algebra (here CALG) terminal in that class; a basic general theorem (in [ARW]) shows that this algebra has indeed the properties required of an observational semantics.

SYST-PLUS = <u>enrich</u> SYST <u>by</u>

<u>opns</u> isres: state × store → bool

<u>axioms</u> isres(<nil,sh>,sh) = true

s ==TAU==>s' ∧ isres(s',sh)=true ⊃ isres(s,sh) = true.

Then we obtain the following result qualifying CALG as the observational semantics of SYST w.r.t. the observations, expressed by the operation isres (here we have chosen the initial model of STORE).

<u>Proposition 0.</u> There exists an algebra CALG with the following properties:
for any srt ∈ Sorts(Sig(STATE))-Sorts(Sig(STORE)), ground terms t,t' ∈ $W_{Sig(STATE)}|_{srt}$
01 CALG |= **D**(t) iff SYST |– **D**(t)
02 CALG |= t = t' iff for any sh ∈ $W_{Sig(STATE)}|_{store}$, any s ∈ $W_{Sig(STATE)}$ $\{x\}|_{state}$ with x of sort srt
[SYST-PLUS |– isres(s[t/x],sh)=true iff SYST-PLUS |– isres(s[t'/x],sh)=true].□

Property 01 says that all the interesting objects of STATE are defined in CALG; by property O2 two terms of sort srt are equivalent if and only if in every context of sort state they satisfy the same observations. It is most important to note that in this way every subcomponent of a program gets an observational semantics: in EL1 this is true of a process; for a language with procedures, that is how a procedure, generally involving processes, gets a denoted value.
(SYST-PLUS$_C$ and CALG$_C$ are defined, starting by SYST$_C$, in the same way.)

3 EQUIVALENCE RESULTS

We have already seen that the two, direct and continuation, semantics differ in the definition of the corresponding behaviours, while they have formally the same transition rules for the systems S-SYST, P-SYST, SYST and S-SYST$_C$, P-SYST$_C$, SYST$_C$; but note that the behaviour components of the states are taken in different domains.
Let us briefly summarize our findings. The equivalence results are centered around a main theorem stating the strong (bisimulation) equivalence denoted by ~, in the sense of Milner and Park (see [M1, M2]), of two behaviours roughly corresponding to a statement in the two semantics (however the technical result is more precise and subtle and will be commented later).
Since the transitions of SYST and SYST$_C$ depend only on the transitions of the component behaviours and on the storage state and not on the behaviour states, from the main result we get the equivalence of two programs, as labelled trees, in which we disregard the intermediate but not the final states (an equivalence stronger than strong bisimulation).
Finally, in the special case that we observe an input/output semantics, as we have done e.g. in this paper, we get the equivalence of the two semantics for an EL1 program.
We now state formally the main results and lemmas.

<u>Theorem 1 (Main Theorem).</u> For every st ∈ STAT; for every $\rho_C \in ENV_C$, $\rho \in ENV$ s.t. $\rho_C(x) = \rho(x)$ for all x ∈ VID; for every θ ∈ *CONT*, bh ∈ *BH*, emap ∈ $CALG_{map(eid,behaviour)}$ such that
i) θ ~ **trap** emap **in** bh
ii) for every exception e, ρ_C(e) ~ emap(e)
iii) the domain of emap includes all the exceptions e such that st has a substatement of the form <u>raise</u> e not enclosed by a block with an handler for e,
we have that S_C[st]ρ_C θ ~ **trap** emap **in** (S[st]ρ ; bh).
(Note that for simplicity here we consider that all the exceptions in a program are different).
<u>Proof</u>. By induction on the structure of st, using Lemma 1 and 2 below.□

<u>Comment.</u> The behaviour bh used in iii) plays in the direct style the role of a continuation (indeed it is the behaviour following ; and hence the execution of the statement st ; however we need to consider **trap** emap **in** bh instead of bh as we do in i), since we have to close both S[st]ρ and bh with the treatment of the exceptions which are going outside of st and bh, guaranteeing that the behaviours corresponding to such exceptions are again strongly equivalent (condition ii).

Lemma 1. For every $e \in$ EXP; for every ρ_C, ρ as in the Main Theorem;
for every $k \in$ *ECONT* and vfunct $\in$ $CALG_{funct(val,\ behaviour)}$ such that ($k(v) \sim$ vfunct(v) for all $v \in$ VAL),
we have that $E_C[e]\rho_C\, k \sim$ **def**$_{VAL}$ $E[e]\rho$ **in** vfunct.
Proof. By structural induction on e.□

Lemma 2. For every decs $\in$ DECS; for every ρ_C, ρ as in the Main Theorem;
for every $\chi \in$ *DCONT*, efunct $\in$ $CALG_{funct(env,\ behaviour)}$
such that ($\chi(\rho_C') \sim$ efunct(ρ') for all ρ_C', ρ' as in the Main Theorem),
we have that $D_C[decs]\rho_C\, \chi \sim$ **def**$_{ENV}$ $D[decs]\rho$ **in** efunct.
Proof. By structural induction on decs.□

Comment. Analogously to what we have in the Main Theorem, where a behaviour corresponding to a statement continuation is used, in Lemma 1 and 2 we have, correspondingly to an expression continuation k and to a declaration continuation χ, a function from expression values to behaviours vfunct and a function from environments to behaviours efunct. Technically we note that we can prove Lemma 1 and 2 apart. Since in EL1 the evaluation of expressions and of declarations does not require the evaluation of statements. For more complex languages, in which e.g. we have function procedures as components of expressions, the obvious and easy generalization of the proof technique is to prove by multiple induction a main theorem including also Lemma 1 and 2 (i.e. using multiple induction on statements, expressions and declarations).
It is also interesting to note that a key role is played in the otherwise straightforward tedious proof, by interesting simple properties of behaviours, of which we give just few examples:

- **trap** emap **in** (a Δ bh) $\sim$ a Δ **trap** emap **in** bh
- **def**$_{VAL}$ (a Δ bh) **in** vfunct $\sim$ a Δ **def**$_{VAL}$ bh **in** vfunct
- (**if** bv **then** bh_1 **else** bh_2); bh $\sim$ **if** bv **then** (bh_1 ; bh) **else** (bh_2; bh)
- **trap** emap **in fix** λ x . bh $\sim$ **fix** λ x . **trap** emap **in** bh. End of comment.

We can now state a corollary establishing the strong equivalence of the behaviours corresponding to a statement in the two semantics.

Corollary 1. For every st $\in$ STAT without raise statements jumping outside of it;
for every $\rho_C \in ENV_C$, for every $\rho \in ENV$ such that ($\rho_C(x) = \rho(x)$ for all $x \in$ VID),
we have that $S_C[st]\rho_C$ **nil** $\sim$ $S[st]\rho$.
Proof. From the Main Theorem, because **trap emptymap in (bh; nil)** $\sim$ bh.□
Now we can state formally the equivalence at SYST level.

Lemma 3. For every $bhc_1,\dots,bhc_n \in W_{Sig(SYST_C)|behaviour}$, $bhd_1,\dots,bhd_n \in W_{Sig(SYST)|behaviour}$,
sh, sh' $\in W_{Sig(STORE)|store}$ s.t. $bhc_1 \sim bhd_1,\dots,bhc_n \sim bhd_n$, we have that

i) for every $bhc_1',\dots,bhc_n' \in W_{Sig(SYST_C)|behaviour}$
$SYST_C \vdash \langle bhc_1|\dots|bhc_n, sh\rangle ==TAU==> \langle bhc_1'|\dots|bhc_m', sh'\rangle$ implies
there exist $bhd_1',\dots,bhd_m' \in W_{Sig(SYST)|behaviour}$ such that
$SYST \vdash \langle bhd_1|\dots|bhd_n, sh\rangle ==TAU==> \langle bhd_1'|\dots|bhd_m', sh'\rangle$ and $bhc_1' \sim bhd_1',\dots, bhc_m' \sim bhd_m'$

ii) converse of i).

Proof. The proof proceeds first proving a similar property for S-SYST and S-$SYST_C$, P-SYST and P-$SYST_C$; and in each case the proof is straightforward by cases on the transition clauses noticing that the actions of the states of the systems depend only on the actions of the component behaviours and the shared storage state and not on the behaviour states.□

Note that the proof technique obviously generalizes to tSMoLCS concurrent systems, where the actions of the states depend only on the actions of the subcomponents and on the global information and not on the subcomponents states.
Finally we can apply the previous results to obtain the equivalence of the two semantics on programs w.r.t. the input / output semantics defined before.
Theorem 2. For every pr_1, $pr_2 \in$ PROG
$CALG_C \models P_C[pr_1] = P_C[pr_2]$ iff $CALG \models P[pr_1] = P[pr_2]$.
Proof. An EL program pr will have the form **program** bl, where bl is a block statement and we have
$P_C[$**program** $bl] = \langle S_C[bl]\rho_0 nil, sh_0\rangle$ $\quad$ $P[$**program** $bl] = \langle S[bl]\rho_0, sh_0\rangle$.
Hence from Corollary 1 and Lemma 3 we obtain that for every sh $\in W_{Sig(STORE)|store}$,
$SYST_C \vdash P_C[pr] ==TAU==> \langle nil, sh\rangle$ iff $SYST \vdash P[pr] ==TAU==> \langle nil, sh\rangle$ and thus we get the result .□

This theorem generalizes to all the cases where observational semantics ($\sim^{o}$) is such that
($s_1 \sim s_2$ and s_1 input/output equivalent to s_2) implies $s_1 \sim^{o} s_2$.

Acknowledgment We gratefully acknowledge the benefits of many discussions and remarks resulting from the practical application of our approach to the Ada trial definition by the other colleagues of the CRAI - Genoa group, A. Giovini, F. Mazzanti, E. Zucca. Moreover we warmly thank Ombretta Arvigo for a very patient Mac typing under pressure and at any time.

Appendix 1: Semantic functions and domains (continuation style)

P_C: PROG $\rightarrow ANSWER_C$
E_C: EXP $\rightarrow(ENV_C \rightarrow(ECONT \rightarrow CONT))$
S_C: STAT $\rightarrow(ENV_C \rightarrow(CONT \rightarrow CONT))$
D_C: DECS $\rightarrow(ENV_C \rightarrow(DCONT \rightarrow CONT))$

$ANSWER_C = (CALG_C)_{state}$
$CONT = (CALG_C)_{behaviour}$ (Continuations)
$ECONT = (VAL_C \rightarrow CONT)$ (Expression continuations)
$DCONT = (ENV_C \rightarrow CONT)$ (Declaration continuations)
$ENV_C = (VID \rightarrow DEN)$ (Environments)
$VAL_C = (CALG_C)_{val}$ (Values of expressions)
$DEN = LOC \cup CONT$ (Denotations)
$LOC = (CALG_C)_{loc}$ (Locations of the shared store)

Appendix 2: Semantic clauses (continuation style)

1 P_C[program bl] = $<S_C[bl]\rho_0 nil, sh_0>$
ρ_0, sh_0 and nil as in fig. 1.

2 $S_C[x := e]\rho\theta = E_C[e]\rho(\lambda\, v.\, UPDATE(\rho(x),v)\ \Delta\ \theta)$

3 S_C[if be then st_1 else st_2]$\rho\theta$ = $E_C[be]\rho(\lambda\, bv.$ **if** bv **then** $S_C[st_1]\rho\theta$ **else** $S_C[st_2]\rho\theta)$

4 S_C[while be do st]$\rho\theta$ = **fix** $\lambda\,\theta'.\ E_C[be]\rho(\lambda\, bv.$ **if** bv **then** $S_C[st]\rho\theta'$ **else** $\theta)$

5 $S_C[st_1; st_2]\rho\theta = S_C[st_1]\rho(S_C[st_2]\rho\theta)$

6 S_C[raise e]$\rho\theta$ = TAU $\Delta\ \rho(e)$

7 S_C[decs begin st when e_1 do st_1 ... when e_n do st_n end]$\rho\theta$ =
$D_C[decs]\rho(\lambda\,\rho'.\ S_C[st]\rho'[S_C[st_1]\rho'\theta/e_1,...,S_C[st_n]\rho'\theta/e_n]\theta)$

8 S_C[send(chid,e)]$\rho\theta$ = $E_C[e]\rho(\lambda v.\ SEND(chid,v)\ \Delta\ \theta)$

9 S_C[rec(chid,x)]$\rho\theta$ = $\underset{VAL}{+}\ \lambda\, v.\ REC(chid,v)\ \Delta\ UPDATE(\rho(x),v)\ \Delta\ \theta$

10 S_C[create process bl]$\rho\theta$ = CREATE($S_C[bl]\rho$ **nil**) $\Delta\ \theta$

11 $E_C[c]\rho k$ = TAU Δ k(C[c])

12 $E_C[e_1\ bop\ e_2]\rho k = E_C[e_1]\rho(\lambda v_1.\ E_C[e_2]\rho(\lambda v_2.\ TAU\ \Delta\ k(Bop[bop](v_1,v_2))))$

C : CONST $\rightarrow VAL_C$, Bop: BOP $\rightarrow ((VAL_C \times VAL_C) \rightarrow VAL_C)$
are the semantic functions for constants and binary operators, which are not given here in full.

13 $E_C[x]\rho k = \underset{VAL}{+}\ \lambda\, v.\ READ(\rho(x),v)\ \Delta\ k(v)$

14 D_C[var x]$\rho\,\chi = \underset{LOC}{+}\lambda\, l.\ ALLOC(l)\ \Delta\ \chi\ (\rho[l/x])$

15 $D_C[decs_1\ decs_2]\rho\,\chi = D_C[decs_1]\rho(\lambda\,\rho'.\ D_C[decs_2]\rho'\,\chi)$

Appendix 3: Definition of BH-SYST$_C$

BEHAVIOUR$_C$ =
enrich ACT + FUNCT(LOC,BEHAVIOUR$_C$) + FUNCT(VAL,BEHAVIOUR$_C$) +
FUNCT(BEHAVIOUR$_C$,BEHAVIOUR$_C$) by
sorts behaviour
opns **nil**: → behaviour
□Δ □: act × behaviour → behaviour
if □ **then** □ **else** □: val × behaviour × behaviour → behaviour
fix□: funct(behaviour,behaviour) → behaviour
{ $+_T$□: funct(t,behaviour) → behaviour | T=VAL, LOC}

where ACT is the same as for BEHAVIOUR.
BH-SYST$_C$= enrich BEHAVIOUR$_C$ by
opns —>: behaviour × act × behaviour → bool
axioms nil $\xrightarrow{\text{BEING-CREATED(bh)}}$ bh
a Δ bh $\xrightarrow{a}$ bh
if true **then** bh$_1$**else** bh$_2$ = bh$_1$ **if** false **then** bh$_1$**else** bh$_2$ = bh$_2$
bhfunct(**fix** bhfunct) = **fix** bhfunct
{ tfunct(t) $\xrightarrow{a}$ bh' ⊃ $+_T$ tfunct $\xrightarrow{a}$ bh' | T = VAL, LOC }.

REFERENCES

(LNCS stands for Lecture Notes in Computer Science, Springer Verlag).

[AMRW] E.Astesiano, G.F.Mascari, G.Reggio, M.Wirsing, *On the parameterized algebraic specification of concurrent systems*, Proc. CAAP '85 - TAPSOFT Conference, LNCS n. 185, 1985.

[AR1] E.Astesiano, G.Reggio, *A syntax-directed approach to the semantics of concurrent languages*, in Proc. 10th IFIP World Congress (H.J. Kugler ed.), North Holland,p. 571-576, 1986.

[AR2] E.Astesiano, G.Reggio, *The SMoLCS approach to the formal semantics of programming languages - A tutorial introduction* - , to appear in Proc. of CRAI Spring International Conference: Innovative software factories and Ada, 1986.

[ARW] E.Astesiano, G.Reggio, M.Wirsing, *Relational specifications and observational semantics*, in Proc. of MFCS'86, LNCS n. 233, 1986.

[BJ] D.Bjorner, C.B.Jones, *Formal specification and software development*, Prentice Hall, 1982.

[BO] D.Bjorner, O.Oest, *Towards a formal description of Ada*, LNCS n. 98, 1980.

[BW1] M.Broy, M.Wirsing, *On the algebraic specification of finitary infinite communicating sequential processes*, in Proc. IFIP TC2 Working Conference on "Formal Description of Programming Concepts II", (D. Bjørner ed.), North Holland, 1983.

[BW2] M.Broy, M.Wirsing, *Partial abstract types*, Acta Informatica 18, 47-64, 1982.

[BW3] M.Broy, M.Wirsing, *Algebraic definition of a functional programming language and its semantic models*, R.A.I.R.O. vol. 17,1983.

[G] M.J.C.Gordon, *The denotational description of programming languages*, Springer Verlag, 1979.

[KCDDH] G.Kahn, D.Clement, J.Despeyroux, T.Despeyroux, L.Hascoet, *Natural semantics on the computer*, I.N.R.I.A. project draft, 1985.

[M1] R.Milner, *A calculus of communicating systems*, LNCS n. 92, 1980.

[M2] R.Milner, *Calculi for synchrony and asynchrony*, TCS 25, 267-310, 1983.

[P] G.Plotkin, *A structural approach to operational semantics*, Lecture notes, Aarhus University, 1981.

[S] J.E.Stoy, *Denotational semantics: the Scott-Strachey approach to programming language theory*, The MIT Press, London, 1977.

EXPRESSIBILITY OF FIRST ORDER LOGIC WITH A NONDETERMINISTIC INDUCTIVE OPERATOR

V. Arvind and S. Biswas
Department of Computer Science and Engineering
Indian Institute of Technology
KANPUR, INDIA

1. INTRODUCTION

Two important applications of the languages of first-order logic of finite structures and its various extensions are as query languages of relational databases and as languages capturing different natural complexity classes. Expressibility of such logics has, therefore, been studied in great depth. See, for example, [1, 2, 5, 6, 7, 8, 9].

First-order logic with equality (FO) with the least fixpoint operator (LFP) and total order predicate is an important logic as it precisely captures the class PTIME. (Hereafter, we refer to this logic as FO + LFP + order. Similarly we use FO + LFP to denote first-order logic with LFP but without order). In this paper we define and study a new operator called NIO (for nondeterministic inductive operator) which can do everything that LFP does, but can dispense with the requirement that order be given as a logical constant for capturing PTIME.

The motivation behind the definition of NIO is the observation (detailed in Section 2) that one reason why FO + LFP needs order to capture PTIME is that it lacks, while inductively defining a predicate, the ability to choose just one out of several candidates. NIO has that power; it nondeterministically chooses one from a set of possibilities. As a result, in general, evaluation of an FO + NIO expression on a structure defines a predicate which is nondeterministically chosen from a set of possible ones. On the other hand, when we consider the set of FO + NIO expressions each of which assigns a unique predicate to every structure of appropriate vocabulary, we find that this set precisely captures the class PTIME. It would appear that we have, therefore, an answer to the problem posed by Gurevich [5]: define an extension of FO which captures PTIME but does not require order to be given as a logical constant. But, unfortunately, the above set of FO + NIO expressions does not have a syntactic characterization. We see in Section 4 that there is no algorithm to decide if a given FO + NIO expression is in this set.

To understand the nature of general FO + NIO expressions, we introduce the language L_α associated with an FO + NIO expression α. We show that, in general, L_α can be NP-complete. We also give sufficient conditions which guarantee L_α to be in PTIME. Finally we give a couple of lower bound results in expressibility when the arity of an FO + NIO expression is considered a complexity measure.

For basic definitions, we refer to [5]. For details on LFP, see [2, 5, 7].

2. A LIMITATION OF FO + LFP

That FO + LFP does not capture PTIME is well known, see e.g. [2]. Here we characterize a limitation of FO + LFP which explains why this logic cannot do certain PTIME tasks. It has been observed in [5] that FO as well as FO + LFP can express only those global predicates which are invariant over isomorphic structures. We look at this idea a little differently to characterize a limitation.

We shall use $\bar{d}$ to denote a tuple of domain elements and $\bar{x}$ to denote a tuple of variables. For a mapping h, and $\bar{d} = (d_1,\ldots,d_k)$, $h(\bar{d})$ will denote $(h(d_1),\ldots,h(d_k))$.

<u>Definition</u>: Let M be a structure of vocabulary τ and let h be a permutation on the domain elements of M. Then h is an automorphism on M if for every predicate symbol R in τ we have that $R(\bar{d})$ holds in M iff $R(h(\bar{d}))$ holds in M for every k-tuple $\bar{d}$ of domain elements, arity of R being, say, k.

<u>Fact</u>: Let π be an FO (or FO + LFP) expressible global predicate which assigns a k-ary predicate P^M to every structure M of vocabulary τ. Now, if such a structure M has an automorphism h defined on it then for every k-tuple $\bar{d}$ of domain elements $P^M(\bar{d})$ holds in M iff $P^M(h(\bar{d}))$ holds in M.

The above can be easily proved by induction. We use this fact to show that FO + LFP cannot do certain simple PTIME tasks.

Let us consider a binary global predicate π which assigns a predicate T^G on every undirected graph G with one labelled vertex such that T^G will define a tree in G rooted at the labelled vertex to span the connected component of G containing the labelled vertex. We claim that π cannot be expressed in FO + LFP.

Consider the graph G of Figure 1. In G the vertex v_1 is labelled.

Define h as: $h(v_1) = v_1$, $h(v_2) = v_3$, $h(v_3) = v_2$, and $h(v_4) = v_4$. It is easily verified that h is an automorphism on G. Therefore, if π had a definition in FO + LFP then we have that T^G contains (v_2, v_4) iff T^G contains $(h(v_2), h(v_4))$ i.e., (v_3, v_4). Similarly, T^G will have either both or none of (v_1, v_2) and (v_1, v_3). Hence T^G cannot constitute a required spanning tree.

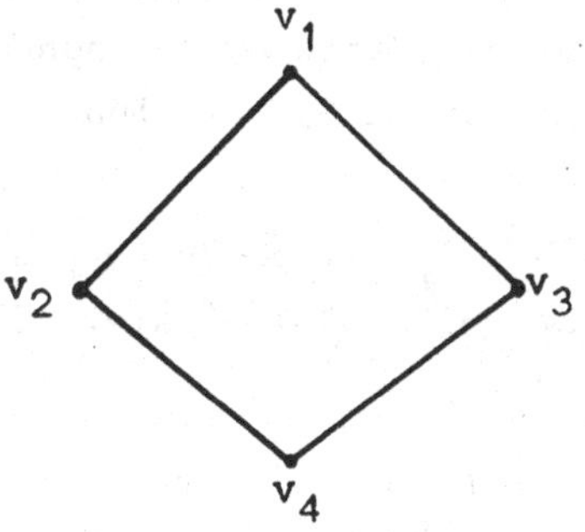

Fig. 1 : The graph G.

3. THE OPERATOR NIO

Notice that because of the availability of the equality predicate we can reckon in FO + LFP that G above has only four vertices. Yet, we are unable to deal with G even as a special case as there is just no way to distinguish between v_2 and v_3. To overcome this problem one approach is to assume that a total order predicate on the domain of the structure is available as a logical constant [5, 7]. The limitation that we have seen then ceases to exist as with order one can distinguish between any two domain elements, the only automorphism then possible is the identity one.

There is, however, one disadvantage: order overcomes the limitation by over-specification. Again looking at the example of Section 2, with order we can select one from the set $\{(v_2, v_4), (v_3, v_4)\}$ by picking up that pair which is, say, least pair of the set in the ordering of all pairs. But we would have been perfectly happy to choose the other one as there was no reason to prefer one pair over the other, all that we wanted was to pick up one and only one from the set. This motivates us to consider an inductive definition, somewhat like the LFP operator, which has the ability of making an arbitrary choice from a set of possibilities.

Definition: Let P be a k-ary predicate symbol and Ψ be a first-order formula of vocabulary $\tau \cup \{P\}$ with k free variables. On a structure S of vocabulary τ let P^S be a predicate defined as follows:

$$P^S = \bigcup_{i \geq 0} P_i^S \qquad \text{where} \quad P_o^S = \emptyset$$

$$\text{and} \quad P_{i+1}^S = P_i^S \cup \underline{\text{oneof}}\ \{\bar{a} \mid \Psi(P_i^S, \bar{a}) \wedge \sim P_i^S(\bar{a}) \text{ is true in } S\}.$$

<u>oneof</u> (A) is empty when A is empty otherwise it is some singleton subset of A. We call P^S to be defined by the <u>nondeterministic inductive operator</u> from Ψ on the structure S, notationally, P^S is NIO (Ψ, P) on the structure S.

We call the sequence P_o^S, P_1^S,... above as the sequence of <u>successive approximations</u> to P^S, the defined predicate. The following are immediate from the definition:

1. For all i, $P_i^S \subseteq P_{i+1}^S$.
2. When the structure S is finite, there is a least j such that for all $i \geq j$, $P_i^S = P_j^S$.

We note that, in general, NIO (Ψ, P) on a structure does not define a unique predicate, rather the predicate is any of a set of possible ones, nondeterministically chosen. As an example, let Ψ be

$$\begin{aligned}&\text{IF } (\forall x)(\forall y) \quad \sim P(x, y)\\ &\text{THEN } E(x, y)\\ &\text{ELSE } E(x, y) \wedge (\exists z)[P(z, x) \vee P(x, z)]\\ &\qquad\qquad \sim(\exists z)[P(y, z) \vee P(z, y)].\end{aligned}$$

then NIO (Ψ, P) defines a spanning tree on connected undirected graphs which are structures of the type {E(.,.)}.

<u>Notation</u>: Let FO + NIO denote the first order language augmented with the NIO operator.

We give below two examples. First is an expression α, in FO + NIO, which is true of connected graphs and false for unconnected graphs. Let Ψ be defined as above, and α be

$$(\forall x)(\exists y)\ [P(x, y) \vee P(y, x)] \tag{1}$$

where $P \Leftarrow \text{NIO}(\Psi, P)$. (We use this extra notation to emphasize that the two references to P in (1) refers to an identical predicate which is, though, nondeterministically obtained). We note that connectedness is not first-order expressible even in the presence of a total order predicate [5].

As another example, we give an FO + NIO formula α such that α is true on a structure iff the cardinality of the domain is even. Let Ψ be

$$\sim(\exists z)\,[Q(x, z) \vee Q(z, x) \vee Q(y, z) \vee Q(z, y)] \wedge (x \neq y)$$

and α be $(\forall x)(\exists y)\,[Q(x, y) \vee Q(y, x)]$ where $Q \Leftarrow NIO(\Psi, Q)$. We note that this is not expressible either in FO + order or in FO + LFP [5, 2].

Observation: Mutual and nested NIO definitions can be collapsed to a single NIO definition using wider arity as done in the case of the LFP operator using similar techniques [3].

4. POWER OF FO + NIO

(We give only sketches of the proofs in most cases due to space limitations. See the full paper for details).

Our first observation is that it is easy to evaluate an FO + NIO formula.

Lemma 4.1: A predicate defined by a FO + NIO formula on a structure S can be obtained in a time polynomial in the size of S.

(As noted before, different evaluation of the same FO + NIO formula may define different predicates on the same structure. The lemma only says that such a predicate can be obtained easily).

The next result shows that in an appropriate sense NIO is a generalization of LFP operator.

Lemma 4.2: Let Ψ be monotonic in P. Then the predicate P^S defined by $NIO(\Psi, P)$ on a structure S is unique and it is precisely the one defined through LFP using the same Ψ.

Proof (Sketch): Let P_o^S, $P_1^S, \ldots$ be the successive approximations to P^S computed using NIO. Similarly for the LFP definition, let Q_o^S, $Q_1^S, \ldots$ be the successive approximations to the predicate Q^S which is computed. We can prove by inductions that for every i there is a j such that $P_i \subseteq Q_j$, and for every k there is an m such that $Q_k \subseteq P_m$, using the facts that Ψ is monotonic and S is finite. ▫

In fact, FO + NIO is more powerful than FO + LFP.

Lemma 4.3: A total order predicate can be defined in FO + NIO.

Proof: Let Ψ be defined on structures S of any vocabulary as follows:

$$\Psi \equiv \text{if } (\forall x)(\forall y)\ \sim P(x, y)$$
$$\text{then true}$$
$$\text{else } (\exists z)\, P(z, x) \wedge (\forall w) \sim P(x, w)$$
$$(\forall w)\, [\sim P(y, w) \wedge \sim P(w, y)]$$

Then NIO(Ψ, P) defines a successor relation using which a total order can be formulated easily. ▫

It is clear from the definition of NIO that the same FO + NIO formula on different evaluations can define more than one predicate on the same structure. Such a formula cannot be said to express any global predicate, as a global predicate by definition assigns a unique predicate to a structure. There are, however, FO + NIO formulas which assign unique predicates to every structure. We have seen two such formulas in Section 3 (one for expressing connected graphs and the other for graphs with an even number of vertices). This leads us to the following:

Definition: Let U be the class of FO + NIO formulas each of which defines a unique predicate on structures of appropriate vocabulary.

Note: We emphasize that a formula in U may have a subformula which is not in U. For example, in the connectedness example of Section 3, for the Ψ given there, NIO(Ψ, P) is not in U but $(\forall x)(\exists y)(P(x, y) \vee P(y, x))$, with $P \Leftarrow$ NIO(Ψ, P), is in U.

It has been shown [7] that FO + LFP + order captures precisely the class PTIME. Therefore, in view of the Lemmas 4.1, 4.2 and 4.3 we immediately have

Theorem 4.4: The set U of FO + NIO formulas expresses all and only the PTIME global predicates.

Unfortunately U is not a syntactic class. Because we have

Theorem 4.5: Given an FO + NIO formula Ψ, it is undecidable if Ψ is in U.

Proof (Sketch): We reduce the blank tape halting problem for Turing machines to the membership problem for U. Given a deterministic Turing machine M, we can define an FO + NIO formula NIO(Ψ, P) that assigns a unique predicate on every structure $S = (D, <)$, where $<$ is a total order relation on the domain D, iff M does not halt on the blank tape. Here, Ψ is such that, for a structure $S = (D, <)$, NIO(Ψ, P) essentially simulates M for $|D|$ steps: the resulting NIO(Ψ, P) for S is a predicate in which codes for instantaneous descriptions of M working on blank tape for $|D|$ steps get constructed. However, if M reaches the halting state within $|D|$ steps, Ψ is such that it allows two distinct tuples as candidates to be chosen, out of which exactly one can be chosen by NIO semantics. Thus NIO(Ψ, P) will not be unique for this S. Hence it follows that NIO(Ψ, P) is unique for each S iff M does not halt on blank tape. ◘

We have seen that the class U captures PTIME. To study the expressibility of FO + NIO in general we first need the following definition.

<u>Definition</u>: Given an FO + NIO formula α of vocabulary τ, the language L_α <u>associated</u> with α is defined as:

$$L_\alpha = \{(S, P^S) \mid P^S \text{ is a predicate defined by } \alpha \text{ on the finite structure } S \text{ of vocabulary } \tau\}.$$

(α can be seen as a relation between structures of vocabulary τ to predicates on such structures. The language L_α is the graph of this relation). Each L_α is clearly in NP.

The simplest kinds of α are NIO(Ψ, P)'s. Even for such α's, associated languages can be NP-complete. In fact,

<u>Theorem 4.6</u>: For any NDTM M running in polynomial time there is a Ψ such that given an input x to M one can construct in time polynomial in $|x|$ a structure S and a predicate P^S on S such that x is accepted by M iff P^S can be defined by NIO(Ψ, P).

<u>Proof (Sketch)</u>: The structure S is meant to be a coding of x. For binary x of length n, such a coding is possible with $S = (\{0, 1, \ldots, n-1\}, <, A)$ where $<$ is a total order on the domain and A is a unary predicate.

Ψ is so defined that NIO(Ψ, P) defines P^S on S by following a computation path of M on x. If in this path at time t the c-th cell contains the -th symbol, and M is in state q at that time, then a tuple representing all this information will be in P^S. Further, this tuple will also record whether the head is scanning the c-th cell at this time t or not. Thus, a certain number of such tuples code an instantaneous description (ID) of M. The construction of the predicate P^S by NIO using Ψ simulates a computation of M on x by including tuples that code an ID for successive ID's. Suppose at some stage of the construction of P^S, all the tuples representing IDs upto time t are already in P^S. Then, since M is a nondeterministic machine, it can go from the ID at time t to one out of the several possible ID's at time (t+1). Now,

Ψ is so constructed that at this point corresponding to the encodings of each of the possible ID's at time (t+1), one representative tuple as argument will make Ψ true. From the semantics of NIO, one and only one of these tuples will next enter P^S. This is how a nondeterministic move of M is simulated. The representative tuple is such that from this tuple and the P^S so far constructed, the rest of the tuples coding the chosen ID at time (t+1) can be included in P^S.

If at any stage in the simulation it is discovered that M has reached an accepting state, then Ψ is so constructed that every m-tuple is brought into P^S, m being the arity of P. Therefore, if we define P^S in the statement of the theorem to be the predicate which is true for every m-tuple of the domain, we have that NIO(Ψ, P) defines this P^S iff M accepts x. □

The following corollary is an immediate consequence.

<u>Corollary 4.7</u>: There is a NIO(Ψ, P) such that the associated language $L_{NIO(\Psi, P)}$ is NP-complete.

<u>Proof</u>: Consider an NP-complete language L and let M be an NDTM accepting L. Let Ψ satisfy the statement of Theorem 4.6 for this M. To know if a string x is in L construct corresponding S and P^S, time for construction is polynomial in $|x|$. Now (S, P^S) is in $L_{NIO(\Psi, P)}$ iff x is in L. Hence $L_{NIO(\Psi, P)}$ is NP-complete. □

From the proof of theorem 4.6 we note that the Ψ defined there satisfies the following: once the accepting state is encountered, it allows all tuples to be put into P^S, even those tuples which were rejected at earlier stages. On the other hand, if we consider Ψ in the NIO definition for either the spanning tree predicate or the total order predicate then we observe the following property: if a tuple is admissible at a certain stage k of the construction and becomes inadmissible at a later stage l, greater than k, then that tuple stays inadmissible at all subsequent stages. Since $L_{NIO(\Psi, P)}$ is an easily recognizable set in these two examples, it leads us to generalize this property into the following theorem.

<u>Theorem 4.8</u>: If Ψ in the definition of NIO (Section 3) satisfies the following for every structure S

(i) For all k-ary predicates A^S, B^S and C^S on S, if $C^S \subseteq B^S$ and $B^S \subseteq A^S$ then for all k-tuples $\bar{d}$, $\Psi(C^S, \bar{d}) \wedge \sim\Psi(B^S, \bar{d}) \rightarrow \sim\Psi(A^S, \bar{d})$, and

(ii) For any k-ary predicate B^S on S, for all $\bar{d}_1$, $\bar{d}_2 \in S^k$,

$$\Psi(B^S, \bar{d}_1) \wedge \Psi(B^S, \bar{d}_2) \wedge \sim\Psi(B^S \cup \{\bar{d}_1\}, \bar{d}_2)$$
$$\rightarrow \sim\Psi(B^S \cup \{\bar{d}_2\}, \bar{d}_1)$$

Then $L_{NIO(\Psi, P)}$ can be recognized in polynomial time by a greedy algorithm.

<u>Proof</u>: Given a Ψ and (S, P^S), our algorithm has to test if (S, P^S) is in $L_{NIO(\Psi, P)}$. The following is a description of the algorithm:

<u>If</u> $\{\bar{d} \mid \Psi(P^S, \bar{d}) \wedge \sim P^S(\bar{d})\}$ is not empty
<u>then</u> (S, P^S) is not in $L_{NIO(\Psi, P)}$, <u>return</u>
<u>else</u> (Construct Q^S in the following manner)

$Q_o^S = \emptyset$

$Q_{i+1}^S = Q_i^S \cup$ <u>Select-one</u> $\{\bar{d} \mid P^S(\bar{d}) \wedge \Psi(Q_i^S, \bar{d}) \wedge \sim Q_i^S(\bar{d})\}$

where $Q^S = \bigcup_{i \geq o} Q_i^S$. (Note: the <u>select-one</u> operator chooses the one which is lexicographically the least of the available tuples at every stage);

<u>If</u> $Q^S = P^S$
<u>then</u> (S, P^S) is in $L_{NIO(\Psi, P)}$
<u>else</u> (S, P^S) is not in $L_{NIO(\Psi, P)}$.

Clearly Q^S is constructed in time polynomial in $|S|$. We omit the proof of correctness of the algorithm. ▫

We note that predicates like spanning tree and total order can be defined with the restrictions of theorem 4.8 on Ψ. The two preceding theorems show how the complexity of the language L_α depends on the structure on Ψ when α is simply NIO(Ψ, P). However if α is allowed to be an FO + NIO expression using NIO(Ψ, P) then L_α can be NP-hard even if Ψ satisfies conditions of theorem 4.8.

<u>Fact</u>: There is a o-ary, FO + NIO expression α using NIO(Ψ, P), where NIO(Ψ, P) assigns a 1-ary predicate with Ψ satisfying conditions of theorem 4.8 such that L_α is NP-hard.

<u>Proof</u>: For a directed graph G = (V, E) consider the following Ψ:

$$\Psi(P, x) \equiv (\forall z)(P(z) \rightarrow \sim E(x, z) \wedge \sim E(z, x)).$$

Clearly any NIO(Ψ, P) is a maximal independent set in G. Also, Ψ satisfies the conditions of theorem 4.8. Let

$$\alpha \equiv (\forall x)(\exists y)\ [P(x) \vee (P(y) \wedge E(y, x))]$$

where $P \Leftarrow$ NIO(Ψ, P).

Clearly $(G, T) \in L_\alpha$ iff G has a kernel [4]. But testing for a kernel in a directed graph is NP-complete [4]. Hence L_α is NP-hard. □

Note: This example is easily extended to the general case where α is m-ary and NIO(Ψ, P) assigns a k-ary predicate and again L_α is NP-hard.

We had observed in Section 3 that mutual and nested NIO definitions can be collapsed into a single NIO definition, by suitable widening of arity. Now the arity of NIO definitions can be considered a complexity measure. A similar approach has also been taken by Chandra and Harel in connection with LFP [2]. We indicate a couple of lower bound results in this direction.

Lemma 4.9: For directed graphs G = (V, E, a, b), where a and b are constants, consider the predicate P(x, y) which constitutes a simple path from a to b if it exists else P is empty. There does not exist a Ψ of arity 2 such that NIO(Ψ, P) defines P on G.

Proof: Suppose that such a Ψ exists.

$$P_o^G = \emptyset$$

$$P_{i+1}^G = P_i^G \cup \underline{\text{oneof}} \{(x, y) \mid \Psi(P_i^G, x, y) \wedge \sim P_i^G(x, y)\}$$

Then consider $\Psi(\emptyset, x, y)$. This is an FO formula with x and y as free variables and relation symbol E(.,.). Clearly, $(\exists x)(\exists y)\ \Psi(\emptyset, x, y)$ is true iff there is a path from a to b. This implies that we can test for a path from a to b using an FO formula. This is impossible since connectedness is not FO expressible [5]. □

Remark: However, the path-defining predicate P can be expressed by an FO+NIO expression $\alpha(Q)$ where $Q \Leftarrow$ NIO(Ψ, Q) and both α and Ψ are 2-ary:

```
Ψ ≡ IF   Q(a, b)
    THEN false
    ELSE IF   (∀z) ~Q(z, b)
         THEN  IF ~(∃x)(∃y) Q(x, y)
               THEN E(x, y) ∧ (x = a)
               ELSE (∃v)(∀w) [Q(v, x) ∧ ~Q(y, w) ∧ ~Q(w, y)
                                      ∧ E(x, y)]
         ELSE (∃u) [Q(u, b) ∧ Q(x, u) ∧ (y = b)].
```

To understand the predicate Q^G that is constructed by Ψ, we note that first a tree rooted at a is constructed till b is reached by the constructed tree. Then for every vertex x in the path from a to b the tuple (x, b) is included in Q.

We can now see that the path defining predicate P can be defined by the following α:

$$\alpha \equiv Q(a, b) \wedge [Q(x, y) \wedge Q(y, b)) \vee ((y = b) \wedge Q(x, y) \wedge E(x, y))]$$

Here, α returns empty predicate when $Q(a, b)$ is false, i.e., when a is not connected to b. Otherwise α is true for a pair (x, y) iff (x, y) is an edge in the unique path from a to b constructed in Q; for, y is certainly on the path as witnessed by Q(y, b) and there is a unique pair in Q with second argument as y.

Suppose arity is restricted to some k. Then a natural question is whether FO + NIO is more expressive than FO + LFP + order. Below is a result to show that the answer is affirmative when $k = 2$.

<u>Lemma 4.10</u>: Let the predicate P(x, y) define a maximal spanning forest for graphs $G = (V, E, <)$. Then there is no LFP definition of arity 2 which constructs the predicate P. But there is an FO + NIO expression of arity 2 which defines P for graphs G.

<u>Proof</u>: Suppose there is an LFP definition of P using some first-order Ψ (by definition). Then for a given graph G, the LFP operator constructs T_o, which is the least fixpoint and is a maximal spanning forest. We have, when we use this T_o in place of P in Ψ, the following first-order formula true on G.

$$F \equiv (\forall x)(\forall y)(\Psi(E, T_o, x, y) \leftrightarrow T_o(x, y))$$

(This simply says that T_o is a fixpoint of Ψ).
Consider the predicate $T_1(u, v, x, y)$ defined as:

$$T_1(u, v, x, y) = E(x, y) \quad \text{if} \quad u \neq x \text{ or } v \neq y$$
and $T_1(u, v, u, v) = \text{false}$.

(T_1 is E with the edge (u, v) removed).
For a given set $v = \{0, 1, \ldots, n-1\}$ with total order <, consider the edge relation E defined as follows:

If $x < n-1$ then $E(x, x+2)$ and $E(n-1, 0)$.

Then for n even, $G' = (V, E, <)$ is a simple path. For n odd it is a disconnected graph with two components: a cycle and a simple path. These graphs are from [5]. From the first order formula F, by substituting T_1 instead of T_o, and then taking existential closure for u and v, we get

$$(\exists u)(\exists v)(\forall x)(\forall y)\,[\Psi(E, T_1, u, v, x, y) \leftrightarrow T_1(u, v, x, y)]$$

Clearly, this formula is true for a graph G' iff $T_1(u, v, x, y)$ is a fixpoint for Ψ, for some u and v. But for n even, it is clear that G' is itself the maximal spanning forest; while for n odd an edge from the cycle in G' has to be removed to get a maximal spanning forest. Therefore,

$$(\exists u)(\exists v)(\forall x)(\forall y)\ [\Psi(E, T_1\ u, v, x, y) \Leftrightarrow T_1(u, v, x, y)]$$

is true on G' iff n is odd. But it is impossible to test if a finite set is even or odd using a first-order formula [5]. Hence no LFP definition of arity 2 for P exists.

The FO + NIO expression which defines a spanning-tree of a connected component in Section 3 is of arity 2. It can be easily modified to define a maximal spanning forest. This proves our lemma. □

5. CONCLUDING REMARKS

In this paper we have introduced a nondeterministic inductive operator to augment first-order logic and studied some of its expressibility and complexity aspects. We have seen that NIO is a generalization of LFP in an appropriate sense. It has been our experience, as the examples of its use in the paper would indicate, that NIO is easy to use and is quite appropriate in many varied situations. However, to assess its role as a programming primitive for query languages, a critical comparison with other such primitives [1] is necessary.

Theoretically, the most interesting question here seems to be to see if a syntactic subclass of U exists which has the same expressive power as U to capture PTIME. To draw a parallel, general LFP definition uses monotonicity, which is undecible to check. But use of positive formulas in place of monotonic ones in the LFP definition retains the ability to capture PTIME when order is externally supplied. Positivity, of course, is easy to check.

Other open problems are to look for improvement over Theorem 4.8, to examine more critically arity as a complexity measure and to contrast NIO with other important operators, e.g., iterated fixpoints.

Acknowledgement

We thank Professor Yuri Gurevich for his insightful remarks on an earlier draft of this paper, especially for pointing out Theorem 4.5.

REFERENCES

1 Chandra, A., (1981)
Programming Primitives for Database Languages,
8th Symposium on Principles of Programming Languages, ACM, pp 50-62.

2 Chandra, A. and Harel, D., (1982)
Structure and Complexity of Computable Queries,
Journal of Comp. and System Sciences, 25, pp 99-128.

3 Chandra, A. and Harel, D., (1982)
Horn Clauses and the Fixpoint Query Hierarchy,
Proc. ACM Symp. on Principles of Database Systems.

4 Garey, M.R. and Johnson, D.S., (1979)
Computers and Intractability: A Guide to the Theory of NP-Completeness, Freeman.

5 Gurevich, Y., (1984)
Toward Logic Tailored for Computational Complexity,
Proc. Logic Colloq. Aachen 1983, Lecture Notes in Mathematics,
Vol. 1104, pp 175-216, Springer-Verlag.

6 Gurevich, Y., (1985)
Logic and the Challenge of Computer Science,
Technical Report, University of Michigan, Computing Research Laboratory, CRL-TR-10-85.

7 Immerman, N., (1982)
Relational Queries Computable in Polynomial Time (Extended Abstract),
14th ACM Symp. on Theory of Computing, pp 147-152.

8 Immerman, N., (1983)
Languages which Capture Complexity Classes (Preliminary Report),
15th ACM Symp. on Theory of Computing, pp 347-354.

9 Vardi, M.Y., (1982)
The Complexity of Relational Query Languages (Extended Abstract),
14th ACM Symp. on Theory of Computing, pp 137-146.

Bounded Nondeterminism

and the Approximation Induction Principle in Process Algebra

(Extended Abstract)

R.J. van Glabbeek

Centre for Mathematics and Computer Science
P.O. Box 4079, 1009 AB Amsterdam, The Netherlands

This paper presents a new semantics of ACP_τ, the Algebra of Communicating Processes with abstraction. This leads to a term model of ACP_τ which is isomorphic to the model of process graphs modulo rooted $\tau\delta$-bisimulation of BAETEN, BERGSTRA & KLOP [2], but in which no special rootedness condition is needed. Bisimilarity turns out to be a congruence in a natural way.

In this model, the Recursive Definition Principle (RDP), the Commutativity of Abstraction (CA) and Koomen's Fair Abstraction Rule (KFAR) are satisfied, but the Approximation Induction Principle (AIP) is not. The combination of these four principles is proven to be inconsistent, while any combination of three of them is not.

In [2] a restricted version of AIP is proved valid in the graph model. This paper proposes a simpler and less restrictive version of AIP, not containing guarded recursive specifications as a parameter, which is still valid. This infinitary rule is formulated with the help of a family B_n of unary predicates, expressing bounded nondeterminism.

1980 Mathematics Subject Classification (version 1985): 68Q10, 68Q45, 68Q55, 68N15.
1982 CR Categories: F.1.2, F.3.2, F.4.3, D.3.1.
Key Words & Phrases: Concurrency, Process algebra, ACP, Approximation Induction Principle, Recursion, Abstraction, Fairness, Liveness, Consistency, Bisimulation, Bounded Nondeterminism.
Note: Sponsored in part by Esprit project no. 432, METEOR.

INTRODUCTION

Concurrency

A process is the behaviour of a system. The system can be a machine, a communication protocol, a network of falling dominoes, a chess player, or any other system. Concurrency is the study of parallel processes. The features studied include communication between parallel processes, deadlock behaviour, abstraction from internal steps, divergence, nondeterminism, fairness, priorities in the choice of actions, tight regions, etc. Processes are mostly studied within a model, capturing some of the features of concurrency. Among these models one finds Petri nets (see for instance REISIG [13]), Topological models (as in DE BAKKER & ZUCKER [3]), Algebraical models (like the projective limit models in BERGSTRA & KLOP [4]), Graph models (as in MILNER [10] and in BAETEN, BERGSTRA & KLOP [2]) and observation models, in which a process is fully determined by its possible interactions with the environment (like Hoare's failures model of Communicating Sequential Processes, see BROOKES, HOARE & ROSCOE [7], and the models used in Trace theory, see for instance REM [14]). Parameters in the classification of these models of concurrency are the features captured by the model, the identifications made on processes and the particular way of representing them. The identification issue deals with the question when two processes are to be considered equal. This is of importance on judging whether or not a certain system correctly implements a specification. The possible answers constitute a broad spectrum of process semantics, ranging from trace semantics, where two processes are identified as soon as their possible sequences of actions coincide, to bisimulation semantics, where all information about the timing of the divergencies of those traces is preserved.

Process algebra

Process algebra is an algebraic approach to the study of concurrent processes. Its tools are algebraical languages for the specification of processes and the formulation of statements about them, together with calculi for the verification of these statements. Process algebra is not to be regarded as a model of concurrency. On the one hand it is a method for specifying processes and proving statements about them without being limited to a particular model; on the other hand it is a method for analysing and comparing the different models of concurrency.

To illustrate the first application, consider a typical example. Suppose a machine is composed out of two components. In order to verify that it behaves as it should, one specifies the behaviour of the two components as well as the intended behaviour of their composition in an algebraical language. This language should be equipped with a composition operator and with a calculus, consisting of laws concerning the equality relation, the composition operator and the operators involved in the specifications of the three processes. In selecting the calculus it should be checked that all its rules and axioms are valid in the environment in which the machine is operating. Now one is able to formulate and prove the statement: the behaviour of the composition of the two components is equal to the intended behaviour of the desired machine.

The creation of an algebraical framework suitable to deal with such applications, gives rise to the construction of building blocks of operators and axioms, each block describing a feature of concurrency in a certain semantical setting. The models of concurrency serve to prove the consistency of the theories built from these blocks, and to illustrate the range of their applicability.

As to the second application, the various models of concurrency can be studied and classified by axiomatising them, and pointing out which axioms constitute the differences between them.

The first axiomatic treatment of concurrency is Milner's Calculus of Communicating Systems [10]. This calculus is closely linked to Milner's graph model (of 'synchronisation trees') with bisimulation semantics, and the axioms are presented as theorems, valid in this model. Other calculi are Milne's CIRCAL [9] and the Algebra of Communicating Processes (ACP) of BERGSTRA & KLOP [4]. The last one is not tied to a particular model. It is the core of a family of axioms systems, fitting in the process algebra methodology sketched above. Its standard semantics is bisimulation semantics, since it identifies the least; any theorem proved in bisimulation semantics remains valid in coarser semantics; but there are building blocks with axioms for more identifications. The present paper examines some rules and axioms, belonging to this family, and employs the notation of ACP. Although it builds further on the research done in [4] and [2], it can be read independently. For further details is refered to the full paper [8].

1. Atomic Actions and Communications

An atomic action is the most elementary component of a process. It is considered not to be divisible into smaller parts and not subject to further investigations. Mostly an atomic action is considered to be observed pointwise in time, for if the time it takes is to be observed, two atomic actions can be distinguished: its beginning and its end. It depends on the level of abstraction, which actions one wants to see as atomic.

Atomic actions are thought to occur simultaneously in a process only if they are communicating, like the actions 'give' and 'receive'. The simultaneous occurrence of actions a and b is denoted by $a|b$. In general $a|b = b|a$ and $(a|b)|c = a|(b|c)$. A multiset $a_1| \cdots |a_n$ (with $n \geq 2$) of communicating atomic actions is called a communication. The presentation of an algebra of communicating processes starts with postulating an alphabet A^0 of atomic actions and specifying which communications can occur.

Formally, an alphabet A of atomic actions and communications is defined as a set of nonempty multisets of symbols, such that if $a \in A$ and $b \subseteq a$ then also $b \in A$. Elements of A are called *actions*. A singleton action is called *atomic*; other actions are *communications*. A^0 is the set of atomic actions in A. Two actions a and $b \in A$ are said to communicate if their union $a|b \in A$.

Example: $A = \{a, b, c, b|c, c|c, b|c|c\}$. There is communication possible between b and c, c and c, $b|c$ and c and between b and $c|c$, while there is no communication possible between a and b or between b and $b|c$.

If $A = \{a, b, a|b\}$ and one wants to use c as an abbreviation for $a|b$, write $A = \{a, b, a|b{=}c\}$. This presentation differs slightly from the presentation in BERGSTRA & KLOP [4,5], where A contains only atomic actions and communication is given by a partial binary function $|: A \times A \rightarrow A$. There the last example would be $A = \{a,b,c\}$ and $a|b = c$.

2. The Algebra of Communicating Processes with Abstraction

ACP$_\tau$, the algebra of communicating processes with abstraction, is the equational theory, presented in the upper blocks of table 2. Its language is built inductively from a set $V = \{x,y,z,...\}$ of variables, and the constants and operators of table 1. The equality predicate = is always present, but never mentioned. An alphabet A of atomic actions and communications occurs as a parameter in ACP$_\tau$.

ACP$_\tau$:	constants:	a	for any atomic action $a \in A^0$
		δ	deadlock
		τ	silent action
	unary operators:	∂_H	encapsulation, for any $H \subseteq A$
		τ_I	abstraction, for any $I \subseteq A$
	binary operators:	$+$	alternative composition (sum)
		$\cdot$	sequential composition (product)
		$\Vert$	parallel composition (merge)
		$⌊⌊$	left-merge
		$\vert$	communication merge (bar)

Table 1

The meaning of these constructs will be given informally below, together with an explanation of the axioms of ACP$_\tau$. In table 2, all axioms are in fact axiom schemes in a,b and c, with a,b,c ranging over $A \cup \{\delta\}$, unless further restrictions are made in the table.

ACP_τ	$x+y = y+x$	A1	$x\tau = x$	T1
	$x+(y+z) = (x+y)+z$	A2	$\tau x + x = \tau x$	T2
	$x+x = x$	A3	$a(\tau x + y) = a(\tau x+y)+ax$	T3
	$(x+y)z = xz+yz$	A4		
	$(xy)z = x(yz)$	A5		
	$x+\delta = x$	A6		
	$\delta x = \delta$	A7		
	$a\mid b = b\mid a$	C1		
	$(a\mid b)\mid c = a\mid(b\mid c)$	C2		
	$a\mid b = \delta$ if $a\mid b \notin A$	C3		
	$x\parallel y = x\lfloor\!\lfloor y + y\lfloor\!\lfloor x + x\mid y$	CM1		
	$a\lfloor\!\lfloor x = ax$	CM2	$\tau\lfloor\!\lfloor x = \tau x$	TM1
	$(ax)\lfloor\!\lfloor y = a(x\parallel y)$	CM3	$(\tau x)\lfloor\!\lfloor y = \tau(x\parallel y)$	TM2
	$(x+y)\lfloor\!\lfloor z = x\lfloor\!\lfloor z + y\lfloor\!\lfloor z$	CM4	$\tau\mid x = \delta$	TC1
	$(ax)\mid b = (a\mid b)x$	CM5	$x\mid\tau = \delta$	TC2
	$a\mid(bx) = (a\mid b)x$	CM6	$(\tau x)\mid y = x\mid y$	TC3
	$(ax)\mid(by) = (a\mid b)(x\parallel y)$	CM7	$x\mid(\tau y) = x\mid y$	TC4
	$(x+y)\mid z = x\mid z + y\mid z$	CM8		
	$x\mid(y+z) = x\mid y + x\mid z$	CM9		
			$\partial_H(\tau) = \tau$	DT
			$\tau_I(\tau) = \tau$	TI1
	$\partial_H(a) = a$ if $a\notin H$	D1	$\tau_I(a) = a$ if $a\notin I$	TI2
	$\partial_H(a) = \delta$ if $a\in H$	D2	$\tau_I(a) = \tau$ if $a\in I$	TI3
	$\partial_H(x+y) = \partial_H(x)+\partial_H(y)$	D3	$\tau_I(x+y) = \tau_I(x)+\tau_I(y)$	TI4
	$\partial_H(xy) = \partial_H(x)\cdot\partial_H(y)$	D4	$\tau_I(xy) = \tau_I(x)\cdot\tau_I(y)$	TI5
PR	$\pi_n(\tau) = \tau$ $\pi_0(ax) = \delta$ $\pi_{n+1}(ax) = a\cdot\pi_n(x)$ $\pi_n(\tau x) = \tau\cdot\pi_n(x)$ $\pi_n(x+y) = \pi_n(x)+\pi_n(y)$			
B	$B_0(x)\quad B_n(a)\quad B_n(\tau)\quad \frac{B_n(x)}{B_n(\tau x)}\quad \frac{B_n(x)}{B_{n+1}(ax)}\quad \frac{B_n(x),B_n(y)}{B_n(x+y)}$			
AIP^-	$\frac{\forall n\in\mathbb{N}\ \pi_n(x)=\pi_n(y), B_n(x)}{x=y}$			
KFAR	$\frac{x=ix+y}{\tau_{\{i\}}(x)=\tau\cdot\tau_{\{i\}}(y)}$			
CA	$\tau_I\circ\tau_J(x)=\tau_{I\cup J}(x)$			

Table 2

a represents the process, starting with an a-step and terminating after some time. (see below)

δ is the action of acknowledging that there is no possibility to proceed. Put $A_\delta = A \cup \{\delta\}$.

τ represents the process terminating after some time, without performing observable actions. Put $A_\tau = A \cup \{\tau\}$.

$x+y$ represents the process that executes either x or y. The choice between x and y is made at the begining of $x+y$. It is not specified by whom. The axioms A1, A2 and A3 state that in a choice the alternatives are regarded to form a set. Axiom A6 states that deadlock only occurs if there are no alternatives.

$x\cdot y$ represents the process x, followed after possible termination by y. The process x fails to terminate if it ends in deadlock (A7), or if it performs an infinite sequence of actions, or if it goes on forever without performing any action. The last possibility is called *divergence*. The axioms A4 and A5 are rather straightforward, but since (at least in bisimulation semantics) the timing of the choices is of importance, there is no axiom $x(y+z) = xy+xz$.

$x \| y$ represents the simultaneous execution of x and y. It starts when one of its components starts and terminates if both of them do. (see below)

$x \lfloor\!\lfloor y$ is as $x \| y$, but under the assumption that x starts first (CM2,3,4, TM1,2).

$x | y$ is as $x \| y$, but starting with a communication between x and y (CM5,6,7,8,9). This communication may be preceded by some silent steps, but these are no part of the process (TC3,4). Silent processes do not take part in communications (TC1,2). Axiom CM1 states that a process $x \| y$ starts either with x or with y or with a communication between x and y. If the first actions from x and y do not communicate (as is always the case if $x = \delta$ or $y = \delta$) the summand $x | y$ can be removed, using C3 and A6,7.

$\partial_H(x)$ represents the process x without the possibility of performing actions from H. ∂_H renames the actions from H into δ (DT, D1-4). Mostly it is used to remove the remnants of unsuccessful communication from a merge, thereby indicating that the process is not at the same time communicating (through H at least) with the environment. This is why ∂_H is called encapsulation.
Example: $A = \{give,\ receive,\ give \,|\, receive\}$; $H = \{give,\ receive\}$.

$$\partial_H(give \| receive) = \partial_H(give \cdot receive + receive \cdot give + give \,|\, receive) =$$

$$= \delta \cdot \delta + \delta \cdot \delta + give \,|\, receive = give \,|\, receive.$$

$\tau_I(x)$ represents the process x, of which the actions from I are not considered important anymore. τ_I renames the actions from I into τ (TI 1-5).

For $a \in A$ the chosen semantics of the expression a can be motivated as follows: a denotes a process executing an action a. Although both the process and the action are denoted by a, they are different entities. We require the process a to take a positive amount of time, since it seems a natural assumption that all activity takes some time. However, in this time interval there should be only one single point where the execution of the action a is recorded (one could take the first moment that evidence is available for the execution of a), for if we would allow an action to manifest itself during a positive time span, then equations as $a \| b = ab + ba$, which hold in ACP$_\tau$, could be refuted on grounds of real-time behaviour. Hence there are three events to be recorded in the life of the process a: its beginning, the occurrence of the action a and its termination. Now the question arises where the second event has to be situated between the other ones. Suppose a process like $a+b$ operates in an environment where a cannot be executed (the process expression $a+b$ appears in the scope of a $\partial_{\{a\}}$ operator); then this option cancels out and the process will perform a b-step. However, if the process a can start without being recognizable as the process a, then it will be too late to do a b-step if the action a turns out to be impossible, and deadlock occurs. So, in order to define a ∂_H operator properly, one has to assume that the identity of a process a is clear from its beginning, at least for an environment $\partial_H(\cdot)$. Therefore the expression a is chosen to denote a process that starts with executing the action a. A process that does the a-step only after some time can be denoted by the expression τa (see figure 1).

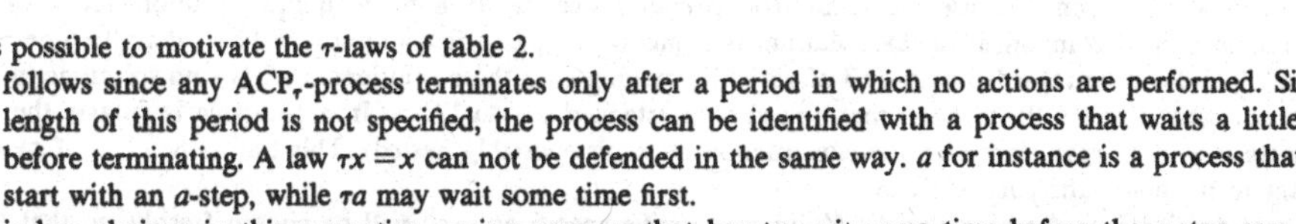

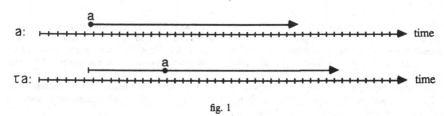

fig. 1

Now it is possible to motivate the τ-laws of table 2.

T1 follows since any ACP$_\tau$-process terminates only after a period in which no actions are performed. Since the length of this period is not specified, the process can be identified with a process that waits a little longer before terminating. A law $\tau x = x$ can not be defended in the same way. a for instance is a process that has to start with an a-step, while τa may wait some time first.

T2 is less obvious in this semantics. τa is a process that has to wait some time before the a-step can be performed, while $\tau a + a$ has the option to perform an a-step immediately. However, in ACP$_\tau$ these processes are identified, since the property 'having to wait some time before an action can happen' is not considered important enough for discriminating between processes. This in contrast with the property 'being able to wait some time before an action happens', which *is* used to discriminate between processes: $\tau a + a \neq a$. The argument is that a $\partial_H(\cdot)$ environment (in which certain actions can not be executed) discriminates only on grounds of the second property: in a sum only those summands can be canceled that are not able to wait some time before an action happens.
Of course it is also possible to use a more subtle semantics in which both properties are used for distinguishing between processes. However, in unrestricted form such a semantics would clash with the axioms CM2

and CM3: $ab = a\|\_b = (a\tau)\|\_b = a(\tau b + b)$. Therefore this option is not pursued in this paper.

T3 is adopted since $a(\tau x + y)$ already has the possibility to start with an a-step and then, after some time, reach a state where only x is possible.

These arguments will be formalised in section 5. Then propositions 4 and 5 of section 9 will tell us that the τ-laws exactly reflect the proposed semantics in the theory.

Using the axioms of table 2 it turns out that $\tau_{\{a\}}(a\|b)$ is equal to τb and hence different from b:

$$\tau_{\{a\}}(a\|b) = \tau_{\{a\}}(ab + ba) = \tau b + b\tau = \tau b + b = \tau b.$$

This fits in with the meaning of $x\|y$, given in section 2. $a\|b$ starts when one of its components starts and terminates if both of them do.

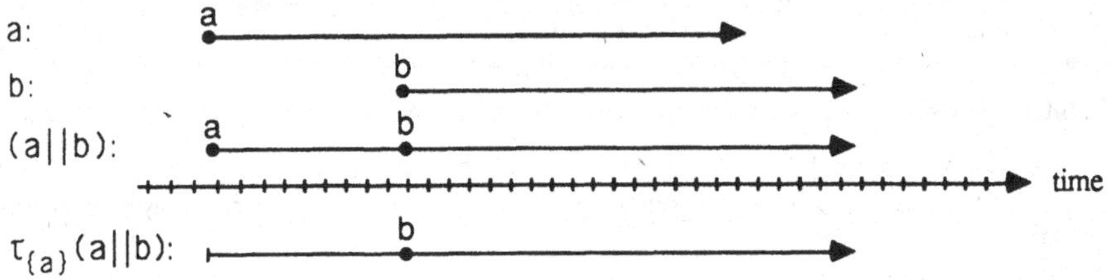

fig. 2

As indicated in figure 2, it is quite possible that the process a starts before b does. After abstraction from a, the resulting process is τb.

ACP_τ was first presented in BERGSTRA & KLOP [5]. In this presentation only axiom C3 is different, as a consequence of the different treatment of communication, mentioned in section 1. The τ-laws T1,T2 and T3 originate from MILNER [10]. In [5] it is proved that ACP_τ is a sound and complete proof system for closed recursion free terms, with respect to the semantical notion of bisimulation. However it is possible to make more identifications (depending on a notion of observability for instance), by adding some axioms. In a completeness proof it is important to know that any finite closed process expression can be rewritten into a process expression, built up inductively, following the scheme τ, ax, τx, $x+y$. Finally note that the axioms CM2,5 and 6 are derivable from the others.

3. RECURSION

A *recursive specification* E is a set of equations $\{x = t_x \mid x \in V_E\}$ with V_E a set of variables and t_x an ACP_τ term for $x \in V_E$. The variables of V_E may appear in t_x. Other variables occurring in t_x $(x \in V_E)$ are called *parameters* of E. Mostly, only recursive specifications without parameters are used. A *solution* of E is an interpretation of the variables of V_E as processes (in a certain domain) (as a function of an interpretation of the parameters of E), such that the equations of E are satisfied.

The Recursive Definition Principle (RDP) tells us that every recursive specification has a solution. In section 9 a model for ACP_τ will be presented, satisfying RDP. RDP cannot be expressed algebraically, since in algebraic languages no existential quantification is permitted.

Recursive specifications are used to define (or *specify*) processes. If E has a unique solution, let $<x \mid E>$ (with $x \in V_E$) denote the x-component of this solution. If E has more than one solution, $<x \mid E>$ denotes 'one of the solutions of E', and can be regarded as a kind of variable, ranging over these solutions. If E has no solutions (possible in a model, not satisfying RDP), then no meaning can be attached to $<x \mid E>$. In a recursive language, the syntactical constructs $<x \mid E>$ may appear in the construction of terms (possibly nested). This limits the class of models of the language to the ones satisfying RDP.

In most applications the variables $X \in V_E$ in a recursive specification E will be chosen freshly, so that there is no need to repeat E in each occurrence of $<X \mid E>$. Therefore the convention will be adopted that once a recursive specifications is declared, $<X \mid E>$ can be abbreviated by X. If this is done, X is called a *formal variable*. Formal variables are denoted by capital letters. So after the declaration $X = aX$, a statement $X = aaX$ should be interpreted as an abbreviation of $<X \mid X = aX> = aa<X \mid X = aX>$.

Let $E = \{x = t_x \mid x \in V_E\}$ be a recursive specification, and t a process expression. Then $<t \mid E>$ denotes the term t in which each (free) occurrence of $x \in V_E$ is replaced by $<x \mid E>$ (avoiding name clashes). In a recursive language all formulas $<x \mid E> = <t_x \mid E>$ (with E as above and $x \in V_E$) may be considered provable. If the above convention is used, these formulas seem to be just the equations of E.

Let T be an equational theory (like ACP_τ) over a signature Σ and e a Σ-equation, both recursion free. The following

notation is employed:
$T \vdash e$: e is provable from T in the recursion free language over Σ.
$T \models e$: e is true in all Σ-algebras, satisfying T.
$T+RDP \vdash e$: e is provable from T in the recursive language over Σ.
$T+RDP \models e$: e is true in all Σ-algebras, satisfying T and RDP.
Now Birkhof's completeness theorem for equational logic reads:

$$T \vdash e \Leftrightarrow T \models e.$$

It can be extended trivially to the case where T contains also conditional equations, and predicates are allowed in Σ. Now the following proposition, whose proof is omitted, justifies the notation $T+RDP \vdash e$.

PROPOSITION 1. $T+RDP \vdash e \Leftrightarrow T+RDP \models e$.

4. THE APPROXIMATION INDUCTION PRINCIPLE

PR is a building block that can be added to ACP$_\tau$. It consists of the unary operators π_n (projection) for $n \in \mathbb{N}$, and the axioms presented in the third block of table 2. $\pi_n(x)$ represents the process x, which is only allowed to perform n visible actions. The next visible action is blocked, i.e. renamed into δ.

The Approximation Induction Principle (AIP) is the infinitary rule

$$\boxed{\text{AIP} \quad \frac{\forall n \in \mathbb{N}\ \pi_n(x)=\pi_n(y)}{x=y}}$$

saying that a process is fully determined by its finite projections. It follows if one choses to identify processes that can not be distinguished by their finite observations.

5. ACTION RELATIONS BETWEEN PROCESSES

If x and y are processes and $a \in A$, then write
$x \xrightarrow{a} y$ if x can evolve into y during a period in which only the action a is performed.
$x \xrightarrow{\tau} y$ if x can evolve into y, taking a positive amount of time in which no visible actions occur.
$x \xrightarrow{a} \surd$ if x can terminate after having done only an a-step, and
$x \xrightarrow{\tau} \surd$ if x can terminate after some time, without performing visible actions.

The involved binary predicates $\xrightarrow{a}$ and unary predicates $\xrightarrow{a}\surd$, both for $a \in A_\tau$, are called *action relations*. A *process expression* is a term in the recursive language of ACP$_\tau$+PR. Let $\mathcal{P}$ be the domain of closed process expressions. On $\mathcal{P}$ the action relations are generated by the *action rules* presented in the upper block of table 3. All these rules are schemes in a and b, with a,b ranging over A_τ, unless further restrictions are made in the table. These action rules provide an alternative explanation of the meaning of the language constructs of ACP$_\tau$+PR+RDP. Note that the τ-laws of table 3 exactly reflect the motivations for the τ-laws of table 2, as given in section 2, in terms of action relations. Also note that the instance $\tau \xrightarrow{\tau} \tau$ of the first τ-law of table 3 does not imply that the process τ may fail to terminate. It only says that after waiting some time on the process to terminate, it may still not be ready. The situation is as in Zeno's paradox: Achilles *will* catch up with the Tortoise.

The action relations can be generalised as follows. If x and y are processes and $\sigma \in A^*$, then write

$x \overset{\sigma}{\twoheadrightarrow} y$ if x can evolve into y during a period (of positive duration) in which (only) the sequence of actions σ occurs.

$x \overset{\sigma}{\twoheadrightarrow} \surd$ if x can terminate after a period (of positive duration) in which (only) the sequence of actions σ occurs.
On $\mathcal{P}$ these generalised action relations are generated by the rules presented in the bottom block of table 3. There $\tau \in A^*$ denotes the empty string, a ranges over A and σ,ρ over A^*.

6. FAIR ABSTRACTION

EXAMPLE (due to F. Vaandrager): A statistician performs a simple experiment in a closed room: he tosses a coin until tail comes up; then he leaves the room to report success. Let p be the probability that, if he tosses the coin, tail comes up. Assume $0<p<1$. The behaviour of the statistician is specified by

$$S = head \cdot S + tail \cdot success$$

Being outside the room, the only part of the process we can observe is the statistician leaving the room to report

a :	$a \xrightarrow{a} \surd$				
$+$:	$\dfrac{x \xrightarrow{a} x'}{x+y \xrightarrow{a} x'}$	$\dfrac{x \xrightarrow{a} \surd}{x+y \xrightarrow{a} \surd}$	$\dfrac{y \xrightarrow{a} y'}{x+y \xrightarrow{a} y'}$	$\dfrac{y \xrightarrow{a} \surd}{x+y \xrightarrow{a} \surd}$	
$\cdot$:	$\dfrac{x \xrightarrow{a} x'}{xy \xrightarrow{a} x'y}$	$\dfrac{x \xrightarrow{a} \surd}{xy \xrightarrow{a} y}$			
$\Vert$:	$\dfrac{x \xrightarrow{a} x'}{x\Vert y \xrightarrow{a} x'\Vert y}$	$\dfrac{x \xrightarrow{a} \surd}{x\Vert y \xrightarrow{a} y}$	$\dfrac{y \xrightarrow{a} y'}{x\Vert y \xrightarrow{a} x\Vert y'}$	$\dfrac{y \xrightarrow{a} \surd}{x\Vert y \xrightarrow{a} x}$	
	$\dfrac{x \xrightarrow{a} x',\ y \xrightarrow{b} y'}{x\Vert y \xrightarrow{a\mid b} x'\Vert y'}$	$\dfrac{x \xrightarrow{a} \surd,\ y \xrightarrow{b} y'}{x\Vert y \xrightarrow{a\mid b} y'}$	$\dfrac{x \xrightarrow{a} x',\ y \xrightarrow{b} \surd}{x\Vert y \xrightarrow{a\mid b} x'}$	$\dfrac{x \xrightarrow{a} \surd,\ y \xrightarrow{b} \surd}{x\Vert y \xrightarrow{a\mid b} \surd}$	(if $a\mid b\in A$)
$⫫$:	$\dfrac{x \xrightarrow{a} x'}{x ⫫ y \xrightarrow{a} x\Vert y}$	$\dfrac{x \xrightarrow{a} \surd}{x ⫫ y \xrightarrow{a} y}$			
$\mid$:	$\dfrac{x \xrightarrow{a} x',\ y \xrightarrow{b} y'}{x\mid y \xrightarrow{a\mid b} x'\Vert y'}$	$\dfrac{x \xrightarrow{a} \surd,\ y \xrightarrow{b} y'}{x\mid y \xrightarrow{a\mid b} y'}$	$\dfrac{x \xrightarrow{a} x',\ y \xrightarrow{b} \surd}{x\mid y \xrightarrow{a\mid b} x'}$	$\dfrac{x \xrightarrow{a} \surd,\ y \xrightarrow{b} \surd}{x\mid y \xrightarrow{a\mid b} \surd}$	(if $a\mid b\in A$)
∂_H:	$\dfrac{x \xrightarrow{a} x'}{\partial_H(x) \xrightarrow{a} \partial_H(x')}$	$\dfrac{x \xrightarrow{a} \surd}{\partial_H(x) \xrightarrow{a} \surd}$	(if $a\notin H$)		
τ_I:	$\dfrac{x \xrightarrow{a} x'}{\tau_I(x) \xrightarrow{a} \tau_I(x')}$	$\dfrac{x \xrightarrow{a} \surd}{\tau_I(x) \xrightarrow{a} \surd}$	(if $a\notin I$)		
	$\dfrac{x \xrightarrow{a} x'}{\tau_I(x) \xrightarrow{\tau} \tau_I(x')}$	$\dfrac{x \xrightarrow{a} \surd}{\tau_I(x) \xrightarrow{\tau} \surd}$	(if $a\in I$)		
π_n:	$\dfrac{x \xrightarrow{a} x'}{\pi_{n+1}(x) \xrightarrow{a} \pi_n(x')}$	$\dfrac{x \xrightarrow{a} \surd}{\pi_{n+1}(x) \xrightarrow{a} \surd}$	(if $a\neq\tau$)		
	$\dfrac{x \xrightarrow{\tau} x'}{\pi_n(x) \xrightarrow{\tau} \pi_n(x')}$	$\dfrac{x \xrightarrow{\tau} \surd}{\pi_n(x) \xrightarrow{\tau} \surd}$			
recursion:	$\dfrac{<t_x\mid E> \xrightarrow{a} y}{<x\mid E> \xrightarrow{a} y}$	$\dfrac{<t_x\mid E> \xrightarrow{a} \surd}{<x\mid E> \xrightarrow{a} \surd}$			
τ - laws:	$a \xrightarrow{a} \tau$	$\dfrac{x \xrightarrow{\tau} y,\ y \xrightarrow{a} z}{x \xrightarrow{a} z}$	$\dfrac{x \xrightarrow{\tau} y,\ y \xrightarrow{a} \surd}{x \xrightarrow{a} \surd}$	$\dfrac{x \xrightarrow{a} y,\ y \xrightarrow{\tau} z}{x \xrightarrow{a} z}$	$\dfrac{x \xrightarrow{a} y,\ y \xrightarrow{\tau} \surd}{x \xrightarrow{a} \surd}$

$\dfrac{x \xrightarrow{a} y}{x \overset{a}{\twoheadrightarrow} y}$	$\dfrac{x \xrightarrow{a} \surd}{x \overset{a}{\twoheadrightarrow} \surd}$	$\dfrac{x \xrightarrow{\tau} y}{x \overset{\tau}{\twoheadrightarrow} y}$	$\dfrac{x \xrightarrow{\tau} \surd}{x \overset{\tau}{\twoheadrightarrow} \surd}$	$\dfrac{x \overset{\sigma}{\twoheadrightarrow} y,\ y \overset{\rho}{\twoheadrightarrow} z}{x \overset{\sigma\rho}{\twoheadrightarrow} z}$	$\dfrac{x \overset{\sigma}{\twoheadrightarrow} y,\ y \overset{\rho}{\twoheadrightarrow} \surd}{x \overset{\sigma\rho}{\twoheadrightarrow} \surd}$

Table 3

success. So the actions from $I = \{head, tail\}$ are hidden, and the observed process is $\tau_I(S)$. Since $0<p<1$, the process S will perform a *tail* action sooner or later, which yields the identity

$$\tau_I(S) = \tau \cdot success.$$

What is needed is an algebraic framework in which one can prove this equation.

An infinite path of a process x is an infinite alternating sequence of labels $a_i \in A_\tau$ and processes x_i $(i \in \mathbb{N})$, such that $x \xrightarrow{a_0} x_0 \xrightarrow{a_1} x_1 \xrightarrow{a_2} x_2 \rightarrow \dots$.

Such a path has an *exit* at $x_i (i \in \mathbb{N})$ if $x_i \xrightarrow{b} y$ with either $b \neq a_{i+1}$ or $y \neq x_{i+1}$. This exit is called a τ-*exit* if $b = \tau$. A path is called *improbable* if it has infinitely many exits. Now a process is said to be *fair*, if for any improbable path the probability that it will be executed is zero. In a theory for fair processes there is room for proof rules stating that certain improbable paths may be discarded. There is however a problem in discarding improbable paths. If a process is placed in a context $\partial_H(\cdot)$ then certain paths may stop to be improbable because their exits disappear. In that case they may not have been discarded. Thus only paths may be discarded which are improbable in all contexts. These are the paths with infinitely many τ-exits. KFAR$^-$ is a proof rule, stating that certain paths with infinitely many τ-exits, which are made invisible by a τ_I operator, may be discarded.

KFAR$^-$	$\dfrac{x = ix + \tau y + z}{\tau_{\{i\}}(x) = \tau \cdot \tau_{\{i\}}(\tau y + z)}$

A version of KFAR$^-$ appeared first in BERGSTRA, KLOP & OLDEROG [6]. It is a restricted version of Koomen's Fair Abstraction Rule (KFAR), which was presented in BAETEN, BERGSTRA & KLOP [2], and will be discussed in the next section.

The last axiom of table 2, the commutativity of abstraction (CA), says that it does not matter in which order actions are considered unimportant (or made invisible). It occurred already as one of the conditional axioms (also abbreviated as CA) in BAETEN, BERGSTRA & KLOP [1], and will play an important role in observations to come.

Using KFAR$^-$ and CA the identity $\tau_I(S) = \tau \cdot success$ from the example of the statistician can be derived formally:

$$\tau_{\{tail\}}(S) = \tau_{\{tail\}}(head \cdot S + tail \cdot success) = head \cdot \tau_{\{tail\}}(S) + \tau \cdot success + \delta,$$

$$\text{so } \tau_I(S) = \tau_{\{head\}} \circ \tau_{\{tail\}}(S) = \tau \cdot \tau_{\{head\}}(\tau \cdot success + \delta) = \tau \cdot success.$$

A theory, containing rules like KFAR$^-$ is only suited for the study of fair processes. For any application it has to be checked that all processes concerned are fair indeed.

7. DEADLOCK = LIVELOCK

EXAMPLE. Choose $A = \{a, b, c, b|c\}$ and $H = \{b,c\}$. Then $\mathrm{ACP}_\tau \vdash \partial_H(aaab \| c) = aaa(b|c)$. So the process c inside the encapsulated merge $\partial_H(aaab \| \cdot)$ waits patiently until it can communicate with $aaab$. If such a communication is not possible, deadlock occurs:

$$\mathrm{ACP}_\tau \vdash \partial_H(aaa \| c) = aaa\delta$$

$$\mathrm{ACP}_\tau \vdash \partial_H(aaac \| c) = aaa\delta.$$

So deadlock occurs in an encapsulated merge if not all components are terminated, and the ones which are not are all waiting for an opportunity to communicate. From this one learns that deadlock, as in $aaa\delta$, should not be interpreted as a violent crash of the system, but as an eternal sleep.

EXAMPLE. Specify X by $X = aX$. Then $\tau_{\{a\}}(X)$ remains active forever (it performs a-steps), but no actions can be observed. This is called *livelock*.

In order to distinguish deadlock from livelock one can assume that processes are noisy. The noise starts at the beginning of a process, and ends if the process terminates or starts waiting. If a component in an encapsulated merge has to wait for a suitable communication it becomes silent until the communication is enabled, but as long as at least one component is making progress (visibly or invisibly) noise is being made. Only if all components are waiting (or terminated), the process becomes silent. This guarantees that no further action is possible and it will remain silent forever. In such a semantics, deadlock is observable (silence is), but livelock is not (one can never know that from some moment on no visible action will be performed). In bisimulation semantics, as employed in this paper, processes are not assumed to be noisy, and no distinction between deadlock and livelock is made. This can be expressed algebraically by the rule:

deadlock = livelock	$\dfrac{x = ix}{\tau_{\{i\}}(x) = \tau\delta}$

In this rule livelock is expressed as $\tau_{\{i\}}(x)$, with x satisfying $x = ix$, and deadlock as $\tau\delta$. Note that livelock can not be expressed as a process x satisfying $x = \tau x$, since also τa satisfies $x = \tau x$. Furthermore deadlock can not be expressed by δ, since in $a \cdot (b + \delta)$ no deadlock occurs.

Equating deadlock and livelock amounts to stating that in a process invisible infinite paths without any exits may be discarded (leaving $\tau\delta$ in place). In combination with fairness this means that any invisible infinite path may be discarded, regardless whether it is improbable or not. This is expressed by Koomen's Fair Abstraction Rule:

$$\text{KFAR} \qquad \frac{x = ix + y}{\tau_{\{i\}}(x) = \tau \cdot \tau_{\{i\}}(y)}$$

The rule *deadlock* = *livelock* can be obtained from KFAR by substituting $y = \delta$. KFAR^- can be obtained by substituting $y = \tau y + z$.

8. Consistency & Liveness

For $p \in \mathcal{P}$ write $p \not\rightarrow$ if $p \xrightarrow{a} q$ for no $a \in A_\tau$ and $q \in \mathcal{P}$. A theory T is said to be *consistent* if $T \vdash p = q$ implies:

(i) $p \overset{\sigma}{\twoheadrightarrow} \surd$ if and only if $q \overset{\sigma}{\twoheadrightarrow} \surd$

(ii) $p \overset{\sigma}{\twoheadrightarrow} p' \not\rightarrow$ if and only if $q \overset{\sigma}{\twoheadrightarrow} q' \not\rightarrow$

for any pair of closed recursion free process expressions p and q. This notion was called 'trace consistency' in Bergstra, Klop and Olderog [6]. A theory T with $T \vdash \tau = \tau + \tau\delta$ for instance is inconsistent. Depending on whether or not one wants to assume fairness and/or *deadlock* = *livelock* there are several ways to define consistency in terms of recursive process expressions as well. The main possibilities are discussed in Van Glabbeek [8]. In order to leave all options open, in this paper consistency is defined in terms of recursion free process expressions only. In this paper process theories are required to be consistent, so that deadlock behaviour can be dealt with properly.

The notions of safety and liveness are frequently used in the literature. Roughly, safety means that something bad cannot happen, while liveness means that something good will eventually happen. Use τ^ω as an abbreviation of $\tau_{\{i\}}(\langle x \mid x = ix \rangle)$. If termination is considered to be something good then $T \vdash \tau = \tau + \tau^\omega$ should be regarded as a violation of liveness (by the theory T). In [8] this concept has been formalised.

9. A Term Model for ACP_τ + PR + RDP + CA + KFAR.

A *bisimulation* is a binary relation R on $\mathcal{P}$, satisfying:

- if pRq and $p \xrightarrow{a} p'$, then $\exists q': q \xrightarrow{a} q'$ and $p'Rq' (a \in A_\tau)$.
- if pRq and $q \xrightarrow{a} q'$, then $\exists p': p \xrightarrow{a} p'$ and $p'Rq' (a \in A_\tau)$.
- if pRq then: $p \xrightarrow{a} \surd$ if and only if $q \xrightarrow{a} \surd (a \in A_\tau)$.

p and $q \in \mathcal{P}$ are *bisimilar*, notation $p \leftrightarrow q$, if there exists a bisimulation R on $\mathcal{P}$ with pRq.

Proposition 2. *$\leftrightarrow$ is a congruence on $\mathcal{P}$.*
Proposition 3. *Any theory for which $\mathcal{P}/\leftrightarrow$ is a model is consistent and respects liveness.*
Proposition 4. *$\mathcal{P}/\leftrightarrow$ is a model of* ACP_τ + PR + RDP + CA + KFAR.
Proposition 5. ACP_τ + PR *is a complete axiomatisation of $\mathcal{P}/\leftrightarrow$ for closed recursion free process expressions.*
Proposition 6. *$\mathcal{P}/\leftrightarrow$ is isomorphic to the graph model* $\mathbb{G}_{\aleph_1}/\leftrightarrow_{r\delta}$ of Baeten, Bergstra & Klop [2].

Proofs. Omitted.

The notion of bisimulation originates from Park [12]. Bisimilarity is similar to the notion of observation congruence of Milner [11] and rooted $\tau\delta$-bisimilarity of Baeten, Bergstra & Klop [2]. If the relations $p \xrightarrow{a} q$ and $p \xrightarrow{a} \surd$ were defined without the τ-laws of table 3, the corresponding version of bisimilarity would be strong congruence, or δ-bisimilarity; if they were defined, using an extra rule $x \xrightarrow{\tau} x$, it would be observation equivalence or $\tau\delta$-bisimilarity. In [11] and [2] observation equivalence or $\tau\delta$-bisimilarity appears as a natural equivalence, with the unpleasant property of not being a congruence. Then a context requirement or rootedness condition is proposed to make it into a congruence. This is not necessary in the present approach: bisimilarity turned out to be a congruence in a natural way.

The model $\mathcal{P}/\leftrightarrow$ can be used to prove that the Recursive Definition Principle holds in the graph model of [2]. RDP holds trivially in $\mathcal{P}/\leftrightarrow$: $\langle x \mid E \rangle / \leftrightarrow$ is the x-component of a solution of E in $\mathcal{P}/\leftrightarrow$. From the last proposition it follows that it holds in the graph model also. Details are omitted here.

As demonstrated already in BAETEN, BERGSTRA & KLOP [2], AIP does not hold in $\mathbb{G}_{\aleph_1}/{\leftrightarrow_{rd}}$ and hence not in $\mathcal{G}/{\leftrightarrow}$: Let $\sum_{n>0} a^n$ be the process $(<x\,|\,x=xa+a>)_{\leftrightarrow} \in \mathcal{G}/{\leftrightarrow}$ and $a^\omega = (<x\,|\,x=ax>)_{\leftrightarrow} \in \mathcal{G}/{\leftrightarrow}$. Then

$$\mathrm{AIP} \models \sum_{n>0} a^n = \sum_{n>0} a^n + a^\omega \text{ but not } \sum_{n>0} a^n \leftrightarrow \sum_{n>0} a^n + a^\omega.$$

Hence it seems worthwhile to look for another model of ACP_τ, in which AIP is valid. However, such an attempt can only succeed at the expense of RDP, CA or KFAR.

10. THE INCONSISTENCY OF BPA* + RDP + AIP + CA + KFAR

In this section it will be proved that the combination of RDP, AIP, CA, and KFAR is inconsistent on top of ACP_τ+PR. Since the operators $\|$, $\lfloor\!\lfloor$, $|$ and ∂_H are not involved in this proof, the result can be formulated more sharply. Let BPA* be the subtheory of ACP_τ+PR consisting of the axioms A, T, TI, and PR of table 2. Assume that the alphabet A contains at least two different actions a and b.

THEOREM 1. BPA*+RDP+AIP+CA+KFAR $\vdash \tau = \tau + \tau\delta$.

PROOF. Declare the following recursive specifications:

$$X_k = aX_{k+1} + b^k \ (k>0) \qquad Y = bY \qquad Z = aZ + \tau$$

Now the theorem follows from the following 6 lemmas:

I.	$\tau_{\{b\}}(X_1) = Z$	an application of AIP
II.	$\tau_{\{a\}}(Z) = \tau$	an application of KFAR, even of KFAR$^-$
III.	$\tau_{\{a,b\}}(X_1) = \tau$	from I and II, using CA
IV.	$\tau_{\{a\}}(X_1) = \tau_{\{a\}}(X_1) + Y$	an application of AIP, using T2
V.	$\tau_{\{b\}}(Y) = \tau\delta$	an application of KFAR; this time of *deadlock* = *livelock*
VI.	$\tau_{\{a,b\}}(X_1) = \tau + \tau\delta$	from IV and V, using CA and III. □

To illustrate the proof, the process graphs of X_1, $\tau_{\{b\}}(X_1)$, Z, $\tau_{\{a\}}(X_1)$ and $\tau_{\{a\}}(X_1)+Y$ are presented in figure 3. In [2,4,5,8] it can be found how process graphs can be obtained from closed process expressions.

In the proof of theorem 1, the equation of deadlock and livelock plays a crucial role. If KFAR is replaced by the weaker proof rule KFAR$^-$, only expressing fairness, the inconsistency disappears:

PROPOSITION 7. BPA*+RDP+AIP+CA+KFAR$^-$ *is consistent.*
PROOF. See VAN GLABBEEK [8].

However this theory has another disadvantage, it violates liveness:

PROPOSITION 8. BPA*+RDP+AIP+CA+KFAR$^-$ $\vdash \tau = \tau + \tau^\omega$.
PROOF. As above, but without using Lemma V, it can be proved that $\tau = \tau + \tau_{\{b\}}(Y)$, where $\tau_{\{b\}}(Y)$ can be written as τ^ω (see section 8).

Furthermore in [8] it is shown that if in BPA*+RDP+AIP+CA+KFAR either RDP or AIP or CA or KFAR is dropped, a consistent theory that respects liveness remains. So in theorem 1 all ingredients are really needed.

11. BOUNDED NONDETERMINISM AND THE VALIDITY OF AIP$^-$

Let B be a new building block that can be added to ACP_τ. It consists of the unary predicates B_n (*boundedness*) for $n \in \mathbb{N}$, and the rules and axioms presented in the fourth block of table 2. $B_n(x)$ states that the nondeterminism displayed by x before its nth visible step is bounded. This means that for any sequence σ of length $< n$ of visible actions there are only finitely many different processes to which x can evolve by performing σ.

Define the predicates $\overset{\sigma}{\twoheadrightarrow}$ on $\mathcal{G}/{\leftrightarrow}$ by: $P \overset{\sigma}{\twoheadrightarrow} Q$ if there are $p \in P$ and $q \in Q$ with $p \overset{\sigma}{\twoheadrightarrow} q$. Now the predicates B_n can be defined on $\mathcal{G}/{\leftrightarrow}$ by: $B_n(P)$ if $\{Q \in \mathcal{G}/{\leftrightarrow} \mid P \overset{\sigma}{\twoheadrightarrow} Q\}$ is finite for any $\sigma \in A^*$ with length $<n$. $P \in \mathcal{G}/{\leftrightarrow}$ is *bounded* (P displays only bounded nondeterminism) if $\{Q \in \mathcal{G}/{\leftrightarrow} \mid P \overset{\sigma}{\twoheadrightarrow} Q\}$ is finite for any $\sigma \in A^*$. Of course P is bounded if and only if for all $n \in \mathbb{N}$ $B_n(P)$.

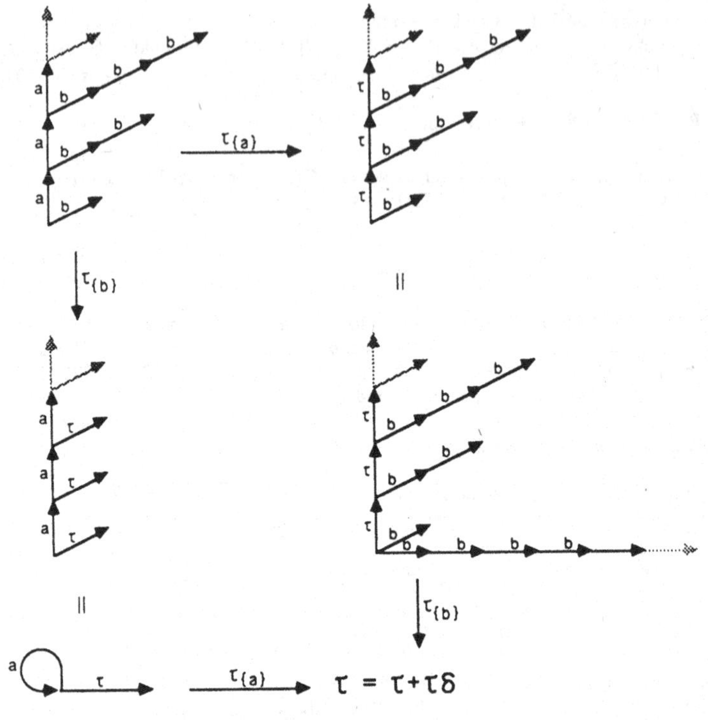

fig. 3

PROPOSITION 9. $\mathcal{P}/\underline{\leftrightarrow} \models B$.
PROOF. Omitted.

A process expression $p \in \mathcal{P}$ is *(syntactically) bounded* if $\{q \in \mathcal{P} \mid p \overset{\sigma}{\twoheadrightarrow} q\}$ is finite for any $\sigma \in A^*$. Note that $(q)_{\underline{\leftrightarrow}} \in \mathcal{P}/\underline{\leftrightarrow}$ is bounded does not imply that $q \in \mathcal{P}$ is bounded.

LEMMA. *If $p \in \mathcal{P}$ is bounded and $p \overset{\sigma}{\twoheadrightarrow} q$, then also $q \in \mathcal{P}$ is bounded.*
LEMMA. *If $P \in \mathcal{P}/\underline{\leftrightarrow}$ is bounded, then there is a $p \in P$ bounded.*
PROOFS. Omitted.

Since AIP is not valid in the model $\mathcal{P}/\underline{\leftrightarrow}$ and even inconsistent in combination with RDP, CA and KFAR, a restricted version AIP$^-$ is proposed in table 2, formulated with the help of the predicates B_n. Now it remains to be proven that $\mathcal{P}/\underline{\leftrightarrow} \models$ AIP$^-$.

The proof below can be viewed as a reconstruction of the proof of BAETEN, BERGSTRA & KLOP [2], that a more restrictive version of AIP$^-$ holds in the graph model $\mathbb{G}_{\aleph_1}/\underline{\leftrightarrow}_{rr}$, which is isomorphic to $\mathcal{P}/\underline{\leftrightarrow}$. It makes use of the lemmas above. As a corollary it follows that all rules of table 2 are satisfied by $\mathcal{P}/\underline{\leftrightarrow}$, and that ACP$_\tau$+PR+B+RDP+AIP$^-$+CA+KFAR is consistent and respects liveness.

THEOREM 2. $\mathcal{P}/\underline{\leftrightarrow} \models$ AIP$^-$.

PROOF. Let $P,Q \in \mathcal{P}/\underline{\leftrightarrow}$, $B_n(Q)$ for $n \in \mathbb{N}$ and $\forall n \in \mathbb{N}$: $\pi_n(P) = \pi_n(Q)$. It has to be proved that $P=Q$. Take $p \in P$ and $q \in Q$, such that q is bounded. Then $\forall n \in \mathbb{N}$: $\pi_n(p) \underline{\leftrightarrow} \pi_n(q)$. It suffices to prove that $p \underline{\leftrightarrow} q$, i.e. that there is a bisimulation R on $\mathcal{P}$ with pRq.
CLAIM: R can be defined by: pRq if $\forall n: \pi_n(p) \underline{\leftrightarrow} \pi_n(q)$ and q is bounded.

- Suppose pRq and $p \overset{a}{\longrightarrow} p'$ (with $a \in A_\tau$). Then put $S_n = \{q^* \in \mathcal{P} \mid q \overset{a}{\longrightarrow} q^* \;\&\; \pi_n(p') \underline{\leftrightarrow} \pi_n(q^*)\}$, and remark that
  I. $S_0 \supseteq S_1 \supseteq S_2 \supseteq ...$, since $\pi_{n+1}(p') \underline{\leftrightarrow} \pi_{n+1}(q^*)$ implies $\pi_n(p') \underline{\leftrightarrow} \pi_n(q^*)$.
  II. $S_n \neq \varnothing$, for $n \in \mathbb{N}$, since $\pi_{n+1}(p) \underline{\leftrightarrow} \pi_{n+1}(q)$.
  III. S_n is finite, for $n \in \mathbb{N}$, since q is bounded.
  From these observations it follows that $\bigcap_{n=0}^{\infty} S_n \neq \varnothing$. Choose $q' \in \bigcap_{n=0}^{\infty} S_n$, then $q \overset{a}{\longrightarrow} q'$ and $p'Rq'$.
- Suppose pRq and $q \overset{a}{\longrightarrow} q'$ (with $a \in A_\tau$). Then put $S_n = \{p^* \in \mathcal{P} \mid p \overset{a}{\longrightarrow} p^* \;\&\; \pi_n(p^*) \underline{\leftrightarrow} \pi_n(q')\}$, and remark that

$S_0 \supseteq ...$ and $S_n \neq \varnothing$ for $n \in \mathbb{N}$ (as above).

Now, for $n \in \mathbb{N}$, choose $p_n \in S_n$. By the first part of this proof, there are $q_n \in \mathcal{P}$ with $q \xrightarrow{a} q_n$ and $p_n R q_n$. But since q is bounded, there must be a process q^* in the sequence $q_0, q_1, q_2, ...$ occurring infinitely many times. Let $I = \{n \in \mathbb{N} \mid p_n R q^*\}$ and choose $i \in I$. It suffices to prove that $p_i R q'$. Let $n \in \mathbb{N}$, then an $m \in I$ exists with $m > n$. So $\pi_n(p_m) \leftrightarrow \pi_n(q')$, since $p_m \in S_m \subseteq S_n$. Furthermore $p_m R q^*$ and $p_i R q^*$, so $\pi_n(p_i) \leftrightarrow \pi_n(q^*) \leftrightarrow \pi_n(p_m) \leftrightarrow \pi_n(q')$. This holds for any $n \in \mathbb{N}$, thus $p_i R q'$.

- If pRq then: $p \xrightarrow{a} \surd \Leftrightarrow \pi_1(p) \xrightarrow{a} \surd \Leftrightarrow \pi_1(q) \xrightarrow{a} \surd \Leftrightarrow q \xrightarrow{a} \surd$.

Thus R is a bisimulation and the theorem is proved. □

12. Conclusion

In this paper a model $\mathcal{P}/\leftrightarrow$ of ACP$_\tau$ has been constructed, satisfying RDP, CA and KFAR, but not satisfying AIP. It has been shown that the price of changing this model in such a way that AIP holds is rather high:

- either RDP has to be dropped, in which case a lot of interesting processes can not be defined anymore,
- or CA has to be dropped, which makes the model very unnatural,
- or KFAR has to be dropped entirely, which makes for instance protocol verification with channels that can make errors almost impossible,
- or KFAR has to be replaced by KFAR$^-$, in which case only safety properties of protocols can be verified, and no liveness properties.

Therefore another strategy has been pursued: to find a restricted version of AIP, valid in the model $\mathcal{P}/\leftrightarrow$, whose computational possibilities approximate those of AIP as close as possible. This was first done in Baeten, Bergstra & Klop [2]. In table 2 of the present paper, a simpler and less restrictive version of AIP, called AIP$^-$, is proposed, not containing guarded recursive specifications as a parameter. For this reason the predicates B_n were introduced.
Finally AIP$^-$ is proved valid in $\mathcal{P}/\leftrightarrow$, which guarantees the consistency of the resulting theory ACP$_\tau$+PR+B+RDP+AIP$^-$ +CA+KFAR.

References

[1] J.C.M. Baeten, J.A. Bergstra & J.W. Klop, *Conditional axioms and α/β calculus in process algebra,* report CS-R8502, Centrum voor Wiskunde en Informatica, Amsterdam 1985, to appear in: Proc. IFIP Conference on Formal Description of Programming Concepts, Gl. Avernaes 1986, (M. Wirsing, ed.), North-Holland.

[2] J.C.M. Baeten, J.A. Bergstra & J.W. Klop, *On the consistency of Koomen's Fair Abstraction Rule,* report CS-R8511, Centrum voor Wiskunde en Informatica, Amsterdam 1985, to appear in Theoretical Computer Science.

[3] J.W. de Bakker & J.I. Zucker, *Processes and the denotational semantics of concurrency,* Information & Control 54 (1/2), pp. 70-120, 1982.

[4] J.A. Bergstra & J.W. Klop, *Algebra of communicating processes,* Proc. of the CWI Symp. Math. & Comp. Sci., eds. J.W. de Bakker, M. Hazewinkel & J.K. Lenstra, Amsterdam 1986.

[5] J.A. Bergstra & J.W. Klop, *Algebra of communicating processes with abstraction,* Theoretical Computer Science 37(1), pp. 77-121, 1985.

[6] J.A. Bergstra, J.W. Klop & E.-R. Olderog, *Failures without chaos: a new process semantics with fair abstraction,* report CS-R8625, Centrum voor Wiskunde en Informatica, Amsterdam 1986, to appear in: Proc. IFIP Conference on Formal Description of Programming Concepts, Gl. Avernaes 1986, (M. Wirsing, ed.), North-Holland.

[7] S.D. Brookes, C.A.R. Hoare & W. Roscoe, *A theory of communicating sequential processes,* Journal ACM 31(3), pp. 560-599, 1984.

[8] R.J. van Glabbeek, *Bounded nondeterminism and the approximation induction principle in process algebra,* report CS-R8634, Centrum voor Wiskunde en Informatica, Amsterdam 1986.

[9] G.J. Milne, *CIRCAL and the representation of communication, concurrency, and time,* Transactions on Programming Languages and Systems (ACM) 7(2), pp. 270-298, 1985.

[10] R. Milner, *A calculus for communicating systems,* Springer LNCS 92, 1980.

[11] R. Milner, *Lectures on a calculus for communicating systems, Seminar on Concurrency,* Springer LNCS 197, pp. 197-220, 1985.

[12] D.M.R. Park, *Concurrency and automata on infinite sequences,* Proc. 5th GI Conference, Springer LNCS 104, 1981.

[13] W. Reisig, *Petri Nets, An Introduction,* EATCS Monographs on Theoretical Computer Science, Springer-Verlag 1985.

[14] M. Rem, *Partially ordered computations, with applications to VLSI design,* Proc. 4th Advanced Course on Foundations of Computer Science, part 2, eds. J.W. de Bakker & J. van Leeuwen, Tract 159, Mathematisch Centrum, Amsterdam 1983.

The Step Failure Semantics

Dirk Taubner, Walter Vogler

TU München, Institut für Informatik, Arcisstr. 21, D-8000 München 2

Extended Abstract

Abstract: The (linear) failure semantics is a well known model for the theoretical version of Hoare's CSP. We generalize this semantics by taking steps (i.e. multisets of simultaneously occurring actions) instead of single actions as the basic execution unit. Hence opposed to the linear semantics, where parallelism is modelled as arbitrary interleaving in order to avoid technical complication, the step failure semantics models true parallelism and is equally easy to manage. Opposed to the linear model here divergence is treated uniformly.

The relation to the linear semantics can be established using our newly introduced deparallelize operator.

0. Introduction

A classical programming language with parallelism, nondeterminism and communication as primitives is Hoare's CSP (Communicating Sequential Processes) [Hoare 78]. Formal semantics have been given for parts of CSP [Francez et al. 79], [Plotkin 83], [Francez, Lehmann, Pnueli 84].

To study the important features of CSP and their semantics an abstract version called TCSP (Theoretical CSP) was developed. By now the failure model [Brookes, Hoare, Roscoe 84], [Olderog, Hoare 86], [Brookes, Roscoe 84] may be seen as a standard semantics for TCSP. In this model parallelism is treated as equivalent to arbitrary choice between sequential executions.

But TCSP can be used as a general model for processes and then this treatment of parallelism is not adequate. Parallelism includes but is more than arbitrary interleaving, it includes the possibility of simultaneous execution as well. For example consider two actions which need the same resource, for instance there is one processor only. It may be possible to execute them in any order (arbitrary interleaving) but it is not possible to execute them simultaneously.

Only if a semantics describes simultaneous execution directly it is possible to study the speed-up by parallelism, to compute the number of processors needed for fastest execution, or to analyze the effect of a limited number of processors.

Some semantics for TCSP with true parallelism have been proposed, [Goltz, Loogen 85], [Loogen 85] using event structures, [Taubner 85] using Petri nets, [Broy 86] using labelled partial orders.

In this paper we give a semantics which stays comparatively close to the (linear) failure model, but describes the execution and refusal of actions in parallel. The basic idea is to consider steps, i.e. finite multisets of actions to be executed simultaneously, instead of single actions. Therefore our model is called the *step failure semantics*. We also take into account null steps which do not contain any action. A null step may be interpreted as an idle step where nothing is done, it must not be confused with an internal τ-action, such τ-actions are not present in our model. Idle steps are necessary if one process has to wait to synchronize with another. And indeed null steps allow an elegant definition of synchronized parallel composition. In the linear model divergence is considered to be catastrophic and is described by an extra set of divergence strings. Now in general every process (even a deadlocking process) can make idle steps, hence the refusal of idle steps may be used to indicate catastrophic behaviour. Using null steps this way allows a uniform treatment of divergence in our model.

Let us mention that despite these advantages one could do without null steps, and our results can be modified accordingly. The close relationship between the two models is established on the one hand by a homomorphism to the linear model, which guarantees consistency. On the other hand all equalities given in [Brookes, Roscoe 84] hold in our model as well, except the one regarding interleaving and parallelism. Since for applications mainly such equalities are needed the step failure model is essentially as easy to manage as the linear model.

Once true parallelism is considered it can be sensible to restrict parallelism in a controlled way, e.g. if only a limited number of processors is available. Therefore we introduce the deparallelize operator, to explicitely disallow the simultaneous execution of certain actions. Since the linear model completely deparallelizes all processes implicitely, the deparallelize operator clarifies the relationship between the linear and the step model. For special cases the deparallelizer corresponds to the restriction operator of CCS [Milner 80]. Moreover it turns out to be technically useful to prove continuity of the hiding operator.

Apart from the deparallelizer we use the syntax of TCSP as in [Olderog, Hoare 86]. The reader is assumed to be familiar with one of [Brookes, Hoare, Roscoe 84], [Brookes, Roscoe 84] or [Olderog, Hoare 86].

The notion step is taken from Petri net theory where subsets [Rozenberg, Verraedt 83] and multisets [Reisig 85], [Kiehn 86] of concurrently firable transitions are investigated. However, the idea to consider collections of simultaneous actions has been used in various models.

Maximal non-conflict sets of statements of concurrent programs with shared variables are examined in [Salwicki, Müldner 81]. Collections of fixed size have been treated: [Elrad, Francez 82] decompose CSP-like programs into n-tuples of program segments with special properties in order to simplify analysis; [Shields, Lauer 75] use vector firing sequences as a semantics for COSY to describe the synchronized behaviour of n sequential processes; and [Nivat 82], [Arnold 82] proceed similarly. In COSY the empty word and in [Nivat 82] the "empty action" e is used in a way we use null steps.

In CIRCAL [Milne 85], a model close to TCSP, an operational semantics with collections of simultaneous events as basic execution unit is given. Opposed to our model simultaneity may even be enforced, and as the alphabets of processes determine the synchronization no two instances of the same event can occur in one step, i.e. sets instead of multisets are used.

1. Preliminaries

We use a countable alphabet Σ of atomic actions denoted by a, b, c... . Σ contains a special symbol $\surd$ (tick), which is interpreted as successful termination. Since several instances of one action may occur concurrently a *step* is formalized by a finite multiset over Σ, i.e. $x: \Sigma \to \mathbb{N}$, where $x(a) \neq 0$ for finitely many $a \in \Sigma$. Intuitively steps have to be finite since no physical machine can execute infinitely many actions at the same time. Also this finiteness assumption appears to be necessary for the proof of welldefinedness and continuity of parallel composition. Let $\mathbf{M}$ be the set of all finite multisets over Σ. $\bar{0}$ is the empty multiset called the *null step* ($\bar{0}(a) = 0$ for all $a \in \Sigma$). We use x, y to range over $\mathbf{M}$, X, Y to range over $\mathbf{P}(\mathbf{M})$, the powerset of $\mathbf{M}$, and v, w to range over $\mathbf{M}^*$, the set of *step sequences*. A step consisting of a single instance of a is written as $\hat{a}$, and called a *singleton step*. From now on the word action is used for both, an element of Σ and an element of a step, i.e. an instance of an action.

A *weakening* of a step sequence $w \in \mathbf{M}^*$ is a step sequence describing the same execution of actions, but with less parallelism. The traces considered in interleaving semantics are the extreme cases of weakening with only singleton steps. $We(w)$, the set of all weakenings of $w \in \mathbf{M}^*$, is defined inductively by

$$We(\varepsilon) := \{\bar{0}\}^*$$

$$We(vx) := We(v) \cdot \{x_1\, x_2 \ldots x_n \in \mathbf{M}^* \mid \sum_{i=1}^{n} x_i = x\}.$$

Thus a step may be decomposed into a sequence of steps with the same actions, including the case that null steps are inserted.

For a set X let $p(x)$ denote the set of finite subsets of X.

As syntax for TCSP we use

$$P ::= DIV \mid STOP \mid SKIP \mid a \to P \mid P\backslash a \mid$$
$$P_1 \text{ or } P_2 \mid P_1 \,\square\, P_2 \mid P_1 \,||_A\, P_2 \mid P_1 \,;\, P_2 \mid p \mid \mu p.P \mid P \,\#_B$$

where $A \subseteq \Sigma$, $a \neq \surd$, $B \subseteq \mathbf{M}$, and p is a process identifier.

For the motivation of these operators the reader is referred to [Brookes, Roscoe 84] or [Olderog, Hoare 86], except for the deparallelize operator $\#_B$, which is new. To save parentheses let unary operators precede over binary operators.

The following example illustrates our semantics. Take the TCSP-term
$P = a \rightarrow STOP \ ||_{\emptyset} (a \rightarrow STOP \ \square \ b \rightarrow STOP)$,
which could be pictured as the Petri net

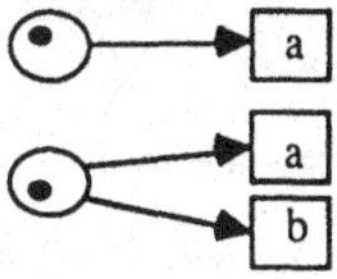

(A formal semantics for TCSP using nets is given in [Taubner 85]). For alphabet $\Sigma = \{a,b,\surd\}$ P has as linear failure semantics

$\{\varepsilon\, \emptyset,\ \varepsilon\{\surd\}\} \cup \{aX,\ bX \mid a \notin X \subseteq \Sigma\} \cup \{aaX,\ abX,\ baX \mid X \subseteq \Sigma\}$,

whereas in the step failure semantics P' s meaning is (we omit null steps which are always possible)

$$\{\varepsilon X \mid X \subseteq \{x \in \mathbf{M} \mid x \geq \begin{bmatrix} b \\ b \end{bmatrix} \vee x \geq \begin{bmatrix} a \\ a \\ b \end{bmatrix} \vee x \geq \hat{\surd}\}\}$$

$$\cup \{\hat{a}X,\ \hat{b}X \mid X \subseteq \{x \in \mathbf{M} \mid x \geq \begin{bmatrix} a \\ a \end{bmatrix} \vee x \geq \hat{b} \vee x \geq \hat{\surd}\}\}$$

$$\cup \{\begin{bmatrix} a \\ a \end{bmatrix} X,\ \begin{bmatrix} a \\ b \end{bmatrix} X,\ \hat{a}\hat{a}X,\ \hat{a}\hat{b}X,\ \hat{b}\hat{a}X \mid X \subseteq \mathbf{M} \setminus \{\hat{0}\}\}.$$

Here the simultaneous execution of several actions is described, for example a and b may be executed in one step and also two instances of a. Not only can actions be executed simultaneously but also the simultaneous execution of actions can be refused, e.g. all steps containing at least two a' s may be refused after a $\hat{b}$ step.

Also note that at the beginning $\begin{bmatrix} a \\ b \end{bmatrix}$ cannot be refused. One could think of an alternative interpretation of P, namely it could be argued that at the beginning P can refuse $\begin{bmatrix} a \\ b \end{bmatrix}$ since it could pick the "wrong" a. But a general idea of failure semantics is that if in a certain "state" something is possible it cannot be refused.

The technique to give the step failure semantics is the same as in [Olderog, Hoare 86]; we give a *denotational model*, i.e. a complete partial order (cpo) as domain and continuous operators on that domain corresponding to the operators of the syntax. This model straightforwardly induces the semantics including recursion. See [Olderog, Hoare 86] for details.

2. The Domain

The domain of the linear failure semantics [Brookes, Roscoe 84] is extended to allow steps instead of single actions. In the following definition conditions (1-6) are adaptions from the linear version, whereas (7-9) specifically treat the parallelism.

Definition 1 $F \subseteq \mathbf{M}^* \times \mathbf{P}(\mathbf{M})$ is an element of our domain $\mathbb{F}$ iff

(1) $\varepsilon\emptyset \in F$

(2) $vw\emptyset \in F \Rightarrow v\emptyset \in F$

(3) $wX \in F \wedge Y \subseteq X \Rightarrow wY \in F$

(4) $wX \in F \wedge (\forall\, y \in Y\colon wy\emptyset \notin F) \Rightarrow w(X \cup Y) \in F$

(5) $(\forall\, Y \in p(X)\colon wY \in F) \Rightarrow wX \in F$

(6) $v\{0\} \in F \Rightarrow vw\{0\} \in F$

(7) $wX \in F \wedge v \in We(w) \Rightarrow vX \in F$

(8) $wX \in F \wedge x \in X \wedge x \lneqq y \Rightarrow w(X \cup \{y\}) \in F$

(9) $v\bar{0}wX \in F \Rightarrow vwX \in F$

Remarks: [Brookes, Roscoe 84] use a separate set of traces without refusal set to indicate divergence. This is not necessary in our semantics. A null step is always possible (cf. 7), so in general it does not make sense to refuse it. But divergence is modelled by allowing arbitrary behaviour so the refusal of null steps is possible. Hence divergence is characterized by the ability to refuse the null step (6). Note that by (6), (8) and (5) in case of divergence every failure pair is possible.

Parallelism is the possibility to execute actions simultaneously but not the necessity so every less parallel execution is possible as well. This means that parallelism is not the same as but includes arbitrary interleaving. As an element of a failure set is interpreted as (the beginning of) a possible behaviour all weakenings have to be included (7).

With this view of parallelism it follows that if at some point a step is possible every smaller step is possible as well. (8) is the other side of the coin: If a step can be refused, every larger step can also be refused.

(9) Null steps represent idle steps but not unobservable internal actions. Although null steps are an elegant way of treating divergence and defining parallel composition they can be avoided easily using the following isomorphism which also brings the domain into a form similar to that of [Brookes, Roscoe 84, p. 290f.]:

$\phi\colon \mathbb{F} \to \mathbb{F}'$,

$$F \to \left[F \cap (\mathbf{M}_1^* \times \mathbf{P}(\mathbf{M}_1)),\ \pi_1(F \cap (\mathbf{M}_1^* \times \{0\}))\right],$$

where $\mathbf{M}_1 := \mathbf{M} \setminus \{0\}$, and π_1 is the projection onto the first component.

The following shows that $\mathbb{F}$ is an appropriate domain.

Theorem 1: $(\mathbb{F}, \supseteq)$ is a cpo with bottom element $\bot = \mathbf{M}^* \times \mathbf{P}(\mathbf{M})$.

For this proof and all others see the full version [Taubner, Vogler 86].

3. The Operators

In this section for every syntactic operator we give the corresponding operator on our domain $\mathbb{F}$ using the same symbol.

$DIV := \mathbf{M}^* \times \mathbf{P}(\mathbf{M})$

$STOP := \{wX \mid w \in \{\overline{0}\}^* \wedge X \subseteq \mathbf{M} \setminus \{\overline{0}\}\}$

$SKIP := \{wX \mid w \in \{\overline{0}\}^* \wedge X \subseteq \mathbf{M} \setminus \{\overline{0}, \hat{\surd}\}\}$

$\quad \cup \{v\hat{\surd}wX \mid v, w \in \{\overline{0}\}^* \wedge X \subseteq \mathbf{M} \setminus \{\overline{0}\}\}$

Recall that a null step is not considered as an activity, it might be interpreted as waiting which is possible even in a deadlock state and after termination.

Let $a \in \Sigma \setminus \{\surd\}$, $F, F_1, F_2 \in \mathbb{F}$.

$a \rightarrow F := \{vX \mid v \in \{\overline{0}\}^* \wedge X \subseteq \mathbf{M} \setminus \{\overline{0}, \hat{a}\}\}$

$\quad \cup \{v\hat{a}wX \mid v \in \{\overline{0}\}^* \wedge wX \in F\}$

For the hiding operator we use the following auxiliary definitions,

for a step x let $(x \setminus a)(b) := \begin{cases} x(b) & \text{if } a \neq b \\ 0 & \text{otherwise}, \end{cases}$

for a step sequence $w = x_1 \ldots x_n$ let $w \setminus a := w_1 \ldots w_n$, where $w_i = \begin{cases} \varepsilon & \text{if } x_i \setminus a = \overline{0} \neq x_i \\ x_i \setminus a & \text{otherwise}. \end{cases}$

Hiding a in a step sequence means in general deleting all a's from every step. But if a non null step consists of a's only we delete it. This realizes the same abstract view of hiding as the linear model, we do <u>not</u> introduce internal actions, such as τ-actions (cf. Definition 1 (9)).

$F \setminus a := \{(w \setminus a)X \mid w(X \cup \{\hat{a}\}) \in F\}$

$\quad \cup \{(w \setminus a)uX \mid \forall n \in \mathbb{N}: w(\hat{a})^n \emptyset \in F \wedge u \in \mathbf{M}^* \wedge X \subseteq \mathbf{M}\}.$

F_1 **or** $F_2 := F_1 \cup F_2$,

$F_1 \,\Box\, F_2 := \{wX \mid w \in \{\overline{0}\}^* \wedge wX \in F_1 \cap F_2\}$

$\quad \cup \{wX \mid w \in \{\overline{0}\}^* \wedge \varepsilon\{\overline{0}\} \in F_1 \cup F_2 \wedge X \subseteq \mathbf{M}\}$

$\quad \cup \{wX \mid w \notin \{\overline{0}\}^* \wedge wX \in F_1 \cup F_2\}.$

Let $A \subseteq \Sigma$. For the parallel operator we use the *synchronisation of steps and step sequences.* Let $x, y \in \mathbf{M}$. The synchronisation $x +_A y$ is only defined if the steps agree on A.

If $x|_A = y|_A$, then $(x +_A y)(a) := \begin{cases} x(a) & \text{if } a \in A \\ x(a)+y(a) & \text{otherwise}. \end{cases}$

For step sequences $v = x_1 \ldots x_n$ and $w = y_1 \ldots y_n$ of equal length with $x_i|_A = y_i|_A$ for $i \in \{1,\ldots,n\}$ we define $v +_A w := (x_1 +_A y_1) \ldots (x_n +_A y_n)$.

This definition is only possible because we use null steps. The synchronisation of step sequences of different length can be established by inserting suitable null steps first (cf. Def. 1 (7)).

$F_1 \,||_A\, F_2 := \{wX \mid \exists\, w_1X_1 \in F_1, w_2X_2 \in F_2 : w = w_1 +_A w_2$

$\quad \wedge X \subseteq \{x \mid \forall x_1, x_2 \in \mathbf{M}: x = x_1 +_A x_2 \neq \{\overline{0}\} \Rightarrow x_1 \in X_1 \vee x_2 \in X_2\}\}$

$\quad \cup \{wuX \mid \exists\, w_1X_1 \in F_1, w_2X_2 \in F_2 : w = w_1 +_A w_2$

$\quad \wedge \overline{0} \in X_1 \cup X_2 \wedge u \in \mathbf{M}^* \wedge X \subseteq \mathbf{M}\}.$

In the parallel composition a step x is possible if there is a decomposition $x_1 +_A x_2 = x$ such that x_1 is possible in F_1 and x_2 in F_2. A step x may not be refused if there is a decomposition into

x_1, x_2 such that F_1 cannot refuse x_1 and F_2 cannot refuse x_2. This means that a step may be refused if for every decomposition F_1 can refuse x_1 or F_2 can refuse x_2.

A step sequence is *tick-free* if no step contains a $\surd$.

$$F_1 \; ; \; F_2 := \{vX \mid v(X \cup \{\hat{\surd}\}) \in F_1 \wedge v \text{ is tick-free}\}$$
$$\cup \{vwX \mid v\{\overline{0}\} \in F_1 \wedge v \text{ is tick-free} \wedge w \in \mathbf{M}^* \wedge X \subseteq \mathbf{M}\}$$
$$\cup \{vwX \mid v\hat{\surd}\emptyset \in F_1 \wedge v \text{ is tick-free} \wedge wX \in F_2\}.$$

In the second part it is enough to consider histories vx where x is a single $\hat{\surd}$ instead of an arbitrary step containing a $\surd$, because in this case $vx'\hat{\surd}$ is also a history (due to Def. 1 (7)) where x' is x without ticks.

As in the linear failure semantics there may be histories, which formally continue after a $\surd$. The interpretation of such histories is dubious, and the ;-operator is not well-defined in [Brookes, Roscoe 84, p.292f.] due to these histories, e.g. consider $P:=((a \rightarrow \mu x.x) ||| SKIP);STOP$ then $\surd a\emptyset \in F[\![P]\!]e$ but $\surd\emptyset \notin F[\![P]\!]e$ contradicting (N2) of [Brookes, Roscoe 84, p.290]. The definition for the linear model should be modified along the lines of the definition above. Such histories, as well as steps containing $\surd$ together with other actions, can be avoided by automatically including $\surd$ in A whenever applying the parallel composition ($||_A$).

Now we introduce the deparallelize operator ($\#_B$), where $B \subseteq \mathbf{M}$ is a set of steps. The effect of $F \#_B$ is that parallel execution of actions is restricted in the following way. Steps in B or larger steps are not possible for $F \#_B$ and can consequently be refused. Of course, if a step which is possible in F is forbidden by B then all weakenings are possible in F and some of them may still be possible in $F \#_B$.

If for example $B = \left\{\begin{bmatrix} a \\ b \end{bmatrix}\right\}$ and $\begin{bmatrix} a \\ a \\ b \end{bmatrix}\emptyset \in F$, then $\begin{bmatrix} a \\ a \\ b \end{bmatrix}\emptyset$, $a\begin{bmatrix} a \\ b \end{bmatrix}\emptyset$, $\begin{bmatrix} a \\ b \end{bmatrix}a\emptyset \notin F\#_B$ but $b\begin{bmatrix} a \\ a \end{bmatrix}\emptyset$, $\begin{bmatrix} a \\ a \end{bmatrix}b\emptyset$, etc. $\in F \#_B$.

Let $B \subseteq \mathbf{M}$, $\overline{B} := \{y \mid \exists\, x \in B : x \leq y\}$.

$$F \#_B := \{w(X \cup Y) \mid w \in (\mathbf{M} \setminus \overline{B})^* \wedge wX \in F \wedge Y \subseteq \overline{B}\}$$
$$\cup \{wuX \mid (w\{\overline{0}\} \in F \vee \overline{0} \in B) \wedge w \in (\mathbf{M} \setminus \overline{B})^* \wedge u \in \mathbf{M}^* \wedge X \subseteq \mathbf{M}\}.$$

This new operator is useful for instance if the simultaneous execution of certain actions would require more resources than available. Especially if the number of processors is limited, say n, let B contain all steps of size $n+1$, then in $F \#_B$ all steps contain at most n actions (unless divergence occurs). Additionally the deparallelize operator is technically useful (see the proof for the continuity of the hiding operator).

A rough correspondence to [Nivat 82, pp.476, 521] can be established for the special case of n synchronized sequential processes by choosing his *synchronization condition* appropriately.

Note that in the special case where B contains a singleton step, say $\hat{a}$, this has the effect of restricting $F \Vert_B$ to executions not containing any a-action. This is like the restriction operator (\x'0'a) in CCS [Milner 80, pp. 27, 68].

We included the case $\bar{0} \in B$ for completeness, then $F \Vert_B = DIV$.

All these operators are well-defined and continuous. Some of the proofs are rather involved and we omit them here, see [Taubner, Vogler 86].

The main problems arise in the treatment of parallel composition and hiding. Naturally for parallel composition the step semantics differs from the linear model. But for the proof of continuity of hiding we can make use of the corresponding result of the linear case. For this we have to apply the following lemmas.

Lemma 1: Let $a \in \Sigma \setminus \{\surd\}$, $H := \{x \in \mathbf{M} \mid x \geq a \wedge x \neq a\}$, then for $F \in \mathbb{F}$ $F \backslash a = (F \Vert_H) \backslash a$.

In other words if we use the deparallelizer to limit occurences of a to singleton steps, hiding a gives the same result.

After deparallelizing hiding a in our model basically means deleting $\hat{a}$ just as in the linear model if we take $\mathbf{M}_1$ as alphabet. Hence we have the second lemma, where $\backslash_l$ denotes the linear hiding operator as defined in [Brookes, Roscoe 84, p. 292f.] and ϕ is the isomorphism from section 2.

Lemma 2: $\phi(F \Vert_H \backslash a) = (\phi(F \Vert_H)) \backslash_l \hat{a}$.

Now the proof of continuity simply is: For a directed family $\{F_i\}$ of $\mathbb{F}$ holds

$$\bigcap_i (F_i \backslash a) = \bigcap_i (\phi^{-1}(\phi(F_i \Vert_H) \backslash_l \hat{a})) \qquad \text{lemmas 1, 2}$$

$$= \phi^{-1}(\phi((\bigcap_i F_i) \Vert_H) \backslash_l \hat{a}) \qquad \text{continuity of } \phi^{-1}, \backslash_l, \phi, \Vert$$

$$= (\bigcap_i F_i) \backslash a \qquad \text{lemmas 2, 1.}$$

4. Comparison to Linear Failure Semantics

The linear failure semantics has widely been considered as a standard model for TCSP [Olderog, Hoare 86], [Loogen 85], [Taubner 85]. Our aim was to distinguish between concurrency and arbitrary interleaving but to stay as close as possible to the linear failure model [Brookes, Roscoe 84].

To show that our model distinguishes at least as fine as the linear semantics, we give a homomorphism between our semantics, which we call $\mathbf{F}$, and the semantics $\mathbf{N}$ (with domain N) of [Brookes, Roscoe 84]. $\mathbf{N}$ does not have the general $||_A$ but only the special cases $||_\Sigma$, $||_\emptyset$ (denoted $||$, $|||$ resp. there) and of course $\mathbf{N}$ does not have $\Vert_B$, hence in this context we have to restrict the syntax given in section 1 accordingly.

For the proof of the homomorphism property we use the following proposition.

Proposition 1: Let $\mathbf{F}$, $\mathbf{N}$ be denotational models and Ψ be a strict continuous homomorphism from $\mathbb{F}$ to N (i.e. for every operator op and for every $d_1, \ldots, d_n \in \mathbb{F}$ we have $\Psi(op_{\mathbf{F}}(d_1, \ldots, d_n)) = op_{\mathbf{N}}(\Psi(d_1), \ldots, \Psi(d_n))$). Then for every closed term P we have $\Psi(\mathbf{F}[P]) = \mathbf{N}[P]$.

Proof: [Prop. 2.2, Olderog, Hoare 86].

For simplicity in the following we will not distinguish between a and $\hat{a}$, and hence not between Σ and the set of singleton steps over Σ.

Then define $\Psi\colon \mathbb{F} \to \mathrm{N},\ F \to [F \cap (\Sigma^* x\ \mathbf{P}(\Sigma)),\ \pi_1(F \cap (\Sigma^* x\ \{\emptyset\}))]$

where π_1 denotes the projection onto the first component. The proofs that Ψ is strict, continuous and respects the operators are straightforward, except for the sequential composition operator, cf. the remark in section 3. The form of the homomorphism indicates the close relationship; it simply reduces a step failure set to its linear part. We can formalize this with the help of the deparallelizer.

Proposition 2: Let $\mathbf{M}_2 := \{x \in \mathbf{M} \mid |x| \geq 2\}$, then for all closed TCSP-terms P_1, P_2

$$\mathbf{N}[P_1] = \mathbf{N}_2[P_2] \quad \text{iff} \quad \mathbf{F}[P_1 \Vdash_{\mathbf{M}_2}] = \mathbf{F}[P_2 \Vdash_{\mathbf{M}_2}].$$

The close relationship to the linear model is substantiated by the fact that all properties listed in [Table 1 and 2; Brookes, Roscoe 84] are also true in our model except the one expressing the equivalence of parallelism and interleaving. Namely we have (where instead of $||$ and $|||$ the more general case $||_A$ for $A \subseteq \Sigma$ is considered):

$$F \,\Box\, F = F$$

$$F_1 \,\Box\, F_2 = F_2 \,\Box\, F_1$$

$$F_1 \,\Box\, (F_2 \,\Box\, F_3) = (F_1 \,\Box\, F_2) \,\Box\, F_3$$

$$F_1 \,\Box\, (F_2 \text{ or } F_3) = (F_1 \text{ or } F_2) \,\Box\, (F_1 \text{ or } F_3)$$

$$F_1 \text{ or } (F_2 \,\Box\, F_3) = (F_1 \,\Box\, F_2) \text{ or } (F_1 \,\Box\, F_3)$$

$$F \,\Box\, STOP = F$$

$$a \to (F_1 \text{ or } F_2) = a \to F_1 \text{ or } a \to F_2$$

$$a \to F_1 \,\Box\, a \to F_2 = a \to F_1 \text{ or } a \to F_2$$

$$F \text{ or } F = F$$

$$F_1 \text{ or } F_2 = F_2 \text{ or } F_1$$

$$F_1 \text{ or } (F_2 \text{ or } F_3) = (F_1 \text{ or } F_2) \text{ or } F_3$$

$$F_1 \,||_A\, F_2 = F_2 \,||_A\, F_1 \qquad \text{for } A \subseteq \Sigma$$

$$F_1 \,||_A\, (F_2 \,||_A\, F_3) = (F_1 \,||_A\, F_2) \,||_A\, F_3 \qquad \text{for } A \subseteq \Sigma$$

$$F_1 \,||_A\, (F_2 \text{ or } F_3) = (F_1 \,||_A\, F_2) \text{ or } (F_1 \,||_A\, F_3)$$

$$\text{If } \{a, b\} \subseteq A \qquad a \to F_1 \,||_A\, b \to F_2 = \begin{cases} STOP & \text{if } a \neq b \\ a \to (F_1 \,||_A\, F_2) & \text{if } a = b \end{cases}$$

$$F \,||_\Sigma\, STOP = \begin{cases} STOP & \text{if } F \neq DIV \\ DIV & \text{if } F = DIV \end{cases}$$

$$F \,||_\emptyset\, STOP = F$$

$$
\begin{aligned}
F_1 ; (F_2 ; F_3) &= (F_1 ; F_2); F_3 \\
SKIP ; F &= F \\
STOP ; F &= STOP \\
F_1 ; (F_2 \textbf{ or } F_3) &= (F_1 ; F_2) \textbf{ or } (F_1 ; F_3) \\
(F_1 \textbf{ or } F_2) ; F_3 &= (F_1 ; F_3) \textbf{ or } (F_2 ; F_3) \\
a \to F_1 ; F_2 &= a \to (F_1 ; F_2) \\
F \backslash a \backslash b &= F \backslash b \backslash a \\
F \backslash a \backslash a &= F \backslash a \\
(a \to F) \backslash b &= \begin{cases} a \to (F \backslash b) & \text{if } a \neq b \\ F \backslash b & \text{if } a = b \end{cases} \\
(F_1 \textbf{ or } F_2) \backslash a &= F_1 \backslash a \textbf{ or } F_2 \backslash a \\
F \,\Box\, DIV &= DIV \\
F \textbf{ or } DIV &= DIV \\
F \,||_A\, DIV &= DIV \\
DIV ; F &= DIV \\
DIV \backslash a &= DIV
\end{aligned}
$$

Remark: In general $F_1 \,||_A\, (F_2 \,||_B\, F_3) = (F_1 \,||_A\, F_2) \,||_B\, F_3$ is not true, even not if one of A, B is the whole alphabet or the emtpy set, as the counter example

$$
\begin{aligned}
STOP &= STOP \,||_\Sigma\, (STOP \,||_\emptyset\, a \to STOP) \\
&\neq (STOP \,||_\Sigma\, STOP) \,||_\emptyset\, a \to STOP = a \to STOP
\end{aligned}
$$

shows.

The law $a \to F_1 \,||_\emptyset\, b \to F_2 = a \to (F_1 \,||_\emptyset\, b \to F_2) \,\Box\, b \to (a \to F_1 \,||_\emptyset\, F_2)$ of [Table 1, Brookes, Roscoe 84] which is missing in the above list allows to eliminate asynchronous parallel composition from terms. Of course this cannot be true in our model. If such an equivalence is wished for, it has to be enforced explicitely by use of the deparallelize operator.

Let $a, b \notin A$ and $\begin{bmatrix} a \\ b \end{bmatrix} \in B \subseteq \mathbf{M} \backslash \{\bar{0}, \hat{a}, \hat{b}\}$ then

$$
(a \to F_1 \,||_A\, b \to F_2) +\!\!+_B = a \to ((F_1 \,||_A\, b \to F_2) +\!\!+_B) \;\Box\; b \to ((a \to F_1 \,||_A\, F_2) +\!\!+_B).
$$

Finally we list some results concerning deparallelizing.

$$
\begin{aligned}
F \,||_A\, STOP &= F +\!\!+_{\{\hat{a} ; a \in A\}} && \text{for } A \subseteq \Sigma \\
DIV +\!\!+_B &= DIV && \text{for } B \subseteq \mathbf{M} \\
F +\!\!+_{\{\bar{0}\}} &= DIV && \\
F +\!\!+_{B \cup C} &= F +\!\!+_B +\!\!+_C && \text{for } B, C \subseteq \mathbf{M} \\
STOP +\!\!+_B &= STOP && \text{for } B \subseteq \mathbf{M} \backslash \{\bar{0}\} \\
(a \to F) +\!\!+_B &= a \to (F +\!\!+_B) && \text{for } B \subseteq \mathbf{M} \backslash \{\bar{0}, \hat{a}\} \\
F \backslash a +\!\!+_B &= F +\!\!+_B \backslash a && \text{for } B \subseteq \mathbf{M} \backslash \{\hat{a}\} \\
(F_1 \textbf{ or } F_2) +\!\!+_B &= F_1 +\!\!+_B \textbf{ or } F_2 +\!\!+_B && \text{for } B \subseteq \mathbf{M} \\
(F_1 ; F_2) +\!\!+_B &= F_1 +\!\!+_B ; F_2 +\!\!+_B && \text{for } B \subseteq \mathbf{M}
\end{aligned}
$$

$$(F_1 \Box F_2) \Uparrow_B \quad = \quad F_1 \Uparrow_B \Box F_2 \Uparrow_B \qquad \text{for } B \subseteq \mathbf{M}$$

$$(F_1 \,||_A\, F_2) \Uparrow_B \quad = \quad F_1 \Uparrow_B \,||_A\, F_2 \Uparrow_B \qquad \text{for } A \subseteq \Sigma,\ B \subseteq \mathbf{M}$$

$$\text{and } \forall x \in B: \exists y \in B: x \geq y \wedge y|_{\Sigma \setminus A} = 0.$$

5. Discussion

With the step failure semantics we have given a model for TCSP which is close to the linear failure semantics but distinguishes true parallelism from arbitrary interleaving.

The step semantics allows both, parallel execution as well as refusal of parallel execution. An alternative would be to consider the parallel execution only. This ***simple step failure semantics*** can easily be derived by taking for $F \in \mathbb{F}$ $\quad F \cap \mathbf{M}^* \times \mathbf{P}(\mathbf{M}^1)$, where $\mathbf{M}^1 := \{x \in \mathbf{M} \mid |x| \leq 1\}$ (i.e. $\mathbf{M}^1$ contains null and singleton steps only).

Another semantics which considers parallel execution only is [Broy 86]. The other semantics with true parallelism mentioned in the introduction are not close to the linear model formally and they violate some of the desired properties listed in section 4, e.g. $F \Box F = F$.

We illustrate the first three semantics, which are structurally close to the linear model, with an example.

Let $P := a \to SKIP \;\; ||_{\{\surd\}} \;\; b \to SKIP$

$\quad Q := a \to b \to SKIP \;\; \Box \;\; b \to a \to SKIP$

Then contrary to the linear model all three distinguish P and Q. But we have

in the simple step failure semantics	$P = P \Box Q = P$ **or** Q,
in the step failure semantics	$P = P \Box Q \neq P$ **or** Q,
and in Broy's semantics	$P \neq P \Box Q = P$ **or** Q.

Broy's semantics for P is different from the right hand side processes since it does not explicitely include the histories ab and ba. For us parallelism includes arbitrary interleaving, hence we have equality. On the other hand P **or** Q can refuse $\begin{bmatrix} a \\ b \end{bmatrix}$ at the beginning, whereas $P \Box Q$ cannot.

Acknowledgement We thank Prof. W. Brauer for the good working atmosphere. Ernst-Rüdiger Olderog and one of the referees are acknowledged for putting some literature to our attention.

References

[Arnold 82] A. Arnold: Synchronized Behaviours of Processes and Rational Relations; Acta Informatica 17, 21-29 (1982)

[Brookes, Hoare, Roscoe 84] S.D. Brookes, C.A.R. Hoare, A. W. Roscoe: A Theory of Communicating Sequential Processes; JACM 31, 560-599 (1984)

[Brookes, Roscoe 84] S.D. Brookes, A.W. Roscoe: An Improved Failures Model for Communicating Processes; in S.D. Brookes, A.W. Roscoe, G. Winskel (eds.): Seminar on Concurrency (1984); LNCS 197, 281-305

[Broy 86] M. Broy: Process Semantics of Communicating Concurrent Programs; Univ. Passau, Report MIP-8602 (1986)

[Elrad, Francez 82] T. Elrad, N. Francez: Decomposition of Distributed Programs into Communication-closed Layers; Science of Computer Programming 2, 155-173 (1982)

[Francez et al. 79] N. Francez, C.A.R. Hoare, D.J. Lehmann, W.P. de Roever: Semantics of Nondeterminism, Concurrency, and Communication; JCSS 19, 290-308 (1979)

[Francez, Lehmann, Pnueli 84] N. Francez, D. Lehmann, A. Pnueli: A Linear-history Semantics for Languages for Distributed Programming; TCS 32, 25-46 (1984)

[Goltz, Loogen 85] U. Goltz, R. Loogen: Towards a Non-interleaving Semantic Model for CSP-like Languages; RWTH Aachen, Bericht Nr. 105 (1985)

[Hoare 78] C.A.R. Hoare: Communicating Sequential Processes; CACM 21, 666-677 (1978)

[Kiehn 86] A. Kiehn: On the Concurrent Behaviour of Petri Nets; Univ. Hamburg, Bericht FBI-HH-B-119/86 (1986)

[Loogen 85] R. Loogen: Ein semantisches Modell für nichtdeterministische, parallele Prozesse; RWTH Aachen, Diploma Thesis (1985) unpublished

[Milne 85] G.J. Milne: CIRCAL and the Representation of Communication, Concurrency, and Time; ACM TOPLAS 7, 270-298 (1985)

[Milner 80] R. Milner: A Calculus of Communicating Systems; LNCS 92 (1980)

[Nivat 82] M. Nivat: Behaviours of Processes and Synchronized Systems of Processes; in: M.Broy, G.Schmidt(eds.): Theoretical Foundations of Programming Methodology; 473-551 (1986)

[Olderog, Hoare 86] E.-R. Olderog, C.A.R. Hoare: Specification-oriented Semantics for Communicating Processes; Acta Informatica 23, 9-66 (1986)

[Plotkin 83] G.D. Plotkin: An Operational Semantics for CSP; in: D. Bjørner (ed.): Formal Descriptions of Programming Concepts II, IFIP 1983, 199-223

[Reisig 85] W. Reisig: On the Semantics of Petri Nets; in: E.J.Neuhold, G.Chroust(eds.): Formal Models in Programming; IFIP 1985, 347-372

[Rozenberg, Verraedt 83] G. Rozenberg, R. Verraedt: Subset Languages of Petri Nets, Parts I and II; TCS 26, 301-326 (1986) and TCS 27, 85-108 (1986)

[Salwicki, Müldner 81] A. Salwicki, T. Müldner: On the Algorithmic Properties of Concurrent Programs; LNCS 125, 169-197 (1981)

[Shields, Lauer 79] M.W. Shields, P.E. Lauer: A Formal Semantics for Concurrent Systems; LNCS 71, 571-584 (1979)

[Taubner 85] D. Taubner: Two Net-oriented Semantics for TCSP; Univ. Hamburg, Bericht FBI-HH-B-116/85 (1985)

[Taubner, Vogler 86] D. Taubner, W. Vogler: The Step Failure Semantics; Techn. Univ. München, Report TUM-I8614 (1986)

ON THE COMPLEXITY OF CONTAINMENT, EQUIVALENCE, AND REACHABILITY FOR FINITE AND 2-DIMENSIONAL VECTOR ADDITION SYSTEMS WITH STATES

Rodney R. Howell[1], Dung T. Huynh[2], Louis E. Rosier[1], and Hsu-Chun Yen[3]

Abstract

In this paper, we analyze the complexity of the reachability, containment, and equivalence problems for two classes of vector addition systems with states (VASSs): finite VASSs and 2-dimensional VASSs. Both of these classes are known to have effectively computable semilinear reachability sets (SLSs). By giving upper bounds on the sizes of the SLS representations, we achieve upper bounds on each of the aforementioned problems. In the case of finite VASSs, the SLS representation is simply a listing of the reachability set; therefore, we derive a bound on the norm of any reachable vector based on the dimension, number of states, and amount of increment caused by any move in the VASS. The bound we derive shows an improvement of two levels in the primitive recursive hierarchy over results previously obtained by McAloon, thus answering a question posed by Clote. We then show this bound to be optimal. In the case of 2-dimensional VASSs, we analyze an algorithm given by Hopcroft and Pansiot that generates a SLS representation of the reachability set. Specifically, we show that the algorithm operates in $2^{2^{c*l*n}}$ nondeterministic time, where l is the length of the binary representation of the largest integer in the VASS, n is the number of transitions, and c is some fixed constant. We also give examples for which this algorithm will take $2^{2^{d*l*n}}$ nondeterministic time for some positive constant d. Finally, we give a method of determinizing the algorithm in such a way that it requires no more than $2^{2^{c*l*n}}$ deterministic time. From this upper bound and special properties of the generated SLSs, we derive upper bounds of DTIME($2^{2^{c*l*n}}$) for the three problems mentioned above.

1. Introduction

The containment and equivalence problems for vector addition systems (VASs) (or equivalently vector addition systems with states (VASSs) or Petri nets) are, in general, undecidable [1, 10]. They are decidable, however, for classes of VASs (VASSs, Petri nets) whose reachability sets are effectively computable semilinear sets (SLSs). Such classes include finite VASs [16], 3-dimensional VASs [30], 5-dimensional VASs (or, equivalently 2-dimensional VASSs) [11], conflict free VASs [6], persistent VASs [9, 18, 20, 25], weakly persistent VASs [32], and regular VASs [8, 31]. For each of these classes, the algorithm which generates the SLS representation of the reachability set is a search procedure that is guaranteed to terminate. However, no analysis of when termination will occur is provided, and thus no complexity results are obtained. The perhaps best studied class is that of symmetric VASs. For this class the equivalence and reachability problems have been shown to be exponential space complete [3, 14, 22]. The best known lower bound for the general reachability problem is exponential space [19]. Few other complexity results appear to be known.

In this paper, we concern ourselves with examining the complexity of the containment and equivalence

[1]Department of Computer Sciences, University of Texas at Austin, Austin, TX 78712.

[2]Computer Science Department, University of Texas at Dallas, Richardson, TX 75083. This author was supported in part by the National Science Foundation under grant number DCR-8517277.

[3]Department of Computer Science, Iowa State University, Ames, IA 50011.

problems for two classes of VASSs -- finite VASSs and 2-dimensional VASSs. Recently, Mayr and Meyer [24] showed that the containment and equivalence problems for finite VASs are not primitive recursive. Subsequently, McAloon [23] showed that the problems are primitive recursive in the Ackermann function, and Clote [5] showed the finite containment problem to be DTIME(Ackermann) complete. Let $f_1(x)=2x$ and $f_n(x)=f_{n-1}^{(x)}(1)$ for $n>1$, where $f_i^{(m)}$ is the m-th fold composition of f_i. Using a combinatorial argument, McAloon showed an upper bound for the time complexity of the finite-containment problem that can be shown to be at least $f_{k+1}(m)$, where k is the dimension and m is the maximum sum of the elements of any vector in the VAS (see also [5]). Clote [5] subsequently used Ramsey theory to give an upper bound of approximately $f_{k+6}(m)$ and posed a question as to whether McAloon's bound could be improved. It follows that these bounds also hold for the size of finite VASs. McAloon's bound on the size of finite VASs is close to optimal. See [20, 24, 26, 31].

Let BV(k,b,n) be the class of k-dimensional n-state finite VASSs where the maximum increase in the norm of a vector (i.e., the sum of the absolute values of its elements) caused by any move is b. (Assume the start vector is **0**.) In Section 2, we use a tree construction technique to derive an upper bound on the largest norm of any vector reachable in BV(k,b,n). The bound we derive for k-dimensional VASs is $f_{k-1}(d^*m^2)$, $k \geq 2$, ($f_{k-1}(d^*m)$ for $k \geq 4$), where m is the maximum sum of the elements of any vector in the VAS, and d is a constant. By then considering the addition of states and the restriction of the start vector to **0**, we derive a bound of $f_k(c^*\max(n,\log b))$ on the norm of the largest vector reachable in BV(k,b,n), where $k \geq 3$ and c is a constant. Furthermore, we show that this bound is tight for b=1. (I.e., we illustrate for each k and m a VASS in BV(k,1,m*(2*k-1)+2) that can generate a vector with norm $f_k(m)$.) These results immediately yield, for the k-dimensional VAS finite containment problem, a bound of $f_{k-1}(d'^*m)$ time, for $k \geq 4$ and some constant d'. This bound represents an improvement of two levels in the primitive recursive hierarchy over McAloon's result, thus answering the question posed by Clote. Since we do not know of any attempts to use tree construction techniques similar to ours in analyzing combinatorial problems, and because our techniques yield better results than the standard combinatorial techniques applied in the past to this problem, we surmise that our techniques may have other applications. Finally, we show that the containment and equivalence problem (for BV(k,b,n)) require at least time $f_{k-c}(d^*n)$ infinitely often for some constants c and d. The proof is such that each position in the constructed VASS can be bounded by $f_{k-c}(d^*n)$. Hence, if we considered the entire class of VASSs whose positions were bounded by $f_k(n)$ (rather than just BV(k,b,n)) our lower bound would be tight. We surmise, therefore, that the constant c can be eliminated. The section concludes by showing the problems for BV(1,1,n) to be complete for $A\Pi_2^L$ -- the second level of the alternating logspace hierarchy [4].

The other class of VASSs we study in this paper is that of 2-dimensional VASSs. The study of VASSs having a specific fixed dimension is interesting because it can be shown, using techniques similar to those in [1, 7, 10], that there exists a k such that the containment and equivalence problems are undecidable for k-dimensional VASSs. Although the best upper bound for k is unknown at this writing, the containment and equivalence problems are known to be decidable for k=2 [11]. 2-dimensional VASSs are of additional interest because the reachability set is not, in general, semilinear when the dimension is greater than two [11]. In Section 3, we utilize the ideas inherent in the previous section to provide an analysis of the algorithm given in [11], which generates from an arbitrary 2-dimensional VASS the SLS representation of its reachability set. As a result of the analysis, we obtain upper bounds for the containment, equivalence and reachability problems in the case of 2 dimensions. Let VASS(2,l,n) denote the class of 2-dimensional VASSs whose integers can each be represented in l bits and such that n is the maximum of the number of states and the number of transitions.

Specifically, we show that the algorithm of Hopcroft and Pansiot [11] operates on any VASS in VASS(2,l,n) in NTIME($2^{2^{c*l*n}}$) for some constant c. Furthermore, there are instances that require $2^{2^{d*l*n}}$ steps for some positive constant d; hence our analysis (of the algorithm) is tight. We then give a minor modification to the algorithm that reduces its complexity to DTIME($2^{2^{c'*l*n}}$) for some constant c'. The SLS constructed by the resulting algorithm contains O($2^{2^{c'*l*n}}$) linear sets. Each of these linear sets has a base with norm O($2^{2^{c'*l*n}}$) and O(2^n) periods with norm O($2^{d'*l*n}$) for some constant d'. From these properties we derive an upper bound of DTIME($2^{2^{c*l*n}}$) for the reachability, equivalence, and containment problems for VASS(2,l,n). Now the best known lower bounds for these problems are significantly smaller (e.g., NLOGSPACE (NP) for the reachability problem of VASS(2,1,n) (VASS(2,l,n)) [27]). Hence, there is still much room for improvement. However, the two algorithms for the general reachability problem in [17, 21] do not appear to yield better upper bounds for 2-dimensional VASSs. Hence, whether or not these bounds can be tightened we leave as an open question.

2. Finite VASSs

Let Z (N, N^+, R) denote the set of integers (nonnegative integers, positive integers, rational numbers, respectively), and let Z^k (N^k, R^k) be the set of vectors of k integers (nonnegative integers, rational numbers). For a vector $v \in Z^k$, let v(i), $1 \leq i \leq k$, denote the i-th component of v. For a given value of k, let **0** in Z^k denote the vector of k zeros (i.e., **0**(i)=0 for i=1, . . . ,k). Now given vectors u, v, and w in Z^k we say: v=w iff v(i)=w(i) for i=1, . . . ,k; $v \geq w$ iff $v(i) \geq w(i)$ for i=1, . . . ,k; v>w iff $v \geq w$ and $v \neq w$; and u=v+w iff u(i)=v(i)+w(i) for i=1, . . . ,k. A k-dimensional *vector addition system* (VAS) is a pair (v_0,A) where v_0 in N^k is called the *start vector*, and A, a finite subset of Z^k, is called the set of *addition rules*. The *reachability set* of the VAS (v_0,A), denoted by R(v_0,A), is the set of all vectors z, such that $z=v_0+v_1+\cdots+v_j$ for some $j \geq 0$, where each v_i ($1 \leq i \leq j$) is in A, and for each $1 \leq i \leq j$, $v_0+v_1+\cdots+v_i \geq \mathbf{0}$. A k-dimensional *vector addition system with states* (VASS) is a 5-tuple (v_0,A,p_0,S,δ) where v_0 and A are the same as defined above, S is a finite set of states, δ ($\subseteq S \times S \times A$) is the transition relation, and p_0 is the initial state. Elements (p,q,x) of δ are called *transitions* and are usually written $p \rightarrow (q,x)$. A *configuration* of the VASS is a pair (p,x), where p is in S and x is a vector in N^k. (p_0,v_0) is the initial configuration. The transition $p \rightarrow (q,x)$ can be applied to the configuration (p,v) and yields the configuration (q,v+x), provided that $v+x \geq \mathbf{0}$. In this case, (q,v+x) is said to *follow* (p,v). Let σ_0 and σ_t be two configurations. Then σ_t is said to be *reachable* from σ_0 iff $\sigma_0=\sigma_t$ or there exist configurations $\sigma_1, \ldots, \sigma_{t-1}$ such that σ_{r+1} follows σ_r for r=0, . . . ,t-1. We then say $\sigma=<\sigma_0, \ldots, \sigma_t>$ is a *path* in (v_0,A,p_0,S,δ). The *reachability set* of the VASS (v_0,A,p_0,S,δ), denoted by R(v_0,A,p_0,S,δ), is the subset of $S \times N^k$ containing all configurations reachable from (p_0,v_0). The *reachability problem* for VASSs (VASs) is to determine, for a given VASS (VAS) V and vector v, whether $v \in R(V)$. The *containment* and *equivalence problems* are to determine, for two given VASSs (VASs) V and V', whether $R(V) \subseteq R(V')$ and whether R(V)=R(V'), respectively.

We find it convenient to define VASS(k,l,n) as the set of VASSs (v_0,A,p_0,S,δ) such that $\{v_0\} \cup A \subseteq Z^k$, l is the maximum length of the binary representation of any integer in the system, and n=max(|S|,|δ|). In this section, we will assume the start vector is **0**. (Note that R(v_0,A,p_0,S,δ)=R(**0**,A$\cup v_0$,q,S$\cup$\{q\},δ') for some $q \notin S$ and some δ'.) Let BV(k,b,n) be the set of all VASSs (**0**,A,p_0,S,δ) such that R(**0**,A,p_0,S,δ) is finite, $A \subseteq Z^k$, |S|=n, and $\max\{\sum_{i=1}^{k} v(i) : v \in A\}=b$. For any $v \in Z^k$, we define the *norm* of v, ||v||, as $\sum_{i=1}^{k} |v(i)|$. (Note that this is often called the *1-norm*.) We define μ(k,b,n) as the maximum norm of any vector reachable by a VASS in BV(k,b,n). Let σ be a path in a VASS. We define the *monotone increasing component* of σ, $\iota(\sigma)$, to be the sequence of configurations σ_i in σ for which all previous configurations in σ having the same state as σ_i have a vector with strictly smaller norm than that of σ_i. If σ is a path in a VASS in BV(k,b,n), then $\iota(\sigma)$ clearly has finite length.

In what follows, we only sketch the main ideas of the proofs. For more details, see [12].

2.1. Bounds on the Sizes of Finite VASSs

The general idea in what follows is to arrange the monotone increasing component of a path in a VASS into a tree in which any proper subtree contains only configurations whose states are the same and whose vectors have identical values in certain positions. In particular, in a subtree rooted at depth i (where the root of the tree is defined to be at depth 0), $i \geq 1$, all vectors will agree in at least i-1 positions. The resulting tree has certain properties which allow us to give a tight upper bound on its size, and hence, on the length of the monotone increasing component. We define $\mathcal{T}$(k,b,n) as the set of trees T having the following properties:

1. T has height $\leq$ k (i.e., the longest path from the root to a leaf is no more than k);
2. The root node of T is labelled 0 and has no more than n-1 children;
3. The nodes in T have integer labels such that for any node labelled $r>b$, there is a node labelled s, $r-b \leq s<r$;
4. The label of any node in T is less than the label of any of its children;
5. The number of children of any node of depth i, $1 \leq i \leq k-1$, is no more than the node's label.

Each node in a tree $T \in \mathcal{T}$(k,b,n) will represent a configuration in $\iota(\sigma)$; the node label will be the norm of the vector in that configuration. Each proper subtree of T will represent a hyperplane having dimension k-j+1, where j is the depth of the root of the subtree. The root of T represents the initial configuration. The remainder of T is divided into subtrees rooted at depth 1, each representing the set of configurations in $\iota(\sigma)$ having some particular state. Suppose some state q is entered for the first time with vector v. Then the configuration (q,v) is represented by a node with depth 1 in T. Now all subsequent configurations in $\iota(\sigma)$ containing q must have a vector v' such that $v'(i)<v(i)$ for some i; otherwise, the path from (q,v) to (q,v') could be pumped, producing infinitely many configurations. Consider the hyperplane of dimension k-1 in which all vectors w are such that $w(i)=v'(i)$. For an arbitrary v, there are at most $||v||$ such hyperplanes, each defined by the values of i and $v'(i)<v(i)$. The subtrees rooted at depth 2 in T represent these hyperplanes, their roots representing the first configuration occurring in that hyperplane. Likewise, the subtrees rooted at depth j represent hyperplanes of dimension k-j+1. It is easily seen that T satisfies properties 1,2,4, and 5 above; furthermore, since b is the maximum increase in norm caused by any transition, property 3 must also hold. We therefore have the following lemma:

Lemma 2.1: Let σ be a path in a VASS in BV(k,b,n), $\iota(\sigma)=<\sigma_0, \ldots, \sigma_t>$. There is a tree $T \in \mathcal{T}$(k,b,n) with t+1 nodes whose labels are the norms of the vectors in $\iota(\sigma)$.

The following lemmas can now be shown:

Lemma 2.2: For any tree $T \in \mathcal{T}$(k,b,n), there is a tree $T' \in \mathcal{T}$(k,b,n) with the same number of nodes as T such that the labels on all nodes of any given depth are nondecreasing from left to right.

Lemma 2.3: For any k, b, and n, $\mathcal{T}$(k,b,n) contains a tree of maximal size (i.e., a tree having as many nodes as any other tree in $\mathcal{T}$(k,b,n)).

Lemma 2.4: Any tree in $\mathcal{T}(k,b,n)$ having maximal size has its node labels arranged in order of a depth-first (preorder) traversal.

Corollary 2.1: Let S(k,b,n,i,x) be the set of subtrees in $\mathcal{T}(k,b,n)$ whose root is at depth i with label x. The largest element of S(k,b,n,i,x) has its node labels arranged in order of a depth-first (preorder) traversal.

Lemma 2.2 can be shown by observing that if a tree $T \in \mathcal{T}(k,b,n)$ has its top j levels ordered, then any subtrees rooted at the next level whose whose roots are out of order may be swapped, resulting in a tree $T' \in \mathcal{T}(k,b,n)$. Lemma 2.3 is shown by induction on k. The idea is to show that if the lemma were false for k but true for k-1, then any tree in $\mathcal{T}(k,b,n_0)$, where n_0 is the smallest integer such that $\mathcal{T}(k,b,n_0)$ has unbounded tree sizes, can be rearranged to form a tree in $\mathcal{T}(k\text{-}1,b,n_0\text{+}u)$ for some u. Finally, Lemma 2.4 is shown by rearranging a tree $T \in \mathcal{T}(k,b,n)$ whose node labels are not in order of a depth-first traversal into a tree T′ that has room for at least one more node. After we rearrange T so that each level has nondecreasing node labels from left to right, we wish to move the smallest node label s which does not appear in depth-first order into its proper place in a depth-first ordering. It is not hard to show that by repeatedly moving the leftmost descendants of s on successive levels upward to replace their parents, we can make room for the node displaced by s and any extra subtrees beneath this node. These subtrees are all moved upward in the tree, so there is room for new nodes at the bottoms of these subtrees.

Since the largest tree T in $\mathcal{T}(k,b,n)$ has its node labels arranged in depth-first order, the value of any given node in T (except the root) and the number of children it has (if its depth is k-1 or less) is simply b plus the largest label in the subtree rooted at its left-hand sibling, or b plus the label of its parent if it has no left-hand sibling. It is therefore a straightforward matter to derive a recurrence relation for the largest node label in T. If we let $\lambda_1(b,n)=n{*}b$, $\lambda_2(b,n)=n{*}\max(\log b,1)$, and $\lambda_i(b,n)=\max(n,\log b)$ for $i \geq 3$, we can easily show the following theorems:

Theorem 2.1: There exist constants c and d (independent of k and b) such that for any k-dimensional finite VAS (v_0,A) with $\max\{\sum_{i=1}^{k} v(i) : v \in \{v_0\} \cup A\} = b$, $k \geq 2$, we have $\forall v \in R(v_0,A)$, $||v|| \leq f_{k-1}(c{*}\lambda_{k-1}(b,||v_0||))$.

Theorem 2.2: There exists a constant c (independent of k, b, and n) such that $\mu(k,b,n) \leq f_k(c{*}\lambda_k(b,n))$.

[12] gives a VASS in BV(k,1,m*(2*k-1)+2) (and also in VASS(k,1,m*(4*k-3))) that can produce a vector with norm $f_k(m)$; hence, our derived bound for $\mu(k,b,n)$ is tight.

2.2. The Finite Containment and Equivalence Problems

In this subsection we concern ourselves with the complexity of the equivalence and containment problems for finite VASSs. If u is an upper bound on the norm of any vector reachable by a k-dimensional VASS (or VAS), clearly u^k is an upper bound on the number of vectors in the reachability set. It then follows that the finite containment and equivalence problems can be solved in time $O(u^{2k})$. Thus, from Theorems 2.1 and 2.2 we have the following result, which represents an improvement of two levels in the primitive recursive hierarchy over the bound provided by [23].

Theorem 2.3 There exists a positive constant c (independent of k, b, and n) such that the containment and equivalence problems can be solved in time

1. $f_k(c{*}\lambda_k(b,n))$ for BV(k,b,n), $k \geq 2$;

2. $f_1^4(c^*n^*b)$ for 2-dimensional finite VASs whose vectors cause increments of no more than b and whose start vectors have norm n;

3. $f_{k-1}(c^*\lambda_{k-1}(b,n))$ for k-dimensional finite VASs, $k \geq 3$, whose vectors cause increments of no more than b and whose start vectors have norm n.

We can also show, by a refinement of the proof in [24], the following:

Theorem 2.4: There exist positive constants a, b and c (independent of k and n) such that the containment and equivalence problems for BV(k,1,n) require $f_{k-a}(b^*n)$ time infinitely often whenever $k>c$.

In the proof of the previous theorem, the construction is such that each position is bounded by $f_{k-a}(b^*n)$. By letting $V_i(n)$ denote the set of finite VASSs whose reachability sets are bounded by $f_i(n)$, we have the following corollary:

Corollary 2.2 There exist positive constants c and d (independent of i and n) such that the time complexity of the containment and equivalence problems for $V_i(n)$ are bounded above (below) by $f_i(d^*n)$ $(f_i(c^*n))$.

Finally, the following theorem, proved by standard techniques, may be of independent interest. (See also [4, 28, 29].)

Theorem 2.5: The containment and equivalence problems for $\cup_n BV(1,1,n)$ are $A\Pi_2^L$-complete.

3. 2-dimensional VASSs

In this section, we closely examine the algorithm provided in [11], which generates an SLS representation of the reachability set of a given 2-dimensional VASS. We first show that this algorithm operates in NTIME($2^{2^{b^*l^*n}}$) for some constant b independent of l and n on any VASS in VASS(2,l,n). We then prove that, for any VASS in VASS(2,l,n), there is a DTIME($2^{2^{c^*l^*n}}$) algorithm to generate a corresponding SLS representation with O($2^{2^{d^*l^*n}}$) linear sets, where c and d are constants independent of l and n. Each of these linear sets has O(2^n) periods with norm O($2^{c'^*l^*n}$) for some constant c′ independent of l and n. These properties allow us to derive upper bounds of DTIME($2^{2^{c^*l^*n}}$) for the reachability, equivalence, and containment problems for VASS(2,l,n). Although we are unable to establish the corresponding lower bounds, we are able to show that the search procedure of Hopcroft and Pansiot requires $2^{2^{c^*l^*n}}$ steps. Thus, our analysis of their algorithm is tight. So far, the best lower bound we know for $\cup_{l,n}$VASS(2,l,n) is NP [27]. Hence, there is still much room for improvement. Now, before continuing to the detailed discussion, the following definitions are required.

For any vector $v_0 \in N^k$ and any finite set $P(=\{v_1,\ldots,v_m\}) \subseteq N^k$, the set $L(v_0,P)=\{x:\exists k_1,\ldots,k_m \in N^k \text{ and } x=v_0+\sum_{i=1}^{m} k_i v_i\}$ is called the *linear set* over the set of *periods* P. The *size* of the linear set $L(v_0,P)$, denoted by $|L(v_0,P)|$, is defined to be $\sum_{i=0}^{m} k^*\log_2 ||v_i||$. (I.e., the number of bits needed to represent the linear set.) A finite union of linear sets is called a *semilinear set* (SLS, for short). The size of a SLS is the sum of the sizes of its constituent linear sets. The *cone* generated by v_0 and P, denoted by $C(v_0,P)$, is the set $\{x:\exists k_1,\ldots,k_m \in R^k, k_1,\ldots,k_m \geq 0, \text{and } x=v_0+\sum_{i=1}^{m} k_i v_i\}$.

Given a VASS=(v_0,A,p_0,S,δ) and a path l in the state graph, $l= s_1 \xrightarrow{v_1} s_2 \xrightarrow{v_2} \cdots s_{t-1} \xrightarrow{v_{t-1}} s_t$ where $s_i \rightarrow (s_{i+1},v_i)$ $(1 \leq i \leq t-1)$ is in δ, l is a *short loop* iff $s_1 = s_t$ and $s_i \neq s_j$ $(1 \leq i < j \leq t)$. The *displacement* of l, denoted by $|l|$, is $\sum_{i=1}^{t-1} v_i$. l is a *short positive loop* (*p-loop*, for short) iff l is a short loop and $|l| > 0$.

In what follows, our analysis heavily depends on the algorithm given in [11]. Hence, for the sake of completeness, the algorithm is listed below. However, only a brief description will be given. The reader is encouraged to refer to [11] for more details. Given a 2-dimensional VASS V, the main idea behind the algorithm is to construct a tree in which each node is labelled by a 3-tuple $[x,p,A_x]$, where $x \in N^2$, $p \in S$ and $A_x \subseteq N^2$, to represent the reachability set generated by V. In what follows, each A_x is called a *loop set*. Each v in A_x is called a *loop vector*. The label $[x,p,A_x]$ indicates that $\{(p,v): v \in \mathcal{L}(x,A_x)\} \subseteq R(v_0,A,p_0,S,\delta)$. The intuitive idea of why the procedure works is the following. The tree is built in such a way that each path, in a sense, corresponds to a computation of the VASS. Each time an executable (valid) p-loop is encountered, that particular p-loop will be added (if necessary) to the loop set since clearly that loop can be repeated as many times as we want. If, along any path of the tree, there is an ancestor $[z,p,A_z]$ of $[x,p,A_x]$ such that $A_x=A_z$ and $x \in \mathcal{L}(z,A_z)$, then that particular path terminates at $[x,p,A_x]$. (This condition will be referred to as the *terminating condition*.) In [11], it was shown that a point (p,v) in $S \times N^2$ is reachable in V iff there exists a node with the label $[x,p,A_x]$ such that $v \in \mathcal{L}(x,A_x)$. (In other words, the reachability set coincides exactly with the SLS associated with the tree construction.) Furthermore, the tree construction will eventually terminate. Now, in order to put complexity bounds on this procedure, some measure of the tree is needed. In particular, we will see later that in order to derive the upper bound of the Hopcroft-Pansiot algorithm, it suffices to consider the following two quantities:

(1) $\max\{||v||: \exists\ [x,p,A_x] \in T \text{ such that } v \in A_x\}$,

(2) $\max\{||x||: [x,p,A_x] \in T\}$.

The first quantity gives an upper bound on the number of periods in each linear set, and the second quantity gives an upper bound on the number of linear sets in the SLS.

<u>Algorithm:</u> (from [11])

Create root labelled $[x_0,p_0,\emptyset]$;
while there are unmarked leaves **do**
begin
    Pick an unmarked leaf $[x,p,A_x]$;
    Add to A_x all displacements of short positive loops from p valid at x;
    if A_x is empty and there exists an ancestor $[z,p,A_z]$ with $z<x$,
    then add x-z to A_z;
    if there exists $c \in N^2$, $c=(0,\gamma)$ or $(\gamma,0)$ such that
        (a) c is not colinear to any vector of A_x, and
        (b) either
            (i) there exists an ancestor $[z,p,A_z]$ of $[x,p,A_x]$ such that $x-z=c$, or
            (ii) for some short nonpositive loop from p valid at x with displacement a and some $b \in A_x$, there exists $\alpha, \beta \in N$ such that $\alpha a+\beta b=c$
    then add c to A_x;
    if there exists an ancestor $[z,p,A_z]$ of $[x,p,A_x]$ such that
        $\mathcal{L}(z,A_z)$ contains x and $A_z==A_x$
    then mark $[x,p,A_x]$
    else
        for each transition $p \rightarrow (q,v)$ **do**
        begin
            Let $A_x=\{v_1,\ldots,v_k\}$

for each a, $a=\alpha_1 v_1+...+\alpha_k v_k$ where
$(\alpha_1,...,\alpha_k)$ is a minimal k-tuple such that $x+a+v \geq 0$,
do construct a son $[y,q,A_y]$ where $y=x+a+v$ and $A_x=A_y$;
end
if $[x,p,A_x]$ has no son **then** mark $[x,p,A_x]$;
end

Now, we are ready to derive an upper bound on the algorithm's complexity. Given a VASS V in VASS(2,l,n) and some path s in the corresponding tree T, one can easily see that there are at most 2^n distinct p-loops in any loop set. In addition to those p-loops, at most one non-axis vector and 2 axis vectors can occur in any of the loop sets in s (in what follows, if they exist, they will be referred to as u_1, γ_1 and γ_2, respectively). Of all the vectors appearing in the loop sets in s, only u_1, γ_1 and γ_2 can have a norm greater than $n*2^l$. Consider an arbitrary path in the tree generated by the algorithm. Let $h_{u_1}(l,n)$, $h_{\gamma_1}(l,n)$ and $h_{\gamma_2}(l,n)$ denote the maximum norm of all the vectors added before u_1, γ_1 and γ_2 are added, respectively. Also, let $h_k(l,n)$ denote the maximum norm of all vectors ever occurring in the system before the k-th loop vector is added. For two arbitrary nodes $d_1=[x_1,p_1,A_1]$ and $d_2=[x_2,p_2,A_2]$, $d_1 \rightarrow d_2$ iff d_1 is an ancestor of d_2 in T. d_2 is said to be *redundant* with respect to d_1, denoted by $d_1 \bullet\!\!< d_2$, iff $p_1=p_2$, $A_1=A_2$, $x_2-x_1 \in \mathcal{L}(\mathbf{0},A_1)$ and $d_1 \rightarrow d_2$. We also say that a node d is redundant iff there exists a d′ such that $d' \bullet\!\!< d$. (Note that, according to the terminating condition, if $d_1 \bullet\!\!< d_2$, then d_2 is a leaf.) A sequence of nodes $d_1=[x_1,p_1,A] \rightarrow d_2=[x_2,p_2,A] \rightarrow \cdots \rightarrow d_t=[x_t,p_t,A]$ is said to be *monotonic* (*strongly monotonic*) if $||x_1|| \leq ||x_2|| \leq \cdots \leq ||x_t||$ ($x_1 \leq x_2 \leq \cdots \leq x_t$). In what follows, we first derive the quantity $\max\{||v||: \exists\, [x,p,A_x] \in T$ such that $v \in A_x\}$, which is one of the two values we are most interested in. Hence, we must derive bounds for $||u_1||$, $||\gamma_1||$ and $||\gamma_2||$. Now notice that according to the algorithm, as long as the loop set remains empty, any path in T corresponds exactly with some path in V containing no pumpable loop. Since u_1 is added only to an empty loop set, it follows from Theorem 2.2 that:

Lemma 3.1: $h_{u_1}(l,n) \leq h_1(l,n)=O(2^{c*l*n})$, and $||u_1|| \leq a*2^{b*l*n}$, for some constants a, b, and c independent of l, and n.

As long as the loop set is empty, a path in T corresponds exactly with a path in the associated VASS. After the first loop vector is added, however, the correspondence no longer remains exact. Therefore, we must find an upper bound on the gain in norm caused by one step in T. The following lemma follows from [13].

Lemma 3.2: Let $u=[x,p,A_x] \rightarrow u'=[x',p',A_{x'}]$ be two consecutive nodes in T. Let $r=\max\{||v||: v \in A_x\}$. Then $||x'-x|| \leq c*(r*2^l)^{d*n}$, for some constants c and d independent of r, and l. (I.e., the maximum gain in one step in T is bounded by $c*(r*2^l)^{d*n}$.)

In deriving bounds for $||\gamma_1||$ and $||\gamma_2||$, the idea is to show that if a monotonic sequence of some specified length exists, then a strongly monotonic sequence of a certain length must also exist. A key fact used is that if $[x_1,p,A]$ is an ancestor of $[x_2,p,A]$ such that $||x_1||>||x_2||$ and if the vector v in A with maximum (minimum) slope in A is not an axis vector, then x_2 must be to the right of (above) the line through x_1 and x_1+v [11]. This fact, together with the pigeon-hole principle and results from [2], can be used to show the following lemmas:

Lemma 3.3: Consider a nonempty loop set $A=\{v_1,...,v_m\}$, where $v_1,...,v_m$ are arbitrary loop vectors. Let $\beta=\max\{||v||: v \in A\}$. If $d_1=[x_1,p,A] \rightarrow d_2=[x_2,p,A] \rightarrow \cdots \rightarrow d_{\beta^2+1}=[x_{\beta^2+1},p,A]$ is a strongly monotonic sequence, then there exist i and j, $1 \leq i,j \leq \beta^2+1$, such that $d_i \bullet\!\!< d_j$.

Lemma 3.4: Let σ: $d \rightarrow d'$ be a path in T. Let A_d be the loop set in d. Assume that $A_d \neq \emptyset$ and no axis vector exists in A_d. If $d_1=[x_1,p,A]\rightarrow d_2=[x_2,p,A]\rightarrow \cdots \rightarrow d_t=[x_t,p,A]$ is a monotonic sequence in σ, then it is also strongly monotonic.

Lemma 3.5: $h_{\gamma_1}(l,n)\leq c'*2^{d'*l*n}$, and $||\gamma_1||\leq c*2^{d*l*n}$, for some constants c, c', d, and d' independent of l, and n.

Lemma 3.6: Consider a loop set $A=\{v_1,\ldots,v_m\}$ that contains a vertical (horizontal) axis vector. (We include the case in which both axis vectors exist.) Let $\beta = \max\{||v||: v\in A\}$. Let b and f be arbitrary positive integers. If $d_1=[x_1,p,A]\rightarrow d_2=[x_2,p,A]\rightarrow \cdots \rightarrow d_{\beta*b+1}=[x_{\beta*b+1},p,A]$ is a monotonic sequence contained in the area $\{<x,y>: f\leq x\leq f+b-1 \text{ and } 0\leq y\}$ ($\{<x,y>: f\leq y\leq f+b-1 \text{ and } 0\leq x\}$), then there exist i and j, $1\leq i<j\leq \beta*b+1$, such that $d_i \bullet\!< d_j$.

Lemma 3.7: $h_{\gamma_2}(l,n)\leq a'*2^{b'*l*n}$, and $||\gamma_2||\leq a*2^{b*l*n}$, for some constants a, a', b, and b' independent of l, and n.

From the above facts and a straightforward application of the pigeon-hole principle, we can show

Lemma 3.8: $h_k(l,n)=O(2^{k*2^{c*l*n}})$, for some constant c independent of k, l, and n.

Since there will be at most 2^n+3 vectors in any A_x, the following theorem is obtained:

Theorem 3.1: For an arbitrary V in VASS(2,l,n) and its corresponding tree T, $\max\{||x||: [x,p,A_x]\in T\}=O(2^{2^{d*l*n}})$, for some constant d independent of V, l, and n.

[12] gives a VASS in VASS(2,l,3*n+4) whose Hopcroft-Pansiot tree can reach a vector with norm $2^{2^{d*l*n}}$, for some positive constant d; hence this upper bound is tight.

We are now ready to construct an algorithm to generate a SLS representation of the reachability set of a given VASS. The reader, at this point, should recall that in the original Hopcroft-Pansiot algorithm, no upper bound is given for the size of the SLS representation, neither does it tell how quickly the SLS can be generated. In what follows, we utilize the results obtained earlier in this section to construct a modified version of the Hopcroft-Pansiot algorithm. The main idea in our modification is that the terminating condition is not checked; instead, no node containing a vector larger than the bound given in Theorem 3.1 is ever added to the tree, and no axis vector larger than the bound derived in Lemma 3.7 is ever added to a loop set. Thus, our tree contains all the nodes in the Hopcroft-Pansiot tree, plus perhaps some additional nodes which are redundant. Furthermore, it is clear that if our tree contains duplicate nodes, then the respective descendants of these nodes are identical. Hence, we can prune our tree by never adding duplicate nodes. Hence, we have the following theorem:

Theorem 3.2: Given a VASS $V=(v_0,A,p_0,S,\delta)$ in VASS(2,l,n) and a state p in S, we can construct a SLS $\mathcal{SL}=\cup_{i=1}^{k}\mathcal{L}_i(x_i,P_i)$ in DTIME($2^{2^{c*l*n}}$), for some constant c independent of V, l, and n, such that,

(1) $\mathcal{SL}=\{x: (p,x)\in R(v_0,A,p_0,S,\delta)\}$,

(2) $k=O(2^{2^{d_1*l*n}})$, for some constant d_1 independent of l and n,

(3) $\forall i$, $1\leq i\leq k$, $||x_i||=O(2^{2^{d_2*l*n}})$, for some constant d_2 independent of l and n,

(4) $\forall i$, $1\leq i\leq k$, $|P_i|=O(2^n)$, where $|P_i|$ is the number of vectors in P_i,

(5) $\forall v\in P_i$, $1\leq i\leq k$, $||v||=O(2^{d_3*l*n})$, for some constant d_3 independent of l and n.

From Theorem 3.2 we want to show that the reachability, containment and equivalence problems for VASS(2,l,n) can be solved in DTIME($2^{2^{c*l*n}}$) for some fixed constant c. While the proof for the reachability problem for VASS(2,l,n) is quite straightforward, the complexity results for the equivalence problem for SLSs [13, 15] do not directly yield the desired upper bound for the containment and equivalence problems for VASS(2,l,n). However, a careful application of the proof techniques in [15] yields the desired upper bound for the containment and equivalence problems also.

Theorem 3.3: For VASS(2,l,n), the reachability, containment and equivalence problems can be solved in DTIME($2^{2^{c*l*n}}$), for some constant c independent of l and n.

Acknowledgment: We would like to thank Professor Vidal-Naquet for pointing out reference [23].

References

[1] Baker, H., Rabin's Proof of the Undecidability of the Reachability Set Inclusion Problem of Vector Addition Systems, MIT Project MAC. CSGM 79, Cambridge, MA, 1973.

[2] Borosh, I. and Treybig, L., Bounds on Positive Integral Solutions of Linear Diophantine Equations, *Proc. AMS 55*, 2 (March 1976), pp. 299-304.

[3] Cardoza, E., Lipton. R. and Meyer, A., Exponential Space Complete Problems for Petri Nets and Commutative Semigroups, *Proceedings of the 8th Annual ACM Symposium on Theory of Computing* (1976), pp. 50-54.

[4] Chandra, A., Kozen, D. and Stockmeyer, L., Alternation, *JACM 28*, 1 (January 1981), pp. 114-133.

[5] Clote, P., The Finite Containment Problem for Petri Nets, *Theoret. Comp. Sci. 43* (1986), 99-106.

[6] Crespi-Reghizzi, S. and Mandrioli, D., A Decidability Theorem for a Class of Vector Addition Systems, *Information Processing Letters 3*, 3 (1975), pp. 78-80.

[7] Davis, M., Matijasevic, Y. and Robinson, J., Hilbert's Tenth Problem. Diophantine Equations: Positive Aspects of a Negative Solution, *Proceedings of Symposium on Pure Mathematics 28* (1976), pp. 323-378.

[8] Ginzburg, A. and Yoeli, M., Vector Addition Systems and Regular Languages, *J. of Computer and System Sciences 20* (1980), pp. 277-284.

[9] Grabowski, J., The Decidability of Persistence for Vector Addition Systems, *Information Processing Letters 11*, 1 (1980), pp. 20-23.

[10] Hack, M., The Equality Problem for Vector Addition Systems is Undecidable, *Theoret. Comp. Sci. 2* (1976), pp. 77-95.

[11] Hopcroft, J. and Pansiot, J., On the Reachability Problem for 5-Dimensional Vector Addition Systems, *Theoret. Comp. Sci. 8* (1979), pp. 135-159.

[12] Howell, R., Huynh, D., Rosier, L., and Yen, H., Some Complexity Bounds for Problems Concerning Finite and 2-Dimensional Vector Addition Systems with States, to appear in *Theoret. Comp. Sci.*

[13] Huynh, D., The Complexity of Semilinear Sets, *Elektronische Informationsverarbeitung und Kybernetik 18* (1982), pp. 291-338.

[14] Huynh, D., The Complexity of the Equivalence Problem for Commutative Semigroups and Symmetric Vector Addition Systems, *Proceedings of the 17th Annual ACM Symposium on Theory of Computing* (1985), pp. 405-412.

[15] Huynh, D., A Simple Proof for the Σ_2^P Upper Bound of the Inequivalence Problem for Semilinear Sets, *Elektronische Informationsverarbeitung und Kybernetik 22* (1986), pp. 147-156.

[16] Karp, R. and Miller, R., Parallel Program Schemata, *J. of Computer and System Sciences 3*, 2 (1969), pp. 147-195.

[17] Kosaraju, R., Decidability of Reachability in Vector Addition Systems, *Proceedings of the 14th Annual ACM Symposium on Theory of Computing* (1982), pp. 267-280.

[18] Landweber, L. and Robertson, E., Properties of Conflict-Free and Persistent Petri Nets, *JACM 25*, 3 (1978), pp. 352-364.

[19] Lipton, R., The Reachability Problem Requires Exponential Space, Yale University, Dept. of CS., Report No. 62, Jan., 1976.

[20] Mayr, E., Persistence of Vector Replacement Systems is Decidable, *Acta Informatica 15* (1981), pp. 309-318.

[21] Mayr, E., An Algorithm for the General Petri Net Reachability Problem, *SIAM J. Comput. 13*, 3 (1984), pp. 441-460. A preliminary version of this paper was presented at the *13th Annual Symposium on Theory of Computing*, 1981.

[22] Mayr, E. and Meyer, A., The Complexity of the Word Problems for Commutative Semigroups and Polynomial Ideals, *Advances in Mathematics 46* (1982), pp. 305-329.

[23] McAloon, K., Petri Nets and Large Finite Sets, *Theoret. Comp. Sci. 32* (1984), pp. 173-183.

[24] Mayr, E. and Meyer, A., The Complexity of the Finite Containment Problem for Petri Nets, *JACM 28*, 3 (1981), pp. 561-576.

[25] Muller, H., Decidability of Reachability in Persistent Vector Replacement Systems, *Proceedings of the 9th Symposium on Mathematical Foundations of Computer Science* , LNCS 88 (1980), pp. 426-438.

[26] Muller, H., Weak Petri Net Computers for Ackermann Functions, to appear in *Elektronische Informationsverarbeitung und Kybernetik.*

[27] Rosier, L. and Yen, H., A Multiparameter Analysis of the Boundedness Problem for Vector Addition Systems, *J. of Computer and System Sciences 32*, 1 (February 1986), pp. 105-135.

[28] Rosier, L. and Yen, H., Logspace Hierarchies, Polynomial Time and the Complexity of Fairness Problems Concerning ω-Machines, *Proceedings of the 3rd Annual Symposium on Theoretical Aspects of Computer Science*, LNCS 210 (1986), pp. 306-320. To appear in *SIAM J. Comput.*

[29] Rosier, L. and Yen, H., On the Complexity of Deciding Fair Termination of Probabilistic Concurrent Finite-State Programs, *Proceedings of the 13th International Colloquium on Automata, Languages and Programming*, LNCS 226 (1986), 334-343.

[30] Van Leeuwen, J., A Partial Solution to the Reachability Problem for Vector Addition Systems, *Proceedings of the 6th Annual ACM Symposium on Theory of Computing* (1974), pp. 303-309.

[31] Valk, R. and Vidal-Naquet, G., Petri Nets and Regular Languages, *J. of Computer and System Sciences 23* (1981), pp. 299-325.

[32] Yamasaki, H., On Weak Persistency of Petri Nets, *Information Processing Letters 13*, 3 (1981), pp. 94-97.

CLOSURE PROPERTIES OF DETERMINISTIC PETRI NETS

Elisabeth PELZ

LRI, CNRS U.A. 410, Université Paris-Sud,

Bat. 490, F-91405 ORSAY Cedex, France

ABSTRACT: Deterministic Petri nets, as introduced in Vidal-Naquet's thesis [V] are studied here. We investigate systematically their closure properties under the standard language theoretical operations and prove in particular that the complement of a lan-guage of a deterministic net is always the language of a Petri net - which improves on both sides Hack's result on the complementation closure of free Petri net languages [H] -.

RESUME: Nous étudions ici des réseaux de Petri déterministes que Guy Vidal-Naquet avait introduit dans sa thèse d'Etat [V]. Nous présentons leurs propriétés de clôture par des opérations usuelles sur des langages formels. En particulier, le complément d'un langage de réseau déterministe est toujours un langage de réseaux de Petri. Cela améliore de beaucoup un résultat de Hack [H] sur la complémentation.

ZUSAMMENFASSUNG: Deterministische Petrinetze, wie Guy Vidal-Naquet sie in seiner Habilitationsschrift einführte, werden hier untersucht. Wir erhalten ihre Abschluss-eigenschaften bezüglich der üblichen sprachtheoretischen Operationen. Im besonderen zeigen wir, dass das Komplement einer deterministischen Petrinetzsprache immer die Sprache eines Petrinetzes ist. Dies verbessert bei weitem einen Satz von Hack [H] über Komplementierungen von freien Petrinetzsprachen.

0 INTRODUCTION:

Deterministic Petri nets have been introduced by Guy Vidal-Naquet [V]. They originated from the following considerations: Petri net problems are often undecidable because at some states of the evolution of the net several choices to fire transitions with the same label are possible. On the other hand, free labeled Petri nets are not powerful enough for appropriated modeling of certain industrial processes, especially those where signals (which are associated to transitions) should be treated. In particular, the languages of free labeled nets do not even contain the rational languages.

Deterministic Petri nets are defined as labeled Petri nets having the additional property that at each marking (which represents a state of the system) and for each label at most one transition with this label is firable. In these nets a sequence of actions leads to a well defined state.

In Vidal-Naquet's thesis [V] several examples of industriel processes modeled by deterministic nets are given. To analyze these nets we dispose of the well known techniques developed for usual Petri nets. Moreover, several improvements were found for the study of the behaviour of deterministic nets.

The behaviour of these nets was essentially studied from the point of view of formal language theory. This approach turn out to be extremely fruitful. Let us mention some of the nicest results:

One way to define the behaviour is to consider all labeled sequences leading to a final marking. For this definition, the class of regular languages as well as the class of free net languages is strictly contained in the class of deterministic Petri net languages. On the other hand, the latter one is strictly included in the class of Petri net languages. The same strict inclusion relations hold for the classes of corresponding firing sequences [V]. Moreover, some problems undecidable for Petri nets become decidable for deterministic nets [V]. We obtain a new result here: the inclusion problem for deterministic nets is decidable.

In their paper on specification problems of the input-output behaviour of control structures of concurrent systems Yoeli and Etzion show some nice results concerning deterministic nets [Y-E]: several formalizations of the concept of behavioural equivalence, initially invented by Milner for CCS, coincide when considering deterministic nets.

More recently, Carstensten studied the infinite behaviour of Petri nets with respect to fairness. He established exactly the relations between the different classes of infinitary languages including those defined on deterministic nets.

Still several questions about deterministic nets have never been treated until now. In particular, the closure properties of the different classes of deterministic net languages stayed unknown. In this paper we achieve a systematic treatment of these problems similar to the work of Hack [H] and Peterson [P] on the closure properties of the classes of Petri net languages, and of Rozenberg and Verraedt [R-V] on those of subset languages of Petri nets.

We prove in particular, that the complements of deterministic Petri net languages are always Petri nets languages. These results need some intermediate observations on different formalizations of the definitions of acceptation with respect to particular marking sets. They imply the decidability of the inclusion problem of the type "$L_2 \subseteq L_1$?", where L_1 is a deterministic Petri net language and L_2 a Petri net language.

In [H], Hack stated that the complementation closure of non-free Petri net languages would imply the undecidability of the Reachability Problem. He had overseen, that the gap between free and usual Petri net languages can be filled by the deterministic ones. Our complementation result which improves on both sides Hack's result on the complementation closure of free Petri net languages, naturally does not cancel the decidability of the Reachability problem, proved by Mayr and Kosaraju.

1 FUNDAMENTAL NOTIONS AND PROPERTIES

First let us remark, that whenever we use the symbols $\subset$ (resp. $<$) strict inclusion (resp. strict order) between the given objects is expressed. When strictness is not established or does not matter, we note $\subseteq$ (resp. $\leq$).

1.1 NOTIONS OF LANGUAGE THEORY

If Σ is an finite alphabet, Σ^* denotes the set of all finite words over Σ. A ***language*** over Σ is a subset L of Σ^*, the ***complement*** of a language L is the set of words Σ^*-L, noted $\complement L$.
The set of ***prefixes*** (or ***left factors*** or ***initial segments***) ***of*** L is noted pref(L) and is defined by pref(L) = $\{w \in \Sigma^* | \exists v \in \Sigma^* \; wv \in L\}$.

A ***class of languages*** is a subset **E** of $\mathcal{P}(\Sigma^*)$, its ***complementary class*** , noted **co-E**, is defined by **co-E** = $\{ \complement L \mid L \in$ **E** $\}$. Its prefix class, noted **pref(E)** is defined by **pref(E)** = $\{$ pref(L) $\mid L \in$ **E** $\}$.

Rat denotes the class of languages recognized by finite automata, also called class of ***rational*** (or ***regular***) ***languages*** .

1.2 DEFINITIONS OF PETRI NETS

When we mention in this paper a ***net*** or a ***Petri net*** N, we always mean a ***λ-free labeled Petri net*** $N = (P,T,A,v,e,M_0,F)$, where $P = \{p_1,...,p_r\}$ is a finite set of ***places*** , $T=\{t_1,...,t_s\}$ a finite set of ***transitions*** , $A \subseteq P\times T \cup T\times P$ a set of ***arcs*** ,
$v: (P\times T \cup T\times P) \rightarrow \mathbb{N}$ a ***valuation*** of the arcs verifying $v(x,y)=0$ if and only if (x,y) is not in A,
$e: T \rightarrow \Sigma$ a ***λ-free labelling*** of T in the alphabet Σ , M_0 a marking of P, called ***initial marking*** , and $F \subset \{M \mid M:P \rightarrow \mathbb{N}\}$ a finite set of markings, called ***final markings*** . We write (N,F) instead of N if the context do not define precisely, which set of final markings is considered.

The input (resp. output) places of a transition t are noted °t (resp. t°), more formally: $°t=\{p\in P \mid (p,t)\in A\}$ and $t°=\{p\in P \mid (t,p)\in A\}$.

The set of markings $\{M \mid M:P \rightarrow \mathbb{N}\}$ and $\mathbb{N}^r$ are generally identified. An partial ordering $\leq$ on markings is defined by $M\leq M'$ iff for all places p $M(p)\leq M'(p)$; we write $M<M'$ if the order is strict for at least one place. A ***partial marking*** m is an application from P to $\mathbb{N} \cup \{\omega\}$ identified with the infinite set of markings $\{ M \mid M(p)=m(p)$ if $m(p)\neq \omega$, and $M(p)\in \omega$ otherwise $\}$. A set of partial markings $\mathcal{F}_p$ can replace the set of final markings F in the definition of a net.

A ***transition*** t ***is enabled*** (we also say: ***occur*** or ***is firable***) at a marking M if and only if for all places $p\in P$, we have $M(p) \geq v(p,t)$, which is written $M(t>$. We write $M(t>M'$ (resp. $M(\overline{t}>M'$) if the occurence of the transition t (resp. of the finite sequence of transitions $\overline{t}$) changes the marking M into the new marking M', defined by $M'(p)=M(p)-v(p,t)+v(t,p)$, for all places p. A ***marking*** M ***is accessible*** in N, if there exists an occurence sequence $\overline{t}$ verifying $M_0(\overline{t}>M$, we also say that M ***is reached*** by $\overline{t}$. The labelling e is canonically extended to sequences of transitions by $e(t_1,t_2,...,t_n) = e(t_1)e(t2) ...e(t_n)$.

A ***deterministic net*** is a Petri net, noted D, whose labelling fonction is deterministic: for each accessible marking M in D and each letter σ of the alphabet Σ, there is at most one transition $t\in T$ labeled σ, which is enabled at M.

A ***free (labeled) net*** is a Petri net, whose labelling function is injective: for each letter σ of the alphabet Σ, there is at most one transition $t\in T$ labeled σ.

An ***arbitrary labeled net*** may have λ-labels on some transitions, i.e. $e: T \rightarrow \Sigma \cup \{\lambda\}$. The fact that λ-labels are allowed will always be mentioned explicitely by the supscript λ. For instance, a deterministic net with λ-labels is noted D^λ; it verifies that at each accessible marking at most one λ-labeled transition may be enabled.

1.3 LANGUAGES ASSOCIATED TO PETRI NETS

The ***finite behaviour of a net*** N can be defined by several conditions on the final markings; we consider the following languages (and classes of languages) over a given alphabet Σ associated to N:

$L(N) = \{w\in \Sigma^* \mid \exists M_f\in F\ \exists \overline{t}\in T^*\ M_0(\overline{t}>M_f \text{ and } e(\overline{t}) = w\}$

is called the ***language of*** N . The corresponding class of languages is noted **L**, and the restriction on deterministic nets **L(det)**; more precisely:

L = {L(N) | N is a λ-free labeled Petri net },
L(det) = {L(D) | D is a λ-free labeled deterministic Petri net },
$\mathbf{L}^\lambda$ = {L(N^λ) | N^λ is an arbitrary labeled Petri net },
$\mathbf{L}^\lambda$(det) = {L(D^λ) | D^λ is an arbitrary labeled deterministic Petri net }.
$\mathbf{L}^f$ = {L(N) | N is a free labeled Petri net },

In the same manner the ***language of*** N ***with respect to a set of final partial markings*** can be defined:

$L(N,\mathcal{F}_p) = \{w\in\Sigma^* \mid \exists\, m\in\mathcal{F}_p\ \exists\, M\in m\ \exists\, \bar{t}\in T^*,\ M_0(\bar{t}>M \text{ and } e(\bar{t}) = w\}$.

$G(N) = \{w\in\Sigma^* \mid \exists M\in \mathbb{N}^r\ \exists M_f\in F\ \exists \bar{t}\in T^*\ M_0(\bar{t}>M,\ M\geq M_f \text{ and } e(\bar{t}) = w\}$
is called the ***weak language of*** N.

We will only consider elements of this class whose set of final markings is fixed to be the zero-marking: $G(N,\{0^r\})$ is the set of all ***labeled firing sequences of*** N. We write $G_0(N)$ instead of $G(N,\{0^r\})$, and the corresponding classes of languages are noted $\mathbf{G_0}$, $\mathbf{G_0(det)}$, $\mathbf{G_0}^\lambda$, $\mathbf{G_0}^\lambda\mathbf{(det)}$. We will also consider the class of labeled sequences of free nets:

$\mathbf{G_0}^f = \{G_0(N) \mid N$ is a free labeled Petri net$\}$.

$\Delta(N) = G_0(N)\text{-}L(N)$ is the ***difference language of*** N; it is the set of all labeled firing sequences of N which do not reach one marking of the final marking set F. The corresponding classes of languages are noted Δ and Δ**(det)**.

1.4 FONDAMENTAL PROPERTIES OF DETERMINISTIC NETS

It is very easy to verify that the following properties are true for each deterministic net D:

P1: If w is in $G_0(D)$, then there is exactly one occurence sequence $\bar{t}$ labeled w and it defines a unique marking M with $M_0(\bar{t}>M$.

P2: If for some words w, v and for all n, wv^n is in $G_0(D)$, then there exist indices $i,j>0$, sequences $\bar{s}$ labeled w, $\bar{t}$ labeled v^i, $\bar{t}'$ labeled v^j and markings M, M', M" such that $M_0(\bar{s}>M(\bar{t}>M'(\bar{t}'>M''$ and $M''\geq M'$.

Mainly these properties are used as in the proofs of the theorems quoted here, cf. [V], as in those of our theorems given in the next sections.

Strict inclusion results between the different classes of languages have been obtained [V] and allow to situate exactly the deterministic classes:

Theorem 1.1: $\begin{matrix} \mathbf{Rat} \subset \\ \mathbf{L}^f \subset \end{matrix}\ \mathbf{L(det)} \subset \mathbf{L} \subset \mathbf{L}^\lambda\mathbf{(det)}$

Theorem 1.2: $\begin{matrix} \mathbf{pref(Rat)} \subset \\ \mathbf{G_0}^f \subset \end{matrix}\ \mathbf{G_0(det)} \subset \mathbf{G_0} \subset \mathbf{G_0}^\lambda\mathbf{(det)}$

These results show that allowing in deterministic nets supplementary transitions which are λ-labeled, makes the resulting classes richer than classes defined on usual nets. This comes from the fact that λ-labelling introduces non-determinism (more details are given in [V]).

As, in this paper, we are interested in deterministic behaviour, we are restricting our further investigations to the deterministic classes **L(det)** and $\mathbf{G_0(det)}$. These two classes are strictly situated between those defined for the corresponding behaviour on finite automata (resp. free labeled Petri nets) and on usual Petri nets.

2 SOME RESULTS ABOUT ACCEPTATION WITH RESPECT TO PARTICULAR MARKING SETS:

First we show, given a net with a finite set $\mathcal{M}$ of markings ($\subset \mathbb{N}^r$), how to find a finite set of of partial markings such that acception in one of these markings is equivalent to the fact to attain a marking which does not surpass all markings of $\mathcal{M}$.

We also give a modified version of a result of Peterson [P], which show how a net N for which a finite set of final partial markings is specified, can be transformed in a net N' with a finite set of final markings in $\mathbb{N}^r$, such that the languages of the two nets are equal. The difference with Peterson's result is that we allow nets having arbitrary valuations.

Proposition 2.1: Let N be a Petri net and $\mathcal{M}=\{ M_1, \ldots, M_n \} \subset \mathbb{N}^r$ a set of markings of N. Then there exists a set of partial markings $\mathcal{F}_p$ such that the following property (*) is true for all markings M :

for all $j \le n$, $M \not\ge M_j$, if and only if for some $m \in \mathcal{F}_p$, $M \in m$. (*)

proof: As usual, $P=\{p_1, \ldots, p_r\}$ is the set of places of N. For all $i \le r$, we define the set of indices of markings of M for which the place p_i is not zero:

$Q_i := \{ j \mid 1 \le j \le n \text{ and } M_j(p_i) > 0 \}$. Let X_i be the powerset of Q_i.

The set X will contain those elements of the cartesian product of the X_i which constitute a partition of $\{1, \ldots, n\}$ in r (eventually empty) buckets $x_1, \ldots, x_r$:

$X = \{ (x_1, \ldots, x_r) \in \prod_{1 \le i \le r} X_i \mid \text{for all } j \le n \text{ there is one and only one } i \le r \text{ such that } j \in x_i \}$

For each element $x \in X$ we define a set of partial markings m_x in the following way:

$m \in m_x$ if for all $i \le r$, we have

- $m(p_i) = \omega$, if $x_i = \emptyset$
- $m(p_i) \in [0, \min\{ M_j(p_i) - 1 \mid j \in x_i \}]$, if $x_i \ne \emptyset$

We define $\mathcal{F}_p$ as the union of these sets m_x of partial markings: $\mathcal{F}_p = \cup_{x \in X} m_x$.

Now the property (*) will be verified:

First note that if one of the markings in $\mathcal{M}$ is the zero-marking then $\mathcal{F}_p$ is empty and property (*) is trivially true. Now, let us suppose that none of the markings in $\mathcal{M}$ is the zero-marking.

"$\Leftarrow$" It suffices to show that, for all $m \in \mathcal{F}_p$ and $M \in m$, $M \not\ge M_j$ holds for all $j \le n$. Let $m \in \mathcal{F}_p$ and $M \in m$, then $m \in m_x$ for some $x \in X$, $x=(x_1, \ldots, x_r)$. By the definition of X, we have for all $i \le r$ and $j \le n$, that $j \in x_i$ implies that $M_j(p_i) > 0$. The marking M verifies that $M(p_i) = m(p_i) < M_j(p_i)$ for all $j \in x_i$. As x defines a partition of $\{1, \ldots, n\}$, it follows that for all $j \le n$, $M \not\ge M_j$.

"$\Rightarrow$" Let M be a marking such that for all $j \le n$, $M \not\ge M_j$. Then there exists for all $j \le n$ a place $q_j \in P$ with $M(q_j) < M_j(q_j)$. Now, for all $i \le r$, the bucket x_i can be defined by $x_i = \{j \mid q_j = p_i\}$. From the definition of the places q_j follows that for all $j \le n$ and $i \le r$, $j \in x_i$ implies that $M_j(p_i) > 0$. Thus $(x_1, \ldots, x_r) \in X$. We define the marking m by setting $m(p_i) = M(p_i)$ if $x_i \ne \emptyset$ and $m(p) = \omega$, otherwise. Then clearly, $m \in m_x$ and $M \in m$.

Proposition 2.2: Let N be a Petri net and m_j a partial marking. Then there exists a net N_j whose final marking set is $F=\{M_j\} \subset \mathbb{N}^r$, where

$$M_j(p) = \begin{cases} 0 & \text{if } m_j(p) = \omega \\ m_j(p) & \text{otherwise} \end{cases},$$

such that $L(N,\{m_j\}) = L(N_j,\{M_j\})$.

proof: As usual the set of transitions of N is $T = \{ t_1, ..., t_s \}$. Let Q be the set of all places for which m_j is ω.

For all $i \le s$ such that $t_i^\circ \cap Q \neq \emptyset$, we define finite sets R_i, S_i and U_i by $R_i = t_i^\circ \cap Q$, $S_i = t_i^\circ - R_i$ and $U_i = \{ u: R_i \to \mathbb{N} \mid 0 \le u(p) \le v(t_i,p) \text{ for all } p \in R_i \}$.

Now we add for all $i \le s$ and all $u \in U_i$ a transition t_{iu} with $e(t_{iu}) = e(t_i)$, ${}^\circ t_{iu} = {}^\circ t_i$, $t_{iu}{}^\circ = S_i \cup \{ p \mid u(p) > 0 \}$ and $v(t_{iu},p) = u(p)$.

This construction does not transform the behaviour of the places s_i with exact final marking, but allows the places of Q in N_j to have less or the same number of tokens as in the original net N. Therefore, for each sequence of $L(N,m_j)$ there is an appropriated sequence firable in N_j which leads to the final marking with zero token in the places of Q and identic to m_j elsewhere. Thus $L(N,m_j) = L(N_j,M_j)$.

3 COMPLEMENTS FOR DETERMINISTIC PETRI NETS

Theorem 3.1: Let D be a deterministic Petri net labeled over a finite alphabet Σ. Then there exists a Petri net N such that $L(N) = \complement G_0(D)$.

Corollary 3.2: The class **co-G_0(det)** is included in **L**.

proof of the theorem: Let D be a deterministic Petri net. For each $\sigma \in \Sigma$ we distinguish a finite set of markings in the following way: let T_σ be the subset of transitions of D which are labeled σ. For each $t \in T_\sigma$ there is a minimal marking M_t at which t is firable (i.e. $M_t(p) = v(p,t)$ at all places p). All Petri nets being monotone, the fact that t is enabled at M_t implies that t is enabled at each marking $M \ge M_t$.

Let be $\mathcal{M} = \{ M_t \mid t \in T_\sigma \}$. By proposition 2.1, there exists a set of partial markings $\mathcal{F}_p(\sigma)$ such that for arbitrary markings M holds:

$$M \not\ge M_t, \text{ for all } t \in T_\sigma, \quad \text{if and only if} \quad M \in m, \text{ for some } m \in \mathcal{F}_p(\sigma).$$

This signifies that each marking, for which σ is **not** firable, is in $\mathcal{F}_p(\sigma)$ and vice versa.

By proposition 2.2, the deterministic net $(D,\mathcal{F}_p(\sigma))$ can be transformed in a net N_σ with a final marking set $F_\sigma \subset \mathbb{N}^r$, such that $L(N_\sigma,F_\sigma) = L(D,\mathcal{F}_p(\sigma))$ (you have to take the union of the nets obtained separately for each one of the partial markings in $\mathcal{F}_p(\sigma)$). As the construction of N_σ add a lot of transitions with the same label which are enabled at the same time, this Petri net is not deterministic (see the proof of prop. 2.2).

Let N_σ' be the Petri net with the following language: $L(N_\sigma') = L(N_\sigma,F_\sigma)\cdot\sigma\cdot\Sigma^*$ which exists because **L** is closed under product of concatenation.

Finally, let N be the Petri net of the union of the nets N_σ' for $\sigma \in \Sigma$, verifying $L(N) = \cup_{\sigma\in\Sigma} L(N_\sigma')$. Now we have to show the following assertion for each word $w \in \Sigma^*$:

$$w \in \complement G_0(D) \quad \text{if and only if} \quad w \in L(N) .$$

$\Rightarrow$: If $w \in \complement G_0(D)$, then there is an initial segment v de w (eventually the empty word) and a letter $\sigma \in \Sigma$ such that $v\sigma$ is also an initial segment of w and the following condition holds:

(*) for each firing sequence $\bar{t}$ labeled v and each transition $t' \in T_\sigma$,
$M_0(\bar{t}>$ and not $M_0(\bar{t}.t'>$

As D is deterministic, such a firing sequence is unique (by **P1**), and the condition (*) is equivalent to "$v \in G_0(D)$ and $v\sigma \notin G_0(D)$". Let M be the unique marking reached after firing the sequence labeled v. As no transition labeled σ is enabled at M, necessarily M is in $\mathcal{F}_p(\sigma)$. Thus v is in $L(D,\mathcal{F}_p(\sigma))$ and in $L(N_\sigma,F_\sigma)$. It follows from the above construction, that $v\sigma$ and w are in $L(N_\sigma')$ and in L(N).

$\Leftarrow$: If $w \in L(N)$ then $w \in L(N_\sigma')$ for some $\sigma \in \Sigma$. As $L(N_\sigma') = L(N_\sigma,F_\sigma)\cdot\sigma\cdot\Sigma^*$, there is a decomposition of the word w, $w=v\sigma v'$ with $v \in L(N_\sigma,F_\sigma)$ and $v' \in \Sigma^*$. Then v is also in $L(D,\mathcal{F}_p(\sigma))$ and by **P1** there is only one sequence labeled v firable in D. Thus v is exactly one of the words which cannot be continued by σ in the deterministic net D. It follows that neither $v\sigma$ nor w are in $G_0(D)$, i.e. $v\sigma$ and w are in $\complement G_0(D)$.

Theorem 3.3: Let D be a deterministic Petri net over a finite alphabet Σ. Then there exists a Petri net N such that $L(N) = \Delta(D)$.

Corollary 3.4: The class **Δ(det)** is included in **L**.

proof of the theorem: Let D be a deterministic Petri net. Let v be a word in the difference language $\Delta(D)$ of D. Then there exists an unique firing sequence $\bar{t}$ of D labeled v (by **P1**) and the reached marking M is not in the set of final markings F. Thus the marking M verifies one of the following conditions:

(i) $M \not\geq M_f$ for all $M_f \in F$, or

(ii) $M > M_f$ for some $M_f \in F$ and $M \neq M_f$ for all $M_f \in F$.

This observation furnishes the idea of the construction in two steps of the net whose language will be $\Delta(D)$.

First we treat all markings M verifying condition (i): we obtain - as in the proof of theorem 3.1 - by the successive application of proposition 2.1 (with $\mathcal{M}$ =F) and 2.2, a Petri net N' such that for all words w,

$w \in L(N')$ iff w is the label of a firing sequence $\bar{t}$ of D such that the marking M with $M_0(\bar{t}>M$ verifies $M \not\geq M_f$ for all $M_f \in F$.

As previously, the net N' we obtain, is generally not deterministic.

For the markings verifying the second condition, we can define a new set F" of final markings of the net D, such that for all words w,

$w \in G(D,F")$ iff w is the label of a firing sequence $\bar{t}$ of D such that the marking M with $M_0(\bar{t}>M$ verifies $M \neq M_f$ for all $M_f \in F$ and $M > M_f$ for some $M_f \in F$.

This set can be obtained by taking the markings M_f of F and increasing the number of tokens in one place by one. Thus each M_f defines $|P|=s$ new markings: For all $M_f \in F$ and all $i \leq s$, let $M_{f,i}$ be the marking defined by

$M_{f,i}(p_i)=M_f(p_i)+1$ and $M_{f,i}(p)=M_f(p)$ for all places $p \neq p_i$.

Thus $F" = \{M_{f,i} \mid M_f \in F \text{ and } 0 \leq i \leq s\}$. As $\mathbf{G} \subset \mathbf{L}$, the net (D,F") can be transformed in a Petri net N" such that $L(N") = G(D,F")$.

Let N be the net of the union of N' and N". Then $L(N) = L(N') \cup L(N") = \Delta(D)$.

Theorem 3.5: Let D be a deterministic Petri net over a finite alphabet Σ. Then there exists a Petri net N such that $L(N) = \complement L(D)$.

Corollary 3.6: The class **co-L(det)** is included in **L**.

proof of the theorem: As $\complement L(D) = \Delta(D) \cup \complement G_0(D)$, we may consider the Petri net N_1 which recognizes $\Delta(D)$ and the Petri net N_2 which recognizes $\complement G_0(D)$ (whose existences are given by Theorem 3.3, resp. 3.1). Let N be the Petri net which is the union of N_1 and N_2.

Thus $L(N) = L(N_1) \cup L(N_2) = \Sigma^*-L(D)$.

These results are a little bit surprising: in generally Petri nets are not closed under complement. In [P] for instance, we give explicitely a methode (inspired by the logical characterization of net-behaviours) to obtain languages which are Petri net languages, whereas their complements are not Petri net languages, and in [P-P] some examples of such languages can be found.

Hack [H] gave a proof of $\mathbf{co\text{-}G_0}^{\mathbf{f}} \subset \mathbf{L}^{\lambda}$, but this result is not at all amazing seen the power brought by λ-labelling. He stated in the same paper ([H], end of §7) that the complementation closure of the non-free Petri net languages would imply the undecidability of the Reachability Problem. He had overseen that the gap between free and usual Petri net languages can be filled by the deterministic ones.

By showing that with λ-free labellings, the complement of a deterministic Petri net is always a Petri net ,we are improving Hack's result on both sides: $\mathbf{co\text{-}G_0}^{\mathbf{f}} \subset \mathbf{co\text{-}G_0(det)} \subset \mathbf{L} \subset \mathbf{L}^{\lambda}$.

And as already mentionned in the introduction, this result naturally does not cancel the decidability of the Reachability Problem.

In the following, we will show that these results cannot be strengthened: The classes **co-**$\mathbf{G_0(det)}$ and **co-L(det)** are not closed by complement because deterministic Petri nets D exists whose complements with respect to L(D) or $G_0(D)$ are non deterministic Petri nets .

Proposition 3.7: The class $\mathbf{co\text{-}G_0(det)}$ is not included in $\mathbf{G_0(det)}$.

proof: This result nearly follows from the definition of $\mathbf{G_0}$, whose languages are prefix-closed . Thus the complement of each such language contains certain words and not their initial segments.

For instance, let us consider $L = \text{pref}\{\, a^n b^n \mid n>0 \,\}$ which is clearly in $\mathbf{G_0(det)}$. The words $a^n b^{n+1}$, for all n>0, belong to its complement $\complement L$, but the set of strict initial segments of this words, which is L, trivially do not.

Proposition 3.8: The class **co-L(det)** is not included in **L(det)**.

proof: Let us consider the language $L= \{\, a^n b^n \mid n>0 \,\}$ which is clearly in **L(det)** and suppose that there is a deterministic net D accepting its complement: $L(D,F)=\complement L$.

First let us assume that the markings obtained after having fired the sequences labeled a^m, for m>0, which are in L(D,F), are not all distinct. Thus there are m,n>0, $\bar{t}$, $\bar{t}'$, M and M', such that $e(\bar{t})=a^m$, $e(\bar{t}')=a^n$, $M_0(\bar{t}>M(\bar{t}'>M'$, $M,M' \in F$ and M=M'. As for all m,i>0, $a^m b^i$ is a firing sequence of D, there are unique $\bar{s}$ and M" such that $e(\bar{s})=b^m$ and $M'(\bar{s}>M''$ (by **P1**). The sequence $a^m b^m$ is not in L(D,F), thus $M'' \notin F$. This implies that $a^{m+n} b^m$ is not in L(D,F), too, contrary to the fact that this word is in $\complement L$.

Therefore, for all m,n>0, $\bar{t}$, $\bar{t}'$, M and M', such that $e(\bar{t})=a^m$, $e(\bar{t}')=a^n$ and $M_0(\bar{t}>M(\bar{t}'>M'$, we have necessarely $M \neq M'$, and by **P2**, even $M<M'$.

It follows that an infinite number of distincts markings belong to F, which is in contradiction with the fact that F is finite. Thus $\complement L$ cannot be in **L(det)**.

4 REMAINING CLOSURE PROPERTIES ON L(det):

In the next two sections we investigate whether the classes **L(det)** and **G_0(det)** are closed for the usual operators of formal language theory. We show that for almost all operators the answer is "no". This implies that we cannot hope to construct deterministic nets by small moduls which could be fit together afterwards.

Remark: Some of these results are easy to prove, thus it is not astonishing, that the facts on union and renaming are already known by several persons working on deterministic nets, cf. [V2] or [C], but actually no trace of these facts can be found in the litterature.

Fact 4.1: **L(det)** is closed under intersection.

proof: It is very easy to see that the usual construction of the intersection net , applied to two deterministic Petri nets furnishs a deterministic Petri net, too.

Fact 4.2: **L(det)** is not closed under union.

proof: Let us consider the two languages $L_1 = \{ a^n b^n \mid n>0 \}$ and $L_2 = \{ a^n b^{2n} \mid n>0 \}$, which are clearly in **L(det)**. Suppose that a deterministic Petri net D=(N,F) exists, whose language L(D) is $L_1 \cup L_2$.

As there are only a finite number of markinge in F, there is some $M \in F$, $k<l$, $\bar{t}$, $\bar{s}$ such that $e(\bar{t}) = a^k b^k$, $e(\bar{s}) = a^l b^l$, $M_0(\bar{t}> M$ and $M_0(\bar{s}> M$. As $a^k b^{2k} \in L_2$, there are $M' \in F$ and $\bar{r}$ such that $e(\bar{r}) = b^k$ and $M(\bar{r}> M'$. But then $M_0(\bar{s}\bar{r}> M'$ also holds and $a^l b^{l+k} \in L(D)$, without being in $L_1 \cup L_2$.
We may conclude that $L_1 \cup L_2$ is not in **L(det)**.

Fact 4.3: **L(det)** is not closed under λ-free renaming (i.e. alphabetic morphisme).

proof: The language $L = \{ a^n b^n \mid n>0 \} \cup \{ c^n b^{2n} \mid n>0 \}$ is clearly in **L(det)**. By the renaming ψ defined by $\psi(c)=a$, $\psi(a)=a$, $\psi(b)=b$, we obtain $\psi(L)=L_1 \cup L_2$ of the previous proof (ii). Thus $\psi(L)$ cannot be in **L(det)**.

Fact 4.4: **L(det)** is not closed under λ-free morphisme.

(consequence of 4.3)

Fact 4.5: **L(det)** is not closed under shuffle product

Let us remark that Hack [H] and Peterson [P] call this operator "concurrency" adopting the notation || . Here we note ⧢ the shuffle operator.

proof: Let us consider $L_1 = \{ a^n c^n \mid n>0 \}$, $L_2 = \{ c^m b^m \mid m>0 \}$, which are clearly in **L(det)**. We will show that $L = L_1 ⧢ L_2$ is not in **L(det)**.

We will suppose the contrary: Let D be the deterministic Petri net which recognize L. In particular, D recognize for all i>0 and j>0 the words $a^i c^{j+i} b^j$ and $a^i c^{j+i} b^{j+i} c^i$. Let us fixe $j \neq 0$; we call, for all i, M_i the unique marking of F such that there exists a firing sequence $\bar{t}_i$ labeled $w_i = a^i c^{j+i} b^j$ with $M_0(\bar{t}_i> M_i$ (its existence follows from **P1**). As F is finite, there existe i and i', i'>i, such that $M_{i'}=M_i$. Let be $\bar{s}_{i'}$ the sequence labeled $b^{i'} c^{i'}$ such that there exists $m_{i'} \in F$ and $M_{i'}(\bar{s}_{i'}> m_{i'}$. But then $a^i c^{j+i} b^{j+i'} c^{i'}$ would be also in L, which is impossible by its definition. Thus L cannot be in **L(det)**.

Fact 4.6: **L(det)** is not closed under concatenation product.

proof: Let us consider $L_1 = \{ a^n b^n \mid n>0 \}$, $L_2 = \{ a\Sigma^* + b^2\Sigma^* + \lambda \}$, which are clearly in **L(det)**, with $\Sigma=\{a,b\}$. Suppose that there is a deterministic Petri net D recognizing $L = L_1 \cdot L_2$. We fixe some n $> |F|$. For each k, we call M_k the unique marking such that there exists $\bar{t}_k$ labeled $a^n b^n$ and $M_o(\bar{t}_k > M_k$ (by **P1**). By the choice of n, there are $i<i'<n$ such that $M_{i'}=M_i$. As $a^n b^{n+1} \notin L$, $M_{n+1} \notin F$ follows. But M_{n+1} is an accessible marking and there existe $\bar{s}$ labeled b^{n+1-i} such that $M_i(\bar{s}> M_{n+1}$. As $M_{i'}=M_i$, $a^n b^{i'} b^{n+1-i}$ is not in L, too, contrary to the definition of L. Therefore, L cannot be in **L(det)**.

Fact 4.7: **L(det)** is not closed under iterated product (star operation).

(Consequence of 4.6)

5 Remaining closure properties on G_0(det):

Fact 5.1: **G_0(det)** is closed under intersection.

(Corollary of 4.1)

Fact 5.2: **G_0(det)** is not closed under union.

proof: Let us consider the languages $L_1=\{ a^n b^i c \mid 0 \leq i<n \}$ and $L_2=\{ a^+ b^* \}$, which are both in **G_0(det)**. Suppose that there is a deterministic Petri net D such that $G_o(D) = L = L_1 \cup L_2$. As $a^+ \subset L$, we call M_i the unique marking such that $M_o(\bar{t}_i > M_i$ and $e(\bar{t}_i)=a^i$ (by **P1**) and there are j,j' such that $M_j \leq M_{j'}$ (by **P2**). As $a^j b^* \subset L$, there are also $l,k>0$ such that there are $\bar{s}_l$ and $\bar{r}_k$ labeled b^l and b^k and markings m,m' in $\mathbb{N}^r$ such that $Mj(\bar{s}_l > m(\bar{r}_k > m'$ with $m' \geq m$ (by **P2**).

Let be p the smallest integer p' such that for $l'=j+p' \cdot j'$ holds $l'>l$, and let q and k' be integers such that $k'=l+q \cdot k > l'$. Clearly, $M_{l'} > M_j$. We call m_l and $m_{k'}$ the markings in $\mathbb{N}^r$ verifying $M_{l'}(\bar{s}_l > m_l$ and $M_{l'}(\bar{s}_l . \bar{r}_k{}^q > m_{k'}$. Then $m_{k'} \geq m_l$. As $L_1 \subset G_o(D)$, there is a transition r labeled c enabled at m_l. But r is also enabled at $m_{k'}$, thus $a^{l'} b^{k'} c$ would also be in $G_o(D)$, which is contrary to the definition of L. Thus L cannot be in **G_0(det)**.

Fact 5.3: **G_0(det)** is not closed under λ-free renaming (i.e. alphabetic morphisme)

proof: The language $L' = \text{pref}\{ a^n b^i c \mid 0 \leq i<n \} \cup \{ d^+ b^* \}$ is clearly in **G_0(det)**. By the renaming ψ defined by $\psi(d)=a$, $\psi(a)=a$, $\psi(b)=b$ and $\psi(c)=c$, we obtain $\psi(L')$ is equal to the language L of the previous proof (ii). Thus **G_0(det)** does not contain $\psi(L')$.

Fact 5.4: **G_0(det)** is not closed under λ-free morphisme.

(Consequence of 5.3)

Fact 5.5: **G_0(det)** is not closed under shuffle product (concurrency).

proof: Let us take $L_1=\text{pref}\ \{a^n b^n c^n \mid n>0 \}$ and $L_2=\text{pref}\ \{b^m c^m d^m \mid m>0 \}$ which are clearly languages of **G_0(det)**. We will show by contraposition that $L=L_1 ш L_2$ is not in **G_0(det)**. Let be n>0. As $a^n b^*$ belongs to L, there are integers m_1,m_2 and markings M_1,M_2 such that there exist sequences $\bar{t}_1, \bar{t}_2$ with $e(\bar{t}_1)= a^n b^{m_1}$, $e(\bar{t}_2)=b^{m_2}$ and $M_o(\bar{t}_1 > M_1(\bar{t}_2 > M_2$ with $M_2 \geq M_1$.

Let us fixe some k,l,m>0 such that $m=l\cdot m_2>n$ and $m_1+l\cdot m_2=k+n$. We consider sequences $\bar{s},\bar{s}'$ and markings M,M' such that $e(\bar{s})=a^nb^{k+n}$, $e(\bar{s}')=b^m$ and $M_0(\bar{s}>M(\bar{s}'>M'$, where necessarely $M'\geq M$. As $a^nb^{n+k}c^{n+k}d^k$ belongs to L, there exists $\bar{r}$ with $e(\bar{r})=c^{n+k}d^k$ and $M(\bar{r}>$. It follows that $M'(\bar{r}>$ too, thus $w=a^nb^{n+k+m}c^{n+k}d^k$ would be in L . We will show that this is not possible.

As the subword a^n comes necessarely from a word w_1 of L_1 we have only two possible constellations:

(i) $w_1=a^nb^{n-i}$ for $0\leq i\leq n$ or (ii) $w_1=a^nb^nc^{n-i}$ for $0\leq i\leq n$

Let us look for the only word w_2 such that $w_1w_2=w$.

For (i) we find $w_2=b^{i+k+m}c^{n+k}d^k$; as $i+m>n$, the word w_2 cannot be in L_2.

For (ii) we find $w_2=b^{k+m}c^{k+i}d^k$; as $m>i$, the word w_2 cannot be in L_2.

Thus, w is not in L and, by consequence, L cannot be in $\mathbf{G_0(det)}$.

Fact 5.6: $\mathbf{G_0(det)}$ is not closed under concatenation product.

proof: We will suppose the contrary.
Thus for $L_1=\text{pref}\ \{a^nb^n \mid n>0\}$ and $L_2=\text{pref}\ \{b^mc^md \mid m>0\}$ which are clearly languages of $\mathbf{G_0(det)}$, there exists a deterministic Petri net D with $G_0(D)= L=L_1\cdot L_2$. Let us fixe n>0; there is an unique sequence $\bar{t}$ and a marking M such that $e(\bar{t})=a^n$ and $M_0(\bar{t}>M$ (by **P1**) . As $a^nb^* \subset L$, there are i>n and j>0 such that there exist unique sequences $\bar{s}$ and $\bar{r}$ with $e(\bar{s})=b^i$ and $e(\bar{r})=b^j$ and $M(\bar{s}>M'(\bar{r}>M''$ with $M''>M'$. Let k>0 be such that i=n+k.

As $a^nb^{n+k}c^kd$ belongs to L, there is an unique sequence $\bar{u}$ with $e(\bar{u})=c^kd$ such that $M'(\bar{u}>$. As $M''(\bar{u}>$ also holds, $w=a^nb^{n+k+j}c^kd$ should be in L. We will show that this is not true: if w_2 belongs to L_2 and $|w_2|_d=1$, then $|w_2|_b=|w_2|_c$. Thus the only choice for taking $w_2\in L_2$ such that there exists w_1 with $w_1\cdot w_2=w$ is $w_2=b^kc^kd$. But then $w_1=a^nb^{n+j}$ and w_1 do not belong to L_2. Therefore, L cannot be in $\mathbf{G_0(det)}$.

Fact 5.7: $\mathbf{G_0(det)}$ is not closed under iterated product (star operation).

(Consequence of 5.6)

6 CONCLUDING REMARKS:

The complementation results of §3 implies in particular that the complement of free labeled Petri net languages are always Petri net languages. Thus the following problem, known as inclusion problem, "$L_2\subseteq L_1$?", becames decidable when L_1 is a deterministic Petri net language, L_2 can be the language of a usual Petri net. Let us remember that the problem is undeciadable if L_1 is also the language of a usual Petri net.

As the emptyness problem for Petri net languages is decidable (as a consequence of Mayr's and Kosaraju's result), and as our inclusion problem is equivalent to the emptyness problem of $L_2\cap \complement L_1$, which is the language of a Petri net (cf. §3), the decidability of the above problem follows.

An other consequence concerns subset languages as studied by Rozenberg and Verraedt [R-V]. We know that the nonclosure result for a class of sequentialized Petri nets implies the analogous nonclosure result for the class of subset languages defined by the corresponding class of Petri nets. Thus the classes of subset languages of deterministic nets with or without final markings are not closed under union, concatenation-product, iterated product, shuffle-product, renaming and morphisme. These result could complete the table of closure results on classes of subset languages given in Rozenberg's and Verraedt's article.

References:

[C] H. CARSTENSEN: "***Fairness bei nebenläufigen Systemen*** ", doctoral thesis, Universität Hamburg, september1986

[H] M. HACK: "***Petri net languages*** " , Comp. Struct. Group Memo 124, Project MAC, MIT, Cambridge MASS., 1975

[P] E. PELZ: "***ω-languages of Petri nets and logical sentences*** ", proceedings of the 7th european workshop on Petri nets, Oxford, 1986

[P-P] M. PARIGOT , E. PELZ: "***A logical formalism for the study of finite behaviour of Petri nets*** ", in Advances in Petri nets 1985, ed. by G. Rozenberg, Springer-Verlag, 1986

[Pe] J.L. PETERSON, "***Petri net theory and the modeling of systems*** ", Prentice-Hall, Englewood Cliffs, NJ, 1981

[R-V] G. ROZENBERG, R. VERRAEDT, "***Subset languages of Petri nets, Part II: Closure properties*** ", TCS 27, pp 85-108, North-Holland, 1983

[V] G. VIDAL-NAQUET, "***Deterministic Languages for Petri nets*** ", in the proceedings of of the first european workshop on Petri nets, Strasbourg, 1980,
also in
Application and theory of Petri Nets, ed. by C. Girault and W. Reisig, Informatik Fachberichte 52, Springer-Verlag, 1982.
This article summarizes the 5th section of his thesis:
G. VIDAL-NAQUET, "***Rationalité et déterminisme dans les réseaux de Petri*** ", thèse d'Etat, Université Pierre et Marie Curie, Paris, 1981

[V2] G. VIDAL-NAQUET, personal communication, 1986

[Y-E] M. YOELI, T. ETZION, "***Behavioral equivalence of concurrent systems*** ", in the proceedings of the third european workshop on Petri nets, Varenna, 1982

Some Results on Fairness: The Regular Case

Lutz Priese
Ralf Rehrmann
Uwe Willecke-Klemme
Fachbereich 17
Mathematik / Informatik
Universität-Gesamthochschule-Paderborn

ABSTRACT

We introduce some steps towards a theory of fairness in ω-regular languages.

1. Introduction

The concept of fairness has attracted much attention in recent years in studies of the behaviour of nondeterministic or concurrent systems or programs. Fairness and several closely related concepts have been introduced, such as starvation-freeness, justice, weak- strong- extreme-fairness, S-T-P-fairness, fair termination, etc. The common idea is that any component of some system that is enabled sufficiently often must eventually be activated.

Unfortunately, as most research on fairness and it's relatives is done in different quite specific models, it becomes quite difficult to distinguish between results about fairness itself and about the underlying model. Some work has been done inside Petri-net theory. E.g. Best[B1] presented a hierarchy of n-fairness that collapses in Simple Nets. Fairness has also been studied in CCS (see [Mi1]) and CCS-like calculi, see e.g. [CS1], where a calculus is presented for exactly the fair expressions in a CCS-like language, or [Da1] with an abstract model of fair computations. Most work on fairness has been done in programming languages, see e.g. [AO1], [DH1], [FK1], [Ha1], or [LPS], where fairness is also connected with temporal logic. A quite general approach was done by Queille and Sifakis [QS1], where fairness is studied in T-Systems. In the style of our following approach a first result, namely that ω-regular languages are closed under fair merge, can be found in Park [Pa1].

In this paper we try to do some steps towards a general theory of fairness in the style of automata and formal language theory. We use multigraphs or automata as a basic model where we can distinguish between actions (transitions, arcs) and their names. Also we restrict our research in this paper on finite structures, i.e. the regular case is studied. Our main purpose is to get deeper insight in these fairness-phenomena without sticking too close to a specific model (such as some concurrent language). However such general results should later lead to conclusions for applied computer science. This work reported here is by no means complete. It is a first approach and will leave the reader with more questions and open problems than with answers. Also this survey contains no proofs that have to be presented in a later, much extended version.

This research was supported by a grant of the DFG.

2. Basic Definitions

In this chapter we just repeat and introduce some simple notations that are requested for our study.

For any set A the cardinality of A is denoted $|A|$. The powerset of A is written as 2^A. $\mathbb{N}$ is the set of all positive, $\mathbb{N}_0$ the set of nonnegative integers.

For an alphabet Σ let Σ^* (Σ^ω respectively) denote the set of all finite (infinite) sequences or ***words*** over Σ (Σ^* is the free monoid). The ***empty sequence*** is denoted λ. For any alphabet Σ we assume $\varepsilon\notin\Sigma$ and define $\Sigma_\varepsilon:=\Sigma\cup\{\varepsilon\}$. $|w|$ denotes the length of a word w, $|w|:=\omega$ for $w\in\Sigma^\omega$, where $\omega>n$ for all $n\in\mathbb{N}$.

As we identify words $w\in\Sigma^*$ with sequences of letters of Σ, w(i) is the i-th element of the sequence w if $|w|\geq i$, and remains undefined otherwise. With w[i] we denote the prefix of length i, so we let $w[i]:=w(1)...w(i)$ if $|w|\geq i$ and $w[i]:=w$ otherwise.

The set of arbitrarily long sequences is $\Sigma^\infty:=\Sigma^*\cup\Sigma^\omega$. For $v\in\Sigma^*$ and $w\in\Sigma^\infty$ the concatenation $v\circ w$ (usually written as vw if no confusion will arise) is defined as the word u that is uniquely determined by $u(i)=v(i)$ for $i\leq|v|$, and otherwise $u(i)=w(i-|v|)$. For $v\in\Sigma^\omega$ and $w\in\Sigma^\infty$ vw remains undefined.

An ***ω-language*** (***∞-language***, ***$*$-language*** respectively) is a subset of Σ^ω (Σ^∞, Σ^*). In the sequel we use the word ***language*** to denote a $*$-language, ω-language or ∞-language.

On Σ^∞ we define a partial order $\leq$ by setting $v\leq w$ if there exists an $i\in\mathbb{N}$, s.t. $v=w[i]$. We will write $v<w$ if $v\leq w$ and $v\neq w$. If $v\leq w$ ($v<w$) v is a ***(proper) prefix*** of w. The set of all prefixes of a word w is abbreviated as ***Pref(w)***, i.e. $Pref(w):=\{u\in\Sigma^* \mid u\leq w\}$. For a sequence $(w_i)_{i\in\mathbb{N}}$ of words in Σ^* with the property $w_i<w_{i+1}$ we define $w := \lim_{i\to\infty} w_i$ to be the word $w\in\Sigma^\omega$ s.t. $\forall i\in\mathbb{N}$: $w_i<w$. For $v,w\in\Sigma^\infty$ we say v is a ***subword*** of w ($v\subseteq w$ for short) iff $\exists u\in\Sigma^*$ s.t. $uv\leq w$. If a subword occurs infinitely often - i.e. if $\exists J\subseteq\mathbb{N}$: $|J|=\omega$, s.t. $\forall j\in J$: $w[j]v<w$ - we will write $v\subseteq_\omega w$. If $|v|=1$ we sometimes write $v\in w$ ($v\in_\omega w$) instead of $v\subseteq w$ ($v\subseteq_\omega w$).

For any language M over Σ we define the following sets:

$Pref(M):=\{Pref(w) \mid w\in M\}$, the ***prefix language*** of M. The set $\overline{M}$ is called the ***closure*** or ***ω-closure*** of M and is defined as

$$\overline{M}:=\{w\in\Sigma^\omega \mid \exists (w_i)_{i\in\mathbb{N}}: \forall i: w_i\in M \text{ and } w_i<w_{i+1} \text{ and } w=\lim_{i\to\infty} w_i\}.$$

Further the ***adherence*** of M is $adh(M):=\overline{Pref(M)}$.

Additionally for any $*$-language M the ***infinite iteration*** is defined as $M^\omega:=\{w\in\Sigma^\omega \mid \exists (w_i)_{i\in\mathbb{N}}: w_i\in(M-\{\lambda\})^i$ and $w_i<w_{i+1}$ and $w=\lim_{i\to\infty} w_i\}$ for $M\notin\{\phi,\{\lambda\}\}$ and $\phi^\omega = \{\lambda\}^\omega = \{\lambda\}$. Also we let $M^\infty:=M^\omega\cup M^*$ and $w^\omega:=\lim_{i\to\infty} w^i$, where w^i is the i-th iterate of w.

Note that Pref(M) is always a $*$-language (i.e. a language in the classical sense), whilst adh(M) and $\overline{M}$ are ω-languages.

For a better understanding of the underlying concepts of ω-languages the reader should refer to [BN1], [Ei1] or [Pe1].

3. Automata

Within this chapter we introduce our model of computation, the multi-graph, which is similar to notions like 'automaton' or 'transition-system'.

3.1. Definition

A ***finite multi-graph*** G is a tuple $G=(V,E,\mu)$ of finite sets V (of vertices), E (of edges), and a mapping $\mu:E\rightarrow V\times V$.

If $\mu(e)=(v_1,v_2)$ we say that e is an edge from vertex v_1 to v_2.

A ***path*** p in G is a finite or infinite sequence $(e_i)_{i\in I}$ of edges $e_i\in E$, s.t. $\mu(e_i)=(v_i,v_{i+1})$, $\mu(e_{i+1})=(v'_{i+1},v'_{i+2})$ implies that $v_{i+1}=v'_{i+1}$ $\forall i,i+1\in I$, where $I=\mathbb{N}$ or $I=\{i|1\leq i\leq k\}$ for some $k\in\mathbb{N}$. We thus regard a path as a word $p\in E^{\infty}$.

We use the standard technical terms for graphs. As $\mu(e_1)=\mu(e_2)$ for $e_1\neq e_2$ may hold, we allow multiple arcs between vertices.

3.2. Definition

An ***automaton*** A is a tuple $A=(S,\Sigma,E,\mu,\Phi,s_A)$ of finite sets S (of states), Σ (of actions), and E of edges, s.t. (S,E,μ) is a multi-graph with a weight-function $\Phi:E\rightarrow\Sigma_\varepsilon$, and an initial state $s_A\in S$.
An ε-edge (i.e. an edge e with $\Phi(e)=\varepsilon$) shall be mapped onto the empty word λ by Φ^λ. Therefore we extend Φ to the fine homomorphism $\Phi:E^\infty\rightarrow\Sigma_\varepsilon^\infty$ as usual via:

$$\Phi(\lambda):=\lambda \quad \text{and } \Phi(ep):=\Phi(e)\Phi(p) \text{ for } e\in E \text{ and } p\in E^\infty.$$

From this we derive the homomorphism $\Phi^\lambda:E^\infty\rightarrow\Sigma^\infty$ by setting $\Phi^\lambda(e):=\Phi(e)$ if $\Phi(e)\in\Sigma$ and $\Phi^\lambda(e):=\lambda$ if $\Phi(e)=\varepsilon$.

In contrast to the classical theory of automata we make a clear distinction between edges $e\in E$ and their names $\Phi(e)\in\Sigma_\varepsilon$. Furthermore it is sometimes important to be able to talk about ε-edges in a different manner than about λ. That is possible in this model because of the use of two morphisms Φ and Φ^λ.

Infinite automata (with an infinite set of states) are a very general model, able to describe T-Systems, Petri-nets, communicating systems of Hoare [Ho1] and Milner's CCS [Mi1] (in part, if one will not use the recursion operator to get dynamically growing automata). Parallel activities are easily described in this model in the standard manner using a diamond construction, as the 'process' of a parallel system is such an infinite automaton.

Our main restriction is that we will deal only with ***finite*** automata in this paper. Thus we try to develop the regular part of a theory of fairness here.

3.3. Definition

Let $A=(S,\Sigma,E,\mu,\Phi,s_A)$ be an automaton. A path p in A is a path in the included multi-graph. Let $p=(e_i)_{i\in N}\in E^{\omega}$ be an infinite path, $p'=(e'_i)_{0\le i\le n}$ be a finite path, with $\mu(e'_i)=(s_i,s_{i+1})$ We say

p' *starts from* s_0, *passes* s_i ($i\in\{0,\ldots,n+1\}$) and ends in s_{n+1}.

p' is called *final* iff $\forall$ $e\in E$: p'e is no path in A.

p' is a *subpath* of p iff p' is a subword of p. We use the notations for words also for paths.

p *passes* a state $s\in S$ *infinitely often* iff

$\exists J\subset \mathbb{N}$: $|J|=\omega$ s.t. $\forall j\in J$: $\exists s_{j+1}\in S$: $e_j=(s,s_{j+1})$.

The *infinity set* of p is the set

$S^{\omega}(p):=\{s\in S \mid p \text{ passes s infinitely often } \}$.

We will need these preliminary definitions of paths and multi-graphs to define fairness, as the property 'fairness' shall state that 'some action that may be done infinitely often will be done infinitely often'. This general idea will be made precise on the abstract level of multi-graphs now.

4. Fairness

4.1. Definition

Let $A=(S,\Sigma,E,\mu,\Phi,s_A)$ be an automaton, $e\in E$, $p\in E^{\infty}$.
The path p is called:

edge-fair (ef)

iff $\forall s\in S^{\omega}(p)$: $\forall e\in E$:($\exists s'\in S$: $e=(s,s') \Rightarrow e\underset{\omega}{\in}p$)

path-fair (pf)

iff $\forall s\in S^{\omega}(p)$: $\forall p_0\in E^{+}$:(p_0 starts from s $\Rightarrow p_0\subset p$)

letter-fair (lf)

iff $\forall s\in S^{\omega}(p)$: $\forall e\in E$:($\exists s'\in S$: $e=(s,s') \Rightarrow \Phi(e)\underset{\omega}{\in}\Phi(p)$)

word-fair (wf)

iff $\forall s\in S^{\omega}(p)$: $\forall p_0\in E^{+}$:(p_0 starts from s $\Rightarrow \Phi(p_0)\subset\Phi(p)$)

Further any final path p is called x-fair for every x∈{edge, path, letter, word}.

In contrast to edge- and letter-fairness it suffices to state $p_0\subset p$ ($\Phi(p_0)\subset\Phi(p)$) for path- and word-fairness as this implies the $\underset{\omega}{\subset}$ relation obviously.

4.2. Definition

Let $A=(S,\Sigma,E,\mu,\Phi,s_A)$ be an automaton. The *languages* induced by A are defined as follows:

$L(A):=\{w\in\Sigma^* \mid \exists p\in E^*$ final and starting in s_A, s.t. $w=\Phi^\lambda(p)\}$

$L^{xf}(A):=\{w\in\Sigma^\infty \mid \exists p\in E^\infty$ x-fair, starting in s_A, s.t. $w=\Phi^\lambda(p)\}$, where x-fair denotes one of the fairness notions from above.

For $F\subseteq S$ let:

$L^\omega(A,F):=\{w\in\Sigma^\omega \mid \exists p\in E^\omega$ starting in s_A, $F\cap S^\omega(p)\neq\phi$, s.t. $w=\Phi^\lambda(p)\}$

$L^\infty(A,F):=L^\omega(A,F)\cup L(A)$

For $°\in\{\phi$,edge-fair,letter-fair,path-fair,word-fair$\}$ we define $Rec^°_\Sigma$ to be the set of all languages M, s.t. there exists an automaton A with $M=L^°(A)$. Rec^ω_Σ is the set of all languages M s.t. there exists an A and F s.t. $M=L^\omega(A,F)$.

Usually the recognizable languages are those accepted by automata with final states. We don't need these because any automaton with ε-edges only needs to have one single final state, and this state may be chosen to be a sink state. This is not true for ω-regular languages, where final states are required. However we will be able to prove our main theorem (Rec and Rat coincide for some fairness conceptions; see 6.5) without any need for final states.

To get an idea of the fair languages of an automaton let's have a look at some very simple examples.

4.3. Examples

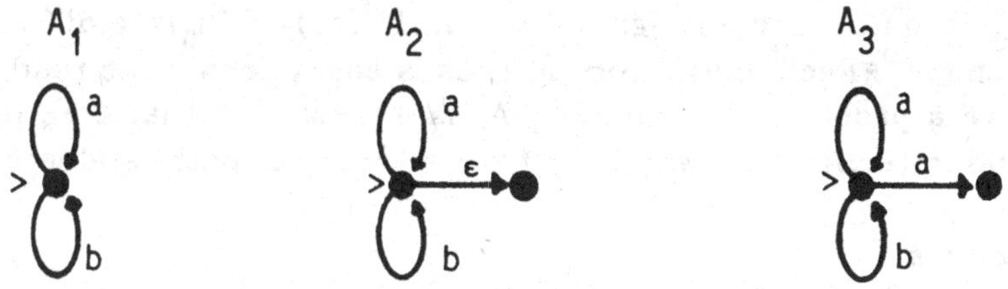

Figure 1

For the automata A_i of figure 1 there holds:

1.) $L(A_1)=\phi$, $L^{ef}(A_1)=L^{lf}(A_1)=(a^*bb^*a)^\omega$ but $(a^*bb^*a)^\omega\neq L^{pf}(A_1)\cup L^{wf}(A_1)$ as the word $(ab)^\omega\notin L^{pf}(A_1)\cup L^{wf}(A_1)$, e.g.. In $(ab)^\omega$ not every enabled subpath (or subword) is used!

2.) $L^°(A_2)=(a+b)^*$ for $°\in\{\phi,ef,lf,pf,wf\}$

3.) $L^°(A_3)=(a+b)^*a$ for $°\in\{\phi,ef,pf\}$, but $(a+b)^*a$ is properly included in the letter-fair as well as in the word-fair language as those also include infinite words, as such a path may always use the a-edge from s_1 to s_1 instead of that to s_2!

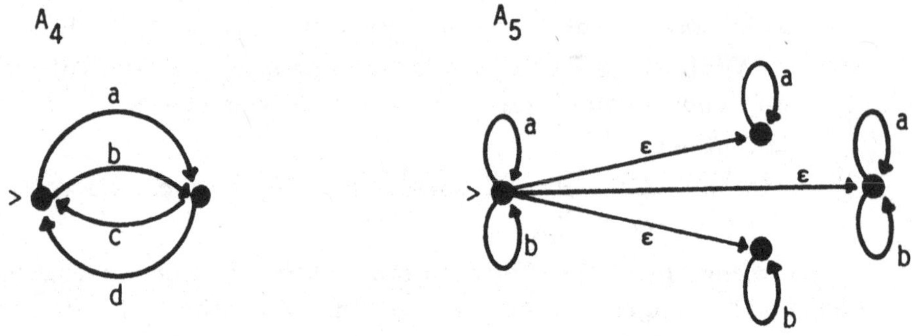

Figure 2

A_4 (see figure 2) shows clearly the differences between edge- or letter-fairness on the one hand and path- or word-fairness on the other hand. The "deterministic" process $(acbd)^\omega$ is a word in $L^{ef}(A_4)$ and $L^{lf}(A_4)$ but not in $L^{pf}(A_4)$ or $L^{wf}(A_4)$! Thus path- and word-fairness force a certain randomness in the behaviour.

pf and wf are closely related to P-fairness of Queille and Sifakis [QS1] and ∞-fairness of Best [B1], whereas ef and lf are related to strong-fairness (of several authors) and to S- and T-fairness of Queille and Sifakis. In fact, T-fairness in finite models is our edge-fairness.

A_5 is quite interesting: Note that $L^{ef}(A_5)=L^{lf}(A_5)=\{a,b\}^\omega$. On the other hand, $\Sigma^\omega \notin Rec_\Sigma^{pf} \cup Rec_\Sigma^{wf}$ for $|\Sigma|>1$, as is easily seen. (The reader may try to give a proof as an exercise.) A_5 is a first hint that treatment of edge- and letter-fairness will differ from a theory of path- and word-fairness.

4.4. Lemma

Let $xf \in \{ef, lf, pf, wf\}$ and A be an automaton.

i) $L^{pf}(A) \subseteq L^{wf}(A)$ ii) $L^{ef}(A) \subseteq L^{lf}(A)$ iii) $Rec_\Sigma \subset Rec_\Sigma^{xf}$

5. Results on Edge- and Letter-Fair Languages

Edge- and letter-fair languages can be treated as ω-regular languages by the following theorem:

5.1. Theorem

For every automaton A there exist automata B_1, B_2, B_3 and sets F_1, F_2:

i) $L^{ef}(A)=L^\infty(B_1,F_1)$

ii) $L^{lf}(A)=L^\infty(B_2,F_2)$

iii) $L^{lf}(A)=L^{ef}(B_3)$

For example regard A_4 (figure 2). There holds:

$L^{ef}(A_4)=L^{lf}(A_4)=(L_{11}aL_{21})^{\omega}\cap(L_{11}bL_{21})^{\omega}\cap(L_{12}cL_{11})^{\omega}\cap(L_{12}dL_{11})^{\omega}=:L$,

where L_{ij} is the language of all finite paths leading from state s_i to s_j in the automaton. Thus L is an ω-regular language. In general this transformation for letter fairness is much more involved.

In the above theorem the step from ef- or lf-languages (or automata) to ω-regular languages is done algorithmically. The main step of this transformation is a decomposition of automata in special strongly connected subautomata. Applying a linear time algorithm of Tarjan [Ta1] to find all strongly connected components in a graph , the above transformation from A to B_1 of theorem 5.1 can be done in linear time. Thus we can embed this fairness theory into the quite reasonably understood theory of ω-regularity. For example, the equivalence problem for edge- or letter-fair languages is thus solved, applying the results of Büchi [Bü1] and Alawain [Al1].

Unfortunately such a theorem is not known for path- or word-fairness, and we will concentrate on this more difficult case in the sequel.

6. Algebraical Treatment of Path- and Word-fairness

Word-fairness and path-fairness have been introduced via automata. Another approach follows Kleene's regular expressions.

6.1. Definition

Let M be a language with $M\neq M^*$. Then

$M^{pf}:=M,\ M^{wf}:=M$

Let M be a language with $M=M^*$. Then

i) $M^{wf}:=\{w\in adh(M)\mid \forall u\in M: u\subset w\}$

ii) $M^{pf}:=\{w\in M^{\omega}\mid \exists\,(w_i)_{i\in\mathbb{N}}: \forall i:(w_i<w_{i+1}$ and $w_i\in(M-\{\lambda\})^i)$ and $w=\lim_{i\to\infty} w_i$ and $\forall u\in M\ \exists\, k,l\in\mathbb{N}: w_k=w_l u\}$

6.2. Definition

Rat_{Σ}, the set of all languages defined through a regular expression over Σ, is defined as usual:

i) $\phi\in Rat_{\Sigma},\ \forall a\in\Sigma: a\in Rat_{\Sigma}$

ii) $\forall x,y\in Rat_{\Sigma}: (x+y),(xy),\ x^*\in Rat_{\Sigma}$

Rat°_{Σ} for $\circ\in\{pf,wf\}$ is defined analogously:

i) $Rat_{\Sigma}\subset Rat^{\circ}_{\Sigma}$

ii) $\forall y,z\in Rat^{\circ}_{\Sigma}\ \forall x\in Rat_{\Sigma}: (y+z),\ (xy),\ x^{\circ}\in Rat^{\circ}_{\Sigma}$

Note that Rat_Σ° are classes of ∞-languages for $^\circ\in\{pf,wf\}$. As Rat_Σ^ω consists of ω-languages only it needs a slightly different definition:

$\forall x,y\in Rat_\Sigma: xy^\omega\in Rat_\Sigma^\omega$

$\forall x,y\in Rat_\Sigma^\omega: (x+y)\in Rat_\Sigma^\omega$

We define an *interpretation* I as a mapping from expressions onto languages as usual:

$$I(0)=\phi,\ I(a)=\{a\},\ I(x+y)=I(x)\cup I(y),\ I(xy)=I(x)I(y),$$
$$I(x^*)=(I(x))^*,\ I(x^\omega)=(I(x))^\omega,\ I(x^{pf})=(I(x))^{pf},\ I(x^{wf})=(I(x))^{wf}$$

We identify expressions with languages and say that M is a Rat_Σ°-language or $M\in Rat_\Sigma^\circ$ for $^\circ\in\{\phi,\omega,pf,wf\}$, iff there exists an expression $x\in Rat_\Sigma^\circ$ with $M=I(x)$.

6.3. Main Theorem

i) $Rec_\Sigma=Rat_\Sigma$ ii) $Rec_\Sigma^\omega=Rat_\Sigma^\omega$

iii) $Rec_\Sigma^{pf}=Rat_\Sigma^{pf}$ iv) $Rec_\Sigma^{wf}=Rat_\Sigma^{wf}$

It should be noted that we have not stated an algebraical counterpart 'Rat_Σ^{ef}' and 'Rat_Σ^{lf}'. In fact we don't have such a definition.

A proof of this theorem operates with 'final' and 'almost final' automata. The key is the following lemma for that we need some preliminary definitions.

6.4. Definition

A *sub-automaton* $A_f=(S_f,\Sigma,E_f,\mu_{/A_f},\Phi_{/A_f},s_f))$ of $A=(S,\Sigma,E,\mu,\Phi,s_A)$ is called

1.) *final* iff

i) A_f is trim, i.e. $\forall s\in S_f$: $\exists\, p,q\in E_f^*$:

p leads from s_f to s,

q leads from s to s_f

ii) $\exists\, e\in E_f$: $\Phi(e)\neq\varepsilon$

iii) $\forall p\in E^*$: $\forall s_1,s_2\in S$:

p leads from s_1 to s_2 and $s_1\in S_f \Rightarrow s_2\in S_f$

2.) *almost final* iff

i) and ii) hold and

iii) $\forall p\in E^*$: $\forall s_1,s_2\in S$:

p leads from s_1 to s_2 and $s_1\in S_f \Rightarrow \exists\, q\in E_f^*$: $\Phi^\lambda(q)=\Phi^\lambda(p)$

For a final or almost final automaton A we define the language

$$\mathfrak{L}(A):=\{w\in\Sigma^* \mid \exists \text{ path } p \text{ from } s_A \text{ to } s_A\text{: } w=\Phi^\lambda(p)\}$$

i.e. the language in the classical sense if the initial state is regarded to be the only final state.

There holds

6.5. Lemma

i) For any final automaton A:

$$L^{pf}(A)=(\mathfrak{L}(A))^{pf}$$

ii) For any almost final automaton A:

$$L^{wf}(A)=(\mathfrak{L}(A))^{wf}$$

With this lemma one proves a canonical representation for fair languages:

For any automaton A there exist finite sets $I,J\subset\mathbb{N}$, automata B_i, B_j', final subautomata C_i and almost final subautomata D_j s.t.

i) $$L^{pf}(A)=\sum_{i\in I} L(B_i)(\mathfrak{L}(C_i))^{pf} + L(B_0)$$

ii) $$L^{wf}(A)=\sum_{j\in J} L(B_j')(\mathfrak{L}(D_j))^{wf} + L(B_0')=\sum_{j\in J} L(B_j')(\mathfrak{L}(D_j))^{pf} + L(B_0')$$

i.e. for every automaton A there exists an automaton B s.t. $L^{wf}(A)=L^{pf}(B)$

6.6. Remark

Using the canonical representation we can prove that $Rat_\Sigma^{pf/wf}$ are closed under intersection. Further Rat_Σ^{pf} is closed under homomorphism and Rat_Σ^{wf} is closed under λ-free homomorphism. As $\Sigma^\omega\notin Rat_\Sigma^{pf/wf}$ for $|\Sigma|>1$ one easily obtains that both classes are not closed under complement, substitution and inverse homomorphism.

Let us now summarize some algebraical properties of path- and word-fair languages.

6.7. Lemma

Let M and N be $*$-languages over Σ with $M=M^*$ and $N=N^*$.
There holds obviously:

i) $M^{pf}=MM^{pf}=M^*M^{pf}$

ii) $(M\subseteq N \text{ or } M^\omega\subseteq N^\omega) \not\Rightarrow (M^{pf}\subseteq N^{pf} \text{ or } M^{pf}\subseteq N^{pf})$;

iii) $(M^{pf}\subseteq N^{pf} \text{ or } M^{pf}\subseteq N^{pf}) \Rightarrow M \subseteq \mathrm{Pref}(N)$;

More involved are:

iv) $\mathrm{Pref}(M)=\mathrm{Pref}(N) \Rightarrow M^{pf}\cap N^{pf}\neq\phi$

v) $\mathrm{Pref}(M)=\mathrm{Pref}(N) \Leftrightarrow \mathrm{adh}(M)=\mathrm{adh}(N) \Leftrightarrow M^{wf}=N^{wf}$

If M and N are additionally regular there holds:

vi) $M^{wf}\cap N^{wf}\neq\phi \Rightarrow \mathrm{Suf}(M^{wf})=\mathrm{Suf}(N^{wf}) \Leftrightarrow \mathrm{Inf}(M)=\mathrm{Inf}(N)$

$$\not\Rightarrow M^{wf}\cap N^{wf}\neq\phi$$

where
$\mathrm{Suf}(L)=\{w \mid \exists u\in\Sigma^*: uw\in L\}$ is the set of ***suffixes of** L* and
$\mathrm{Inf}(L)=\{w \mid \exists u,v\in\Sigma^*: uvw\in L\}$ is the set of ***infixes of** L*.

The result vi) is a hint that these fair languages are quite sparse within the topology of ω-languages. By Lemma v) we have a decision procedure for $M^{wf}=N^{wf}$ for regular $*$-languages M and N. However this does not solve the fair-language equivalence problem. In fact, we have no algorithms to decide $L^{pf}(A)=L^{pf}(B)$ or $L^{wf}(A)=L^{wf}(B)$ for given automata A,B. The results mentioned are just steps towards such an algorithm.

7. A Hierarchy Result

A canonical question rises at once, whether edge-fairness and path-fairness are two endpoints of a hierarchy of "n-fairness". Suprisingly this is not true for a straightforward definition of "n-fairness".

7.1. Definition

For $n\in\mathbb{N}$ a path p in some automaton is called ***n-path-fair*** (n-pf) iff

p is final or $\forall s\in S^\omega(p)$: $\forall q\in E^n$ q a path starting in s $\Rightarrow q\subseteq_\omega p$.

$L^{n\text{-}pf}(A) = \{w\in\Sigma^\infty \mid \exists$ n-pf path p in A starting from s_A s.t. $\Phi^\lambda(p)=w\}$

A language M is n-pf iff $M=L^{n\text{-}pf}(A)$ for some automaton A.

$Rec_\Sigma^{n\text{-}pf}$ is the set of all n-pf languages over a fixed alphabet Σ.

Clearly, $L^{m\text{-}pf}(A) \subset L^{n\text{-}pf}(A)$ for $1 \le m \le n$ for any automaton A, as any n-pf path is also m-pf for $1 \le m \le n$. More involved are inclusions between the $Rec_\Sigma^{n\text{-}pf}$ classes.

7.2. Theorem

i) $\forall\, m,n \in \mathbb{N}: 1 \le m \le n : Rec_\Sigma^{ef} = Rec_\Sigma^{1\text{-}pf} \supsetneq Rec_\Sigma^{m\text{-}pf} \supsetneq Rec_\Sigma^{n\text{-}pf}$.

ii) $\forall\, n \ge 1 : Rec_\Sigma^{n\text{-}pf} \subset Rec_\Sigma^{2n\text{-}pf}$.

iii) $\forall\, n \ge 1 : Rec_\Sigma^{ef} = Rec_\Sigma^{n\text{-}pf}$.

Obviously iii) is a simple consequence of i) and ii). Our proof for ii) implies some tricks with ε-edges. For a deeper understanding whether those ε-edges are essential, we introduce classes of ε-free languages.

7.3. Definition

An ε-free automaton is an automaton $A=(S,\Sigma,E,\mu,\Phi,s)$ with $\Phi: E \to \Sigma$ (instead of Σ_ε).

$$Rec_{\Sigma,\varepsilon\text{-free}}^{n\text{-}pf} = \{M \subset \Sigma^\infty \mid \exists\ \varepsilon\text{-free automaton A s.t.: } M=L^{n\text{-}pf}(A)\}$$

Part i) of the previous theorem holds also for ε-free classes. A quite involved construction allows to transform any ε-free automaton A for any n into some ε-free automaton B for any $m \ge n$ s.t. $L^{n\text{-}pf}(A) = L^{m\text{-}pf}(B)$. However, this transformation leads to an automaton B of exponential size (in m and A) such that a theory of n-path-fairness cannot be embedded into the theory of ω-regularity as easy as before.

7.4. Theorem

i) $\forall\, m,n \in \mathbb{N} : 1 \le n \le m : \forall$ automata A : $\exists$ automaton B :
$L^{n\text{-}pf}(A) = L^{m\text{-}pf}(B)$.

ii) $\forall\, n \ge 1 : Rec_{\Sigma,\varepsilon\text{-free}}^{n\text{-}pf} = Rec_{\Sigma,\varepsilon\text{-free}}^{1\text{-}pf}$

iii) $\forall\, n \in \mathbb{N} : \forall$ automata A : $\exists$ automaton B : $\exists\, F \subset S_B$:
$L^{n\text{-}pf}(A) = L^\infty(B,F)$.

Thus this canonical approach collapses and leads to no hierarchy. Also any other attempt of hierarchies cannot have Rec_Σ^{ef} and Rec_Σ^{pf} as two end-points, as $Rec_\Sigma^{pf} \not\subset Rec_\Sigma^{ef} \not\subset Rec_\Sigma^{pf}$.

It should be noted that 7.4 iii) holds also in the inverse direction, as for any automaton B, any $F \subset S_B$ and any $n \ge 1$, there exists an automaton A s.t. $L^{n\text{-}pf}(A) = L^\infty(B,F)$. However, again A is of exponential size in n and B, but needs no ε-edges. Thus there holds suprisingly :

7.5. Theorem

$$\forall\, n\geq 1 : Rec_{\Sigma}^{\infty} = Rec_{\Sigma}^{n\text{-}pf} = Rec_{\Sigma,\varepsilon\text{-}free}^{n\text{-}pf}$$

8. Discussion

There may rise some criticism why we studied fairness for a new 'exotic' type of automaton instead of standard automata for ω-languages like Muller- or Büchi-automata. However all these approaches coincide in many important cases, as final states are not required for fairness.

A Büchi-automaton (Muller-automaton) is an automaton A (of definition 3.2) together with a set $F\subseteq S$ ($\Gamma\subseteq 2^S$, respectively) . An accepting path p now is a final path or an infinite path with $S^{\omega}(p)\cap F \neq \phi$ (or $S^{\omega}(p)\in\Gamma$, resp.) starting from the initial state (see Park [Pa1]). This leads to several classes of fairness :

$$L^{B\text{-}xf}(A) = \{\, w\in\Sigma^{\infty} \mid \exists \text{ path } p : w = \Phi^{\lambda}(p);\ p \text{ is Büchi-accepting and x-fair}\}$$

$$L^{M\text{-}xf}(A) = \{\, w\in\Sigma^{\infty} \mid \exists \text{ path } p : w = \Phi^{\lambda}(p);\ p \text{ is Muller-accepting and x-fair}\}$$

One may define now canonically :

$$Rec_{\Sigma}^{B\text{-}xf} \quad , \quad Rec_{\Sigma}^{M\text{-}xf}$$

and also

$$Rec_{\Sigma,\varepsilon\text{-}free}^{B\text{-}pf} \quad , \quad Rec_{\Sigma,\varepsilon\text{-}free}^{M\text{-}pf}$$

if one operates only with ε-free automata.

Note that $Rec_{\Sigma,\varepsilon\text{-}free}^{M\text{-}pf}$ coincides with the class of strongly 3-accepted languages of Rosier and Yen [RY1] . However we researched quite a lot of these classes also, as there holds for $x\in\{edge,path\}$:

$$Rec_{\Sigma}^{xf} = Rec_{\Sigma,\varepsilon\text{-}free}^{xf} = Rec_{\Sigma,\varepsilon\text{-}free}^{M\text{-}xf} = Rec_{\Sigma}^{M\text{-}xf} = Rec_{\Sigma}^{B\text{-}xf} = Rec_{\Sigma,\varepsilon\text{-}free}^{B\text{-}xf} .$$

This important result shows that final states are not required in a theory of fairness. As it is well-known, this is not true for the theory of ω-regularity. The language $(ab^{*})^{\omega}$ e.g. cannot be recognized without final states. This fact forced the introduction of concepts like Muller- or Büchi-automata for a study of ω-regularity, with all difficulties arising in a proof of the Main-Theorem that can be avoided in our approach.

References

[AO1] *K.R.Apt, E.R.Olderog* **Proof rules and transformation dealing with fairness** Science of Computer Programming 3 (1983) 65-100

[B1] *Eike Best* **Fairness and conspiracies** Imformation Prossesing Letters 18 (1984) 215-220

[BN1] *L.Boasson, M.Nivat* **Adherences of languages** JCSS 20 (1980) 285-309

[Bü1] *J.R.Büchi* **On a decision method in restricted second order arithmetic** Logic, Methodology and Philosophy of Science; Proc. 1960 Int. Congr. for Logic; Stanford University Press 1-11

[CS1] *Gerado Costa,Colin Stirling* **A Fair Calculus Of Communicating Systems** Acta Informatica 21 (1984) 417-441

[Da1] *Ph.Darondeau* **About fair asynchrony** Theoretical Computer Science 37 (1985) 305-336

[DH1] *Ido Dayan, David Harel* **Fair termination with cruel schedulers** Fundamenta Informaticae IX (1986) 1-12

[Ei1] *S.Eilenberg* **Automata, Languages and machines Vol A** Academic Press, New York 1976

[FK1] *N.Francez, D.Kozen* **Generalized fair termination** ACM Symp. of Prog. Languages (1984)

[Ha1] *David Harel* **Effective transformations on infinite trees, with application to high undecidability, dominoes and fairness** Journal of the ACM 33 (1986) 224-248

[HN1] *M.Hennessy,R .de Nicola* **Testing Equivalences for Processes** Theoretical Computer Science 34 (1984) 83-133

[Ho1] *C.A.R.Hoare* **Communicating Sequential Processes** Comm.ACM 21 (1978) 666-677

[LPS] *D.Lehmann, A.Pnueli, J.Stavi* **Impartiality, justice and fairness** LNCS 115 (1981) 264-277

[Mi1] *Robin Milner* **A Calculus of Communicating Systems** Lecture Notes in Computer Science 92 (1980)

[Mu1] *D.E.Muller* **Infinite sequences and finite machines** Proc.4th Ann.Symp.on Switch.Circuit Theory and logical Design 3-16 IEEE (1963)

[Pa1] *D.Park* **Concurrency and automata on infinite sequences** LNCS 104 (1981)

[Pe1] *D.Perrin* **Recent results on automata and infinite words** LNCS 176 (1984) 134-148

[Po1] *Lucia Pomello* **Some Equivalence Notions for Concurrent Systems** Arbeitspaiere der GMD 103 (July 1984)

[QS1] *J.P.Queille, J.Sifakis* **Fairness and related properties in Transition Systems - A temporal logic to deal with fairness** Acta Informatica 19 (1983) 195-220

[RY1] *L.E.Rosier, Hsu-Chun Yen* **Logspace hierarchies, polynomial time and the complexity of fairness problems concerning ω-machines** University of Texas Dep.of Comp.Sciences, Techn. Report No. 85-08 (1985)

[Ta1] *R.Tarjan* **Depth-First Search and Linear Graph Algoritms** SIAM J. Comp. ,Vol.1 (1972) 146-160

Decidability Questions for Fairness in Petri Nets

Heino Carstensen

Universität Hamburg, Fachbereich Informatik
Rothenbaumchaussee 67/69, D-2000 Hamburg 13

1 Introduction

The infinite behaviour of Petri nets, especially the fair behaviour, is investigated. Fairness of concurrent systems includes two different approaches. One may give criteria for a modelled problem under which the Petri net behaves fair. E. g. certain actions must appear again and again in every sequence, but it is not said how this can be achieved. The other approach gives criteria for a fair execution of the net, i. e. the selection of concurrently enabled transitions is done in a fair manner. In [Carstensen, Valk 85] these two approaches were investigated and compared to each other.

For languages with problem fairness some decidability results are given in [Valk, Jantzen 85]. E. g. for a Petri net it is known to be decidable if it exists an infinite firing sequence in which a certain transition appears infinitely often. In this paper it is shown that the question if there is an infinite firing sequence which has the finite delay property for one group of transitions is decidable, too. A firing sequence has the finite delay property for a group of transitions, if infinitely often all transitions of this group are simultaneously not activated or some of them appear infinitely often. This criterion for fairness is sometimes called justice or weak fairness. There is also a stronger criterion: an infinite firing sequence is fair for a transition, if it appears infinitely often or is only activated finitely often. It turns out to be undecidable if a net allows an infinite firing sequence which is fair for one transition as well as for all transitions. An analysis of the complexity of the mentioned decidable questions shows that they are all hard for DSPACE(exp).

To prove the undecidability and the hardness of the complexity we show that these problems for Petri nets correspond to known problems for the universal program machine with counters introduced in [Minsky 67]. The proof of the undecidability is based on a theorem of Vidal-Naquet in [Brams 85].

The following section gives the definitions of Petri nets and of universal program machines. Then the connections between them and effects for the complexity of the problems are shown. In the third section the problems for exection fairness, i. e. the finite delay property and (strong) fairness are investigated.

2 Basic definitions and results

In this section we want to give the formal definition of Petri nets and some notations which will be used later. After an introduction of the universal program machine a comparison between this model and the Petri nets will be made. Finally we will define the infinite behaviour of Petri nets.

First some mathematical notations will be needed.

Definition 1 The positive integers are denoted by $\mathbb{N}^+$ and $\mathbb{N} = \{0\} \cup \mathbb{N}^+$. The cardinality of $\mathbb{N}$ is ω, i. e. $|\mathbb{N}| = \omega$.
The quantors $\exists$ and $\forall$ will be extended to $\underset{\infty}{\exists}$ and $\underset{\infty}{\forall}$, there are infinitely many and for all but infinitely many. Let A be a set and p a predicate, then $\underset{\infty}{\exists} a \in A : p(a)$ means $|\{a \in A \mid p(a)\}| = \omega$. And $\underset{\infty}{\forall}$ is defined by $\underset{\infty}{\exists} a \in A : p(a) \Leftrightarrow \neg \underset{\infty}{\forall} a \in A : \neg p(a)$.

Definition 2 A *Petri net* $N = (S, T; F, W, m_0)$ is given by two finite and disjunct sets, the set of *places* S, and the set of *transitions* T, a *flow relation* $F \subseteq (S \times T) \cup (T \times S)$, a *weight function* $W : F \to \mathbb{N}^+$, and an *initial marking* $m_0 : S \to \mathbb{N}$. A *marking* m is a mapping $m : S \to \mathbb{N}$, and it is given by a vector over $\mathbb{N}^S$.

For this definition we do not consider labels of transitions because they are not needed in the context of this paper. The dynamic behaviour of a Petri net is described by the firing rule.

Definition 3 Let N be a Petri net. A transition $t \in T$ is *activated* by a marking $m \in \mathbb{N}^S$, written $m\ (t\rangle$, if on every input place s of t, $(s,t) \in F$, there are at least $W(s,t)$ tokens, i. e. $\forall s \in S : (s,t) \in F \Rightarrow W(s,t) \leq m(s)$.
An activated transition may fire and it produces a *follower marking* m', $m\ (t\rangle\ m'$, by subtracting $W(s,t)$ tokens from every input place and adding $W(s',t)$ tokens on every output place s' of t, $(t,s') \in F$, i. e.

$$\forall s \in S : m'(s) = \begin{cases} m(s) - W(s,t) + W(t,s) & , \text{if } (s,t) \in F \wedge (t,s) \in F \\ m(s) - W(s,t) & , \text{if } (s,t) \in F \wedge (t,s) \notin F \\ m(s) + W(t,s) & , \text{if } (s,t) \notin F \wedge (t,s) \in F \\ m(s) & , \text{if } (s,t) \notin F \wedge (t,s) \notin F. \end{cases}$$

A sequence $v = t_1 t_2 \ldots t_n$ of transitions is called *firing sequence* from m, if it exists a sequence of markings $\delta(v,m) = m_1 m_2 \ldots m_{n+1}$ with $m = m_1\ (t_1\rangle\ m_2\ (t_2\rangle \ldots (t_n\rangle\ m_{n+1} = m'$, written $m\ (v\rangle\ m'$. The sequence $\delta(v,m)$ is the *corresponding marking sequence* of v starting from m, if it starts from the initial marking, it is defined: $\delta_0(v) = \delta(v, m_0)$.
For an arbitrary sequence α, $\alpha(i)$ denotes the ith element of α and $\alpha[i]$ the prefix of length i of α, i. e. $\alpha[i] = \alpha(1) \ldots \alpha(i)$.

Some notations for Petri nets will be given.

Definition 4 Let N be a Petri net. A marking m' is *reachable* from m, $m\ (\rangle\ m'$, if it exists a firing sequence v from m with $m\ (v\rangle\ m'$. If it holds that $v \in T^+$ we write $m\ (+\rangle\ m'$.
N is called *k-bounded*, $k \in \mathbb{N}$, if for every reachable marking m' it holds $\forall s \in S : m'(s) \leq k$. N is *bounded*, if it exists a $k \in \mathbb{N}$ so that N is k-bounded.
N is said to be in a *deadlock* by m if no transition is activated by m.

Now the definition of an universal program machine, described in [Minsky 67], will follow.

Definition 5 A *universal program machine* (UPM) M with $k \in \mathbb{N}^+$ counters is given by
— k counters: $c_1, \ldots, c_k$ and
— a program with finitely many steps, each step consists of a step number and an instruction.
There is one BEGIN-instruction and at least one END-instruction in every program. The other instructions are
— $c^+(m)$: Increase the value of counter c and go to step number m,
— $c^-(n,m)$: Decrease the value of counter c and go to step number m, if the value of c was greater than zero, otherwise go to step number n.

In [Minsky 67] it was shown, that for every Turing machine a UPM can be built with two counters, which simulates the Turing machine, i. e. the contents of the tape can be coded into the two counters. Moreover, if the working space of the Turing machine is limited by 2^k then the two counters of the UPM can be bounded by 2^{2^k}.

2.1 Simulation of a UPM by a Petri net

Since a UPM can simulate Turing machines, in general it is impossible to simulate a UPM by a Petri net. For Petri nets it is decidable if a given marking can be reached from the initial marking — for Turing machines this problem corresponds to the halting problem, which is known to be undecidable.

Nevertheless, for a UPM which counters are bounded by 2^{2^k} it was proved by [Lipton 76] that it can be simulated by a Petri net.

Theorem 1 *A UPM with two counters bounded by* 2^{2^k}, *for* $k \in \mathbb{N}^+$, *can by simulated by a Petri net, which has a size limited by a linear function of* k.

The simulation of a UPM by a Petri net means, that the net consists of places which correspond to the counters of the UPM and of a place p_{END} on which a token indicates that the simulation is finished. It is required that there is a reachble marking in the net for a successful computation in the UPM, so that the number of tokens on the places representing the counters is equal to the value of the counters and a token is on p_{END}. In the net there are no other markings reachable in which p_{END} contains a token. The size of a net is bounded by a linear function of k, if this holds for the power of sets of transition and places, the values of the weight funtion, and the initial marking.

We will not give the entire proof of this theorem, but since its idea will be used later, some comments of the transformation in [Lipton 76] are given.

A UPM operates on counters by changing their values, i. e. by adding or subtracting one. In a Petri net this can be simulated by adding tokens to places or removing them. The only difficulty is that an unbounded net cannot test if there are no tokens on a place. If a place s is bounded by n, then it is possible to test if it contains no token by introducing a complementary place $\bar{s}$ and testing if there are at least n tokens on $\bar{s}$. The initial marking for this place must be $n - m_0(s)$. If we use this idea for constructing the net simulating a UPM bounded by 2^{2^k}, neither the values of the weight function nor the initial marking is limited by a linear function of k. Hence the crucial part of the proof was to show that one can build a subnet which has the desired size and indicates if there is no token on s. This subnet may bring a token on a place s_{yes} iff s contains no token and on s_{no} otherwise. It is not required that every firing sequence in the subnet reaches a marking with a token on s_{yes} or on s_{no}, but then the sequence will lead the net eventually into a deadlock.

A more exactly investigation of the transformation in [Lipton 76] shows that the net is 2^{2^k}-bounded and that every test on zero only consists of a finite firing sequence — either properly finishing the test or reaching a deadlock. With this transformation the following statement can be shown.

Theorem 2 *The reachability problem for Petri nets is hard for deterministic, exponential space (DSPACE(exp)), even if only bounded nets are considered.*

2.2 Infinite firing sequences of Petri nets

The behaviour of Petri nets will be described by its set of possible firing sequences. Since we are interested in the infinite behaviour, it is necessary to define infinite firing sequences.

Definition 6 Let N be a Petri net. Then $v \in T^\omega$ is an *infinite firing sequence* of N, if $v[i]$ is a finite firing sequence for every $i \in \mathbb{N}$. The set of all infinite firing sequences of N will be denoted by $\mathrm{F}_\omega(N)$.

We will mention that the problem, if a Petri net has at least one infinite firing sequence is decidable, also if a certain transition can appear infinitely often. But both problems are hard for DSPACE(exp). The simulation of a UPM by a Petri net means that for every computation of the UPM there is a corresponding firing sequence. Hence there is an infinite firing sequence in the net, iff the UPM has an infinite computation.

For every problem in DSPACE(exp) there is a deterministic Turing machine with exponentially limited space, so that for every input the machine has a finite computation. With the transformation mentioned above one can build a (deterministic) UPM simulating the Turing machine which also has only finite computations and which counters are bounded by a double exponential function.

Theorem 3 *For a Petri net N and a set of transitions $E \subseteq T$ the problems $\mathrm{F}_\omega(N) \neq \emptyset$? and $\exists v \in \mathrm{F}_\omega(N) : \underset{\infty}{\exists} i \in \mathbb{N}^+ : v(i) \in E$? are both decidable. They are hard for DSPACE(exp), even in the case of bounded nets.*

Proof: 1) The decidability can be shown by using a property of Petri nets called monotonicity. If it exists an (infinite) firing sequence from a marking m then this sequence is also possible from every marking which is greater than m. In [Valk, Jantzen 85] a procedure is given to calculate the set of all minimal markings from which an infinite firing sequence is possible, and from which a certain transition can be fired infinitely often.

2) For an arbitrary problem in DSPACE(exp) we take the UPM described above, which halts on every input. Then the Petri net N simulating this UPM has no infinite firing sequence. Without restriction, let the UPM have two END-instructions, one which is reached if an input is accepted and the other if it is not accepted. The net N is extended by a transition t which can fire infinitely often if there is a token on the place which corresponds to the accepting END-instruction. Now the new net has an infinite firing sequence, iff the UPM accepts. In every infinite firing sequence t appears infinitely often.

3 Execution fairness in Petri nets

An infinite firing sequence in a Petri net will be called execution fair, if no transition is treated in an unfair manner. In this paper two different definitions of execution fairness will be given. A sequence fulfills the finite delay property, if there is no transition which is permanently activated but will not fire. And a sequence is called fair, if every transition which is infinitely often activated fires infinitely often.

Definition 7 Let N be a Petri net, then an infinite firing sequence $v \in \mathrm{F}_\omega(N)$ fulfills the *finite delay property*, or v is *fdp*, if
$\forall t \in T : ((\exists i \in \mathbb{N}^+ : \forall j \in \mathbb{N}^+, j \geq i : \delta_0(v)(j)\ (t\rangle\,) \Rightarrow (\underset{\infty}{\exists} i \in \mathbb{N}^+ : v(i) = t))$.
And v is *fair*, if
$\forall t \in T : ((\underset{\infty}{\exists} i \in \mathbb{N}^+ : \delta_0(v)(i)\ (t\rangle\,) \Rightarrow (\underset{\infty}{\exists} i \in \mathbb{N}^+ : v(i) = t))$.
We define the following languages for N:
$\mathrm{L}_\omega^{fdp}(N) = \{v \in \mathrm{F}_\omega(N) \mid v \text{ is fdp}\}$ and $\mathrm{L}_\omega^{fair}(N) = \{v \in \mathrm{F}_\omega(N) \mid v \text{ is fair}\}$.

3.1 Fair firing sequences

In this subsection it will be shown that it is undecidable if there is an infinite firing sequence in a net which is fair, i. e. if $\mathrm{L}_\omega^{fair}(N) \neq \emptyset$. We will prove this for the very special case, that fairness is only required for one single transition. Then also a proof for the general case will be given, but at first an undecidable problem will be stated.

In [Brams 85] it was shown, that for a Petri net N and a set of transitions $E \subseteq T$ it is undecidable if there is an infinite firing sequence, which never activates one of the transitions of E, i. e. no marking during this infinite sequence activates a transition of E. The proof gives a transformation for a UPM with two counters into a net N, so that a firing sequence never activating a transition of E simulates a computation of the UPM. Thus such an infinite firing sequence exists, iff the UPM does not have a finite computation. This problem is undecidable for UPMs. Here we will prove that even if E is a singleton, i. e. $E = \{t\}$, for $t \in T$, the problem remains undecidable. The idea of the proof is similiar.

Theorem 4 *For a net N and a transition $t \in T$ it is undecidable, if there is an infinite firing sequence $v \in \mathrm{F}_\omega(N)$ so that $\forall i \in \mathbb{N}^+ : \neg(\delta_0(v)(i)\ (t\rangle)$.*

Proof: Consider an arbitrary UPM M with two counters. A net N with a transition t will be constructed, so that it simulates the UPM if markings activating t are not allowed, i. e. every firing sequence in N passes only through markings which do not activate t. The two counters c_1 and c_2 will be represented by places. For each step i of the program a place p_i will be introduced, initially p_1 contains a token. The action of the step $i : c_k^+(i')$ will be done by a transition which takes a token from p_i and puts one on c_k and on $p_{i'}$. For the steps $i : c_1^-(i'', i')$ and $j : c_2^-(j'', j')$ a transformation according to the figure 1 will be done. The places outside of the dashed boxes will be used for all transformations of program steps.

It is easy to see, that in any case the alternative $= 0$ is used, although there is a token on the corresponding counter, the transition t will be activated. In the net N there is thus an infinite firing sequence never activating t, exactly if the UPM had an infinite computation.

Note that this construction may be easily extended to UPMs with more than two counters. The additional counters are also represented by places and have analogous arcs with the other transitions, e. g. the first transition of the alternative $= 0$ of $c_k^-(j'', j')$ puts a token on each $c_{k'}$, $k' \neq k$.

In this proof we have not allowed that t ever will be activated. Now we will investigate the differences if the firing sequence must only be fair with respect to t, i. e. t may only be activated finitely often without being fired. For the net in figure 1 a firing of t would cause a deadlock of the net.

Definition 8 Let N be a Petri net and $\mathcal{T} \subseteq \wp(T)$ a set of subsets of transitions, then an infinite firing sequence $v \in \mathrm{F}_\omega(N)$ is called *fdp with respect to* $\mathcal{T}$, if
$\forall \hat{T} \in \mathcal{T} : ((\underset{\infty}{\forall} i \in \mathbb{N}^+ : \exists t \in \hat{T} : \delta_0(v)(i)\ (t\rangle) \Rightarrow (\underset{\infty}{\exists} i \in \mathbb{N}^+ : v(i) \in \hat{T}))$
and *fair w. r. t.* $\mathcal{T}$, if
$\forall \hat{T} \in \mathcal{T} : ((\underset{\infty}{\exists} i \in \mathbb{N}^+ : \exists t \in \hat{T} : \delta_0(v)(i)\ (t\rangle) \Rightarrow (\underset{\infty}{\exists} i \in \mathbb{N}^+ : v(i) \in \hat{T}))$
The languages of these sequences are given by
$\mathrm{F}_\omega^{fdp}(N, \mathcal{T}) = \{v \in \mathrm{F}_\omega(N) \mid v \text{ is fdp w. r. t. } \mathcal{T}\}$ and
$\mathrm{F}_\omega^{fair}(N, \mathcal{T}) = \{v \in \mathrm{F}_\omega(N) \mid v \text{ is fair w. r. t. } \mathcal{T}\}$.

It is not possible to use the proof of theorem 4 directly for fair languages. A firing sequence which is fair with respect to the transition t would not simulate a computation of the UPM correctly. But it holds that a fair sequence simulates a computation in which there are only finitely many failures. Every fair sequence in the net may only choose an alternative $= 0$ though the counter contains a token finitely often.

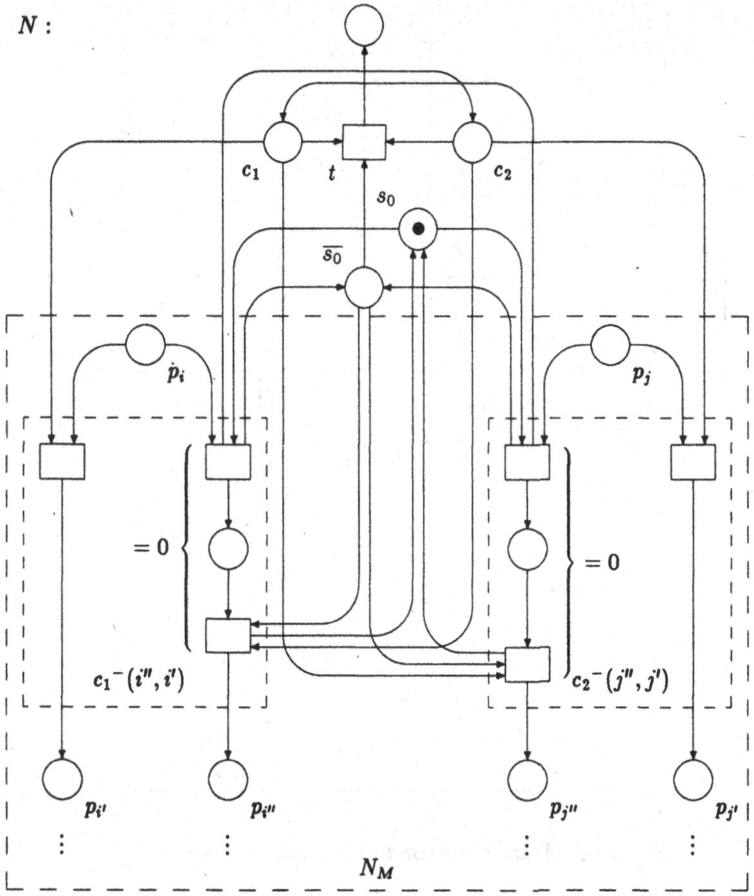

Figure 1: Transformation to the proof of theorem 4

In the next proof it will be shown that the problem, if there is an infinite fair firing sequence with respect to t, remains undecidable and is equivalent to the halting problem of UPMs. Again we will construct a Petri net for an arbitrary UPM. The idea of this construction is to determine a (finite) number $n \in \mathbb{N}$ of steps in which the UPM reaches an END-instruction. If it has reached this instruction it will be started again with the old input on the counters and may go n steps to reach an END-instruction, and so on.

A fair infinite firing sequence simulates infinitely many finite successful computations of the UPM. Since the test on zero may only be wrong finitely often, infinitely many times there are totally correct simulations of successful computations. Thus there is a fair (infinite) firing sequence, iff the UPM has a halting computation.

Theorem 5 *For a Petri net N and a transition $t \in T$ it is undecidable if* $\mathrm{F}_\omega^{fair}(N, \{\{t\}\}) \neq \emptyset$.

Proof: Let M_0 be an arbitrary UPM with two counters c_1 and c_2. We build a UPM M_1 with six counters c_1,c_2, c_1',c_2', c_1'', and c_2'', which executes the program of M_0 but at the end it writes the initial values on the counters. At the beginning M_1 has the same values on c_1' and c_2' as M_0 on c_1 and c_2. M_1 has the following program:

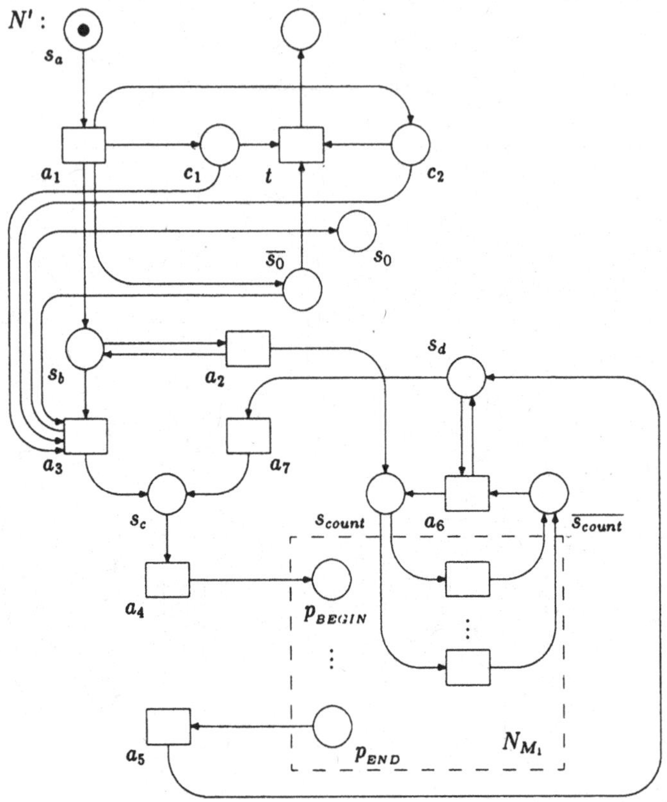

Figure 2: Transformation to the proof of theorem 5

$M_1 =$ 0 : BEGIN;

1 : $c_1'^-(4,2)$; 2 : $c_1^+(3)$; 3 : $c_1''^+(1)$;

4 : $c_2'^-(7,5)$; 5 : $c_2^+(6)$; 6 : $c_2''^+(4)$;

7 : $c_1''^-(9,8)$; 8 : $c_1'^+(7)$;

9 : $c_2''^-(11,10)$; 10 : $c_2'^+(9)$;

11 : Start M_0 and when the END-instruction is reached goto 12;

12 : $c_1^-(13,12)$; 13 : $c_2^-(14,13)$ {c_1 and c_2 are set to zero};

14 : END;

Note that in every computation of this UPM M_1 the sum of the values of c_k' and c_k'' is invariant, also if wrong alternatives are chosen by the tests on zero.

According to the transformation in the proof of theorem 4 (see also figure 1) a net N_{M_1} is constructed. With this subnet we build the net N' as it is sketched in figure 2. In this sketch again only two counters are shown, the others must be introduced as it is described in the proof of theorem 4. The arcs between transitions of N_{M_1} and the places c_1, c_2, s_0, and $\overline{s_0}$ remain unchanged, though they also are not shown.

We will prove that N' has the behaviour mentioned in the introduction of this proof. At the beginning only transition a_1 can fire. Then a_2 may fire arbitrarily often, until a_3 takes the token away, this also deactivates the transition t. In an infinite firing sequence t may not appear, thus in a fair sequence it may only be activated finitely often. This will ensure that a_3 must fire after finite time, hence on s_{count} will be put finitely many tokens. Let this be n

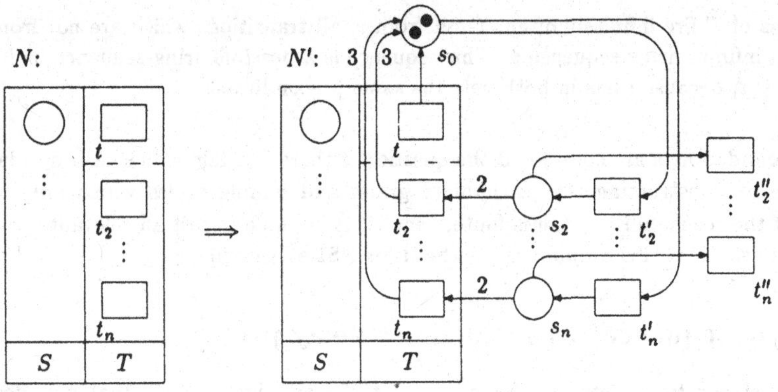

Figure 3: Transformation to the proof of theorem 6

tokens. Then a_4 transports a token on p_{BEGIN} and starts the simulation of M_1. At least n transitions of N_{M_1} may fire until a token lies on p_{END}.

By the transitions a_5, a_6, a_7, and a_4 again n tokens can be brought back on s_{count} and a new simulation of M_1 is started.

It is easy to see that an infinite firing sequence, which is fair w. r. t. t, must infinitely often execute transitions a_4 and a_5, because of the place s_{count}. Hence a fair firing sequence simulates infinitely many computations of M_1. As it was mentioned, infinitely many of these simulations are correct. If there is an infinite, fair firing sequence, M_1 has a halting computation.

For the reverse, consider a halting computation in M_1, i. e. a computation which reaches an END-instruction after finitely many steps. Let this be n steps. During the simulation in the net N' at least two transitions fire for each step. Therefore let a_2 put $2 \cdot n$ tokens on s_{count} at the beginning. Later on a correct simulation will never activate transition t. Hence there is an infinite firing sequence which is fair w. r. t. t in the net N'.

Altogether it follows, that there is a fair sequence w. r. t. t, iff M_1 and by that also M_0 has a halting computation.

With this theorem we can show that it is also undecidable if there is an infinite sequence in a net which is fair for all transitions.

Theorem 6 *For a Petri net N it is undecidable if* $\mathrm{F}_\omega^{fair}(N) \neq \emptyset$.

Proof: For a given net N and a transition t, we will show a transformation into a net N', so that $\mathrm{F}_\omega^{fair}(N, \{\{t\}\}) \neq \emptyset$ iff $\mathrm{F}_\omega^{fair}(N') \neq \emptyset$.

Build the net N' from the net N according to the figure 3.

Let v be a fair firing sequence w. r. t. t in the net N. Then this sequence is also possible in the net N', if before every transition t_i twice t'_i was inserted. For the firing of a transition t_i two tokens from s_0 are needed, but three are returned. So arbitrary many tokens may be collected on the place s_0. Hence for every i it is possible to insert the sequence $t'_i t''_i$ infinitely often, without activating t_i. Such an infinite firing sequence, built from v with these two extensions, is fair for all transitions in N'. The transitions $t'_2, \ldots, t'_n$, and $t''_2, \ldots, t''_n$ fire infinitely often and the transitions $t_2, \ldots, t_n$ will only be activated if they should fire. Of course this sequence will remain fair with respect to t.

On the other hand for every fair sequence v' in N' we can find a sequence in N which is fair w. r. t. t. The transitions $t'_2, \ldots, t'_n$, and $t''_2, \ldots, t''_n$ can only appear infinitely often if also transitions of T fire infinitely often. Omit from v' all transitions which are not from T, then we get an infinite firing sequence v. This sequence is a possible firing sequence in N and it is fair w. r. t. t, because t has in both nets the same preconditions.

If only bounded nets are considered the question if there is a fair sequence is decidable. This can be done by constructing the reachability graph and finding cycles which are fair. For a bounded net the reachability graph is finite, hence it is possible to test all relevant cycles. But it is also easy to see that this problem is also hard for DSPACE(exp).

3.2 Firing sequences with the finite delay property

It will be shown for a Petri net N and one set of transitions $E \subseteq T$ that it is decidable, if $F_\omega^{fdp}(N, \{E\}) \neq \emptyset$, i. e. if there is an fdp firing sequence w. r. t. E. The proof of this statement is mainly based on the calculation of the residue set markings, i. e. the set of minimal markings, of a right closed set. Hence we will first give the definition of a residue set and the condition under which it can be computed. Then two technical lemmata which use this residue set are needed to prove the statement.

Definition 9 Let N be a Petri net. Then an *extended marking* is an element of $(\mathbb{N}_\omega)^S = (\mathbb{N} \cup \{\omega\})^S$, i. e. there might be infinitely many tokens on the places.
For $x \in (\mathbb{N}_\omega)^S$ we define the *region* of x by $\mathrm{reg}(x) = \{y \in \mathbb{N}^S \mid y \leq x\}$.
A set $K \subseteq \mathbb{N}^S$ is called *right closed* if $\forall x \in K : \forall y \in \mathbb{N}^S : y \geq x \Rightarrow y \in K$. For a right closed set K the set of its minimal elements is called the *residue* of K, i. e.
$\mathrm{res}(K) = \{x \in K \mid \neg\exists y \in K : x \geq y\}$.

The residue of a right closed set can be computed iff a condition holds ([Valk, Jantzen 85]):

Lemma 1 *Let $K \subseteq \mathbb{N}^S$ be a right closed set. Then* $\mathrm{res}(K)$ *can be computed iff* $\mathrm{reg}(x) \cap K \neq \emptyset$ *is decidable for* $x \in (\mathbb{N}_\omega)^S$.

We will need the following two lemmata.

Lemma 2 *For a Petri net N and a set $\hat{S} \subseteq S$ of places the residue of $K \subseteq \mathbb{N}^S$ can be computed, where K is defined by*
$\forall m' \in K : \exists v \in T^+ : \exists m'' \in \mathbb{N}^S, m' \ (v\rangle\ m'' : (m' \leq m''$ *and* $\forall s \in \hat{S} : m'(s) = m''(s))$.

Proof: With the previous lemma we have to show that the question $\mathrm{reg}(x) \cap K \neq \emptyset$ is decidable for $x \in (\mathbb{N}_\omega)^S$.

This problem will be reduced to the reachability problem, which was shown in [Mayr 84] and [Kosaraju 83] to be decidable. First the net N will be modified. Put on every $s \in S$ $x(s)$ tokens if $x(s) \neq \omega$, otherwise introduce the following extension in the net N for the place s:

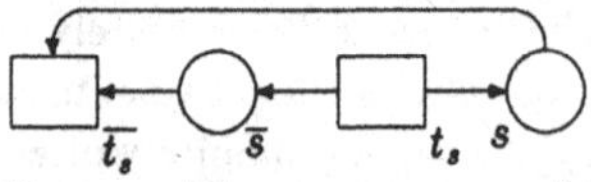

The transition t_s may put arbitrarily many tokens on s, but to eliminate tokens on $\bar{s}$ the same number of tokens must be eliminated on s.

Further add to every place $s \in S$ which does not belong to $\hat{S}$ a transition, which can take tokens from s. It holds $\mathrm{res}(K) \cap K \neq \emptyset$, iff in the new net the initial marking can be reached with a firing sequence containing at least one old transition.

Let v' be such a firing sequence, then it holds for a marking m with
$m = \begin{cases} x(s) & \text{for } x(s) \neq \omega \\ |v'|_{t_s} & \text{otherwise} \end{cases}$, that $m \in K$ and $m \in \text{reg}(x)$.
On the other hand, if $\text{reg}(x) \cap K \neq \emptyset$, then let m be the marking with $m \in \text{reg}(x) \cap K$. In N' let every transition t_s fire $m(s)$ times for $x(s) = \omega$. Then execute the firing sequence $v \in T^+$ which was mentioned in the statement of this lemma and fire $\overline{t_s}$ $m(s)$ times. Finally take away the tokens which are added to the places of $S/\hat{S}$ and the initial marking is restored.

Lemma 3 *For a Petri net N and a set $\hat{M} = \{d_1, \ldots, d_k\}$ of markings it can be decided, whether there are markings m' and m'' with*
$m_0 \langle\rangle\, m' \langle + \rangle\, m''$, $m' \leq m''$ and $\forall d \in \hat{M} : \neg(d \leq (m' + \omega \cdot (m'' - m')))$.

Proof: It holds $m' \leq m''$ and $\neg(d \leq (m' + \omega \cdot (m'' - m')))$, iff $\exists s \in S : d(s) > m'(s) = m''(s)$, i. e. there is at least one place s for which $m(s)$ is smaller than $d(s)$ and the number of tokens remains unchanged in m''. For $d \in \hat{M}$ let s_d be some place with $d(s_d) > m'(s_d) = m''(s_d)$. There are only finitely many possibilities to attach a place s_d to the marking d. Let us consider one of the possible choices for all $d \in \hat{M}$ and let $\hat{S} = \{s_d \in S \mid d \in \hat{M}\}$ be the set of these places for all markings of $\hat{M}$.

Calculate for the net N and $\hat{S}$ the residue of the set K of the condition in the previous lemma. For every marking m' which is greater or equal an element of $\text{res}(K)$ there is a m'' with $m' \langle + \rangle\, m''$ and $\forall s \in \hat{S} : m'(s) = m''(s)$. Hence it must be tested, if such a marking m' can be reached, with $\exists r \in \text{res}(K) : m' \geq r$ and $\forall d \in \hat{M} : m'(s_d) < d(s_d)$. For the places of $\hat{S}$ it is easy to see that there are only finitely many possibilities to distribute tokens on them. For all other places we have a lower bound for the marking m'. For the new net we introduce transitions for these places which can eliminate unnecessary tokens. For this net we have to test, if a marking m' is reachable with
$\exists r \in \text{res}(K) : [\forall d \in \hat{M} : r(s_d) < m'(s_d) < d(s_d) \text{ and } \forall s \in S/\hat{S} : r(s) = m'(s)]$. Hence the reachability must only be tested for finitely many markings. Additionally there were only finitely many possibilities to construct the set $\hat{S}$ for which the residue must be calculated and tested in the described way.

Theorem 7 *For a Petri net N and a set of transitions $E \subseteq T$ it is decidable if*
$F_\omega^{fdp}(N, \{E\}) \neq \emptyset$.

Proof: 1) Every sequence in which at least one transition of E appears infinitely often is fdp w. r. t. E. By theorem 3 this problem is decidable.

2) If such sequence does not exist, there is still one possibility for an fdp sequence. A sequence v, in which no transition of E appears infinitely often, is fdp w. r. t. E, if there are infinitely many situations, in which no transition of E is activated. Let $\hat{M}$ be the set of (minimal) markings in which a transition of E is activated, i. e.
$\hat{M} = \{m \mid \exists t \in E : \forall s \in S : (s,t) \in F \Rightarrow m(s) = W(s,t)\}$. Then it holds for v:
$\overset{\infty}{\exists} i \in \mathbb{N}^+ : \forall d \in \hat{M} : \neg(\delta_0(v)(i) \geq d)$.
Let (m_i), $i \in \mathbb{N}^+$, be an infinite sequence of markings with $m_i \langle + \rangle\, m_{i+1}$ and $\forall d \in \hat{M} : \neg(m_i \geq d)$. Without restriction, we can assume that additionally $m_i \leq m_{i+1}$. (Every infinite sequence of vectors of nonnegative integers has an infinite increasing subsequence, see [Dickson 13]).

For every marking m_i let S_i be the set of minimal subsets of places for which it holds:
$\hat{S} \in S_i \Rightarrow (\forall d \in \hat{M} : \exists s \in \hat{S} : m_i(s) < m(s))$. Here minimal means that for two sets A and B with $A \subset B$, which both fulfill the conditions, only set A is considered.

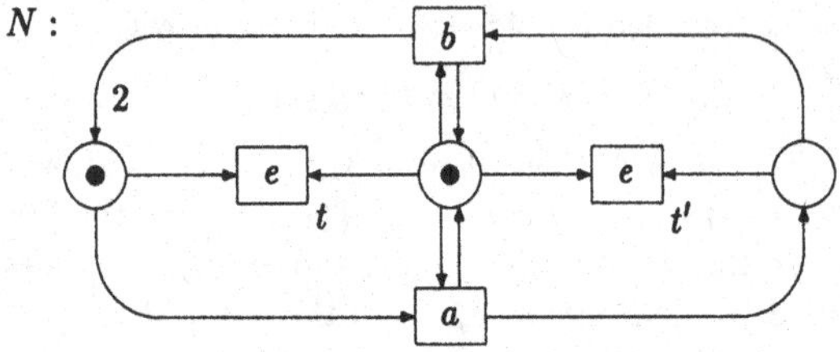

Figure 4: A Petri net with $\mathcal{T} = \{\{t\}, \{t'\}\}$

There are only finitely many subsets of S and the sequence of markings (m_i) is increasing, hence it exists an $i \in \mathbb{N}^+$ and a set $\hat{S}$ with $\forall j \in \mathbb{N}^+, j > i : \hat{S} \in S_j$. Then there is also an $l \in \mathbb{N}^+$ with $\forall s \in \hat{S} : m_l(s) = m_{l+1}(s)$.

Let $u \in T^*$ be the firing sequence with $m_0\ \langle u \rangle\ m_l$ and $v \in T^+$ the sequence with $m_l\ \langle v \rangle\ m_{l+1}$. It is easy to see that the sequence $w = uv^\omega$ is possible in N and fdp w. r. t. E. Hence if there is an fdp sequence w. r. t. E, in which transitions of E do not appear infinitely often, then there is also a sequence of the form $w = uv^\omega$, $u \in T^*$ and $v \in t^+$, which is fdp w. r. t. E.

By lemma 3 it is decidable if such a sequence is possible in a net.

It is not known, if for two or more sets of transitions in $\mathcal{T}$ the problem $\mathrm{F}_\omega^{fdp}(N, \mathcal{T}) \neq \emptyset$ is still decidable. But we can state that the idea of the previous proof cannot be extended to more than one set of transitions. The reason can be shown by the net in figure 4. It holds $\mathrm{F}_\omega^{fdp}(N, \{\{t\}, \{t'\}\}) \neq \emptyset$, because the sequence $w = \prod_{i=0}^{\infty} a^{2^i} b^{2^i} = abaabbaaaabbbb \ldots \infty$ is fdp w. r. t. $\{\{t\}, \{t'\}\}$. For the place s_1, as well as s_2, there are infinitely often no tokens on it. But there is no fdp sequence of the form $w = uv^\omega$, for $u \in T^*$ and $v \in T^+$.

A restriction on bounded nets would lead to the decidability of the problems. But again the problems are hard for DSPACE(exp).

4 Conclusions

For a Petri net and a group of transitions E a procedure is given to decide if there is an infinite firing sequence which is fdp w. r. t. E. An analysis of the complexity shows that even the problem if there is an arbitrary infinite firing sequence in a bounded net is hard for DSPACE(exp). If (strong) fairness is required the problem becomes undecidable, this is even shown for the question if there is an infinite firing sequence which is fair w. r. t. one transition t.

An open problem remains the question if there is an infinite firing sequence which is fdp w. r. t. more than one group of transitions.

References

[Brams 85] G. W. Brams: *Réseaux de Petri: Théorie et Pratique — Tome 1: théorie et analyse*; Masson, Paris 1983.

[Carstensen, Valk 85] H. Carstensen, R. Valk: *Infinite Behaviour and Fairness in Petri Nets*; In G. Rozenberg (ed.): *Advances in Petri Nets 1984*; Lecture Notes in Computer Science 188, (S. 83 - 100), Springer, Berlin 1985.

[Dickson 13] L. E. Dickson: *Finiteness of the Odd Perfect and Primitive Abundant Numbers with n Distinct Prime Factors*; American Journal of Mathematics 35, (S. 413 - 422), 1913.

[Kosaraju 83] S. R. Kosaraju: *Decidability of Reachability in Vector Addition Systems*; Proc. 14th Ann. Symp. on Theory of Computing, (S. 267 - 281), 1982.

[Lipton 76] R. J. Lipton: *The Reachability Problem Requires Exponential Space*; Yale University, Department of Computer Science, Research Report 62, 1976.

[Mayr 84] E. W. Mayr: *An Algorithm for the General Petri Net Reachability Problem*; SIAM J. Comput. Vol. 13, (S. 441 - 460), 1984.

[Minsky 67] M. L. Minsky: *Computation: Finite and Infinite Machines*; Prentence Hall, New Jersey 1967.

[Valk, Jantzen 85] R. Valk, M. Jantzen: *The Residue of Vector Sets with Applications to Decidability Problems in Petri Nets*; Acta Informatica 21, (S. 643 - 674), 1985.

Optimal Sorting on Multi-Dimensionally Mesh-Connected Computers

Manfred Kunde*
Institut für Informatik
TU München
Arcisstr. 21
D-8000 München 2

Abstract

An algorithm is presented sorting $N = n_1 n_2 \ldots n_r$, $r \geq 2$, elements on an $n_1 \times n_2 \times \ldots \times n_r$ mesh-connected array of processors within $2(n_1 + \ldots + n_{r-1}) + n_r + 0(n_1^{1-\varepsilon} + \ldots + n_r^{1-\varepsilon})$, $\varepsilon > 0$, data interchange steps. Hence this algorithm asymptotically matches the quite recently given lower bound for r-dimensional meshes. The asymptotically optimal lower bound of $(2r/2^{1/r})\, N^{1/r}$ interchange steps can only be obtained on r-dimensional meshes with aspect ratio $n_i : n_r = 1 : 2$ for all $i = 1,\ldots,r-1$. Moreover, for meshes with wrap-around connections the slightly altered algorithm only need $1.5(n_1 + \ldots + n_{r-1}) + n_r + 0(n_1^{1-\varepsilon} + \ldots + n_r^{1-\varepsilon})$ data interchange steps, which asymptotically is significantly smaller than the lower bound for sorting on meshes without wrap-arounds.

1. Introduction and notations

The design and analysis of fast parallel algorithms has become more and more important by the advancements of VLSI-technology. Especially for VLSI-architectures, where a regular net of simple processing cells and local communication between these cells are required [FK,KL], several parallel algorithms for fundamental problems as matrix arithmetic, signal and image processing, sorting and searching etc. have been proposed [U]. It has turned out that for so-called VLSI algorithms data movement is very often the significant performance factor. In this paper we present sorting algorithms on certain mesh-connected computers where the number of parallel data transfers is asymptotically minimal.

A simple model of parallel computers - well-suited for VLSI implementation - is the two-dimensional mesh-connected array or mesh of processors. For this model several sorting algorithms have been proposed [KH,LSSS,NS,SI,SS,TK]. Some of these two-dimensional algorithms have been generalized to algorithms suitable for r-dimensional cubes, $r \geq 3$, [NS,TK] and quite recently two further approaches for sorting on three or more dimensional meshes have been proposed [Ku2,S].

* This work was supported by the Siemens AG, München.

An $n_1 \times n_2 \times \ldots \times n_r$ mesh-connected array or mesh of processors is a set mesh$(n_1,\ldots,n_r)$ of $N = n_1 n_2 \ldots n_r$ identical processors where each processor $P = (p_1,\ldots,p_r)$, $1 \leq p_i \leq n_i$, is directly interconnected to all its nearest neighbours only (Figures 1 and 2). A processor $Q = (q_1,\ldots,q_r)$ is called a nearest neighbour of P if and only if the distance fulfills $d(P,Q) = |p_1 - q_1| + \ldots + |p_r - q_r| = 1$.
For example, for $r = 2$, that is in the plane, every processor has at most 4 nearest neighbours. Note that no "wrap-around" connections are allowed. At each time step each processor can only communicate with one of its nearest neighbours. That is, at most N/2 communications can simultaneously be performed. For the sorting problem we assume that N elements from a linearly ordered set are loaded in the N processors, each receiving exactly one element. The processors are thought to be indexed by a certain one-to-one mapping from $\{1,\ldots,n_1\} \times \ldots \times \{1,\ldots,n_r\}$ onto $\{1,\ldots,N\}$. With respect to this function the sorting problem is to move the i-th smallest element to the processor indexed by i for all $i = 1, \ldots, N$.

Figure 1 a x b x c mesh

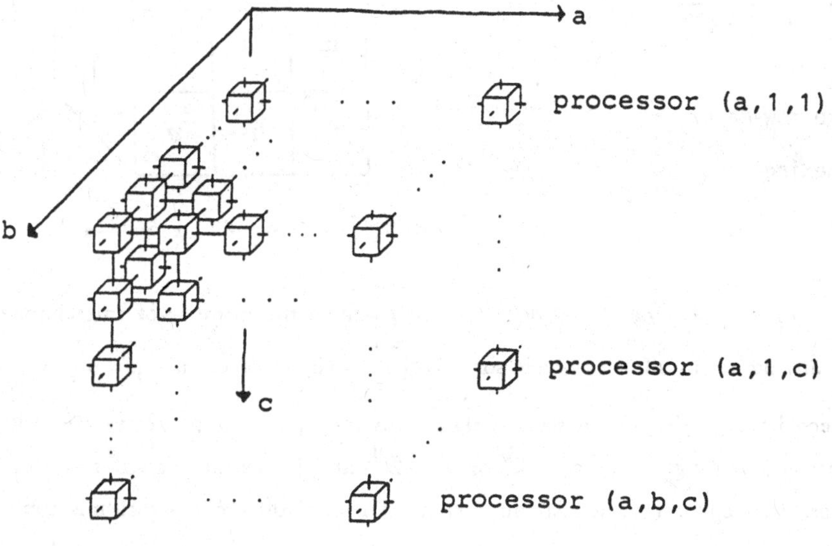

In this paper we assume the index function snake_r to be a snake-like ordering where higher dimensions have more weight than lower ones. More precisely, let $\text{snake}_1(p_1) = p_1$ for every p_1, $1 \leq p_1 \leq n_1$, and for all $r \geq 2$, all $i = 1,\ldots,r$ and all $p_i = 1,\ldots,n_i$ define:

$$\text{snake}_r(p_1,\ldots,p_r) = n_1 \ldots n_{r-1}(p_r - 1) + \begin{cases} \text{snake}_{r-1}(p_1,\ldots,p_{r-1}) & \text{if } p_r \text{ is odd} \\ n_1 \ldots n_{r-1} + 1 - \text{snake}_{r-1}(p_1,\ldots,p_{r-1}) & \text{if } p_r \text{ is even.} \end{cases}$$

For the two-dimensional case this ordering is equivalent to the snake-like row-major indexing [TK] (Figure 2).

Clearly, the sorting problem can be solved by a sequence of comparison and interchange steps. It is well-known that data movement is a significant performance measure for sorting algorithms on mesh-connected architectures. Therefore, in this paper we concentrate on the number of data interchange steps which may be caused by a comparison or not. Note that one interchange step is equivalent to two routings and optionally one comparison in [TK].

Figure 2

a) 4 x 3 mesh

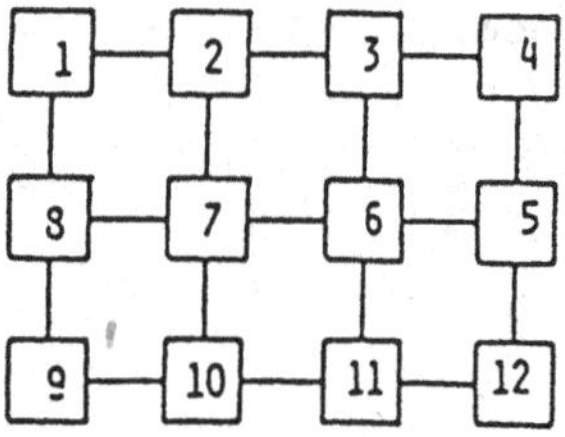

snake-like row-major indexing

b) 3 x 3 x 3 mesh-connected cube

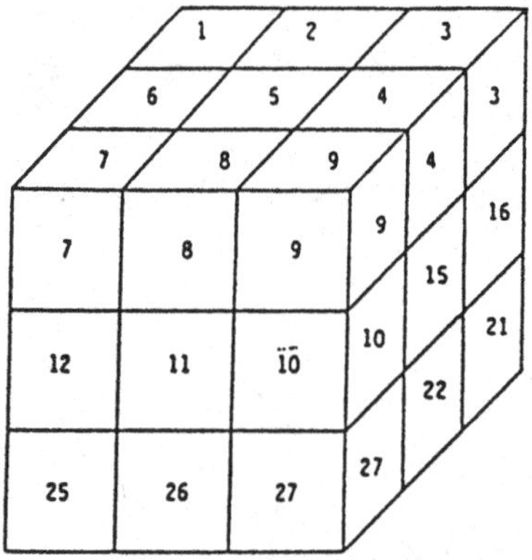

snake-like indexing (snake_3)

For the rest of the paper let $\text{SORT}(n_1,\ldots,n_r)$ denote the number of interchange steps needed by an algorithm SORT which sorts $N=\prod_{i=1}^{r} n_i$ elements on a $n_1 \times n_2 \times \ldots \times n_r$ mesh-connected array. Very often sorting algorithms for $n_1 \times \ldots \times n_r$ arrays are well suited only for special side lengths like $n_i = 2^k$ or $n_i = 2^{2k}$ and for certain aspect-ratios $c_1 : c_2 : \ldots : c_r$ where $n_i = c_i m$ for some real number m. To make different algorithms comparable to each other we normalize the aspect-ratio $c_1 : c_2 : \ldots \; c_r$ such that for the product $c_1 c_2 \ldots c_r = 1$ holds. That is, if $N = n_1 n_2 \ldots n_r$ elements are to be sorted, we obtain $n_i = c_i N^{1/r}$ for all $i = 1,\ldots,r$. Then the asymptotic linear factor of a sorting algorithm SORT for r-dimensional mesh-connected arrays with aspect-ratio $c_1 : c_2 : \ldots : c_r$ is defined by

$$\text{ALF}(\text{SORT},c_1,\ldots,c_r) = \lim_{m\to\infty} \inf \,(\text{SORT}(c_1 m,\ldots,c_r m)/m).$$

Quite recently it has been shown that in the two-dimensional case for an arbitrary sorting algorithm SORT the asymptotic linear factor is ALF(SORT, c_1, c_2) $\geq 2c_1 + c_2$ [Ku1,SS]. If $c_1/c_2 = 2^i$ then this bound is matched by the s^2-way-merge of Thompson and Kung [TK]. Schnorr and Shamir [SS] demonstrated that their t-way-unshuffle sorting algorithm is asymptotically optimal for aspect ratios, where c_1/c_2 is any rational number. Moreover, for sorting n^2 elements the minimal number of interchange steps asymptotically is $2\sqrt{2}n$, which can only be obtained on processor meshes with aspect-ratio 1:2, whereas on n x n meshes at least 3n interchange steps are necessary.

For r-dimensional arrays it has been shown that the asymptotic linear factor generally is larger than or equal to $2(c_1 + \ldots + c_{r-1}) + c_r$ [Ku1]. For the 3-dimensional case sorting algorithms for an n x n x n mesh-connected cube have already been proposed in [TK,NS]. Both algorithms asymptotically need 15n interchange steps whereas Schimmler [S] recently developed a simpler sorting algorithm on a cube with 19n interchange steps. In [Ku2] a method is presented for obtaining sorting algorithms on arbitrary a x b x c arrays based on arbitrary sorting algorithms for mesh-connected rectangles. By using one of the optimal 2-dimensional algorithms [SS,TK] a sorting algorithm for an n x n x n cube can be constructed needing only 12n interchange steps (neglecting low order terms). An improvement of this method gave an algorithm for an n/2 x n x 2n mesh which one sorts n^3 elements within 10.5 n interchange steps. All of these 3-dimensional algorithms have asymptotic linear factors which are more than twice as big as the recently obtained lower bound of $2c_1 + 2c_2 + c_3$, which is 5 for the above mentioned cases. For r-dimensional meshes, $r \geq 4$, the only proposed sorting algorithms [Ku2,NS,TK] lead to asymptotic linear factors which are at least 3/4r times bigger than the general lower bound of $2(c_1 + \ldots + c_{r-1}) + c_r$.

In the second section we show that sorting on an r-dimensional mesh, $r \geq 3$, with arbitrary aspect ratio $c_1 : c_2 \ldots : c_r$, c_i/c_r a rational number for all i=1,...,r-1, can be done with an asymptotic linear factor of exactly $2(c_1 + \ldots + c_{r-1}) + c_r$. Hence both the proposed algorithm and the previously derived bound are asymptotically optimal.

Moreover, as proven for the 2-dimensional case [Ku1,SS], the sorting problem for three- and more-dimensional meshes turns out to be asymmetric with respect to the different dimensions. The best possible asymptotic factor of $2r/\sqrt[r]{2}$ can be obtained only on $n_1 \times \ldots \times n_r$ meshes with aspect ratio $n_i : n_r = 2$ for all i = 1,...,r-1 [Ku1].

In the third section it is demonstrated how to improve the asymptotic linear factor, if wrap-around connections are allowed. In this case a processor $P = (p_1,\ldots,p_r)$ is nearest neighbour of $Q = (q_1,\ldots,q_r)$ if the wrap-around-distance fulfills $d_{wrap}(P,Q) = |(p_1-q_1) \bmod n_1| + \ldots + |(p_r-q_r) \bmod n_r| = 1$. It is shown that for wrap-around meshes with aspect ratios $c_1 : \ldots : c_r$, $r \geq 2$, sorting algorithms exist having asymptotic linear factor of $1.5(c_1 + \ldots + c_{r-1}) + c_r$. Therefore, under the assumption that wrap-around connections need nomore time for data transport than ordinary connections asymptotic linear factors for sorting algorithms can be obtained which are provable better than those ones for algorithms on meshes without wrap-arounds. On wrap-around meshes the best asymptotic linear factor $(1.5)^{1-1/r} \cdot r$ can only be obtained with aspect ratio $c_i : c_r = 2 : 3$ for all $i = 1,\ldots,r-1$. Hence the best asymptotic linear factor of $2^{1-1/r} \cdot r$ for meshes without wrap-arounds is at least $(4/3)^{1-1/r}$ times larger than the best linear factor for the wrap-around case.

2. An optimal multi-dimensional sorting method

In this section we present an asymptotically optimal sorting algorithm for r-dimensional meshes, $r \geq 2$, with arbitrary aspect ratios. Before going into details of the algorithm we briefly introduce the notations used for the rest of the paper.

Notations

1. $[a,b] = \{a,\ldots,b\}$ denotes the interval of integers between a and b.
2. Let $cont_t(P)$ be the contents of processor $P \in mesh(n_1,\ldots,n_r)$ at time $t \geq 0$.
3. For all $i = 1,\ldots,r$ let u_i and v_i be integers with $u_i v_i = n_i$, u_i dividing v_i and $(u_1+2(u_2+\ldots+u_{r-1}))u_1\ldots u_r < v_1$. That is, the u_i's have to be rather small compared to the v_i's. Moreover, we demand that there is a real number ε,
   $0 < \varepsilon \leq 1/(r+2)$, such that $u_i \geq n_i^{\varepsilon}$ and $v_i \leq n_i^{1-\varepsilon}$ for all $i=1,\ldots,r$. As an abbreviation we call such n_i's ε-composite integers.
4. For all $r \geq 1$, all $i = 1,\ldots,r$ and all $k_i = 1,\ldots,u_i$ r-dimensional blocks are defined as follows:

   $$B(k_1,\ldots,k_r) = [(k_1-1)v_1 + 1 \ , \ k_1 v_1] \times \ldots \times [(k_r-1)v_r + 1 \ , \ k_r v_r]$$

   Note that a block contains $v_1\ldots v_r$ processors and $mesh(n_1,\ldots,n_r)$ consists of $u_1\ldots u_r$ blocks. As an abbreviation we will use

   $$B(k_1,\ldots,k_{i-1},*_i,\ldots,*_r) = \bigcup_{j=i}^{r} \bigcup_{k_j=1}^{u_j} B(k_1,\ldots,k_{i-1},k_i,\ldots,k_r).$$

5. If the initial loadings of the processors consist of zeroes and ones only, that is, $cont_0(P) \in \{0,1\}$ for all $P \in mesh(n_1,\ldots,n_r)$, then let $one_t(M) = \sum_{P \in M} cont_t(P)$ denote the number of ones contained in subset M of processors at time $t \geq 0$. The number of zeroes is then given by $zero_t(M) = |M| - one_t(M)$. (The time index t will often be omitted if it

is clear which time point t is meant.)

6. A modified snake-like ordering is sometimes used within the algorithm. For all $i = 1,\dots,r$ let

$$\text{low}_i - \text{snake}_r(p_1,\dots,p_r) = \text{snake}_r(p_i,p_1,\dots,p_{i-1},p_{i+1},\dots p_r),$$

which describes a snake-like ordering where the i-th coordinate is the lowest one. Hence $\text{low}_1 - \text{snake}_r \equiv \text{snake}_r$.

7. We say that a subset A of $\text{mesh}(n_1,..,n_r)$ is ordered according to the total snake if A is ordered with respect to an index function $g : A \to \{1,..,|A|\}$ where for all P,Q in A : $g(P) < g(Q)$ iff $\text{snake}_r(P) < \text{snake}_r(Q)$.

The correctness of the proposed algorithm will be shown by the help of the zero-one principle [Kn] telling us that an algorithm sorts an arbitrarily given initial loading of arbitrary integers if and only if all initial loadings only consisting of zeroes and ones are sorted correctly. We therefore will restrict our attention to meshes where the processors contain either zeroes or ones at the beginning.

For the algorithm proposed in the following we distinguish two stages: 1. data distributing or unshuffle stage and 2. special sorting stage. These two stages were already used to abtain optimal sorting algorithms for the 2-dimensional case [SS, TK]. The algorithm proposed in the following may be viewed as a generalization of the sorting algorithm of Schnorr and Shamir [SS] where distributing the data is done by presorting of blocks and mainly by the help of the m-way unshuffle operation.

Definition m,n positive integers with m dividing n. Then for all $j = 1,\dots,n$:

$$m - \text{unshuffle}(j) = ((j-1) \bmod m) \cdot \frac{n}{m} + \lceil j/m \rceil .$$

The permutation m-shuffle distributes the elements of each intervall of length m in such a way that each intervall of length n/m is hit.

We are now ready to formulate the sorting algorithm which is called r-dimensional distribution sort.

r-Dimensional-Distribution-Sort (r-DDS)

r-DDS($n_1,\dots,n_r,u_1,\dots,u_r$)
begin
UNSHUFFLE ($n_1,\dots,n_r,u_1,\dots,u_r$)
SPECIALSORT ($r,n_1,\dots,n_r,u_1,\dots,u_r$)
end

UNSHUFFLE $(n_1,.., n_r, u_1,.., u_r)$
begin

U1. **for** i=1 **to** r−1 **do**

begin

1. for all h=1,...,r and all k=1,.., u_h in parallel:

   Sort all $v_1 \times \ldots \times v_r$ blocks $B(k_1,.., k_r)$ according to index function low_1 − $snake_r$

2. u_i-way unshuffle along the i-th axis:

   for all h=1,..,r, h≠i and all j_h=1,.., n_h perform an u_i-way unshuffle on $\{j_1\} \times .. \times \{j_{i-1}\} \times [1,n_i] \times \{j_{i+1}\} \times .. \times \{j_r\}$

end

U2. for all h=1,..,r and all k_h=1,.., u_h in parallel:

Sort all blocks $B(k_1,..,k_r)$ with respect to low_1 − $snake_r$.

end

For all h, $2 \leqq h \leqq r$:
SPECIALSORT $(h, n_1,.., n_r, u_1,..., u_r)$

begin

S1. Sort all h-columns according to the total snake. For all i=1,...,r , i≠h , and all j_i=1,.., n_i in parallel:

Sort $\{j_1\} \times .. \times \{j_{h-1}\} \times [1,n_h] \times \{j_{h+1}\} \times .. \times \{j_r\}$ according to the total snake.

S2. Sort h-dimensional subblocks.

For all l=1,..,h , and all k_1=1,..,u_1, all i=h+1,..,r and all j_i=1,..,n_i in parallel:

1. Sort $B(k_1,..,k_h) \times \{j_{h+1}\} \times .. \times \{j_r\}$

2. Sort $B(k_1,..,k_{h-1}) \times [(k_h-1)v_h - v_h/2+1 \ , \ k_h v_h - v_h/2] \times \{j_{h+1}\} \times .. \times \{j_r\}$ according to the total snake.

S3. SPECIALSORT $(h-1, n_1,.., n_r, u_1,.., u_r)$

S4. Garbage collection

For all i=h+1,...,r and all j_i=1,..,n_i in parallel:

perform $2v_1$ parallel steps of the odd-even transposition sort on each h-dimensional subarray

$mesh(n_1,.., n_h) \times \{j_{h+1}\} \times .. \times \{j_r\}$ according to the total snake

end

Remark: If $h = r$, then blocks $B(k_1,..,k_r)$ and $mesh(n_1,..,n_r)$ are considered in step S2 and S4.

SPECIALSORT $(1, n_1,\ldots,n_r, u_1,\ldots, u_r)$

begin

Sort all 1-columns (rows) according to the total snake. For all $i = 2,\ldots,r$ and all $j_i = 1,\ldots,n_i$ in parallel:

Sort $[1,n_1] \times \{j_2\} \times .. \times \{j_r\}$

end

Theorem 1

For all $r \geq 2$ and all ε, $0 < \varepsilon \leq 1/(r+3)$, the algorithm r-DDS sorts $N = n_1 \ldots n_r$ elements, n_i an ε-composite, on an $n_1 \times \ldots \times n_r$ mesh-connected array within

$$2(n_1 + \ldots + n_{r-1}) + n_r + 0(n_1^{1-\varepsilon} + \ldots + n_r^{1-\varepsilon}) \text{ interchange steps.}$$

Corollary

a) The asymptotic linear factor of r-DDS is optimal, that is

$$\text{ALF}(\text{r-DDS}, c_1,\ldots,c_r) = 2(c_1 + \ldots + c_{r-1}) + c_r$$

for all aspect ratios $c_1 : c_2 : \ldots : c_r$, $c_1 c_2 \ldots c_r = 1$ and c_1/c_i a rational number for all $i = 2,\ldots,r$.

b) The minimal asymptotic factor of $2r/\sqrt[r]{2}$ can only be obtained on r-dimensional meshes with aspect ratio $c_i : c_r = 1 : 2$ for all $i = 1,\ldots,r-1$.

For the sake of brevity the proof of the corollary and the complexity analysis of the algorithm is omitted here.

For proving that r-DDS really sorts assume that from now on there is an arbitrary, but fixed initial zero-one loading. For a mapping $g : \mathbb{N}^k \rightarrow \mathbb{N}$ say that a set of blocks MB is block-g-sorted iff each block of MB is sorted with respect to the same index function and for all blocks $B,C \in MB$ $|\,one(B) - one(C)\,| \leq g(n_1,\ldots,n_r)$ hold. The proof of the correctness of r-DDS can be done with help of the following four lemmata of which the proofs are omitted here and can be found in a full version of this paper.

Lemma 1

Let s(i) be the starting time and t(i) the finishing time of the i-th call of the loop of step U1. Then for all $j = 1,\ldots,r$ and all $k_j = 1,\ldots,n_j$:

$$a_i\,(k_1,\ldots,k_{i-1},\, k_{i+1},\ldots,k_r)$$

$$= \sum_{j=1}^{u_i} \lfloor \mathrm{one}_{s(i)}\,(B\,(k_1,\ldots,k_{i-1},j,k_{i+1},\ldots,k_r)\,)\,/\,u_i \rfloor$$

$$\leq \mathrm{one}_{t(i)}\,(B\,(k_1,\ldots,k_i,\ldots k_r)\,) \leq a_i\,(k_1,\ldots,k_{i-1},\, k_{i+1},\ldots,k_r) + u_i.$$

For $i = 1,\ldots,r$ define mappings $g_i\colon \mathbb{N}^r \rightarrow \mathbb{N}$ in the following way: $g_1(n_1,\ldots,n_r) = u_1$ and $g_i(n_1,\ldots,n_r) = u_i + u_i \lceil g_{i-1}(n_1,\ldots,n_r) / u_i \rceil$ for $i \geq 2$. Then the following lemma holds:

Lemma 2

After the i-th call of U1., $1 \leq i \leq r-1$, for all $j = i+1,\ldots,r$, all $k_j = 1,\ldots,u_j$ and for all blocks B,C in $B(*_1,\ldots,*_i,k_{i+1},\ldots,k_r)$ we have

$$|\; \mathrm{one}_{t(i)}(B) - \mathrm{one}_{t(i)}(C) \;| \leq g_i(n_1,\ldots,n_r).$$

By lemma 2 and step U2. it is now easily seen that the following lemma hold:

Lemma 3

After the unshuffle phase for all $k_r = 1,\ldots,u_r$ the sets of blocks $B(*_1,\ldots,*_{r-1},k_r)$ are block-g_{r-1}-sorted.

Lemma 4

Let $M = \mathrm{mesh}(n_1,\ldots,n_r)$ consists of block columns $B(*_1,\ldots,*_{r-1},k_r)$, $k_r = 1,\ldots,u_r$, such that all $B(*_1,\ldots,*_{r-1},k_r)$ are block-g-sorted with respect to a mapping $g : \mathbb{N}^r \rightarrow \mathbb{N}$ with $g(n_1,\ldots,n_r) < v_1/(u_1\ldots u_r)$. Then SPECIALSORT$(r,n_1,\ldots,n_r,u_1,\ldots,u_r)$ sorts M.

For proving the theorem observe that by point 3 of the notations $(u_1\ldots u_r)g_{r-1}(n_1,\ldots,n_r) < v_1$ is valid for function g_{r-1}. Hence by lemma 3 the assumptions of lemma 4 are fulfilled and our theorem is proven.

3. Sorting on meshes with wrap-around connections

The basic ideas of r-DDS can be applied to meshes with wrap-around connections. That is, two processors $P = (p_1,\ldots,p_r)$ and $Q = (q_1,\ldots,q_r)$ are directly neighboured if and only if the wrap-around distance d_{wrap} fulfills $d_{wrap}(P,Q) = |(p_1 - q_1) \bmod n_1| + \ldots + |(p_r - q_r) \bmod n_r| = 1$. The indexing function of such a mesh is assumed to be the same as in the case where no wrap-arounds are allowed.

The idea now is to use the wrap-around connections during the data distribution phase in such a way that the element placed in processor $P_1 = (p_1,\ldots, p_{i-1}, j, p_{i+1},\ldots, p_r)$ has to be transported with respect to the u_i-unshuffle to the processor $P_2 = (p_1,\ldots,p_{i-1}, u_i$-unshuffle(j), $p_{i+1},\ldots,p_r)$ on the shortest way as possible. It is easily seen that $d_{wrap}(P_1,P_2) \leq n_i/2$, meaning that only $n_i/2$ interchange steps are sufficient to perform the u_i-unshuffle along the i-th axis. A simple execution of the data transport by interchange steps can be obtained with help of the following operation called the bi-way-unshuffle. Let m,n be integers with m dividing n. Then for all j = 1,...,n define

$$\text{m-bi-unshuffle}(j) = (\lceil jm/n \rceil + j \bmod m - m/2 - 1) \frac{n}{m} + \lceil j/m \rceil .$$

It is easily seen that the bi-unshuffle operation distributes the data as well as the unshuffle operation. The element j then has to reach the position pos(j) = m-bi-unshuffle(j) mod n. If m-bi-unshuffle(j) $\leq$ j, then the element has to be transported into the left direction, whereas in the other case it has transported to the right. Note that for each intervall [am+1, (a+1)m] the first (m/2-1) elements are always transported to the left and while the last m/2-1 elements always must go the right. The transport direction of the m/2-th and the (m/2+1)-st element depends on the actual value of a. It can be shown that the data movement can be done by at most n+n/m data interchange steps.

According to the above discussion let for meshes with wrap-around BI-UNSHUFFLE($n_1,\ldots,n_r,u_1,\ldots,u_r$) be defined in the corresponding way as UNSHUFFLE in the last section. Then the r-dimensional distribution sort for meshes with wrap-around connections is given as follows:

r-DDS-WRAP($n_1,\ldots,n_r,u_1,\ldots,u_r$)

begin

BI-UNSHUFFLE($n_1,\ldots,n_r,u_1,\ldots,u_r$)

SPECIAL SORT(r, $n_1,\ldots,n_r,u_1,\ldots,u_r$).

end

Theorem 2

a) For all $r \geq 2$ the asymptotic linear factor of r–DDS–WRAP is

$$\mathrm{ALF}(\text{r-DDS-WRAP}, c_1,\ldots,c_r) = 1.5(c_1 + \ldots + c_{r-1}) + c_r$$

for all aspect ratios $c_1 : c_2 : \ldots : c_r$, $c_1 \ldots c_r = 1$, and c_1/c_i rational numbers for all $i = 2,\ldots,r$.

b) r–DDS–WRAP can reach a minimal asymptotic linear factor of $r\cdot(3/2)^{1-1/r}$ only on meshes with aspect ratio $c_i : c_r = 2 : 3$ for all $i = 1,\ldots,r-1$.

It is still an open question which minimal asymptotic linear factor can be reached on meshes with wrap–arounds. A lower bound in this case is $c_1 + \ldots + c_{r-1} + c_r/2$, a bound which can be easily derived from the corresponding bound for sorting on meshes without wrap–arounds [Ku1, SS]. Therefore the r–DDS–WRAP is asymptotically optimal within a factor of $1 + (c_1 + \ldots + c_r)/(2c_1 + \ldots + 2c_{r-1} + c_r)$ which is smaller than 2 and about 3/2 in the interesting cases.

By theorem 2 a question of Schnorr and Shamir [SS] is partially answered. An optimal lower bound for sorting on meshes with wrap–arounds is smaller than the corresponding bound for meshes without wrap–arounds. By theorem 1 and 2 we know that asymptotically optimal sorting algorithms on meshes without wrap–arounds are at least $(4/3)^{1-1/r}$ times slower than those ones on wrap–around meshes.

4. Conclusion

In this paper we presented a sorting algorithm for r–dimensional mesh–connected arrays without wrap–around connections which turns out to be asymptotically optimal. For meshes with aspect ratio $c_1 : c_2 : \ldots : c_r$, $c_1 \ldots c_r = 1$, the algorithm r–DDS was proven to have an optimal asymptotic linear factor of $2(c_1 + \ldots + c_{r-1}) + c_r$. In a certain sense this means that the sorting problem is asymmetric with respect to the different dimensions. More precisely, an absolute minimal asymptotic linear factor of $r\cdot 2^{1-1/r}$ can only be obtained if and only if the aspect ratio fulfills $c_i : c_r = 1 : 2$ for all $i = 1,\ldots,r-1$.

Moreover, it could be shown that for meshes with wrap–around connections an modification of the r–DDS led to an algorithm r–DDS–WRAP having an asymptotic linear factor of $1.5(c_1 + \ldots + c_{r-1}) + c_r$ which is significantly better than the optimal factor in the corresponding case without wrap–arounds. The absolute minimal asymptotic linear factor for this algorithm is $r\cdot(3/2)^{1-1/r}$ and can only be obtained on wrap–around meshes where the aspect ratios fulfill $c_i : c_r = 2 : 3$ for all $i = 1,\ldots,r-1$. This again indicates that the sorting problem on wrap-around meshes is also asymmetric with respect to the different dimensions. It is still an open question, whether r-DDS-WRAP is an optimal algorithm. Finally, it should be mentioned that the complexity of the algorithms include so called low order terms which are significant in the cases where the side lengths of the meshes are small. But it seems that the basic ideas of distributing the data and then sorting along the axes can also be useful for designing algorithms for meshes with relatively small sidelengths.

References

[FK] Foster, M.J., Kung, H.T., The design of special-purpose VLSI-chips. IEEE Computer (1980), 26-40.

[KH] M. Kumar and D.S. Hirschberg, An efficient implementation of Batcher's odd-even merge algorithm and its application in parallel sorting schemes, IEEE Trans. Comp., Vol. C-32, 254-264 (1983)

[KL] Kung, H.T., Leiserson, C.E., Systolic arrays for VLSI. Symposium on Sparse Matrix Computation 1978, Proceeding, eds.: I.S. Duff, C.G. Stewart, (1978).

[Kn] D.E. Knuth, The art of computer programming, Vol. 3: Sorting and Searching, Addison Wesley, Reading, 1973, pp 224-225.

[Ku1] M. Kunde, Lower bounds for sorting on mesh-connected architectures, Proceedings AWOC 86, VLSI Algorithms and Architectures, LNCS 227, Springer, Berlin, 1986, 84-95.

[Ku2] M. Kunde, A general approach to sorting on 3-dimensionally mesh-connected arrays. CONPAR 86, Proceedings, LNCS 237, Springer, Berlin 1986, 329-337

[LSSS] H.-W. Lang, M. Schimmler, H. Schmeck and H. Schröder, Systolic sorting on a mesh-connected network, IEEE Trans. Comp., Vol. C-34, 652-658 (1985)

[NS] D. Nassimi and S. Sahni, Bitonic sort on a mesh-connected parallel computer, IEEE Trans. Comp., Vol. C-28, 2-7 (1979)

[S] M. Schimmler, Fast sorting on a three dimensional cube grid, Bericht 8604, Institut f. Informatik, University of Kiel, Germany, 1986

[SI] K. Sado and Z. Igarashi, A fast parallel pesudeo-merge sort algorithm, Technical Report, Gunma University, Japan, 1985

[SS] C.P. Schnorr, A. Shamir, An optimal sorting algorithm for mesh connected computers, STOC 1986, Proceedings

[TK] C.D. Thompson and H.T. Kung, Sorting on a mesh-connected parallel computer, CACM Vol. 20, 263-271 (1977)

[U] J.D. Ullmann, Computational aspects of VLSI, Computer Science Press, Rockville, 1984

On the contact-minimization-problem

(Extended Abstract)

Paul Molitor

Fachbereich 10, Universität des Saarlandes

D-6600 Saarbrücken, FRG

Abstract

The contact minimization problem is the problem of determining which layers should be used for wiring the signal nets of a circuit, such that the total number of layer changes (called contacts or via holes) is minimized. In this paper we show how to use a polynomial-time algorithm to find a maximum matching for a graph to solve the contact minimization problem for two layers. Furthermore we show that the contact minimization problem for n layers is NP-complete for all fixed $n \geq 3$.

1. Introduction

As improvements in VLSI-technology make it possible to put increasingly large numbers of components on a chip, it becomes important to be able to automate the design of integrated circuits. A leading feature of such VLSI-design systems is the placement and routing aspect, which consists of two phases: in the first phase, the planar wire "layout" is determined, i.e. which wires occupy which regions in the plane; in the second phase, each wire segment is assigned a layer ([BB]).

A special case of the **layer-assignment problem** is studied in [BB],[Li],...: Given a collection of edge-disjoint wires in a rectangular grid (knock-knee mode), decide on which layers each wire will run on condition that contacts (layer changes or via holes) are allowed only at grid points. Brady and Brown ([BB]) show that any wire layout can be wired in four layers. This result is optimal in the sense that it is NP-complete to determine whether a given wire layout is three-layer wirable ([Li]). Unfortunately the algorithm presented in [BB] does not minimize the total number of via holes. But, as the total number of via holes influences the performance of the circuit and its manufacturing costs, an important optimization goal of the layer assignment phase is to minimize the total number of contacts. This problem is called the **contact-minimization problem (CM-problem)**

The CM-problem is stated as follows: Given a circuit in the Euclidian plane, we want to assign layers to the segments of the signal nets such that the total number of layer changes is minimized.

The problem is called **topological**, if there is enough room to place a contact on any wire segment and **geometrical** if there are some wire segments on which there is not enough room to place a contact.

The literature published so far ([CK],[Ka],[Mo],[Pi],...) only studies the special case that there are only two layers available to embed the signal nets (**2-CM-problem**). This restriction is justified by technology: in order to avoid layers of different types (⇒ different performance), the signal nets are embedded into two metal layers.

In 1981 Ciesielski and Kinnen ([CK]) gave an exponential integer programming solution to the topological 2-CM-problem. In [Pi] the geometrical 2-CM-problem is reduced to the max-cut problem for planar graphs with arbitrary weights, which itself can be reduced to the minimum weight matching problem ([Ba]).

In this paper, we show how to reduce the geometrical 2-CM-problem to the minimum weight matching problem directly (without using the max-cut problem). The treatment presented here constitutes a better understanding of the problem than was obtained before and leads furthermore to the solution of the following problems. These problems were open until now.

- The solution of the contact minimization problem is global, i.e. by minimizing the total number of contacts it may happen that one signal net is burdened with an excessive number of contacts. In section 6 we show how to change our algorithm such that no signal net can be burdened too much. Notice, that by trying to minimize the maximum number of contacts on one signal net this may incur more contacts in the whole circuit.
- In the same manner we can change our algorithm such that there are signal nets (like power supply), on which contacts are placed only if no other solution exists.
- The topological **n-CM problem** is NP-complete for all fixed $n \geq 3$. The problem even remains NP-complete for signal nets having no vertex degree exceeding 4.

2. The n-CM-problem

In the following let $n \geq 2$ be a fixed natural number.

We represent the signal nets of a circuit by a planar undirected graph $G = (V, E)$, which is always possible if the crossovers are considered as vertices of the graph. Let $E_v := \{\{v, w\}; \{v, w\} \in E\}$ be the set of edges adjacent to vertex $v \in V$.

For any vertex $v \in V$ there exists a relation $x \sim_v y$ $(x, y \in E_v)$ expressing whether x and y have to be embedded into the same layer. Formally

$$x \sim_v y \iff x, y \text{ have to be assigned the same layer.}$$

A layer assignment of vertex v into n layers is described by a mapping $s_v : E_v \to [0 : n-1]$ expressing by $s_v(x) = i$ that edge x is (locally) embedded into layer i. Obviously s_v has to satisfy the condition:

$$(\forall x, y \in E_v)\ s_v(x) = s_v(y) \iff x \sim_v y.$$

Therefore such a mapping s_v only exists if E_v is partitioned (by the relation $\sim_v$) into m classes with $m \leq n$. Hence we assume that this supposition holds. It is easy to see that the relation $\sim_v$ does not determine s_v in an unique way: for any permutation $\pi : [0 : n-1] \to [0 : n-1]$, $s'_v = \pi \circ s_v$ is a layer assignment of v under condition that s_v is a layer assignment of v.

A **n-layer assignment of G with respect to** $\{\sim_v;\ v \in V\}$ is described by a set $s = \{s_v;\ v \in V\}$. Obviously it is possible that there is some edge $\{a,b\} \in E$ which is embedded into two different layers, i.e. $s_a(\{a,b\}) \neq s_b(\{a,b\})$. Such an edge is called **s-critical.** Let $c(s) := card\{e \in E;\ e \text{ is } s\text{-critical}\}$ be the amount of s-critical edges of G.

The **topological n-CM-problem** can now be formulated as follows:
Find a n-layer assignment s of G with respect to $\{\sim_v;\ v \in V\}$ *such that for any other n-layer assignment* s' *of G with respect to* $\{\sim_v;\ v \in V\}$: $c(s') \geq c(s)$.

Let $Y \subseteq E$ be the set of edges on which there is not enough room to place a contact, i.e. which must not be 'critical'.A n-layer assignment s of G with respect to $\{\sim_v;\ v \in V\}$ is called $(G,\sim,Y)$**-n-layer-assignment**, if each edge $e \in Y$ is not s-critical.

Then the **geometrical n-CM-problem** can be formulated as follows:
Find a $(G,\sim,Y)$*-n-layer-assignment s such that for any other* $(G,\sim,Y)$*-n-layer-assignment* s': $c(s') \geq c(s)$.

Remark 1

(1) It is obvious that the topological n-CM-problem is a special case of the geometrical n-CM-problem ($Y = \emptyset$).

(2) The restriction that a contact may only be placed onto an edge signifies that the contact minimization problem for 2 layers only handles internal three-way splits. (The reduction made in [Pi] only works under this restriction too.) It is an open problem how to handle four-way splits.

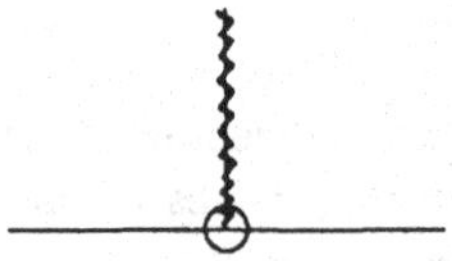

$\equiv$

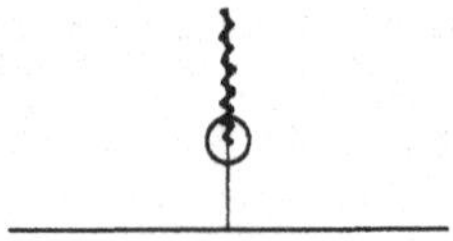

via hole placed on a three-way-split — via hole placed on the respective edge

In the case of more than two layers, this restriction is unimportant, as we show that the problem whether there exists a layer-assignment needing no contact is NP-complete.

3. Some theoretical results on the 2-CM-problem

Let $n = 2$, $\delta := \{\delta_v;\ v \in V\}$ a set of mappings $\delta_v : E_v \times E_v \to \{0,1\}$ defined by

$$\delta_v(x,y) = 0 \iff x \sim_v y.$$

Then the following lemma holds because of the supposition made in section 2 that for any vertex $v \in V$ the number m of classes of E_v defined by the relation $\sim_v$ is less or equal than the number of available layers.

Lemma 1

$(\forall v \in V)(\forall x, y, z \in E_v): \quad \delta_v(x,y) + \delta_v(y,z) = \delta_v(x,z) \; mod \; 2.$

Definition 1

$(e_0, v_1, e_1, v_2, e_2, \ldots, e_{m-1}, v_m, e_m)$ is called **path** of G, if
(1) $(\forall\, i \in \{0, \ldots, m\})\; e_i \in E$
(2) $(\forall\, j \in \{1, \ldots, m\})\; v_j \in V$
(3) $(\forall\, k \in \{1, \ldots, m-1\})\; e_k = \{v_k, v_{k+1}\}$
(4) $e_0 \in E_{v_1}$ and $e_m \in E_{v_m}$

Definition 2

Let $p = (e_0, v_1, e_1, \ldots, v_m, e_m)$ be a path.
- p is called **cycle**, if $e_0 = e_m$, $e_o = \{v_1, v_m\}$.
- p is called **simple**, if $v_i \neq v_j$ for $i \neq j$ and $(e_i = e_j \;\Rightarrow\; i = j$ or $i, j \in \{0, m\})$.

Definition 3

An edge $e \in E$ is called **bridge**, if there is no simple cycle containing e.

Example 1:

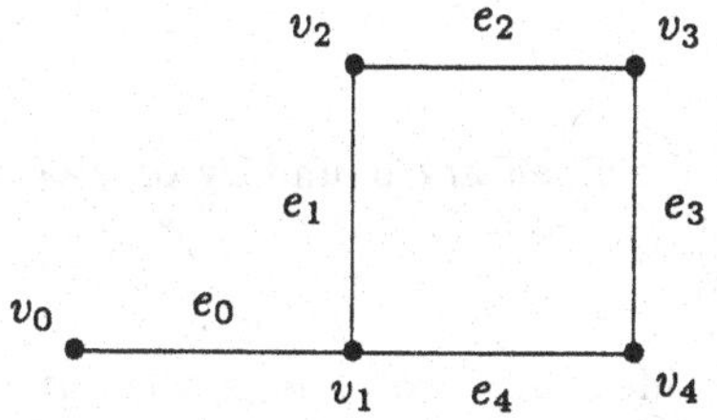

- e_0 is a bridge.
- $p = (e_1, v_2, e_2, v_3, e_3, v_4, e_4, v_1, e_1)$ is a simple cycle.
- $p' = (e_1, v_2, e_2, v_3, e_3, v_4, e_4, v_1, e_0, v_0, e_0, v_1, e_1)$ is not a simple cycle.

Lemma 2

If G is a finite graph without simple cycle, then there exists a $(G, \sim, Y)$-2-layer-assignment s such that $c(s) = 0$.

Proof:

As G is a forest with a finite number of vertices, the statement of lemma 2 follows by induction on the cardinality of V. ■■

Definition 4

A path $(e_0, v_1, e_1, \ldots, v_m, e_m)$ is called **even (odd)**, if $\sum_{i=1}^{m} \delta_{v_i}(e_{i-1}, e_i)$ is even (odd).

Lemma 3

Let $p = (e_0, v_1, e_1, \ldots, v_m, e_m)$ be a path of G, s a $(G, \sim, Y)$-2-layer-assignment with $c(s) = 0$. Then: $s_{v_1}(e_0) = s_{v_m}(e_m) \iff p$ is even.

(*Proof*: by induction on m.)

Corollary 1

There exists a $(G, \sim, Y)$-2-layer-assignment such that $c(s) = 0$ iff each cycle in G is even.

Proof:

"$\Rightarrow$" follows by lemma 3.

"$\Leftarrow$" (by induction on the cardinality k of E)

Let $G = (V, E)$ be a planar, finite graph with k edges.

If $k < 2$ then there is nothing to show.

If $k \geq 2$, an edge e is removed from G. If e is a bridge, it is obvious that the corollary is right. Otherwise the corollary follows because of lemma 3. ■■

Let $\chi(G)$ be an arbitrary planar embedding of G in the Euclidian plane. $\chi(G)$ divides the plane in **elementary regions**. To each elementary region belongs an **elementary boundary** $(e_0,\ v_1,\ e_1, \ldots, e_m,\ v_{m+1},\ e_0)$. Notice, that each elementary boundary is a cycle.

Remark 2

If G is biconnected, then each elementary boundary of $\chi(G)$ is simple.

Example 2

In example 1 the plane is divided into two regions, the outer face and the inner face. p is the elementary boundary of the inner face, p' the elementary boundary of the outer face.

Definition 5

An elementary region is called **even** (**odd**), if its elementary boundary is even (odd).

Corollary 2

There exists a $(G, \sim, Y)$-2-layer-assignment s such that $c(s) = 0$ iff each elementary region of $\chi(G)$ is even.

Sketch of the proof:

"$\Rightarrow$" follows by corollary 1.

"$\Leftarrow$" Claim: There is an odd cycle in G iff there is an odd cycle in a biconnected component of G.

Proof of claim:
We assume that there is an odd cycle C in G containing a bridge. Then we have the following situation:

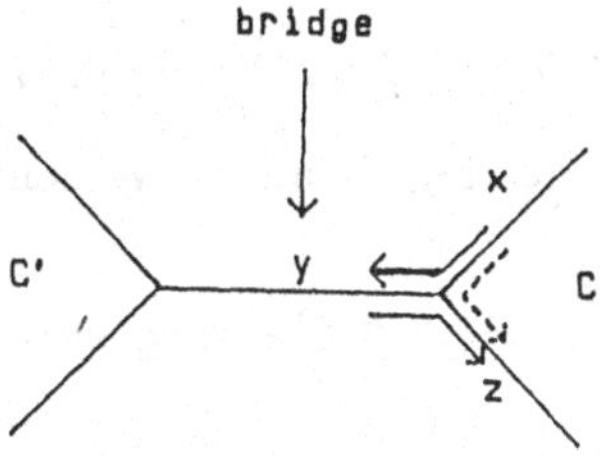

Because of lemma 1 it follows that $\delta_v(x,y) + \delta_v(y,z) = \delta_v(x,z)$ *mod* 2. Thus the whole cycle C is odd iff either cycle C' or C'' is odd. ■

By the above claim we can assume w.l.o.g. that G is biconnected. Thus each elementary boundary is simple. By lemma 1 it follows that each simple cycle is even (see the Theorem of MacLane ([ML]). It is obvious that each cycle is even if each simple cycle is even. Thus the statement follows by corollary 1. ■■

Let $R_{\chi(G)}$ be the set of the elementary regions of $\chi(G)$. Then the following lemma holds.

Lemma 4
$card(\{r \in R_{\chi(G)}; r \text{ is odd}\})$ is even.

In the next section we still need the two following definitions.

Definition 6
A multigraph $G_{(d)} = (V_{(d)}, E_{(d)})$ is called **dual graph of** $\chi(G)$ if
(1) $V_{(d)} = R_{\chi(G)}$
(2) For any edge $x \in E$ adjacent to the faces f_1, f_2 in $\chi(G)$, there exists an edge $e_x \in E_{(d)}$ with the endpoints $f_1, f_2 \in V_{(d)}$.
(3) $e_x = e_y \iff x = y$
Notice that $card(E_{(d)}) = card(E)$.

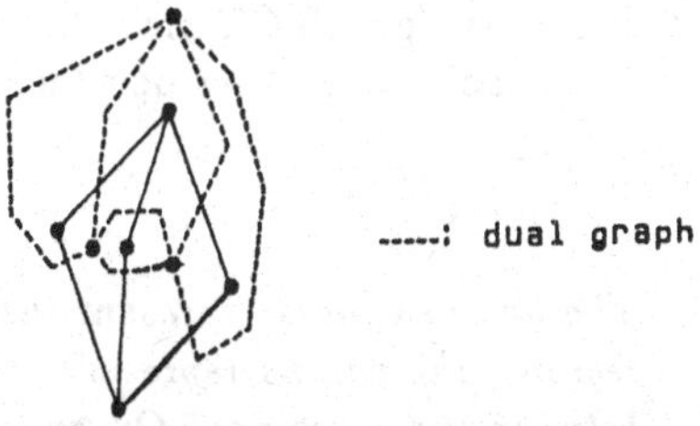

In the following let $Y_{(d)} = \{e_x;\ x \in Y\} \subseteq E_{(d)}$ for any subset $Y \subseteq E$.

Let $G_{(d)}$ be the dual graph of $\chi(G)$ and $G^Y_{(d)} = (V_{(d)}, E_{(d)} \setminus Y_{(d)})$. Then we define:

Definition 7

Let f, f' be two elementary regions of $\chi(G)$. The distance $d^Y_{\chi(G)}(f, f')$ is the length of the minimum length path connecting f and f' in the graph $G^Y_{(d)}$.

If there does not exist a path connecting f and f', we define $d^Y_{\chi(G)}(f, f') = +\infty$.

4. An algorithm for the topological 2-CM-problem

In order to guarantee a $(G, \sim, \emptyset)$-2-layer-assignment s such that $c(s) = 0$, it is obvious that one has to transform odd elementary regions into even ones by inserting vias, i.e. by substituting some edge $\{a, b\} \in E$ by edges $\{a, x_{\{a,b\}}\}$ and $\{x_{\{a,b\}}, b\}$ $(x_{\{a,b\}} \notin V)$, where $\{a, x_{\{a,b\}}\} \not\sim_{x_{\{a,b\}}} \{x_{\{a,b\}}, b\}$.

Example 3

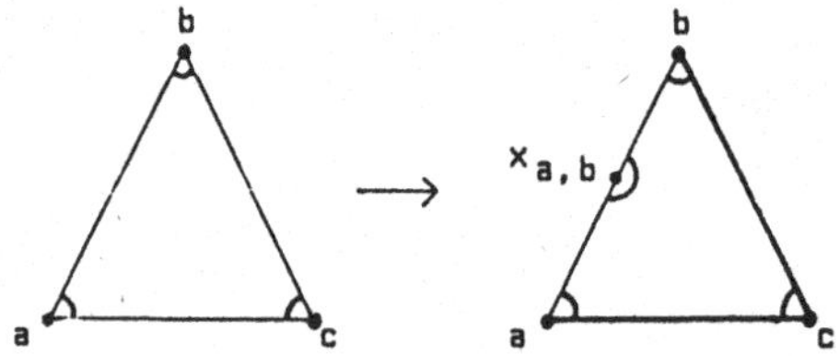

(There is an arc between two adjacent edges $x, y \in E_v$ $(v \in V)$, iff $x \not\sim_v y$)

It is clear that if s is a $(G, \sim, \emptyset)$-2-layer-assignment ,then we can transform G into a graph G' by inserting $c(s)$ contacts, such that there exists a $(G', \sim, \emptyset)$-2-layer-assignment s' with $c(s') = 0$.

Remark 3

Let $\chi(e)$ be an edge of $\chi(G)$, such that e is not a bridge. Then there exists exactly two faces f_1,f_2 adjacent to $\chi(e)$. By placing a contact onto $\chi(e)$, the faces f_1, f_2 change their states: if f_i $(i = 1, 2)$ is even (odd), then it becomes odd (even).

Therefore in order to transform a graph G into a graph G', such that any face of G' is even, one has to 'connect' any odd face of G to exactly one other odd face of G.

Example 4:

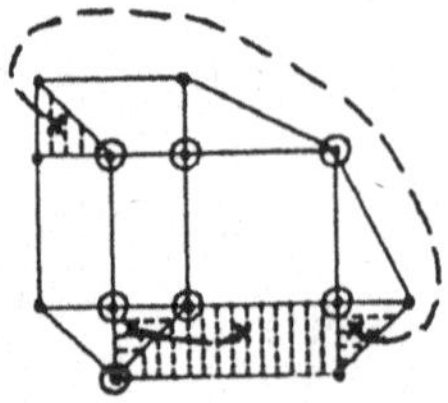

The hatched faces represent the odd elementary regions, the chains represent the 'connections' between these regions. On any edge, which is crossed by such a chain, a contact will be placed.

Let $O_{\chi(G)}$ be the set of the odd elementary regions of $\chi(G)$. The problem of finding an optimal $(G, \sim, \emptyset)$-2-layer-assignment is solved by the following algorithm (see also corollary 1):

(1) Partition the set $O_{\chi(G)}$ into sets $O_1, \ldots, O_k$, such that (a) and (b) holds
(a) $(\forall i \in \{1, \ldots, k\})$ $card(O_i) = 2$
(b) $\sum_{i=1}^{k} d_{\chi(G)}(f_i, f_i')$ is minimal with respect to condition (a). $(O_i = \{f_i, f_i'\})$.

(2) If $O_i = \{f_i, f_i'\}$, then find the respective path p of length $d^{\emptyset}_{\chi(G)}(f_i, f_i')$ connecting f_i and f_i'. Place on the respective edges of G via holes.

<u>*Remark 4*</u>
The total number of contacts placed by the algorithm does <u>not</u> depend on the special embedding $\chi(G)$.

Obviously (2) can be solved in $O(|V|^2)$.

The partitioning problem of (1) can be formulated as follows

Let $G" = (O_{\chi(G)}, E", \omega)$ be a weighted complete graph, where
(a) $O_{\chi(G)}$ represents the set of vertices.
(b) $E" = \{\{a, b\}; a \neq b\} \subset O_{\chi(G)} \times O_{\chi(G)}$ represents the set of edges.
(c) $\omega : E" \rightarrow \mathbf{N_0}$ is a mapping defined by $\omega(\{a, b\}) = d^{\emptyset}_{\chi(G)}(a, b)$, which represents the weights of the edges.

Find $E_1 \subseteq E"$ such that E_1 is a minimum weight matching in G''.

<u>*Remark 5*</u>
The minimum weight matching problem can be solved in $O(|V|^3)$ ([Ga]).

5. An algorithm for the geometrical 2-CM-problem

If there exists a solution to the geometrical 2-CM-problem, we only have to apply the algorithm presented in chapter 4 to find an optimal solution by replacing $d^{\emptyset}_{\chi(G)}$ by $d^{Y}_{\chi(G)}$ (see definition 7).

In linear time we can tell whether there exists a solution: If the problem turns out to be non-solvable, we can find a connected component of $G^{Y}_{(d)}$ which contains an odd number of vertices of $O_{\chi(G)}$.

6. Extension

It is possible to alter the algorithm to the case that there are signal nets, for instance signal nets for power supply, on which via holes are placed only if no other solution exists:

Let $Z \subseteq E$ be the edges on which contacts are undesired ($Z \cap Y = \emptyset$). We associate with any edge $e \in E$ a weight $\lambda(e)$:

$$\lambda(e) = \begin{cases} 1 & \text{, if } e \notin Z \\ m & \text{, if } e \in Z \quad (m \geq 1) \end{cases}$$

Then the distance $d^{Y,Z}_{X(G)}(f, f')$ is defined as the minimum weight path connecting f and f'. It is obvious that the algorithm proposed in section 4 computes an optimal solution to our problem with respect to m, by substituting in the algorithm $d^{Y}_{X(G)}$ by $d^{Y,Z}_{X(G)}$.

In the same manner we can prevent that some signal net is burdened by an excessive number of contacts by giving large weights to the great signal nets and smaller weights to the little signal nets.

It is clear that by applying the proposed extensions we may incur more contacts in the whole circuit.

7. The n-CM-problem is NP-complete

First we investigate the following problem for all fixed $n \geq 3$:

Instance: Undirected planar graph $G = (V, E)$ and relations $\sim$.
Question: Does there exist a $(G, \sim, \emptyset)$-n-layer-assignment s such that $c(s) = 0$.

We call the above problem the **zero-contact problem for n layers.**

Theorem 1
The zero-contact problem for 3 layers is NP-complete.

Proof: (Transformation from Graph-3-Colorability ([GJ]))
Claim 1: The problem whether there exists a function $f : V \rightarrow \{0, 1, 2\}$ such that $f(u) \neq f(v)$ whenever $\{u, v\} \in E$ is NP-complete for planar graphs $G = (V, E)$.

(*Proof of Claim 1*: see ([GJ] pp.191).) ■

Let $G = (V, E)$ be a planar graph. We transform G into a graph $G' = (V', E')$ by substituting each edge $\{a, b\} \in E$ by two edges $\{a, x_{\{a,b\}}\}$ and $\{x_{\{a,b\}}, b\}$ ($x_{\{a,b\}} \notin V$)

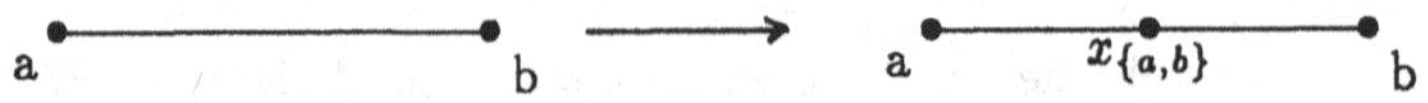

We define $\sim_v$ for all $v \in V'$ as follows:

$$x \sim_v y \iff v \in V \text{ or } x = y$$

Claim 2: There exists a $(G', \sim, \emptyset)$-3-layer-assignment s with $c(s) = 0$ iff there exists a mapping $f : V \rightarrow \{0, 1, 2\}$ such that $f(u) \neq f(v)$ whenever $\{u, v\} \in E$.

Proof of Claim 2:

"$\Leftarrow$" For all $v \in V$ we define s by $s_v(x) = f(v)$ $(\forall x \in E'_v)$ and for all $x_{\{a,b\}} \in V' \setminus V$ by $s_{x_{\{a,b\}}}(\{a, x_{\{a,b\}}\}) = f(a)$ and $s_{x_{\{a,b\}}}(\{x_{\{a,b\}}, b\}) = f(b)$.

By construction it follows that s is a $(G', \sim, \emptyset)$-3-layer-assignment without s-critical edge.

"$\Rightarrow$" Because of the above definition of $\sim$, $s_v(x) = s_v(y)$ $(\forall v \in V)(\forall x, y \in E'_v)$.

We define $f : V \rightarrow \{0, 1, 2\}$ by $f(v) = s_v(x)$ for some edge $x \in E'_v$.

By construction it follows that $f(u) \neq f(v)$ whenever $\{u, v\} \in E$ ■

Because of Claim 2 the theorem follows. ■■

Corollary 3

The topological 3-CM-problem is NP-complete.

Corollary 4

Because of the NP-completeness of the Graph-3-Colorability problem for planar graphs having no vertex degree exceeding 4 ([GJ]), the 3-CM-problem remains NP-complete, if we only consider planar graphs having no vertex degree exceeding 4.

Theorem 2

The zero-contact problem for n layers is NP-complete for all fixed $n \geq 3$.

Proof: (by induction on n)

$n = 3$ see proof of theorem 1.

$n \geq 4$ Let $G = (V, E)$ be an undirected planar graph, let $\sim = \{\sim_v;\ v \in V\}$ be a set of relations as described in section 2.

We transform G into a graph $\overline{G} = (\overline{V}, \overline{E})$ by inserting for all adjacent vertices a, b a new vertex $v_{a,b}$ and edges $\{a, v_{a,b}\}$, $\{v_{a,b}, b\}$.

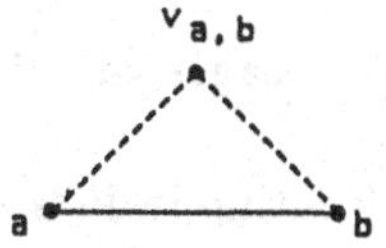

We define for all $v \in \overline{V}$ and for all $x, y \in \overline{E}_v$:

$$x \overline{\sim}_v y \iff (x, y \in E \text{ and } x \sim_v y) \text{ or } x, y \in \overline{E} \setminus E.$$

Let $\overline{\sim} = \{\overline{\sim}_v;\ v \in \overline{V}\}$ be the corresponding set of relations. Then it follows:

There exists a $(G, \sim, \emptyset)$-(n-1)-layer-assignment s with $c(s) = 0$ iff there exists a $(\overline{G}, , \overline{\sim}, \emptyset)$-n-layer-assignment $\overline{s}$ with $c(\overline{s}) = 0$. ■■

Corollary 5

The topological n-CM-problem is NP-complete for all fixed $n \geq 3$.

Corollary 6

The topological n-CM-problem remains NP-complete ($\forall n \geq 3$) for planar graphs having no vertex degree exceeding 4.

Proof:

Instead of inserting for all adjacent vertices a,b a new vertex $v_{a,b}$ and edges $\{a, v_{a,b}\}$, $\{v_{a,b}, b\}$ which blocks one layer (see proof of theorem 2), we insert the following signal net which also blocks one layer:

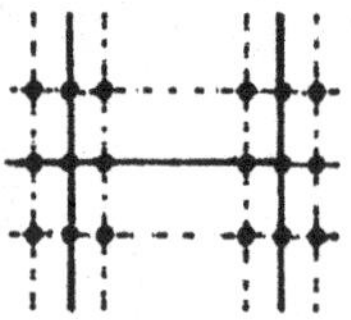

∎

8. Acknowledgement

I would like to thank Dr. Bernd Becker, Jean Paul Bertrand, Ursula Fissgus, Prof. Dr. Günter Hotz, Reiner Kolla and Dr. Hans-Ulrich Simon for their comments and suggestions.

9. References

[Ba] F. Barahona:
"Sur la complexité du problème du verre de spins"
Rapport de Recherche 171, Octobre 1979, Université Scientifique Et Medicale et Institut National Polytechnique de Grenoble, Mathematiques Appliquées et Informatique.

[BB] M. Brady, D. Brown:
"VLSI Routing: Four Layers Suffice"
Advances in Computing Research, vol. 2 pages 245-257, JAI Press Inc London.

[CK] M. Ciesielski, E.Kinnen:
"An Optimum Layer Assignment for Routing in IC's and PCB's"
Proceedings of the 18th Design Automation Conference, June 1981, pp. 733-737.

[Ga] H. Gabow:
"Implementation of Algorithms for Maximum Matching on Non-Bipartite Graphs"
Ph.D. Dissertation, Stanford University 1973.

[GJ] M. Garey, D. Johnson:
"Computers and Intractability: A Guide to the Theory of NP-completeness"
W.H.Freeman & co., San Francisco, 1979

[Ka] Y. Kajitani:
"On Via Hole Minimization of Routing on a 2-layer Board"
Proceedings of the ICCC 1980, pp.295-298

[Li] W.Lipski:
"An NP-complete problem related to three layer channel routing"
Manuscript, Institute of Computer Science, PAS, Warsaw, Poland 1982.

[ML] S.MacLane:
"A combinatorial condition for planar graphs"
Fundamenta Math. 28, 22-32 (1937)

[Mo] P.Molitor:
"Layer Assignment by Simulated Annealing"
North-Holland, Microprocessing and Microprogramming 16 (1985), pp.345-350

[Pi] R.Y.Pinter:
"Optimal Layer Assignment for Interconnect"
Proceedings of the ICCC 1982, pp.398-401

MAKING DISTRIBUTED SPANNING TREE ALGORITHMS FAULT-RESILIENT

(Extended Abstract)

Reuven Bar-Yehuda, Shay Kutten,
Yaron Wolfstahl and Shmuel Zaks[1]
Department of Computer Science, Technion, Haifa, Israel.

ABSTRACT

We study distributed algorithms for networks with undetectable fail-stop failures, assuming that all of them had occurred before the execution started. (It was proved that distributed agreement cannot be reached when a node may fail during execution.) Failures of this type are encountered, for example, during a recovery from a crash in the network. We study the problems of leader election and spanning tree construction, that have been characterized as fundamental for this environment. We point out that in presence of faults just duplicating messages in an existing algorithm does not suffice to make it resilient; actually, this redundancy gives rise to synchronization problems and also might increase the message complexity. In this paper we investigate the problem of making existing spanning tree algorithms fault-resilient, and still overcome these difficulties. Several lower bounds and optimal fault-resilient algorithms are presented for the first time. However, we believe that the main contribution of the paper is twofold: First, in designing the algorithms we use tools that thus argued to be rather general (for example, we extend the notion of token algorithms to multiple-token algorithms). In fact we are able to use them on several different algorithms, for several different families of networks. Second, following the amortized computational complexity, we introduce amortized message complexity as a tool for analyzing the message complexity.

1. INTRODUCTION

The design of algorithms for distributed networks plays an important role in the study of distributed computing; particularly, a lot of research has been recently performed in models that assume certain faults in the networks. This study suggests a systematic design of fault-tolerant distributed algorithms for the basic problem of spanning tree construction, with the hope that extensions for general problems will follow.

1.1 Preliminaries

The basic model consists of a distributed network of n identical processors, except their distinct identities, k of which start the algorithm, and m bidirectional communication links connecting pairs of processors. The network is asynchronous (the time to transmit a message is unpredictable). The processors all perform the same algorithm, that includes operations of (1) sending a message over a link, (2) receiving a message from a pool of unserviced messages which arrived over links, and (3) processing information locally. Any subset of the processors may start the algorithm. No information is known to any processor, except for the information we explicitly

[1] The work of this author was supported in part by a Technion grant no. 121-641.

assume it has (e.g. that a node knows its own identity). We view the communication network as an undirected graph, where nodes represent processors and edges represent communication links. To measure the efficiency of an algorithm, we use the common measure of the maximal possible number of messages transmitted during any execution, where each message contains at most $O(\log MaxId)$ bits (see e.g. [GHS83]).

In the *leader election* problem (e.g. [GHS83]) it is required that the nodes co-operate to distinguish one of them. Electing a leader, and the related spanning tree construction problem, are fundamental in many distributed algorithms, and have been studied for various models and cost measurements in reliable networks. *Termination detection* applies to a given distributed algorithm; it is required that some node will know that this algorithm has already computed its output, even though this output is distributed among the nodes. This problem is a generalization of the termination detection problem, which was also thoroughly investigated in reliable networks (e.g. [F80]).

Real systems, however, are not reliable. They are subject to faults of different types.

Consider the possibility that some edges or nodes in the network may be faulty. A faulty edge is an edge, every message which is transmitted over which, in either direction, is lost. A faulty node is a node all of its incident edges are faulty. Because our basic model is asynchronous, it cannot be distinguished whether a message is delayed or lost.

For the case where nodes can fail *during* the execution of an algorithm it was proved that no protocol for reaching distributed agreement (hence election) can be devised [FLP85]. Other types of faults are also hard or impossible to cope with [F83]. However, the presence of faults was pointed out as a motivation for leader election (as a method to reorganize the network) [G82]. (It was also pointed out there, that it is suffucient to deal with limited types of faults, since reliable hardware equipment makes failures of the more general type quite rare [G82].) We assume that no failure occurs during the execution of the algorithm.

Even with these assumptions about faults, it can be shown that no fault-tolerant leader-election algorithm can guarantee termination. Thus additional assumptions are needed. This includes, for example, knowledge about synchrony in the network ([G82]), its topology ([KW84,SG85]), or its size ([SG85]). Alternatively we can omit the requirement for termination detection and do with a spanning tree construction (rather than leader election).

We develop in this paper some new fault-resilient algorithms. However, our main contributions are the tools we use: First, we believe that our techniques to make existing algorithms fault resilient are rather general. In fact we are able to use them on several different algorithms, for several different families of networks. The applicability of our method to some other algorithms is straightforward (e.g. applying it to the algorithm of [HS80] for cycles will yield an algorithm which is resilient to many faults.) Second, we introduce a method we have found useful in analyzing the complexity of such algorithms.

1.2 Our Assumptions and Results

In spanning tree construction algorithms, trees are merged to eventually span the whole network. Every tree has a unique *center of activity*, which is a node, or a token, that decides on the tree expansion or merging. This method seems essential to prevent contradicting decisions (like two trees merging via two edges and creating a cycle). This center always tries to expand the tree in exactly one direction, both in order to ensure correctness and to save messages. From the correctness point of view it seems that expanding in more than one direction can either create a cycle or cause two trees to be deadlocked (waiting for each other's response). From the complexity point of view it seems that if actions corresponding to the two directions do contradict, at least one of them has caused redundant work.

In the presence of undetectable faults the above "One-expanssion-direction" approach can cause the algorithm to be deadlocked, waiting for an answer from a faulty node, or over a faulty edge. If expansion, however, is tried only over an edge which has been proved to be non-faulty, high complexity can be caused, since it may happen that the next edge to be proved non-faulty is always far from the center of activity.

In our algorithms we use more than one token in a tree. Most decisions are done locally (without consulting the center), and contradicting actions are prevented by the following method: each token acts according to the global information it has about the state of the tree. Thus the center must be consulted only when this information does not suffice to make the decision. This information is a lower bound on a certain value that represents the status of the tree (and remains true even when the exact value is updated); this value may be the size of the tree (Section 2), its phase (Section 3.1) or some criterion to know which of the new non-faulty edges were already reported to the center (Section 3.2).

Using this method we also show that the complexity of a resilient algorithm is not always higher (in order of magnitude) than the complexity of a non-resilient algorithm for the same problem, even though duplicating messages is used.

A t-resilient algorithm is an algorithm that yields the correct answer when at most t processors are faulty. We first derive an $\Omega(n \log k + k\, t)$ lower bound for the message complexity of any t-resilient election algorithm in complete networks, and show how to modify an existing election algorithm ([H84]) to achieve a t-resilient election algorithm (for any $t < \frac{n}{2}$) the complexity of which matches the lower bound. It also improves on existing resilient algorithms in terms of message, bit, space and computational complexity measures. Note that when t is $O(\log k)$ the message complexity is the same as for reliable networks. On the other hand, for a larger t the message complexity must be higher than that for reliable networks (where it is $O(n \log k)$ [KMZ84]). We also consider the cases where edges may fail and where every node's identity is known to its neighbors. In order to analyse the message complexity of the algorithm we introduce the notion of *amortized* message complexity, derived from that of *amortized* computational complexity in [FT84]. It is suggested that this technique may prove useful in analyzing the complexity of distributed algorithms in similar situations. This is done in section 2.

Next we present (in section 3.1) an optimal resilient spanning tree construction algorithm for general graphs. For this we modify the non-resilient algorithm of [KKM85].

As explained above, the termination cannot be detected in this model without additional knowledge. We therefore add (in section 3.2) the assumption that n is known, with which termination can be detected by the above algorithm, but with a higher message complexity. We then modify another non-resilient algorithm ([G]) and get a resilient version of it, improving the message complexity of the termination detection. In a complete network the message complexity of this algorithm is also optimal. As exemplified by this algorithm, termination detection in this model is a different (generalized) problem than the thoroughly investigated termination detection problem in reliable networks, and needs different solutions.

In [G82, M84] election in unreliable networks is investigated for the synchronous case, while we investigate the asynchronous case. Fault-resilient consensus in the presence of partial synchrony is discussed in

[DLS84]. An $\lceil n/2 \rceil - 1$-resilient consensus algorithm for a complete network is presented in [FLP85]. $O(n^2)$ messages are sent in any execution of this algorithm; however, since most messages contain $O(n \log MAX\_ID)$ bits, the bit complexity is $O(n^3 \log MAX\_ID)$ and the message complexity, in terms of our model, is $O(n^3)$ (our result implies an $O(n^2)$ algorithm for this case).

A (rather complicated) 1-resilient election algorithm for complete networks is presented in [KW84]. A method to generalize it for a larger t is hinted, but for $t = \lceil \frac{n}{2} \rceil - 1$ the message complexity of a generalized algorithm would be $O((t \log t)(n \log n)) = O(n^2 \log^2 n)$. An $\Omega(n \log n)$ and $O(n \log n)$ lower and upper bounds for 1-resilient election in a ring are found in [SG85].

2. RESILIENT ALGORITHMS IN COMPLETE NETWORKS

2.1 Informal description of the t-resilient algorithm

Here we assume that the communication graph is complete, and only nodes may fail. In [KWZ86] we show that in the case where also edges may fail similar results hold. We modify the simple algorithm of [H84] (which is similar to that of [AG85a]) that elects a leader in a non-faulty complete network. In this algorithm some nodes are candidates for leadership, called *kings*. Each king tries to *annex* other nodes to its *domain* (initially containing only itself). An annexed king ceases to be a king, and stops trying to annex other nodes, but those already annexed by it remain in its own domain. The *size* of a node is the size of its domain, which is initially zero, becomes 1 when the node wakes up spontaneously, and may only grow. The size and identity of node A are denoted by *size(A)* and *id(A)*, respectively. A node may belong to several domains, but it remembers the edge leading to its *master*, that is the last node by which it was annexed (a node that has not been annexed by another node is considered its own master). Each king owns one *token*, which is a process representing it, and carrying its size and identity, as well as an additional message, which is one of the following:

a. an ASK message, originated by the node that owns the token.

b. an ACCEPT message, originated by a node that was annexed by the token.

In order to annex a neighbor B, king A sends its token to visit B (with an ASK message). The token proceeds from node B to B's master C (may be B itself). The next actions taken by the token depend on *(size(A), id(A))* and the information it finds in C and B, as follows:

Case 1. *((size(A), id(A)) > (size(C), id(C))* [2]:

Node C ceases to be a king [3], but does not join A's domain. The token returns to node B. If by now any token of another node D has passed B and *(size(D), id(D)) > (size(A), id(A))*, then the token (of A) is killed. Otherwise, B joins A's domain, and the token returns to A (with an ACCEPT message), and *size(A)* is incremented (by 1).

Case 2. *((size(A), id(A)) < (size(C), id(C))*:

The token is killed.

A token that returns safely repeats the process of attempting to annex a new neighbor. The algorithm terminates when one node A has *size(A) = n*.

---

[2] Lexicographically, namely $size(A) > size(C)$ or $size(A) = size(C)$ and $id(A) > id(C)$.

[3] Note that that a node may "cease to be a king" more than once; we use this convention throughout the paper.

In our t-resilient version each king owns $t+1$ tokens that are initially sent to different neighbors. In addition to the types of messages used above, there is a third type:

c. a REJECT message, originated by a node that refused to be annexed by the token. The actions taken by a token of node A that arrives at a master C of a neighbor B of A, depend on *(size(A), id(A))* and the information it finds in C and B, as follows:

Case 1. *((size(A), id(A)) > (size(C), id(C))*:

Node C ceases to be a king, (but does not join A's domain). The token returns to node B, and proceeds according to the following:

Case 1.1. A token of node D has meanwhile passed B and *(size(D), id(D)) > (size(A), id(A))*:

Node A's token is not killed, but returns to A (with a REJECT message), carrying *size(D)* and *id(D)*. *size(A)* may have increased while waiting for this token to return. If *(size(A), id(A))* is still smaller than *(size(D), id(D))* (note that for *size(D)* we use the lower bound carried in the token), then node A ceases to be a king (without joining any other domain). We term this REJECT message a *relevant* REJECT. Otherwise *(size(A), id(A)) > (size(D), id(D))* and we say that this REJECT message is *irrelevant*. Node A now starts a *war* with C (unless it is currently involved in another war). Any of A's tokens returning during a war are not sent again until the war is over (we term these tokens *suspended*). In the war A sends again the token to B (with an ASK message). The war with C continues until the token returns from B to A with an ACCEPT message, or until A loses (as a result of a relevant REJECT message or a leader announcement message). During this war, king A's token may return several times from B with irrelevant REJECT messages, in which case it will be sent back to B (with the updated size of A). If A wins it increments *size(A)* and all the currently suspended tokens are sent over unused edges, unless one of them is an irrelevant REJECT message, in which case another war starts.

Case 1.2. No token of another node D, such that *(size(D), id(D)) > (size(A), id(A))*, has passed B:

B joins A's domain, the token returns to A (with an ACCEPT message), and *size(A)* is incremented.

Case 2. *((size(A), id(A)) < (size(C), id(C))*

The token returns to node B and then to A (with a REJECT message), carrying *size(C)* and *id(C)*, and proceeds according to the following:

Case 2.1. *(size(A), id(A)) < (size(C), id(C))* (using the lower bound for *size(C)* carried in the token):

Node A ceases to be a king (without joining any other domain).

Case 2.2. *(size(A), id(A)) > (size(C), id(C))* (as carried in the REJECT message; this REJECT message is also called *irrelevant*):

Node A starts a war with B as in Case 1.1.

A token that returned safely repeats the process of attempting to annex a new neighbor. When a node A has *size(A)* $> \frac{n}{2}$, it announces its leadership, and the algorithm terminates.

2.2 Correctness and complexity analysis

In [KWZ86] we prove the correctness:

Theorem 1: In every execution of the t-resilient algorithm in a network with no more than t faulty processors, exactly one node declares itself a leader.

For the complexity analysis we define the *amortized message complexity* as the actual message complexity plus the *potentials* of the nodes, which are non-negative integers (defined in the sequel). Thus the amortized message complexity is an upper bound for the message complexity. In some events during execution the amortized message complexity does not change, although the actual one increases. This is because other components of the amortized message complexity decrease. Thus the amortized message complexity is a useful tool when we want to have an upper bound on the number of messages sent, even though the number in each case is not known. (This makes the method especially attractive when dealing with distributed algorithms, and especially in the presence of faults. In this environment the "uncertainty" is especially high.)

We use the following notations denoting values up to (and including) the τ-th reception event in a node A (including its treatment and the messages sent as a result), for a particular execution of the algorithm.

(1) $\#send(A,\tau)$ denotes the number of times a token has been sent by KING A. This is A's part in the actual message complexity of a prefix of that execution of the algorithm.

(2) $\#wars(A,\tau)$ is the number of wars in which A was involved.

(3) $\#susp(A,\tau)$ is the total number of times a token was suspended in A.

(4) $\#held(A,\tau)$ is the total number of currently suspended tokens.

(5) $\#inc(A,\tau)$ is the increment in the size of A since the beginning of the current war, if such exists.

(6) $\#IRR(A,\tau)$ is the number of irrelevant REJECT messages received by A from B (the node with which it is currently involved in a war, if such exists) since the beginning of the current war.

(7) $SIZE(A,\tau)$ is the size of A's domain.

(8) The $potential(A,\tau)$ of A is $\#held+(SIZE-\#wars)+(SIZE-\#susp)+(\#inc-\#IRR)$

(we omit the (A,τ) notation in all terms).

Lemma 1: Let A be any node that initiated the algorithm and is still a KING after its τ-th reception in a particular execution. Then

$$3SIZE+t+1 > \#send+potential \qquad (*)$$

Sketch of Proof: First we note that the following is clear from the definition:

$$\#inc-\#IRR \geq 0 \qquad (**)$$

We continue by induction on τ.

Induction Basis: On initiating the algorithm, node A sends $t+1$ tokens. By that time:

$3SIZE+t+1=4+t>(t+1)+0+1+1+0-0=\#send+\#held+(SIZE-\#wars)+(SIZE-\#susp)+(\#inc-\#IRR)$

and (*) holds.

Inductive Step: Assuming (*) holds after the τ-th reception, we show that it holds after the $\tau+1$st reception. From the formal description of the algorithm we have to consider seven cases, only three of which are discussed here:

Case 1: A token that successfully accomplished a capture (i.e. a token with an ACCEPT) is received and A is not involved in a war. The token is sent for another capture attempt, both $SIZE$ and $\#send$ are incremented (by 1), so (*) holds.

Case 2: A token with an ACCEPT message is received while A is involved in a war. The token is suspended,

SIZE ,*#susp* , *#held* and *#inc* are incremented and (*) holds.

Case 3: A token has returned with an ACCEPT from some processor with which A is in a war. If no other REJECTs are suspended then *SIZE* is incremented and all suspended tokens are now sent on unused edges. For each token sent, *#send* is incremented and *#held* is decremented. Also, *#inc–#IRR* $=0$, so by (**) the right-hand side does not increase.

Corollary 1: The total number of ASK messages sent by a processor is bounded by $3 \cdot s+t$, where s is the final size of the processor.

Now that we have bounded the number of tokens a KING sends, by the KING's final size, we can use a technique similar to the one used in e.g. [AG85a, G, H84], using the following lemma:

Lemma 2: If there are $l-1$ KINGs whose final size is larger than that of KING A, then the latter is bounded by n/l.

The message complexity can now be computed:

Theorem 2: The number of messages used by the algorithm is $O(n \log k + k\, t)$.

Sketch of Proof: Let s be a final size of a KING that has initiated the algorithm. By Corollary, 1 the number of times this KING has sent a token with an ASK message does not exceed $3 \cdot s + t$. Each time the token used at most 4 messages (2 to arrive at the neighbor's master and 2 to come back). The final size of the nodes that were never awakened by the high-level protocol is one. Other $n-1$ messages are needed for the LEADER announcement. Thus by Lemma 2 the total number of messages is bounded from above by $pn-1+4(3n\,(1+1/2+1/3+...+1/k)+k\,t)=O(n \log k + k\,t)$.

The following theorem implies that our algorithm is optimal:

Theorem 3: The message complexity of election in complete networks containing at most t faulty processors is at least $\Omega(n \log k + k\, t)$.

The proof of Theorem 3 appears in [KWZ86]. For the case where every node knows its neighbors' identities, a variation of the above proofs can be used to prove (see [KWZ86]):

Theorem 4: The message complexity of election in complete networks containing at most t faulty processors where every node's identity is known to the node's neighbors is $\Theta(k\, t)$.

3. RESILIENT ALGORITHMS IN GENERAL NETWORKS

3.1 Constructing a spanning tree in general networks

We make the algorithm of [KKM85] resilient and optimal. As in the case of complete networks, the idea is to make decisions (as long as possible) using information which may not be up-to-date. Here this policy leads to enabling many nodes of a tree to locally decide in parallel, to add neighbors to the tree. Thus a tree may annex new leaves, while other nodes of that tree (even the root) are being captured by other trees. We give here a brief description of the algorithm. (This problem was independently investigated in [AG85b]. Another algorithm for this problem was lately announced [AS86].)

First we explain the basic principle of the algorithm. Initially every node sends *test* messages over all its edges. Thus if an edge is not faulty, its endpoints will eventually know it, and mark the edge *non-faulty*. Each edge may receive the following marks in each of its endpoints (or in both): *non-faulty, tree-edge-to-father, tree-edge-to-son,* and *deleted.* Initially no edge is marked. Every node is a part of a rooted tree, initially containing only itself. Each tree has an associated value called *generation* (or *phase*), initially 0, and is set to 1 if its root node spontaneously starts the algorithm.

Each tree has also a single *main* token which usually resides in the root. Main tokens of trees are used to create new trees in such a way that the creation of a new tree (main token) in generation $g+1$, involves the destruction of at least two main tokens in generation g. We defer the explanation of the exact method by which such a new main token is created. For now it suffices to note that since each tree has only one main token, the number of trees in generation $g+1$ is at most half the number of trees in generation g.

Each node in a tree generates a *local* token, whose task is to annex the node's neighbors to the node's current tree. Several local tokens of a tree T may simultaneously annex nodes to the tree (in a method to be explained). At the same time, local tokens of other trees may annex nodes of T to the other trees. Each local token always carries the correct tree's generation, and root, since both values never change (as long as the node doesn't join another tree). The tree information that the local token may not have is the answer to the question "does the main token still exist?" For example it may happen that the root has been annexed by a tree in a higher generation, and the main token has thus been destroyed in the root. Thus the local token must consult the tree root only when the local token arrives at a node that belongs to another tree of the same generation. In this case the local token must consult the tree root, since the main tokens of the two trees may be used to create a tree in a higher generation.

We now outline the algorithm. A more detailed description appears in [K86].

The main token of each tree waits in the tree root until it is awakened by a local token of the same tree. The local token generated by a node, v, tries to annex v's neighbors to v's current tree. To annex a neighbor, the local token travels to the neighbor, carrying the generation of v's tree, and the identity of its root. If the generation of the neighbor's tree is lower, then it is annexed as v's son. If the generation of the neighbor's tree is higher, then v's local token is destroyed. If the generations are equal (and the neighbor belongs to another tree) then a meeting must be arranged between the main tokens of the two trees. The local token arranges that meeting only if the *id* of its root is higher than the *id* of the other tree's root. (Otherwise the arrangement is the "responsibility" of the other tree.) To arrange the meeting it goes to its tree root and wakes the main token. The main token then travels to the root of the other tree. If it arrives and finds the other main token, then the two main tokens are destroyed, and a main token of a higher generation is created. The tree of the new main token first contains only one node- the root of the second mentioned tree. A local token is also generated at that node, and the new tree starts to grow as described above. Some time must pass until all the nodes of the two trees of the lower generation are captured by trees of higher generations (not necessarily this new tree). Each of the two old trees may still exist, and even grow. Eventually, only one tree remains in every connected component.

Some care must be taken in implementing the algorithm, to limit its message complexity, and still not violate its correctness. When a local token arrives at a node which was annexed by another local token of the same tree, it "deletes" that edge from the graph. (It is shown in [K86] that such an edge is not needed to maintain the connectivity.) Also, a local token is destroyed when it finds that another token of the same generation (or a higher generation) has preceded it on the way to the root. Also, a main token is destroyed when it finds that another main token of the same (or higher) generation has preceded it on its way to meet another main token.

In [K86] we prove the correctness of the algorithm and its optimality:

Theorem 5: Let G be an undirected graph, containing faulty nodes and edges. Let G' be the graph of the non-faulty nodes and edges of G. The above algorithm weakly constructs a spanning tree in any connected component of G', using $O(m+n \log k)$ messages.

3.2 Leader election with termination detection in general networks

In order to elect a leader and detect termination, we now assume that every node knows n. (Thus, like in the case of complete graphs, termination can be detected when more than $\frac{n}{2}$ nodes are captured by some node.) We also assume that there are non-faulty edges which, together with the non-faulty nodes, form a connected non-faulty component which contains more than $\frac{n}{2}$.

A relatively simple (but having a high message complexity) method is to use the algorithm of Section 3.1 and add some a subroutine that counts the nodes. Each node which joins a tree can send a message to the tree root and when there are more than $\frac{n}{2}$ nodes the root becomes a leader. One problem with this scheme is that nodes may also leave trees. However, even if this problem is solved, the message complexity could be $O(n)$ for each node to join a tree. Since there are n nodes, and each may join $O(log\ n)$ trees, the message complexity is $O(n^2 \log n)$. By modifying the algorithm in [G] we derive an $O(n^{2)}$ fault-resilient algorithm. This matches the lower bound of $\Omega(m+n \log k)$ messages in the case of dense graphs, and is therefore not worse than that of existing non-resilient algorithms. The description of the algorithm follows. (The formal proofs appear in [BK86].)

We start with a main token which traverses its tree in order to find an edge leading to a node which belongs to another tree. This must be an edge which is known not to be faulty, otherwise the token may be lost, and the algorithm will be deadlocked. Once the token traverses such an edge, the conventional methods can be used in order to decide what happens to the two trees; for example, they can be merged, as in Section 3.1. The problem is to find such an edge using a small number of messages.

Each node initially contains a "sleeping" *king* token identified by the node's *Id*, and is considered as a one-node rooted "territory" tree. The *king* and its tree have an associated *IdOfKingdom* which is the *king*'s *Id*. The *king*'s role is to expand its "territory" tree in order to occupy a majority of the nodes. Each edge end-point contains a *scout* token. The role of a *scout* token is to test its edge and notify a *king*. When a *king* is notified by a *scout*, it starts a traversal "battle." In each "battle", the king traverses only tested edges and eventually returns to its root. While the *king* traverses these edges, it is rebuilding its territory tree. When the *king* enters an "enemy territory" (a node with a different *IdOfKingdom*), the *Id*s of the enemy tree and the *king* are compared in order to find out who wins. If the *king*'s *Id* is lower, it becomes a "loser," which eventually causes the *king*'s "death." Otherwise, the *king* assigns its *Id* to the node's *IdOfKingdom*, thereby annexing the node to its "territory" tree.

In refining the above scheme we aimed to guarantee:

(1) Once a king has a majority, no other king will ever have a majority. (This is needed to prove the partial correctness.)

(2) In every "battle" traversal the king visits an enemy territory. (This is needed to prove termination.)

(3)

(3a) In its "battle" traversal a king blocks edges that are not needed for connectivity. Once an edge is blocked by a king, no other kings will ever traverse it.

(3b) For each king's "battle" traversal, every node forwards at most one scout on its way to notify the king. (These are needed in order to reduce the messages complexity.)

Each "battle" consists of two traversals. In the first the king *freezes* every node it annexes. A king which enters an enemy frozen node, waits until either the node is unfrozen, or the king has become a "loser". When the king counts a *Majority* nodes it has frozen in this "battle", it stops after broadcasting a leadership message. (This guarantees (1).) In the second traversal of its "battle", the king unfreezes all the nodes it has frozen, and returns to sleep in its initiating node.

The traversals are performed according to the Depth First Search (DFS) strategy, specifically, that of Tremaux (see e.g. [E79]). The king traverses only edges which are tested and not blocked. An edge is blocked by the king when it is a DFS *back edges*. (This, together with the freezing mechanism, guarantees (3a).)

The scout makes a round trip on the edge it tests. according to the information it finds in both endpoints it decides whether the king should be notified. If so the scout climbs up the tree built by the king. It stops when its notification is guaranteed to reach the king (either by this scout, or by another). (This, together with the two-traversals mechanism, will be shown to guarantee (2) and (3b).)

The Formal Algorithm

Each node contains:

Constants: *Id* = the identity of the node; {The only difference between nodes' programs}
Majority = any integer greater than $n/2$; {n - total number of nodes}

Variables: *IdOfKingdom* initially *Id* ;
Counter : initially 1 ;
Date : initially 0 ;

Token: *king* : initially in status *Sleep*, and associate 4-touple:
(*KingId*, *KingCounter*, *KingShouldWake*, *KingHasLost*)
initially (*Id*, 1, *false*, *false*) ;

Each edge entry in a node has:

Variable: *mark*: (*CLOSE*, *OPEN*, *USED*, *UNUSED UP*, *BLOCK*) initially *CLOSE* ;

Token: *scout*: initially in status *test*, and associate variables:
ClimberDate and *CompareId*, initially undefined;

When a node wakes up {spontaneously or by a token's arrival} each *scout* token is sent through its entry.

The Algorithm of a Scout x-->y

test Status:

Travel from x through edge (x,y) ;
When arrives to y: Mark edge (x,y) *OPEN* if marked *CLOSE* ;
Go to *compare* Status ;

compare Status:

CompareId := *IdOfKingdom* {of y} ;
Carry with you *CompareId*, travel back to x ;
{Compare} When arrives x: If *IdOfKingdom* {of x} = *CompareId* {of y} then stop {vanish} ;
{Wait} Wait Until x is not frozen ;
{Check} If edge (x,y) in x is not marked *OPEN* then stop {vanish} ;
{Set} *ClimberDate* := *Counter* {of x} ;
Go to *Climber* Status ;

```
climber Status:
                    While ClimberDate = Counter and ClimberDate > Date {in x} do begin
    {UpDate}            Date := ClimberDate ;
    {Arrived? Stop!}    If x is frozen or no edge in x is marked UP then stop {vanish} ;
    {Climb up}          Travel the edge (x,v) marked UP, and assign x:=v ;
                    end {While}
                    Stop {vanish} ;
```

The Algorithm of a King initiated in node *r*

```
Sleep Status: {Initially and after Unfreeze}:
                    If KingHasLost then stop {vanish} ;
    {Should wake}   If KingShouldWake then Go to Freeze Status ;
    {Sleep}         Wait Until r is frozen or Date = Counter ;
    {Wake}          If r is frozen then stop {vanish} else Go to Freeze Status ;
Freeze Status: {From status Sleep}
    {Initiate}      Freeze r; KingCounter:=1; x := r;
    {Main}          Repeat
    {Go up}             If x ≠ r then travel the edge (x,y) marked UP, and assign x:=y ;
    {Deep down}         While exist an OPEN or UNUSED edge in x do begin
    {Freeze edge}               Let (x,y) be such an edge. Mark (x,y) USED and travel to y ;
    {Old node?}                 If y is frozen and belongs to your kingdom then begin
    {Block}                         Mark (x,y) in y BLOCK ;
    {Go back}                       Travel back to x ; Mark (x,y) in x BLOCK; end {if}
    {New node}                  else begin
    {Wait}                          Wait Until y is not frozen or a higher identity is known to y ;
    {Lost?}                         If a higher identity is known to y
    {Lost!}                         then begin
    {Back off}                          Travel back the edge (x,y) ; Mark (x,y) in x UNUSED
                                        ;
    {Give up}                           KingHasLost := true ; Go to Unfreeze Status ; end
                                        {Lost!}
    {Take over}                     else begin
    {Freeze node}                       Freeze the node and increment KingCounter ;
    {Majority?}                         If KingCounter ≥ Majority then Go to Leader Status ;
    {Update father}                     If an edge in y is marked UP then mark it UNUSED;
                                        If y ≠ r then mark (x,y) UP ;
                                        Assign x:=y;
                                    end {Take over}
                                end {New Node}
                        end {while}
    {Till finish}   Until ( x = r )
                    Go to Unfreeze Status ;
Unfreeze Status: {From status Freeze}
    {Main}          repeat
    {Melted by you?}    If x is not frozen then
    {Unfreeze edge}       Travel the edge (x,y) marked UP and Mark (x,y) in y UNUSED ;
    {Deep down}         While exist a USED edge in x do
```

Let (x,y) be a *USED* edge: Travel to y, and assign $x:=y$;

{Should wake?} If *Date* = *Counter* then *KingShouldWake* :=*true*

{Update node} *Counter* :=*KingCounter* ; Unfreeze x ;

{Till finish} Until ($x=r$)

Go to *Sleep* Status ;

Leader Status: {From status *Freeze* when *KingCounter* =*Majority* }

{Election} The current node is the leader.

{Notify}

Perform a broadcast over non-*BLOCK* ED EDGES, to notify all nodes.

{termination} When a node forwards this broadcasts it records the edge over which it has received the broadcast, and stops all algorithm activity.

In [BK86] we prove:

Theorem 6: Let G be an undirected graph, containing faulty nodes and edges. Let $G'=(V',E')$ be a connected subgraph of G containing only non-faulty nodes and edges, s.t. $|V'| > \frac{n}{2}$. The above algorithm elects a leader in G using $O(n^2)$ messages.

REFERENCES

[AG85a] Afek, Y., and Gafni, E., Time and Message Bounds for Election in Synchronous and Asynchronous Complete Networks, *4-th ACM Symposium on Principles of Distributed Computing*, Minaki, Canada, August 1985, pp 186-195.

[BK86] Bar-Yehuda, R., and Kutten, S., Fault-Tolerant Leader Election with Termination Detection, in General Undirected Networks, Technical Report #409, Computer Science Department, Technion, Haifa, Israel, April 1986, Revised August 1986.

[AG85b] Awerbuch, B., and Goldreich, O., private communication.

[AS86] Afek, Y., and Saks, M., An Efficient Fault Tolerant Termination Detection Algorithm (draft), unpublished.

[DLS84] Dwork, C., Lynch, N., and Stockmeyer, L., Consensus in the Presence of Partial Synchrony, *3th ACM Symposium on Principles of Distributed Computing*, Vancouver, Canada, August 1984, pp 103-118.

[F83] Fischer, M. The Consensus Problem in Unreliable Distributed Systems (a Brief Survey), YALE/DCS/RR-273, June 1983.

[FLM85] Fischer, M.J., Lynch, N.A., and Merritt, M., Easy Impossibility Proofs for Distributed Consensus Problems, *4-th ACM Symposium on Principles of Distributed Computing*, Minaki, Canada, August 1985, pp. 59-70.

[FLP85] Fischer, M., Lynch, N., Paterson, M., Impossibility of Distributed Consensus with One Faulty Process, *JACM*, Volume 32(2), April 1985.

[F80] Francez, N., Distributed Termination, *ACM-TOPLAS*, January 1980.

[FT84] Fredman, M.L., and Tarjan, R.E., Fibonacci Heaps and Their Uses in Improved Network Optimization Algorithms, *25th FOCS* Singer Island, Florida, October 1984.

[G] Gallager, R.G., Finding a Leader in a Network with $O(|E|)+O(n \log n)$ messages, Internal Memo, Laboratory for Information and Decision Systems, MIT, undated.

[G82] Garcia-Molina, H., Election in a Distributed Computing System, *IEEE Trans. on Computers*, Vol. c-31, No 1, 1982.

[GHS83] Gallager, R.G., Humblet, P.M., and Spira P.M., A Distributed Algorithm for Minimum-Weight Spanning Trees, *ACM TOPLAS*, January 1983, Vol. 5, No. 1.

[H84] Humblet, P., Selecting a Leader in a Clique in $O(n \log n)$ Messages, internal memo., Lab. for Information and Decision Systems, M.I.T., February, 1984.

[HS80] Hirshberg, D.S., and Sinclair, J.B., Decentralized Extrema-Finding in Circular Configurations of Processes, *CACM*, November 1980.

[K86] Kutten, S., Optimal Fault-Tolerant Distributed Spanning Tree Weak Construction in General Networks, Technical Report #432, Computer Science Department, Technion, Haifa, Israel, August 1986.

[KKM85] Korach, E., Kutten, S., and Moran, S., A Modular Technique for the Design of Efficient Distributed Leader Finding Algorithms, *4-th ACM Symposium on Principles of Distributed Computing (PODC)*, Minaki, Canada, August 1985, pp. 163-174.

[KMZ84] Korach, E., Moran, S, and Zaks, S, Tight Lower and Upper Bounds For Some Distributed Algorithms for a Complete Network of Processors, *3th ACM Symposium on Principles of Distributed Computing (PODC)*, Vancouver, B.C., Canada, August 1984, pp. 199-207.

[KW84] Kutten, S., and Wolfstahl, Y., Finding A Leader in a Distributed System where Elements may fail, *Proceeding of the 17th Ann. IEEE Electronic and Aerospace Conference (EASCON)*, Washington D.C., September 1984, pp. 101-105.

[KWZ86] Kutten, S., Wolfstahl, Y., and Zaks, S., Optimal Distributed t-Resilient Election in Complete Networks, Technical Report #430, Computer Science Department, Technion, Haifa, Israel, August 1986.

[M84] Merritt, M., Election in the Presence Of Faults, *3th ACM Symposium on Principles of Distributed Computing*, Vancouver, Canada, August 1984, pp. 134-142.

[SG85] Shrira, L., and Goldreich, O., Electing a Leader in the Presence of Faults: a Ring as a Special Case, to appear in *Acta Informatica*.

THE DERIVATION OF ON-THE-FLY GARBAGE COLLECTION ALGORITHMS FROM DISTRIBUTED TERMINATION DETECTION PROTOCOLS

(EXTENDED ABSTRACT)

Gerard Tel[1], Richard B. Tan[2], and Jan van Leeuwen.

Department of Computer Science, University of Utrecht,
P.O. Box 80.012, 3508 TA UTRECHT, The Netherlands.

Abstract: In this paper a close relation is worked out that exists between two distinct problems in the area of distributed computations, namely "on-the-fly" garbage collection and distributed termination detection. It is demonstrated how "on-the-fly" garbage collecting algorithms can be derived from termination detection protocols by applying a few standard transformations. Virtually all existing on-the-fly garbage collecting algorithms can be obtained in this way. Also some new, highly parallel garbage collecting algorithms are easily obtained in this way.

1. Introduction.

In modern high performance computing systems parallel processing is used. One of the problems in this field is that of parallel/concurrent garbage collection. Assume there is a *mutator program* or user program that changes the structure of a linked data structure or graph. Doing so, the mutator may create *garbage cells*, which are cells (nodes) that are no longer reachable from one or more designated cell(s) called *root(s)*. To avoid the memory from becoming exhausted, the task of a garbage collecting system or garbage collector is to identify these garbage cells and recycle them to a pool of free cells. We say a garbage collecting system is *concurrent* if it allows the mutator to continue its operation concurrently with it. The advantage of concurrent systems is that no "freeze" of the mutator is needed. We speak of a *parallel* collector (or mutator) if the garbage collector (or the mutator) is a parallel process in itself. Dijkstra et.al. [Dij78] introduced the first concurrent garbage collector, using one processor for the mutator and another processor for the collector. Ever since several concurrent or "on-the-fly" garbage collectors have been proposed [Be84,HK82,Hu85,KS77]. For a more complete treatment of the garbage collecting problem, see eg. Cohen [Co81].

Typical garbage collectors operate in two phases. First, all cells accessible from the root(s) are marked, and next all unmarked (and hence inaccessible) cells are collected. The collection phase is quite straightforward and will not be dealt with in this paper, but the marking phase requires a graph marking algorithm which can be

---

[1] The work of this author was supported by the Foundation for Computer Science of the Netherlands Organization for the Advancement of Pure Research (ZWO)

[2] Author's address: Dept. of Mathematics and Computer Science, University of Sciences & Arts of Oklahoma, Chickasha, OK 73018, USA. The work of this author was partially supported by a grant from the Netherlands Organization for the Advancement of Pure Research (ZWO).

quite intricate in the case of a concurrent system. The correctness proofs given by Dijkstra et.al. [Dij78] and Hudak and Keller [HK82] are long and tedious.

According to Dijkstra [D622] it was C.S. Scholten who first noticed the analogy between the problem of graph marking and a problem now known as termination detection in distributed systems. In fact it turns out, as we will show, that suitable solutions to the latter problem can be almost mechanically transformed into solutions of the former. The contributions of this paper are a description of the heuristics of one transformation and its application to several existing solutions for the termination detection problem. The approach will enable us to obtain a clear and transparant derivation of both existing and exciting new concurrent graph marking algorithms.

For the termination detection problem, assume there is a set $\mathbb{P}$ of processes, each of which can be either *active* or *passive*. An active process can become passive at any time, a passive process can become active only by interaction with an active process. We say $\mathbb{P}$ is *terminated* when all processes in $\mathbb{P}$ are passive. It is easily seen that this state is stable. A *termination detection protocol* is a protocol that detects this stable state. For a more complete treatment of the termination detection problem, see eg. [TL86].

In section 2 we present the heuristics behind our transformation. Section 3 applies this heuristic to transform a well-understood termination detection protocol for a ring of processes [DFG83] into the garbage collector of Dijkstra et.al. [Dij78]. In section 4 we transform the Dijkstra/Scholten termination detector for diffusing computations [DS80] into the Hudak/Keller marking-tree graph marking algorithm [HK82]. The rest of the paper introduces new marking algorithms by transforming various termination detection protocols. See [TTL86] for a more detailed presentation.

2. Graph Marking.

For the purpose of graph marking, assume that each cell of the computer's memory contains an extra field: *color*, and that initially all *color* fields contain the value *white* (i.e., all cells are unmarked). The aim of the marking phase is to color all cells reachable from the root (or one of the roots) *black*. Later the collecting phase will collect all unmarked cells as garbage.

2.1. The marking system. For the moment, assume that during the activities of the marking system the mutator does not change the graph structure at all. Define for each memory cell i the following process:

```
MARK(i) :
    { Wait until activated by external cause }
    for all j ∈ children(i) do
        if j was not activated before (* i.e., in this "round" of the collector *)
            then activate j ;
    color(i) := black ;
    stop. (* i.e., become passive *)
```

and let $\mathbb{P}$ = {MARK(i) | i is memory cell }. In the rest of this paper we will identify a cell i with its associated process MARK(i). Assume that initialy all processes in $\mathbb{P}$ are passive. We run the following program fragment:

```
MARK-ROOTS:
    for all r ∈ roots do activate r.
```

Definition: *INV* is the property that no passive black cell has a passive white child.

We can state the following claims:

Lemma 2.1: *INV* holds before the execution of MARK_ROOTS and after this execution, when processes in *IP* are active.

Proof: Initially there are no black cells, and MARK_ROOTS does not introduce any. MARK(*i*) eventually colors *i* black, but only after its children have been activated. Hence MARK(*i*) does not cause *i* (nor any other cell) to be a black cell with a white child. □

Lemma 2.2: The system will terminate in finite time.

Lemma 2.3: When the system terminates, all reacable cells are black.

Proof: There are no white roots, because they have all been activated (it is easy to see that any activated process must be black upon termination). There are no active cells, so the lemma follows by *INV*. □

So, when we can detect termination of the system, we can easily construct a graph marking algorithm. We obtain the following heuristic:

> One can obtain a graph marking algorithm by superimposing a termination detection protocol on the set of processes {MARK(*i*) | *i* is a cell in the memory}.

2.2. Concurrent mutator actions. When the mutator adds an edge to the graph during the execution of the marking system it may violate *INV*. Hence we implement the action of adding an edge from *i* to *j* as:

> ADD_REF (*i,j*):
>
> *children (i) := children (i) + {j} ;*
>
> **if** *j* has not been activated yet **then** activate *j*.

We assume that this piece of code is always executed "indivisibly" by the mutator, and then it obviously does not violate *INV*. Hence we obtain the following heuristic:

> One can obtain a concurrent graph marking system by (1) superimposing a termination detection protocol on the set of processes {MARK(*i*) | *i* is a cell in the memory} and (2) letting the mutator activate targets of newly added edges.

3. Derivation of a marking algorithm due to Dijkstra et.al.

In [Dij78], Dijkstra et.al. presented an on-the-fly garbage collector. We shall demonstrate in this section how one can obtain this marking algorithm (the "coarse-grained" version) by simply transforming a suitable termination detection algorithm. The termination detection algorithm is the one presented by Dijkstra et.al. in [DFG83].

3.1. The algorithm of [DFG83]. We describe briefly the algorithm of [DFG83] in a slightly more efficient form. It assumes that the network contains a ring as a subnetwork and that the number of processes, *N*, is known. Also, there must be one unique process called the leader. Besides active and passive states a third state called *blue* (called passive-black in [DFG83]) is introduced. A process that finishes its task first enters the blue state (instead of the passive state). The leader starts the termination detection by sending a token <0> over the ring.

- A passive process increases the value of the token by one.
- A blue process which receives the token, first sets its state to passive and then sends out a token <1>.
- An active process that receives the token will not do anything with the token until it turns blue. Then it

behaves as a blue process (i.e., it turns passive and sends out a token <1>).

If a token <k> is on the ring, it has "seen" k consecutive passive processes without encountering a blue one. It is proven in [DFG83] and [TTL86] that there is termination when the value of the token reaches N.

3.2. Derivation of the marking system. For the purpose of graph marking, we can use one color-field in each cell to represent the state of the process (*active, passive, blue*) as well as the progress of the marking phase (*white, black*). We use the color

gray for active processes,
blue for blue processes,
white for passive processes whose cells are unmarked,
black for passive processes whose cells are marked.

We arrange the memory cells as a ring by going cyclically through it. Then the DFG-algorithm is simulated by the following program fragment (for the "basic computation" we substitute the process MARK):

```
token := 0 ; place := 0 ;
repeat
      if color(place) = gray then
            begin (* run MARK(place) *)
                  for all j ∈ children(place) do
                        if color(j) = white then color(j) := gray;
                  color(place) := blue
            end;
      if color (place) = blue then
            begin (* a blue cell is entered *)
                  color (place) := black ; token := 0
            end ;
      token := token + 1 ; place := (place + 1) mod N
until token = N.
```

While this program is executing, gray cells can "spontaneously" execute MARK and become blue (see sec. 6). If this is not done, the marking system progresses only in cells where the token arrives. It can be proven however, that the system terminates also in that case (be it in $O(N^2)$ time worst case). But then the blue color for processes is only an "intermediate" color that a cell gets in the first **if**-statement and looses again in the second. In fact, the color blue is used only to "trigger" the second **if**-statement. So we can combine these two if-statements into one. Further, we assume that "**if** *color(j) = white* **then** *color(j) := gray*" is one indivisible operation, henceforth referred to as "*shade(j)*" (as in [Dij78]). The entire marking system now becomes:

```
for all r ∈ roots do shade(r) ; (* MARK-ROOTS *)
token := 0 ; place := 0 ;
repeat
      if color(place) = gray then
            begin
                  for all j ∈ children (place) do shade(j) ;
                  color (place) := black ;
                  token := 0
            end;
```

token := *token* + *1* ;
place := (*place* + *1*) *mod N*
until *token* = *N*.

It turns out that we arrive at a marking algorithm, that was presented as early as in 1975 by Dijkstra et.al. [Dij78]. But, where Dijkstra et.al. needed a considerable effort to find it, we obtained it by a "mechanical" transformation from another algorithm.

3.3. Concurrent mutator actions. According to section 2.2, the graph marking algorithms will also work when there is a concurrently active mutator process that executes the following code indivisibly when it adds an edge:

ADD(*i,j*):
children(i) := *children(i)* + {*j*} ;
shade(j).

No overhead for deletion of edges is needed.

4. Derivation of a marking algorithm due to Hudak and Keller.

Hudak and Keller [HK82] presented a garbage collecting system that can be run on an arbitrary number of garbage collecting processors in parallel, and allows concurrent activities of arbitrarily many mutator processes. Also its memory may be distributed, see figure 1. We show how their marking system can be obtained by transforming the Dijkstra/Scholten termination detection protocol (DS-protocol).

4.1. The DS–protocol. Again we start with a description of the DS-termination detection protocol. This description is very brief. For more details, see [DS80] or [TTL86]. In the DS-protocol each active process remembers by whom it was activated (its *father*) and how many other processes it has activated. When a process p and all of p's children are ready, p sends a "signal" to its father. When an active process receives another activation message, it signals immediately. p keeps a counter $D(p)$, which is the number of activation messages sent minus the number of signals received. When p has finished its computational tasks, it remains *engaged* until it has received enough signals so $D(p) = 0$. Then p signals to its father and becomes *neutral*. It is assumed that all activity is started (indirectly) by one special process E, which has no father at all: it is the "root" of all activities. Dijkstra and Scholten [DS80] proved that for any system behaving according to these

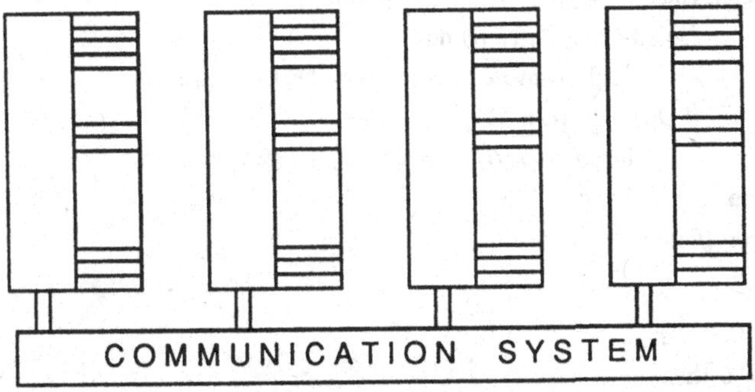

Figure 1

rules we have:

Theorem 4.1: A finite time after all computational tasks are finished, $D(E) = 0$.

Theorem 4.2: If $D(E) = 0$, all computational activities have terminated.

4.2. Derivation of the marking system. In the following the statement "*activate (i, father)*" means: "send an activation message to *i*, bearing "*father*" as sender". When *i* receives this message, it does the following.

```
ACTIVATE (i, father) :
    if i was not activated before then
        begin
            for all j ∈ children (i) do
                begin activate (j, i) ; D(i) := D(i) +1 end ;
            color (i) := black;
            while D(i) > 0 do
                begin await receipt of a signal ;
                    (* Meanwhile handle incoming activation
                        messages as normal *)
                    D(i) := D(i)-1
                end ;
            signal (father)
        end
    else signal (father).
```

Again, we represent "engaged" cells by the color gray. Then "*i* was not activated before" can be replaced by "*color(i) = white*". Further we defer "*color(i) := black*" to the time of neutralization of *i*. This of course does not affect the correctness or termination properties of the algorithm. The reason we do this will soon become clear: we will use one statement to describe the coloring of *i* as well as its neutralization. Observe that all activities of a process are "message driven". So we can store relevant information about the process in the cell, and quit ACTIVATE. When a signal is received, we restart the process. The system then transforms into the following:

```
ACTIVATE (i, father):
    if color (i) = white then
        begin color(i) := gray; father (i) := father ;
            for all j ∈ children (i) do
                begin activate (j, i) ; D(i) := D(i) + 1 end;
            if D(i) = 0  then
                begin color (i) := black ; signal (father (i)) end
        end
    else signal (father).

SIGNAL (i) :
    D(i) := D(i)-1 ;
    if D(i) = 0 then
        begin color(i) := black; signal (father (i)) end.
```

Hudak and Keller assume that there is only one root. They start the marking system by activating this root with a "fake" father E, which triggers termination when signalled:

```
MARKING-SYSTEM:
      activate (root, E) ;
      wait until done.

SIGNAL (i) :
      if i = E
            then done := true
            else  begin D(i) := D(i)-1 ;
                        if D(i) = 0 then
                              begin color(i) := black ; signal (father(i)) end
                  end.
```

Actually Hudak observed that this "marking-tree" algorithm was developed independently of Dijkstra-Scholten's DS-protocol but later found to be similar.

5. A highly parallel collecting system.

As in section 3, assume that the mutator is one sequential process, running on a non-distributed memory. The parallel collector derived in this section is a generalization of the collector derived in section 3.

5.1. A highly parallel termination detection protocol. The basis of the marking algorithms derived in this section is the following termination detection protocol skeleton:

```
repeat
      success := true ;
      for all processes p ∈ IP do
            if p was active since the previous visit to p
                  then success := false
until success.
```

This skeleton is also the basis of the DFG protocol (section 3). In the DFG protocol the inner loop is executed sequentially, but this is not crucial for its correctness. By supplying a parallel scheme according to which processes are visited, one obtains a fast termination detection algorithm. Examples can be found in eg. [TL86], a clear correctness argument in [CM85].

5.2. A highly parallel graph marking system. In order to turn the protocol skeleton for distributed termination detection into a graph marking system, three things need be done:

- Add the code for MARK_ROOTS,
- Specify what is meant by visiting a process,
- Supply a scheme according to which cells are visited.

Using the same color and notations as in section 3, the code for MARK_ROOTS is of course:

```
MARK_ROOTS:
      for all i ∈ roots do shade(r).
```

A "visit" will have about the same meaning as in section 3. Again we combine the termination detection protocol with a scheduler, to execute the code for MARK in gray cells. So, let *visit(i)* be the following routine:

```
VISIT(i):
    if color(i) = gray then
        begin
            for all j ∈ children(i) do shade(j) ;
            color(i) := black ;
            success := false
        end.
```

We will now supply a parallel visiting scheme to complete the garbage collecting system. Assume that there are k processors available for garbage collection. The simplest traversal scheme for the processes is to partition the set $\{0..N-1\}$ of cells in k parts, and give each garbage collection processor a part. So, let $\{S_i \mid 1 \le i \le k\}$ be a partition of $\{0..N-1\}$. The marking system is given by:

```
for all r ∈ roots do shade(r) ;
repeat
    success := true ;
    for all i ∈ {1,..,k} pardo
        for all p ∈ S_i do visit(p)
until success.
```

6. Garbage collection in a ring of processors.

If in a system as in section 4 the processors can be arranged in a ring, its is also possible to arrange all memory cells in a ring, see figure 2. This means that we can run the marking system from section 3 on it, with some interesting changes:

- In order to let garbage collecting processors proceed with the marking in "their" regions even if they don't

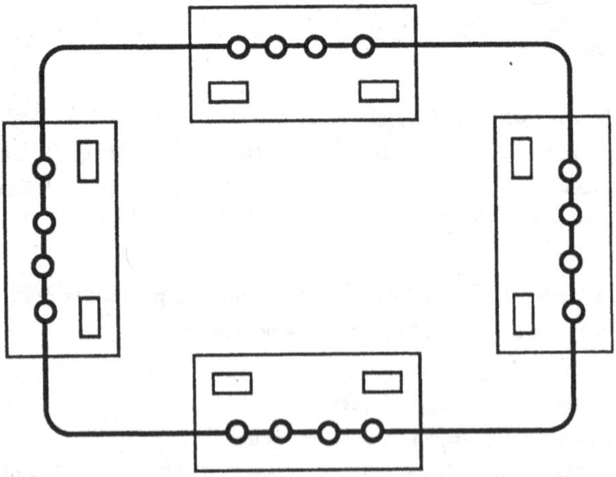

Figure 2

have the token, we reintroduce the blue color.

- The simulated token has to be sent really as a token when the algorithm continues on the next processor.

The resulting system is the following (Assume processor P has N_P cells, locally addressable as $1...N_P$):

```
1. (* MARK_ROOTS *)
      all P do
            for all r ∈ roots do shade(r).

2. (* Local progress of marking *)
      all P do
            repeat
                  i := ... ; (* a gray cell in processor P *)
                  for all j ∈ children(i) do shade(j) ;
                  color(i) := blue
            until there is termination.

3. (* Start of DFG protocol *)
   (* Only one processor, the leader l, executes: *)
      send <0> to S(l).

4. (* Scheduling and termination detection *)
   (* Upon receiving the token <v>, P executes: *)
      val := v ;
      for i:=1 to N_P do
            begin
                  if color(i) = gray then
                        begin
                              for all j ∈ children(i) do shade(j) ;
                              color(i) := blue
                        end ;
                  if color(i) = blue then
                        begin
                              val := 0 ;
                              color(i) := black
                        end ;
                  val := val+1 ;
                  if val=N then (* there is termination *)
                        begin .... (* take appropriate action *) end
            end ;
      send <val> to S(P).
```

7. Graph marking in an arbitrary network.

Assume the same architecture as in the previous section, except that the processors are not arranged in a ring, but in an arbitrary network G.

7.1. "Hierarchical" termination detection. Suppose there is a termination detection algorithm T for processes arranged according to G. (See e.g. [TL86] for termination detelection algorithms for arbitrary networks G.)

Now we define a *group* of processes to be the set of processes residing in one processor. We say a group is active if any of its members is active, and passive if none of its members are active. We can construct a *two level* termination detector for this system:

- a low level detector runs within every group to see if all processes in the group are passive (i.e., if the group is passive),
- a high level detector is run among the groups to see if the system has terminated as a whole.

It can be shown that on the high level termination detection algorithm T can be used. For details, see the full paper [TTL86].

7.2. Hughes' collector. In Hughes' collector [Hu85] the idea in the previous section is used to construct a rather complex collecting system. In fact, an infinite number of marking systems is run in parallel. Each of these is labeled by a timestamp. "Local" marking actions contribute to all marking systems at the same time. Rana's corrected termination detection protocol [Ra83] is used to detect which marking systems have terminated. Again we refer to the full paper [TTL86] for a more complete synthesis of the collecting system.

8. Conclusion.

We have exploited an observation due to C.S. Scholten, saying that there is a close relation between on-the-fly garbage collection and the termination detection problem for distributed systems. We specified a transformation that can be applied to any termination detection protocol to obtain a graph marking algorithm. Both the on-the-fly garbage collector [Dij78] due to Dijkstra et.al. and Hudak and Keller's multiprocessor "marking-tree" collector [HK82] can be easily and transparently obtained by transforming existing detection protocols. Several new and highly parallel algorithms were derived by transforming suitable termination detection protocols on various networks.

The distributed termination detection problem has been given considerable attention in the last few years. It has turned out that this problem has connections not only to on-the-fly garbage collection, but also to election [TL86] and deadlock detection [Na86]. Thus it seems worthwhile to make a more thorough study of the mechanisms underlying termination detection.

By exploiting the connections between different problems in distributed computing and using program transformation techniques as in this paper, one can build upon existing distributed algorithms to derive intricate solutions to new problems in a clear and transparant fashion.

Acknowledgement: We thank C.S. Scholten for his comments on an earlier version of this paper.

9. References.

[Be84] : M. Ben-Ari, Algorithms for on-the-fly garbage collection, ACM ToPLaS 6 (june 1984), pp. 333-344.

[CM85] : K.M. Chandy and J. Misra, A paradigm for detecting quiescence properties in distributed computations, In: K.R. Apt (ed), Logics and models of concurrent systems, Springer Verlag, pp 325–341.

[Co81] : J. Cohen, Garbage collection of linked datastructures, Comp. Surv. 13 (sept. 1981) pp. 341-367.

[D622] : E.W. Dijkstra, On making solutions more and more fine-grained, EWD622, in: E.W. Dijkstra,

Selected writings on computing, a personal perspective, Springer Verlag, Heidelberg 1982.

[DFG83] : E.W. Dijkstra, W.H.J. Feijen and A.J.M. van Gasteren, Derivation of a termination detection algorithm for distributed computations, Inf. Proc. Lett. 16 (june 1983), pp. 217-219.

[DS80] : E.W. Dijkstra and C.S. Scholten, Termination detection for diffusing computations, Inf. Proc.Lett. 11 (aug. 1980), pp. 1-4.

[Dij78] : E.W. Dijkstra, L. Lamport, A.J. Martin, C.S. Scholten and E.F.M. Steffens, On-the-fly garbage collection : An exercise in cooperation, Comm. ACM 21 (nov 1978), pp. 966-975.

[HK82] : P. Hudak, R.M. Keller, Garbage collection and task detection in distributive applicative processing systems, in : Proceedings of the ACM Symp. on LISP and functional programming, Pittsburg, 1982.

[Hu85] : J. Hughes, A distributed garbage collection algorithm, in : J.P. Jouannaud (ed.), Functional Programming Languages and Computer Architecture, LNCS vol. 201, Springer Verlag, Heidelberg, 1985, pp. 256-272.

[KS77] : H.T. Kung and S.W. Song, An efficient parallel garbage collection system and its correctness proof, in: Proceedings 18th Annual IEEE Symp. on Found. of Comp. Sc., 1977, pp. 120-131.

[Na86] : N. Natarajan, A distributed scheme for detecting communication deadlock, IEEE Trans. on Softw. Eng. SE 12 (apr. 1986), pp. 531-537.

[Ra83] : S.P. Rana, A distributed solution to the distributed termination problem, Inf. Proc. Lett. 17 (1983) pp. 43-46.

[TL86] : R.B. Tan and J. van Leeuwen, General symmetric distributed termination detection, Techn. Rep. RUU-CS-86-2, Dept. of Computer Science, University of Utrecht, 1986. (Submitted to Computers and Artificial Intelligence.)

[TTL86] : G. Tel, R.B. Tan and J. van Leeuwen, Derivation of graph marking algorithms from distributed termination detection protocols, Techn. Report RUU–CS–86–11, Dept. of Computer Science, University of Utrecht, Utrecht, 1986. (Submitted for publication.)

ON THE EXPECTED COMPLEXITY OF DISTRIBUTED SELECTION

Nicola Santoro[1], Jeffrey B. Sidney[2], Stuart J. Sidney[3]

(1) School of Computer Science, Carleton University, Ottawa, Canada
(2) Faculty of Administration, University of Ottawa, Ottawa, Canada
(3) Department of Mathematics, University of Connecticut, Stout, U.S.A.

1. INTRODUCTION

1.1 The Problem

The classical problem of selecting the k-th smallest element of a set F drawn from a totally ordered set has been extensively studied in serial and parallel environments. In a distributed context, it has different formulations and complexity measures.

A *communication network* of size d is a set $S=\{S_0, \dots , S_{d-1}\}$ of *sites*, where each site has a local non-shared memory and processing capabilities. In the *point-to-point* model, associated with S is a set $L \subseteq S \times S$ of direct communication lines between sites; if $(S_i,S_j) \in L$, S_i and S_j are said to be *neighbours*. Sites communicate by sending messages; a message can only be sent to and received from a neighbour. The couple G=(S,L) can be thought of as an undirected graph; hence, graph-theoretical notation can be employed in the design and analysis of distributed algorithms in the point-to-point model.

A *file* of cardinality N is a set $F=\{f_1,\dots,f_N\}$ of records, where each record $f \in F$ contains a unique key k(f) drawn from a totally ordered set *F*; in the following, $f_i > f_j$ will denote that $k(f_i) > k(f_j)$.

A *distribution* of F on S is a d-tuple $X=<X_0,\dots,X_{d-1}>$ where $X_i \subseteq F$ is a subfile stored at site S_i, $|X_i| \le c$, $X_i \cap X_j = \emptyset$ for $i \neq j$, and $\cup_i X_i = F$.

Order-statistics queries about F can be originated at any site and will activate a query resolution process at that site. Since only a subset of F is available at each site, the resolution of a query will in general require the cooperation of several (possibly all) sites according to some predetermined algorithm. Since local processing time is usually negligible when compared with transmission and queueing delays, the goal is to design resolution algorithms which minimize the amount of communication activity rather than the amount of processing activity.

The *distributed selection problem* is the general problem of resolving a query for locating the K-th smallest element of F. The tuple <N, K, N[0], ..., N[d-1]> is called the problem *configuration*, and $\Delta = \mathrm{Min}\{K,N-K+1\}$ is called the problem *size*, where N[i] is the cardinality of X_i. Any efficient solution to this problem can be employed as a building block for a distributed sorting algorithm [11].

The complexity of this problem (i.e., the number of communication activities required to resolve an order-statistics query) depends on many parameters, including the number d of sites, the size N of the file, the number N[i] of elements stored at site S_i, the rank K of the element being sought, the topology of the network. This work deals with applications for which the size of the file is much greater than the number of sites; i.e., N»d.

1.2 An Historical Prospective

The current definition of the distributed selection problem is the result of a synthesis of two distinct types of investigations carried out in the past, each having its own motivations and assumptions.

The first type of investigations on the distributed selection problem and the related *ranking* problem [5,6,19] were generalizations of the studies on the *minimum-finding* (or *election*) problem in the point-to-point model, where it was assumed that each site contained one element. Several solutions have been presented [3,8,17]; in all these investigations, the focus was on the *worst-case* complexity; the only exception is the distributed translation by Shrira, Francez and Rodeh [17] of the well-known serial algorithm for random selection.

A different motivation came from the investigations by Yao [18] and Abelson [1] on the amount of communication needed to evaluate a smooth Boolean function whose arguments were stored at two different sites. The case where the arguments of the function are elements from a totally ordered set, and the result of the function is the median of the arguments was independently studied by Rodeh [9] and Santoro & Sidney [14] who proved a Θ(log N) bound on the problem for d=2; the constant in the bound was later improved [2]. The generalization to the case d>2 was then the object of several investigations in the so-called *shout-echo* model (a topology-independent model allowing broadcast-type primitives) [7,10,12,14-16]. Almost all solutions obtained in this model are easily convertible to solutions in the more common point-to-point model (used in the other class of investigations). Also these investigations have focused on the *worst-case* complexity.

One important fact learned in the investigations with the shout-echo model is about the nature of the distributed selection problem itself. Since it is assumed that the cost of local processing is negligible, is it reasonable to assume that the elements stored at a site are sorted; thus, the distributed selection problem can be seen as the distributed equivalent of the serial problem of *selection in an array with sorted columns* where each column correspond to a subfile. Based on this observation, a distributed version of the optimal serial algorithm by Frederickson and Johnson [4] was developed leading to a Θ(d log(k/d)) algorithm for complete and star graphs in the point-to-point model and to a Θ(log(k/d)) algorithm in the shout-echo model [16]. Again, these bounds apply to the *worst-case* complexity.

In this paper, the *expected* communication complexity of the distributed selection problem is analysed.

1.3 Main Results

All existing solutions in both models have a similiar structure, in that a sequence of iterations is performed whose effect is to reduce the "size" of the problem (e.g., the number of file elements among which the sought element can be found), until the elements is finally located or another (possibly, brute-force) method can be effectively employed.

The main contribution of this paper consists in the design and analysis of a new *reduction technique*. The proposed algorithm is shown to drastically reduce the size of the problem (occasionally, it also locates the element being sought). More specifically, it transforms the problem of locating the K-th smallest among N elements distributed among d sites to the problem of locating the k=O(d) smallest element (recall, N»d). To perform this reduction, the algorithm is shown to require O(log log Min {K , N - K + 1}) iterations on the average; each iteration can be implemented using O(d) message exchanges in the point-to-point model, and only a constant number of communication activity in the shout-echo model. This bound is derived subject to a standard type randomness assumption on the distribution of the elements among the sites.

This result implies an O(d loglog Min{K,N-K+1} + d log d) and an O(loglog Min{K,N-K+1} + log d) upper-bound on the expected communication complexity of the distributed selection problem in the point-to-point and in the shout-echo models, respectively; these new bounds must be contrasted with the existing O(d log N) and O(log N) bounds on the expected case without randomness assumptions for the point-to-point [17] and the shout-echo [13] models, respectively.

To the reader familiar with the literature in data structures, it will not escape the similiarity (but not equivalence) between the new and existing bounds on one hand, and the bounds on the expected serial complexity of interpolation search and of binary search on the other hand.

2. THE REDUCTION TECHNIQUE

The proposed reduction technique consists of a sequence of iterations; at the beginning of each iteration, an element expected to be "close" to the sought element is choosen; its overall rank is then determined and, based on this result, some elements are removed from consideration. This process is repeated until either the sought element is located or the amount of elements still under consideration has fallen below a pre-determined threshold (the parameter s below).

Let f_K be the K-th smallest element in F, and let $X_i=\{x_{i,j} : 1 \le j \le N[i] \}$ be the set of elements stored at site S_i, where $N[i] \ge 0$ and $\Sigma_i N[i] = N$. Without loss of generality, let $x_{i,j} < x_{i,j+1}$ for all values of the indices for which the relation is defined; and let S_0 be the site initiating the algorithm (e.g. the site at which the order-statistics query has been originated). The following notation is used to describe the problem under consideration at the start of an iteration:

$\{x_{i,j} : L[i]<j\le H[i]\}$ is the set of elements under consideration at site S_i, where $0\le L[i]\le H[i]\le N[i]$;

$n[i] = H[i] - L[i]$ is the number of elements under consideration at site S_i;

$n=\Sigma_i n[i]$ is the total number of elements still under consideration;

$k=K-\Sigma_i L[i]$ is the rank of f_K among the elements still under consideration.

The point-to-point version of the proposed algorithm for reducing the size of the problem of determining f_K (the K-th smallest element) is described below.

REDUCTION ALGORITHM

The algorithm is composed of two phases: Initialization and Iteration.

Initialization phase:

each site S_i, upon reception of a 'start' message from S_0, initializes the local variables $n[i] := N[i]$, $L[i] := 0$, $H[i] := N[i]$, and starts the Iteration phase.

The *Iteration* phase is composed of three stages: Collection, Ranking and Update.

Collection stage:

the values n, m, n[m], L[m], $\Sigma_i L[i]$, and k are collected at site S_0, where m is such that $n[m] = Max\{n[i]\}$, $n =\Sigma_i n[i]$, and $k = K- \Sigma_i L[i]$. If $Min\{k, n-k+1\} > s$, site S_0 computes the value $h=\lceil k (n[m] + 1) / (n+1) - 1/2 \rceil + L[m]$ and sends it to site S_m which starts the Ranking stage; if, instead, $Min\{k,n-k+1\} \leq s$, the amount of elements still under consideration has fallen below the pre-determined threshold and the algorithm terminates (the execution of some other selection algorithm may now start).

Ranking stage:

the value $x_{m,h}$ is sent by S_m to all sites; upon reception, the value $r = \Sigma_i r[i]$ is collected at S_0 which starts the Update stage, where $r[i] = |\{j : x_{i,j} < x_{m,h}\}|$. (i.e., r is the rank of $x_{m,h}$ in the entire file).

Update stage:

S_0 compares r with K. If $r = K$, then $x_{m,h}$ is the sought value and the algorithm terminates. If, instead, $r \neq K$ then site S_0 notifies all sites of whether $r > K$ or $r < K$, and starts the entire Iteration phase again; upon notification, each site updates its local variables n[i], L[i], H[i] accordingly (i.e., if $r < K$, then $L[i]:= r[i]$; if $r > K$, then $H[i]:= r[i]$, except for S_m where $H[m]:= h-1$; in either case, $n[i]:= H[i] - L[i]$) and starts the entire Iteration phase again.

Theorem 1 (Worst-case complexity) The reduction algorithm terminates after at most 1.386 d $\log((N+1)/d)+1$ iterations. Furthermore, at the end of each execution of the Collection stage, the value k represents the rank of f_K among the elements still under consideration.

Proof. Consider an execution of the Update stage and assume that the value k represents the rank of f_K among the elements still under consideration before this execution. If $x_{m,h}$ is not the sought element (i.e., $r \neq K$), all and only the elements smaller than or equal to $x_{m,h}$ (greater than or equal to $x_{m,h}$) are removed from consideration if $r<K$ ($r>K$); thus, the new value k' of k determined in the next Collection stage will be the rank of f_K among the elements still under consideration. Let n' be the value of n after this execution of the Update stage. If $r<K$, then at least $h \geq k\,((n[m]+1)\,/\,(n+1)) - 1/2 > (k/d) - 1/2$ additional elements are eliminated from consideration, from which follows that $k' \leq ((d-1)/d)\,k + 1/2$ and $n'-k'+1=n-k+1$. If $r>K$, at least $n[m]-h+1 \geq n[m] - (k\,(n[m]+1)/(n+1) + 1/2) + 1 \geq (n-k+1)/d - 1/2$ additional elements are eliminated from consideration, from which follows that $n'-k'+1 \leq ((d-1)/d)\,(n'-k'+1) + 1/2$ and $k=k'$. That is, after an iteration not resulting in termination, either k or n-k+1 is reduced by approximately a (d-1)/d factor. Let t_1 (t_2) denote the maximum number of executions where $r<K$ ($r>K$); thus, the maximum number t of iterations to termination is $t \leq t_1 + t_2 + 1 \leq 2\,\log((N+1)/d)\,/\,\log(d/(d-1)) + 1 < 1.386\,d\,\log((N+1)/d) + 1$. □

3. ALGORITHM ANALYSIS

In the following, the proposed reduction technique is first reformulated in a purely combinatorial manner eliminating the communication steps. The reformulated algorithm will be analysed, and the results will be interpreted in the context of the reduction technique.

3.1 Reformulation of Problem and Solution

To motivate the reformulation, note that the reduction technique deals with a set of fixed parameters: $x_{i,j}$ ($1 \leq j \leq N[i]$, $0 \leq i \leq d-1$); and a set of "state" variables n[i], L[i], H[i], n, k. The state variables are initially set and undergo transformations in each iteration until termination. The effect of the $x_{i,j}$'s on the transformations is felt only through the r[i]'s. It is easy to see that for any monotonic strictly increasing function $f: F \rightarrow \Re$, if each $x_{i,j}$ is replaced by $f(x_{i,j})$, then the values of m and h calculated in the Collection stage remain unchanged. Hence, the transformations effected during the execution of the reduction technique are invariant under monotonic strictly increasing transformations of the problem data $x_{i,j}$. In particular, the function $f(x_{i,j})$= rank of $x_{i,j}$ in F converts the original problem into one defined on a data set consisting of the integers 1 to N. Algorithm A below may be viewed as dealing with exactly this transformed problem; i.e., the problem in which $x_{i,j}$ is replaced by $f(x_{i,j})$.

Define a *scheme* of dimension d to be a tuple V=(n, k, n[0], ..., n[d-1]) where n and k are positive integers with k<n, {n[i]} is a sequence of non-negative integers whose sum is n, and W(a,b]={a+1,a+2,...,b-1,b} where a is an integer and b=a+n.

A *distribution* with scheme V is a function π:W→ {0,...,d-1} such that |{j: π(j)=i}|= n[i], 0≤i≤d-1. Let Π(V) be the set of all distributions with scheme V; the number of elements in Π(V) is the multinomial coefficient $|\Pi(V)| = \binom{n}{n[0] \ldots n[d-1]}$.

Primes shall be used consistently to refer to additional schemes. Thus, if V' is a second scheme, it will be automatically denoted as V'=(n',k',{n'[i]},W') with W'=(a',b'], and a typical member of Π(V') will be denoted by π'.

Following is the reformulation of the reduction technique presented in the previous section.

ALGORITHM A

(given a scheme V of dimension d, a distribution $\pi \in \Pi$(V), and a parameter s>d)

1. If Min{k, n-k+1} < s terminate the algorithm.

2. Let q be the h-th smallest integer in {j: π(j) = m}, where $h=\lceil k(n[m] + 1) / (n+1) -1/2 \rceil$ with m the smallest index such that n[m] = Max{ n[i] }.

3. (a) If q=a+k, set n[m]:=1, n[j]:=0 (j≠m), V := (1, 1, n[0], .., n[d-1], (k-1,k]) and terminate the algorithm.

   (b) If q<a+k, set n[i]:= |{j: j>q and π(j)=i}| (0≤i≤d-1), V:= (b-q, a+k-q, n[0], ..., n[d-1], (q,b]), a:= q, π:= π|(a,b]; and return to step 1.

   (c) If q>a+k, set n[i]:= |{j: j<q and π(j)=i}| (0≤i≤d-1), V:=(q-a-1, k, n[0], ..., n[d-1], (a,q-1]), b:=q-1, π:= π|(a,b]; and return to step 1.

That algorithm A is a translation of the reduction technique can be seen by noting that the set of elements eliminated in the Update stage consists of just those elements still under consideration which are different from, no greater than, or no smaller than $x_{m,h}$ in F, depending on whether case (a) or (b), or (c) holds.

Each iteration of algorithm A decreases n and W (so the algorithm must eventually terminate) and does not decreases the value of a nor increases the value of b or n[i]; an iteration does not change the value a+k. $\langle V,\pi\rangle$ will denote a scheme V and a distribution $\pi \in \Pi$(V). For a non-negative integer t, $\langle V,\pi\rangle \rightarrow_t \langle V',\pi'\rangle$ means that V and V' have the same dimensions and t iterations of algorithm A convert $<V,\pi>$ into $<V',\pi'>$. Let $V \rightarrow_t V'$ mean that $<V,\pi> \rightarrow_t <V',\pi'>$ for some π and π'.

The scheme V is said to have the *randomness property* if all $\pi \in \Pi(V)$ have the same probability $P[\pi]=1/|\Pi(V)|$, where P[e] denotes the probability of event e. Having selected a probability measure on V, an induced (conditional) probability measure on V' if $V \rightarrow_t V'$ is obtained; the following lemma says that with this probability measure, V' inherits the randomness property from V.

Lemma 1 If $V \rightarrow_t V'$ and V has the randomness property, then V' also has the randomness property.

Proof. It is sufficient to prove that the number $D(V,t,\pi')=|\{\pi \in \Pi(V) : <V,\pi> \rightarrow_t <V',\pi'>\}|$, which is defined for each $\pi' \in \Pi(V')$, is independent of the choice of π'; the proof will be by induction on t.
The result is trivial for t=0. Let t=1; suppose n'>1 (so case (a) does not hold in step 3) and that there is some π_0' for which $D(V,1,\pi_0') > 0$, for otherwise the result is trivial. Choose π_0' such that $<V,\pi_0> \rightarrow_1 <V',\pi_0'>$. Assume case (b) holds in step 3 (the argument for case (c) is similar). Evidently, $W'=(q_0,b]$ where q_0 is calculated in step 2; Let $W'' = (a,q_0]$, $n''[i] = n[i]-n'[i]$, $n''= n-n'= q-a$, so $\Sigma_i n''[i] = n''$, $n''[i] \geq 0$, $|W''|=n''$, $|\{j \in W'' : \pi_0(j)=i\}| = n''[i]$; $\pi_0(q_0) = m$ implies $n''[m]>0$. Let Π'' denote the set of functions $\pi'':W'' \rightarrow \{0,...,d-1\}$ such that $|\{j \in W'' : \pi''(j)=i\}|=n''[i]$ and $\pi''(q_0)=m$. Then $\pi' \in \Pi(V')$ and $\pi \in \Pi(V)$ satisfy $<V,\pi> \rightarrow_1 <V',\pi'>$ precisely if $\pi|W' \in \Pi'$ and $\pi|W'' \in \Pi''$. Thus, $D(V,1,\pi')=|\Pi''|$ for all $\pi' \in \Pi(V')$ and the result is proved for t=1.
Suppose the result holds for all t, $1 \leq t \leq T-1$, where $T > 1$. Choose $\pi' \in \Pi(V')$, and let V'' be any scheme of dimension d. By induction assumption, there are exactly $D(V'',1,\pi') = D(V'',1,V')$ distributions $\pi'' \in \Pi(V')$ such that $<V'',\pi''> \rightarrow_1 <V',\pi'>$, and for each such π'' there are exactly $D(V'',T-1,\pi'') = D(V,T-1,V'')$ distributions $\pi \in \Pi(V)$ such that $<V,\pi> \rightarrow_{T-1} <V'',\pi''>$. That is, there are exactly $D(V,T-1,V'')\ D(V'',1,V')$ distributions $\pi \in \Pi(V)$ such that $<V,\pi> \rightarrow_T <V',\pi'>$ and $<V,\pi> \rightarrow_{T-1} <V''$, distribution in $\Pi(V'')>$; summing over all possible V'' gives $D(V,T,\pi') = \Sigma_{\text{all } V''}$ $D(V,T-1,V'')\ D(V'',1,V')$ and this sum is independent of the choice of π'. □

Until further notice, V will be a scheme which has randomness property. The expected number of iterations of algorithm A will now be bounded. Let $\Delta=\text{Min}\{k, n-k+1\}$.

Lemma 2 Suppose algorithm A performs an iteration on V resulting in scheme V' (which depends on $\pi \in \Pi(V)$). Let $\Delta'= \text{Min}\{k',n'-k+1\}$, a random variable. Then, for all $r>0$, $P[\Delta' < c(r)\,\Delta^{1/2}] \geq 1-(1/r^2)$ where $c(r) = (r + 1/2)\ (3\,(d-1)/2)^{1/2}$.

Proof. Let $Z_{i,q}$ be the random variable defined on $\Pi(V)$ so that $Z_{i,q}(\pi)$ is the rank in W of the q-th smallest integer in $\{j \in W : \pi(j) = i\}$, $1 \le q \le n[i]$, $0 \le i \le d-1$. The mean $\mu(Z_{i,q})$ and variance $\sigma^2(Z_{i,q})$ of $Z_{i,q}$ are easily calculated [15]: $\mu(Z_{i,q}) = q (n + 1) / (n[i] + 1)$ and $\sigma^2(Z_{i,q}) = q(n + 1) (n - n[i]) (n[i] - q + 1) / (n[i] + 2) (n[i] + 1)^2$, $i \le q \le n[i]$, $0 \le i \le d-1$. Let $\mu = \mu(Z_{m,h})$ and $\sigma = \sigma(Z_{m,h})$; it is not difficult to show that $\sigma^2 < 3 (d-1) \Delta / 2$. Observe that $\Delta' \le | Z_{m,h} - k| \le |Z_{m,h} - \mu| + |\mu - k|$. Using the definition of $\mu(Z_{i,q})$ with $i = m$, $q = h$ and $|h - k (n[m] + 1) / (n + 1)| \le 1/2$, it follows that $|\mu - k| = |h (n + 1) / (n[m] + 1) - k| \le (n + 1) / 2 (n[m] + 1) < d/2$. Using the observed inequality on Δ' and Chebyshev's inequality, $P[\Delta' < u + d/2] \ge P[\Delta' - |\mu - k| < u] \ge P[|Z_{m,h} - \mu| < u] \ge 1 - \sigma^2/u^2$, for any $u > 0$. Since $\Delta \ge d+1 \ge 3$, it follows that $d < (3 (d-1) \Delta / 2)^{1/2}$; hence, $c(r) \Delta^{1/2} = (r - 1/2) (3 (d-1) \Delta/2)^{1/2} > r \sigma + d/2$. Setting $u = r\sigma$, it follows that $P[\Delta' < c(r) \Delta^{1/2}] \ge P[\Delta' < r\sigma + d/2] \ge 1 - 1/r^2$. □

Thus, a single iteration of algorithm A reduces a scheme of size Δ to one of size $\Delta' < c(r) \Delta^{1/2}$ with probability at least $1 - (1 / r^2)$. Of course, this is of interest only when $r>1$, so assume $r>1$ from now on. In the development below, the subscript i refers to the scheme V_i which results after i iterations of algorithm A (the initial scheme is V_0).

Consider a scheme $V=V_0$ (of dimension d) and apply algorithm A, starting with a (random) $\pi \in \Pi(V)$. For each non-negative integer t, either the algorithm terminates in fewer than t iterations, or it produces after t iterations a scheme V_t of size Δ_t. By Lemma 2 applied to V_{t-1}, if the algorithm performs $t \ge 1$ iterations,

$$P[\Delta_t < c(r) (\Delta_{t-1})^{1/2}] \ge 1 - (1 / r^2). \quad (1)$$

Let the random variable T be the number of iterations required for termination; that is, $\Delta_T < s$ and (if $T>0$) $\Delta_{T-1} \ge s$. If $\Delta = 1$, no iterations are necessary, so assume $\Delta \ge 2$. Fix $r > 1$ and $\theta > 1$ such that $\theta \le \Delta$, and set $s = \theta c(r)^2$. Necessarily $s > 27 (d-1) / 8$ since $d > 2$.

Iteration $t \ge 1$ will be called an *r-success* if either $\Delta_t < c(r) (\Delta_{t-1})^{1/2}$ or step 3(a) occurs. Let T_0 be the number of r-successes until termination of algorithm A.

<u>Lemma 3</u> Let $r > 1$, $\Delta \ge \theta > 1$, and $s = \theta c(r)^2$. Then the expected number E(T) of iterations of algorithm A satisfies $E(T) \le (r^2 / (r^2-1)) T_0$.

Proof. By relation (1), the expected number of iterations before an r-success is at most $(r^2 / (r^2-1))$. □

Lemma 4 Let $r > 1$, $\Delta \geq \theta > 1$, and $s = \theta\, c(r)^2$. Then the number of r-successes until termination of algorithm A is at most $T_0 = \lfloor \log\log \Delta - \log\log \theta + 1 \rfloor$.

Proof. Suppose r-successes occur at iterations $t_1 < t_2 < ... < t_p$, where $t_1 \geq 1$. Since $T_0 \geq 1$, it can be assumed that $p \geq 2$. For $1 \leq j \leq p-1$, step 3(a) cannot occur; hence $\Delta_{tj} < c(r)\,(\Delta_{tj-1})^{1/2}$. Letting Δ_0 be the original value of Δ, by induction it follows that

$$\Delta_{tj} < c(r)^{2-2^{-(j-1)}} (\Delta_0)^{2^{-j}} < c(r)^2\, \Delta^{2^{-j}}$$

In particular, for $j=p-1$,

$$\theta\, c(r)^2 = s \leq \Delta_{tj} < c(r)^2\, \Delta^{2^{-(p-1)}}$$

which yields $p-1 < \log\log \Delta - \log\log \theta$. □

3.2 Communication Complexity of The Reduction Technique

Return now to the reduction technique. After the Initialization phase, site S_0 knows the problem configuration < N, K, N[0], ..., N[d-1] >, to which the initial scheme V = (N, K, N[0], ..., N[d-1], {1,...,N}) can be associated. The unknown manner in which F is distributed into subfiles $X_0, ..., X_{d-1}$ according to the configuration corresponds to a distribution $\pi \in \Pi(V)$ via the rule $\pi(j) = i$ precisely if $f_j \in X_i$. After t iterations, algorithm A yields a scheme $V_t = (n_t, k_t, \{ n_t[i] \}, W_t)$ and a distribution $\pi_t \in \Pi(V_t)$, and the reduction technique yields a problem whose configuration is $<n_t, k_t, \{n_t[i]\}>$. In particular, algorithm A applied to V and π terminates exactly after the same number of iterations as does the reduction technique applied to the given problem. The *randomness assumption* is that, given the problem configuration, all allocations of F into $X_0, ..., X_{d-1}$ are *a priori* (i.e., before execution of the reduction technique) equally likely; that is, given the problem configuration , associated scheme V, and correspondence between the given configurations and distributions $\pi \in \Pi(V)$, the scheme V has the randomness property.

Theorem 2 Let a problem have $d \geq 2$ sites and size $\Delta \geq 2$. Let numbers r and θ satisfying $r > 1$ and $1 < \theta \leq \Delta$ be given, and let $s = 3\,(d-1)\,(r+1/2)^2 / 2$. Under the randomness assumption on the given problem configuration, in order to reduce the problem to a problem of size $\Delta' < s$, the reduction technique requires, on average, no more than $(r^2/(r^2-1)) \lfloor \log\log \Delta - \log\log \theta + 1 \rfloor$ iterations.

Proof. By lemmas 3 and 4. □

For a fixed r and θ, s=O(d) and T_0=O(log log Δ). Observing that an iteration can be implemented using two shout-echoes [15], it follows that:

Corollary 1 The reduction technique reduces a problem of size Δ to a problem of size Δ'=O(d) using on the average O(loglogΔ) communication activities in a shout-echo network.

Observing that an iteration can be implemented exchanging 5(d-1) messages in a point-to-point network, it follows that

Corollary 2 The reduction technique reduces a problem of size Δ to a problem of size Δ'=O(d) using on the average O(d loglog Δ) messages in a point-to-point network.

Choose r = θ = 2; thus s = 18.75 (d-1). Since a problem on s elements can be solved using 1.387 log s + O(1) shout-echoes on the average [13], it follows that

Corollary 3 There is an algorithm which will solve a problem of size Δ in the shout-echo model using no more than 2.667 $\lfloor$loglog Δ + 1$\rfloor$ + 1.387 log ($\lfloor$ 18.75 (d -1) $\rfloor$) + O(1) communication activities on the average.

Similiarly, choosing r = θ = 2 and using the expected (d-1) (2 log s + 1) bound for solving a problem on s elements in the point-to-point model [17], it follows that

Corollary 4 There is an algorithm which will solve a problem of size Δ in the point-to-point model using no more than (d-1) (6.667 $\lfloor$loglog Δ + 1$\rfloor$ + 2 log ($\lfloor$ 18.75 (d -1) $\rfloor$) + O(1)) messages on the average.

4. CONCLUDING REMARKS

The results presented here can be generalized in several ways. In particular, the assumption of the absence of any redundancy in the file ($X_i \cap X_j = \emptyset$ for $i \neq j$) can be removed with simple modifications to the algorithm and mantaining the same complexity [15]. Note that by allowing replications in the file, the model is extended to include the case in which every element at every site may be regarded as an independent draw from the identical distribution.

Because of the correspondence between distributed selection and K-selection in matrices with sorted columns, the bounds established here immediately imply bounds on the expected complexity of this and related problems (e.g., selection in X+Y); no such bounds were previously known.

A drawback of the proposed algorithm is its worst-case complexity; it is an open problem the design of a technique that yields a lower worst-case while still offering an expected complexity comparable to the one achieved here.

Another interesting open problem is the derivation of a lower bound on the expected communication complexity of distributed selection for the two models. A lower-bound on the worst-case complexity in the shout-echo model has been recently established by Marberg and Gafni [7]; in the point-to-point model, the only known lower bound is the one for complete binary trees established by Frederickson [3].

ACKNOWLEDGMENT

This work has been supported in part by the Natural Sciences and Engineering Research Council of Canada.

REFERENCES

[1] H. Abelson, "Lower bounds on information transfer in distributed systems", *J. ACM 27*, 2, April 1980, 384-392.

[2] F. Chin, H.F. Ting, "A near-optimal algorithm for finding the median distributively", *Proc. 5th IEEE Conf. on Distributed Computing Systems*, Denver, May 1985.

[3] G.N. Frederickson, "Tradeoffs for selection in distributed networks", *Proc. 2nd ACM Symp. on Principles of Distributed Computing*, Montreal, Aug. 1983, 154-160.

[4] G.N. Frederickson and D.B.Johnson, "The complexity of selection and ranking in X+Y and matrices with sorted columns", *J. Computer and System Science 24*, 2, April 1982, 197-208.

[5] E. Korach, D. Rotem, N. Santoro, "Distributed algorithms for ranking the nodes of a network", *Proc. 13th SE Conf. on Combinatorics, Graph Theory and Computing*, Boca Raton, Feb. 1982, 235-246.

[7] J.M. Marberg, E. Gafni, "An optimal shout-echo algorithm for selection in distributed sets", *Proc. 23rd Allerton Conf. on Comm., Control and Computing*, Monticello, Oct. 1985.

[8] T.A. Matsushita, "Distributed algorithms for selection", Master Thesis, Department of Computer Science, University of Illinois, Urbana, July 1983.

[9] M. Rodeh, "Finding the median distributively", *J. Computer and System Science 24*, 2, April 1982, 162-167.

[11] D. Rotem, N. Santoro, J.B. Sidney, "Distributed sorting", *IEEE Transactions on Computers C-34*, 4, April 1985, 372-376.

[12] D. Rotem, N. Santoro, J.B. Sidney, "Shout-echo selection in distributed files", *Networks 16*, 1986, 77-86.

[13] N. Santoro, M. Scheutzow, J.B. Sidney, "New bounds on the communication complexity of distributed selection", *J. Parallel and Distributed Computing*, to appear.

[14] N. Santoro, J.B. Sidney, "Order statistics on distributed sets", *Proc. 20th Allerton Conf. on Communication, Control and Computing*, Monticello, Oct. 1982, 251-256.

[15] N. Santoro, J.B. Sidney, S.J. Sidney, "On the expected complexity of distributed selection", Tech. Rep. SCS-TR-69, School of Computer Science, Carleton University, Ottawa, Feb. 1985.

[16] N. Santoro, E. Suen, "Reduction techniques for selection in distributed files", *Proc. Int. Conf. on Parallel Processing*, St. Charles, 1986, 1003-1009.

[17] L. Shrira, N. Francez, M. Rodeh, "Distributed k-selection: from a sequential to a distributed algorithm", *Proc. 2nd ACM Symp. on Principles of Distributed Computing*, Montreal, Aug. 1983, 143-153.

[18] A.C.C. Yao, "Some complexity questions related to distributive computing", *Proc. 11th ACM Symp. on Theory of Computing*, Atlanta, 1979, 209-213.

[19] S. Zaks, "Optimal distributed algorithms for sorting and ranking", *IEEE Transactions on Computers C-34*, 4, April 1985, 376-379.

LPG : A generic, logic and functional programming language

D. Bert, P. Drabik, R. Echahed
LIFIA
BP 68 - 38402 Saint Martin d'Hères Cedex
FRANCE

LPG is a programming language designed to implement and to experiment new concepts in the field of specification languages. In LPG, programs are "theories" in Horn clause logic with equality [3] [4]. Syntactically, a program is a theory presentation TP = (S, Σ, Π, E, C) in which sorts (S), operators (Σ) and predicates (Π) can be declared; operators are specified by conditional equations (E), and predicates are specified by Horn clauses (C). Litterals of a clause body may be equalities on terms. There are three kinds of presentations : (i) presentations of "properties" (i.e. class of structures like group theory, ring theory, etc); (ii) presentations of data types (i.e. definitions of sorts, operators and/or predicates) where the semantics is given by initial models; (iii) presentations of enrichments (i.e. hierarchical definitions of new operators and/or predicates on data types previously defined). Moreover, data type and enrichment presentations may be parameterized by properties [1], thus providing generic data types, and generic enrichments. It is also possible to relate theories between themselves by declaring theory-morphisms inside presentations. Those declarations are helpful for the instantiation mechanism which is needed because of genericity. Up to now, the following tools are already available :

- An interpreter : this tool is designed to reduce ground terms to their normal form, with respect to the rewriting system deduced from the equations. This interpreter is an abstract machine which deals with compiled programs. It also uses buit-in procedures for operators over predefined data types like natural numbers, strings, etc. Taking advantage of the instantiation mechanism of generic operators, the interpreter is a good tool for testing specifications, prototyping, and functional programming.

- A logical evaluator (called "solver") : given a list of litterals and/or equalities on terms (i. e. a goal), the solver tries to find the values of the variables which satisfy the goal. The underlying algorithm combines the resolution principle and the conditional narrowing [2]. It has been shown sound and complete for a canonical rewrite rule system, but termination is not guaranteed for every goal.

- An interactive theorem prover : we have developed an interface with the OASIS system [5] in order to prove theorems. Implemented strategies are equational rewriting, case analysis, and proofs by induction. This system is also used to verify semantic correctness of specifications, like the validity of theory morphisms.

Current developments include a completion algorithm, and analysis of properties as sufficient completeness of the operators, or persistency of the parameterization functors. Most of the implementation programs are written in Pl/I, under the Multics operating system. A version running on Sun workstations is planned for 1987.

The presentation of LPG can be sketched as follows :

1- Generic and functional programming : examples of interpretations and presentation of the instantiation mechanism.
2 - (Generic and) logic programming : resolution of equations on terms, and evaluation of goals.
3 - Interactive proofs of theorems.

References

[1] D.Bert, R.Echahed, *Design and Implementation of a generic, logic and functional Programming Language*, Proc. of the European Symposium on Programming, Saarbrücken, LNCS 213, pp. 119-132.
[2] R.Echahed, *Prédicats et sous-types en LPG. Réalisation de la E-unification*, RR IMAG-550-LIFIA-29, Juillet 85.
[3] J.A.Goguen, R.M.Burstall, *Introducing Institutions*, Proceedings Logics and Programming Workshop, pp. 221-256, 1984.
[4] J.A.Goguen, J.Meseguer, *Equality, Types, Modules and Generics for Logic Programming*, Proc. of International Conference on Logic Programming, Uppsala 1984.
[5] E.Paul, *Manuel OASIS*, Note technique NT/PAA/CLC/LSC/959, CNET, Fév. 1985.

CEC

Hubert Bertling
Harald Ganzinger
Hubert Baumeister

Universität Dortmund
Informatik V
Postfach 50 05 00
4600 Dortmund 50

CEC (Conditional Equations Completion) is a system for manipulating parametric conditional equational specifications. Its main components at the moment are a completion procedure according to what is described in Ganzinger's STACS 87 paper, a recursive path decomposition ordering, a polynominal ordering and AC-unification.

At the user level it provides the following operatons on parametric specifications:

- union of specifications
- application of specification morphims
- parameter passing
- enrichment
- completion
- term normalization
- proving of equational and inductive theorems
- observing the automatic and user requested critical pair computations
- saving and restoring completion states

The whole system is implemented in C-Prolog under Unix System V on a 68000 based workstation.

ASSPEGIQUE

An integrated specification environment

Michel Bidoit, Francis Capy, Christine Choppy, Marie-Anne Choquer, Stéphane Kaplan, Françoise Schlienger, Frédéric Voisin.

Laboratoire de Recherche en Informatique
C.N.R.S. U.A. 410 "Al Khowarizmi"
Université Paris-Sud - Bât 490
F - 91405 ORSAY Cédex
FRANCE

Asspegique is an integrated environment for the development of large algebraic specifications and the management of a specification data base. The aim of the **Asspegique** specification environment is to provide the user with a "specification laboratory" where a large range of various tools supporting the use of algebraic specifications are closely integrated. The main aspects adressed in the design of **Asspegique** are the following : dealing with modularity and reusability, providing ease of use, flexibility of the environment and user-friendly interfaces. The **Asspegique** specification environment supports (a subset of) the specification language Pluss.

The tools available in the **Asspegique** specification environment include a special purpose editor, modification tools, a compiler, a symbolic evaluator, theorem proving tools and an assistant for deriving Ada implementations from specifications. All these tools are available to the user through a full-screen, multi-window user interface and access the specification data base through the hierarchical management tool. Most of these tools also use Cigale, a system for incremental grammar construction and parsing, which has been especially designed in order to cope with a flexible, user-oriented way of defining operators, coercion and overloading of operators.

REVEUR4 : A Laboratory for Conditional Rewriting

Wadoud BOUSDIRA, Jean-Luc REMY
Centre de Recherche en Informatique de Nancy
Campus scientifique BP 239
54506 VANDOEUVRE-LES-NANCY FRANCE

REVEUR4 is the implementation software of the mechanism of contextual rewriting. This form of conditional rewriting has been systematized by Rémy (REM 82) and considers hierarchical systems. The principle consists in replacing term conditional rewriting by a contextual rewriting in order to study the confluence of a system on ground terms that satisfies properties so called sufficient completeness and well coveredness.

Contextual rewriting is a hierarchical method with two levels : the first one is constituted of boolean calculus, it is the primitive level, and the second one is constituted of conditional operations. This method allows for case raisonning, with each case being associated with a context formed of hypotheses.

The kernel of REVEUR4 is constituted of two classes of modules, the first one is constituted of the modules which are inherited from REVE, a classical rewrite rule laboratory, without any conditions, and the second one is proper to conditional rewriting.

The aim of REVEUR4 is to extend Knuth-Bendix completion procedure (K&B 70) to conditional theory using contextual rewriting. This rewriting is defined on contextual terms (or c-terms) noted c :: t, where c and t are themselves terms. Moreover, c is of sort boolean and is called context.

A c-term (c :: t) can then be rewritteen to different c-terms (c_i :: t_i). Consequently, contextual rewriting relation admits several normal forms for a same c-term and we shall not talk anymore about normal forms but about sets of contextual normal forms.

From a finite set of equations in input, REVEUR4 provides decision procedure for word problem on ground terms in conditional theory (ZHA 84). This proof is realized by checking that every contextual critical pair converges and proceeds if necessary to a completion of the system.

Nevertheless, the contextual rewriting is a form of conditional rewriting which needs a careful use. Indeed, problems relative to constraints underlying its definition can arise and it is then necessary to proceed some verifications during the completion procedure. On the one hand, we have to check that properties of hierarchy and well coveredness of the system are still satisfied. Indeed, the reduction of system rules by rules recently introduced and the calculus of set of contextual normal forms of a c-term are no more valid if the system is not well covered. On the other hand, REVEUR4 manipulates equations denoted p :: g == d where every variable of p has to be contained either in g or in d. A problem arises if a contextual critical pair is generated during procedure which does not satisfy this condition and the system then abort (Z&R 85) (B&R 86).

In order to etablish the c-termination of hierarchical rewriting system, REVEUR4 uses RDOS ordering (Recursive Decomposition Ordering with Status) (LES 84). It is a simplification ordering ; its property of incrementality makes the use of system and allows for automatic proofs.

REVEUR4 has been implemented in CLU and it runs on VAX and SUN3 under UNIX system (R&Z 84). This laboratory is an experimental version and it is still under development.

(B&R-86) **BOUSDIRA. W, REMY. J.L,**
Complétion des systèmes de réécriture conditionnelle, Rapport de recherche 86-R-120, C.R.I.N

(LES-84) **LESCANNE. P,**
Uniform Termination of Term Rewriting Systems- Recursive Decomposition Ordering with Status, Proceedings 9th CAAP, Bordeaux, 1984

(K&B-70) **KNUTH. D, BENDIX. P,**
Simple Word Problems in Abstract Algebra, Leech J.ed, Pergamon Press, pp. 263-297, 1970

(REM-82) **REMY. J.L,**
Etude des systèmes de réécriture conditionnelle et applications aux types abstraits algébriques, Thèse d'Etat, I.N.P.L, Nancy, 1982

(R&Z-84) **REMY. J.L, ZHANG. H,**
REVEUR4 : A system for validating conditional algebraic specifications of abstract data types, Proc. of 6th ECAI Conference, Pisa, Italy, 1984

(ZHA-84) **ZHANG. H,**
REVEUR4: Etude et mise en oeuvre de la réécriture conditionnelle, Thèse de 3ème cycle, Université de Nancy 1, 1984

(Z&R-85) **ZHANG. H, REMY. J.L,**
Contextual rewriting, Proc. of the 1st Conf. on Rewriting Techniques and Applications, Lect. Notes in Comp. Sci., 202, Dijon, France, 1985

An Interactive, Incremental and Portable Computer Algebra System for λ-Calculus and Combinatory Logic based on Video Edition and Rewriting Techniques

Nelly GIRARD

LITP-Paris VI
(couloir 45-55, 2e étage)
4 place Jussieu
75252 Paris Cedex 05
FRANCE

The fifteen last years have seen an incresing need for computer algebra systems (Macsyma, Reduce, Scrachtpad). Simultaneously, λ-Calculus and Combinatory Logic revealed to be a privileged tool for modelling functional languages.

We present ECOLE: a new, totally interactive, completely video-oriented, self-documented, extensible, redefinable and portable computer algebra system devoted to λ-calculus and Combinatory Logic.

ECOLE takes λ-terms or combinatory expressions and transforms them interactively, according to the standard rewriting rules. Each rule and command is bound to a unique key.

The screen is divided in several windows, displaying such calculus and commands. In the calculus window, the term is written with the standard notation (implicit association to the left). Positioning the blinking cursor allows to specify the implicit parenthesis and to select a subterm.

New combinators may be interactively created during a session: their λ-definition, considered as pattern, is compiled into procedures realising their optimized abstraction and application rules. Also, the system may be extended with new algorithms, such as reduction or abstraction strategies. Extensions are integrated in the same way than the standard commands, insuring the homogeneity of the system.

An on-line documentation provides key-bindings, available commands, definition of combinators and others. Its consistency and completeness are automatically maintained at each extension. Defining a new combinator induces a complete analysis, featuring a canonical representation, its free variables and its effects (associative, duplicative ...).

ECOLE is implemented in Le_Lisp, a LISP system available on most machines under UNIX.

The Passau RAP System: Rapid Prototyping for Algebraic Specifications

Heinrich Hussmann
Universität Passau
Fakultät für Mathematik und Informatik
Postfach 2540
D-8390 Passau
F. R. G.

Abstract

The Passau RAP system provides machine support for the development of algebraic specifications formulated by conditional equations. The system has been developed at the University of Passau, partially sponsored by the "Sonderforschungsbereich 49 Programmiertechnik" at the Technical University of Munich and the ESPRIT project 432 "METEOR". RAP is in use since the end of 1984, a revised version has been released in summer 1986. There are a number of installations at other sites.

The aim of the system is to supply a most flexible prototyping facility for algebraic specifications.This means that the specification is given an operational semantics with a logic-programming flavour, comprising
- systematic test of the specification
  (and hence a comparison with the informal requirements behind it)
- automatic generation of test data for later implementations
- proof of simple algebraic properties of the specified functions.

RAP uses hierarchical algebraic specifications ([Wirsing et al. 83]) as a specification language. A modularisation mechanism is contained within this language as well as the concept of sorts (types). The axioms of specifications are in general of the form

$t_1 = s_1$ & ... & $t_n = s_n$ => $l = r$

(where the t_i, s_i, l, r are terms); they are interpreted by the system as conditional rewrite rules.

The main component of the system is the so-called "conditional narrowing algorithm". This algorithm combines (conditional) term rewriting and resolution techniques, offering the functional evaluation of terms as well as a PROLOG-like mechanism for answering queries. Such queries are formulated in our framework as systems of equations containing unknown variables. The conditional narrowing algorithm enumerates substitutions for these variables such that the equations hold in the first order theory defined by the given axioms. For more theoretical results on the algorithm see [Hussmann 85] and [Fribourg 85].

In RAP, the conditional narrowing algorithm can be observed and controlled using a powerful interactive debugger. Moreover, a number of system parameters are adjustable, in particular:
- search strategy within the proof tree (breadth-first, depth-first, limited depth-first)
- redex selection strategy (full, leftmost-innermost)
- usage of various optimizations (e.g. subsumption, conditional rewriting).

In addition to the conditional narrowing algorithm, the system contains tools for testing useful properties of algebraic specifications:

- finite termination of the corresponding term rewriting relation
- complete definition of function symbols by case analysis over constructor terms.

The conditional narrowing algorithm may be applied to specifications even when these properties do not hold, but the result of the tests is used automatically to optimize the narrowing process.

The system is written in portable PASCAL (approx. 9000 l.o.c), it is currently available for the VAX/VMS, UNIX 4.X BSD and VM/CMS operating systems. The experimentation done in Passau with the system includes classical abstract data types as well as rather large and new specifications. The most complex specification tested with RAP up to now is a functional description of the INTEL 8085 microprocessor which contains about 250 axioms.

Experimentation with RAP lead to interesting conclusions (see [Geser, Hussmann 86]), among them:

- A functional algebraic language together with an interpreter based on leftmost-innermost narrowing and rewriting may become an alternative to existing logic-programming systems. To reach Prolog´s efficiency, some of the implementation techniques used there have to be taken over.
- Breadth-first search is a powerful and valuable tool for systems like RAP because of its property to enumerate the solutions in a fair manner. For testing small examples, as typical in RAP applications, breadth-first search may be even superior in performance to depth-first search.

References:

[Fribourg 85]
L. Fribourg, Handling function definitions through innermost superposition and rewriting. Proc. RTA 85 Conf., Lecture Notes in Computer Science 202, pp. 325-344, 1985.

[Geser, Hussmann 86]
A. Geser, H. Hussmann, Experiences with the RAP system - a specification interpreter combining term rewriting and resolution. Proc. ESOP 86 Conf., Lecture Notes in Computer Science 213, pp.339-350, 1986.

[Hussmann 85]
H. Hussmann, Unification in conditional-equational theories. Proc. EUROCAL 85 Conf., Lecture Notes in Computer Science 204, pp. 543-553, 1985.

[Wirsing et al. 83]
M. Wirsing, P. Pepper, H. Partsch, W. Dosch, M. Broy, On hierarchies of abstract data types. Acta Informatica 20, pp. 1-33, 1983.

SPRAC: A SOFTWARE ENGINEERING ENVIRONMENT

M. LEMOINE, R. JACQUART, G. ZANON

ONERA-CERT-DERI
2, ave E. BELIN
31055 TOULOUSE CEDEX (FRANCE)

ABSTRACT

SPRAC is an Integrated Computer Assisted Software Development System. It interacts with the user for the expression of formal specifications, for the purpose of producing and validating software components. SPRAC is concerned with the development of classical programs, e.g. programs written in imperative languages such as PASCAL or ADA.

Date: 27/08/86
Ref: stacs87.1
File: stacs.nro

SPRAC: A SOFTWARE ENGINEERING ENVIRONMENT

M. LEMOINE, R. JACQUART, G. ZANON

ONERA-CERT-DERI
2, ave E. BELIN
31055 TOULOUSE CEDEX (FRANCE)

The main characteristics of SPRAC are the following:

1) the ability to describe the software objects at three distinct levels, corresponding to definition levels more and more close to the computer.

2) the existence of a project data base (PDB) which presents a structured working area. The schema of the PDB is relational.

3) the existence of a set of tools providing an active assistance in the framework of a transformational approach.

At the level of design languages, we find an assertional language, called LF, which is based on a typed first order predicate logic. LF permits specification of functions, abstract data types, and representation of abstract data types. All these objects can be generic.

At the second level, LA is an applicative language used to describe algorithms.

The last level is called the LM level, and corresponds to the level of programming languages. In practice all software produced with the help of SPRAC must have an operational level in LM.

SLOG: A LOGIC INTERPRETER FOR EQUATIONAL CLAUSES

Laurent Fribourg
L.I.E.N.S., 45 rue d'Ulm, 75005 Paris - France
Laboratoires de Marcoussis, Route de Nozay, 91460 Marcoussis - France

This work has been supported by the Laboratoires de Marcoussis and by the METEOR ESPRIT project 432. SLOG (pronounce S-Log) is a Prolog-like language developed at Laboratoires de Marcoussis [1][2][3]. One important difference with Prolog is that it uses a **functional** formalism instead of a **relational** one. A Prolog program is made of Horn clauses containing symbols of variables, functions and predicates. An equivalent SLOG program is made of equational clauses, i.e. Horn clauses where the only predicate is equality and where the head is an equation oriented from left to right. The function symbols of the Prolog program are kept as such and are called **constructors** in the SLOG program. On the other hand, the predicate symbols of the Prolog program are replaced by function symbols called **defined operators** in the SLOG program. A Prolog goal is made of a set of predicates, whereas an SLOG goal is made of a set of equations. In SLOG, the repartition of the function symbols between constructors and defined operators has to be given by the programmer. Given a goal, the solution found by the interpreter contain only constructors and variables (no defined operators). An SLOG program is composed of two parts: the **axioms** and the **simplification set.**

The Axioms

The axioms are the essential part of an SLOG program: it is the logical part which allows the deduction of the solutions from the submitted goal. The inference rule which is used for this deduction is called "narrowing" and corresponds to the Prolog resolution. As Prolog resolution, narrowing is applied only to the leftmost equations of the goals.

Any Prolog program can be executed by SLOG, once the clauses of the Prolog program have been translated into a functional form and written into the part "AXIOMS" of the SLOG program. For example, one can define the sum on natural numbers built over the constructors zero and s, by the following set of axioms:

```
+(X,zero) = X.
+(X,s(Y)) = s(+(X,Y)).
```

and the predicate less-than-or-equal-to on natural numbers built over the constructors zero and s, by the following set of axioms:

```
le(zero,X) = true.
le(s(X),s(Y)) = true:-le(X,Y) = true.
```

The Simplification Set

The simplification set is a set of equations (oriented from left to right) called simplifying clauses, which makes the execution of the program more efficient. It contains additional information which is consistent with the axioms. This information is not necessary to compute the solutions but is helpful for speeding up the computation or pruning fruitless paths of computation. This is achieved through an inference rule called "simplifications". Unlike narrowing, simplification replaces goals by equivalent ones. Therefore, simplification is backtracking free. Simplification has priority over narrowing and is performed on all the goal equations (not only the leftmost one).

For example, in the sum program above, it can be useful to add the following properties in the simplification set:

+(zero,X) = X.

+(s(X),Y) = s(+(X,Y)).

Likewise, in the less-than-or-equal-to program above, it is generally useful to add the negative information: *le(s(X),zero) = false* . Suppose indeed that the interpreter is trying to compute the solutions of a local subgoal of the form *le(t1,t2) = true* , thanks to the negative information *le(s(X),zero) = false* , it may realize that the subgoal reduces to the contradictory equation *false = true*. It then rejects the current path of computation and backtracks. The negative information thus makes more efficient the computation of the *positive* goal *le(t1,t2) = true* .

Were there no mechanism of simplification in SLOG, then SLOG would exactly behave as a Prolog interpreter running with the program corresponding to the axioms. Thanks to its mechanism of simplification and the rules contained in the simplification set, SLOG is able to **control** the execution of programs in a more flexible and efficient way than Prolog (see examples in [3]).

References

[1] Fribourg L., "Oriented Equational Clauses as a Programming Language", J. Logic Programming 1:2, August 1984, pp. 165-177.

[2] Fribourg L., "SLOG: A Logic Programming Interpreter Based on Clausal Superposition and Rewriting", IEEE Symp. on Logic Programming, Boston, July 1985, pp. 172-184.

[3] Fribourg L., Holvoet Y., Mauboussin A., Vargenau M.E., "SLOG 1.1: User's Manual", Technical Report, Laboratoires de Marcoussis, 1986.

An Algebraic Transformation System for occam Programs

M. Goldsmith, A. Cox, G. Barrett

Oxford University Computing Laboratory Programming Research Group, 8-11 Keble Road, Oxford OX 1 30D, UK

Occam is a programming language which combines considerable expressive power, particularly tailored towards concurrent problems, with relatively simple semantics well founded in mathematics. The Oxford University Programming Research Group has been associated with the development of the language from the outset, through the close connection between occam and the pure mathematical notation of Communicating Sequential Processes (CSP). The semantics of both occam and CSP have been the subjects of considerable research at PRG. We are a project working under Bill Roscoe to develop and apply this knowledge to practical uses, especially the mechanised (or machine assisted) transformation and verification of occam.

We have available two forms of semantic description of occam: denotational and algebraic. The denotational semantics [1] are most suitable as a basis for analysing the relationship between an occam program and its specification, and for formal verification. The algebraic semantics [2] take the form of laws, derived from the denotational semantics, which relate equivalent forms of program fragment; this is clearly the essential prerequisite for any transformation system.

The desired final shape of the program will, of course, depend on its intended application. On the one hand, one might wish to optimise a program for execution on a single processor or a given array of transputers. Alternatively, the program might represent a VLSI design, in which case the transformations would be geared towards decomposing the program into implementable modules and minimising silicon area, path lengths, etc. This would typically take the form of transformations from general occam programs into a restricted subset of occam with, for example, patterns of communication that have a known silicon implementation.

The pilot transformation system is based on the complete set of laws for a subset of occam given in [2] and generally relies heavily on direction from its user. The laws given there are specialised in that they are best adapted to transforming programs into normal form, and the normal form strategy has been fully automated using higher-order functions to combine them. We expect to supplement these with laws directed towards such goals as increasing efficiency, parallelism introduction and elimination, etc. Even in its rudimentary form the system has been put to practical use, where INMOS Ltd have used it in the rigorous development of the floating point IMS-T800 Transputer, transforming micro-code back to a form more obviously equivalent to the software emulation of floating-point operations.

References:

[1] Roscoe, A. W.: Denotational Semantics for occam, July 1984 NSF/SERG Seminar on Concurrency, CMU, Springer Verlag LNCS 197.

[2] Roscoe, A. W.: and C. A. R. Hoare: The Laws of occam Programming, PRG monograph PRG-53.

REVE a Rewrite Rule Laboratory

Pierre LESCANNE

Centre de Recherche en Informatique de Nancy
Campus Scientifique BP 239
54506 Vandoeuvre Cedex France

1 — System Sumary

REVE is a rewrite rule laboratory intended to conduct experiments in equational theories based on rewriting techniques. It was built to provide both convenient tools for an experimented user and to make experiments using the most recent techniques in the field. Among others, it offers tools to compute convergent rewriting systems i.e., confluent and noetherian and to perform proofs by induction based on the method of proof by consistency.

REVE has four versions, REVE-1 was the prototype [LES,83], REVE-2 is a robust software for working on term rewriting systems, REVE-3 is a laboratory for equational rewriting based on Jouannaud and Kirchner's completion algorithm [J-K,84], [K-K,85], REVEUR-4 [R-Z,84] is a laboratory for conditional rewriting based on Remy and Zhang's ideas.

2 — Applications

REVE has its main applications in equational algebra [LES-83] and abstract data type specifications. It has also applications in Petri nets properties [C-J,85] and data base theory [C-K,85].

3 — Implementation

REVE is written in CLU and is available on VAX/UNIX and SUN workstation. Its architecture in described in [FOR-84]

4 — Developments

The main developments are currently on termination algorithms, proof by induction, introduction of new equational theories through unification algorithms, efficiency of equational rewriting, introduction of new strategies for conditional rewriting.

5 — List of participants

REVE-2 Alhem Ben Cherifa (CRIN), Dave Detlefs (MIT), Randy Forgaard (MIT), John Guttag (MIT), Azzedine Lazrek (CRIN), Pierre Lescanne (CRIN).

REVE-3 Claude Kirchner (CRIN), Hélène Kirchner (CRIN), Jalel Mzali (CRIN), Kathy Yelick (MIT).

REVEUR-4 Jean-Luc Remy (CRIN), Hantao Zhang (CRIN).

6 — References

[FOR,84] R. FORGAARD, "A program for generating and analyzing term rewriting system", Master of science in computer science MIT 1984. Jouannaud Kirchner

[C-J,85] C. CHOPPY, C. JOHNEN "Petrireve: Proving Petri Net Properties With Rewriting Systems", Proc. 1st Conference on Rewriting Techniques and Applications, Dijon (France), Lecture Notes in Computer Science vol. 202, Springer Verlag, pp. 271-286, 1985.

[C-K,85] S.S. COSMADAKIS, P.C. KANELLAKIS, "Two Applications of Equational Theories to Data base Theory", Proc. 1st Conference on Rewriting Techniques and Applications, Dijon (France), Lecture Notes in Computer Science vol. 202, Springer Verlag, pp. 107-123, 1985.

[J-K,84] J.P. JOUANNAUD, H. KIRCHNER, "Completion of a set of rules modulo a set of equations", Proceedings 11th ACM Conference of Principles of Programming Languages, Salt Lake City (Utah, USA), 1984.

[K-K,85] C. KIRCHNER & H. KIRCHNER, "Implementation of a general completion procedure parameterized by built-in theories and strategies", Proceedings of the EUROCAL 85 conference, 1985.

[LES,83] P. LESCANNE "Computer Experiments with the REVE Term Rewriting System Generator" 10th POPL, Austin, Texas, January 1983, pp 99-108

[R-Z,84] J.L. REMY, H. ZHANG, "REVEUR 4: a System for Validating Conditional Algebraic Specifications of Abstract Data Types" Proceedings of the 5th ECAI Pisa, 1984.

Author Index